5/24

ART, ARTISANS
& APPRENTICES

George Scharf detail of Fig. 25 showing a young apprentice leaving a colourman's shop with his master. Within the shop, faintly visible through the open door, an apprentice may be seen grinding pigment.

Art, Artisans & Apprentices

Apprentice Painters & Sculptors
in the Early Modern British Tradition

JAMES AYRES

Oxbow Books
Oxford & Philadelphia

Published in the United Kingdom in 2014 by
OXBOW BOOKS
10 Hythe Bridge Street, Oxford OX1 2EW

and in the United States by
OXBOW BOOKS
908 Darby Road, Havertown, PA 19083

Hardcover Edition: ISBN 978-1-78297-742-1
Digital Edition: ISBN 978-1-78297-743-8

A CIP record for this book is available from the British Library

Library of Congress Cataloging-in-Publication Data

Ayres, James.
  Art, artisans and apprentices : apprentice painters & sculptors in the early modern
British tradition / James Ayres.
    pages cm
  Includes bibliographical references and index.
  ISBN 978-1-78297-742-1
 1. Art–Study and teaching–Great Britain–History–18th century. 2. Art–Study and
teaching–North America–History–18th century. 3. Painters–Training of–Great Britain–
History–18th century. 4. Painters–Training of–North America–History–18th century.
5. Sculptors–Training of–Great Britain–History–18th century. 6. Sculptors–Training of–
North America–History–18th century. 7. Great Britain–Social conditions–18th century.
8. North America–Social conditions–18th century. I. Title.
  N185.A94 2014
  707.1'55–dc23
                              2014017592

Printed in the United Kingdom by Berforts Information Press

For a complete list of Oxbow titles, please contact:

UNITED KINGDOM
Oxbow Books
Telephone (01865) 241249, Fax (01865) 794449
Email: oxbow@oxbowbooks.com
www.oxbowbooks.com

UNITED STATES OF AMERICA
Oxbow Books
Telephone (800) 791-9354, Fax (610) 853-9146
Email: queries@casemateacademic.com
www.casemateacademic.com/oxbow

Oxbow Books is part of the Casemate Group

CONTENTS

INTRODUCTION

Biographies of Early Modern painters and sculptors in Britain and Colonial America show that whilst some individuals were "articled" to a successful studio many, perhaps most, were apprenticed to a particular trade of varying degrees of relevance. In general these "lives of the artists" touch on matters of training before moving on to what are perceived to be the substantive concerns in the life and work under review.[1] Understandable though this position may be the brevity of information on training too easily gives insufficient importance to an historical reality. Before the full emergence of schools of art, an apprenticeship in a trade with some aesthetic values provided an important means to an end for those who had artistic aspirations or were to develop them.

For individuals who escaped the limitations of an exclusively trade training their workshop experience, when transferred to a studio, equipped them to realise their artistic aspirations. Many of the founder members of the Royal Academy of Arts in London sprang from such a background. One such was the first, and sadly the last, Royal Academician to serve as that institution's house painter (see p. 197). Such a direct line, between the trade and the art, was a feature that gave that body a vitality, in its early years, that it has never quite recaptured.

This is a sprawling subject which I shall endeavour to centre on the very "long eighteenth" century (at its most extended *c.* 1660–1837) but which will be reviewed in terms of what preceded and succeeded it. For example, the high standard of craftsmanship that characterise the material culture of Georgian Britain had its origins in the apprenticeship system which stemmed from the medieval guilds. The decline in that method of training coincided with, or maybe attributed to, the rise of consumerism, industrialisation and the emergence of Empire: an age of both evolution and revolution.

Beyond, or rather within, the wider historical context the principal concern of the chapters that follow are the particulars of each of a given series of crafts. In these accounts consideration will be given to tools and materials, the nature and length of apprenticeships and the extent to which a tyro was expected to produce a "proof piece" or "masterpiece" at the conclusion of "his time". As a "craft history" rather than an "art history" the emphasis will be on the processes rather than the products. Not that the intention is to produce a *manual* in the exact meaning of that word. On the contrary, the focus will be on the nature of the training in different crafts as reflected in the skills that they involved. From that starting point the way in which some tradesmen evolved into sculptors and painters will be considered.

Down to the third quarter of the seventeenth century there was little distinction between the so-called "fine" and "decorative" arts. Even so the evolution from artisan to artist could stem from the restrictive practices of a given craft or from some admissible relaxations of such regulations. Why, and for what reasons, were plumbers to be permitted by Guild authority to apply oil paint and how did some members of that craft emerge as easel painters? How was it that plasterers became entitled to apply lime-wash and distempers and, in some instances, become mural painters? What was the motivation that persuaded some woodcarvers to transfer their allegiance to marble? In what ways did some chasers inform the wider artistic community?

The crafts of the visual arts, in common with other trades in general, were regulated in major urban centres by the guilds or livery companies. These fraternities were at their most specialist and powerful in the City of London. For this reason the reach and influence of the capital was formidable and extended across the Atlantic.[2] The crafts, like the arts, were inevitably and indelibly metropolitan – urbanity was, by definition, urban. In Britain this was mitigated by the custom amongst the aristocracy and gentry of spending only "the season" in town. Much of the year was spent in country houses where the elite became ambassadors of sophistication. A comparable situation obtained in the North American Colonies. In the Old South individual plantations were equipped with wharfs from which tobacco, indigo and cotton were exported direct to Britain and to which the latest fashionable goods from London, Bristol and Liverpool were imported.

In representing special interest groups the guilds were therefore at their most powerful in the larger towns and cities. For this reason many of the craft fraternities emerged in association with the urbanisation on which they were dependent. In England the first challenge to guild authority occurred in early Tudor London. It was then that Italian Renaissance artists reached these shores at the behest of the king – a situation that left guild members as impotent onlookers. Although the gradual decline of these fraternities as trade organisations did not begin until the seventeenth century their wavering authority was to have a deleterious impact on apprenticeships as a system of training.

The number of craft trades involved in the visual arts was legion. The range and extent of training that was expected, demanded and met was truly remarkable. Although we may too easily presume an understanding of the activities that constitute "painting" we are less familiar with the "staining" of cloths and "transparencies" or the defining nature of "limning". Similarly "sculpture" once possessed an exact meaning in which "die-sinkers", "gem engravers" and "chasers" occupied an honourable position. The understanding of these crafts in the visual arts receded as training in an apprenticeship was displaced by education in an art school. All these issues were to have an impact not only on artists but on the work that they produced. In this sequence of events artisans become affiliated to the "Combinations" (proto-Trade Unions) as artists aspired to a professional status under the diktats of academies.

Until the 1840s some painters and many sculptors emerged in their art from a trade background. Of the painters, Peter Monamy (1681–1749), Charles Catton RA (1728–1798) and Robert Smirke RA (1752–1845) had begun their careers as house, sign or carriage painters. And what was true for painters was also the experience of many sculptors. Sir George Frampton RA (1860–1928) was in his early years a trade stone carver who was sometimes reduced to venturing forth as a "field ranger". By these means the craft-based visual arts survived, here and there, down to the First World War.

The widening chasm between "fine" and "applied" art may have begun in the eighteenth century. Sir Joshua Reynolds certainly saw a distinction between the "intellectual dignity ... that ennobles the painter's art; that lays the line between him and the mere mechanic".[3] When confronting such prejudices it is reassuring to recall Oscar Wilde's assertion that: "there are moments when art almost attains the dignity of manual labour".[4]

Notes

[1] An example being Ronald Paulson's *Hogarth*, 1991, where the subject's apprenticeship as a silver engraver is outlined in vol. I, pp. 38–39

[2] Arms of the Painter-Stainers of London used as a sign by the English-born, London-trained painter and decorator Thomas Child in Boston, Massachusetts, fig. xxx

[3] Joshua Reynolds 1778, p. 72

[4] Oscar Wilde "The Model Millionaire" in Isabel Murray ed. *The Collected Shorter Writings of Oscar Wilde*, London, 1979, p. 90

Part 1

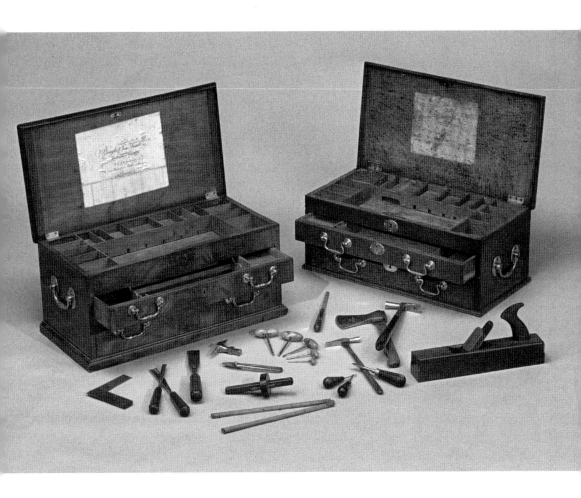

CRAFTS, TRADES, ARTISANS
& GUILDS

Chapter 1

ART & MYSTERY

The words "Art & Mystery" occur, with some regularity, in the indentures or agreements that were drawn up between a master and the parents or guardians of a prospective apprentice. In the language of Early Modern Britain "Art" was understood as the craft and "Mystery" as the secrets of the trade in which the master agreed to provide instruction.

If "craft" has been seen in differing ways the word "art" has enjoyed, or been subject to, a promiscuous range of interpretations, few of which are objective. Its etymology may be traced via old French to the Latin route in which *ars* signified that which was "put together, joined or fitted".[1] This was precisely the sense in which Horace used the word in one section of his *Ars Poetica*. In that work he describes a series of limbs from different animals being put together to form one "assemblage".[2] It seems that this physical and practical understanding of *Ars* or *Art* persisted down to early seventeenth century London. In 1637 the Button Makers Company petitioned the Privy Council regarding their concerns about the intrusion of aliens into their craft. In their Petition these tradesmen were seeking to establish a closed-shop with "all lawful powers grantable to *artists* of like condition" (my italics).[3] This usage survives in the now outmoded "artificer" and continues in the term "artisan". In these circumstances it was perfectly reasonable that many youths would be apprenticed to trades relating to painting and sculpture and that some would later emerge as artists in the modern sense of the word.

In simple terms medieval England was a cultural continuum for despite the tiny elite the vast bulk of the other ranks were party to, if not members of, the one tradition. There was also a parallel continuity between art and craft, manual activities for which God himself could be claimed as the first creator.[4] On such a basis, and with the authority of the Almighty, the Gothic tradition maintained its vigour to the last and exhibited no symptoms of decline. Indeed the great innovation, now known as the "Perpendicular" style, gave it an added impetus. Consequently when the Italian Renaissance reached these shores it confronted a strong pre-existing religious and cultural tradition. The most obvious, and certainly the first, example of this collision of aesthetic outlook may be seen in Henry VII's chapel at Westminster Abbey. This supreme example of Perpendicular Gothic was completed in 1512, the very year that Pietro Torrigiano began work on the king's bronze tomb that was to occupy the centre of the self-same building.[5] A remarkably pure example of the high Italian Renaissance in an alien Northern setting. Perhaps inevitably, for such a revolutionary work in England, Torrigiano's activities did not go unnoticed amongst English artisans. By 1516 hand-bills were pasted up anonymously on the walls in London streets accusing the king of favouring foreign craftsmen to the detriment of those who were native-born.[6] Possibly as a somewhat tardy response to such pressure a Proclamation was issued in 1523 which excluded all but the elite from employing foreign artisans. This elite was defined as a Member of Parliament or individuals with an annual income of £100 or more.[7] In effect this was a sumptuary law which probably had the effect of making work by foreign artisans and artists all the more desirable and fashionable. This may have given the new Renaissance idiom the driving force which ultimately eclipsed the late Gothic tradition. By the mid-sixteenth century artists and craftsmen, with something of a classical taste, began arriving in England from the Low Countries. These immigrants settled in areas like Southwark, south of the Thames in Surrey, and therefore beyond the control of the London guilds. As a consequence classicism in England was, for several generations, to be mediated through Dutch eyes. In addition to Southwark there were, in the London area, a number of free-trade zones which enabled foreigners to practice their craft irrespective of the provisions of the Proclamation of 1523. By 1678 the corporate memory of that Proclamation appears to have faded from memory. On 16 November of that year the sculptors John van der Stein (fl. 1678–1700) and Arnold "Luellan" (Quellin 1653–1686) and their servants (probably apprentices) were granted a dispensation to work for the crown – a "Licence to Forainers employed at Windsor [Castle] to remain here without molestation." Some of these individuals may have been Roman Catholics which could, possibly, account for this extra measure against the protectionism of native artisans. In 1708 an act of Parliament was passed "for naturalizing of foreign Protestants". Under this provision the German-born painter Johann Zoffany RA (1733–1810), obtained letters of denization despite being a Catholic. Far less liberal was the prohibition that the Corporation of London placed on Freemen who, from 1731, were not to be permitted to take on black apprentices.[8]

The Proclamation of 1523, as a form of sumptuary law, established two cultural registers; one for the elite and another for the vast majority of the English population. This is a feature that Robert Redfield, writing in the 1930s, defined as the "great tradition" which he contrasted to the "little tradition".[9] This thesis has more recently been developed by Peter Burke who argues that the aristocracy and gentry continued to participate in the "little tradition" down to the seventeenth century. Burke also notes that craftsmen, like agricultural workers, spoke what was, in effect, a dialect of specialist terms within their largely visual culture with its oral component. More to the point Burke goes on to assert that craftsmen were inevitably "better at using their hands than using words ... The artefacts which they produced are our most immediate contact" but that it is necessary to translate this material culture "from paint, or wood, or stone, into words." It also explains why, in 1798, some surprise was expressed that a carver and gilder like Jackson could write so well.[10] These issues are surely part of the timeless conundrum that things are more difficult to read than words. In this respect many of the writers on the visual arts, from Vasari (1550) to Hogarth (1753) were well placed as practitioners, to provide a bridge between the visual and the verbal. This direction of travel, this sequence of thinking, could also operate in reverse; from the lexicons of the written word to the practicalities of the man-made object. Such was the position of the great Dr Samuel Johnson (1709–1784). It was he who, when praising a group of canvases by James Barry (1741–1806), went on to observe that; "Whatever the hand has done the mind has played its part."[11]

The biographical approach to art history which Vasari may be seen to have established, has proved to be remarkably persistent. However, as a painter and architect, an important feature of his encyclopaedic work is that it was prefaced by an account of the materials and procedures deployed by the artists whose lives he chronicles. This important element is often omitted from later editions of the *Lives*.[12] To Vasari we should perhaps attribute "the cult of the individual" with regard to painters and sculptors. This was inevitably followed by the rise in anecdotal evidence, a corpus of information which, compared with statistical analysis, is often viewed with suspicion. Certainly economic historians like John Michael Montias and Lorna Weatherill have done much to widen and deepen our understanding of art and artisans within a wider socio-economic framework.[13] In retrieving the past, statistical findings have their value, but so too does the recorded word of mouth. Surely those who bore witness to the events of their own time, the mood of the moment, the character of their contemporaries, have valuable evidence to offer? The utility of such testimony is evident in J. T. Smith's *Nollekens and His Times* (1828) and in Joseph Farington's *Diary* (1793–1821). Indeed Horace Walpole (pub. 1762–1771) and Edward Edwards (1808) identify their respective publications on *Painting* as *Anecdotes.*[14]

In Early Modern Europe many of the artists who wrote about their vocation were not above describing the rudiments of their craft. In contrast a painter like Reynolds was so anxious to emphasise the intellectual dignity and social status of easel painting and painters that he elided the details of the "mechanic" parts of his art. Such disdain did not go unrecognised by his contemporaries. For John Williams, under the alias of Anthony Pasquin (1796), the great Sir Joshua was as "injurous to the true principles of painting as a fine prostitute to the establishment of morals."[15]

Although "Oil & Colourmen" were long established in London, Sir Joshua and his contemporaries in the capital were amongst the first to be able to purchase ready-made, industrially produced, oil paints. Consequently he and his contemporaries were in a position to distance themselves from the craft of their art. For Reynolds such hauteur was near disaster. His pigments on the one hand had a tendency to fade or, alternatively, his use of bitumen caused them to darken and crack. Most seriously this was an attitude which made him an easy victim of the "Venetian Secret" with its promise of an elixir of everlasting Titian.[16] In the deployment of materials and techniques failures, like successes, serve to demonstrate the importance of the artist's craft in realising a given concept.

As noted above, those artists who functioned in a pre-industrial situation were profoundly aware that the crafts that brought handmade objects into existence were an integral part of their presence. Analogy may offer a usefully oblique approach to the visual arts in a way that by-passes the drifting meaning of words. In some senses these arts may be characterised as a combination of the material (the utilitarian or secular) with a concept which may be described as the spiritual component of a work of sculpture or painting. These problems of usage and definition may involve an ostensibly simple noun like "patron". And yet in the Anglo-French of medieval England a patron signified a pattern – a maquette or a model for a work of art.[17] Only later did the "patron" also come to signify the client. As late as the seventeenth century these "patrons" or patterns would form part of a detailed specification which the maker or artist was to follow in accordance with the contract.[18] By these means the client formed an active part in the creative process. In contrast the purchase of a ready-made object was not patronage but commerce.

This raises important questions as to the degree to which a patron might have sufficient knowledge and discernment to discharge his or her responsibilities

FIGURE 1. Francis Hayman (1708–1776 *The Artist and his Patron c.* 1748–50, oil on canvas (71.8 × 91.4 cm). This image demonstrates the active participation of the client in the creation of a picture in a largely pre-consumerist age. (National Portrait Gallery, London)

effectively. Inevitably clients possessed various levels of understanding and expertise and therefore their involvement as patrons differed. On an architectural scale many of the prelates in medieval England were described as "builders" of their respective abbeys or cathedrals – although this was generally little more than a courtesy offered to these individuals as patrons in both senses of the word. In some cases though the princes of the church are known to have participated more actively as craftsmen or, more generally, as labourers. For example, St Hugh of Avalon (1140–1200) as Bishop of Lincoln "often bore the hodload of hewn stone or binding lime" to assist with the construction of the Cathedral. By the sixteenth century the wider availability of paper encouraged patrons to become involved in the design process. In 1539 a fort at Cowes, on the Isle of Wight, was to be built "according to the platte devised by the King", although this plan may well have been drawn up by others and received little more than Henry VIII's imprimatur it nevertheless received his visual approval.[19] Certainly many royal or aristocratic clients, on the basis of a "liberal" education, were very well informed. Take, for example Queen Elizabeth I's instructions to her limner Nicholas Hilliard (*c.* 1547–1619) that he should take her portrait "in the open alley of a goodly garden" where there would be no "shadowe".[20] This demonstrates that the queen was well aware that such a location would offer the most flattering light. A similarly active engagement existed amongst patrons in relationship to monumental sculpture. In common with many aristocrats, both before and since, the sixth Earl of Shrewsbury spent much of his time in his last years in the late 1580s working on the design of his own tomb.[21] In the following century Lord Arundel went so far as to argue that "one who could not design a little would never make an honest man".[22] For some grandees their responsibilities as clients were not particularly active but their visual perception could remain acute: "A man of Polite Imagination ... can converse with a Picture, and find an agreeable companion in a Statue". One such was the antiquarian and libertine 1st Earl of Charlemont (1728–1799) who was quick to condemn Richard Dalton's drawings of Halicarnassus as "faint and inadequate copies", a view that was shared by many of his contemporaries.[23] For others the role of the patron was little more than administrative. Horace Walpole (1717–1797) on a visit to Northamptonshire considered it:

> "a great sacrifice for I quit the gallery [at Strawberry Hill] almost at the critical minute of consumation. Gilders, carvers, upholsterers and picture cleaners are labouring at their several forges, and I do not love to trust a hammer or brush without my own supervisal ..." [24]

Alternatively patronage could be far more "hands-on" than was the case with an aesthete like Walpole. This was particularly true of the applied arts. In the preface to Joseph Moxon's *Mechanic Exercises or Doctrine of Handy Works* (published in parts from 1678) its author states that: "it is very well known, that many Gentlemen in this Nation, of good Rank and high Quality, are conversant in Handy-Works: And other Nations exceed us in numbers of such." Although Moxon fails to identify the "Nations" or individuals he had in mind a number of possibilities might be considered. Among these was the Swedish nobleman Carl Gustaf Wrangle (1613–1676) who worked at a lathe in his workshop in Skokloster Castle.[25] In this activity Wrangle may have been following royal precedence for turnery was the craft that was indulged in by Christian IV (1588–1648) of Denmark. Examples of this work, allegedly by the king, can be seen in Rosenborg Castle, Copenhagen. In France, no less a figure than the "Sun King", Louis XIV, gained a reputation as an amateur lock-smith. As Moxon was evidently aware, European precedent permitted the elite to work at a craft. At the very least this would have enabled them to have an informed insight into the quality of what was made for them. Some such individuals appear to have made the "patrons" or "patterns" that were used as the basis for the works they commissioned – a far more practical basis than a mere drawing. For example the landowner Sir George Savile MP (1726–1784) went so far as to make a scale model (1 inch: 1 foot) in oak of a five-bar gate which was passed to his estate carpenters to make-up at full size (Fig. 2). This may have been unusual but it was by no means exceptional since there was a market in London for "Gentlemen's Tool Chests" which contained implements for working wood of the type sold in the 1770s by William Hewlett (Fig. 3). By 1785 *The Daily Universal Register,* the precursor of *The Times,* included an advertisement for the sale of such tool kits.[26] These are not isolated examples. Dr Bartholomew Moss, the Dublin physician and amateur cabinet-maker left, on his death in 1761, a "set of tools fit for a gentleman or nice mechanic." One such "gentleman" was William Windham (1717–1761) of Felbrigg Hall, Norfolk who was such an enthusiastic wood turner, boat builder and book-binder that he reserved two large rooms in his house as workshops.[27] In the early nineteenth century the involvement of the gentry and aristocracy in these activities was probably quite widespread, they were, after all, members of the leisured classes. In 1817 Capt. Sherston of Stowbury near Wells was described as: "a good mechanic ... [with] an excellent lathe; at present he is busily occupied in completing a musical clock".

By 1830 the Rev John Skinner who recorded this observation in his Journal would go on to describe Owen, one of his two sons, "amusing himself with his lathe" which was installed in the Rectory at Camerton in North Somerset. Similarly Henry Peyto Verney (1773–1852) of Compton Verney House, Warwickshire, is known to have purchased tools and lathes for making the prototypes of the various mechanisms he devised. In North America an inventory of George Washington's possessions (taken in 1799) recorded "1 Chest of Tools" in his study. In 1786 Thomas Jefferson purchased "a chest of tools" from Thomas Robinson in London.[28]

In some rare instances it seems that such interests were not confined to gentlemen. For example the aristocratic Mary Talbot (1776–1855) owned a couple of woodworking lathes. One of these was purchased for her in 1811 by her husband from "Mr Hotzapful" (Holtzapffel of London) for £24-6s-6d and included a "tool case".[29] These were sent to Penrice Castle their country house in south Wales. The second lathe was located in their other establishment, Melbury House, Dorset. These two lathes were used by Mary Talbot for making dolls in their house in Wales whilst the device in Dorset was employed for the production of "beautiful beads for necklaces, bracelets etc. etc." made from the bark of a Scotch fir tree.[30] Although these skills were of varying relevance to our theme they demonstrate that potential patrons might well have a hands-on understanding as to how things were made. Such individuals would have pronounced views on the quality of the craftsmanship in the works of art they commissioned or purchased and a practical understanding of the work of the artists they employed. In these circumstances "Sculptors of eminence [would] not submit to the directions of the *ignorant* employer … however powerful his station in life may be".[31]

From about 1716, if not before, artists in London had access to ready-made oil paints, manufactured by horse mills, the products of which were sold by oil and colourmen to both house and easel painters. For many decades this trade was dominated by the Emerton dynasty of "Colourmen". By the 1770s the Reeves brothers had devised their watercolour cakes – the first of what might be described as "convenience paints" to be marketed.[32] The ramifications of this innovation would be extensive and long lasting. Professional artists who were not specialist limners could now use watercolour out-of-doors and paint landscapes in the presence of nature. In addition amateurs, in both the exact and inexact meaning of the word, could now more easily participate in an art that had previously been largely the preserve of specialists. Amongst architects their drawings could now more often be given polychromatic washes – a feature that may well have influenced the type of light and airy colour schemes that came into fashion for interiors at about this time. For aspiring naval and army officers drawing had long been part of their training in various military academies – now these range finding landscapes and coastal studies sprang into lively colour. In all these circumstances an active participation in the visual arts was not only possible, but almost compulsory for the elite. Queen Charlotte was a student of Gainsborough and George III was tutored in architecture (and architectural drawing) by Chambers. Amongst the aristocracy the 2nd Lord Harcourt (1736–1809) exhibited his etchings with the Society of Arts and for some families easel painting could become a feature of their shade of blue blood – as was the case with the 3rd, 5th and 6th Dukes of Rutland. Despite such aristocratic precedent the north Somerset rector the Rev John Skinner (1772–1834) was ambivalent with regard to the social position of painters. In noting his son Joseph's "natural talents for drawing" he fleetingly thought of placing him with Benjamin Baker of Bath (1776–1838) "for his learning to paint in oils" but concluded that "this profession of an artist is infra-dig". The contradictions inherent in that phrase were probably widely shared at that date

FIGURE 2. *Model gate* made of oak by Sir George Savile (1726–1784): his marble bust by Nollekens is illustrated as Fig. 124. This 5-bar gate is made to a scale of 1 in : 1 ft, producing, what remains to this day, a standard width of 10 ft 4 in (215 cm) (Author's Collection)

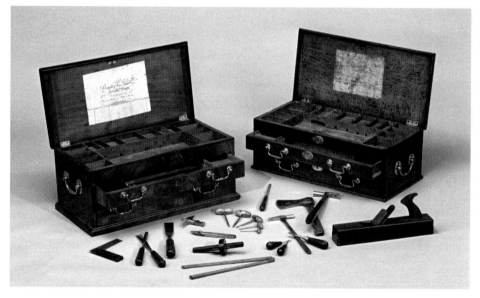

FIGURE 3. Two "*Gentlemen's tool chests*" retailed by the London ironmonger William Hewlett in *c.* 1773. A number of potential patrons of the visual arts possessed a hands-on understanding of a craft (Colonial Williamsburg Foundation, Virginia)

(2 August 1830) – easel painting may, by this time, have been a profession but it was not quite "proper".[33]

With industrialisation and the rise of consumerism the traditional notions of patronage were in decline.[34] By gradual increments the well informed patron of the past gave way to purchasers who acquired works of art from dealers who sold "old masters" or contemporary works that were speculatively produced. As early as the 1750s some regretted that:

"generally speaking [many artists had become] the property of picture dealers (at that time their chief employers) and held by them in somewhat the same kind of vassalage and dependence that many authors are by booksellers."[35]

This situation was fraught with potential conflict. The Swiss-born painter Jean André Rouquet (1701–1758) observed that English artists fought against the interests of the picture dealers.[36] As the nature of patronage changed so too did the relationships between clients and artists which were, in part, a consequence of the intervention of art dealers. Despite this quiet revolution old attitudes persisted. When King George III visited the Academy exhibition on 22 April 1796 it was his presumption that the works on show were commissioned by true patrons.[37] Only a few months later, on 9 July 1796, Henry Fuseli RA (1741–1825) admitted that he had trouble working "on given subjects which he is employed to paint. His best exertions are when he had only to consider how he shall satisfy himself."[38] In much the same vein George Morland (1763–1804) was compelled, through his profligate lifestyle, to submit to the "drudgery" of undertaking commissions.[39] In general portraiture was, almost by definition, the product of a commission – a role not necessarily enjoyed by all such clients.

"Of all the miseries under the sun to which poor mortal man is heir, Heaven preserve, or rather release me from those of a patron … Scarcely a year passes but I am to be found stuck up somewhere [in an exhibition] about the walls of Somerset House."[40]

With the rise of consumerism art was increasingly acquired "off the peg" in exhibitions – paintings and sculptures which were ready-made and available for purchase. In the historic sense of the word patronage was all but dead.

The seeds of this change, from patronage as a prospective activity, to consumption as a passive indulgence, date back before the Reformation – but in medieval England such transactions were the exception.[41] Mass, or at least bulk production, continued as a minor feature in the arts of Tudor and Stuart England. For example, once canvas sizes were standardised, carvers and gilders were able to produce picture frames in anticipation of their sale. A similar situation prevailed in early Georgian London amongst the sign-makers, a specialist trade involving painters, carvers and blacksmiths. These tradesmen were centred on Harp Alley off Shoe Lane, Fleet Street.[42] This was where Thomas Proctor (Fig. 62) stocked "all sorts of *Signs, Bushes, Bacchus's, Bunches of Grapes and Show-Boards*" from what he claimed was "The Oldest Shop" in the Alley.[43] These were clearly standard products for which bulk production made sense. As such, this aspect of Proctor's trade is a clear, and rather early, example of consumerism in the visual arts. However, he and others in the Harp Alley workshops, also worked on commission. In this way these craftsmen straddled two distinct approaches in the sale of their work. An awareness of these changes may have been present in the minds of those who were responsible for the foundation of the Society for the Encouragement of Arts, Manufacturers and Commerce in 1754 (now the Royal Society of Arts, RSA). One the most significant figures behind this Society was the drawing teacher William Shipley (1715–1803) who was well placed to propose that this organisation should give:

> "Rewards for the Encouragement of Boys and Girls in the Art of Drawing, and it being the opinion of all present that the Art of Drawing is absolutely necessary in many Employments, Trades and Manufactures and that the Encouragement thereof may prove of great utility to the Public, it was resolved to bestow Premiums on a certain number of Boys and Girls under the age of Sixteen, who shall produce the best Pieces of Drawing ..."[44]

By 1797 the link between art and manufacture was also noted by Academicians like the chaser George Michael Moser (1704–1783), the sculptor John Flaxman (1755–1826) and the painters Joseph Farington (1747–1821), John Hoppner (1758–1810) and Benjamin West (1738–1820) (see pp. 88–89 below).[45]

In a list of premiums, drawn up by the Society of Arts in 1758, prizes were offered for drawings that related to the polite arts which included such subject matter as the human figure, "Beasts, Birds, Fruit or Flowers" (although some of these prizes were reserved for those who attended the St Martin's Lane Academy). The same list also offered premiums for design drawings for weavers, calico-printers, cabinet-makers (see Fig. 9) and coach-makers as well as for manufacturers working in iron, brass, porcelain, earthenware or "any other Mechanic Trade that requires Taste".[46]

Of the various materials used for drawing in both art and industry, for both aesthetic and technical purposes, charcoal and ink have a long history and these were joined by silver-point and the humble lead pencil. The latter was in fact composed of graphite which, being brittle, was encased in wood. In Britain graphite was found in the Lake District where it was known as "wadd", and in New England the source of this black-lead, as it was also known, was in Rhode Island. In neighbouring Massachusetts pencils using this mineral were manufactured by the family of the writer Henry Thoreau (1817–1862) who took an active part in the business.[47] In the 1750s the graphite mines in Borrowdale near Keswick were owned by "an Irish Gentleman by the name of Shepherd". He ensured that this mineral was only extracted in an occasional summer simply because enough could be extracted "to satisfy the small demand in England for several years".[48]

In Hanoverian England references to the association between art and industry refer to "manufactures", simply because these early manifestations of industrial development were the "manual factories" that preceded the more fully mechanised enterprises.[49] Consequently, the distinction between an early industrialist's manufactory and an artist's studio (fully staffed with apprentices, journeymen, and other assistants) may have been less evident than they subsequently became.

The practical approach that saw the "fine arts" as the basis for the production of the "applied" or "decorative arts" seems to have been a widely held, if not unchallenged, view. Joseph Farington recorded both positions in his *Diary* in 1797. He notes that although there was a general belief that "the fine arts [could be an] elegant amusement purchased at considerable expense" it was important for a "Commercial People" to remember that these arts "will enrich as well as embellish" the nation.[50] This was a time when the fine arts were increasingly being purchased as pre-existing objects, a situation made possible by the burgeoning number of exhibitions of contemporary art.

The first collection of contemporary paintings in England that was fully accessible to the public was formed by the Foundling Hospital in London (est. 1739) although it should be added that by this date country house tourism was already in place offering access to numerous private collections.[51] A number of artists contributed their works to the Foundling Hospital including Hayman, Highmore, Hudson, Hogarth and Ramsay and their canvases were later joined by those of Gainsborough, Reynolds and Benjamin West (see p. 433 below).[52]

By 1760 the first annual exhibition of contemporary art was shown in the rooms of the Society of Arts. Then on 25 April 1769 the Royal Academy followed this precedent with the opening of their first such show, a tradition that continues to this day. The Academy's regulations for their exhibitions stipulated that "No copies Nor any Pictures without Frames will be admitted." It was also determined that an entrance fee would be payable to prevent the gallery from becoming too crowded "by improper Persons." The works for sale were to be marked in the catalogue by an asterisk suggesting that a majority of works were commissioned.[53] With the exception of portraiture, that was generally created for a specific client, these shows were, in the long run, to be dominated by speculative productions.

The Academy's exhibitions became, with their royal patronage, an immediate success with the London social season, but their impact on the visual arts was not always welcomed. In 1781 an article appeared in *The Morning Chronicle* that noted their adverse effect in "their tendency to make the artist force his effects ... making their work more assertive."[54] Exhibitions were not seen simply as neutral undertakings for the encouragement of the arts but events that played an active role in influencing the work that was produced to show in them. A similar tendency was noted in the competitions that were held for students at the Royal Academy Schools. In 1772 the student sculptor Thomas Englehart (1745–1809) won the gold medal for a relief and triumphed over his contemporary in the schools: John Flaxman (1755–1826). Englehart's success was not universally applauded. One critic favoured Flaxman's submission and observed that: "What is original seems at first to many merely outré, and every deviation from the beaten track must needs be error."[55]

Here the implication is that the gold medallist worked to the taste, the received opinion, of the judges whereas Flaxman's more "outré" work was more "original". From these attitudes it is evident that in the changed circumstances in which artists now functioned they were not simply at liberty to experiment, they would eventually be all-but compelled to do so.

In previous generations successful artists would employ a whole studio of assistants; be they apprentices, journeymen or specialists in particular aspects of their art or its craft. By these means a given work of art, though emanating from an individual, was in fact the product of a team working under the aegis of the studio. The autographed work was then less central to the concerns of the age than it would later become. This position is reflected in the surviving inventories for the great houses of eighteenth century England. In 1710 Drayton House, Northamptonshire was graced by "One Picture of a girl with a lamb. Thirty seven other Pictures of Several sorts and Sizes." Similarly the 1743 inventory for Ditchley Park, Oxfordshire, lists "prints … of harlots progress … in Pear tree frames wth Gilt Edges and a whole length of Queen Elizab[th] in a Gilt frame."[56] In the age of patronage the emphasis was on the subject, and even the picture frames, but not on the artist. The "Queen Elizab[th]" was the famous "Ditchley Portrait" by Marcus Gheeraerts the Younger (1561/2–1636).[57] By 1772 this outlook had changed and the Ditchley inventory for that year lists among other pictures "19 Hogarth's Prints of Marriage a la Mode the Harlots Progress &c and 4 others" thus giving primacy to the artist's name.

The presence of signatures on works of art in Britain is, generally speaking, a phenomenon that followed the Reformation.[58] Once introduced the autographed work was to acquire, over time, more social prestige and consequent financial value. These intrinsic and extrinsic properties would eventually offer mutual advantage to both the purchaser and the maker. One of the earliest examples of a signature on an English statuary's work dates to 1573. In that year John Guldon of Hereford placed his name on the monument to John Harford in Bosbury Church in the county.[59] This whole question of the identification of the maker occurs in the 1581/82 *Book of Ordinancies* of the Painter Stainers of London. Article 8 in this list of regulations states that all works produced by members of the fraternity were to carry "the marks of the house [studio/workshop] ... to be appointed by the Master and Wardens [of the Guild]... to be known for good work. One penny to be paid for every piece so marked".[60] It is not known if this type of "hallmark", such as that which had for long been administered by the Goldsmith's Company, was ever introduced on a regular basis. Furthermore, although the approved mark was presumably recorded by the Company, it would probably have taken an enigmatic abstract form that did not reveal a name – rather like a mason's mark. Such a "mark of the house" would have done nothing to foster the "cult of the individual" amongst painters and sculptors in the way that signatures would later do.

The workshop system, in which artists and artisans not only produced an item but also provided a service, persisted into the eighteenth century and beyond.[61] In other words a portrait painter would not simply create a likeness on the canvas, but would organise its framing, crating, dispatch and hanging. The sense of a contractual obligation is implicit in the following receipt issued by the painter Joseph Wright of Derby (1734–1797) in 1783.

RECEIPT for the Coke Conversation Piece

Dan¹. Parker Coke Esq	£75 – 12 – 0
Frame for Dº	6 – 5 – 5
Case	1 – 0 – 9
Portage	0 – 1 – 0
Carriage	0 – 10 – 6
	83 – 9 – 8
Joiner	2 – 2 – 5
	£85 – 12 – 1

Received 7th Jan 1783[62]

The employment of the joiner, being something of an afterthought, suggests that this tradesman uncrated the painting and hung it on arrival. This receipt for a painting is comparable to a bill dated 12 June 1821 for a mirror frame supplied by George Cooper of Piccadilly ("opposite St James's Church") to Thomas Stevens Esq.

Chimney Glass in carved and gilt frame	£50 – 00 – 0
Packing case to Dº	3 – 06 – 0
Insurance on the Plate	1 – 16 – 0
Agreed Nett Price	55 – 02 – 0[63]

In comparing these two transactions the similarity between art and artefact is obvious. Significantly only the typically high value of the plate glass for the mirror is covered by an insurance premium.

As we shall see an artist's workshop in Early Modern Britain employed apprentices, journeymen and other assistants. Only some of these individuals could hope, in the long term, to become master craftsmen and still fewer would evolve into artists in their own right. Whatever their aspirations this was a system in which all could maintain some sort of employment. For a minority with connections, luck, skill or ability (in roughly that order) success could beckon. Apprenticeships for trades of many kinds conformed well to the needs of studio practice. Numerous crafts offered skills that were relevant to either painters or sculptors. For this reason the following three or four chapters will consider, in some detail, the Guilds and the apprentices they supervised. This will show how, in the years following the Civil War and into the mid-eighteenth century, the power of the Guilds as trade organisations declined as that of Academies rose in influence and the social position of artists changed. These events were accompanied by a parallel and associated transition from empirical training to a theoretical education in the fine arts. In other words there was a discernable shift from an apprenticeship to a pupilage. During this move from one system to the other there was some inevitable overlap. For this reason establishments like the St Martin's Lane Academy or the Duke of Richmond's cast gallery offered part-time schooling. Most significant was the demand for "drawing from the naked", something that was not hitherto available to apprentices and seldom affordable for their masters. The life classes, in the St Martin's Lane establishment, were therefore conducted during the evenings at the end of the working day and those who attended ranged from youthful apprentices to established artists.

As has been noted this evolution in art education was coupled with the rise of consumerism and the potential this gave artists to produce works in anticipation of selling them. In this respect the foundation of the Royal Academy with its annual market place (the exhibitions) may be seen as the response, by a collective of artists, to industrialisation and consumerism.[64] With speculative production and the availability of industrially produced oil paints it was both necessary and possible for painters to keep costs to a minimum. This probably had a deleterious impact on the workshop system amongst painters. Whilst these studios were now able to employ far fewer assistants the autographed work grew in importance. Now that artists were functioning as largely solo performers the presentation of their work to the public gained in importance. For this reason private galleries, or "show rooms" as they were known, were attached to the studios of successful artists – or space was rented for this purpose. A considerable income could be generated by the "show-rooms". In 1781 some 20,000 individuals paid one shilling each to view John Singleton Copley's *Death of Chatham*. Some decades later in January 1813 Copley's fellow American Benjamin West PRA took the "Great Room" at 125 Pall Mall (a former home of the RA) to exhibit his enormous canvas (34 × 16 ft/1036 × 488 cm) *Christ Rejected by the Jews*. The picture was shown beyond a proscenium arch to increase its already theatrical effect still further (Fig. 136).[65] These "show Rooms" were not confined to painters for both Chantrey and Westmacott displayed their sculpture in such galleries.[66]

Sculpture was always a capital intensive activity. This was one reason why the most successful practitioners continued to employ a large number of assistants well into the nineteenth century. Furthermore sculptors like Flaxman maintained the tradition of "fine artists" making "applied art" – as, for example, chimneypieces. The equivalent decorative work by "liberal painters", items like chimney boards and overmantel pictures, gradually fell into disfavour amongst them whilst sculptors remained oblivious to this kind of apartheid in the visual arts. Not that these diverse activities were always necessarily seen with such equanimity by their potential clients. Lady Luxborough's opinion of Prince Hoare of Bath (1711–1769) may have been typical. Hoare, she observed, "although a statuary … deigns to exercise his art in sculpture on humble paper [-mâché] ceilings" although her ladyship had the good grace to acknowledge that his work was "very handsome".[67]

As we have seen the availability of mass produced paints, especially in London, enabled painters to function with the aid of very few assistants – particularly by comparison with past practice. For this reason a landscape or history painting could be a speculative venture involving the minimum of financial risk. Consequently commissions were to become the exception. By the 1790s the painter Sir Peter Francis Bourgeois (1756–1811) was resistant to more contractural obligations and consequently sold his canvases by auction where "some sold better, some worse" as is usual with such sales. By 1796 "many works" in the Academy's annual show were "painted purposely for exhibition."[68] As noted above this led to the assumption that the remaining works on show were commissions. These approaches to the making and marketing of a particular canvas could be undertaken in one of two ways. In 1796 Robert Smirke RA (1752–1845) agreed to paint Shakespeare's *Seven Ages of Man* "on speculation" and then, a couple of years later in 1798, accepted a commission to portray *Otahite* for a fee of £300.[69]

The use of ready-made and prepared canvases by painters led, inexorably, to standardised dimensions for these and the frames that encompassed them. This seems to have occurred at a surprisingly early date. The physician Sir Theodore de Mayerne (1573–1655) was given a recipe for priming canvas by a Walloon, living in London in the early seventeenth century, who was a specialist imprimeur. At this time Dutch painters were using ready-made oak panels imported from the Baltic – a trade with which English merchants were certainly engaged. A century later, when Kneller painted his series of portraits of members of the Kit-Cat dining club between 1702 and 1717 they were painted on canvases that, even then, were considered to be of an unusual dimension – 36 × 28 in (91.5 × 71 cm). So standardised had canvases become that oddities of this dimension have been known ever since as "Kit-cats".[70]

The availability of ready-made oil paints was, as noted above, followed in the 1770s by the watercolour cakes developed by the Reeves Brothers and finally, in 1841, by John G. Rand's collapsible metal tubes for oil paint.[71] In the wake of these innovations a vast army of amateur artists were, for the first time, able to work in these media. Because bladder colours, the precursors to tube oil paint, were difficult to use (or rather reuse) professional painters were, more often than not, compelled to have their paints and pigments prepared "in house". Once manufactured paints became widely available this became an aspect of their craft that many painters were able to abandon. For Reynolds, and his contemporaries in London, painting could be freed from the bondage of manual craft and accepted as a "liberal art" with cerebral aspirations. Freed from these practical considerations, and with far fewer (if any) assistants, successful painters could now work long and curious hours. In 1796 Benjamin West was "subject to so many interruptions in the day, of late He paints most by Candle light after tea till 12 o'clock [midnight] or later and that the strong light from his lamp enables him to see better than by day light".[72] Working in this way could result in rather theatrical effects, not that this discouraged Sir Thomas Lawrence (1769–1830) from following West's example. Lawrence was known, whilst "residing in Jermyn Street", and later in Bond Street: to paint by "the overpowering blaze of a large screen reflecting several Argand lamps, from nine or ten at night until three or five in the morning; and, after a few hours rest, go to his palette again."[73]

In Stuart England a few knighthoods were bestowed on foreign artists – although in the case of Peter Paul Rubens this honour may have had more to do with his activities as an international diplomat than his prodigious gifts as a painter.[74] The first English artist to be so honoured by the Hanoverians was Sir James Thornhill (1675–1734) but he came from a gentry family in Dorset so his knighthood (of 1720) scarcely marks the rising status of artists at that time. This was an age in which social position mattered. Nevertheless personal demeanour could advance some fortunate individuals. Take, for example William Kent (1685–1748). Although his training was limited and his background modest he emerged from provincial Yorkshire as a figure of consequence on the national design scene. From humble beginnings, probably as a coach painter, he became the archetypical self-made man. Perhaps there was a streak of envy that led one commentator to remark that Kent was:

> "among those fortunate men who, without high qualities of mind or force of imagination, obtain wealth and distinction through good sense, easy assurance, and that happy boldness of manner which goes rejoicing along the way where original merit often hesitates and stumbles"[75]

Although the alleged lack of a "high quality" of mind must remain a matter of opinion, Kent certainly became dependent upon the patronage of the "high born" Richard Boyle 3rd Earl of Burlington which conferred some reflected status.

In the century in which Kent was born social class was an unavoidable issue although in this respect the professions held a distinct position. For the Quaker George Fox (1624–1691), who had been apprenticed as a shoe-maker, there were just three professions: the clergy, physicians and lawyers. Not that their situation was unassailable. For Nicholas Culpeper writing in 1649 "the liberty of our Commonwealth [was] most infringed by three sorts of men: Priests, Physitions, Lawyers". Late in the century Gregory King identified six degrees of persons which suggests a more subtle social gradation, and therefore the mobility in status, of which Kent may have been one of the beneficiaries. Certainly, in the London of Queen Anne, Peter Earle estimated that about one fifth of the population had a claim to be categorised as middle class.[76] Across the Atlantic, in the American slave-owning state of Virginia, Patrick Henry (1736–1799) identified four classes of people: the "well-born" planters, the "hearty yeoman", the "lower orders" of landless poor whites and the slaves (who represented about 40% of the population).[77] For later generations of artists the potential for crossing these social divides increased. The painter John Opie RA (1761–1807), from far off Cornwall, was one such. After his move to London it was said of him that "His habitual ruggedness of address was stigmatised by the courtly observer" despite which many of the members of polite society accepted this "with a kind of joyful astonishment".[78]

Anecdotes of this kind are inevitably more concerned with the artist than with the art. It would seem that as painters emerged from their obligations to their patrons they could more easily develop as personalities in their own right. One rather superficial manifestation of this related to matters of clothing and personal appearance. In this respect artists were now able to be as varied as any other group of individuals. Richard Wilson, when attending the St Martin's Lane Academy was always "superbly dressed" and his waistcoat was "of the richest green satin, ornamented with gold lace". Some, like George Henry Harlow appeared in "the extreme of fashion" so that he became "the laughing stock of his brother artists".[79] The young George Morland (1763–1804)[80] was known for "the very extreme of foppism" in dress but even he was outdone by the effete appearance of Richard Cosway RA (1740–1830). Cosway was highly respected as a painter by his contemporaries although as a person Sir Thomas Lawrence (1769–1830) referred to him as "that little being we have been accustomed never to speak or think of but with contempt."[81] W. H. Pyne was more forgiving in arguing that the quality of Cosway's work "shall stand recorded long after his harmless eccentricities have been forgotten and all his ghosts quietly laid in the Red Sea."[82] For a slightly earlier generation it was said of the portrait painter Thomas King that he was "… one of those men who suppose an eccentric line of conduct to be the mark or privilege of genius."[83]

Eccentricity of dress, then as now, could be deployed for promotional effect. To some extent John Opie's appearance was stage-managed. On being asked why the rustic Opie was not presented in a more polished guise Wolcot responded:

> "No! No! You may depend on it, in this wonder-gaping town [London], all curiosity would cease if his hair were dressed and he looked like any other man. I shall keep him in this state for the next five years at least".[84]

Outside the inevitable grime of their studios sculptors were no less various in their dress. Flaxman, for example, never wore powder in his wig or hair "nor did he ever attempt to exhibit ornaments of finery". In contrast "Mr Wilton … always dressed in the height of fashion [but] his manners … were perfectly gentlemanlike"[85] (Fig. 94).

From the standpoint of the twenty-first century, with its supposed egalitarianism, questions of social standing, if not appearance, may seem irrelevant. Nevertheless with the foundation of the Royal Academy of Arts in 1768, an officer class was established amongst painters, sculptors and architects. An Academician was now expected to be an artist and a gentleman (or lady, as the case may have been). As with a commission in the army or navy "the diploma granted to every Academician, on his becoming a member, … has the king's sign manual and gives him the rank of Esquire".[86] Despite their improved social standing artists now emerged from a great variety of backgrounds and foregrounds in terms of birth, training or education; differing circumstances which had the potential to place the Academy in something of a dilemma. For example, it was noted that its President's "pronunciation was tinctured with the accent of Devonshire, his features coarse and his outward appearance slovenly." In a courtly age these were seen as serious disadvantages. However, Sir Joshua Reynolds' redeeming features included a "mind that was certainly not inelegant".[87] A more significant predicament for the Academy occurred in 1797 when John Rossi (1762–1839) was proposed as an Associate RA. According to his fellow sculptor Sir Joseph Wilton RA (1722–1803), Rossi was a "very ingenious Artist but not a cultivated man." To its credit the Academy elected him an Associate RA in 1798. Despite this, in 1800, just as Rossi was on the verge of being promoted to full RA, the question of his demeanour arose again. Wilton repeated his opinion that "Rossi wanted gentlemanly and suitable manners" although his claims as an artist were high.[88] Once again the Academy got its priorities right and the candidate was elected to full membership. On the other hand Rossi's lack of urbanity may have inhibited his professional advancement. In the 1790s he was commissioned to model a small portrait of the Prince of Wales from life. On one of his visits for this work the Prince kept him waiting three hours while he first saw his shoemaker and tailor. Even worse, on a subsequent visit the sculptor waited in vain for five hours.[89]

Perhaps the most obvious example of the unity of art and craft as manifest in the English language is the noun "masterpiece". This word is defined in the *Shorter Oxford English Dictionary* (2 vols 2003) as: "A work of outstanding artistry or skill; a masterly production; a consummate example of some skill or other kind of excellence … a person's best piece of work". This rather schizophrenic interpretation is biased in favour of the historical definition rather than the modern understanding that a "masterpiece" is a supreme example of artistic endeavour. In the exact, the historic, the pre-industrial, sense of the word a "masterpiece" was a specimen of skill. This was the object that an apprentice submitted to the guild, to which he was registered, as a demonstration of his abilities in his chosen *métier* at the conclusion of "his time". If the guild accepted this physical example of his abilities the youth could proceed to employment as a journeyman and, ultimately, gain his freedom to practice his chosen craft (but see pp. 66–67 below for exceptions).[90] Some of these apprentices went on to become master craftsmen of such exemplary quality that, in a well-worn eighteenth century phrase with still earlier origins, they were described as "artists in their trades."[91] Although this was generally a figure of speech it could also be, or become, a literal truth as was the case with the many highly skilled craftsmen who evolved into eminence as artists. This was certainly true of the one-time silver engraver William Hogarth (1697–1764) who as a painter is fully established in the English artistic cannon.[92] Similarly John Bacon RA (1740–1799), following an apprenticeship with Nicholas Crisp, the jeweller and Bow porcelain manufacturer, emerged as a sculptor (Figs 19, 95 and 99).[93]

This kind of metamorphosis from a trade to an art is regularly noted in the biographies of Early Modern artists. There was, in short, nothing particularly unusual in a craft training resulting in an individual becoming a painter or sculptor although the ability to become a true artist has always been the exception. The following chapters are, therefore, a very tentative review of a theme that is wide in historical, craft and artistic terms. To reduce these issues to somewhat more manageable proportions the focus will be on "the long eighteenth century" which, at its longest, may be dated from the Restoration (1660) to the death of William IV (1837). Despite this more reasonably narrow horizon the penumbra is wide. The apprenticeship system and guild structure is medieval in origin and it was then that many of the eternal verities of craftsmanship were established. If the crafts are seen to have reached a plateau of achievement in Early Modern Britian we are brought down to earth by industrialisation which displaced hand wrought artefacts with items produced by machine. In the visual arts "training" gave way to "education", and "making" was accorded less significance than the "concept".

In a pre-industrial context the great number of crafts that were relevant to painting and sculpture was wide and, at times, disconcerting. Furthermore the progression from a given trade did not always follow a logical trajectory. For example: Edward Edwards (1738–1806) John Fernley (1782–1860) and George Romney (1734–1802) built solid reputations as easel painters but all began as apprentices in one of the woodworking trades. Another, rather perplexing, case is that of Edward Burch RA (1730–1814). Quite how he made the transition from being a Thames waterman, to adopting that most difficult of skills in becoming a die-sinker and gem engraver, is unknown but he may have been a waterman by guild affiliation rather than by trade. Certainly watermen were known to develop a spirit of "truculent egalitariasm",[94] a useful outlook for a craftsman such as Burch.

More typically training was both relevant and thorough. In general an apprenticeship in a trade that was applicable to the visual arts would equip a youth with an eye for *line* (e.g. engraving), for *colour* (e.g. sign-painting) or *form* (e.g. wood carving). The association between engraving and drawing skills is obvious. William Blake (1757–1827) was fortunate to be apprenticed to James Basire (1730–1802) a member of a whole dynasty of Huguenot engravers with a very wide experience in this calling.[95] Similarly, the Scottish engraver John

a

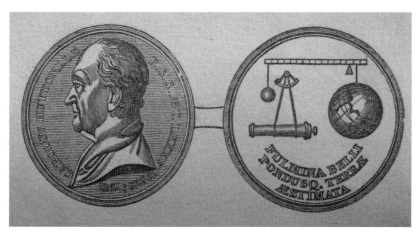

b

FIGURE 4. a) Woodcut by Thomas Bewick (1755–1828) and b) the corresponding image as printed. Note the depth of cuttung for the reverse of this medallion to ensure a white background when printed. This wood engraving formed the frontispiece of John Bruce's *Memoir of Charles Hutton*, Newcastle, 1823 (John Gall & Rosy Allan Collection)

Hunter did much of his early work "upon pewter pots, dog collars, door plates, visiting cards, etc".[96] This was paralleled in the north of England where Thomas Bewick (1753–1828) was apprenticed to the copper plate engraver Ralph Beilby of Newcastle in 1767, at the traditional age of fourteen years, at a premium of £20. Bewick's first essays in engraving included items like coffin plates, door plates and collars for dogs; exactly the same type of products that the American engraver David Claypoole Johnston (1799–1865) began work on. Only later did Bewick make his name as a wood engraver and naturalist with his publications on *Quadrupeds* (1790) and *British Birds* (2 vols 1797; 1804).[97] Although the work of an engraver was often wide in scope it could, in large population centres, be a highly specialist activity. James Gillray (*c.* 1757–1815), whose incisive satirical engravings were to terrorise the establishment figures of his day, was apprenticed to a writing engraver – a man named Ashby who lived at the lower end of Holborn Hill, London. It was there that young Gillray learnt to cut in copper choice specimens "of penmanship ... in sweeping flourishes ... from the incomparable pen of Tomkins of Sermon-lane". Gillray later moved on to work for Bartolozzi where he further developed his graphic line for figure subjects.[98]

The sort of specialisation amongst artisans that was possible in large urban centres could result in workshops adopting almost industrial methods even though they could scarcely be described as manufactories. This prompted Bewick, on one of his few visits to London in 1776 to note that "one man does one branch of business & and another another... & it is by this division of labour they thus accomplish so much and so well." This was taken to extremes in the watchmaking trade where a single timepiece could involve the skills of as many as twenty-one craftsmen.[99] On Bewick's visit to the capital he must have seen, or have been aware of, the great canvases by artists such as Benjamin West. Despite such distractions the Northumbrian remained loyal to his work "in little." It could be argued that Bewick's tight focus carried him further within the confines of the wood-block than did the vaunting ambition of a West, Barry or a Fuseli. Perhaps because his aim was less Bewick's relative achievement is greater. His work certainly goes far beyond the sort of wood-cuts that decorated the public prints of his day. The subtleties of his art-form may have been dependent on craft skill but mysteriously move beyond such utilitarianism. What was true for Bewick was applicable to others. This was surely the message contained in John Clare's paean of praise for the English watercolour landscapes of Peter de Wint (1784–1849) which he contrasts with those artists: "where common skill sees nothing deemed divine."[100]

Notes

[1]   *Shorter Oxford English Dictionary* (2003), see also George Unwin (1908) 1966, p. 62
[2]   For Horace's *De Arte Poetica* see Thomas 2009, p. 70 footnote, and Ronald Paulson 1979, p. 35
[3]   George Unwin (1908), 1966, p. 330
[4]   This cultural continuum in medieval Europe is noted by Philip Ziegler in *The Black Death*, London, (1969) 2010 – eg p. 67. Walter Cahn 1979, pp. 40, 41
[5]   Margaret Whinney 1964, p. 4 and Howard Colvin ed. *et al.* 1976, pp. 210–222
[6]   George Unwin (1908) 1966, p. 247
[7]   Nicholas Cooper 1999, pp. 23–24

8   Ingrid Roscoe *et al.* 2009; Martin Postle ed. 2011, p. 29; Jerry White 2012, p. 133
9   A thesis first published by Robert Redfield and reprinted in *Peasant Society and Culture,* Chicago, 1956
10 Peter Burke (1978) 1994, pp. 58, 80. Burk's study is European-wide – I have substituted 'agricultural workers' for Burk's "peasants": Joseph Farington, p. 1112, 16 December, 1798
11 G. B. Hill and L. F. Powell eds (1934) 1971, p. 224
12 Giorgio Vasari *Lives of the most excellent Painters Sculptors and Architects* (1550) – see Louisa S. Maclehouse transl. *Vasari on Technique* intro by G. Baldwin Brown (1907)
13 John Michael Montias 1982; Lorna Weatherill (1988) 1996
14 Horace Walpole *Anecdotes of Painting in England* (1762–86) – Edward Edwards 1808
15 Anthony Pasquin (alias of John Williams) 1796 cited by Richard Wendorf 1996, p. 61
16 A good account of the "Venetian Secret" can be found in Robert C. Alberts 1978, pp. 225–239
17 Lawrence Stone 1955, pp. 179, 193
18 Walter Cahn 1979, p. 55–58
19 L. F. Salzman (1952) 1992, pp. 3, 5, 15 – Salzman cites many such examples
20 Thornton and Cain eds of Hilliard's *Treatise* 1981, p. 86
21 Mary S. Lovell *Bess of Hardwick ...* (2005), London, 2009 p. 359. This tomb was placed in what is now Sheffield Cathedral
22 Horace Walpole, 1786, Vol. II, p. 129 quoting from John Evelyn 1662, p. 103
23 Addison: *Spectator* No. 411; Jason M. Kelly 2009, pp. 116–117. In 1756 Robert Adman was of the opinion that Dalton was "esteemed" one of the "most ignorant mortals [which] entitled him to the name of 'Dulton'"
24 George E. Haggerty "Strawberry Hill: Friendship and Taste" in Michael Snodin ed. 2009, p. 79, Peter Inskip *Review Architecture Today*, March 2010, issue 206
25 For Moxon see Derek A. Long 2013; for Sweden see Maita di Niscemi *et al. Manor Houses & Castles of Sweden* Woodbridge, 1988, p. 130 which illustrates this workshop
26 James M. Gaynor and Nancy L. Hagedorn 1993, p. 20 – *The Daily Universal Register* (1 January 1785). The first copy of what three years later became *The Times*
27 Richard Wilson and Alan Mackley *The Building of the English Country House,* London (2000) 2011, pp. 72–76. Howard and Peter Coombs 1971; Knight of Glin and James Peill 2007, p. 89
28 Historical *Guide* to Compton Verney House, 2nd edn, 2008, p. 5; James M. Gaynor 2001
29 James Ayres 1998, p. 165
30 Joanna Martin 2004, p. 232
31 J. T. Smith (1828) 1919, Vol. I, p. 137
32 James Ayres 1985, pp. 105–110, 130–132
33 Howard and Peter Coombs 1971; W. T. Whitley 1928, Vol. II, pp. 73–74. Anthony Gerbino and Stephen Johnston 2009, p. 133. According to Joseph Farington (29 April 1797) Lord Harcourt "gave a picture of his painting to the picture gallery at Oxford"
34 Neil McKendrick *et al.* 1983
35 W. T. Whitley 1928, Vol. I, pp. 156–157
36 W. T. Whitley 1928, Vol. I, p. 160
37 Joseph Farington p. 527, 22 April 1796 – the "drawings" were almost certainly watercolours. They were probably not marked in the catalogue with an asterix, indicating they were not for sale

[38] Joseph Farington p. 597 9 July 1796

[39] Allan Cunningham 1830, Vol II, p. 218

[40] *Library of Fine Arts* 1831, Vol. II, p. 120 The Royal Academy was then located in Somerset House 1780–1837

[41] The Nottingham alabasterers not only worked to commissions, on the basis of tightly worded contracts, but would also produce items in bulk. In 1491 Nicholas Hill of Nottingham produced no less than 58 severed heads of John the Baptist at 1 shilling and 1s 6d each. Lawrence Stone 1955, p. 216

[42] Jacob Harwood and John Camden Hotten 1866

[43] British Museum, Dept of P&D: Trade Labels

[44] D. G. C. Allan and John L. Abbott 1992, p. 92: see also W. T. Whitley 1928, Vol. II, p. 249

[45] W. T. Whitley 1928, Vol. I, p. 373 – for the reference to Moser

[46] The list includes prizes for drawings of "statues" and "casts" – D. G. C. Allan and John L. Abbott 1992, 102–103

[47] R. D. Harley (1970) 1982, pp. 136–157, James Ayres 1985, fig. 80

[48] Torsten and Peter Berg 2001, p.289

[49] Maxine Berg 1995, pp. 169–171

[50] Joseph Farington *Diary* 27 Dec 1797 and, for a similar observation: 12 Jan 1799

[51] Ian Ousby 2002, pp. 51–59

[52] Founding Hospital – see W. T. Whitley 1928, p. 163: *Chambers Encyclopaedia* 1862; William Sandby 1862, p. 32; Sidney C. Hutchinson 1968, pp. 34–35 and Kit Wedd 2004, p. 25

[53] Sidney C. Hutchinson 1968, pp. 54–56

[54] W. T. Whitley 1928, Vol. I, p. 373

[55] Allan Cunningham 1830, Vol. III, p. 286

[56] James Ayres "Review" of Tessa Murdoch ed. *Noble Households: 18th Century Inventories ...* Adamson, Cambridge, 2006 in the Georgian Group Magazine Issue 2, 2007, p. 31

[57] Karen Hearn ed. 1995, p. 89, Cat 45

[58] In pre-Reformation England a work of art was generally made to the greater glory of God – even in a secular context. Such works could scarcely be affronted by the presence of a signature. The cult of the individual was largely the product of Humanism

[59] Margaret Whinney 1964, p. 234 n. 39

[60] W. A. D. Englefield (1923) 1936, p. 68

[61] The decline in this dual role for painters may be seen to have begun in 1841, the date when collapsible metal tubes for oil paint was patented

[62] Exhibited as item 142 in *Wright of Derby*, Tate Britain, 1990 – *Not* in catalogue

[63] The bill is dated 12 June 1821, Author's collection

[64] McKendrick *et al.* 1983, but not for this extension to this thesis

[65] Jerry White 2012, 286, Ruth S. Kraemer *Drawings by Benjamin West*. Pierpont Morgan Library, New York, 1975, pp. 55–56, Cat 94

[66] J. T. Smith (1828) 1919, Vol. I, p. 159

[67] W. T. Whitley 1928, Vol. I, p. 107. The social position of Hoare was unusual in that he had married money and was in a position to select his commissions

[68] Joseph Farington, p. 822 8 August 1797 and p. 556, 24 May 1796

[69] Shakespeare's *Seven Ages of Man* from *As You Like It*, Joseph Farington, pp. 537–8 1 May 1796 and p. 1046 16 August 1798

[70] Ernst van de Wetering (1997) 2004, pp. 8–22. For standard canvas/frame sizes see James Ayres 1985, p. 213

[71] James Ayres 1985, p. 132

[72] Joseph Farington, 25 March 1796

[73] *Library of Fine Arts* 1831–2, Vol. II, p. 182

[74] Hugh Trevor-Roper *Europe's Physician ... Sir Theodor de Mayerne*, Yale University Press, New Haven and London, 2006 pp. 301–302

[75] Allan Cunningham 1830, Vol. V, p. 300

[76] Rosemary O'Day 2000; For Fox see pp. 3 and 25 for Culpeter see p. 15, for King see p. 255 and for Earl p. 256

[77] Douglas R. Egerton, *Gabriel's Rebellion: The Virginia Slave Conspiracies of 1800 & 1802*, Chapel Hill, 1993, p. 3

[78] Allan Cunningham 1830, Vol. V, p. 300

[79] J. T. Smith (1828) 1919, Vol. II, pp. 268, 331

[80] *Ibid.*, p. 216 also Vol. II, 319–320

[81] W. T. Whitley 1928, Vol. II, pp. 113–116

[82] W. H. Pyne 1824, Vol. II, p. 39

[83] King was a pupil of George Knapton (1698–1778) Edward Edwards 1808, p. 28

[84] *Ibid.*, Vol. II, p. 220. See also *Library of Fine Arts* 1832, Vol. IV

[85] J. T. Smith (1828) 1919, Vol. II, 359, 115

[86] Prince Hoare 1813, p. 14. In April 1797 Hoppner proposed at a meeting of the Academy that "Esq" be added to all printed lists of RAs. Joseph Farington, p. 827 25 April 1797

[87] W. T. Whitley 1928, Vol. II, p. 300 quoting a "Miss Knight"

[88] Farington *Diary*, p. 759, 29 Jan 1797, p. 1337 1 Jan 1800

[89] Joseph Farington, p. 621 27 July 1796

[90] Walter Cahn 1979

[91] This seems to have been a seventeenth century phrase that gained wide usage in the eighteenth century and in Colonial and Early Federal America. Abbott Lowell Cummings 1979, p. 40

[92] Ronald Paulson 1991, Vol. I, p. 38

[93] D. G. C. Allan and John L. Abbott eds 1992, chapter 4

[94] Mostly cited by Edward Edwards 1808, who also makes reference (pp. 49–50) to a painter named Hannan "A native of Scotland [who] was put apprentice to a cabinet maker", Jerry White 2012, p. 103

[95] Museum of London, exhibition catalogue: *The Quiet Conquest: The Huguenots 1695–1985*, London, 1985 pp. 161–164. This dynasty of engravers included Isaac Basire (1704–1748) his son James (1730–1802) another James (1769–1822) and another James (1796–1869) plus a John (n.d.)

[96] J. T. Smith (1828) 1919, Vol. I, p. 161

[97] Thomas Bewick *My Life* (1862), 1981, Jenny Uglow 2006, pp. 39–40. As a wood engraver Bewick influenced the Dorset engraver & poet William Barnes (1801–1886). Bewick was visited by the American John James Audubon in 1827

[98] Cited by Jenny Uglow 2006, p. 100

[99] W. H. Pyne 1824, p. 409; Jerry White 2012, 215

[100] Jonathan Bate ed. *John Claire: Selected Poems*, Faber & Faber, London 2003, 198

Chapter 2

THE GUILDS
& LIVERY COMPANIES

In pre-Reformation England there were two significant types of fraternity: the secular craft guilds and the religious guilds. The former were town centred but the latter, being parish-based, were both urban and rural. Although spiritual and benevolent activities were also a feature of the craft guilds their *raison d'être* was focussed upon trades or occupations. These craft guilds were most fully organised, and therefore best documented, in London. What follows is consequently largely concerned with the capital and its considerable influence on both provincial and colonial trade organisations.

Many of the crafts may be viewed as the hub on which the visual arts turned. In parallel with this the "closed-shops" established by the guilds reserved to themselves "all lawful powers granted to *artists* of like condition" (my italics).[1] Here "artists" is used in the sense of "artisan". In the twenty-first century the crafts may be seen either as fundamental (e.g. to the building trades) or as trivial (e.g. candle making) occupations, but they are consistently viewed as manual. For this reason many trades are seen to occupy a social ghetto in which they are regarded as the antithesis of the occupations of the mind. As such they are too easily viewed as of secondary importance to the "professions" – an attitude that presumes an easily defined distinction between the manual and the theoretical. Despite this prejudicial mind-set George Unwin noted, over a century ago, "that the word 'craft', like 'art' or 'mystery' ... had no such limited meaning in the middle Ages". As Unwin went on to say a craft then:

> "signified a trade or calling, generally, and a typical member of a craft was well-to-do ... Often it is true, he had gone through an apprenticeship to the manual side of his craft, and this fact was of greatest importance as it brought manual labour under the influence of the professional spirit."

The social position that membership of a trade guild offered is
of relevance to the career of the
dramatist and poet Ben Jonson
(1572–1637) in a number of ways.
An example of this relates to his
celebrated walk to Scotland of 1618.
When he arrived in Edinburgh from
London he was received by the city
fathers as an "inglishman burges and
guild brother in communi forma".
In other words, as a bricklayer and
freeman of the relevant London
Company, Jonson was seen to share
a common bond with the citizens
of the Scottish capital and that this
was of greater consequence than
his position as a writer. Neither
should we suppose that Jonson's
membership of the Company of
Tylers and Bricklayers was honorary
for his writings sometimes reveal
a practical understanding of the
building trades – such as the specific
uses for which lime plaster and loam
were deployed.[2]

FIGURE 5. *Plumber's Sign* carved and polychromed wood. This plumber is shown
holding a dresser and a roofers hammer.
In addition many of these tradesmen also
worked in oil paint. (Private Collection)

In many ways industrialisation has separated us from the handmade
object and its maker to the extent that Ben Jonson's career path may seem
all-but incomprehensible. By the mid-nineteenth century Henry Mayhew
may sometimes have registered a distinction between artisans and unskilled
labourers (see pp. 39–40 below) but it was a distinction that was not always
evident in his *London Labour and London Poor* (1862). This ambivalence
presented few problems for what was, in effect, an oral history. But how was
a historian relying on documentary sources to proceed in an attempt to
record the lives of the great mass of undereducated indigent poor? Although
economic historians have found statistical analysis of value in this respect E. P.
Thompson, in his seminal book on *The Making of the English Working Class* (1963)
was compelled to focus on workers who were engaged in a craft – hence the
miss-match between the title of his book and its contents. It is my contention

that "the working class" were distinct from the skilled tradesmen and that the latter, though distanced from the elite of church and state were, as citizens, members of a privileged minority.

That tradesmen were from reasonably "well-to-do" backgrounds is substantiated by the often considerable premiums that a parent or guardian was compelled to pay a prospective master to take an apprentice. Once a youth emerged from his bondage to become a journeyman and ultimately a master, the rewards could be considerable. Physical evidence for this is reflected in the magnificent marble monument that commemorates the stonemason Christopher Kempster (1625–1715) in Burford Parish Church, Oxfordshire. The inscription on this mural tablet describes Kempster as "a person Eminent in his profession" and as a "Freeman of the City of London and of ye Company of Masons."[3] That phrase effortlessly acknowledges that admission to a Company entitled an artisan to two privileges – to practice a "profession" and the right to vote as a citizen. On 10 March 1768 the politician John Wilkes gained the freedom of the Joiners Company by redemption (31 shillings fee) and by this means became a citizen which enabled him to stand as a Member of Parliament for one of the four City of London seats.[4]

One of the principal functions of the trade guilds was to preserve the privileges of their brethren. The threat of immigrant competition was only one of a number of issues with which they were concerned. In particular the merchant guilds, in a public-spirited way, did much to restrict forestalling and to protect consumers from regrating.[5] Accordingly the guilds were not only concerned with the good conduct and well-being of their membership, but were also conscientious in maintaining the quality of the work and the interests of their customers. The extent to which this was achieved was inevitably associated with the degree of specialisation represented by a guild. In this respect the relatively large population of London enabled the Livery Companies in the capital to maximise the unique nature of a given craft. In provincial and colonial towns and cities these fraternities were often somewhat generalised and their powers circumscribed. Even in a significant regional centre like York the Carpenters Company comprised a whole variety of woodworkers including: joiners, carvers, wheelwrights and sawyers in addition to carpenters.[6]

The power of the guilds, and thus the strength of their regulations, also differed over time as did the extent of their geographical reach. Furthermore individual crafts rose and declined in response to demand. Now recondite specialisms like the Heaumers (helmet makers) emerged, declined and disappeared.[7] The particular nature of the best regulated guilds inevitably led to demarcation disputes with related crafts. Conflicts of this kind were most likely to arise between trades using the same or similar materials (as between joiners and carpenters) or providing similar products or services (as between Painter Stainers and the College of Heralds).[8] Arbitration in such disputes was, by the sixteenth century, a matter of law and regulation but physical violence could erupt.[9] In smaller communities where skill was often at a premium, as in Colonial America, there was more than enough work to go round to keep the peace. Also, in smaller urban settlements, where related trades were united under one banner, as with the York Carpenters Company, a more amicable state of affairs prevailed. In contrast the London Carpenters (Charter 1477) and the Joiners (Charter 1571) were distinct Livery Companies. Not so in Colonial and Early Federal America where the Carpenters Company of Philadelphia represented both trades.[10]

Because the separate yet twin cities of London and Westminster, together with their suburbs, formed much the largest conurbation in medieval and Early Modern England the practical reach of the guilds could be considerable. An example of this is the Weavers (Charter 1184) whose jurisdiction extended to Southwark on the south bank of the River Thames in Surrey "and to other places pertaining to London." This orbit of control was extended still further by the Cordwainers (Charter 1438) to "twenty leagues [$c.$ 60 miles/$c.$ 100 km] around the capital."[11] Southwark was a contentious location, with regard to the authority of the City's guilds, being across the river in a different county (Surrey). For this reason the Bakers, late in the reign of Edward III, petitioned Parliament with the complaint that:

> "false workers at diverse trades … who eschew the punishments of the City, repair to the vill of Southwark where the City officials cannot arrest and punish them because the Court of the Marshalsea will not suffer them [the City officials] to exercise any jurisdiction there."[12]

The City Companies were evidently keen to exert their authority over as wide a geographical area as possible. These rights were jealously guarded. A rather dramatic late medieval example of this involved a "foreign" butcher who attempted to sell what was claimed to be sub-standard meat in the City of London – that "foreign" butcher was from the nearby village of West Ham, now well within east London.[13]

In response to these questions of jurisdiction the Charters granted to the guilds after the accession of Elizabeth I extended well beyond the City. For example the Broderers (embroiders Charter 1564) had rights of regulation in the City and its suburbs, in Westminster and Southwark and the in the borough of St Katherine's. The mighty Goldsmiths Company solved these issues in an almost imperial fashion from the first. Their Charter of 1327 states unequivocally that: "the rest of the trade shall come to London to be ascertained [assayed] of their touch [hallmark] of gold and to receive the puncheon with the Leopard's head to mark their work."[14]

Despite this clause a number of provincial assay offices were to be established in cities distant from London – Exeter for example. Even so, in 1733 no less than 12 Birmingham goldsmiths registered their personal marks in London and the centralising tendency of this Livery Company persists.[15]

An important feature of guild control was the power of search. This enabled the individual Companies to maintain a monopoly over their respective trades and ensure that the standards of work, materials and terms of employment and training were maintained. Consequently the guilds may be seen as representing not only the interests of their brethren, the masters, but also those they employed and trained and the customers who purchased their goods or services. So important were these powers that the Inspeximus or the exemplification of ordinances was, in medieval London, almost as effective as a full Charter since it conferred on these bodies the all-important right of search.[16] The presence of these rights shows that many of these fraternities had an existence long before they were Chartered. Despite the very evident importance of this right of search, this authority was briefly removed from the guilds in 1711. By this date these inspections may have already been in decline. The last recorded search by the Painter Stainers took place on the 10 July 1707. Nevertheless the decline or the loss of these on-site reviews of trade workshops represented a serious threat to the future of the Livery Companies as trade organisations.[17]

For as long as the guilds maintained their privileges and authority they were in a position to influence the Civic bodies to which they were notionally subservient. Furthermore in addition to the Inspeximus, many of these fraternities owed their authority not to a Charter but to long-held custom – "time out of mind". There were therefore a number of ways in which a guild could claim its pedigree back beyond the date of its Charter. In addition there were also the unlicensed or Adulterine Guilds. Despite these various forms of authority, with or without documentation, the municipal corporations eventually exercised some sort of control over these bodies that functioned within their civic jurisdiction.

Although the "closed shop" in a defined geographical area was an important privilege it was most effective in London and its environs. Even within the capital there were some zones that were outside the dominion of these fraternities. These enclaves of free trade were known as "liberties" and as such came under private jurisdiction. Among these were St Martins' le Grand, Holy Trinity (later known as Duke's Place) and Blackfriars which, despite its monastic origin, long survived the Reformation as a "peculiar". In addition the Steelyard was, until the late fourteenth century, an extra-territorial outpost of the Hanseatic League.[18] The importance of these autonomous districts is that they offered a haven for both foreigners and aliens (individuals from outside London) and thus maintained the vitality of the City's trade and commerce. These Liberties generally retained their traditional role even as Elizabeth I developed a rather more liberal policy with regard to outsiders. Certainly in late Tudor and Stuart London these free trade areas became a haven for immigrant artisans. In particular Southwark was the location of the homes and workshops of the Johnson and Cure families from the Low Countries who in the mid-sixteenth century plied their trade as "image makers" or sculptors – (see pp. 302, 304 Chapter 14).[19] Others who were attracted to these Liberties included the French limner and cartographer Jacques le Moyne de Morgues (*c.* 1533–1588) who spent the last six years of his life in Blackfriars in lodgings provided by his patron Sir Walter Raleigh. This part of London had well established links with France for it was in that district that the Confraternity of the Immaculate Conception was established in 1503 by French Dominicans. A medicant order of this kind was self-governing and was outside the jurisdiction of the Bishop's see – a level of autonomy that this quarter seems to have retained following the Reformation. On le Moyne's death in 1588 his widow sold her late husband's watercolour drawings of the flora and fauna of what is now South Carolina to Théodore de Bry (1527/8–1598). This Frankfurt-based Flemish goldsmith and engraver was then visiting London. These watercolours formed the basis for the engravings, by de Bry and his sons, which illustrated the Frankfurt edition of the René Loudonnière's *Florida*. In the absence of such free-trade areas, in and about London, this kind of European wide cooperation, on this highly significant publication on the New World, would not have been possible.[20] In other urban centres, beyond the reach of the capital, the situation for aliens could be very different. As late as the 1780s the shipwrights and weavers of Newcastle upon Tyne swore "to take no Scotsman born or other alien apprentice." Furthermore trade solidarity in that great northern port extended to an embargo on Quakers who were excluded from being coiners or armourers: the fine for breaching this regulation being £100.[21]

Religion permeated most aspects of medieval life and for this reason there was considerable overlap in the spiritual objectives of the parish guilds with their charitable and community work; and the craft guilds with their trade and civic activities. Both types of fraternity had their patron saints. Amongst the craft guilds the Painter Stainers sought the intercession of St Luke, the Goldsmiths that of St Dunstan. Consequently these brotherhoods, and in particular the religious guilds, had chapels or chantries, in parish churches and also supported almshouses and the construction of bridges. In Tavistock, Devon, a donation was made in 1442 for the construction of a Clothworkers' aisle in the church. This type of ecclesiastical association was destined to outlive the Reformation. Even today the printers' unions refer to their various chapters as "chapels", a term redolent of pre-Reformation England. Furthermore a profanity like "St Monday" the unofficial "Saints Day" when little work was done, harks back to another age.[22] Despite their similarities these two species of guild, the religious and the civic, maintained their distinct objectives. The Salters remain the only known example of a City Livery Company which originated in a parish fraternity – that of Corpus Christi – in All Hallows, Bread Street.[23]

As Phillip Lindley (2007) has pointed out the Reformation removed the notion of Purgatory as an article of faith. Consequently the chantries, on which the parish guilds lavished so much of their spiritual conviction, were "deprived of their doctrinal rationale."[24] In 1547 all chantries were placed in the hands of the king, their funds appropriated. In London 18 such chantries were compelled to close once they were deprived of the financial support of the parish guilds.[25] In some cases these parish organisations re-emerged, often under a different name, to resume their charitable and spiritual activities. An example was the Guild of the Holy Cross, Abingdon. This religious Guild built the Burford Bridge in the town and, in 1446, established the extant Long Alley Almshouses. In this case the Guild was inevitably abolished in 1547 but as early as 1553 was reconstituted under new Governors as Christ's Hospital – an interregnum of just half a dozen years.[26] The demise of such a body and its rapid re-emergence as a charity was relatively unusual.[27] With the decline of the religious fraternities and the abolition of their chantries the craft guilds advanced their position, although some adjustments were made to their religious affiliations. The Pewterers of London ceased to be known as the Fraternity of St Michael but as a craft organisation they continued to function much as before. Indeed, it could be argued that, the position of the craft guilds were much enhanced by the *Statute of Artificers* of 1563 (which itself had its origins in a similar Act of 1495 and in turn may be related to the *Statute of Labourers* of 1351).[28] Furthermore after the break with Rome the Crown saw the Livery Companies as a useful countervailing force in relationship to the residual powers of "the overmighty lords temporal".

There were two basic types of civic guild, those that represented trading or mercantile activities and others whose membership was craft-based. Inevitably the so-called Twelve Great Companies of London were dominated by the affluent merchant companies.[29] Some of these fraternities were simultaneously representative of both craft and trading guildsmen. For example some brethren in the Goldsmiths Company functioned as both bankers and makers. In most cases these Livery Companies served as friendly societies supporting those of their membership who were in need, corporate or personal. The Mercers, as a great mercantile guild, came to the aid of those amongst them who had suffered losses through shipwreck – Lloyds coffee-house on Tower Street was not established as an insurance centre until 1688. As a profession the underwriter was as new as the beverage sold by Edward Lloyd. The needs of individual master craftsmen were also met by the guilds. This is exemplified by the Goldsmiths' which supported brethren "who by fire and smoke of quicksilver [mercury] have lost their sight – no wonder St Dunstan was also the patron for the blind."[30] Loss of sight was a significant health issue. In 1683 Nicholas Paris was concerned about the effect of using *aqua fortis* (nitric acid) in connection with regilding the mid-fifteenth century bronze effigy of Richard Beauchamp Earl of Warwick on his tomb in the chapel at St Mary's Church, Warwickshire. In fire gilding this figure Paris would have used mercury oxide. An awareness of these toxic materials was widely understood in early Jacobean London. In Jonson's play *Eastwood Ho* (1605) a goldsmith's apprentice is named Quicksilver and his master was named Touchstone – the jasper used to test gold.[31] Like quicksilver the lead oxide used to cure beaver skins was also toxic, rendering hatters proverbially mad.

The spiritual affiliations of the guilds explain why it was that they often conducted their meetings in a church – where they also held services of thanksgiving. Alternatively they met in a tavern, much as the "Combinations" (early trade unions) would later do in George III's reign.[32] At the close of the fourteenth century only the Tailors and the Goldsmiths are known to have been in possession of their own halls in London. Just half a century later there were about 28 such establishments.[33] These halls were on an aristocratic scale and indeed some had previously been the town houses of such personages. Once in possession of a splendid headquarters a fraternity would, in the spirit of a great lord, clothe its retinue in a uniform which brethren were expected to don on ceremonial occasions – hence Livery Companies.

Having survived a succession of major historical transitions in the political, economic, theological, and aesthetic history of England the Livery Companies of London were, by the second half of the sixteenth century, in their pomp.[34] Their image was more than a mirage. The guilds were backed by the Statute of 1351, the Act of 1495 and by the *Statute of Artificers* of November 1562.[35] These measures regularised a tradesman's hours of work and insisted that only those who had served their time as apprentices could gain their freedom to practice a given craft and train others in their "art and mystery".[36]

Curiously George Unwin (1908) has little, if anything, to say about the *Statute of Artificers*. He does though acknowledge the "renaissance of the crafts" in the sixteenth century, particularly in the reign of Elizabeth I.[37] Somewhat whimsically this view is not based on his interpretation of the quality of the work produced at this time, or upon the workshop conditions within which craftsmen functioned. On the contrary, Unwin focusses upon the number of demarcation disputes that took place at that time. In other words he measures the "renaissance of the crafts" in terms of their economic and political power and in doing so pays silent tribute to the *Statute of Artificers* on which that power rested.

About half the Livery Companies that survive in London were formed in Queen Elizabeth's reign. Many that existed then, or earlier, represented callings that are now unknown or whose goods and services have fallen into disuse. Others have emerged in response to new technologies or discoveries. In the seventeenth century various innovations led to the foundation of the Tobacco-pipe Makers, Fanmakers, Coach builders and Gun Makers Companies.

FIGURE 6. Portrait of *Sir Henry Sidney* (1529–1586) from the workshop of an English artist. Pattern portraits (or patrons as they were known) were provided to create official representations of the elite. Such a cut-out image could be transferred to innumerable panels or canvases to create many official versions of the original. (National Portrait Gallery, London)

Even as the guilds gloried in their statutory protection and luxuriated in their halls, symptoms of their decline as trade organisations began to appear. Gradually the direct connection between a guild and its ostensible craft would be diluted. Some have argued that it took little more than a century of formal existence (a Charter) for a guild to begin to lose its connection with its trade origins. A number of explanations have been sought for this. Certainly "London Practice" permitted a man who was free of one Company to practice the craft of another. More pernicious was "Patrimony" whereby the eldest son could join his father's livery on the payment of a fee or "fine" without going to the trouble of serving an apprenticeship. A third method of avoiding seven years "servitude" was by means of "redemption" – the payment of a substantial fee.[38] Perhaps more important were the underlying antagonisms within a guild between the "working masters" with little leisure and less money; and the trading masters who were in possession of more of both. Inevitably power tended to coalesce around the latter category amongst the brethren.[39] The problems of harmonising such conflicting interests were insuperable and many of the guilds became, what they remain to this day, the representatives of capitalism deployed for social and charitable purposes.

In 1624 the guilds, among other organisations and individuals, were faced with the problems and occasional opportunities offered by the *Statute of Monopolies*. In effect these Monopolies were a form of royal largess issued for a period of 14 years. This span of time was related to two seven-year apprenticeships and thereby emphasised the trade-based nature of such a privilege. A case may be made for arguing that these Monopolies were the precursors of the Patents that were to be issued in connection with "intellectual property rights". The Monopolies of the early seventeenth century were, in reality, a pragmatic means by which the Stuart crown raised "stealth taxes" without the inconvenience of seeking Parliamentary approval – a measure that established the system of indirect taxes that is with us still.[40] With these monopolies in place all sorts of injustices could ensue. For example a foreigner in Southwark, possibly Abraham Baker (see p. 123), devised a good blue starch. His secret was then purloined by an Englishman who secured a monopoly on its production. However, the quality was so inferior that the brethren of the Painter Stainers were compelled to import this material from the Continent. In breaking the monopoly on this English-made blue starch the Painter Stainers were summoned to explain their actions to the City authorities.[41] Despite problems of this kind it was rumoured that the guilds were, in some cases, conniving in these monopolies and the income they generated. The taxes based on these exclusive rights may have been a fiscal success but they were a political disaster, a contributing factor that culminated in the Civil War, "the world turned upside down." It is perhaps no coincidence that these Monopolies, issued by the crown, were abolished following the Glorious Revolution of 1688.

After the Restoration (1660) and following the Great Fire of London of 1666 much more than the physical fabric of the City had suffered. In the interests of reconstructing the capital the "closed shop", one of the principal manifestations of guild power, was suspended and aliens and foreigners were permitted to ply their trades within the "square mile" and beyond.[42] This measure was inevitably of particular concern to the building trades and therefore impinged on statuaries working in wood or stone. Master Carpenters were instructed by their Company, to free apprentices before their time and indenture new ones to replace them. Trade secrecy lost much of its force and the whole notion of an "art & mystery" fell victim to the trade manuals that slowly began to appear.[43] At the same time the magisterial folio volumes on architectural design, that had once been confined to the elite, were now supplemented by small quarto editions that would fit in the pocket of a craftsman's apron.[44]

These trends were observable in other urban regional centres. In Bristol the decline in the influence of the various trades seems to have resulted in an attempt to re-impose some regulation. In 1696 by-laws were introduced which prohibited any person who was not a freeman of the city from practicing a trade or opening a shop. Those who transgressed were compelled to pay a fine of £5 a day which, in 1721, was increased to an even more punitive £20. By 1740 these regulations were comprehensively breached by craftsmen from neighbouring Bath in building the Exchange in Bristol – namely John Wood the Elder and his contractor William Biggs. Nevertheless some residual respect for the "closed shop" was to persist. When the carver (wood and stone) and architect James Paty I moved to Bristol (probably from Somerton) he paid a fine in 1721 to become a burgess (free man or citizen) which gave him the liberty to practice his art and craft in the city. An alternative was to become a burgess by marriage as did Paty's nephew James Paty II (1718–1779). In his turn the nephew of Paty II, namely John Paty II (1754–1789), was admitted as an architect: "to the Liberties of this City for that he married Elizabeth the daughter of William Perry, Mariner, deceased, and hath taken the oath of obedience and paid £0-4-6".[45]

With the Act of 1667 for rebuilding London after the Great Fire the guilds lost their full authority over such matters as training and the closed shop. They were therefore not well placed to re-establish their control once the emergency in the capital was over. What was true for London would eventually be replicated elsewhere. The fire in Warwick of 1694 resulted in legislation for its rebuilding that was based on the measures that were taken in London.[46] Much the same was true following the fire of Blandford Forum of 1731.[47] Such events contributed towards the "rationalisation" of the Livery Companies, with or without the precipitous effects of a great fire. In the city of Bath the guilds processed their ancient privileges for the last time in 1765.[48] Not that this spelt an end to trade processions although their purpose was to change. In 1830 the trades in Bath paraded in support of the *Reform Bill* carrying banners variously inscribed: "The United Trades" – "We are All Agreed" – "The Bill or Nothing Else". This then was a political rather than a craft event. Significantly a later march, held on 28 May 1832 in honour of the passing of the *Reform Act*, was organised not by "The United Trades" but by the "Bath Political Forum".[49]

Collectively "The custom of London", "Patrimony", "Redemption" and, in 1711, the abolition of the "right of search" all conspired to reduce the power and influence of the guilds. By George III's reign the resulting vacuum was filled, in part, by the "Combinations" and the Friendly Societies each of which offered support for artisans who were in difficulty of one kind or another. In addition these organisations sometimes served as a cover for political or trade union activity.[50] By 1814 the clauses concerning apprenticeships were removed from the *Statute of Artificers* of 1563.[51] With the decline of apprenticeships in a craft, the role of the various professional bodies that were now emerging became important in relationship to training and education. Among these organisations was the Royal Academy founded in 1768 which was to run its Schools of Painting, Sculpture and Architecture for the purposes of educating students in those three professions. Unofficially the scope of the Academy in its early decades was far wider by virtue of the numerous trades that its founder members had once been engaged in. If this is taken into consideration the Academy encompassed carriage and sign painting, masonry and woodcarving, silver smithing, chasing, die-sinking and engraving. Where the guilds had once, as trade bodies, enjoyed the authority of the *Statute of Artificers* the Academy benefitted not only from its Royal patron, but also from George III's active involvement in its affairs.[52]

Although the Combinations (proto-trade unions) were disconcerting organisations for employers and caused disquiet amongst legislators they were far from extreme for they excluded labourers and were thus confined to highly skilled and therefore thoughtful craftsmen. Francis Place (b. 1771), who had served an apprenticeship as a breeches-maker, noted the respectable nature of such individuals. Place recognised "the difference between skilled workmen and common labourers" which he argued could not be more "strongly marked".[53] The social gulf between craftsmen and labourers was noted with some force in the mid nineteenth century by Henry Mayhew, who nevertheless regarded the craftsmen as radical in the extreme.

> "The artisans are, almost to a man, red-hot politicians. They are sufficiently educated and thoughtful to have a sense of their importance in the State... the unskilled labourers are a different class of people. As yet they are as impolitical as footmen ... they appear to have no political opinions whatever."[54]

To a gentleman like Mayhew these "educated and thoughtful" artisans may have been something of a revelation, perhaps even a "red-hot" threat. From a twenty-first century perspective the artisans of Regency and early Victorian England appear moderate. Almost by definition the Combinations represented a minority of the workforce – namely the skilled craftsmen. These bodies were consequently different in membership, and therefore in character, to the mass labour movements of the twentieth century that were dominated by semi- and unskilled workers. One of the earliest leaders of the craft unions was the Bristol born John Gast (1772–1837) – a shipwright and carpenter by trade who eventually became the leader of the London Carpenters. Gast is therefore typical of this kind of early Union leader.[55] Despite the reasonable nature of these craft unions, attempts were made to restrict the Combinations which had the effect of driving these bodies towards the Jacobins.[56] From 1825 with the repeal of the *Combination Acts* (1799–1800) these organisations were once again free to process their banners through the streets of London and elsewhere.

Of the many causes that led to the decline of the guilds as trade bodies (outlined above) the rise of the so-called pauper apprenticeships was probably significant. These had first been devised in post-Reformation Tudor England as a form of "job creation scheme" to resolve the rising tide of unemployment – one of the unintended consequences of the Dissolution of the Monasteries. These so-called pauper apprenticeships not only removed children of the poor from the responsibility of the parish but, by the late eighteenth century, had become a means of supplying cheap child labour for the burgeoning industrialisation of Britain. This was an abuse of a once proud system of instruction. Indeed even the poor had once been better served in this respect. In the early seventeenth century premiums for apprenticeships were sometimes met by rich benefactors. For example Hugh Sexey's Almshouses (1638) in Bruton, Somerset, accommodated 12 men, 12 women and 12 poor boys. When each of these youths reached the age of 14 "they were bound apprentices to tradesmen at the expense of the charity, £6 being the sum given with each to the master at the time of binding".[57] Despite the decline in the apprenticeship system as policed by the guilds, and the corresponding rise in academies of art, the old values persisted in the quality of much of the work produced by the practitioners of individual crafts and in the language of the wider public. This is reflected in a number of Charles Dickens' novels. For example in *Great Expectations* (1861) he satirically describes a young labourer who had followed his father's "art & mystery" as a grave digger and thus confirms that this phrase was so well understood that it could be used satirically.[58] At their best apprenticeships had offered the finest possible training and education in an "art & mystery" for a given trade, a privilege that, most certainly, did not extend to labourers.

Notes

[1] George Unwin (1908) 1966, p. 330
[2] *Ibid*, p. 62. Ian Donaldson 2011, pp. 90, 338. Donaldson quotes from Jonson *Discoveries*: "What difference is between us (adults) and them (children) but that we are dearer fools, coxcombs at a higher rate. They are pleased with cockleshells, whistles, hobby-horses, and such like; we with statues, marble pillars, pictures, gilded roofs, where underneath is lath and lime, perhaps loam"
[3] The monument is illustrated in James Ayres 1998, fig. 111
[4] Marcia Evans *The Place of the Rural Blacksmith in Parish Life 1500–1900*, Somerset & Dorset Family History Soc. A998, p. 27. Jerry White 2012, 523
[5] Introduction by William F. Kahl p. xxvi to the 1966 edition of George Unwin (1908)
[6] James W. P. Campbell 2002, table i, p. 219
[7] John Harvey 1975, p. 49
[8] Phillip Lindley 2007, pp. 31–32 and p. 91
[9] Hentie Louw 1989
[10] Charles E. Peterson *The Rules of the Carpenters Company* ... 1786, reprint, Mendham, N.Y. 1992
[11] A provision established in the reign of Henry II, George Unwin (1908) 1966, pp. 44, 45, 84
[12] The anomalous position of Southwark was not sorted out until the mid-sixteenth century. Its last emblem of legal autonomy, the Marshalsea, was not abolished until 1849 – time enough to appear in Dickens's novels. George Unwin (1908) 1966, p. 135
[13] The meat came from two carcasses of beasts that, or so it was claimed, came from animals that died a natural death. The meat was confiscated and burnt in the Stocks Market. George Unwin (1908) 1966, p. 90. No date given by Unwin who cites the Calendar of Letter Book E.110
[14] George Unwin (1908) 1966, pp. 79–80, 244
[15] Joan Lane 1996, p. 164
[16] W. A. D. Englefield 1936, p. 40; George Unwin (1908) 1966, chapter iv
[17] Geoffrey Beard 1997, p. 8; Alan Borg 2005, p. 91
[18] George Unwin (1908) 1966, pp. 42, 137–188, 245
[19] Phillip Lindley 2007, pp. 32–33
[20] Kim Sloane 2007, pp. 81, 133 and Peter Mancall 2007, p. 172; Jessie Poesch 1983, p. 4; Scot McKendrick *et al.* 2011, p. 177

21 John Brand *The History & Antiquities ... of Newcastle upon Tyne*, 1789, Vol. II, pp. 342, 343, 349, cited by Jenny Uglow 2006, p. 55
22 Warwick Rodwell 2012, 57, 58; John Rule in Tim Harris ed. 1995, pp. 170, 180, 181
23 George Unwin (1908) 1966, pp. 56–57, 183
24 Phillip Lindley 2007, p. 20
25 George Unwin (1908) 1966, pp. 201, 229
26 Arthur Preston *Christ's Hospital Abingdon* (1929) Oxford University Press, 1994, pp. 25–26. The so-called Exchequer Chamber of the Chantry survives as a separately accessed room over the porch of St Helen's Church – see Steane and Ayres 2013
27 Relative to the large number of chantries that this type of guild had once supported
28 George Unwin (1908) 1966, p. 230; Dan Jones 2012, 493. The Statute of 1351 was drafted as the Ordinance of Labour in 1349
29 Wencelaus Hollar's engraving of 1667 represents the arms of these 12 companies: Cloth workers, Drapers, Fishmongers, Goldsmiths, Grocers, Haberdashers, Ironmongers, Mercers, Merchant Tailors, Skinners and Vintners
30 Joan Lane 1996, p. 44
31 Paris was a goldsmith in Warwick but also did much of the ironwork in the church. The effigy was made by John Massingham in 1449–50. For nitric acid see Martindale, *Extra Pharmacopea* ed. by R. G. Todd, London, 1967, p. 653. *Eastwood Ho* was written collaboratively by George Chapman, John Marston and Ben Jonson – see Ian Donaldson 2011, pp. 206–207
32 Iorwerth Prothero 1979
33 George Unwin (1908) 1966, pp. 176–178
34 These transitions included the following: Plantagenet to Tudor, the Reformation and the Renaissance
35 Dan Jones 2012, 493; Keith Thomas 2009, p. 84 citing II Hen, 1495. c. 22 and the Statute of 1562
36 O. Jocelyn Dunlop 1911, pp. 30, 54
37 George Unwin (1908) 1966, p. 266
38 James W. P. Campbell 2002, p. 221. See also Marcia Evans in note 4, 1997, p. 4
39 George Unwin (1908) 1966, pp. 262, 327–328
40 George Unwin (1908) 1966, chapter xvii "Monopolies"
41 *Ibid.*, p. 311
42 Elizabeth McKellar *The Birth of Modern London ... 1660–1720*, Manchester University Press, Manchester, 1999
43 For example Joseph Moxon from 1677
44 Starting with Godfrey Richards's edition of *Palladio* (the first book) 1663 – and many subsequent editions down to the 1730s
45 Gordon Priest 2003, pp. 14–15, 95, 96
46 Michael Farr *The Great Fire of Warwick 1694*, Hertford, 1992, p. 573
47 James Ayres 1998, pp. 16–18
48 R. S. Neal 1981, p. 68
49 *Ibid.*, pp. 337–338, 343. A similar procession of Tradesmen took place in Bristol in 8 September 1831 to celebrate the coronation of William IV
50 E. P. Thompson (1968) 1991
51 Joan Lane 1996, p. 6; E. P. Thompson (1968) 1991, p. 279
52 George III's engagement with the Academy's balance sheet was such that "the King

passed a morning examining the Academy's accounts." Joseph Farington, p. 523 13 April 1796

53 Vic Gatrell 2006, pp. 580–582
54 Henry Mayhew *London Labour and London Poor* 1862, Vol. III, p. 243 cited by E. P. Thompson (1968) 1991, p. 266
55 Iorwerth Prothero 1979; W. J. Rorabaug 1986; E. P. Thompson (1963) 1991
56 E. P. Thompson (1963) 1991, pp. 199, 466
57 McDermott and Berry eds 2011, 60; Joan Lane 1996, chapter 4, pp. 81–93
58 Charles Dickens 1861, chapter 14

Chapter 3

GUILD REGULATION
OF TRAINING

Central to the responsibility of the guild was the regulation of its "art & mystery". In discharging that duty the supervision of apprenticeships was essential. In theory, if not always in practice, apprentices were expected to be registered with the relevant guild from the point at which the indenture was drawn up and signed. Furthermore, in the centuries before decline set in, a master was only permitted to train a limited number of apprentices at a time – two or three in most trades, although they could, in addition, employ a number of journeymen. The guilds policed their regulations by means of the "power of search"; inspecting a master's workshop or premises and establishing the quality of the work and materials. Through these searches the officers of the guild (fellow craftsmen) were able to check on the number of apprentices, and the conditions in which they, the journeymen and other employees, worked.[1]

Apprenticeship was based on the simple belief that example was better than precept; that seeing how to make or do something was far more effective than a multitude of words. This was certainly the view of Joseph Moxon who, writing in 1683/84, argued that "*Craft* of the Hand … cannot be taught by Words, but is only gain'd by Practice and Exercise" and that this was the most effective way to "inure the hand". So satisfactory was this method of training that in some respects it persists to this day in serious disciplines like sport and music. All these activities are physical and their dextrous demands are best acquired in youth and so apprenticeships traditionally began at the age of 14 years.[2] Even this relatively youthful start is rather late in life if compared, even today, with disciplines like ballet.

Drudgery added much to the effectiveness of apprenticeships. The often utilitarian chores that these youths were expected to undertake took place within a relevant ambiance in which experience and knowledge were absorbed as much unconsciously as consciously. As Matthew Crawford (2009) has pointed out it was in these circumstances that an apprentice's "submission to the judgements of a master felt ennobling rather than debasing".[3] After years of obeying orders, standing around, being the butt of workshop jokes, doing menial jobs like sweeping the floor, an apprentice would eventually be invited to do something skilful such as the sharpening of tools. This was a very challenging aspect of the job, particularly with regard to edged woodworking tools, and was therefore recognised by the novice as a considerable advance, a privilege even. The next step in the hierarchy of skill would be to actually use the tools in question on some modest aspect of the work in hand. Not that the master always offered his trainees an adequate quality of work to hone their skills. As the Irish stone carver Seamus Murphy (1907–1975) recalled "if you don't get the work when you're serving your time, there's no hope for you."[4] By these means, and in these circumstances, workshop experience was sometimes either limited or brutal but it was more often generous in spirit. In general much skill and understanding was developed in the course of a seven year apprenticeship.

That seven years was based on a six day working week and long hours. These hours were first regularised nationally by the *Statute of Labourers* of 1351. This measure was drafted in 1349 as the Ordinance of Labour and was a direct consequence of the Black Death which reduced the population by over one-third. Faced with the prospect of a difficult labour force the authorities sought to set wages at the levels of 1347. The Statute applied to both freemen and serfs, to both craftsmen and labourers.[5] English law, being based on precedent, a comparable Act of 1495 (II Hen.VII.c.2) was further refined by the Act of 1515, and both were influenced by the Statute of 1351. These Acts of Parliament established a working day from 5 am to 7 or 8 pm from mid-March to 29 September (Michaelmas) with half an hour for breakfast and 1½ hours for lunch.[6] The length of the working day was further defined by the *Statute of Artificers* of 1563.[7] Although the hours of working were dependent upon daylight, and were correspondingly shorter in the winter months, these details reveal that in the summer the working week was in excess of 100 hours. By the first decade of the nineteenth century a less arduous regime was in place. According to the Swedish industrial spy Eric Svedenstierna (1802–3) work began in the Hull shipyards "at 7 o'clock in the morning and finished at 6 o'clock in the evening."[8] In this context it should be added that some historians have recently advanced the opinion that, in the past, work was conducted at a more leisurely pace than is usual today.[9]

The long working week and the extended working lives of many craftsmen did much to enhance an apprentice's training. In an age that was innocent of pensions and other benefits many tradesmen, health permitting, would continue working well into their 80s. Having begun work at the age of 14 this could result in a working life of over 65 years.[10] In this way the average workshop or building site would accommodate a very wide range of ages, a spectrum of experience and skill that could easily encompass more than 100 years. This was of the utmost importance because the full realisation of a given art and mystery was dependent on more than a single lifetime. In terms of aesthetic evolution, not to mention the fickle whims of fashion, this breadth of understanding may be contrasted with the narrow bands of time into which phases in art history are too often confined. In the Early Modern past the long hours and years of toil established a strong sense of stylistic continuity that had the potential to inhibit innovation. In these circumstances it is all the more remarkable that fresh ideas, new aesthetics, did emerge. Clear evidence for this can be seen in the three generations of the Abbott family of Frithelstock, Devon. Before the Reformation Frithelstock was the centre of an important Augustinian Priory, ruins of which survive adjacent to the parish church. The founder of this family of artisans John Abbott I (1565–1635) may well have been brought up in a craft tradition with origins in this ecclesiastical establishment before the Reformation. His grandson certainly gives an account in his notebook of how to paint rood screens (see p. 123 below). John Abbott the first was followed by his son, also John II (b. 1612) and he was succeeded by John Abbott III (1639–1727). As an 18 year old apprentice house painter and plasterer it was this last Abbott whose sketch book dated 1665 contains drawings of strapwork ornament typical of the early years of the century.[11] As an apprentice

FIGURE 7. Design for *strapwork ornament* from the 1665 sketchbook of the Devon plasterer John Abbott III (1639–1727). Abbott was the third generation in his family to serve as both a plasterer and a painter. This probably explains why his work as an apprentice was distinctly *retardataire* in contrast to the Baroque ornamental plasterwork created in his mature years (see Fig. 8). (Devon Record Office, Exeter)

the youngest Abbott was evidently strongly influenced stylistically by earlier generations of his family. At the close of the century, as a decorative plasterer, he would make his name working in an up-to date if provincial Baroque idiom.

The example of John Abbott III emphasises that whilst training was thorough and highly traditional it did not necessarily inhibit innovation. This was the basis on which, apprenticeships, at their best, were highly respected as a system of training. William Cobbett (1763?–1835), the radical auto-didact son of a labourer, shared this belief in such empirical instruction. Indeed, as the author of a whole series of published polemics, he was not above arguing against book learning. He was in favour of the young being put to a trade:

> "The taste of the times is, unhappily, to give children something of book-learning, with a view of placing them to live, in some way or other, upon the labour of other people ... what disappointment, mortification and misery to both parent and child! The latter is spoiled as a labourer; his book-learning has only made him conceited; into some course of desperation he falls; and the end is but too often not only wretched but ignominious ... I am wholly against children wasting their time in the idleness of what is called education; and particularly schools over which the parents have no control, and where nothing is taught but the rudeness of servility, pauperism, and slavery."[12]

Cobbett was clearly against the inadequacies of what passed for "education" in too many schools – in contrast to the real training that was offered by numerous workshops. In view of his background and the nature of his writings Cobbett's position in this matter carries great authority and may be contrasted with the views of "Sir Alan Gardiner" who, in 1797, feared that some members of the proletariat might gain an "education disproportionate to the[ir] situation."[13]

Cobbett would have known that trades differed in their levels of skill and education, that many required literacy but others like carpentry, masonry and bricklaying demanded an understanding of applied mathematics and solid geometry which were important components of their art and mystery. The theoretical and empirical problems that confronted a carpenter in setting-out and making the centring for a Welsh groin were considerable.[14] Those who were capable of solving such problems were well positioned to become architects.

In effect all these expectations could make an apprenticeship a rather exclusive form of training and education, a privilege which included the parent or guardian's ability to pay the premium – the fee which a master received on agreeing to train a youth and provide him with board and lodging. In many ways an apprenticeship was paralleled by the custom amongst the aristocracy and gentry of sending their children away to serve in comparable households.

Even amongst the elite a premium was paid for what was, in effect, "an informed apprenticeship in the art of the courtier".[15] Although at a far less exalted level the trade apprentice was nevertheless a member of a privileged minority far removed from the labouring masses and indigent poor. Some studies have suggested that, in the early eighteenth century, as many as one in four apprentices came from county gentry stock. To some extent the premium that was paid on behalf of an apprentice reinforced this status although it could be circumvented where a youth was apprenticed to his or her family; which was permissible provided they were registered with the relevant guild in the customary way. The *Binding Booke of the Company of Painter Stainers* includes numerous and apposite examples of this. For example on 2 November 1726 Thomas Steynor was apprenticed to his father Noah Steynor for seven years and on 5 August 1730 Thomas Painter was bound to his father. In both cases the surname evidently derives from the trade they practiced and in neither example did the parent demand a premium. Nevertheless Registration with the relevant guild was widely demanded (hence the *Binding Book* held by the appropriate authority) although the details differed somewhat from one jurisdiction to another. In Exeter in 1535 "Every *Freeman* that takes an Apprentice ought to Inrole his Indenture with the *Town Clark* on pain of five shillings" – but no reference is made to registration with the relevant guild.[16]

The cost of the premium did not exclude all youths from becoming apprentices for some were the beneficiaries of patronage. However others were denied such training because they were unfree, were bastards or had been born with physical deformities. Those born outside England were also debarred, a regulation that conveniently excluded Scottish and Irish rebels. By 1731 by-laws were in place in London that prohibited masters of a trade from

FIGURE 8. Ornamental plaster ceiling in The Customs House, Exeter. In 1681 Abbott was paid £35 for this elaborate work. For such high relief, in which much of the detailing is fully three dimensional, an armature of timber, rags and strips of lead was necessary.

accepting black apprentices.[17] There was also a property qualification which confined apprenticeships to the sons or wards of householders although the sons of farmers were excluded to keep them on the land. It is not known how fully the latter policy was implemented but the *Statute of Artificers* (1563) insisted that men and women under the age of sixty should work in agriculture if they had no other means of subsistence.[18] Certainly, in smaller communities many craftsmen also farmed small-holdings as was the case with the carpenter father of the sculptor Sir Francis Chantrey RA (1781–1841). In some trades outside the capital (beyond the "Custom of London") a further prohibition excluded those who had followed another vocation even when, in other respects, the individual met all the other requirements.

As we have seen, not all members of a guild had served their time in a relevant, or even irrelevant, trade. Furthermore some had not been accredited to the appropriate guild within their home town. One rather curious case concerns the mason Arthur Morris (d. 1744) of Lewes, East Sussex. In 1712 he was admitted to the Mason's Company of London as a "foreign member" on the payment of £1-16s.[19] This relatively low fee may have been connected with the fact that his father was also a mason by trade (patrimony?) and because he was, in effect, a "country member." With regard to the "Custom of London" which permitted those who were "free" of one trade to practice another, a number of examples could be cited. The case of the dramatist Ben Jonson (1572–1637) is a fairly early manifestation of this. He was born the posthumous son of a Church of England parson and, on his mother's remarriage, became the stepson of the bricklayer Robert Brett. By the time of his death in 1609 Brett had risen to become Master of the Tylers' and Bricklayers' Company, a trade that his stepson was to follow. Accordingly both his education at Westminster School and his training as a bricklayer were abbreviated. Despite this he was admitted a freeman of the Company by June 1596, very possibly by patrimony. By paying his quarterage, sometimes retrospectively, Jonson continued to enjoy the privileges that guild membership conferred. Consequently on 1 May 1612 he was in a position to bind John Catlin of Birmingham as an apprentice bricklayer for a term of eight years. Furthermore the playwright was able to derive a fee for passing on young Catlin as an apprentice actor to one of the London playhouses as was permitted by the "Custom of London".[20] Another example of this "Custom" concerns John Longland who was notionally a Haberdasher, perhaps by patrimony. He certainly served an apprenticeship from 1658 with Thomas Bates of London who was almost certainly a carpenter by trade if not necessarily by affiliation. By March 1666 Longland gained his freedom of the Haberdashers. Then, on September 2 of that year the Great Fire destroyed much of the City. The "Custom of London" would have permitted Longland to have practiced his true *métier* but in any event the great conflagration was to result in many tradesmen being freed from many long-standing regulations.[21] Longland must have been exceptionally proficient in his craft for he was to serve Wren as master carpenter to St Paul's whilst becoming Master of the Haberdashers Company in 1701.[22]

Patromony was a flexible device which enabled a son to join his father's Livery Company irrespective of any trade that he may, or may not, have been apprenticed to. A good example of this heritable guild membership is that of Giles Dance (d. 1751) a mason by trade but a Merchant Tailor by affiliation. On 2 June 1725 his son the builder-architect George Dance Snr (1695–1768) joined the Livery by patromony. In the next generation of the family the architect George Dance Jnr (1741–1825) was also of the fellowship and by 1794 "walked in the City procession as Master of the Tailors Company" as Farington noted of his fellow Royal Academician in his *Diary* on 11 November.[23]

The fee, or premium, that a parent or guardian was expected to pay a master craftsman on behalf of an apprentice varied widely according to the trade or occupation in question. In general though, these payments were sufficient to establish a social gulf between apprentices and the great mass of youths who enjoyed no such advantage. In this respect there was a significant rise in the number of younger sons of gentlemen who were placed in apprenticeships following the Restoration as families sought to recoup losses incurred during the Civil War and interregnum.[24] Another explanation for this feature may be that after 1660 Catholics and dissenters were denied access to the universities although dissenting academies were established.[25] Contemporaries were aware of the social mobility, down as well as up, that these circumstances engendered. In 1691 the well-connected Celia Fiennes noted in her travels around Britain that she "called on an old acquaintance" in Newbury who was "marryed to a tradesman Mr Every".[26] A generation later a French visitor to Britain observed that it was "rare for Peers to put their younger sons out as apprentices as 'tis said they used to do."[27] Certainly some trades were held in higher esteem that others. Ultimately the church and the growth of Empire would provide careers for younger sons of the aristocracy; the victims of primogeniture.

The very high premiums levied by masters in the more prosperous occupations, coupled with the impact of the *Stamp Act* (see p. 62 below), confined some trades and professions to the more affluent members of society. Inevitably these young gentlemen were far less biddable than earlier generations of trainees. This resulted in a potential for insolent behaviour which was recorded by Daniel Defoe who found that apprentices, especially after the *Stamp Act* was passed in 1709 would not "condescend to open or shut the shop windows, much less sweep the shop or warehouse floor."[28]

At about this time premiums for apprenticeships to civil lawyers could range between £70 and £200.[29] By Act of Parliament, in the second year of George II's reign only attorneys, who had been bound apprentice and served their time, could be sworn to practice in court.[30] Premiums for apprenticeships were not only high for lawyers and merchants (mercers for example) but also for those crafts that employed high value raw materials. In pre-industrial Britain metal goods and textiles were extraordinarily expensive with a knock-on effect for those trades that used them. The primacy of the Upholder (Upholsterer) in the fitting-up of rooms may be attributed to the cost of their materials. In this situation the Upholder became the principal contractor on interiors – they were, in short, the interior decorators of their day. As such they were in command of regiments of cabinet-makers, carvers and gilders, joiners, glaziers, painters and many others. The easel painter Edward Edwards (1738–1806) began his career working for the great Upholder William Hallett of Long Acre, London as an apprentice carver and gilder.[31] The potential that Upholders enjoyed for developing substantial wealth resulted in fairly high premiums. In mid-eighteenth century London an Upholder might demand £70 as a down payment for taking on an apprentice – although this would have been less in the provinces.[32]

In the city of Bath a distinct hierarchy is discernable, in the 1760s, between the various trades and occupations as indicated by the range of fees levied as premiums. The Surgeon Henry Wright demanded £262-10-0 to take on an apprentice. This contrasts with other occupations in the Spa such as an Apothecary who asked for £100, a Plumber £70, a Haberdasher £40, a House-Painter £20–£25 and a carpenter between £5 and £25.[33] Medicine in its various disciplines, was the Spa's local industry, but the high premiums to train as a Haberdasher or a Plumber was related to the cost of the materials even though textiles and lead were local products.

The fluctuating level of these premiums may also be used to chart the rise and fall of a particular trade. For example the development of the leaf-spring for wheeled vehicles in Stuart England saw a burgeoning demand for carriages which in turn inspired road improvements. This was a virtuous circle in which the development of the one saw the growth of the other. Furthermore during times of war with France sea travel and transport was avoided creating further incentives for more reliable inland routes.[34] As a consequence coach builders prospered. In about 1730 Thomas Godsal (1716–1763) was apprenticed to the London coachmaker Thomas Basnet for a premium of £35.[35] By 1787 the

FIGURE 9. *A Cabinet Maker's Office c.* 1770, artist unknown. Drawing formed a central role in such a business. A number of sculptors began their careers in woodworking shops but so too did some individuals who subsequently emerged as easel painters. Among the latter were George Romney (1734–1806) and Edward Edwards (1738–1806). (Victoria & Albert Museum, London)

London coachbuilder John Browne demanded a premium of £200 and, just four years later this increased to a remarkable £525.[36]

These figures indicate the extraordinary and rapid rise in the prosperity of coachbuilders during the course of George III's long reign. In this respect the Godsal dynasty is a case in point: Philip Godsal 1689–1762, Thomas Godsal 1716–1763, Philip Godsal 1747–1826. Of these Thomas would have completed his apprenticeship in about 1737 but his son Philip the younger was not formally bound but was admitted to the Company of Coachmakers and Lorimers in 1770 by Patrimony. Thomas Godsal married Susannah the daughter of Henry Lake (d. 1766) another coachbuilder who, via his mother (Frances Webb) was a grandson of a Fellow of All Souls, Oxford, and the great-grandson of a chaplain to Charles II. These particular tradesmen clearly belonged to a well-connected family. Thomas Godsal died in 1763 at the relatively early age of 47. His widow's background, in both social and craft terms, meant that she was well placed to run her late husband's business.[37] In 1768, a couple of years before he was admitted to the Coachmakers Company, the 21 year old Philip Godsal took over running the firm. It was Philip who was to prosper mightily as a gentleman and coachbuilder. By 1818 his total assets were in the region of £149,572 which, it has been argued, was 0.05% of the Net National Income at that time, Godsal's £149,572 representing perhaps £430 million in today's terms although the 5% would not equate to the twenty-first century economy.[38] With such wealth Godsal became a substantial patron of the arts commissioning work from a number of Royal Academicians including: Francis Wheatley, John Hoppner, Isaac Pocock and John Flaxman.[39]

Wealth on the scale achieved by Godsal was dependent upon two fundamentals of economics – a high demand and a large workforce to meet that need. His business was on such a scale that his premises could accommodate 76 carriages at any one time. Even so the company was compelled to pay parking fines on other carriages that pressure of work compelled them to park in the street. In terms of the work force we know that another large carriage builder named John Hatchett employed several hundred men in 1786 – and Godsal's workforce would have been similar, if not greater.[40] Godsal's business was one of a triumvirate of large scale coach-builders in London at this time, the others being Messrs. Wright & Lukin and also Hatchett. All these master coachbuilders were so successful that they were able to give their sons polite educations and leave them with ample means to live as leisured gentlemen.

The evidence provided by a coachbuilder's business like Godsal's enables us to view coach painters in a context that accounts for the high level of artistry that many of these tradesmen achieved. This explains how Charles Catton (1728–1798), a coach painter by trade, could emerge to become a founder member of the Royal Academy. Although Catton was in the possession of the necessary skills the industrialisation of his craft, in the form of paint manufacture, was to prove, in the long run, both a help and a hindrance.

Large workforces seem to have been a feature of many trade-based businesses by the second half of the eighteenth century. Not only coachmakers but also Upholders and Cabinet makers employed considerable numbers of craftsmen and labourers. Furthermore, to maximise profits the division of labour into specialisms within these trades was advancing rapidly. The place of the independent craftsman was in decline. This may have offered an incentive for some individuals to exchange labour in a large workshop for a vocation in a studio as independent artists.[41]

The building trades may have been something of an exception to these overarching trends. Almost by definition the construction industry is of no fixed address and was therefore less easily organised into capitalist enterprises. One of the first to bring the numerous and various building tradesmen within the comfortable yet stifling embrace of year round employment was Thomas Cubitt (1788–1855). The age of the general contractor had arrived at the expense of the independent working master.[42]

In Early Modern Britain the potential profitability of a trade or occupation could, as we have seen, be measured in relationship to the fees or premiums that masters levied to take on an apprentice. In this respect the merchant trades were, inevitably, highly placed. In 1783 the orphaned son of a Suffolk gentleman was placed with a silk Mercer in Aldermanbury London for a premium of £1,000.[43] By contrast the "fine arts" of painting and sculpture may have been seen as fashionable careers despite which the premiums were modest, as compared with capitalist trades. Francis Hayman (1707/8–1776) was apprenticed, in *c.* 1722, to the history painter Robert Browne in London for the sum of £84.[44] In fashionable yet provincial Bath portraiture was much in vogue amongst those who visited the Spa to enjoy ill-health. Among the artists who met this demand was William Hoare (*c.* 1707–1792). He would take an apprentice for a comparatively modest £105 although the same figure would secure training with the London engraver Charles Grignion (1721–1810). In far-off Lancashire the Preston portrait painter Arthur Devis (1711–1787) would only take an apprentice if he was endowed with natural talent – but he still expected to receive a premium of 150 guineas. The guineas in this case denoting the "professional" nature of the vocation.[45] In much the same way a pupilage could involve an annual fee. According to Farington a civil servant named Walker placed his son for three years under the care of the painter Robert Smirke RA (1752–1845). The terms for this were "100 guineas down and 100 guineas a year board etc. The young man [being] between 15 & 16 years of age" at the commencement of his pupilage.[46] The same source states that some five years later Smirke continued to take pupils at this fee but "boarding" was no longer included.[47]

In general premiums for apprenticeships were higher in London and fairly significant in fashionable cities like Bath and York or in major ports such as Bristol. Much the same was probably true for studentships in an artist's studio in such fashionable or commercial centres. In contrast those aspiring painters, sculptors and architects who attended the Academy schools from 1769, after its foundation in 1768, did so *gratis.* Consequently, because the Academy did not charge tuition fees, the traditional premiums or fees that were imposed for apprenticeships or pupilages were placed under some scrutiny with regard to those trades that were of relevance to the visual arts. This matter was certainly discussed in 1799 by the Academicians: Benjamin West, James Barry and Joseph Farington who:

> "talked of the unprepared young men who are admitted [to the] Plaister Academy [of the RA to draw from the Antique] as students. Many (Barry says) of their parents could not give £20 for their learning a trade, and could put them into the Academy for nothing..."[48]

As we shall see (Chapter 9) "liberal" painting gradually emerged from its trade origins requiring an apprenticeship to become a polite profession for which a "pupilage" and, eventually, attendance at an academy became customary. Ultimately these pupilages declined and students were to be largely confined to art schools. This was to be one of the contributing factors that was to distance painters from their craft although the more traditional modes of training persisted into the nineteenth century particularly for the various branches of sculpture (carving, chasing, die-sinking). The premiums that continued to be levied for these activities helped to maintain their status.

The whole question of status was reflected in the high standards of clothing that apprentices, journeymen and masters were expected to maintain. Inevitably this was particularly true of the textile trades and tradesmen for whom it was in their vested interests, and personal disposition, to dress well. The Merchant Tailors of London regularly fined those brethren or their apprentices who did not acquit themselves well in this respect.[49] In 1747 Campbell argued that the Mercer "must dress neatly and affect a Court Air" but then adds mischievously, "however far distant from St James's."[50] Although medieval sumptuary laws had attempted to confine the excessively fashionable, not to say outlandish, dress to the elite the guilds generally expected masters, journeymen and apprentices to look "respectable" rather than up-to-the-minute.[51] They certainly deplored "Apish Affectation and Vanity of Dress."[52] In this respect the attitude of the Painter Stainers of London became evident in 1634 when the Company noted, with some concern, that some of the brethren had been seen wearing:

> "Spotted Clothes and Aprons abroad in the Cittie to the discredit as well of this Companye as of the Art, it is this day ordered that whosoever shall be met in the street by the Master, Wardens or any Brother of this Companye or officer of the same with a Spotted Apron or Clothes without a Cloake, shall be warned to the Hall, the next Court and there be fyned for the first tyme XIId ..."[53]

This seems to have been an ongoing problem for the Painter Stainers as, just two years earlier, a "search" by the company resulted in a report that objected to:

> "the slovenly and indiscreet apparel worn by divers freemen of this Company and their apprentices in wearing fylthy aprons, carrying culler pots openly, to the disgrace of the profession of the Company."[54]

With such a trade clothes spattered by paints or stains were an occupational hazard. In these circumstances artisans were often identifiable by their personal appearance. A good example of this concerned the Scottish-born stonemason Samuel Kevan. On his move to London in 1783 he saw a "Master Slater & some men, knowing them by their tools". These men and their master gave the young Scot employment. The recognition of the attributes of a trade or profession could take various forms. For Mark Twain an individual's trade or occupation could also be discerned by the metaphors employed in their conversation.[55]

In late Stuart Britain, and certainly by the time of the Hanoverians, many easel painters had asserted their independence of guild regulation – not least because the Painter Stainers had lost full command of their craft. These "liberal"painters reflected a whole range of attitudes towards personal appearance; some were casual, others excessively fastidious. As noted above (p. 20) the young George Morland (1763–1804) was known for his "ultra dandyism" … "his head ornamented, according to his own taste, resembled a snow-ball … to which attached a short thick tail, not unlike a painters brush" – in fact a wig with a cue.[56] In contrast James Barry RA (1741–1806) was infamous for his casual appearance which was only exceeded by the tumble-down chaos of this own home at 36 Castle Street, London. When Edmund Burke visited Barry's painting room he found that it "had undergone no alteration whatever from the period when it had been used as a carpenters workshop".[57]

In comparison to the later academies the position of the guilds regarding these matters of personal appearance was unequivocal and long-standing. In 1498 the Ironmongers Company of London introduced a regulation that their apprentices should be well-dressed and not permit their hair to grow so long.[58] This whole question, particularly with regard to apprentices, was based on the fear that disorderly dress could lead to lawless conduct. Apprentices in London certainly had a fearsome reputation for insolent and even violent behaviour, especially on May Day. This could include assault and stabbings, with foreigners being a particular target.[59] A generalised concern for the behaviour of apprentices and their masters resulted in a number of legal measures being taken. In Elizabeth I's reign apprentices were prohibited from taking part in military training for fear that it might encourage "idleness and insolency" –

quite the contrary effect that National Service was believed to have had in the first decade of the reign of Elizabeth II. It seems that either apprentices were believed to be too active or too indolent. As the saying would have it: one boy equalled one day's work, two boys did half a day's work and three boys did no work at all.[60]

As for the "insolency" of master craftsmen, this could often have been a misreading of a tradesman's pride in his work. The diarist John Evelyn (1620–1706) recorded a conversation between himself and a master-builder whom he regarded as "conceited". With the benefit of hindsight it is evident that Evelyn seriously underestimated the training and education of this artisan who responded accordingly: "Sir, I do not come hither to be taught my trade. I have served my apprenticeship, and have wrought ere now with gentlemen that have been satisfied with my work".

Unapologetically the diarist went on to note that he had "frequently met … [such] language of reproach" and that on occasion an artisan would even throw "down his tools … going away in wrath."[61] An employer's sense of superiority could, at times, be matched by a craftsman's pride in his work and the years of practice that it had taken to achieve high objective standards.

Notes

1. Guy Hadley 1976, pp. 27, 28, 63, 64
2. For Moxon see Derek A. Long 2013, p. 78. There has been some debate concerning the age at which an individual began an apprenticeship. However this debate is based on the records of just one Company – the Carpenters of London which refer to actual registrations and may therefore be misleading. Cited by James W. P. Campbell 2002, endnote 60
3. Matthew Crawford 2009, 2010, p. 160
4. Perhaps one of the problems with today's education is that this sequence of events is reversed. An architectural student will be given a "modest" project like designing an airport terminal or a museum. Then, once in the real world that student will be asked to devise something small yet complex like a window catch. See also Seamus Murphy (2005) 2010, p. 146.
5. Joan Lane 1996, p. 52. Dan Jones 2012, 493. The craftsmen itemised in the Ordinance included "Saddlers, skinners, white-tawers, cordwainers, tailors, smiths, carpenters, masons, tilers, shipwrights, carpenters and all other artisans and labourers"
6. Rosemary O'Day 2000, p. 24
7. James W. P. Campbell 2002, pp. 226–227
8. Eric T. Svedenstierna (1802–3), 1973, p. 103
9. Keith Thomas 2009, p. 99

[10] The author's father, the architectural sculptor Arthur J. J. Ayres (1902–1985) enjoyed a working life of about 70 years. Also, in the early 1950s the author worked with a mason and carver named Woollett who, in his turn, had begun his trade as a 14 year old apprentice working on the installation of Cleopatra's "Needle" on the Thames Embankment, London in 1878

[11] The two small manuscript books by John Abbott (the recipes and the drawings) are in Devon Record Office, Exeter: 404M/81,82. Mike Baldwin 2006; I share Baldwin's view that these two small manuscript books are by John Abbott III. Anthony Wells-Cole, 1997, p. 160 appears to be of the opinion that they are the work of an earlier generation – possibly John Abbott II.

[12] William Cobbett (1821) 1979, pp. 6–7

[13] Joseph Farington *Diary* p. 951 20 Dec 1797 with reference to Sunday schools

[14] Peter Nicholson's *Carpenters New Guide* 1823, p. 28

[15] Mary S. Lovell *Bess of Hardwick* ... (Little Brown 2005) Abacus, London, 2009 pp. 18–19. Bess of Hardwick (1527–1608) was about 12 years old when she was sent away from home to serve the Zouche family of Codnor Castle, Derbyshire

[16] Jerry White 2012, p. 90 citing Peter Earle 1989, pp. 3–5. Samuel Izacke, *Antiquities of the City of Exeter*, London, 1741, p. 118

[17] O. Jocelyn Dunlop 1911, pp. 43–44; Jerry White 2012, p. 133

[18] Keith Thomas 2009, p. 89

[19] Rupert Gunnis 1953; Ingrid Roscoe *et al.* eds 2009

[20] Ian Donaldson 2011 pp. 65, 89, 90

[21] Joan Lane 1996, p. 59

[22] James W. P. Campbell 2002, pp. 218–219, 221

[23] Howard Colvin 1995; Joseph Farington *Diary*, p. 259

[24] Joan Lane 1996, p. 20

[25] William Rosen 2010, p. 29

[26] Christopher Morris ed. (1947) 1982, p. 61

[27] François Misson *Memoirs and Observations in his Travels over England* (1729) 1967 transl. John Ozell,

[28] Daniel Defoe 1715, II, p. 261

[29] Rosemary O'Day 2000, pp. 156, 165, 167

[30] *Ibid.*, p. 170

[31] Edward Edwards 1808, p. xxxix; Geoffrey Beard 1997, p. 162

[32] *Ibid.*, p. 6

[33] R. S. Neal 1981, pp. 50–52

[34] James Ayres 1998, p. 55

[35] John Ford 2005, p. 13; Ford gives the date of 1747 as the start of Thomas Godsal's apprenticeship – which must be a mistake

[36] Joan Lane 1996, p. 24

[37] John Ford 2005, p. 13, 30, family tree p. 210

[38] *Ibid.*, p. 9. This total being comprised of £98,130 plus a further £51,442 which he had passed to his children

[39] *Ibid.*, p. 10

[40] *Ibid.*, p. 22–23 – regarding Sophie de la Roche's visit to Hatchett's workshop in 1786

[41] Charles Catton RA (1728–1798) the one-time coach painter is an obvious example

[42] Hermione Hobhouse 1971. Mid-eighteenth century building tradesmen are known to

have contracted for trades other than their own. Also Ralph Allen of Bath, as a quarry owner, provided year round employment and housing for his quarrymen and banker masons – see James Ayres 1998, pp. 4, 71–72

43 Joan Lane 1996, p. 22
44 W. H. Pyne 1823, Vol. I pp. 77–78. Browne may have been Hayman's uncle, his mother's maiden name was Browne. Edward Edwards 1808, Vol. I, p. 50
45 Joan Lane 1996, p. 22
46 Joseph Farington p. 442 14 December, 1795
47 *Ibid.*, p. 1406 17 June, 1780
48 *Ibid.*, p. 1124 1 Jan, 1799
49 O. Jocelyn Dunlop 1911, p. 30 no dates given
50 R. Campbell 1747, p. 197
51 Joan Lane 1996, pp. 27–28
52 S. Richardson 1734, p. 35
53 W. A. D. Englefield (1923) 1936, p. iv; Alan Borg 2005, p. 58
54 *Ibid.*, p. 101
55 Jerry White 2012, 98 citing Kevan *Autobiographical Memoir and Diary*. Kevan was born in 1764 and apprenticed to his brother in 1779. Charles Neider ed. *The Autobiography of Mark Twain*, New York 1990, p. 126
56 Allan Cunningham 1830, Vol. II, pp. 216–218
57 J. T. Smith (1828) 1919, Vol. II, p. 279
58 J. Nicol *Some Account of the Worshipful Company of Ironmongers,* London, 1866, p. 221
59 Thomas Burke 1941, p. 15
60 Keith Thomas 2009, pp. 68–69, 99. I am grateful to John Steane for the gift of this thought provoking book.
61 *Ibid.*, p. 100 citing John Evelyn 1707

Chapter 4

INDENTURED
APPRENTICESHIPS

We sometimes catch a glimpse of people at work in the past in topographical drawings (Figs 10, 25). These may show the tender age at which apprentices began their servitude – children amongst men. Written accounts are less common. One of the best in conveying a sense of this abrupt departure from childhood, to the grown-up world of work, is to be found in Christopher Thomson's (1799–1871) *Autobiography of an Artisan* (1847).[1]

> To be "bound prentice" is usually an event of no small importance in juvenile history. It is the April of life – "tears and smiles," hope and fear, alternate. The aspirant will sometimes venture to look back upon his boy-days, and with mock gravity, call them foolish – an age of trifles. He now fancies himself of importance in the world – is about to become a great man – lectures his former playmates with assumed dignity – yet is the struggle great within him, as to which class, the boy or the man, he really does belong. Often, when in the hey-day of his air-castle building, some trifling incident suddenly throws him back again to the green-fields and play-grounds, and for the moment, he sighs to join his old companions at ball, or hoop, or spinning top; then again he struts, but mimics the man awkwardly; albeit he may be "much older than he looks," it is all in vain. Nature steps in and asserts her rights, and whether he will or no, he must be boy, and man, by turns.

This is the theme of William Hogarth's *Industry and Idleness* (1747) which contrasts the indolence of one apprentice weaver with the "grown-up" efforts and rewards of another. In Trusler's (1778) "explanation" of this series of engravings it is evident that the value of this "modern moral subject" was that it was based on the reality that "example is far more convincing, and, perswasive, than precept." These prints were therefore "an excellent lesson to such young

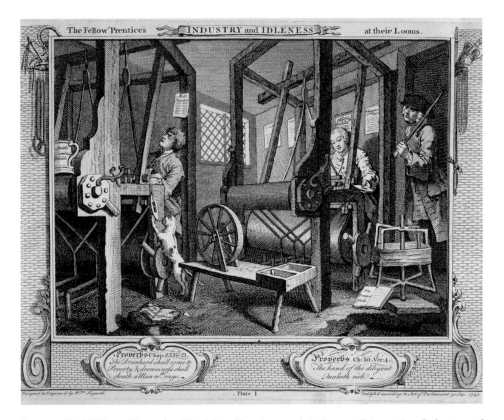

FIGURE 10. William Hogarth, *The fellow 'Prentices at their Looms; Representing Industry and Idleness* – the preparatory sketch for this engraving of 1747 names the three figures shown here very faintly in pencil. The master (right) was Goodchild, the hardworking apprentice (centre) is identified as Barnwell, whilst the sleeping youth is named as Thomas Taylor. The book on the floor in front of Barnwell is *The Prentices Guide* possibly Sir John Barnard's manual published in the same year as Hogarth's engraving. (British Museum, London)

men as are brought up to business ..."[2] And "example" rather than "precept" was the whole basis on which the apprenticeship system functioned.

The terms of an apprenticeship were set out in an "indenture". This was any legal document, written or printed out in duplicate, generally on one sheet of parchment or paper. There were exceptions to this. For example the indenture of 1504 between Henry VII and John Islip, Abbot of Westminster, is in book form and was drawn up in four parts, two of which survive. One edge of all the pages in these books is indented (from the French: *endenture*: toothed).[3] More usually a single sheet was divided by means of an irregular cut – the indent (Fig. 11). In the event of a dispute the two halves (the two copies) could be brought together and, if the erratic cut did not agree (the agreement) one with the other, at least one of the documents was invalid. If the two documents agreed any dispute consequently related to the text of the indenture. These documents were generally drawn up on parchment although paper was gradually introduced for this purpose from the mid-seventeenth century. Early in the following century printed agreements began to appear with suitable spaces in the text for the particulars of the contract. For an apprenticeship this would include the name of the master and his apprentice and the obligations to which both parties were subject. With the introduction of the Stamp Act in 1709 a stamp formed part of these agreements. As a result the State was directly involved in these contracts for the first time. This excise duty was imposed on a sliding scale related to the cost of the premium – 6d in the £1 for those under £50; 12d (1s) in the £1 for those over that sum plus an extra 6d duty. In these circumstances it is likely that few premiums exceeded £49-19s. It is certainly the case that this legislation resulted in the under registration of apprentices with the relevant authorities – despite the requirement that only those youths who were so accredited could, in theory, officially gain the freedom to practice their craft as independent tradesmen – but there were exceptions.[4]

These indentures soon adopted a fairly consistent form of words, possibly a by-product of the increasing use of the printing press for these documents (see Appendix I for an example). A comparison of the wording in two printed indentures emphasises this compatibility. In one such document of 1788 the decorative plasterer John Flaxman the Elder (1726–1803) agreed to train Isaac Dell as a "Moulder and Caster of Plaister Figures." With such agreements the master kept one copy and the apprentice or his family the second. It is therefore most unusual for both copies to survive together as with the Flaxman/Dell example (Fig. 11).[5] In keeping with custom the standardised provisions are printed but the particularities were written-in by a clerk (shown in italics in the transcript Appendix I). Another example is, the 1760 agreement between Henry Phillip (son of William Phillip of Monmouth, labourer) who "hath put himself Apprentice to Charles Rowbotham of the City of Bristol, Brush-maker and Sarah his wife".[6] From this it is evident that Henry Phillip placed himself in a trade – perhaps because his labourer father lacked the resources to pay his premium. In theory no youth was to bind himself to a master without parental consent although by the early seventeenth century this was regarded as "more usual than lawful."[7] Phillip evidently had this parental permission since the document is countersigned by his father using his mark "X". The reverse of this indenture carries a codicil concerning the supply of clothing to Phillip by

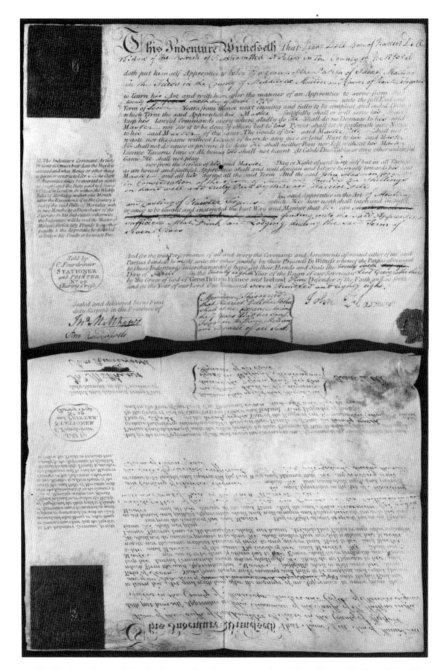

FIGURE 11. Both halves of the *Indenture* for the apprenticeship of Isaac Dell to John Flaxman Snr (1726–1803) – to be instructed in the art and mystery of "Moulder and Caster of Plaister Figures" – dated 1788 (see Appendix I for the full text). (National Art Library, London)

his friends and relatives. In contrast to his father young Phillip was evidently literate and signed the agreement in full in a clear hand.

Characteristically this Bristol indenture required the master to "diligently teach, instruct and inform, or cause to be informed by others, in the craft of brush making." Although the number of apprentices that a master was entitled to accept was limited to no more than three at any one time these trainees often received instruction from journeymen and others, rather than the master. As was customary until the nineteenth century only masters who were married could accept apprentices[8] and a youth was expected to "dwell" with his master and his wife and to obey all "lawful commands", maintain "the secrets of his said master and mistress [and] to keep their goods safe". Such a youth was not to frequent "Taverns" play "Dice" or "commit Fornication". With respect to "Taverns", Innkeepers in Colchester in 1549 forbade their apprentices from entering their establishments on a Sunday as customers – and they would have been at work on the other six days of the week.[9] With marriage prohibited the embargo on fornication was probably a forlorn hope. That was certainly Campbell's (1747) opinion of apprentices in whom: "the Blood runs warm in their Young Veins and they are naturally prone to gratify the new-grown Appetite ....".[10] In common with most such indentures the brush-maker's agreement goes on to state the obligations of the master and his wife in providing the apprentice with "good and sufficient Meat, Drink, *Washing, Lodging and all other necessities Apparel Excepted*". It concludes with the stipulation that the master will pay the apprentice "Four shillings and Six pence towards his Freedom of Bristol in lieu of his Salary."

These documents demonstrate that the master was expected to act towards the apprentice in *loco parentis*. This partly explains why the *Statute of Artificers* (1563) ordained that masters were to be limited to taking no more than three apprentices at a time.[11] Despite these benign intentions apprentices in early Stuart London developed an awareness of their collective power – they numbered some 30,000 individuals. In 1641 these youths objected that they were bound only to their masters "yet of late mistresses had gotten the predominancy over them also."[12] This presumably explains why later indentures like the 1760 Bristol example cited above, generally include reference to the master's wife.

Apprentices were not usually paid, quite the contrary it was the trainee or rather his parent or guardian, who paid for the privilege of his training – the premium. From the master's point of view an apprentice, in his first years, was of little value and might even have been viewed as a hindrance. Clearly in these circumstances it was in the interests of both the master and the apprentice that this training was effective. The burgeoning value of an apprentice was well-exemplified in 1488 when John Bell was appointed as the master mason at Durham Cathedral. Bell was to employ one apprentice whose work was valued at 4 marks yearly in the first three years, 6 marks in each of the following three years and 7 marks in his final and seventh year.[13] Something of this situation is reflected in Caroline Herschel's (1750–1848) reminiscence of the help she gave her astronomer brother casting and polishing lenses. She, with some modesty, recalled that: "I became in time as useful a member of the workshop as a boy might be to his master in the first year of his apprenticeship." In terms of bed and board many of a master's obligations to his apprentices were, by the late eighteenth century, commuted to cash. Take, for example, William Tongue's apprenticeship in *The Art of Manufacturing and Erecting Engines*. This indenture concerned a period of servitude from 1797 to 1804 and was signed by both Matthew Boulton and James Watt. The document states that in lieu of "Meat, drink, lodging and other necessaries" Tongue was to be paid 8 shillings a week for the first year, rising to 14 shillings a week for the seventh and final year.[14] Towards the end of his time the increasing value of a youth to his master may have resulted in some recognition of this in the shape of payments, or payments in kind. Barter certainly occupied an important place in Early Modern Britain. Isaac Ware (1756) describes how master building craftsmen, working as property developers on a terrace of urban houses, would exchange their respective skills.[15] Another feature of this partly cashless economy was the trade perquisites which often took the form of off-cuts from the materials of a given craft. So common did this become that each trade developed a vocabulary to describe, and obscure, these "perks". In this way tailors claimed their "cabbage", the hatters their "bugging" the weavers their "thrums", the shipwrights their "chips" and the gilders their "skewings".[16] What may have begun as a reasonable bonus, became, in the course of time, theft. For example when shipwrights emerged at the end of the working day from the yards that employed them they might be seen staggering under the weight of large baulks of timber carefully described as "chips". As perquisites, or as illegal appropriations, these items had value "in kind". This was a black economy that has left few records but one in which apprentices were doubtless involved.

The progression from an apprenticeship to the freedom to practice a trade was, by no means, assured. Most youths began their servitude at the age of fourteen years and were bound to their masters for seven years. There were exceptions in the age at which this type of training began and the number of years served. In London an apprenticeship to a goldsmith could last as long as ten years.[17] In 1796 a young man was apprenticed to the engraver Byrne at a

premium of £100 but by this date the apprenticeship system was in decline so
he signed up to just five years of servitude.[18] In the past this would have been
prohibited. The city of Exeter took action in 1540 against "John Postell [who]
was dis-franchised for making his *Apprentice* free before the end of his term."[19]
Having served his time the registered apprentice was, in theory, eligible to
become a candidate for membership of the guild although this was normally
delayed by some years spent as a journeyman (a craftsman paid by the day:
journée). Some unfortunate individuals remained in a state of servitude even
after the completion of their time.[20]

In much of Continental Europe an apprentice who had completed his
training would submit a *chef d'oeuvre* to the relevant guild as a demonstration
of his skill.[21] To what extent these were required by English guilds is uncertain.
In London there is no reference to "masterpieces" or "proof pieces" as they
were more generally known in the City, until the late sixteenth century. Unwin
(1908) was of the opinion that this requirement had become general in the
capital by the seventeenth century.[22] Certainly by 1608 physical specimens of
work were demanded in the City by the Embroiderers and the Curriers. Other
guilds would later insist on such evidence including the Weavers, Saddlers and
Joiners. The York guilds made similar provisions for the production of samples
of work. By 1619 the woodworking trades of the northern province required
a "humbling piece" – a term which aptly conveys the humility with which a
young artisan placed his work before the masters of his craft.[23]

By the mid-seventeenth century the proof piece, for all its practical value in
terms of quality control, appears to have been in decline in England although
this pragmatic method of maintaining craft standards persisted in much of
Continental Europe. An indication of the declining place of proof pieces in
the City concerned the Clockmakers which, at the time of its incorporation in
1631demanded masterpieces. A few years later, in 1656, the Company began
to express a concern that proof pieces were no longer a requirement. If this
was a general malaise amongst the guilds at this time it may have been one
of the many consequences of the Civil War. More encouragingly the record
of the Tin-Plate Workers of London show that proof pieces continued to be
submitted down to the last decades of the eighteenth century; but then this
Company was not incorporated until 1670 well after the interregnum.[24]

In the Low Countries the painter Carel van Mander (1604) objected to "the
shameful laws and narrow rules" that the guilds wished to impose on artists.
Mander was of the opinion that painters and sculptors should be exempt
from the need to produce masterpieces "in the same fashion as the works of
cabinet makers and other tradesmen."[25] This sort of resistance may explain the

relaxation of explicit obligations for the production of masterpieces by artists and the less formal arrangements that were adopted for them. In 1667 the sculptor Edward Woodruff was to be admitted a freeman of Oxford provided he could, "in a workmanlike manner, cutt or carve the King's Arms or such other signs for the use of the City as the Mayor or his brethren shall direct."[26] A comparable example concerned the Danish-born sculptor Caius Cibber (1630–1700). This foreigner applied to join the Leather Sellers Company by redemption in 1668 but had some difficulty in finding the fee of £25. The problem was resolved when the Company agreed to accept in lieu "a stone mirmayd over the pumpe" in the courtyard of their hall.[27] Such accreditation was, of course, a greater problem for a foreigner. There is some evidence that the Painter Stainers of London expected a masterpiece to be submitted by aliens who wished to join the Company. On 30 July 1647 the Court of the Painters ordered that the Dutch-born Jacobus Hausman should submit a proof piece within three months. In September 1682 Peter van der Muler was "admitted a foreign member" of the Painter Stainers of London for a payment of 40 shillings and the promise of a proof piece.[28] The submission of a masterpiece remained a constant, if intermittent, refrain into the eighteenth century. On 25 September 1712 the sculptor John Hunt (d. 1754), who had been apprenticed to Grinling Gibbons (1648–1721), became a freeman of Northampton "gratis for carving King Charles's statue", now above the portico of All Saints Church (Fig. 12).[29] Another instance of this form of masterpiece relates to the portrait painter Mary Beale (1632/3–1699). Her father John Cradock, the rector of Barrow in Suffolk, was an amateur painter of some ability. In July 1648 he presented the Painter Stainers Company of London with:

> "a piece of painting of his own making, which he gave into this company, consisting of varieties of fruits: viz. apricocks, quinces, ffilberts, Grapes, Apls and other sorts of fruits, and was also at this court made free of the said company."[30]

This still life was effectively a proof piece, see also p. 184. An echo of these traditions for a masterpiece survives in the shape of the "Diploma work" that Royal Academicians are expected to present to that institution following their election.

With or without such physical evidence of skill the candidate for acceptance into the guild was expected to pay a fee, although this would be considerably less than that paid by those admitted by patrimony or redemption. In the city of Bristol this was traditionally paid by the apprentice's master; as was the case for Phillip Robotham cited above (p. 64,). This fee was also one of the

FIGURE 12. John Hunt (d. 1754) stone figure of *Charles II* which surmounts the west front of All Saints Church, Northampton. This figure was presented to the County Town by the sculptor on 25th Sepember 1712. It served as his proof piece, or master piece, and thus gained him the Freedom of Northampton and the associated right to practice his art and mystery in the town. (National Monuments Record)

impediments deployed by the guilds to regulate the number of craftsmen in a given trade so as to ensure that the supply did not exceed the demand. Another means to this end was the regulation that an apprentice who was not registered with the guild or the city authorities could not qualify for membership. In addition many fraternities began to insist on a delay of at least three years before an apprentice, who had completed his time, would be considered for membership of the brotherhood. In this phase these youths were known as "improvers" or "journeymen"[31] and were expected to remain unmarried.[32] With regard to accreditation by a guild the position of an immigrant was problematic but not insuperable in the capital thanks to the presence of various free trade zones in and around London. Despite such regulations the Danish-born sculptor Christian Carlsen Seest (fl. 1734–1757) travelled and worked in Germany, Holland and England and, presumably in order to circumvent problems over "work permits", he was described in his passport as a "Sculptor Apprentice."[33]

The journeyman was a tradesman who, having completed his apprenticeship was, as noted above, paid daily (*journée*). It should be added that this was the stage at which young artisans often travelled to gain experience and widen their horizons. Sadly many individuals remained in this limbo as journeyman, a situation close to servitude. It was these "yeoman tradesmen" who, with a dwindling opportunity of ever becoming master craftsmen, established what were in effect parallel guilds. Under these circumstances the regulations that journeymen, like apprentices, should remain unmarried was, inevitably, ignored. This was just one of the motivating factors behind the formation of the unofficial "Adulterine Guilds".[34]

On admission to the guild an apprentice was traditionally presented with a gift by his parent or guardian and, sometimes, his master. In 1747 Sir John Barnard published his *A Present for an Apprentice* which was presumably written with this market in mind. However Sir John evidently intended that his book should have as wide a sale as possible. This publication includes much advice to a youth who is about to become an apprentice with an emphasis on his relationship with his master in whose business and domestic household he served. Barnard also proffers the recommendation that a newly free craftsman should defer setting up in business. His reasons centred on his view that "young men prosper best when they have either served as Journeymen to some wary stagers, or have the happiness to be taken in as [business] partners to such" individuals. The book concludes with suggestions on the choice of a wife, the rearing of children and the employment of servants.[35]

Sir John Barnard, whose bust appears in William Kent's Temple of British Worthies at Stowe (1735), was a former Lord Mayor of London and the sub-title to his book promotes it as "a sure Guide to Gain Esteem and Estate wth Rules for his Conduct to his Master and in the World." This publication appeared in the same year (1747) that William Hogarth issued his series of engravings with the collective title *Industry and Idleness* (Fig. 10). This pictorial novel chronicled the failures of a lazy apprentice in contrast to the achievements of a conscientious one. These prints were sold by Hogarth at what he conceived to be the modest price of one shilling so that "the purchase of them became within the reach of those for whom they were intended".[36]

Of more immediate concern to the newly trained artisan were the tools of his trade. In contrast to the workshop equipment like benches etc., which were provided by employers, hand tools were owned by their users who were thus responsible for their maintenance and care. Some of these tools would be made by the artisan who used them but most were purchased. When Thomas Bewick was apprenticed in 1767 to the Newcastle engraver Ralph Beilby his master showed him how to make graving implements. His skill as a toolmaker was to become so significant that this was noted by Audubon, the American naturalist and artist, when he visited the Northumbrian's workshop in April

1827. These tools varied in size from large "scorpers" to the smaller "spitstickers" and "bullstickers". Bewick himself states that these were sharpened on "A good Turkey oil stone [which] may be got at any of the Hardware Shops – but I fear it will require a good deal of practice before you are able to sharpen your tools properly."[37] Turkey stones were from Smyrna in Asia Minor and would have been stocked by hardware stores for sale to a wide range of workers in wood.[38] In Newcastle another likely customer for Turkey Stones was Bewick's good friend, the carver and gilder Walter Cannaway.[39]

In many cases the tools of a given trade were presented to a young craftsman by his parents or guardian, and sometimes by his master, to celebrate the completion of his time. In London, Eton and York apprentice masons were presented with a set of tools at this juncture. In Norwich in 1559/60 newly qualified masons were given a kit of tools that would include a trowel, a hammer-axe, a brick-axe, a pick-axe and a plumb rule. This demonstrates that by this date masons in East Anglia, where stone is scarce, had made the transition to brick. In Oxford there is evidence that between 1513 and 1632 woodworkers emerging from their apprenticeships were more likely to be given the tools of their *métier* than was typical for other trades in the city.[40]

A superb example of a gift to a newly qualified artisan is the set of cabinet makers tools that were presented to Benjamin Seaton to mark both the completion of his apprenticeship and his twenty-first birthday in 1796 – two events which generally coincided, hence this being the traditional "age of majority". This tool kit was given to young Benjamin by his father Joseph Seaton of Chatham, Kent (Rochester Museum). The tools were purchased from Christopher Gabriel of Banner Street, London. They remain as a complete set in the chest designed to house them which, in itself, is a supreme example of cabinet-making. The stark simplicity of the its outer soft-wood carcass with its rope carrying handles contrasts with the veneered mahogany interior which is given visual definition by boxwood stringing and turned ivory drawer knobs – an object that may well have been made by young Seaton as his masterpiece.[41] At a later date these gifts to graduating artisans, like the board and lodging that was once provided for apprentices, were commuted to cash in lieu which consequently dwindled in value.

Up to this point regular reference has been made to an apprentice and "his master". This raises the question regarding the position of girls and women in relationship to the apprenticeship system and their subsequent employment. Traditionally trades like millinery and dressmaking were seen as female occupations. In contrast Joan Lane (1996) has argued that "girls .... were rigorously excluded from apprenticeships in the building or leather

trades and the heavy metal skills ..."[42] There were exceptions but this may well
have been the general situation in London and elsewhere although women
were often employed as labourers. In Newcastle, for example, girls and women
worked as hodcarriers for bricklayers and slaters in the 1820s but it was hoped
that "employment more suitable and becoming for these poor girls" should
be found "than that of mounting high ladders and crawling over the tops of
houses."[43] In general women most typically worked as either labourers or as
employers. Despite this it is known that, even in London, some women were
involved in the building trades in a hands-on sense. This would inevitably mean
that they would have served an apprenticeship.[44] As long ago as 1887 Jupp
and Pocock noted that in Stuart London women were, at times, admitted to
the Wheelwrights Company by right of apprenticeship and the same was true
for the Clockmakers Company in the capital.[45] By 1911 Jocelyn Dunlop cites
two examples of young women claiming and being granted admission to the
Carpenters Company of London in 1675 and 1712, for the good reason that
they had completed their apprenticeships and attained the appropriate level
of skill.[46] More recently Peter Guillery (2000) has followed the extraordinary
story of Mary Lacy (1740–after 1771). Lacy went to sea disguised as a boy, an
apprentice ships' carpenter and later continued in that trade in London as a
house carpenter and property developer, whilst living with her "niece".[47]

The degree to which women were involved, or were permitted to engage, in
the crafts needs further research. As things stand the impression that may be
gleaned, from various sources, is that outside the traditional female occupations
women were generally excluded. The exception to that general position is
that the widows of craftsmen were permitted to continue their late husband's
business in which capacity they were running a commercial enterprise rather
than making "things". In this respect the widows of plumbers, and also painters,
are over represented in the historical record simply because the toxic nature
of lead, and lead-based paints, brought their husbands to an early death.[48] In
taking over the concern of a disabled or deceased spouse many, perhaps most,
female silversmiths with registered hallmarks, were business women rather
than artisans.[49] Of all the women associated with the building trades the most
remarkable was probably "Mrs" Eleanor Coade, a single woman who ran a
very large business manufacturing her eponymous "stone" – in fact a type of
ceramic, a stoneware. The manufactory in Lambeth flourished from 1769 to
1840 and during that time employed some of the most significant sculptors
of the day in the production of master patterns for statuary and architectural
ornament (see p. 327 and Fig. 100).[50]

In view of the difficulties that women generally encountered in apprenticing themselves to a trade their involvement in the visual arts is all the more remarkable since many young men were compelled to approach these arts via a training in a trade. And yet, despite these impediments, no less than two of the founder members of the Royal Academy of Arts were women, although both were from artistic families and foreign backgrounds. In the context of the day (1768) this was doubly enlightened. Of these two Angelica Kauffman (1741–1807) was Swiss and Mary Moser (1744–1819) was the daughter of the chaser George Michael Moser (1704–1783) who was also Swiss-born. Perhaps it was their alien backgrounds that enabled them to confront the English art establishment blithely unaware of any prejudice that may have been present. Even so in Johann Zoffany's group portrait of the Academicians of *c.* 1772 we are given the image of an all-male club, with these two women making their appearance as portraits hung on the wall in the life class with its male model. Despite their presence as founder members of the Academy women were not to be admitted to the RA Schools before 1860 and none was elected as an Academician until the twentieth century.[51]

Following the opening of the Academy Schools in 1769 many individuals who had completed their time as apprentices, with a thorough training in their craft, went on to attend the Schools to enhance their education as artists. This was a generation that enjoyed the benefits of receiving both a training and an education.[52] Of the 77 students who enrolled in that first year 52 were identified as painters, sculptors, architects or engravers but the remaining 25 are not listed by vocation – perhaps they had yet to acquire one? Among this first intake of students was Edward Edwards an ex-apprentice carver and gilder before becoming a painter, and John Bacon, who had been apprenticed in the Bow porcelain manufactory before developing as a sculptor.[53] In 1769 both these men would have been about 30 years of age and, even today, would be regarded as mature students. It is therefore probable that they confined themselves largely to the life classes which took place in the evening. Others who availed themselves of the RA schools included James Gillray and William Blake who had each served their time as apprentice engravers. When William Blake looked back on his formative years as an artist it was not the drudgery of an apprenticeship that he recalled. It was, rather, his time at the RA Schools where he "spent the vigour of [his] youth & genius under the oppression of Sir Joshua & his gang of cunning hired knaves."[54] Blake certainly had a point for even Malone, Reynolds's first biographer (1797), states that the President argued that the students should follow "an implicit obedience to the Rules of Art."[55]

This suggests that students were less stifled by the disciplines of an

FIGURE 13. Johann Zoffany (1734/5–1810): *John Cuff in his Workshop* (1772). Cuff was Master of the Spectacle Makers' Company of London in 1748. The pleasures of making are reflected in this portrait although the assistant, who may have been in a state of perpetual subordination, seems less than enthused. (Royal Collection Trust/ © Her Majesty Queen Elizabeth II 2014)

apprenticeship than by the imposed aesthetic conventions of the Academy. A workshop training equipped an artisan with the tools, both metaphoric and real, of his trade. Consequently a journeyman or freeman was fully able to express his thinking in his chosen medium. Thus emancipated the tradesman possessed a joyful exaltation in his work. This agreeable situation is fully visible in the face of John Cuff in Zoffany's portrait of this master craftsman – although his assistant appears to be less than thrilled (Fig. 13). For those who coupled this sort of assured skill with the visual arts, the pleasures of making were united with "The Pleasures of the Imagination" the subject of a series of essays by Addison (1712).[56] In this way artists who functioned within the craft-based tradition enjoyed, what even economists acknowledge as: "psychic income".[57]

* * * *

In British North America the tradition for trade guilds and their associated apprenticeships were relatively informal but loosely approximated to English precedent.[58] Of these guilds one of the best organised was the Carpenters Company of the City of Philadelphia. Their extant "guildhall" on Chestnut Street was built in 1770–1773 to the designs of Rob Smith one of its brethren. Following American independence the Company published its *Rules of Work* in 1786. This is, in effect, a price book which itemises what the membership was expected to charge for particular jobs – with the prices given in £-s-d. The great rarity of this publication suggest that it had a short print-run implying not only some residual respect for the secrets of the "mystery" of the trade, but also the confidential nature of the prices which were written-in by hand.[59] Another feature of this publication is that it promiscuously mixes prices for carpentry with those of joinery. Whilst this combination of trades within a single Company was out of the question in London at this time it would have been acceptable in the smaller towns of many English regions. Despite the somewhat flexible attitude regarding the demarcation between the crafts in a major city like Philadelphia a sense of trade solidarity prevailed in North American cities. In 1788 the Pewterers and other craft organisations proudly carried their banners in the New York Federal procession of that year.[60]

In the American south the presence of slavery placed the manual crafts in a curious position. A select few slave youths would be apprenticed to a trade, but on the completion of their time they remained in a state of perpetual servitude working for white masters. One such master was Thomas Elfe the cabinet maker of Charleston, South Carolina. His account books for the years 1768–1775 survive and show that his workers included four slave sawyers and five slave joiners and cabinet makers. Despite these "commercial" advantages Elfe nevertheless remained dependent upon the occasional immigrant tradesman such as the "very good upholsterer from London" that he advertised as employing in 1751.[61] Craftsmen from Britain brought with them up-to-date fashions, a feature that we shall see in relationship to painting and sculpture. The trade of house painting was one in which some slaves were also trained. On 26 June the *Maryland Gazette* published an advertisement for the recapture of a runaway "Convict Servant Man named John Winter". This tradesman was described as "a very compleat House Painter; he can imitate Marble or Mahogany very exactly and can paint Floor Cloths". Although, in the bias of this advertisement, Winter is described as "a very impertinent Fellow" he clearly possessed considerable skill since "the last work he did was a House for Col. Washington near Alexandria".

The ratio of slave workers to free masters in workshops in Virginia is clearly illustrated by the following figures taken from the Richmond census of 1782:

> 3 Carpenters owned between them 28 slaves
> 5 Tailors owned between them 14 slaves
> 2 Smiths owned between them 7 slaves

Where such craftsmen were held in a state of thraldom on a plantation the situation was somewhat different. In these circumstances there was insufficient year-round employment for such specialist skills. For this reason owners of plantations hired-out these chattel slaves from time to time, a situation which could result in a modicum of freedom for those in bondage. In general slave craftsmen followed their father's trade with even greater regularity than was typical of freeborn apprentices. This was certainly true of the smith known as Gabriel (b. 1776) of the Brookfield Plantation near Richmond, Virginia. It was he who was to lead one of the most significant slave rebellions in 1800. As Douglas Egerton (1993) has observed Gabriel "was as an artisan a radical, but as a slave artisan he was a revolutionary." Nevertheless labour solidarity could and did exist between the free and unfree craftsmen, between black and white. On the other hand competition with highly skilled slave craftsmen encouraged many free artisans to migrate to the Northern States. This became most evident in border areas just to the south of the Mason Dixon Line where free tradesmen represented just 6% of the population.[62]

By the nineteenth century the position of the trades in the "New World" had become even more fluid than in the past. On his visit to America in 1842 Charles Dickens overheard a conversation between two young English artisans: "This is the country ... You have only to choose a trade, Jem, and be it ... At present I haven't quite made up my mind whether to be a carpenter – or a tailor."[63] Despite these somewhat relaxed attitudes towards training in the trades a later writer, Samuel Clemens, (1835–1910), served a brief apprenticeship as a printer in Missouri where he was bound in 1847 to "Mr Ament" the editor and proprietor of the Hannibal Courier. In his two years there he received the "usual emolument" for such a trainee of "board and clothes but no money." He, and the other two apprentices "slept on pallets on the floor" of the printing office. Clemens afterwards began the peripatetic life of a journeyman printer for newspapers in St Louis, New York, Philadelphia and finally back to the banks of the Mississippi. It was there that he was to apprentice himself as a riverboat pilot to a man named Bixby for a premium of $100.00 of borrowed money. His transformation into Mark Twain had begun and was to be completed during his years as a newspaper reporter in the American west. Abbreviated though these two spells of training may have been they offered Mark Twain an insight into the life of an apprentice which explains his belief in that system of instruction. He was, for example, acutely aware that many individuals believed that they were capable of writing prose even though they had not been subject to the years of drudgery that were necessary for that high calling. This he considered strange since these self-same individuals acknowledged "that an apprenticeship is necessary in order to qualify a person to be a tinner, bricklayer, stonemason, printer, horse-doctor, butcher, brakeman, car conductor, midwife …" and many other occupations.[64]

Because of the paucity of fully trained craftsmen in Colonial and Early Federal America those that practiced a trade there were often involved in a bewildering variety of activities. Amongst painters one of the most obvious examples of this extraordinary diversification is Charles Wilson Peale (1741– 1827). Peale was first bound apprentice to a saddler in Annapolis, Maryland, "attempted coach-making, and soon added clock and watch-making besides working as a silver-smith and beginning to try his hand as a painter." And it was as a portrait painter that Peale (and indeed his progeny) was to build his reputation. As a result of his sojourn in London (1770–1774) Peale's somewhat provincial work gained a modicum of sophistication.[65] Diversification of this kind persisted into nineteenth century New England. Take, for example, the case of Rufus Porter (1792–1884). His chief occupation was that of a house painter which extended to the creation of murals and easel portraiture. This range of work was evidently insufficient for his fecund imagination. As a designer, Porter was the primary inventor of the revolver (selling his patent to Samuel Colt), and an airship; furthermore as a writer he was the founder in 1845 of *The Scientific American* – a journal that is with us to this day.[66] In the young Republic individuals with enterprise were functioning within a fertile environment. The carpenter Ezra Cornell (1807–1874) installed the first telegraph line in the US between Baltimore and Washington DC over which the painter Samuel F. B. Morse (1791–1872) transmitted his code.[67] Cornell was to make a fortune out of the Western Union Telegraph Company, sufficient to endow the University that bears his name.

For the reasons outlined above not only American-born craftsmen but also many from Europe were in a strong position to thrive in the New World. Take for example an individual like Thomas Chambers (1808–1869) who had been brought up in the artisan tradition for easel painting in England. The demand for his type of work faded in Britain but persisted in Early Federal America, so Chambers's move across the Atlantic was opportune. Certainly his work embodies the values of the vernacular tradition that were fast falling out of favour in his native Whitby.[68]

Generally speaking a craft imported to North America in the shape of an individual immigrant seldom survived more than that first generation. This situation was identified in 1806 by the Rev William Bentley who observed that: "the arts were better understood in the first generation at Salem than in any succeeding."[69] Significantly this New England clergyman refers to the "arts" in the ancient Classical sense of the word to describe the crafts (see p. 2 above). By Bentley's day a craftsmen in Massachusetts was more likely to be a Jack-of-all-Trades. This he attributed to the reality that: "In a new Country they had only the necessities of life to provide for … An ingenious Carpenter made rakes, a good mason laid cellar rocks and bricks in clay. A good painter became a glazier …". He concluded this peroration with a splendidly oblique and withering observation that young tradesmen in New England were trained by those who "taught what they practiced, not what they knew."[70]

Notes

[1] Christopher Thompson 1847, opening of chapter iii, p. 57–59. Thompson was apprenticed to a Hull shipbuilder in January 1813 – he worked in the mould lofts
[2] John Trusler, *Hogarth Moralised* 1768, p. 73
[3] Scot McKendrick *et al.* 2011, p. 180
[4] Joan Lane 1996, pp. 4, 19
[5] National Art Library: Victoria & Albert Museum: A builder's contract of 1436 showing both halves of the indenture is illustrated as pl. 20 by L. F. Salzman (1949) 1992
[6] Author's collection
[7] Keith Thomas 2009, p. 34 citing William Gouge (1578–1653)
[8] Marcia Evans *The Place of the Rural Blacksmith in Parish Life 1500–1900*, Somerset & Dorset Family History Soc. 1997, p. 27
[9] O. Jocelyn Dunlop 1911, p. 35
[10] R. Campbell 1747, p. 315. Campbell goes on to refer to the risk of diseases if the apprentice "embraces a common woman"
[11] Joan Lane 1996, p. 3
[12] George Unwin (1908) 1966, p. 335
[13] L. F. Salzman (1949) 1992, p. 49
[14] Robert Holmes *The Age of Wonder*, London, 2008, p. 86; Shena Mason ed. 2009; p. 209 Cat. 251[b].
[15] Isaac Ware 1756, p. 347
[16] John Rule in Tim Harris ed. 1995, pp. 178, 180, 187 – but Rule does not cite "skewings" – these skewings (fragments of gold leaf) were often collected at the end of the year to pay for a "works outing" – pers. comm. A. J. J. Ayres
[17] Joan Lane 1996, pp. 14–16; O. Jocelyn Dunlop 1911, p. 34

[18] Joseph Farington, p. 670 3 Oct 1796
[19] Samuel Isacke 1741, p. 120
[20] George Unwin (1908) 1966, p. 91
[21] Walter Cahn 1979
[22] George Unwin (1908) 1966, pp. 264, 347, 348
[23] James W. P. Campbell 2002, p. 221 endnote 65 and p. 219, table I
[24] George Unwin (1908) 1966, pp. 347–348
[25] Walter Cahn 1979, pp. 86–87 citing Carel van Mander *Schilderboek* (1604);
[26] Rupert Gunnis 1953; also Ingrid Roscoe *et al.* eds 2009
[27] Margaret Whinney 1964, pp. 48–49, the "mirmayd" is now lost
[28] Alan Borg 2005, p. 99 endnote 33. W. A. D. Englefield (1923) 1936, p. 147
[29] Rupert Gunnis 1953; also Ingrid Roscoe *et al.* eds 2009
[30] Alan Borg 2005, p. 53. Cited in the Magazine of the Merchant's House Marlborough,
      No. 44, April 2010: This masterpiece was destroyed in the London bombing in 1940 –
      see W. A. D. Englefield (1923) 1936, p. 113
[31] John Harvey 1975, p. 49
[32] George Unwin (1908) 1966, p. 228
[33] Rupert Gunnis 1953; Ingrid Roscoe *et al.* eds 2009. On 16 September 1748 Seest was
      appointed as the Danish Court Sculptor
[34] George Unwin (1908) 1966, chapter iv "The Adulterine Guilds", pp. 47–60
[35] *Ibid.*, pp. 224–229 and John Harvey 1975, p. 39. Christopher Hussey 1967, 102. Sir John
      Barnard's interest in apprenticeships may be contrasted to his hostility to the "iniquitous
      Practice of Stock-jobbing".
[36] Vic Gatrell 2006, p. 245
[37] Thomas Bewick (1862) 1981; Jenny Uglow 2006, pp. 391, 238
[38] Brian Read and Doug Morgan 2010, p. 59
[39] Jenny Uglow 206, p. 121
[40] Douglas Knoop and G. P. Jones (1933) 1967, pp. 59, 77; Michael Fleming 2012, 111.
      This is based on the records of 668 apprentices of whom 46% were in wood-working
      trades 63% of whom were presented with tools at the conclusion of their time.
[41] Jane and Mark Rees *et al.* (1994) 2012. The chest with its tools and original receipts for
      the same are now in the Guildhall Museum, Rochester, Kent
[42] Joan Lanc 1996, p. 39
[43] E. Mackenzie, *Description & Historical Account … of Newcastle* 1827, cited by Jenny Uglow
      2006, p. 57
[44] James Ayres 1998, pp. 7, 90, 93, 102, 109, 212
[45] E. B. Jupp and W. W. Pocock 1887, pp. 16, 151, 155, 161
[46] O. Jocelyn Dunlop 1911, p. 151
[47] Peter Guillery 2000, pp. 61–69
[48] James Ayres 1998, p. 78
[49] Philippa Glanville and Jenifer Faulds Goldsborough 1990
[50] Alison Kelly 1900
[51] Holger Hoock (2003) 2009, pp. 32, 53. Exclusion from the RA Schools may have been
      connected with the question of working from the nude model – there was certainly nothing
      in the Academy's regulations concerning the exclusion of women from its schools
[52] Sidney C. Hutchison 1968, p. 52
[53] Edward Edwards 1808, p. I and for Bacon see Ingrid Roscoe *et al.* eds 2009

54 Vic Gatrell 2006, pp. 262–3, 275
55 Edmund Malone, *The Works of Sir Joshua Reynolds*, London, 1797, Vol. I, p. 12; Sidney Hutchison 1968, p. 50
56 The title of a series of essays by Joseph Addison which were published regularly from 21 June 1712. John Brewer 1997
57 Irwin Stelzer *The Daily Telegraph* 19 August 2009
58 W. J. Rorabaugh 1986
59 Charles E. Peterson ed. (1796) 1992. A similar price list – but fully in manuscript – was prepared in Providence R.I in 1750. In 1754 *The Carpenter Rules of Work in the Town of Boston* was published.
60 Charles F. Montgomery 1973, pp. 20–21
61 Charles F. Montgomery *American Furniture: The Federal Period ...*, 1966, pp. 12–13
62 Douglas R. Egerton *Gabriel's Rebellion: The Virginia Slave Conspiracies of 1800 &1802*, Chapel Hill, 1993, pp. 21, 24–25, 27, 31
63 Charles Dickens (1842) *c.* 1910, p. 132
64 Charles Nieder ed. *The Autobiography of Mark Twain*, New York, 1990, pp. 115–116, 123, 124–125, 306–307, 373–374
65 William Dunlap (1834) 1969, Vol. I, pp. 136–137
66 Jean Lipman (1968) 1980
67 W. J. Rorabaugh 1986, p. 60 and William Dunlap (1834) 1969, Vol. II, Pt II, pp. 308–319. Morse was educated at Yale and moved to London in 1811 to develop as a painter in association with Benjamin West's "American School". He returned to America in 1815
68 Kathleen A. Foster 2009
69 Abbott Lowell Cummings 1979, p. 42
70 *Ibid.*, p. 42

Chapter 5

THE CRAFT TRADES
& THE VISUAL ARTS

The craft-based trades represented a whole range of skills which resulted in a built-in hierarchy both between and within them. In 1837 it was noted that, as a consequence there was, amongst craftsmen, "a species of aristocracy to which other workmen looked with feelings half of respect, half of jealousy."[1] This highly significant statement occurs in W. B. Adams's book on carriage building. According to this source the "body makers" were the most skilful. Then, in descending order, they were followed by "the trimmers ... the smiths ... the spring-makers ... the wheelwrights, painters, platers, brace-makers and so on". Evidently this had become an industry with clear divisions of labour. It also implies that the painters of coach bodies occur rather low down on this table of precedence. This lowly position is reflected in the weekly levels of pay. For example the high ranking body-makers were paid £2–£3 per week. In contrast the body and line painters were on a wage of about £2, but the respected herald and decorative painters received as much as £3–£4: potentially more than the highly esteemed body-makers. These were the rates of pay in carriage building workshops – an independent herald painter would have earned rather more. These distinctions within such a trade were as nothing as compared with those that emerged between the trade and the art of painting following the establishment of the Royal Academy of Arts in 1768. By 1813 Prince Hoare felt the need to observe that:

> "... so little have the distinctive provinces of Painting been hitherto made the subject of attention by the discriminating classes of society, that its mental part, and its mechanical, continue to be spoken of under the same denomination; and a *Painter* is a term, equally expressive of the man who

fills the aweful [awe inspiring] exhibitions of the Sistine Chapel and of him who covers the wainscot or walls of our houses, to secure them from the injuries of smoke and rain." [2]

The trade of painting was the background from which some emerged to become artists of consequence. In England one could cite the one time carriage painter Sir William Beechey RA (1753–1839) and his fellow tradesman in America, John Neagle (1796–1865).[3] For our purposes it is those trades which demanded some co-ordination of hand and eye that are of relevance. This range of activities could extend from tailoring to turnery, from potting to house-painting. Of the 75 London Livery Companies with Charters dating before 1700 about 50 demanded visual ability and tactile skill. Such a ratio of some 50 to 75 goes part way to explain the high standards of craftsmanship that were achieved in the post-medieval pre-industrial past. Not only were tradesmen well trained but their educated eye made them discriminating customers when purchasing items from brother craftsmen. A chair-maker was working to a form defined by ergonomics much as a tailor's cutter was drawing in relationship to a human figure. A possible example of the latter may be exemplified in the career of John Jackson RA (1778–1831). He began as an apprentice tailor with his father (who was possibly an "Arras" or tapestry tailor – see pp. 98–99 below) in Yorkshire. After serving five years of his time the remaining two years of his apprenticeship were bought-out by the Earl of Carlisle and the artist Sir George Beaumont (1753–1827). This patronage enabled young Jackson to study painting in London.[4] A very similar career path was followed by the former Arras tailor Francis Guy (1760–1820) whose vocation as a painter developed after his emigration to early Federal America (see p. 153 & Fig. 31 below). For those artists who emerged from a trade background the essential disciplines of craftsmanship and materials tended to override the taste of an age or the fashion of the moment.[5]

Although apprenticeships, at their best, offered an effective training various difficulties could arise. Sometimes a youth was "turned over" to another craftsman, due to the master's death – a master who, in some cases, was the apprentice's own father. Alternatively a change of master could result from misbehaviour (on either side) or for reasons of choice. An example of the latter concerned the woodcarver Thomas Johnson (1723–1799). Johnson's father was a London bricklayer and a successful property speculator who died young. The orphaned youth then followed his father's trade by being apprenticed to a bricklayer – but young Johnson was accident prone.[6] In the interests of self preservation he was "turned over", on 29 August 1737 for the modest premium of £9, to his cousin Robert Johnson, the carver and gilder.[7] Another example of a change of master, but not of direction, concerns the sculptor William Smith (fl. 1765–1770) who was apprenticed in 1765 to Thomas Vidgeon. Then, in 1768 he was "by order of the Lord Mayor and Court of Alderman discharged from the said Thomas Vidgeon, for his neglecting to enrol him" in the Mason's Company of London. There must have been some underlying problem, or young Smith was extraordinarily unlucky. He was "turned over" again to George Freshwater but this new master "turned him out of service and refused to receive him therein again." Eventually Smith completed his time as a mason with John Wynn.[8]

Changes in circumstance could result in an apprentice being put to another trade. In 1804 John Gibson (1790–1866) was apprenticed as a cabinet maker with Southwell and Wilson of Liverpool. It was there that he began to develop his *métier* as a woodcarver. His skill in this field was recognised by the sculptor F. A. Legé who recommended him to the Liverpool carvers Samuel and Thomas Franceys. As a consequence of this introduction Gibson was bought-out of his indentures by Messrs Franceys for the high fee of £70. It was they who employed Gibson who was to emerge, in due course, as an independent sculptor and Royal Academician.[9]

Inevitably, not all masters looked after and trained their apprentices as they were obliged to do under the terms of the indenture. Once the guilds began their slow decline as trade organisations in the late seventeenth century the treatment of some apprentices may have worsened. In 1704 Charles Waters, an apprentice barber in Bath reported his master, Samuel Lansdown, to the Mayor and Justices of the Spa. Apparently Lansdown had "not taken care of his apprentice either for meat, drink, lodging or for the instructing him in his trade." In response to this comprehensive failure the authorities placed Waters with another master.[10] As complaints grew in number regulations to deal with such areas of dispute seemed to have increased as the century wore on. By 1780 an Act was passed which reiterated the need for masters to abide by the terms of the indentures to which they and their apprentices were party.[11]

The contrasting yet necessary characteristics that an apprenticeship demanded were shared by most neophytes and were well summarised by George Vertue (1684–1756). His observations were based on his own experience training as an engraver, a skill which "requires much labour, study, juvenile strength and sight to arrive at excellence."[12] Poor health in some form could bring careers to a premature conclusion. In 1797 the painter Francis Wheatley RA (1747–1801) became so afflicted with rheumatism that it prevented "him from using his hands."[13] In the same year Ozias Humphry RA (1742–1810) "complained of bad eyes" and decided to give up his "profession except for twelve to fifteen pictures a year." By the next month he had secured "a place under government" and never intended to practice painting again. [14] Much the same misfortune befell a drawing and music teacher of the name Malchair who complained in August 1800 that "His eye sight was become so bad that glasses could not assist him ..."[15]

Some trades were recognised health hazards. Campbell (1747) describes how the labourers who worked for a paint manufacturer in Whitechapel, East London "are sure in a few Years to become paralytic ... and seldom live a dozen Years in the Business." He goes on to state that glaziers, who used lead-based paint: "are subject to the Palsey" whilst a plumber might also suffer "the Effects of the Lead ... [which] is apt to unbend his nerves and render him paralytic."[16] Of all the building trades it is very noticeable that plumbers widows are most frequently recorded as running their late husband's businesses. For banker masons, particularly those who worked the grit stones of Yorkshire, there was the ever present danger of developing silicosis. Perhaps most grotesque of all were the "red eyes and green hair" to which brass workers were subject.[17] As craftsmen aged so their strength inevitably declined and eyesight failed. Mary Moser RA (1744–1819) "was so near sighted that her nose, when she was painting was within an inch of the canvas".[18] In 1796 Joseph Farington noted in his diary that the 66 year old Edward Burch RA (1730–1814) showed him a gem he was engraving which Farington thought was "feeble as if his eyes failed him" which Burch subsequently acknowledged to be the case.[19]

The strictures involved in observing the secrecy of the mystery inhibited the publication of craft manuals and workshop pattern books until the 1720s. For example John Abbott's manuscript note and sketch books of 1665 were probably typical products of many craft based artists. They are redolent of the art (drawings) and mystery (secret recipes) of the plasterer's trade which included the use of distemper. In much the same way Charles Beale's manuscript notes on *Experimental Secrets found in the way of Painting* (1647–1663) were invaluable to their author as a commercial colourman and to his wife the fashionable portrait painter Mary Beale (1632/3–1699). As manuscripts the confidential nature of these notebooks was maintained although they may well have been lent to fellow masters of the mystery. There is even some evidence that documents of this kind were circulated amongst artisans and artists across Europe (see p. 250). An oblique mid-eighteenth century reference to this need for secrecy occurs in a letter that John Sharman, a local builder sent to Earl Fitzwilliam concerning the rebuilding of the south front of Milton House, Northamptonshire. Sharman was concerned that the "particulars" given in

FIGURE 14. Trade card of *Biggerstaff & Walsh* of Islington *c.* 1791. House painters traditionally undertook a wide range of activities. Shown here are tradesmen engaged in the manufacture of floor cloths, inn signs, easel painting, paper hanging and the grinding of pigments. (British Museum)

his letter were so extensive that: "if it be made publick, I must expect to be condemn'd, both by Surveyors & Workmen ... for setting forth the Mystrey of every man's Business in so clear a light."

Concerns of this nature were brought to a head in 1671 when John Smith, a Clockmaker, published his *The Art of Painting, wherein is included the whole Art of Vulgar Painting according to the best rules for preparing and laying on the Oyl Colours.* To the consternation of the Painter Stainers this publication revealed many of the secrets of their art and mystery. In response later editions of the book sought to mitigate such concerns arguing that "professed Painters whose knowledge [is] supposed to out-strip these first Rudiments of their own Profession" had no cause to be apprehensive.[20]

In relationship to architecture, design books (often Italian in origin), were present in the libraries of the elite in Stuart England; but pattern books were far less available for tradesmen.[21] One of the exceptions was Walter Gedde's *Sundry Draughtes Principally Serving for Glaziers* (1615–1616). Significantly the title of this book of designs goes on to add that it would not be *Impertinent for Plaisterers and Gardiners: be sides sundry other professions*.[22] In other words such manuals were so exceptional that this one small book could be equally useful in determining the pattern of the lead cames in a glazed window, the ribs of a plaster ceiling, or the knots in a garden. The paucity of pattern books and trade manuals amongst working master craftsmen in the late seventeenth century is emphasised by the case of the "the learned bricklayer" Venterus Mandey (1645–1701) himself the author of the *Marrow of Measuring ... glazing, painting, plastering* (1682). When Mandey's library was sold in March 1713/14 it comprised no less than 557 lots, some of which consisted of a number of volumes. For the time this was an extraordinarily large collection of books and yet only a few of them related to design – among them Jean Tijou (London 1693), Lomazzo (English edn, Oxford 1598) and Andrea Pozzo (Rome 1693).[23] No wonder Abbott, in the then distant north Devon of the 1660s, was dependant upon making his own pattern book, much though it might have owed to other publications including Gedde's. Neither was he alone in creating such a manuscript. The decorative painter John Martin produced a similar crib book (*c.* 1699–1701; Fig. 45), which in turn derives, in part, from William Salmon's *Polygraphice* of 1672.[24]

Where Abbott and his contemporary Martin itemise recipes and various "tricks of the trade" they are venturing into areas of knowledge that, at this time, less often saw the light of day in the English printed word. An exception in this respect is Joseph Moxon's *Mechanic Exercises* which began to appear in segments from 1677 – significantly after the Great Fire of London of 1666 when the restrictive practices of the guilds were set aside in the interests of reconstructing the capital. This was certainly the objective of Godfrey Richards's 1668 edition of *Palladio* (the first book) which contains many more illustrations than Moxon's publication. The dedication to the king in Richards's book expresses the hope that his quarto volume will assist in constructing "the new and great City [which] is to be built ... a second happy restoration, inferior only to that of your majesty's person & Government."[25]

Despite the presence of these publications there appears to have been, even in the following century, some residual sense of a need for trade secrecy. When John Elsum published his *Art of Painting* in 1704 he expressed the hope that it would not cause "offence to the Masters of the Mystery."[26] By way of mitigation for revealing these mysteries in print the vital detailed recipes and other information is written-in by hand. This is also true of Thomas Bardwell's *The Practice of Painting* (1756) and, as noted above, is a feature of the *Rule Book* published by the Carpenters Company of Philadelphia in 1786.

a

b

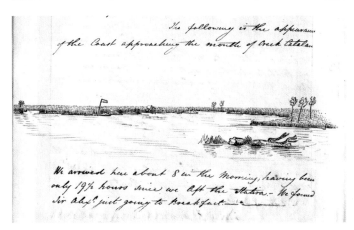

c

The manuscript note books of both John Abbott and John Martin demonstrate that each was capable of drawing. All such craft-based artisans were dependant on this skill and vocation. This was fully recognised on 22 March 1754 when a group of "Noblemen, Clergy, Gentlemen and Merchants" met at Rawthmell's Coffee-house, Henrietta Street, Covent Garden, London.[27] It was their purpose to establish a Society for the Encouragement of Arts, Manufacturers and Commerce: the (R)SA. In this context drawing was seen as central to their objectives which is why, at its foundation, the Society decided to offer prizes to "boys and girls" to encourage this art and skill (see p. 12 above). Even after the advent of the camera in 1833 William Henry Fox Talbot (1800–1877) saw his device as *The Pencil of Nature* (1844). Important though this innovation undoubtedly was shutter and film speeds remained slow and, for this reason, drawing remained central to many aspects of human endeavour down to the twentieth century.[28] Furthermore this is a graphic skill that may be used to interpret rather than simply record – which is why medical and archaeological illustration remain essential.

Although apprenticeships in Early Modern Britain offered a sound training in a particular "trade" or "manufacture" they were often deficient in terms of instruction in drawing, a skill with very wide applications. Furthermore the trades and professions that an organisation like the Society of Arts had in mind with regard to drawing could well have ranged from manufacturers in industry to officers in the army and navy. Military academies certainly included drawing in their prospectuses. Drawing was, in short, a vital component for a great variety of trades and professions. And so it remained into the twentieth century. When Eric Blair (George Orwell) sat the colonial Indian Civil Service

---

FIGURE 15. a) Watercolour from Maj. Gen. Sir William Congreve's (1772–1828) sketchbook showing the disposition of ordnance in a wooded landscape. Note the dotted lines showing the potential trajectory of cannon balls. Although the cannon are shown on plan the trees are represented on elevation in a strangely effective way. (Royal Artillery Museum, Woolwich); b) Watercolour drawing from the same sketchbook, showing a method of carrying a cannon and its gun-carriage – unsigned. As Comptroller of the Royal Laboratory General Sir William Congreve organised the firework display in St James's Park, Hyde Park and Kensington Gardens to mark the "general peace" in 1814 following the Napoleonic Wars. In that administrative role Congreve's artistic sensibilities would have been of value. (Royal Artillery Museum, Woolwich); c) This sketch appears in Col. Sir Alexander Dickson's (1777–1840) manuscript *Journal of Operations in 1814 and 1815 in Louisiana*, part of the War of 1812. The text in the except illustrated here implies that Dickson was not the sole author of "his" *Journal*. Slight though this drawing is it demonstrates the military value of such a record. Significantly many of the place names given in this account are in Spanish rather than French. (Royal Artillery Museum, Woolwich)

exam in July 1922 there were five compulsory papers and three optional ones – namely drawing, Latin and Greek. Drawing was therefore long seen as an important tool for both officers and artisans.[29]

In all these circumstances the committee for the nascent (Royal) Society of Arts (RSA) was finely attuned to the spirit and therefore the needs of the age. Its founders were also somewhat prophetic in recognising the demands of an emerging industrialisation which, in 1754, was yet to be fully evident. At its foundation this Society was composed of eleven members under the chairmanship of Viscount Folkestone.[30] This committee owed much to another of its members, the socially well connected William Shipley (1715–1803) a particularly significant teacher of drawing.[31] Representing the "manufacturers" was Nicholas Crisp the Jeweller and the proprietor of the Bow porcelain works. The founders of the Society were therefore well advised in terms of the quality and standards of drawing that were of central importance in relationship to manufacturing. Neither should we suppose that Crisp's presence at these deliberations was simply a sop towards the needs of commerce and industry for the early minutes of the Society's first meetings state that he was "listened to with due attention."[32]

Crisp was something of an entrepreneur and may not have been, as claimed, a working jeweller and silversmith. There is no record of him having registered a personal hallmark with the Goldsmith's Company but he is known to have employed, among others, the chaser George Michael Moser in connection with this aspect of his business. At Crisp's porcelain factory at Bow the young John Bacon worked as a modeller. For this reason, once Bacon and Moser had made their reputations as artists and Academicians, they were well placed to recognise the relationship between art and manufacturing industry. Bacon was to work closely with Eleanor Coade and her eponymous "stone" and also with Wedgwood and his jasper ware. Similarly Moser was quick to recognise the potential for manufacturers of Angelica Kauffman's (1741–1807) picture of Lawrence Sterne's *Mari*. This canvas was so popular that it became the inspiration for numerous prints from it which:

> "were circulated all over Europe. In the elegant manufactures of London, Birmingham, etc., it assumed an incalculable variety of forms and dimensions, and was transferred to numerous articles of all sorts and sizes from a watch-case to a tea waiter."[33]

Although the Society of Arts accepted that the relationship between the "fine arts" and "manufacturing" were fundamental, the position of the Royal Academy at its foundation in 1768 could be ambiguous. Both organisations recognised the importance of drawing but Reynolds was anxious to establish a distinction between "liberal" easel painters and the "mechanics" who daubed houses. In contrast the American-born Benjamin West (1738–1820), Reynolds's successor in 1792 as President of the RA, recognised that art and industry could be two sides of the same coin. In December 1797 West, together with Hoppner and Farington, attended a meeting with George Canning, at that time the Under-Secretary of State. This lobby, comprised of a group of painters, gave the Academy's backing for a "national School of Art." Their reasoning was clear and to the point, for they believed that such an establishment would result in a "consequent improvement on the designs of all our Manufacturers."[34]

Remarkably Reynolds anticipated this view in the dedication of the published *Discourses* (1779) where he makes reference to: "those Arts by which Manufactures are embellished, and Science is refined."[35] Elsewhere in that publication the President of the RA reveals some contempt for his craft which explains why he lacked the judgement to confront the false promises of the "Venetian Secret". The seductive charms of the "intellectual dignity" of "liberal" painting that Reynolds espoused had its origins in the prejudices born of the contradictory position of the slave owning "democracies" of Classical antiquity. For free-born men the speculations of the mind were respectable occupations – manual activities being reserved for slaves or serfs. The "liberal arts", in which patricians engaged, were comprised of the *trivium*: of grammar, logic and rhetoric, and the *quadrivium*: arithmetic, geometry, astronomy and music. Neither painting nor sculpture were included as "Liberal Arts" because of their fundamentally manual nature – although architecture became, in effect, an associate member of this select group based on the importance of arithmetic and geometry to that profession. This is the historical background that offers part of the explanation for Reynolds's insistence on the "intellectual dignity" of painting.

For all his protestations, Reynolds may have ignored but he could not deny the manual, the "mechanic" aspects of his art. Furthermore the visual arts inevitably involve repetitive work – or "drudgery" as it was often referred to. For example, some thought it strange that Edward Rooker the Elder could work as an engraver by day and, "in the evening play Harlequin on the Stage." At the time this was explained by reference to those details in engraving a plate which involved the repetitious ruling of lines, an activity that "was not to be considered as an effort of mind but a dexterity of hand."[36]

Although Reynolds spoke in terms of the "intellectual dignity" of the visual arts it was social prestige that he sought for artists. In effect an officer class had been established amongst Academicians for their Diploma, like a Commission in the armed services, was signed by the monarch.[37] This probably explains

FIGURE 16. Detail of a *Cut Paper Picture*, signed and dated "J. Reynolds, 1739". Although it is not known if this item is indeed the work of the 16-year-old Joshua Reynolds it is certainly the sort of object that was to be prohibited from the Royal Academy. (See *The Connoisseur* 81, 1931 for a discussion of this picture). (Ex. Collection: Dallas Pratt, New York City)

Joseph Farington's proposal of 1793 that Academicians should wear a specially designed uniform at their formal meetings, a suggestion that was rejected possibly because such a garment might too closely resembled the Livery of a trade guild or, for that matter, the Windsor livery worn by the RA's servants.

The question of "civilian" dress was certainly an issue for the Painter Stainers of London who were concerned that some of the brethren appeared in the streets with paint stains on their garments.[38] As we have seen (pp. 20 & 56) liberal painters and sculptors could be equally casual about their dress or, conversely ultra fashionable. The Irish-born American engraver John James Barralett (*c*. 1747–1815) was described as a "beau of much pretensions, powdered to the extent of fashion of the day, and ruffled to the finger ends. In later life he was a sloven to as great a degree." In 1771 the painter John Trumbull recalled visiting the portraitist John Singleton Copley in Boston at the time of his marriage: "He was dressed on the occasion in a suit of crimson velvet, with gold buttons, and the elegance displayed by Copley in his style of living, added to his high repute as an artist" in his native Massachusetts.[39] Clothes were, of course, but one measure of worldly success. When the sculptor John Deare (1759–1798) wrote home to his brother Joseph on 13 July 1791 he reported that:

> "I have several men at work for me and a boy who acts as my servant. I have the best study in Rome and live like a gentleman; keep a handsome saddle-horse to ride out on every evening after I am tired of application".

Just six days later he wrote again to his brother, perhaps mindful of their early years in Liverpool: "We Romans enjoy the appearance of religion and the reality of art". [40] The possession of a "saddle-horse" was of little consequence as compared with an entire equipage. Take for example the case of John Astley (1720/29–1787). He was recorded as "painting his way back to London [from north west England] in his own post-chaise, with an outrider". On his return journey it seems that Astley could not resist loitering in all this splendour in his "native neighbourhood". This proved to be a sound investment. At the Nutsford assembly in Cheshire he met the widowed Lady Daniel who was "so won by his appearance" that she commissioned Astley to paint her portrait. She then "made him the offer of her hand, a boon which he did not think prudent to refuse". Lady Daniel herself was no less prudent since "by marriage articles [she] reserved her fortune to herself".[41] A carriage or even a landaulet was an enormously expensive vehicle to purchase, run and maintain not to mention the annual tax on the vehicle and the horses.[42] Not that Astley was alone amongst artists in possessing such a vehicle – another was Richard Cosway RA (1740–1821).

Money was not, of course, the only indicator of status. The gentleman painter Joseph Farington RA (1747–1821) did not own a coach and his diary makes regular reference to being given a ride in Cosway's vehicle.[43] Farington was well placed, as a man of independent means, to note social nuance. He records, for example, that the architect James Wyatt RA (1748–1813), although of humble birth, was "treated with great respect at Windsor [Castle]. He always dines at the Equerries Table".[44] Benjamin Wyatt (1709–1772) the founder of that dynasty of architects was, in origin, a simple Staffordshire yeoman farmer and timber merchant who became a builder-architect. This whole question of social status was a matter of great anguish for the Academicians despite, or perhaps because of, their very diverse backgrounds. As noted above (p. 21) despite Joseph Wilton's admiration for the work of his fellow sculptor John Rossi (1762–1839) he described him as a "very ingenious Artist [but] not a cultivated man".[45]

In some respects, and in ways that may not have been discerned by artists who shared Reynolds's outlook, the establishment of the Royal Academy may now be seen as a manifestation of industrialisation. Through its annual exhibitions of contemporary art, speculatively produced works could now be purchased "off the peg". Although this had to some extent always been possible, art in the past was more often a matter of patronage than consumerism. In the last quarter of the eighteenth century, largely under the auspices of the RA, a change in the making and acquisition of works of art was about to dawn. The process was gradual but the trajectory can be followed in the pages of Joseph Farington's *Diary*. On 22 April 1796 he records the visit to the Academy exhibition by King George III and other members of the royal family. It seems that the king gravitated towards Richard Westall's (1765–1836) "drawings" (probably watercolours) and remarked that he had "never seen anything like them" and wanted to know "who they had been made for."[46] In other words the presumption was that these "drawings" had been commissioned and were therefore examples of good old fashioned patronage. Just over a year earlier the Fawkes family of Yorkshire commissioned William Hodges RA (1744–1797) to paint a group of four pictures although, somewhat unusually, the subject was to be "chosen by the artist" rather than the patron.[47] By 24 May 1796 Farington was able to state that "many of the works" displayed in the Academy's annual show were "painted purposely for exhibition" a new and faintly suspect situation that was worthy of record. In some ways this "merchandise" was not seen as quite "proper" so it was not entered in the catalogue as being available for sale but was marked by a discreet asterisk. This somewhat decadent category of art, produced in this brazenly speculative way, had reached a point where it had become evident that Fuseli's "best exertions are when He has only to consider how He shall satisfy himself" without the inconvenience of meeting the demands of a client. For a painter of independent means like the Swiss-born Sir Peter Bourgeois (1756–1811 who bequeathed the collection amassed by Desenfans to establish Dulwich Picture Gallery), none of the normal conventions concerning "production" and "reception" applied which was both how and why he "did not care for Commissions" and sent his paintings for sale by auction.[48]

In general the rise of consumerism in the visual arts, as in so much else, would eclipse patronage as the client economies of the past dwindled. Inevitably portraiture remained one of the exceptions. To some extent it was the dominance of commissioned portraiture, in the exhibitions of the day, that obscured the rise of consumerist art.

Another feature that was influenced by the advent of these regular exhibitions of contemporary work was the time pressure that artists were now placed under. This was of a quite different character to the deadlines to which they had always had to conform in relationship to their clients. In pre-modern Europe it was apparently accepted that the creation of a building, a sculpture or a painting took time – and this despite the shorter life expectancy.[49] The Academy's annual exhibitions were, for artists, a pressure of an altogether different order, particularly for Academicians who were under an obligation to exhibit annually. In October 1796 the sculptor John Bacon RA (1740–1799) proposed "that on acct. of the nature of their work, Sculptors should be allowed once in 3 years to exhibit." This was agreed and extended to painters who were also permitted to send their works to the RA no more regularly than the sculptors.[50] Even these intervals could look somewhat trivial compared with the time taken to produce a single major engraving. For example James Heath's plate for John Singleton Copley's *Major Pierson* was "upwards of 9 years in hand" – but then Heath charged 2000 guineas for this work. Accordingly some perspective may be placed upon Trumbull's distress that the engraver Sharp was "3 years over time" in delivering the plates for the American painter's *Gibralta* and his representations of the military *Actions* in the War of Independence. The clamour from painters for the completion of such plates was driven by the very significant income they derived from the official engravings of their works. An edition of 200 "pulls" from Copley's *Chatham* were sold for some 12 guineas each – a potential total of £2,520.[51]

This conflict between financial urgency and a slow moving craft applied to other aspects of the visual arts. In 1796 Lewis Pingo (1743–1830) estimated that it would take him 6–7 months to cut the die for a medal to commemorate the foundation of the RA. Similarly the sculptor Thomas Banks (1735–1805) having completed the plaster model for his figure of Lord Cornwallis estimated, in May 1796, that it would take a year and a half to enlarge and translate into marble with the aid of a pointing machine. Bacon's plea, in that same year (1796), that sculptors be permitted to send works to the RA's annual exhibitions once every three years was well founded.[52]

Although there were a number of precursors to the RA Schools of Painting, Sculpture and Architecture the advent of such an institution was not always seen as an unalloyed benefit. To some, the Academy was seen as fostering a dictatorship of taste in which aesthetic values were promulgated top-down rather than emerging from the bottom-up (see p. 453). In pre modern Europe "dictatorship" of this kind had been in the hands of the elite, the patrons – but patrons were numerous and subscribed to many points of view with the position and wealth to maintain an independence of outlook. This multiplicity of tastes was to be lost with the relative monoculture of consumerism, a collective aesthetic promulgated by the Academy. For this reason William Blake, who had served his time apprenticed to the engraver James Basire (1730–1802) argued that Englishmen should "know that every man ought to be a judge of pictures, and every man is he who has not been connoisseured out of his senses."[53] A more analytical less populist approach to these problems was raised by the aesthete Richard Payne Knight (1750–1824) who was concerned that the academic outlook "would result in a 'corporate' taste and spirit."[54] This was an opinion shared by William Hazlitt a painter long before he emerged as an essayist.[55] In 1814 he expressed the somewhat arrogant view that "The diffusion of taste is not the same thing as the improvement of taste ... it is lowered by every infusion it receives from common opinion."[56]

In contrast to the Academies of Art the Guilds did not presume to inculcate a "taste". Their ambitions were, by comparison, far more modest. They confined their undoubted authoritarianism to the practicalities of their craft, the good name of their brethren as tradesmen and the interests of their customers. The decline of these guilds was gradual but became most evident in the course of the eighteenth century – when the Academies were to fill part of the resulting vacuum. As a slow moving change its radical nature has been obscured. In essence this was a revolution that saw a shift in emphasis from "training" to "education" from means to ends. In this respect The Age of Reason presided over a contradiction. The apprenticeships that related to the visual arts had provided for the accomplishment of a finite craft. In contrast art, which the academies presumed to teach, is far from finite and may therefore be seen as beyond such a pedagogical approach. At its foundation in 1768 the Royal Academy's membership provided living proof that the old apprenticeship system could offer a viable form of training for artists. Many of these individuals had, in the well-worn phrase of the time, "been bred" to a relevant trade. The coach painter John Baker RA (1736–1771) and the carpenter turned architect John Gwynn RA (1713–1786) spring to mind.[57] Neither was this breadth of experience confined to Academicians or artists based in London.

Following the foundation of the RA a generation of young painters, sculptors and architects were fortunate to have emerged from apprenticeships to become students at these Schools – the best of both worlds. These were individuals who may have begun as decorative painters, furniture carvers, chasers, die-sinkers or building tradesmen but were to emerge as "artists" and/or "designers". In the autumn of 1769 77 students were enrolled at the RA Schools. The first intake included the painter Edward Edwards (a former ornamental carver), the sculptors John Bacon (a modeller for Bow porcelain) and Thomas Banks (apprentice ornamental carver).[58] This variety of backgrounds is all the more remarkable when contrasted with the decided views of what was considered as "Art" for acceptance in the Academy's exhibitions. In 1769 this institution determined that "No needlework, artificial flowers, cut paper, shell work or any such baubles should be admitted to its exhibitions"[59] (see Fig. 16).

In painting and sculpture this shift from patronage to consumerism, from apprenticeships to academies, from craft to art, may not at first have been total but the trend was irreversible. This mutation in emphasis was to be recorded by William Sandby (1862) who observed that "it will be found that it was about the period of the decline of these guilds that most Art academies arose." That may be a fairly neutral identification of an historical reality but then Sandby went on to add that "the arts, like water, will find their level."[60]

Notes

[1]   W. B. Adams 1837, p. 188. So important is this passage that is cited by E. P. Thompson (1963) 1991, p. 262 who in turn cites E. Hobsbawm and A. Briggs. See also John Ford 2005, p. 24 for the remainder of this quote

[2]   John Ford 2005, p. 26; Prince Hoare 1813, pt I, p. 148

[3]   William Dunlap (1834) 1969, Vol. II, pt II, pp. 372–373

[4]   Holger Hoock (2003) 2009, p. 59

[5]   Jacob Hall Pleasants (1943) 1970, pp. 55–89; James Ayres in Henig and Paine 2013

[6]   He fell from a scaffold and on another occasion a brick fell on his head

[7]   Jacob Simon 2003

[8]   Ingrid Roscoe *et al.* eds 2009

[9]   *Ibid.*

[10] R. S. Neal 1981, pp. 51–52

[11] Joan Lane 1996, pp. 4–5

[12] George Virtue quoted by Ronald Paulson 1979, Vol. I, p. 59

[13] Joseph Farington, p. 908 18 Oct 1797; p. 1416 6 July 1800

[14] *Ibid.*, p. 835 9 May 1797; p. 850 6 June 1797

[15] *Ibid.*, p. 1425 1 August 1800

[16] R. Campbell, 1747 – for paint manufacturers p. 107, for glaziers p. 164 and plumbers p. 190

[17] Joan Lane 1996, pp. 45–46

[18] J. T. Smith (1828) 1919, Vol. I, p. 20

[19] Joseph Farington, p. 473 18 Jan 1796; p. 722 17 Dec 1796

[20] Richard Wilson and Alan Mackley *The Building of the English Country House*, London (2000) 2011, p. 130. John Abbott's two manuscript books of recipes and designs are in Devon Record Office, Exeter, 404 M/BI B2, Beale's notebook: Glasgow University Library (MS Ferguson 134); Tabitha Barber 1999, 77; Alan Borg 2005, pp. 83–84

[21] James Ayres 1998, p. 17 which lists the few books of this kind owned by the Bastards of Blandford in 1731

[22] James Ayres 2003, pp. 69, 75, 144

[23] James Ayres 1998, p. 13. A copy of this auction catalogue is in the British Library BL:SC 301(2)

[24] James Ayres 1985, fig. 86, p. 62, James Ayres *The Artist's Craft*, Phaidon, Oxford 1985.

[25] James Ayres 1998, p. 15. Richards's first edition of *Palladio* was published in 1663.

[26] James Ayres 1985, p. 13

[27] Allan and Abbott eds 1992, pp. 91

[28] The author's grandfather, the Danish-born ornithologist Henrik Grönvold (1858–1940) drew illustrations of birds throughout his working life. In some cases these coexist with rather muddy photographs in publications such as F. T. Townend *Pheasants* … London, 1912

[29] Kevin Jackson 2012, 224. The compulsory papers were English, History, Geography, Mathematics and French. In that year the candidates were expected to make representations of a chair, bucket or hut. Of that group of candidates 26 passed and Blair/Orwell was placed a creditable seventh.

[30] Allan and Abbott eds 1992, p. 16

[31] Shipley's brother was the Bishop of St Asaph

[32] Allan and Abbott eds, 1992, pp. 56, 62

[33] W. T. Whitley, 1928, Vol. I., p. 373

[34] Joseph Farington, p. 955 27 Dec 1797, the meeting took place in John Hoppner's (1758–1810) house

[35] Joshua Reynolds 1778; dedication to the king

[36] Joseph Farington, p. 638 12 August 1796. Edward Rooker was the father of "Michaelangelo" Rooker (1743–1801)

[37] Prince Hoare 1818, p. 143. Although not an RA Hoare was for a while the Academy's secretary for foreign correspondence

[38] W. A. D. Englefield (1923) 1936 Introduction, p. iv regarding the Painter Stainers minutes of October 1634

[39] Allan Cunningham 1830, Vol. ii p. 216–7. For Barralett see William Dunlap (1834) 1969, Vol. II, Pt I, p. 43; for Copley see *ibid.*, Vol. I, p. 107

[40] J. T. Smith (1828) 1919, Vol. II, pp. 152–153

[41] Edward Edwards 1808, p. 124. On his wife's death Astley inherited the Duckenfield estate that was estimated to be worth £5,000 p.a.

[42] John Ford 2005, pp. 40, 41, 42

[43] Joseph Farington, p. 261 21 Nov 1794 "Cosway called and took me in his coach to the Royal Academy Club"

[44] *Ibid.*, p. 162 14 Feb 1794

[45] *Ibid.*, p. 759 29 Jan 1797 and p. 621 27 July 1796.

[46] *Ibid.*, p. 527 22 April 1796

[47] *Ibid.*, p. 276 17 Dec 1794

[48] *Ibid.*, p. 882 8 August 1797

[49] In Germany Cologne Cathedral was begun in 1248 and not completed until the late 1800s. Rembrandt spent most of 1642 painting his admittedly very large canvas *The Night Watch*. See Colin Platt (2004) 2005, pp. xviii and caption to the illustration of *The Night Watch*

[50] Details from Farington's Diary – in this sequence p. 674 7 Oct 1796, pp. 467–8 5 June 1796, p. 1057 12 Sept 1798, p. 646 20 Aug 1796, p. 976 1 Feb 1798

[51] Details from Farington's Diary – in this sequence p. 674 7 Oct 1796, pp. 467–8 5 June 1796, p. 1057 12 Sept 1798, p. 646 20 Aug 1796, p. 976 1 Feb 1798

[52] *Ibid.*, p. 725, 22 Dec 1796, p. 556, 25 May 1796

[53] William Blake in the *Monthly Magazine* 1 July 1806 quoted by Trevor Fawcett 1974, p. 138

[54] Northcote's *Life of Reynolds* in the *Edinburgh Review* XXIII (1814), pp. 280, 291, quoted by Trevor Fawcett 1974, p. 10

[55] For an account of the Hazlitt family in America see Nina Fletcher Little (1952) 1972, p. 37. The Hazlitts arrived in Howe, New York from Ireland in 1783 and moved to Massachusetts in 1784 before sailing for England in 1787. In those American Years Hazlitt worked as a decorative painter

[56] *The Champion* 11 Sept 1814 also the *Annals of Fine Arts* 1820, pp. 284–298

[57] Joseph Farington, p. 729 23 Dec 1796

[58] Sidney C. Hutchison 1968, p. 52

[59] RA exhibition regulations cited by Robert C. Alberts 1978, p. 96

[60] William Sandby 1862, Vol. I, pp. 18, 27

PART 2

PAINTERS

Chapter 6

THE ART OF PICTURE CRAFT[1]

The two dimensional pictorial arts encompass numerous methods and materials deploying an extraordinary range of craft skills. In a late medieval context painting on a "table" (a panel) was just one aspect of the craft but, as the precursor of easel painting, was yet to assume dominance.[2]

Consequently the oil paints of the Painters, the size-based media of the Limners and the dyes and stains of the Stainers were just some of the wide range of materials, and therefore crafts, that were involved in the production of the pictorial arts. Additionally the designing, if not the making, of stained glass, tapestry, embroidery, mosaic and sgraffito plaster mural work were all part of the pictorial artists repertoire.[3] As for those other activities, defined by the materials they employed, we discover that in addition to Painters and Stainers, the Plaisterers and also the Plumbers were, by the seventeenth century if not before, engaged in making pictorial works. In these cases it is important to emphasise that the Plaisterers were, in theory, confined to a size medium, the Plumbers to oil paint. This was an important distinction in which, generally speaking, only oil paint could survive when applied to work out-of-doors.

Specialisation in a given craft was probably most pronounced in late medieval and sixteenth century England. This tendency persisted into the seventeenth century with a parallel drift towards a restricted diversification of some specific tasks. For example plasterers continued to create sgraffito mural schemes, a tradition that was maintained in Colonial America.[4] Similarly painters continued their practice of providing designs to be carried out by other craftsmen in various media. By the eighteenth century this role of painters as designers became even more entrenched and extended to sculpture. In textile design the Florentine-born Francesco Zuccarelli RA (1702–1789), "painted a set of designs for tapestry which were executed in the manufactory of Paul Saunders … [in] about the year 1759" for the Earl of Egremont's town house in Piccadilly. Saunders was the "Yeoman Arras worker and Arras Tailor" to the king and his premises were, at that time, on the corner of Soho Square and Sutton Street, London. These tapestries were dyed-in-the-wool labour intensive and highly expensive products which, although woven in yarn were, at this time made to resemble paintings. That this was the objective is confirmed by John Evelyn. While the diarist was in France in 1683 he visited "the new fabrique of ... [Gobelins] Tapissry for designe, tendernesse of worke & incomparable imitation of the best paintings ..."[5] The alternative to pictorial woven tapestries were the stained hangings which, in their turn, were made to resemble woven furnishings of this kind. These less expensive forms of textile mural decoration ranged artistically from the sophisticated to the vernacular and had an extraordinarily wide social distribution from the palaces of kings to the "cots" of the peasantry.[6]

An apprenticeship to a Painter Stainer was a reasonably direct route to becoming a "liberal" or "polite" painter but there were other means to this end. In this respect, and of continuing relevance, was the goldsmith's trade. This was the art and mystery to which Robert Peake (*c.* 1551–1619) was put in London in 1565, becoming a freeman in 1576 although he ultimately emerged as a portrait painter.[7] Similarly, Nicholas Hilliard (*c.* 1547–1619) followed the craft of goldsmith which he was to practice concurrently with his work as a limner. The association between gold and silversmithing and painting in miniature is quite logical in that the one was generally housed in the other.

The engraving of metal for print-making in Early Modern Europe dates back to the use of this technique for decorating armour in Germany in the late fifteenth century. This type of embellishment began with the use of a line cut direct in the steel but later an etched process was adopted using a "resist" (wax etc) in conjunction with acid.[8] Samples of this work were then probably printed on paper and sent to the clients for their imprimatur. Much the same was true for a, now lost, late sixteenth century lettered brass plate at Glastonbury Abbey. This commemorated St Joseph of Arimathea and, in 1639, was illustrated in a publication by Sir Henry Spelman – his plate being printed in reverse direct from the brass.[9] For print-making this basic technique persists along with earlier procedures like wood-block (side grain) and wood-engraving (end grain). By 1642 Ludwig von Siegen of Utrecht devised mezzotint engraving which may have been introduced to England by Prince Rupert of the Rhine (1619–1682).[10] A hundred and fifty years were to elapse before a further method of printing graphic images was developed. In 1798 it was found that a very fine, smooth limestone, quarried in Bavaria, could be used to make what became known as lithographs. These methods, Teutonic in origin, were very rapidly adopted in Britain and elsewhere. In England, more locally available limestone like the white lias of Somerset was sometimes used for lithography as a cheaper alternative.[11]

Among the many artists who began their careers as commercial engravers were James Gillray[12] (*c.* 1757–1815) and Sawray Gilpin. Gilpin "came to London [age 14 in 1747] to a relation, a silversmith" but a couple of years later was passed on to the painter Samuel Scott.[13] Another painter who served his time as an apprentice engraver in London whilst attending the St Martin's Lane Academy was Samuel Wale RA (d. 1786).[14] This alternative route to the visual arts was followed by others. For example, the painter James Northcote RA (1746–1831) was the son of a watchmaker and his father was determined that his son should follow him and apprenticed him to his own trade.[15] Fortunately for the young Northcote the association between watchmaking and engraving was close, due to the engraved and chased details in watches and clocks. Another artist with a similar background was Charles Grignon (1721–1810) whose father Daniel was also a watchmaker.[16]

Engraving silver could easily be extended to include the production of copper plates for printing trade cards and similar ephemera (eg Fig. 21). Work of this kind may be seen as Hogarth's first venture into the graphic arts.[17] As Hogarth was to recall he:

> "soon found this business [engraving], in every respect too limited. The paintings … [in] St Paul's and Greenwich Hospital [by his future father-in-law Thornhill], which were at the time going on, ran in my head, and I determined that silver-plate engraving should be followed no longer than necessity obliged me to it. Engraving on copper was, at twenty years of age, my utmost ambition".[18]

Although Hogarth found engraving "too limited" he was by no means alone in beginning his career in this way. According to the engraver Grignon, who was himself apprenticed to Hubert Gravelot (1669–1773), the portrait painter Thomas Gainsborough (1727–88) "received the first rudiments of his art from the same master" – namely Gravelot.[19] Another example of an apprentice making the transition from engraving to painting was also followed by Michael "Angelo" Rooker RA (1743–1801) who began his training apprenticed to his father the engraver Edward Rooker.[20]

Printed books enjoyed the protection of copyright since 1709 and all print-makers together with others concerned with "intellectual property rights", owe a great debt of gratitude to William Hogarth. It was he who, among others, made representations on this matter which eventually led to the *Engravers*

Copyright Act of 1735.[21] This not only gave print-makers rights over their work, protecting them from pirated editions but, in so doing, provided painters with additional potential earnings. As mentioned above this encouraged painters to invest heavily in commissioning engraved reproductions of their work which became a considerable source of additional income. Although print-making is not central to this account its importance in relationship to painting is too significant to be entirely overlooked.

Mezzotints were to become the principal vehicle for reproducing paintings because their richness, and depth of tone, best interpreted the oil paintings that they followed, an essential consideration. Joseph Farington was of the view that "Reynolds [*sic*] the Engraver [was] unqualified" for such work because "His prints are not sufficiently like pictures ..."[22] In this context the diarist noted that John Singleton Copley (1737–1815) was dissatisfied with Francesco Bartolozzi's (1727–1815) plate after his *Death of Chatham* from which only 1200 impressions had been taken.[23] Copley's step-father in Boston, Massachusetts was Peter Pelham, a painter and engraver, so it is probable that Copley had some knowledge of this craft.[24] By 1799 he turned to another mezzotint artist for his *Lord Chatham*. This was a man named Sharp who agreed to produce the plate for 1200 guineas and finish the work in four years. For such a time-consuming commission Sharp expected to receive an advance on that total of £200 a year "while he was about it".[25] For a smaller scale engraving of the same subject Copley employed a man named Jean Marie Delattre who agreed to do the work for 800 guineas. The resulting engraving was not approved of by Copley and a court case ensued. At these proceedings a group of painters including Benjamin West, Sir William Beechey, Richard Cosway, Sir Peter Francis Bourgeois and Henry Bone gave evidence on behalf of Copley. This litigation was, in a sense, more than an encounter between two individuals, but a conflict between the two communities: on the one hand the painters, and on the other the engravers. Furthermore their mutual dependence seems to have made the clash all the more intense – a civil war. Consequently "The manner in which the painters treated the Engravers, describing them as 'Mechanics', incensed that body greatly".[26] The vehemence of that discord was doubtless enhanced by the sums of money involved. If Sharp's fee of 1200 guineas in 1794 sounds high then Heath's 2000 guineas in 1798 for engraving Copley's *Death of Major Pierson* is astonishing.[27] Needless to say this level of expenditure by painters was undertaken in anticipation of a considerable return on their investment.

The way in which the trade craft of engraving could form the bridge-head from which some individuals could develop as easel painters is most easily

FIGURE 17. Detail showing the very large iron staple above William Hogarth's enormous canvas *The Pool of Bethesda* (164 × 243 in/416.6 × 668 cm) completed 1735/1736. For this work Hogarth employed the theatre scene painter George Lambert (1710–1765) to assist with the landscape backgrounds and the mural spandrels. Such an amanuensis would have possessed the experience to mix paint in large quantities and to lift immense "flats" into position – hence the significance of the iron staple. (St Bartholomew's Hospital, London)

FIGURE 18. The staircase well in the Gibbs Building at St Bartholomew's Hospital, London, showing the Hogarth canvases in position – to the left *The Good Samaritan* – completed in 1737. (National Monuments Record)

followed in the case of William Hogarth. In 1713/14, at the slightly advanced age of 16, he was placed with Ellis Gamble of Blue Cross Street, Leicester Fields, "a silver plate engraver" with whom he "served a prentiship". The delay in Hogarth's engagement with Gamble may have been because his father, Richard Hogarth, was living as bankrupt within the rules of the Fleet Prison. According to the painter's autobiographical notes, the young Hogarth had "an early access to a neighbouring painter [who] drew my attention from play [and so] every opportunity was employed in attempts at drawing."[28] There has been much speculation as to the identity of this "neighbouring painter". It is very possible that he was one of the sign-painters who were located in Harp Alley, reasonably close to the Fleet Prison where his father languished.[29]

If engraving was one approach to the polite art of painting, gold and silversmithing remained, what they had been in the sixteenth century, an important alternative means to that end. This was certainly the trade to which the young Sir Henry Raeburn (1756–1823) was apprenticed in Edinburgh. From goldsmithing he naturally gravitated, as others had done before him, to painting in miniature before painting full size oils on canvas. Such a background fully justified Cunningham's (1830) nicely expressed opinion that "to say that he [Raeburn] was self-taught is an audacious assertion".[30] Audacious or not the American brothers Anson (1779–1852) and Daniel Dickinson (b1795) were both apprenticed to silversmiths before becoming limners of portrait miniatures.[31] In contrast to the apparent amity between the Goldsmiths and the Painter Stainers the latter were, by 1619 in conflict with the newly formed Goldbeaters Company. This Company claimed a monopoly on the production and sale of gold and silver leaf which the Painters had traditionally imported from abroad. By 1772 the interests of these two Companies may have merged for on 8 January that year the Painter's *Binding Book* records that Thomas Smith was apprenticed to Thomas Wickstead, Goldbeater, for seven years. This could be explained by affiliation to a given guild whilst practicing another craft – as was permitted by "the Custom of London". On the other hand the application of leaf metal by means of oil gilding was an accepted aspect of the Painters craft. At the Restoration, and certainly before 1665, the Company ruled that all but Painter Stainers be prohibited from "gilding with gold or silver or making flock-worke".[32] This almost certainly related to oil gilding which, like "flock-worke", involves the use of an oil size as a mordant. In contrast water gilding was confined to work on interiors and, as a trade, was often associated with woodcarving.

At the slightly advanced age of 15 years Edward Edwards RA (1738–1806) was apprenticed as a woodcarver and gilder "to work with his father at the

FIGURE 19. *Silver Salver* by Paul de Lamerie (1688–1751) engraved by William Hogarth in 1728–1729. (Victoria & Albert Museum, London)

shop of Mr [William] Hallet [*sic*] an upholsterer at the corner of Great St Martin's Lane, Long Acre, where he continued till he was 18 years of age". Having removed his son from this apprenticeship his father then encouraged him to take "lessons at a drawing school; in 1759" and three years later "he was deemed qualified to be admitted as a student at the Duke of Richmond's Gallery" before graduating to the St Martin's Lane Academy.[33] Edwards was by no means the only polite painter to have begun a career in the fine arts via one of the woodworking trades. Another was George Romney (1734–1802) who came from a family, of yeoman stock in Appleby-in-Westmoreland, who were compelled to move to Lancashire during the Civil War. It was there that Romney was apprenticed for about four years in "the united trades of carpenter joiner and cabinet maker. Subdivisions in labour prevailed less than now" – or at least that was the case in much of provincial England. In about 1753 he transferred himself to a master painter named Steele where he was bound apprentice for just "four years" to learn "the art or science of painting" for a premium of £20. His first work of art was "a hand holding a letter for the Post Office window at Kendal".[34] The emphasis accorded to drawing and design in a cabinet makers workshop is reflected very fully in a painting by an unknown artist, showing the office of such an establishment in *c.* 1770 (see Fig. 9). Perhaps even more remarkable than Romney is the case of John Ferneley (1782–1860) who was apprenticed to his father, a Leicestershire wheelwright.[35] In this context young Ferneley would have developed a knowledge of the horses which, as a painter, were to become his primary subject matter.

In this utilitarian tradition Zoffany, on his first arrival in England, in 1760, found employment in London decorating clock dials.[36] Some painters virtually specialised in this type of work. In the 1760s James Bunk was "chiefly employed by those who required subjects for mechanical movements, such as clocks for the East Indies (see Fig. 46), in which figures are represented that are put in motion by the machine which they decorate."[37] Other aspiring artists found work as pattern drawers an employment that Thomas Stothert RA (1755–1834) first engaged in.[38] Even more remarkable were those individuals who, despite trade regulations and other considerations, seemingly arrived from nowhere. One such was George Budd who had "been bred a hosier but afterwards pursued painting" including portraiture, landscape "and sometimes still life [1830]".[39]

In Early Modern Britain two dimensional pictorial work was applied to a wide variety of supports and surfaces other than framed pictures. Accordingly trade painters worked on carriages, shop signs, chimney boards, overmantel and over-door panels all of which called forth artistic imagination in the use of paint. In this way a wide diversity of skills were both deployed and developed. These were skills that John Jackson RA (1778–1831) had presumably acquired since having been "apprenticed to a business [as an arras-tailor which was] little congenial to his graphic taste" was later enabled to purchase his release from his indenture through a subscription organised by the painter Sir George Beaumont (see Fig. 45).[40]

In the course of the seventeenth century two trades, that of the Plaisterers and also the Plumbers of London, attempted to establish some limited access to aspects of the work of the Painter Stainers. In response the Painter Stainers placed before Queen Elizabeth a petition which gave voice to their concern that: "now for lack of good orders both Plaisterers and others doth entermeddle in the same science." A bill based on this petition was put before Parliament and passed into law in 1580. By 1599 a bill was presented to the Court of Common Council in the City pointing out that the Plaisterers had formally confined themselves to "lathing, daubing, plaistering and liming."[41] This last item probably signifies limewash or distemper, an aspect of the plasterers trade that, by the eighteenth century occurs under the heading of "washing and stopping"[42] – the association between lime plaster and limewash was inevitably close.

Despite some residual objection the bill of 1599 granted a degree of latitude regarding the range of work that plasterers were to be permitted to undertake. They would however be restricted to a limited group of pigments and media – namely "Whiting, Blacking, Redlead, Redoker, Yellow Ochre and Russet mingled with size only" – the distempers. Evidently the Painter Stainers kept a close eye on this evolving situation for in May 1646 they fined a plasterer £20 "who was using the Art of Painting." By April 1664 the Painter Stainers reiterated their strictures on the Plaisterers who were expected to confine themselves to six colours using "plain size only" and that the work itself should be as "plain as necessary to their profession about the seilings of rooms and such like". These restrictions may have contributed to the Tudor and Stuart fashion for sgraffito decoration in which two colours or tones of plaster were used, the one layer being cut back to reveal the other to decorative effect – an activity well within the scope of the plasterers trade. From the vantage point of the Painter Stainers Company a palette of six colours, and the combinations of the same, should have offered the plasterers an adequate selection of colours. Perhaps for that reason the brethren of the Painter Stainers came to the conclusion that:

FIGURE 20. John Singleton Copley's (1738–1815) portrait of the silversmith, engraver and American patriot *Paul Revere* – oil on canvas *c.* 1768–1770. The painting, with its strong chiaroscuro, is typical of Copley's work in Massachusetts – but then his step-father was the English-born mezzotint engraver Peter Pelham. (Museum of Fine Arts, Boston)

> "… the Plaisterers being altogether unskilful in that Art, pretend to do several paintings which are so ill done as that … [they] … tended to the scandal and disgrace of the Art of Painting within our English nation".[43]

This bill of 1664 did not pass perhaps because the Plaisterers pleaded poverty, besides by 1666 The Great Fire of London was to have the effect of reducing the significance of these demarcation disputes in the building trades. Although the tools and materials used in a given craft could help to define an art and mystery there was some inevitable overlap. For example joiners might use oil paint as an informal glue. This probably explains the will of the King's Joiner William Lee who, on his death in 1483 left "my feleschipp of Joynours of London ij lidgers Colour stones to remayne to the Feleschip of Joynours of London for ever". These mullers and ledger stones were to be made available for loan for fourteen days for use by members of the Company. [44]

As noted above the other trade which provoked conflict with the Painter Stainers was that of the Plumbers. In contrast to the Plaisterers who were, as we have seen, permitted by increments to apply some pigments in a size medium the Plumbers would, by degrees, be entitled to apply oil paint. At first glance the association between the plumbers trade and that of oil painting may seem disconcerting. In fact, by a process known to economists as "backward linkage", there was some logic in this connection. Certainly plumbers would have been involved in the production of lead-based paints and this

FIGURE 21. *Trade Card* for the silversmith Ellis Gamble engraved in *c.* 1723 by his former apprentice William Hogarth (1697–1764). (British Museum, London)

activity almost certainly extended to the making of other lead-based products – red lead, white lead and the siccatives.[45] More important was the role of plumbers in the making of leaded windows and their glazing. With the introduction of joiner-made sash windows in late 17th century England the plumbers retained their role as glaziers. In such windows the glass was held in place, within the timber glazing bars by means of iron sprigs and putty made from linseed oil and whiting. For this purpose it was of utmost importance that the putty retained its flexibility for as long as possible so that the timber, of which the joinery was made, could settle. To facilitate this, the putty was sealed by paint. In this progression of events plumbers added painting in oil to their portfolio of responsibilities. A reflection of all this may be seen in the 1792 inventory for Houghton Hall, Norfolk. There, the Glaziers shop included "… a Casement & a quantity of old iron, 14 brass pullies with iron hooks … sundry iron, lead & brass, A Table with some paint pots &c, a Box of plate Glass, New and old lead …"[46]

All workers who used lead, including lead-based paints, were handling a material that was a recognised health hazard. In 1781 John Stock's bequest of £4,200 to the Painter Stainers of London on 3% stock stipulated that £100 of income be used as grants to ten poor journeymen in London or within 20 miles (*c*. 32 km), either house or ship painters "who by the bad effects of working with paint were lamed in the use of their hands and incapable of doing much business".[47]

In the later seventeenth century the Painter Stainers were less inclined to acquiesce in a situation in which Plumbers impinged on their preserves. Sometime before 1665 the Painter's included the Plumbers in a long list (cited in full on p. 141) of trades that "did break out into the Art of Painting to the great deceit of the people of this nation."[48] The Painters disputes with the Plumbers continued in a desultory way for some time. As late as September 1817 the Painters took action in the Court of the Lord Mayor of London against a glazier who had been working as a painter. This situation was eventually resolved in a strangely benign way, in 1823 the glazier in question joined the Painter Stainers Company.[49] By this date the Guilds were more anxious to recruit members then reject outsiders. Furthermore, by the late eighteenth century the rise of the Combinations (proto- Trade Unions) had diverted the trades into becoming a more overtly political force unconnected with the guilds. In May 1794 William Pitt determined that Parliament would suppress the London Constitutional Society (LCS) and its leaders were arrested. In that same year the Dublin-born plumber John Binns joined the LCS and rose to become its Chairman.[50]

Well into the nineteenth century plumbers continued to work as house and sign painters. As an extension to these activities they also produced easel paintings – as, for example, the plumber William Bagshaw of Rugby who, in 1846, painted a pair of portraits of *The White Ram* and *The White Ewe*. Two surviving plumbers' trade signs, and the trade label of Dobie of London, further demonstrate that this linkage between plumbing and painting persisted into the nineteenth century.[51] This sort of diversification, including the painting of pictures, was even more possible in the provinces, the colonies and ex-colonies. In Liverpool, Joseph Desilva (1816–*c*. 1875) advertised his services as a "Painter, Plumber and Glazier … Paint Oil and Colour Dealer" adding, for good measure, that he also did "Portraits of Ships taken in any situation."[52]

Of all these artistically creative plumbers perhaps the most remarkable was the Dunthorne family of Suffolk and Essex. Of these James Dunthorne's *John Sidey and His Hounds* of 1765 is a particularly enjoyable example of their work (Fig. 49).[53] This connection between leadwork and oil paint serves to explain the association between the landscape painter John Constable (1776–1837) and the plumber-painter John Dunthorne. This was a friendship commemorated in the timber model of a windmill that the artisan gave to the artist as a studio "prop" (Fig. 50).[54] The two men evidently shared the same language in terms of their craft.

By the late nineteenth century the link between the art and the trade of painting had all but passed into history. In the 1870s some academic artists began to look across the divide between easel painters and trade painters with a modicum of respect. In his lectures on painting the American artist William Morris Hunt (1824–1876) urged his students to "Try to get flat, even surfaces. People who paint for a living, house-painters, etc always get flat surfaces. They don't stop to niggle".[55]

For Hunt's generation this was something of a revelation born of the distinction, that by then existed, between the "trade" and the "art" of painting. In the previous century a demarcation of this sort was either absent or imperceptible in North America. Take for example a jobbing painter like the immigrant Ignatius Shnydore. On the 6 June 1788 he advertised that having ceased working as a scene painter for "The Old American Company of Comedians [he was] desirous of becoming a Citizen" as this would enable him "to carry on the painting business in all its branches" as an independent master painter. From his address at 65 Maiden-lane at the corner of Nassau-street, New York he advertised his services in an extraordinarily comprehensive list:

> "Coach and Sign Painting
> Ship and House Painting, Gilding and Glazing,
> Rooms painted in the Italian mode on canvas,
> Transparent Painting, &c. &c."

Shnydore concluded this advertisement by stating that he "flatters himself he will give general satisfaction to all those who may honor him with their commands."[56] For such a tradesman "self expression" was not a concern – they worked to fulfil the demands of their clients.

Much of the work done by these painters and decorators and, for that matter, those who claimed to be "artists", could be relative humdrum. The portrait painter John Opie RA (1761–1807) sympathised with those, less fortunate than himself, who "skulk through life as a hackney likeness-taker, a copier, a drawing-master or a pattern drawer to young ladies".[57]

Some individuals approached the "fine arts" by way of a craft but for others the arts could offer an alternative to a university education. For Catholics and Non-Conformists who were denied access to the Universities, a pupilage with a "liberal" painter provided some form of higher education. This was the course taken by the poet Alexander Pope (1688–1744) who spent six months or so as a pupil of the portrait painter Charles Jervas (1675–1739). Furthermore the poet's friendship with Kneller and Jonathan Richardson Snr (1665–1745) reinforced his understanding of the visual arts. In a letter of 23 August 1713, addressed to John Gay, Pope acknowledged that thanks to the tutelage of "Mr Jervas" he had begun "to discover beauties that were till now imperceptible to me. Every corner of an eye, or turn of a nose or ear, the smallest degree of light or shade on a cheek or in a dimple, have charms to distract me."[58] Pope's poem in praise of Kneller may be an exaggerated tribute but it has the virtue of having been written by someone who knew what it was to paint.

> "Kneller by Heav'n and not a master taught
> Whose art was Nature and whose pictures thought."[59]

Notes

[1]   Horace Walpole 1786, Vol. II, p. 207. According to Walpole "Mr Hieronymo Laniere" the painter, picture cleaner and faker who worked in England was "adept in all the arts of picture-craft"

[2]   Theophilus *On Diverse Arts* (1963) 1979, chapter 17, p. 26. Cennino Cennini (1437) 1933; reprint n.d p. 64

[3]   Maclehose and Baldwin Brown 1907, pp. 91, 243, 265

[4]   James Ayres 2003, pp. 138–159; George P. Bankart (1908) 2002, chapter iv "Sgraffito, or Scratched Ornament", pp. 37–44; Maclehose and Baldwin Brown 1907, chapter xii "Sgraffito-work"

[5]   Edward Edwards1808, pp. 127–129; Geoffrey Beard 1997, p. 12; Colin Platt 2004, p. 145 citing De Beer, *Diary of John Evelyn*, Oxford, 1955, pp. 756–757

[6]   James Ayres 2003, pp. 173–176

[7]   Karen Hearn 1995, pp. 185–186

[8]   Claude Blair 1958, pp. 173–176

[9]   Henry Spelman *Concilia, decreta, leyes …* (1639), London, 1939, see Phillip Lindley 2007, pp. 140, 141. This plate was reversed so Spelman included a mirror image the right way round

[10] 1642 is the earliest dated mezzotint by von Siegen

[11] Trevor Fawcett 2008, p. 100 citing lithographs by Henry Banks

[12] For Gilray see W. H. Pyne 1824, p. 409

[13] For Gilpin see Joseph Farington, p. 1164 26 Feb 1799

[14] For Wale see Edward Edwards 1808, p. 116

[15] *Library of Fine Arts* 1831, Vol. II, pp. 6, 2

[16] Hans Hammelmann 1975, p. 46. The elder Grignon arrived in England in 1688

[17] Ronald Paulson 1991, Vol. I, pp. 38–39. Ann Forester 1963

[18] Allan Cunningham 1830, Vol. I, p. 59

[19] *Ibid.*, Vol. I, p. 322

[20] Edward Edwards 1808, p. 264 see also Hans Hammelmann 1975, pp. 38–66. It is possible that Rooker's early life as an engraver contributed to his poor eyesight in later years

[21] Ewan Clayton 2013, pp. 195–199; Hans Hammellmann 1975, p. 3; Holger Hoock (2003) 2009, p. 227

[22] Joseph Farington, pp. 251–252 8 Oct 1794

[23] *Ibid.*, pp. 261–262 21 November 1794

[24] Exhibition booklet *John Singleton Copley's Watson and the Shark*, National Gallery of Art, Washington DC, 1993

[25] Joseph Farington, p. 1238 15 June 1799

[26] *Ibid.*, p. 1570 1 July 1801 and p. 1573 5 July 1801. For Delattre see Hanns Hammelmann 1975, p. 69. It seems that the evidence given by Hoppner and Opie was not objected to

[27] *Ibid.*, p. 1057 12 Sept 1798

[28] Ronald Paulson 1991, Vol. I, pp. 38–39; Jerry White 2012, p. 101; Ann Forester 1963

[29] Paulson, Vol. I, p. 25 has suggested that this painter was Egbert van Heemskirk who died in London in *c.* 1704 – but it is arguable that the real influence is likely to have been a native Englishman

[30] Allan Cunningham 1830, Vol. V, pp. 204–206

[31] William Dunlap (1834) 1969, Vol. II, Pt I, p. 217, Vol. ii, Pt ii, p. 333

[32] Alan Borg 2005, p. 57; W. A. D. Englefield (1923), 1936, pp. 68 (Article 9), 84

[33] Edward Edwards 1808, pp. 1–2. For William Hallett the Elder see Geoffrey Beard 1997, pp. 162–163. For Hallett's trade label see Ambrose Heal (1953) 1988, pp. 73–74

[34] Allan Cunningham 1830, Vol. V, pp. 50–61

[35] Arts Council of Great Britain, *British Sporting Painting 1650–1850*, 1974, p. 74

[36] Martin Postle ed. 2011, p. 20; J. T. Smith (1828), 1919, Vol. ii, p. 68 "Zoffany graduated from painting clock faces to painting faces"

[37] Edward Edwards 1808, p. 32

[38] Joseph Farington, p. 155 4 Feb 1794. Also Alan Cunningham 1830, Vol. V, p. 46

[39] Edward Edwards 1908, p. 8

[40] Library of Fine Arts 1831, Vol. I, pp. 445–447

[41] W. A. D. Englefield (1923) 1936, pp. 56, 57, 74

[42] *Plaisterers's Price Book* published by The Master Plaisterers, London 1798; copy in Soane Museum, London, also James Ayres 1998, p. 208

[43] W. A. D. Englefield (1923) 1936, pp. 74, 122, 124

[44] John Harvey 1975, p. 155

[45] Max Doerner (1963) 1979

[46] Tessa Murdoch ed. 2006, p. 200

[47] W. A. D. Englefield (1923) 1936, p. 177; Alan Borg 2005, pp. 122–123. See also Joan Lane 1996, pp. 145–146

[48] *Ibid.*, p. 95. In this respect the Plasterers were seen as even more of a threat

[49] *Ibid.*, p. 191

[50] Iorwerth Prothero 1979 – Combinations. For the LCS see E. P. Thompson (1963) 1991, pp. 144, 153

[51] For Bagshaw's work see James Ayres 1980, figs 111 and 112. This pair of paintings is now at Compton Verney, Warwickshire. For trade signs etc, see James Ayres 1998, figs 266, 267, 285

[52] A. S. Davidson 1986, pp. 85–86

[53] Paul Mellon Collection, Upperville, Virginia – now in New Haven, Connecticut

[54] Illustrated: James Ayres 1985, fig. 65

[55] Charles Movalli ed. 1976, p. 17. On p. 124 Hunt gives the following advice: "If you have
     a large surface to paint over get sash tools [brushes] from the paint shop, and do it at
     once. I believe that the old painters used these brushes, certainly for skies, backgrounds
     and draperies. At any rate, they painted broadly and frankly, and they couldn't have
     done it with brushes as we buy nowadays – long, flimsy, weak things, or else stiff and
     unyielding. If you want to know what brushes to use, watch the painters at work on
     windows and doors"

[56] William Kelby (1922) 1970, p. 33

[57] Trevor Fawcett 1974, p. 38, fn.131

[58] W. H. Pyne 1823–24, Vol. II, p. 10

[59] W. T. Whitley 1928, Vol. I, p. 20 – where the poem is quoted in full. See also Peter
     Quennell, *Alexander Pope; the Education of a Genius 1688–1728*, London, 1968

Chapter 7

THE MATERIALS OF PAINTERS

In his *Essay on the Mechanics of Oil Colours* published in Bath in 1787 William Williams argues that a painter should:

> "make himself well acquainted with the qualities and hues of the different pigments in their dry state, that he may judge of the goodness or deficiency of them when ground in oil; it is a pity, but it is true, there are many, and some of much merit, that scarce know the difference of umber and oker in their crude state; seldom if ever seeing them but in bladders."[1]

This account demonstrates that by the 1780s easel painters tended to purchase ready-made paints in bladders (the precursors of tube oil colours) and that they therefore lacked an empirical understanding of pigments and media. Some, amongst that generation of artists, were prepared to acknowledge this deficiency in their knowledge. Henry Tresham RA (1756–1814) "lamented not having practiced the mechanical part of painting before he went to Italy."[2] This was the very type of understanding of materials that an apprenticeship in the art and mystery would have prioritised. For painters pigments and media were the fundamental secrets (mysteries) of the trade. It is therefore no coincidence that much of the early modern documentation on these confidential practicalities is in manuscript form, documents that were to become more numerous from the late fifteenth century.[3] In the reign of Elizabeth I, Nicholas Hilliard prepared his manuscript on limning but such documents were to become more commonplace in Stuart England.[4] As we have seen these include the notebooks of Theodore de Mayerne (dated 1623 and 1644), Richard Symonds (1617–1660), Charles Beale (who recorded much technical detail concerning the pigments and paints used by his wife, Mary Beale: 1633–1699), John Abbott (1630/4–1727) and John Martin (active late seventeenth century).[5]

Many of these manuscripts, not least Hilliard's, were concerned with limning. One of the earlier printed publications regarding this type of information was

Henry Peacham's *The Art of Drawing with the Pen* (1606). In a later edition this appeared as the *Graphice* (1612) with the subtitle *The Gentleman's Exercise* in which the author argues that limning is more appropriate for the amateur (in both the exact and inexact meaning):[6]

> "Painting in Oyle is done I confesse with greater judgement, and is generally of more esteeme then working in water colours; but then it is more Mechanique and will robbe you of over much time from your excellent studies. It being sometimes a fortnight or a month ere you can finish an ordinary piece ... Beside, oyle nor oyle-colours, if they drop upon apparell, will not out; when water-colours will with the least washing."[7]

As Peacham includes information on painting in both watercolour and oil paints he may well be attempting, in that passage, to absolve himself of blame for revealing such secrets. In presenting his publication as being intended for amateurs it was less likely to be seen to compete with those whose trade, whose means of livelihood, was painting. In general both oil and watercolour were media that were beyond the scope of amateurs in pre-industrial Britain.[8] In this respect an aristocratic figure like Sir Nathaniel Bacon (1585–1627) may have been an exception in that, in his capacity as a painter of pictures he used oil paint, possibly aberrant behaviour for a gentleman. In medieval England the knightly class may have served as patrons but the tiltyard and the hunting field was their natural habitat – writing and painting were generally left to others. This puts Thomas Usk's striking comparison, of 1384/5, between a writer's use of words and a painter's selection of colours in context.

> "Some men there ben [be] that peynten with colours ryche and some with vers [verse] as with red ynke and some with coles [charcoal] and chalke; and yet is there good matere [content] to the leade [lay] people of thilke [the like] chalky purtryeyture, as hem [him] thynketh for the tyme, and afterward the sight of the better colours yeven [given] to hem more joye for the first leadenesse [former lack of skill]."

By the early seventeenth century Sir Nicholas Bacon (1585–1627) was sufficiently assured of his place in the world that his skilful work as an easel painter was unlikely to jeopardise his status. Indeed later in the century this sort of activity had extended down to the gentry. For example Thomas Flatman (1635–1688), with his small estate at Tishton near Diss in Norfolk, a lawyer and a poet, nevertheless retained his position as a member of the gentry by confining himself to limning in watercolour.[9] It was though the artist members of the elite that were seen to be jeopardising painting as an art and mystery – an activity with trade secrets. In the 1676 edition of John Smith's *The Art of Painting in Oyl* the author is careful to state that "those that are professed Painters, whose knowledge in these affairs must be supposed to out-strip first Rudiments" would not therefore be concerned with the information contained in his publication – or that was the hope. In fact the Painter Stainers Company expressed strong reservations on his publication (see p. 84 above).[10]

Of the later Stuart miniature painters Alexander Browne has gained some posthumous fame as it was he who taught Mrs Samuel Pepys the art of "limning". Browne was also the proprietor of one of the earlier colourmans' shops in Long Acre, London. He was also the author of *Ars Pictoria* the second edition (1675) of which included what was tantamount to an advertisement:

> "Because it is very difficult to procure the Colours for Limning rightly prepared, of the best and briskest Colours, I have made it part of my business any time these 16 years, to collect as many of them as were exceeding good, not onely here, but beyond the Seas. And for those Colours that I could not meet with all to my mind, I have taken the care and pains to make them my self. One of which Collection I have prepared a sufficient Quantity, not onely for my own use, but being resolved not to be Niggardly of the same, am willing to supply any Ingenious Persons that have occasion for the same at a reasonable rate, and all other Materials useful for Limning, which are to be had at my Lodging in Long-acre, at the sign of the Pestel and Mortar, an Apothecary's Shop; and at Mr Tooker's Shop, at the sign of the Globe, over against Ivie Bridge in the Strand."[11]

Colourmen's shops were therefore present in Stuart London but in provincial Devon: "All sorts of pencels [brushes] and collouers for painting and lynseed oyle, are to be soulde at the Iremongers; Also leafe gold, Shell gold and leaf Silver."[12] This contrasts with the capital where specialist Colourmen's businesses included in addition to Browne's those of John Calfe, "without Temple Bar" (active before 1703) and John Savage (active *c.* 1680–1700).[13] At about this time John Martin states that "most of the Collars a foresaid you may Buy in Little Bladders and the rest in powders with oyles, Shilles [shells] and varnish att Mr Coopers at the sign of the three pidjohns in Bradford Street [London]; a printshop."[14] Cooper's shop was taken over by Robert Keating who sold "Keatings fine Varnish formerly call'd Coopers Picture Varnish". By this date the business dealt "in all the colours for the house-painter, but his chief business consists in furnishing the liberal painters with their fine colours."[15] Keating who abandoned the sign of the Three Pigeons in favour of the White Hart, Long Acre, was followed under the new emblem by Nathan Drake, who may have been related to the Lincoln easel painter of the same name.[16] This kind of continuity is also found with the colour shop of Jos. Pitcher of St Giles, London (Trade *Directories*

1768–1770) whose premises were later occupied by the oil and colourmen Thomas Waddell & ·Son (*c.* 1783–1793). For Campbell (1747), colourmen were seen as "Apothecaries to the Painter" and in Bristol this could almost literally be the case. In that great port city's *Directory* (Sketchley's) for 1775 James Morgan and Son are listed as "druggists and colourmen"[17] This association between art and science was reinforced, even in Protestant England, where St Luke remained the patron saint of both painters and physicians.

Even in a pre-eminent urban centre like London some diversification in the merchandise was inevitable. In addition to the painters' materials sold by ironmongers and print shops some stores, of the kind we would now term delicatessens, were also involved in this retail business and were described in 1747 as

FIGURE 22. *Trade Card* of Joseph Pitcher the *Colour Man*, 1764, at the "Sign of the Good Woman". This emblem may derive from the Biblical parable of the five foolish or heedless (headless) virgins who had no oil in their lamps – and colourmen traditionally stocked oils. (British Museum, London)

follows: "the common Colour-man [who] generally sells Oyls, Pickles and several things that are sold in what are properly called Oyl-Shops."[18]

These then were the sources of pigments and media but outside London the conversion of these raw materials into paint generally remained the responsibility of the painter and a suitable job for his apprentices. In 1764 Robert Dossie described these procedures as involving "sublimation, calcination, solution, precipitation, filtration and levigation."[19] Processes of this kind would have begun by pounding in a mortar and pestle followed by grinding the pigment on a ledger with a muller. Artisan or artist, "mechanic" or "liberal", painters possessed an empirical rather than a theoretical chemical understanding of the properties of their materials.

Until 1841 the nearest approximation to ready-prepared and packaged oil paints were bladder colours. These were paints that were contained in air-tight bladders of sheep or oxen and thus offered a reasonable method of preservation. One of the earlier references to these may be found in John Smith's *The Art of Painting in Oyl* (1676) in which he describes:

> "a parcel of Colours given me in the year 1661 by a Neighbouring Yeoman that were … left at his house by a Trooper … in the time of the Wars about the year 1644. This Man was by profession a Picture-Drawer, and his Colours were all tied up in Bladders … when I opened them, I found them in very good condition".[20]

In general the paint in bladders was customarily accessed by means of a drawing-pin or thumb-tack. However once opened in this way the paint deteriorated rapidly. The collapsible metal tubes for oil paint that were patented in 1841 by John G. Rand were a vast improvement on the old bladder colours. Tube oil paint could last almost indefinitely.[21]

The first major innovation with regard to paint production occurred in 1718 when Marshall Smith patented his "Machine or Engine for the Grinding of Colours … with a Muller or a Flatt stone by Mocion …. exactly Imitating those of Hands."[22] By manual or mechanical means colour was reduced from its lump state in a mortar and pestle and then ground with its medium to produce paint. Alternatively pigment was ground with water or a volatile oil to form, after evaporation, powder colour for subsequent conversion into paint. By 1734 Marshall Smith's patent had been eclipsed by horse mills of the kind used by the Emerton dynasty of colourmen (*c.* 1720–1796).[23] These horse mills did not imitate the movement of the hands in grinding pigment but more closely resembled the mills used to crush apples in preparation for the cider press. This industrialisation of paint manufacture in London was seen by Campbell (1747) as having brought house painting to a "Low Ebb". He does not record their impact on "liberal" painters but, as noted above, William Williams acknowledged that, with the sale of these cheap paints to artists, the preparation of pigments and media ceased to be part of

FIGURE 23. A collection of three hard-stone mullers for grinding pigments – most commonly with a medium – overall height on average 5½ in (14 cm). (Author's Collection)

studio practice. This tended to remove easel painters from an understanding of their materials.

Campbell certainly identified the impact of these cheap products on trade painters. However as early as 1676 John Smith in his *Art of Painting in Oyl* asserts the needs of the clients at the expense of the trade painters. Smith argued that because "the Gentry live far remote from great Cities, where Painters usually reside" they will, with the aid of his book, be able "to play the good Husband in preserving such Ornaments of their Habitations by instructing their servants to paint "Timber Work in Oyl Colours" by using his directions. This was perhaps the inspiration that was to be adopted on a commercial scale by the Emertons. It was their products that were sold: "ready mixed at a low

FIGURE 24. *Trade Card* of Joseph Emerton the Colourman. The Emerton dynasty supplied both liberal and artisan painters through much of the eighteenth century. Their horse mills made possible the production of large quantities of cheap paints. This trade card illustrates such a machine. The items resembling bunches of grapes are bladder colours – the precursors of tube oil paint, which was first patented in London in 1841. (British Museum, London)

Price, and by the Help of a few printed Directions, a House may be painted by any common Labourer at one third the Expence."[24]

As early as 1736 Richard Marten, a house, sign and ship painter advertised in the *South Caroline Gazette* that: "Gentlemen in the Country may be furnished with all sorts of Colours ready mixt and directions to use them."[25] This strongly suggests that Marten was importing these paints direct from the Emertons in London. Whatever the connection may or may not have been it was the Emertons who, in simplifying the work of painters, had deprived them of one aspect of their employment. For this reason Campbell (1747) advised that:

> "no parent ought to be so mad as to bind his child Apprentice [to a house painter] for Seven Years to a Branch that may be learned in as many Hours, in which he cannot earn a subsistence [and] when he has got it [his freedom] runs the risk of Breaking his Neck every Day, and in the end turns out a mere Blackguard."[26]

In addition to horse mills, windmills were used to grind pigment as was the case at Wheatley near Oxford. It was there that two such mills stood at the edge of the quarry where the famous "Oxford ochre" was obtained.[27] In New York City on 20 April 1785 John Morgan advertised that he had "erected a mill for the sole purpose of grinding colours", although no information is offered as to the type of mill, water-mills were certainly used for this purpose.[28]

William Williams's reference to the importance of understanding ground colours in their "dry state" (lump or powder colours) was of particular importance in relationship to the more valuable pigments. In that state colours could less easily be adulterated than when mixed with a medium. The most obvious case where this was a serious concern was with ultramarine, ground from lapis lazuli from distant Afghanistan.[29] As the most costly of pigments it could, in some contexts, be used to establish a chromatic hierarchy within a pictorial composition. In this way, representations of the Virgin Mary's blue robe assumes, for much the same reasons of cost, the character of the imperial purple of Ancient Rome. Ultramarine was not only much the most expensive of colours in general, but its cost exceeded all other blue pigments. On 3 May 1676 Mary Beale "made exchange with Mr Henry, a half an ounce of ultramarine for four pound [weight] of his Smalt [a cheaper substitute] which he valued at eight shillings a pound" – which gives a value of £3-4-0 for one ounce (28 g) of ultramarine. A couple of years earlier in August 1674 "Mr Lely had an ounce of Ultramarine, the richest, at £4-10s per oz".[30] By 1798 Brandroms, the colourman, stocked three grades of ultramarine at "7 guineas, some of 5 and some of 4 guineas an ounce".[31] Henry, Mrs Beale's colourman, was located at what became much later No. 96 Bedford Street, Convent Garden, London. This shop was to be occupied by the colourman Edward Powell and he was followed in the same business and location by Edward Prascey Allen (Fig. 25).[32]

In London, and to some extent in centres trading with the capital, the rise in the use of industrially produced paints and pigments coincides with the gradual decline in the quality of apprenticeships.[33] This was just as well since the preparation of these materials had been central to the work of a youth bound to a painter. In country districts, even those adjacent to London, the old ways of working persisted amongst trade painters well into the Victorian age. The wheelwright George Sturt (1863–1927) recalled that, as a young apprentice working in the paint shop he lacked the strength:

> "in my arm to grind Prussian blue for finishing a waggon body. Ah, the old muller and [ledger] stone under the skylight in the loft, where in summer time one or two cabbage butterflies would be fluttering. All the edges of the [ledger] stone were thick encrusted with dry paint, left behind by the flexible palette knife … The bench and roof-beams all round were covered too with thick paint where brushes had been rubbed out".[34]

Sturt would have begun his apprenticeship at about the age of 14 in 1877. His wistful memories are typical of the many who began their training in a workshop

FIGURE 25. *Allen's Colourman's Shop* in St Martin's Lane, Westminster: drawing of 1829 by George Scharf. A master painter can be seen leaving the premises with his young apprentice. (British Museum, London)

– a combination of details like a youth's lack of strength for the job in hand and even the lack of concentration – those butterflies. Such an account offers a real insight into the experience of a typical apprentice but one that is best understood by some awareness of the processes involved. Not that this is the place to examine these procedures in detail but some outline of them is essential.[35]

FIGURE 26. Suggested reconstruction of the painters cabinet that Richard Wilson (1714–1782) is known to have owned. It was based on a segment of Inigo Jones's Covent Garden piazza of 1631. In this example of eighteenth century case furniture "the rustic work of the piers was divided into drawers and the arches were filled with pencils [brushes] and oil bottles". (Drawing: James Ayres)

Sturt's reminiscences of a paint shop demonstrates the way in which pigments were generally ground with a vehicle or the full medium – hence the accumulation of old paint on the sides of the ledger stone. If, alternatively, powder colour was to be produced other methods were used. For the large quantities that trade painters might wish to stock the pigment was ground with water; slow to evaporate, but cheap. For the smaller volumes of pigment required by "liberal" painters a volatile oil was used which, by definition, was quick to evaporate and expensive. Poppy oil or oil of spike (lavender) were often used for this purpose because of their clarity. The production of powder colour was, for these reasons, either slow or expensive, but it did offer a means of storing pigment for future use by subsequent rapid conversion into various paints or distempers in a choice of media. The production of powder colours inevitably necessitated some form of storage. These were generally simple pieces of furniture in which the drawer size denoted the value of the pigment – the smaller the drawer the more valuable its contents. The landscape painter Richard Wilson owned a painting cabinet that was something of an architectural edifice being based on a segment of "the Piazza" – Covent Garden where he lived, this splendid "storage unit" measured:

> "about six feet from the floor, including the stand. This he used as a receptacle for his painting implements; the rustic work of the piers [of the stand?] was divided into drawers and the arches were filled with pencils [brushes] and oil bottles."[36] (Fig. 26)

It is likely that most pigments were ground with their media, the vehicle and the binder, to form paints – which brings us to the whole question of the various media. These were listed by Richard Haydocke in his "Englished" version (Oxford 1598) of Lomazzo's *Trattoto dell'arte della pittura, scoltura et archittura* (Milan 1584). In this volume painting is divided into three sorts according to "those moistures where with they are ground."[37] Those seven words make two points effortlessly. Paints were regularly ground with a "moisture" and they are defined by their "medium". In this way oil paint might have a vehicle like turpentine and a binder such as linseed oil – which together formed the medium. Turpentine was the principal vehicle for most oil paints although it could have its disadvantages. For example, "The celebrated astronomer Robert Hooke was first placed", so it was said as an apprentice with "Sir Peter Lely, but soon quitted him from not being able to bear the smell of oil colours".[38] For a volatile oil like turpentine painters in Britain would have been dependent upon imports. In 1754 when the Swedish industrial spy Angerstein was visiting Bristol he describes the imports of:

> "The resin secreted by spruce and fir trees in Carolina and New York [which cost 6s.6d per hundredweight]. But the spirits of turpentine that is distilled from it sells for 36s per hundredweight ... For each barrel of turpentine resin brought over from America, the Government pays a bounty for 'encouragement' of 1s.6d ..."

This was very evidently a highly profitable trade. Because the turpentine used in Britain was sourced in the North American colonies the War of Independence resulted in a shortage of this raw material. As a result the Painter Stainers Company held an emergency meeting in July 1779 to discuss the high cost of turpentine. By 17 August members of the Company had submitted samples "for a substitute for turpentine" but none were considered suitable. [39]

With distempers the vehicle would be water and the binder a size. For these distempers, in progressive order of refinement, the sizes were derived from boiled animal bones (Scotch glue) rabbit-skin and parchment. Other glue-like substances used for this purpose included isinglass (fish), glair (white of egg) and the caseins (cheese and milk). The latter was often mixed with ammonia, in the convenient form of urine, to reduce the possibility of it turning sour. In addition to these binders were the gums which William Salmon (1701) stated comprised "chiefly these four: Gum Arabic, Gum Lake, Gum Hedera and Gum Armoniak."[40]

Although the preparation of these paints and distempers could, in a pre-mechanised circumstance, be labour intensive their production necessitated knowledge and experience. Some colours could lose their chromatic value if ground too much, others suffered less in this respect. For example, "Indigo; will grind very fine, and lie with a good body …"[41] Another difficulty was the tendency of ingredients like linseed oil, with its yellow cast, to turn blue into green. To avoid this a clear oil like walnut was used by easel painters but was generally too expensive for trade painters.[42] Alternatively smalt (powdered blue glass) was cast or "strewn" over gold size – a form of *post hoc* medium. Smalt may have been a relatively late introduction to Britain. In 1618 Abraham Baker was granted a monopoly "to make work and compound certayne stuffe called smault … during the term of one and thirty years".[43] A 1662–63 description of how to apply smalt is instructive:

> "First lay white led somewhat thicke then presently [immediately] befor it be dry cast the smalt or strewing blue against it, or upon it & it will sticke fast onto ye white led and shew a pure Azure colour, it is the colour, and thus done yt, you see so excellent a blew in Rood lofts done many years agone …"

If that last statement is true then smalt was used in England at a far earlier date than is sometimes recognised. A possible late medieval example of this method of applying smalt, as described above, was recently identified in a scheme of heraldic paintings found on reused timbers in the Rectory at Ducklington, Oxfordshire.[44]

All these materials formed part of the art & mystery of the painting trades. For example, John Abbott offers as a secret, the use of "Juice of Garlicke" as a "resist" although the Italian Cennino Cennini (born *c.* 1370) attributes the opposite property to garlic – its use as mordant.[45] Such "tricks of the trade" long remained of value to artists. In 1797 Thomas Daniel RA (1749–1840) "calcined [gamboge] to three different degrees; producing warm and cool tints." Another such stratagem was referred to by John Opie RA (1761–1807) who found "a great advantage from warming his oil while using it" arguing that "the colour incorporates better."[46]

A further ingredient sometimes added to paints, to retard the tendency of two or more colours on a support to merge, was megilp. This was described by Whittock (1827) as "a compound of various ingredients mixed together to the consistence of a thick treacle",[47] which is why in German this is known as *Malbutter*: literally "paint butter".[48] The "various ingredients" for oil megilp could include: beeswax and rotten stone, but for distempers soap and stale beer, as well as wax, were included.[49] These compounds were invaluable for trade painters when graining and marbling but were also employed by easel painters like Benjamin West PRA.[50] When Thomas Sully (1783–1872) was visiting

England for nine months in 1809–1810 he met Sir Martin Archer Shee RA (1769–1850) who gave the American painter his recipe for megilp.[51] According to William Dunlap (1834) the artist Benjamin Trott (*c.* 1770–1834) who had "visited the western world beyond the [Appalachian] mountains" became so fixated with what he termed "megrim" (megilp?) that it took "possession of his brain" to the extent that he spent more time "experimenting with this medium than working on his paintings".[52]

So complex were all these matters concerning pigments and their media that some youths were apprenticed, or at least tied, for as long as 13 years of which six were "given exclusively to the manufacture of colours". [53] The centrality of pigments and media to the artists' craft were such that when Godfrey Kneller came to England in 1674/5 he brought with him a servant "whose sole employment was to prepare colours and materials." This assistant was later set up in business by Kneller as an oil and colourman. [54]

By modern standards sales in these oil and colour shops was so small that their stock in trade extended well beyond those two commodities. These shops certainly sold brushes although there were specialists who stocked a wide range of these. One such was William Lyon "At the Sign of the Black Boy, St Michael's Crooked-lane", London who made and sold "all Sorts of Brushes, Wholesale and Retail." Although he may have bought-in sable brushes the ones he made were relatively coarse as indicated by his offer of ready "Money for Hogs-Bristles and Horse-Hair".[55] Brushes, particularly the larger ones, were bound to the handle with twine or wire, those with a metal ferrule being generally a latter innovation. Limewash brushes were usually made of grass held onto the wooden handle by a strip of leather secured by copper rivets – materials that were thought to survive the caustic nature of lime for longer. For smaller brushes birds quills were used which had the virtue of indicating the gauge of the brush in relation to the size of the bird. In this way, in descending order: swan, goose and duck quills were used. There was, furthermore, a belief that aquatic birds provided the best quills for this purpose. Fine, long-haired brushes were reserved for such purposes as sign writing, striping carriages or drawing-in the rigging on shipping pictures. These brushes were known, for obvious reasons, as "writers" and "stripers".[56] In some ways these various types of brush tended to define the nature of the work and thus reinforced the trend towards the division of labour found in carriage making workshops. Maul-sticks (from the Dutch *mahlstick*: painter's stick) were often used in association with these brushes to steady the hand. Implements such as maul-sticks were generally made by those who used them.

Palettes of ivory and porcelain (used by painters working in miniature), were probably made by specialist artisans as were wooden palettes which were made by joiners. In general palettes have increased in size through history, possibly in relationship to the dwindling cost of paints.[57] Their shape has also evolved. According to Ozias Humphrey (1742–1810) Kneller was seen working in London in 1693 using a small palette shaped "like a battledore or hornbook". This he held upright on the same plane as his canvas so that a direct comparison could be made between the paint on the palette and that which he was contemplating incorporating in the picture.[58]

Canvas supports were slow to be adopted perhaps because they were associated with what, in early Stuart England, were perceived to be the lowly products of the Stainers. Ultimately, as mural schemes declined and moveable pictures grew in size, the more easily made and more portable nature of canvas, was seen to be an advantage as compared to paintings on panel. It is noticeable that many of the larger English portraits by Marcus Gheeraerts the Younger (1561–1635) are painted on canvas.[59] Not that panel painting was ever fully outmoded although, by the eighteenth century, mahogany had generally displaced quarter-sawn oak for this purpose. Reynolds was one of the many artists who occasionally painted on mahogany panels.[60]

Canvas was certainly regarded as a relatively new type of support for easel painting as is confirmed by Richard Symonds (1617–1660). His notebooks have much to say about the priming of panels but offer only a few remarks about preparations for canvas. Despite which, and even at this date, artists would purchase pre-prepared canvases. According to Symonds the painter Robert Walker purchased them in London prepared by a man from Liège named Fenn with an address in Purpoole Lane.[61] Prepared linen canvases at this date were almost certainly sold fixed to a frame or even to a picture frame.[62] By the mid-1750s canvas was stretched on frames which were not fixed at the mitres but were wedged so that the canvas could be stretched – hence the term stretchers for these later devices. At first these were regarded as such an innovation that they were known as "drive-up" frames. To what extent pre-prepared canvases were available from seventeenth century oil and colourmen is not easily determined.[63] De Mayerne stated that they were available in early seventeenth century London and by the close of the century the colourman John Savage (active *c.* 1680–1700) sold "prim'd Cloths" from his premises "without Temple Bar".[64] By 1747 *The London Tradesman* states that some colourmen "prepare canvases of all sizes ready stretched on frames which is quite foreign to the business of the ordinary shop,"[65] and yet by 1797 this was standard merchandise for such emporia. Sir Francis Bourgeois usually painted "on canvas as it comes from [the] Colourmen". These linen canvases were generally prepared with gesso (or "Jess") grounds and were sold toned or untoned. Some artists believed that if this ground was washed over with a solution of honey and water it would prevent the "colour from absorbing too fast", although sugar dissolved in water achieved similar results.[66]

The production of these pre-prepared canvases was yet another way in which the apprentice in a painter's workshop was deprived of an area of responsibility. A further and even more significant consequence of these ready-made canvases was that it was now possible, by the closing decades of the seventeenth century, for picture sizes and the frames that encompassed them, to be made to standardised dimensions. By 1733 Gerrard Howard was making architrave frames for Sir Godfrey Kneller's portraits of members of the Kit-Cat Club, so called because the tavern where they met was presided over by Christopher Cat. This series of portraits, now in the National Portrait Gallery, London, were painted between *c.* 1702 and 1717. The dimensions of these frames was 36 × 28 in (91.5 × 71 cm). Canvas and picture frame sizes had become, by the early eighteenth century, so regularised that any departure from the normal dimensions was very evident. Consequently the 36 × 28 in picture size became known by its soubriquet as "a Kit-cat" – a term that survives to this day.[67] Once pictures were being painted to standard sizes they could more easily be created in advance of a purchaser, and frames could be constructed, carved and gilded in anticipation of either. Standardised components were one of the first steps towards art as a consumerist product.

To what extent these ready-made artists' materials were available in the provinces and in the Colonies is an important question that is likely to produce miscellaneous answers. Certainly the practitioners of many crafts were also in business as small-scale retailers. This is another instance of the kind of situation known to economists as "backward linkage". For example, many artisans in the pre-industrial building trades were involved in retailing the materials of their craft. In this way carpenters would sell timber and bricklayers would retail bricks. Similarly a number of easel painters sold pigments, media and paints: among them Mary Beale (1633–1699) and Alexander Browne (fl. 1659–1706).[68] In 1688 Stalker and Parker refer to "the shops which supply us" with artists' materials implying that, like London, there was no problem with obtaining them in Oxford where their book on Japanning was published.[69] By contrast, in March 1734, Maurice Johnson in Northamptonshire was compelled to send to London for a box of oil colours for easel painting via the Peterborough carrier.[70]

＊ ＊ ＊ ＊

In Colonial America the young Benjamin West PRA (1738–1820) obtained his first pigments from "a party of roaming Indians then visiting Springfield", Pennsylvania. These were the earth colours to which he later added indigo so that he was then "possessed of the three primary colours."[71] In general Colonial and Early Federal America was dependent upon imported supplies of this kind. In 1728 the Scottish-born John Smibert (1688–1751) sailed to Newport, Rhode Island, as part of Dean Berkeley's (1690–1763) entourage. Smibert later settled in Boston where he prospered as a portrait painter and opened a colour shop. His understanding of pigments and media would have been considerable as he had served his time as an apprentice "with a common house painter" in Edinburgh before his artistic ambitions developed in London. By the 1740s his surviving American correspondence shows that he imported much of his stock from the London artist and art dealer Arthur Pond (1701–1758).[72] In 1749 Smibert wrote to Pond with a lengthy shopping list which included "Three quarter cloths [canvases for portraits] one dozen … Dark Prussian Blue 3lbs [and also] fan mounts".[73] In North America as in Britain some sense of continuity was maintained through the premises occupied by such businesses. The artist and polymath Charles Wilson Peal (1741–1827) recalled visiting the colourman Moffatt in Boston in 1769 in a shop which had previously been Smibert's.[74] Even before Smibert established his business it is likely that the house painter Thomas Child supplied artists with paints from his Boston workshops. Child was born in England in the 1650s and it is thought he was made free of the Painter Stainers of London in 1679. He is known to have been in Massachusetts by 1685. On his death his widow Katherine continued the business which was later taken over by her nephew from 1714–1725 (see Fig. 29).[75]

* * * *

The continuity of these colourshops on both sides of the Atlantic is strongly related to the importance of goodwill in the craft-based trades. Both artists and artisans would need to have faith in the materials that they purchased. Presumably for this reason Richard Cosway RA (1740–1821) was a regular customer of Newman of Garrard Street whereas Richard Wilson RA (1714–1782) only purchased his brushes there.[76] Loyalty to a particular colourman is possibly discernible in Farington's *Diary* entry of 31 July 1801 where he notes that "Middleton the colourman called & solicited my orders, Poole [another such retailer] being dead."[77] This outlook was also true of Sir Henry Raeburn RA (1756–1823). In Edinburgh his colourman was Taylor & Norrie a shop later patronised by Sir David Wilkie (1785–1841). It seems that Taylor & Norrie purchased much of their stock from Thomas Brown of High Holborn.[78] In such circumstances a Scottish born painter like Raeburn could remain loyal to the same ultimate source of his materials when working in either Edinburgh or London.

* * * *

The limners worked in solid watercolour (gouache) but for maps, printed or manuscript, a translucent wash that would not obscure drawn or printed detail, was essential. Significantly both Thomas Sandby RA (1721–1798) and his more famous younger brother Paul Sandby RA (1725–1809) began their careers as surveyors and map makers before building their reputations as watercolourists.[79] The washes used for this purpose could include Chinese Ink (also known as Indian ink) but alternatives to these imports were also available. In the decade or so either side of 1800 William Jones of 103 Leadenhall Street, London was still stocking "Liquid Colours in Bottles for Prints, Maps, Plans &c ..."[80] The breakthrough in the quest for easily used watercolours had in fact occurred some years earlier. In the 1770s Thomas and William Reeves devised their easily soluble watercolour cakes. The inspiration for these watercolours had come from the far less easily dissolved Chinese (stick) Inks which is doubtless why the brothers named their product Reeves British Ink – (their partnership was dissolved in 1783).[81] As noted above, the final step towards what might be termed "convenience paints" occurred in 1841 when the American portrait painter John G. Rand (1801–1873), then working in London, patented his collapsible metal tubes for oil paint.[82] This innovation brought in its train consequences that Rand was unlikely to have anticipated. *Plein air* painting became more possible and an impasto more easily established and therefore both became more usual. Above all the availability of easily used industrially made paints was to result in vast numbers of Sunday painters and other amateurs. Towards the end of the century Oscar Wilde in *The Model Millionaire* makes reference to a fictitious painter named Alan Trevor who lived in Holland Park: "Trevor was a painter. Indeed, few people escape that nowadays".[83]

* * * *

Innovations in the manufacture and packaging of paint were to distance artists from the craft of their art. Curiously it was at just this time that sophisticated colour theories were being widely developed. As long ago as 1672 Isaac Newton

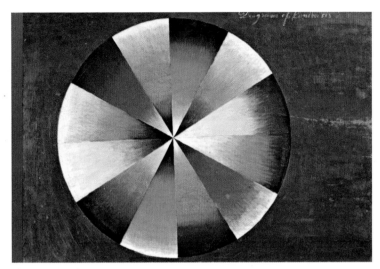

FIGURE 27. Thomas Cole (1801–1848): *Diagram of Contrasts*, 1835. A rather curious colour wheel shows that this Hudson school American landscape painter was moving towards an understanding of colour theory. (Ex. Collection: Barbara Johnson, New Jersey)

had demonstrated that, by passing a beam of white light through a refracting prism, the light could be divided into its component chromatic rays.[84] It seems that this anatomy of colour took some time to be recognised by painters. By 1766 Moses Harris published a volume which included his colour triangle and colour wheel.[85] Despite Harris's endeavours and the even earlier monographs, these theories were not widely circulated amongst artists until the opening decades of the following century. In 1807 J. H. Clarke's manual on watercolour painting included a simple, hand coloured, colour wheel.[86] By 1835 Thomas Cole (1801–1849) in America painted his *Diagram in Contrasts* (oil on board) (Fig. 27).[87] Intriguingly the title of Cole's painting anticipates, by some years, Michel-Eugène Chevreul's *De la loi du Contraste Simultane de Couleurs* (Paris, 1839) which was first published in England in 1854 as *The Principles of Harmony and Contrast of Colour and their Application to the Arts*. Its influence was prodigious. For example the writer Thomas Hardy (1840–1928), in his early years as an architect, lists a dozen examples of "Harmonious Contrasts in Col[d]. Decoration" in his sketchbook.[88] Chevreul's whole theory emerged on the basis of his role as a chemist employed by the Gobelins tapestry workshop. His book was probably the first systematic attempt to promulgate the "laws of simultaneous contrast" – the notion of complementary colours. At the very point that these theories were developing, the ability of painters to achieve those objectives, with precision and permanence, was in decline.

Notes

[1] William Williams 1787, pp. 35–36. At least two painters at this time shared the tautologically Celtic names. In this case the most likely author is the Bristol-born William Williams (1721–1791) who was Benjamin West's first teacher of painting in Pennsylvania. Moreover Williams was an experienced writer as the author of an autobiographical novel (*The Journal of Mr Penrose* 1815) and was back in England by 1787

[2] Joseph Farington, p. 1016 4 June 1798

[3] R. D. Harley (1970) 1982, pp. 2–3

[4] Edinburgh University Library Ms Laing III, 174. See Thornton and Cain 1981

[5] For de Mayerne see R. D. Harley (1970) 1982, p. 9; for Symonds see Mary Beale 1984; for Abbott see Baldwin 2006; the John Martin manuscript is in the Sir John Soane Museum, London

[6] In the historic sense a lover of (the arts) or, in modern usage, an amateur activity – a hobby

[7] R. D. Harley (1970) 1982, p. 7; Peacham was one of the earliest English writers to publish details on oil painting methods

[8] Watercolour cakes devised by Reeves Brothers in the 1770s, tube oil paint patented by John G. Rand in 1841 – see James Ayres 1985, p. 132

[9] David Crystal *The Stories of English* Penguin, London (2004) 2005, p. 174; Horace Walpole 1786, Vol. III, pp. 49–50; Karen Hearn 1995, pp. 222–223 for Bacon and Katherine Coombs 1998, pp. 67–74, 123 for Flatman

[10] John Smith 1676, p. 1; Alan Borg 2005, pp. 83–85

[11] Katherine Coombs 1998, pp. 11, 76, 78. The first edition of Browne's *Ars Pictoria* appeared in 1669, see also Kim Sloan 2000, p. 57

[12] John Abbott *Notebook* 1662–3, Devon Record Office, Exeter

[13] James Ayres 1985, p. 130. See trade labels in British Museum Dept of P & D, 89.26

[14] John Martin manuscript *c.* 1699–1700, pp. 129–130, Sir John Soane Museum, London

[15] R. Campbell 1747, p. 105

[16] Arts Council of Great Britain 1974, Cat. 38–40. Nathan Drake of Lincoln (1726–1778) was probably a relative of Francis Drake (*c.* 1696–1771) the York surgeon and author of *Eboracum* (1736) a history of York. See Diana and Michael Honeybone eds 2010, pp. 225–226

[17] James Ayres 1985, pp. 129–130; R. Campbell 1747, p. 105

[18] R. Campbell 1747, p. 105

[19] Robert Dossie 1764, Vol. I, p. 31

[20] John Smith, 1676, chapter viii and p. 4

[21] James Ayres 1985, p. 132

[22] Ian Bristow 1996, pp. 91–94

[23] Emerton trade labels in British Museum Dept of P & D, reproduced By James Ayres 1998, fig. 316. Also Ian Bristow 1996, p. 93 who refers to Emerton and Manby in 1796

[24] R. Campbell 1747, p. 103–104

[25] Nina Fletcher Little (1952) 1972, p. 4

[26] R. Campbell 1747, p. 103–104

[27] James Ayres 1985, p. 127 – the one surviving windmill on this site has been recently restored

[28] Nina Fletcher Little *Neat & Tidy*, New York, 1980, p. 112

29   R. D. Hartley (1970) 1982, pp. 43–46; Ian Bristow 1996, p. 21

30   Horace Walpole 1786, Vol. III, p. 137 quoting the Beale *Notebooks*

31   Joseph Farington, p. 1076 26 Oct 1798

32   Peter Jackson 1987, p. 32; J. T. Smith (1828) 1919, Vol. ii, pp. 162–163 states that the shutters in this shop "slid in grooves". Edward Powell is listed in Kent's *Directory* of 1792

33   W. T. Whitley 1928, Vol. I, p. 65

34   George Sturt (1923) 1993, pp. 84–85

35   For an overview of these technicalities see James Ayres 1985

36   J. T. Smith (1828) 1919, Vol. II, p. 269

37   Richard Haydocke, 1598 "Third Book of Colours", pp. 125–126

38   Horace Walpole 1786, Vol. III, p. 35. Walpole goes on to add that although Hooke "gave up painting, his mechanic genius turned, among other studies to architecture" including his plan for London after the Great Fire of 1666"

39   Torsten and Peter Berg transl. *Angerstein's illustrated Travel Diary 1753–1755*, 2001, p. 131; Alan Borg 2005, pp. 129–130

40   William Salmon (1672) 1701, Vol. II, chapter xv, para iii

41   Anon (George Jameson?) (1773) 1992. Although published in Scotland this seems to derive from an English manual as references to stone all relate to the south of England – e.g. Portland Stone

42   Ian Bristow 1996 cites some exceptions

43   W. A. D. Englefield (1923) 1936, p. 77

44   John Abbot notebook, 1662–1663 Devon Record Office, Exeter; Kurt Wehlte 1982, p. 150 which states that smalt was a mid-sixteenth century innovation. For Ducklington Rectory see John Steane and James Ayres 2013. The heraldic devices painted on these reused timbers at Ducklington implied that they may well have come from Minster Lovell Hall

45   John Abbott, p. 6; Cennini (1437) 1933, n.d., p. 97

46   Joseph Farington, p. 926 22 November 1797

47   Ian Bristow 1996, p. 134

48   Max Doerner (1963) 1979, p. 108

49   James Ayres 2003, p. 128

50   Joseph Farington, p. 1522 15 March 1801

51   William Dunlap (1834) 1969, Vol. II, Pt i, p. 121

52   *Ibid.*, Vol. I, p. 415

53   William Sandby 1862, p. 18

54   W. T. Whitley 1928, Vol. I, p. 330. The same sources (Vol. I, p. 105) states that Worsdale Snr was one of Kneller's colour grinders

55   Early eighteenth century trade label, Museum of London

56   James Ayres 1985, pp. 123–126

57   This progression in the size of palettes can be seen in the collection of these in the Royal Scottish Academy, Edinburgh

58   W. T. Whitley 1928, Vol. II, p. 237

59   Karen Hearn 2002

60   Joseph Farington, p. 148 26 Jan 1794

61   Mary Beale 1984, pp. 85, 88

62   Example illustrated in James Ayres 1985, p. 82, fig. 115

63   Ernst van de Wetering 2004 p. 22 citing T. Brachert who argued that canvas stretchers were introduced in *c.* 1753–57; Ayres 1985, p. 83

[64] Ernst van de Wetering 2004, p. 117; James Ayres 1985, p. 130. See trade label in British Museum Dept of P & D, 89.26

[65] R. Campbell 1747, pp. 105–106

[66] Joseph Farington, p. 762 3 Feb 1797, p. 1160 17 Feb 1799

[67] The Club met in a tavern near Temple Bar, London that was run by Christopher Cat – hence its name. For a list of standard English and Continental frame sizes see James Ayres 1985, p. 213 and Jacob Simon 1996, p. 61 and figs 133 and 134

[68] James Ayres 1985, p. 129

[69] J. S. Stalker and G. Parker (1688) 1971

[70] Diana and Michael Honeybone eds 2010, p. 87. The paints were sent to Johnson by William Bogdani (1699/1700–1771) a Clerk of Ordnance at the Tower of London and the son of an immigrant Hungarian painter

[71] Allan Cunningham 1830, Vol. II, p. 5

[72] Horace Walpole 1786, Vol. IV, p. 60; Louise Lippincott 1983

[73] William Dunlap 1834, Vol. I, p. 27–31. John Smibert's son Nathaniel (1734–1756) followed his father "in the imitative art" of portraiture. For the Smibert/Pond correspondence see W. T. Whitley 1928, Vol. I, pp. 64–67

[74] W. T. Whitley 1928, Vol. I, pp. 330. Smibert's business was adjacent to a mill which may have ground his pigments

[75] Abbott Lowell Cummings 1979, pp. 198–199

[76] W. T. Whitley 1928, Vol. I, p. 330

[77] Joseph Farington, p. 1580 31 July 1801

[78] W. T. Whitley 1928, Vol. I, pp. 334–335

[79] John Bonehill and Stephen Daniels eds 2009 for examples of manuscript maps see Cat. 10 and 11

[80] Heal Collection, British Museum Dept of P & D 89.85

[81] James Ayres 1985, p. 130–131

[82] *Ibid.*, p. 132

[83] Isobel Murray ed. 1979, p. 89. Holland Park was then the centre of the artistic community in London under the leadership of Lord Leighton PRA (1830–1896)

[84] Martin Kemp 1990, p. 285

[85] *Ibid.*, p. 291

[86] J. H. Clarke *A Practical Essay on the Art of Colouring and Painting Landscapes in Watercolour*, 1807. Colour wheel reproduced in James Ayres 1985, fig. 129

[87] Barbara E. Johnson Collection, New Jersey

[88] Thomas Hardy's *Architectural Notebook* is in the collection of the Dorset Natural History & Archaeological Society, Dorchester see C. J. P. Beatty 2007, p. 207. On p. 100 of the sketchbook Hardy lists the following examples of Harmonious Contrasts:

Black & warm brown	Maroon & warm green
Violet & pale green	Deep blue & pink
Violet & light rose colour	Chocolate & pea green
Deep blue & golden brown	Maroon & deep blue
Chocolate & bright blue	Claret & buff
Deep red & grey	Black & warm green

Chapter 8

PAINTER STAINERS

The craft-based trades are customarily defined by the tools and materials that they employ. These materialistic concerns formed the basis for determining the scope of each trade. In many crafts this involved complex issues with ample potential for demarcation disputes between artisans. In relationship to the Painters and the Stainers no less than two further trades had developed rights to apply colour in late Stuart London. For this reason the various pigments, media and other materials, rather than the implements used to apply them, were used to place more precise limits in the otherwise generalised regulations instituted by the guilds.

As early as 1575 the Painter Stainers of London submitted a Petition to Queen Elizabeth complaining that many painters produced works that were "not so substantially wrought as by skilful men" and that now "for lack of good orders both Plaisterers and others doth entermeddle in the same science". The Petition sought protection from competition by those who were not trained in their art and mystery. The Painter Stainers specialism was identified in their *Book of Ordinancies* of 1581/2 which identified the media used by members of the guild as "oil, size, gum, gleere [glair], glue or any such thing". The *Ordinancies* goes on to define the work itself as the:

> "washing or laying ... or working any kind of colours ... with oil size or gum or any other kind of temperature [tempera] or mixture, or gilding with gold or silver or the colouring, painting or staining upon any silk, cloth, wool, leather, stone, iron, lead, tin, plaister, paper, parchment, vellum or other thing."[1]

In addition to the Painter Stainers the two further trades to develop some rights to this kind of work were, in addition to the Plaisters mentioned above, the Plumbers. By the seventeenth century the Plumbers and glaziers were permitted to apply oil paint whilst the Plasterers were entitled to use limewash and other distempers employing a restricted range of pigments. To the extent that these demarcations were applied in London they were certainly less rigorously imposed elsewhere. For example, a painter in far-off Wales could do whatever work came his way. One such was Thomas ffrancis of Montgomery, a late seventeenth century house, sign and herald painter. As such ffrancis painted inscriptions in churches and he is also known to have produced "3 landskips for chimney peeces" at £2-10s each.[2] The term "herald painter" could be interpreted in a number of ways but in Stuart London could easily have raised objections from the College of Arms which was likely to have regarded artisans engaged in such work as poaching on its preserves.

In London much of the authority of the Painter Stainers derived from their origins as two separate and independent guilds, a history that has been thoroughly chronicled by W. A. D. Englefield (1925 and 1936) and also by Alan Borg (2005). It might be added that Englefield's account is sequential rather than thematic whereas Borg's is the reverse. The latter approach is adopted here so that the regular conflicts between the Heralds and the Painter Stainers are described as a continuous, if intermittent saga. Much the same method has been employed with regard to the Plumbers and Plasterers and also those painters who were described as "working to the life".

* * * *

The Painters as an independent guild are mentioned as being represented at a meeting of the Common Council of the City of London in 1376. In contrast the earliest reference to the Stainers does not occur until *c.* 1400 although, of course both trades are substantially earlier. For example the Painters were granted Ordinances by the Lord Mayor of London in 1283. At this early point in their history the Painters were seen as subordinate to the Saddle Makers whose products they decorated. Eventually the two guilds that represented the tradesmen who used either stains or paints were destined to unite. On 19th October 1502 these two fraternities were: "kynt, joined and unyd to giders as one body and one craft and one ffanship and be re puted, taken and called by the name of Payntour Steynors"[3]

Although the two guilds, once amalgamated, operated under one Master he was flanked by two Wardens representing each of the twin crafts. By 1580 this triumvirate was supported by 24 Assistants and there were 136 Liverymen. These various totals of Liverymen and others, being divisible by two, were designed to establish an equity between Painters and Stainers. This is evident in the arms of the united Company which was quartered to reflect the marriage of the two crafts. However as the Stainers do not appear to have been in possession of a coat of arms the achievement of the Painters was repeated to produce a form of quartering. Despite this intended equality, and as is the way with mergers, one party to the agreement was to gain the ascendancy – namely the Painters.[4] By September 1532 the Company acquired its "private Common Hall", which was conveyed to the Painter Stainers by Alderman John Browne, who was Serjeant Painter to Henry VIII from 1511 to 1532.[5]

In 1580 the Painter Stainers listed the type of work undertaken by the brethren which included face-, history-, arms- and house-painting. This early reference to history painting is one that would return to haunt the visual arts in Georgian Britain. With regard to arms-painting the Painter Stainers were on a collision course with the College of Arms. A couple of years earlier on 16 July 1578 the Company petitioned Lord Burghley arguing that "tyme out of mind" the members of the guild had painted "sundrie sorts of armes". Now, they went on to assert "her highness Heralds at armes late seeking their owne private gayne … [to] thutter ympoverishment of yo L[ordship's] orators." For these reasons, the petition argued that the heralds should "s'cease workmanship and depicting of any sorts of armes or purtrayctes aforesaid"[6]

Possibly in response to these various representations the Charter that was granted to the Company by Elizabeth I in 1581 gave the brethren the right to practice "the art or mystery of … the Painter Stayners" exclusively to those "persons as heretofore have been brought up and instructed … by some one of the same art or as apprentice … for the term and space of seven years." At the conclusion of that "term" such an apprentice was to be "diligently examined" to ensure that the appropriate level of skill had been achieved. The Charter specifically includes Arms painting as falling within the purview of the Company; a passing reference to an aspect of their trade that was a burning issue at this time. The self-made men of Tudor England were keen to demonstrate their ancient pedigree for which, if not always present, a fictional version was concocted.[7] The most effective and certainly the most visible means of achieving this was by the production of a coat of arms. Herald painting therefore provided a potential source of employment, but where was the line of demarcation between the Heralds and the Painter Stainers? Although the Charter of 1581 offered some security to the Company their relationship with the College continued to be fraught with difficulties, not least because the Heralds had the ear of the Court. As Phillip Lindley (2007) has pointed out heraldry was ultimately a question for the armigerous class who, in the 1570s and 1580s, sought to add false quarterings to their arms in the quest for a sometimes spurious antiquity for their pedigree and status. As a learned body the College of Arms refused to connive in such commercialism, or that was the impression the Heralds sought to convey. In reality there was money to be made out of their profession. Between 1560 and 1589 the College issued no less than 3,320 new coats of arms but they achieved that total by granting heraldic achievements to those who were below the armigerous class. These included the bricklayer William Middleton, who was granted his arms as early as 1568 and "Shakespear the player". By 1597 the Earl Marshall of England, in his capacity as head of the College of Heralds, determined to regularise matters. In October of that year William Camden was appointed Clarenceux Herald from 1597 to 1623 for, despite a limited knowledge in that field, he was renowned for scholarship and integrity. By good fortune his father, Sampson Camden, was a Painter Stainer and so his son was able to negotiate a compromise which lasted for some years (see p. 137 below).

One indication of government intervention in some of these issues was the warrant that was issued for the arrest of one W. Dawkyns "a notable dealer in arms and false pedigrees". Even more significant was the reduction in the number of arms granted – between 1590 and 1639 a total of 1,760. This despite the great increase in the number of knights created by James I – a serious source of additional revenue for the crown. In the first four months of his reign (in England) he dubbed 906 new knights each of whom would require a coat of arms. Nevertheless the overall decline in the number of arms drawn-up by the College of Arms reduced the Heralds income. It was probably for this reason that the College sought, with renewed vigour, to protect their professional expertise from tradesmen such as those represented by the Painter Stainers. [8]

With the death of Elizabeth I in 1603 the Heralds determined to re-examine what they saw as "encroachments" by a trade on their learned profession. Even before litigation ensued between the two parties to this dispute the king's Serjeant-Painter John de Critz Snr (before 1552–1642) painted the armorials and banners for the funeral of Henry, Prince of Wales, following his early and calamitous death on 6 November 1612. As a foreigner working for the crown de Critz sailed blithely on between these warring factions seemingly unnoticed by either side; although the artist was to lose his life on the Royalist side in the Civil War.[9] By 1648, in an effort to control what the Heralds perceived to be the errors of the Painter Stainers a Proclamation was issued by the Earl Marshall. This insisted that every design for a memorial should be submitted to the "King of Arms" for approval; and if accepted should be entered in a "Book of Monuments". For this service the College of Arms was to charge a fee. If this procedure was ignored and the arms on the monument were unauthorised or incorrect they were to be officially defaced.[10] This aspect of the agreement was to prove effective and long-lasting. In 1736 a carriage was repainted for a total cost of £85-8s which included a coat of arms – hence the £8 for the "search in the Herald's Office" – see p. 225 below (Carriage Painting).

By 1621 the Painters Stainers appear to have believed that they had reached a compromise position with the Heralds. As noted above this truce owed much to the discrete diplomacy of the Clarencieux King of Arms William Camden. The resulting agreement provided for eight named Liverymen of the Painter Stainers to be permitted to emblazon coats of arms. All those selected were prominent members of the guild.[11] A couple of years later this dispensation was cast into doubt when, in 1624, James I wrote to the Earl Marshall stating that it had been drawn to this attention that "certain Painters and other Tradesmen have now of late taken boldness as of themselves to paint and marshal the coates of armes for funerals of diverse persons of this our Realm ..." The King condemned these "tradesmen" and directed the Earl Marshall to summon the delinquents and, if found guilty, to punish them "by imprisonment or otherwise." Somehow the Painter Stainers survived and, in July 1631, a reworking of the agreement of 1621 was signed by the Heralds and Pursuivants on the one hand, and on the other by Thomas Babb, John Taylor, Henry Lilley and five others, on behalf of the Painter Stainers.[12] These eight individual Painter Stainers were to be permitted to paint arms.

Despite the agreements of 1621 and 1631 the Painter Stainers petitioned Parliament in 1640 "to show our gryvances against the Herralte". There may

The Painters, &c.

13. The Painters Joyners, Carpenters, Masons, and Glasiers, were first Incorporated by the like grant, 44 Eliz, 1602. The Painters give Azure a Cheuron between 3. Phenixes heads erazed Or. The Joynfers & Carpenters give Argent a cheuron engrailed between 3. Compasses dilated sable. The Masons give sable on a Cheuron between 3. towers Argent a pair of Compasses dilated sable. The Glasiers give Argent two crossing Iron in Salvier sable between four Nails on a chief Gules a demy Lyon Passant Gardant Or. Per-

FIGURE 28. *Arms of The Painter Stainers of London.* This woodcut in Samuel Izacke's *Antiquities of Exeter* (1741), shows the use of these arms in Devon and demonstrates the reach of this London guild. (Author's Collection)

Amor quæst Obedientia.

FIGURE 29. *The Arms of the Painter Stainers of London* carved in London in *c.* 1697. It later served in Colonial America, as the shop sign for the London trained house painter Thomas Child. He, together with his wife Kathy, established their business in Boston, Massachusetts in 1701. Their initials and the date have resulted in the removal of the Company's crest – the phoenix. (Bostonian Society, Massachusetts)

have been some abatement of this dispute during the Civil War and the interregnum that followed it. Between 1648 and 1649 Randle Holme (1627–1699) wrote and drew *An Academie or Store House of Armory and Blazon* although it was not published until 1688.[13] In effect, this work was an emblem book suitable for the preparation of coats of arms. In far off Chester, where Holme was based, guild regulation was probably fairly relaxed. Besides in the confusion of the times, with the world turned upside down, Holme described himself as a gentleman. At the Restoration it was found that so many documents had been destroyed in the years of conflict that, in many cases, tangible evidence of genealogy was only to be found in church monuments, stained glass windows and comparable examples of material culture. Items such as these were often the only surviving proof that a family could offer of their pedigree.[14]

The dispute between the learned College and the trade guild rumbled on and re-emerged at the Restoration. As early as October 1660 the Heralds observed that "some few years before 1640, when those times began to be agitated" the Painter Stainers "having the bridal between their teeth, took upon them the name and title of Herald Painters." For their part the Painters argued that they were entitled (or at least eight of the brethren were permitted) to paint "arms and effigies" in contrast to the "heralds whose proper right is only to Blaz but not to paint coats of arms." Here the term to blazon was presumably used to signify the limning of arms on vellum, rather than the portrayal in oil paint, of an heraldic achievement.

Reading between the lines in this ongoing dispute the financial and academic implications, as to who was allowed to do what, was only part of the problem. In particular the Heralds classed the Painter Stainers as simple artisans whom they described as "a sort of illiterate mechanics and so far unknowing in the science and faculty of heraldry that they are to be looked on in no higher consideration than mere day labourers"

The charge of illiteracy was presumably made to emphasise the scholarship of the Heralds. The dispute had descended into class conflict; between the Heralds who were learned gentlemen and the Painters who were stigmatised as tradesmen, or worse, "day labourers" (journeymen). To exaggerate their claim the Heralds asserted that "these Painter Steyners comprehend no Painters of any other denomination than Steinors … a race of mechanical artificers so very low" as to be beneath contempt.[15]

A generation later much of the hostility that this dispute had aroused was dissipated. In 1684 renewed discussions took place between these two bodies which resulted in an agreement that resembled the compact of 1631. This revived truce came into effect in 1686 and, as before, permitted a select few of the brethren of the Painter Stainers to work as "Herald Painters". This compromise was evidently viewed with some suspicion by the College of Arms who were determined that the agreement should be obeyed to the letter. Soon after this truce was implemented (1686) the College took action against William Shiers. Although Shiers was a Painter Stainer, and a future Master of the Company, his offence was that he had painted an heraldic achievement although not being one of the named members of the Company who were permitted to do such work. Extraordinarily enough trouble erupted once more between the old antagonists in 1738, the very year that Shiers became master of the guild. The College of Arms once more petitioned the crown for a new Charter which would give the College a monopoly on arms painting. This petition was rejected – a long running saga was at an end. This is exemplified by "Jnº Bromley" who, at about this time, advertised as a "Coach, Sign and House Painter; In Parker's Street, Lincoln's Inn Fields, London." Significantly he concludes his trade card by adding "NB Arms neatly Painted on Vellum & all Other Herald Painting." The reference to vellum is particularly significant as being the stuff of legal documents and the support favoured by heralds for emblazoning arms.[16] Any wounds that may have been inflicted between the Painter Stainers and the College of Arms in the past were to be healed. By the third quarter of the century the portrait and drapery painter Peter Toms RA (d. 1776) had become Portcullis Pursuivant at the College of Arms.[17]

Despite protestations of the learned nature of the work of the College of
Arms, the Heralds were competing with the Painters over a profitable line of
employment. In early modern Britain heraldic devices were widely deployed at
funerals and figure prominently on church monuments. In addition painted
funeral hatchments were hung on the house frontage of the deceased (Fig.
30) and were subsequently displayed in the church where the burial took
place, a tradition which continued into the nineteenth century. In Porny's
Elements of Heraldry (1771) the author takes a partisan position on the side of
the Heralds. According to Porny the hatchments executed by Painter Stainers
often revealed an ignorance of the range of coronets to which the various
degrees of nobility were entitled. Porny concludes this chapter on regulations
and social conventions by stating that "Herald-painters ... do generally ensign
those [hatchments] of Peers with Coronets, and that of a Maiden Lady with
a knot of Ribbands."[18]

Heraldry was not confined to funerals but was of equal importance to the
living: on carriages, household liveries, bookplates, porcelain and silver. For
the affluent it offered the perfect means of identification and was also highly
decorative. Inevitably these emblems extended their reach to British North
America where they were relatively free of regulation – yet were to remain in
use after the Independence of the young Republic.[19] The American painter
Robert Weir (1803–1889) recalled that he received his first instruction in the
workshop of an English Herald Painter named Robert Cook. It was there that
Weir "devoted from six to eight o'clock in the morning ... three times a week for
three months" learning the painter's trade, and the rest of his time working as
a clerk. He later became a teacher of drawing at West Point Military Academy.[20]

In London, even as the Painter Stainers were in their protracted dispute
with the Heralds they were simultaneously seeking to preserve their monopoly
of heraldic work from encroachments by the "ship painters, escutcheon and
coach painters, leather gilders, goldsmiths, engravers, carvers and other
artificers." In their petition to the Queen of 13 November 1575 the Painter
Stainers objected that "now for lack of good orders both Plaisterers and others
doth intermeddele in the same" art and mystery.[21] This may account for the
sgraffito plaster decoration of the sixteenth and seventeenth centuries; work
which in terms of its materials was clearly within the province of the Plaisterers.
By 1606 an Act of Parliament (4 Jac.I.c20) was passed which protected the
interests of the Painter Stainers. This Act singles out the Plaisterers as having
strayed onto the preserves of the Painters. It refers to the Plaisterers who had
once confined their activities to "lathing, daubing, plaistering and limning" all
of which were permissible but, it was objected, they were now, in addition to

working in distemper, applying oil paint. By an earlier Act of 1603 (I Jac.I.c4) the Plaisterers had gained the statutory right to use size media for distempers and had for long applied limewash which was, in effect, an extension of their lime plasters. They were, however, confined to a restricted range of pigments: "Whiting, Blacking, Redlead, Redoker, Yellow Oker and Russet mingled with size only".[22] Consequently the Painters, as distinct from the Stainers, were granted a monopoly in the use of oils and varnishes amalgamated with pigments of all kinds. At the same time, as established by the *Book of Ordinancies* of 1581/2 (see p. 133 above), Article 4 gave them the right to paint on all manner of supports and surface priming. The one exception to these monopolies appears in Article 7 of the *Ordinancies* which excluded "gentlemen exercising the art for recreation or private pleasure."[23]

Early in the 1660s the Painter Stainers listed various grievances in a document containing nine paragraphs. The first two of these concerned immigrants and "much bad work done by strangers and others". Paragraph four reads as follows:

> "…the following artificers did break out into the Art of Painting to the great deceit of the people of this nation viz. Bricklayers, Carpenters, Wyermakers, Boxmakers, Imbroydermakers, Turners, Joyners, Drum makers, Coachmakers, Virginal makers, Plumbers, Glaziers, Armourers, Hottpressers and more especially Plaisterers or Daubers."[24]

It should perhaps be noted here that the noun like the verb *to daub* derives from the Old French to whitewash or plaster. This term was, for plasterers, simple objective usage of the language and only became a term of contempt when applied to easel painting.[25] Elsewhere in this manuscript the breaking of the closed shop by some of the trades that it lists may, at first sight, seem disconcerting. However the "Joyners" sometimes used oil paint as an informal glue and the "Drum makers" like the Virginal-makers may have decorated the instruments they made rather than sub-contracting such work to the specialists as the Painter Stainers would have expected. Certainly the "Imbroidermakers" would doubtless have regarded their decorative work as so closely related to that of the Painter Stainers that they would have been oblivious to any perceived transgression. As for the Plumbers and Glaziers they, as we shall see, would eventually gain the right to apply oil paint. In the 1660s coachbuilding, as a significant manufacturing trade was relatively new. In this document the Painter Stainers were therefore contending with an evolving situation with regard to "Coachmakers" and other tradesmen.

The most significant problem that the Painter Stainers confronted in early modern London concerned those foreign artists and artisans employed by the king and others who worked beyond the control of the guilds and the City authorities. These independent craftsmen were generally based in the various "Peculiars" in and around the capital. Following some agitation (see pp. 32, 33 above) a Proclamation was issued in 1523 which forbade anyone from employing foreigners except Members of Parliament and those with a minimum annual income of £100.[26] In effect this was a sumptuary law which must have made the work of foreign artists and artisans all the more fashionable. This Proclamation may even have had the unintended consequence of accelerating the adoption of the Renaissance aesthetic in England.

Just three years after the Proclamation of 1523 Hans Holbein arrived in England on his first visit of 1526–1528; his second was in 1532–1543. Like so many artists of his time Holbein worked as both a designer and a painter of panel pictures. The Italianate frieze at Acton Court (c. 1535) may well have been drawn up by the German painter although the actual work would have been carried out by a studio or workshop such as that run by Andrew Wright the then Sergeant Painter to the King.[27] Holbein certainly produced a portrait of Sir Nicholas Poyntz, the owner of Acton Court.

In terms of artists such as Holbein, working for aristocratic and regal patrons, the Painter Stainers were impotent bystanders. This probably intensified the guild's wish to impose their authority where they could. The thirty-seven article submission of 1581, that was translated into the Charter of 1582 stipulated in Article 4 that: "… no person, Englishman or Stanger, denizen or no denizen, freeman or foreign, should at any time work as Painter Stainers, unless qualified to do so through membership of the guild."

Despite this clause these activities were to be extended to those who were known to be skilful and approved by the Master and Wardens of the Painter Stainers. In other words this covered those who had completed an appropriate apprenticeship. In this way the Livery Company was not simply declaring its monopoly on the trade, with some flexibility, it was also aiming to maintain the high standards in the craft. In short the intention, so fully spelt out in Article 4. Nevertheless the document goes on, in Article 24, to demonstrate a pliable approach. It states that "Aliens and strangers using the art in the City were to bear all duties to which they were duly assessed by the Master and Wardens" just like "any other person being a brother of the Company." In other words if foreigners were to creep under the embargo against them the Company would still receive financial compensation. This clause was probably inserted for those painters who were working "for or about the Queen's Majesty" – artists and artisans who were exempted from guild restrictions under the terms of the Proclamation of 1523.[28]

FIGURE 30. The deployment of a funeral hatchment on the house of the deceased prior to its installation in the church at the time of burial; Porny (1765) 1771. Despite the concerns of the College of Heralds hatchments were generally the work of coach and sign painters. (Author's Collection)

In December 1632 the Company made some attempt to institute a search to establish how many "strangers" were working as Painter Stainers in the City. Twenty-eight years later, at the Restoration, the problem of immigrant tradesmen had reached a point where it was all but impossible for the guilds to control the situation. In some desperation the Painter Stainers simply agreed that "all strangers and aliens be compelled to come to the Hall and put themselves under the Government of the Company". To regularise their position an amnesty was declared on these aliens who were nevertheless expected to have "their names and addresses ... registered."[29]

The other and closely related predicament to confront the Painter Stainers, from the sixteenth century onwards, was the emergence of "artist painters" as distinct from "trade painters". Many of the former were foreign born, whilst others were native Englishmen but not freemen of London. It was with regard to this problem that, in 1634, the Master of the Painter Stainers announced that he had met two artists: "Messrs Peake and Gwinbury".[30] As a result of this meeting those "picture makers" who were not yet free of the Company would be permitted to take up their freedom with the Painter Stainers. Despite this apparent amity difficulties persisted for these artists with William Peake (c. 1580–1639) appearing before the Court of the Painter Stainers in January 1636 concerning a letter from "Mr Inigo Jones". By 17 March that year the situation had resolved itself and Inigo Jones "very lovingly came and dined with the Company." The following year this hospitality was extended, at the

St Katherine's Dinner, to Sir Anthony Vandyck and to "the Serjeant Painter, [John de Critz Snr], Mr Surveyor [Inigo Jones] and Mr Dean" (Christopher Wren Snr?).[31] It seems that the Painter Stainers had concluded that discretion rather than confrontation was advisable. The Company therefore determined to accept a limited number of these "professors of that part of our art which they call 'to the life'" to some sort of affiliated status. By 18 October 1647 Thomas Rawlins the die-sinker (and therefore a sculptor) and Sir Peter Lely (1618–1680) were admitted to the Company.[32]

Despite these various compromise agreements the Painter Stainers did not entirely relinquish all control over their twin trades. Even after the Restoration the Company agreed, in 1664, that all who were admitted to the fraternity should be free to practice their art or trade – which, by implication included foreigners. In contrast "All aliens not licenced … were to be recquired to depart the Realm, or work as Journeymen to a Freeman of the Company and register in the Hall". It was under these terms that Peter van der Muler [*sic*] was "admitted a foreign member". For this privilege he paid a fee of "redemption" of 40 shillings (£2) but was also expected to provide a "proof piece".[33]

The Restoration of the Monarchy brought mixed fortunes for the Painter Stainers. Despite the numerous negotiations, agreements, Proclamations and Acts of Parliament the position of the twin crafts remained insecure. Furthermore other interests were intervening. In 1667, 1668 and 1670 a "lacquary patent" was granted to Sir Philip Howard and Francis Watson. This concerned a proprietary lacquer for preserving the hulls of ships that was believed to be "cheaper and more smooth and durable than … pitch tarr, rosin" and similar materials.[34] This was a clear infringement of the sort of work that lay within the scope of the Painters. "Japanning", as the Anglicised version of Oriental lacquer was known, was also within their craft preserves. It should be noted that English Japanning was based on gilding and the use of gesso (for relief work). Although the Painters doubtless claimed ownership of Japanning it was not long before they were in competition with the gentry who indulged in this craft as an "amusement". This was the market that Stalker and Parker's *Treatise on Japaning & Varnishing* (Oxford 1688) was designed to meet.[35] A more fundamental problem for the Company, and indeed other fraternities was Charles II's infamous *quo warranto* which came into effect in 1684 – a measure which insisted that the Livery Companies should relinquish their Charters.[36] Mercifully this legislation was reversed under William and Mary but it occurred at a time when the Guilds began their slow decline as craft organisations.

By the eighteenth century the actions of the Painter Stainers Company of London appear, in retrospect, to have been far from consistent – a possible symptom of that decline. In 1743 a Fishmonger applied to be admitted, but was rejected. By 1766 attitudes had softened when it was proposed (as in 1664 – see p. 146) that all who wished to work as Painters should apply to the Company – a policy that was once again adopted the following year. Perhaps most revealing of all was the Livery's attitudes when it came to the maintenance of their own Hall. In 1776 the columns in the Court Room of the Hall were "underpitted" (underpinned) by Ezekiel Delight who had been appointed in 1774 as District Surveyor for London. In this restoration the decoration of the hall, including marbling and graining, was carried out by Stephen Newman, a citizen and Spectacle Maker but, in accordance with the Custom of London, a painter by trade. As the case of Thomas Johnson demonstrates the Spectacle Makers Company was, at this time, a recognised "flag of convenience". All the same in working in the heart of the government of his craft (the Court Room no less), Newman's position was to be regularised and he was admitted a freeman of the Painter Stainers by Patrimony.[37]

In some respects the Company's policies were relaxed by this time although an occasional attempt was made to regain lost powers. In 1786 a non-freeman and foreigner was "admonished not to exercise the business" of a painter until such time as he was naturalised and made free of the Company. In September 1817 action was taken against a glazier who was working as a painter – a situation that was resolved when he joined the fraternity. This case is anomalous in that glaziers were generally permitted to work as painters. Just ten years later in 1827 Nathaniel Whittock published his *Decorative Painters's and Glaziers's Guide*, a title which acknowledged this linkage. More problematic was the case of James Jaumard le Cren of Coleman Street, London. He refused to explain on whose authority he worked as a painter although not free of the Company. In 1824 the case was heard and then in 1825 and again in 1827 on each occasion being referred to the King's Bench. It was in that court that the Guild's case was finally heard and rejected in 1829 by Lord Tenderden on the grounds that the Court could not be seen to be restraining trade.[38] The "closed shop" controlled by the Painter Stainers, the members of the Livery (the employers), was at an end. This power was briefly usurped by the employees (the workers) but was destined to be taken over by large scale capitalist contractors.

Although restrictive practices had always been a significant feature of the guilds, the rise of the "Combinations" probably revived their importance. At a meeting of the Painter Stainers in 1799 it was agreed

> "that fair, equitable and liberal wages ... between Master and Journeyman should be paid ... at a rate of one guinea per week for good and able

workmen – a day's work being reckoned from 6 o'clock in the morning till 6 o'clock in the evening – and inferior workmen according to their abilities".

The payment of a guinea (£1-1s) was emblematic of the professional status accorded to superior craftsmen. Significantly the next clause in this document related to "the Act to prevent unlawful combinations of workmen", the group solidarity with which the *Unlawful Societies Act* of 1799 was concerned (39 Geo. III, c79). In their own interests the Painter Stainers, as employers or "masters", agreed to help enforce the Act but they did so by means of establishing a reasonable level of remuneration for employees. From this it would seem that these proto trade unions (combinations) had exerted some influence over the older, more traditional, trade bodies concerning working hours and pay. Certainly the Painters of Canterbury conformed with their London brethren in these matters.[39]

Commercial price lists relating to the building trades had been published for some time. A good example being William Salmon of Colchester's *The London and Country Builders ...* price book of 1745 which compares the prices in the capital with those in the provinces – in particular Colchester, Essex.[40] The first such list to be prepared by the Painter Stainers did not appear until February 1783. This may have had something to do with the emergence of the Combinations but was more likely to have been associated with the rising cost of materials. In particular the price of turpentine had soared in the aftermath of the American War of Independence. Consequently the list of 1785 was followed by others in 1803, 1816, 1824–25 and 1831.

In 1831 the Guild was still doing its best to maintain the traditional regulations of the trade. This is reflected in the duties that were laid down in that year for the Beadle:

> "He will be furnished at the commencement of each year with a list of apprentices; their periods of whose servitude will expire therin, and he is to wait on them and ascertain their determination as to taking up their freedom and explain the disadvantages and increased quarterage they will incur by protracting their admission to the Company."

That last substantive point concerning subscriptions to the Company illustrates the inducements that were offered to encourage painters, who were out of their time, to join the guild – a reversal of the situation in earlier centuries when to join the fraternity was a privilege.[41]

The *Great Reform Act* of 1832 required Livery Companies to provide information on their membership. As a result we know that in 1833 the Painter

Stainers of London was composed of 370 Freemen and 117 Liverymen. Of the Freemen 128 had been admitted by redemption and 115 by servitude implying 127 joined by other means. These numbers demonstrate that although apprenticeships were still in place the balance of power was shifting. Of the Freeemen 79 had, in effect, been co-opted and 46 were accepted via Patrimony and two by "gift" producing that total of 127 such individuals. Among later "Honary Freemen" by gift were Sir Joshua Reynolds (in 1781) Sir Frederick Leighton (1889), Sir John Millais (1896) and Sir Edward Poynter (1896). From this we may conclude that the Painter Stainers had made their peace with those who painted "to the life". Even the long fraught demarcation disputes with the College of Arms seem to have faded from memory. In 1828 a Liveryman named George Bishop, who described himself as a herald and painter, presented the Company with its original grant of arms dated 1486.[42]

By 1911 it seems that so few of the brethren were practicing painters that "reduced fees" would apply "to those who practice the Craft of Painting whether as an art … or as a trade".[43] In England at this time the distinction between a "trade" and an "art" could be drawn with confidence.

* * * *

In America by contrast William Dunlap (1834) was enlightened enough to observe that "the mechanic arts have accompanied and assisted the fine arts in every step of their progress". All the same many of the class structures of the Old World persisted in the Young Republic.[44] A case in point concerns Dunlap's inclusion of biographical information on John Vanderlyn (1775–1852) supplied by a friend of the latter's. In this account Vanderlyn's "attainments" are described as so formidable they would "have qualified him for the pursuit of the liberal professions." In mitigation of that remark Dunlap enquires in a footnote "Does the writer mean that he did not pursue a liberal profession?"[45] Dunlap's publication is on surer ground in his account of the career of Thomas Sully (1783–1872). Sully was born into modest circumstances in England where "Painting is considered a mechanical art, and the man of rank would be considered to loose caste by following it". At the age of nine young Sully escaped this situation when he emigrated, in 1792, with his parents to Charleston, South Carolina.[46] He later moved on to Norfolk, Virginia where he began to emerge as the portrait painter he was to become when he moved to Philadelphia in 1808.[47]

The true social and artistic flexibility of society in early Federal America was, as noted above (p. 76), most fully reflected in the life of Rufus Porter

(1792–1884) – a painter about whom Dunlap says nothing. Porter was a Massachusetts-born house and portrait painter who also produced remarkable murals in imitation of French scenic wallpapers. Porter's emergence from his role as a humble house painter, to the true polymath that he became, would probably not have been possible in Britain at that time.[48]

Notes

[1]   Alan Borg 2005, pp. 31–33; W. A. D. Englefield (1923) 1936, p. 67 quoting Article 5 in the *Ordinancies* of 1581/82

[2]   Richard Bebb 2007, pp. 255, 295. The double "ff" as in ffrances was used in the seventeenth century as an alternative to a capital letter

[3]   Alan Borg 2005, p. 5; W. A. D. Englefield (1925) 1936, pp. 13–14. In 1268 the Painters of London, in alliance with the Tailors did battle with the Goldsmiths, a conflict that resulted in 500 deaths. For Saddle Makers see Englefield pp. 24–25. For the agreement of 1502 see Englefield p. 46

[4]   Alan Borg 2005, pp. 18, 23; W. A. D. Englefield (1923) 1936, pp. xi, 46–51

[5]   H. M. Colvin *et al.* 1975, Vol. III, Pt I, p. 38. The Serjeant Painters at this time received an honorarium of £10 p.a. … Brown was followed by Andrew Wright (1532–1543) the Italian Antonio Toto (1544–1554) and the Frenchman Nicholas Lizard (1554–1571)

[6]   W. A. D. Englefield (1923) 1936, pp. xiii, 46, 47, 57, 58

[7]   Phillip Lindley 2007, p. 64

[8]   Ian Donaldson 2011, pp. 160–165, 206. Members of the armigerous class signified their status on legal documents by adding the word "Armiger" after their surnames. William Middleton, the bricklayer, was the father of Thomas Middleton the dramatist. Philip Lindley 2007, pp. 30, 31 citing M. Noble *History of the College of Arms,* London, 1805, p. 162; Alan Borg 2005, pp. 28, 42 for Sampson Camden etc.

[9]   Geoffrey Beard 1997, p. 53; H. M. Colvin *et al.* 1975, Vol. III, Pt I, p. 126. The younger de Critz was also to lose his life in the Civil War (at Oxford); Jennifer Potter 2006, p. 288

[10] Phillip Lindley 2007, pp. 73, 91

[11] W. A. D. Englefield (1923) 1936, p. 82 the named guildsmen were Richard Kimby, Thomas Babb (Master 1636), William Winshell, John Taylor (Master 1643), Ralph Creswell, Richard Prisse, Richard Munday (Upper Warden 1639) and Henry Lilley

[12] *Ibid.,* p. 82

[13] Manuscript: British Library: Harl. Ms. 2026–2035. Also Victor Chinnery 1979, pp. 545–549

[14] Phillip Lindley 2007, p. 213 citing Sir William Dugdale's Heralds Visitations written 1677–1686

[15] W. A. D. Englefield (1923) 1936, pp. 107, 117, 119, 120; Alan Borg 2005, p. 92

[16] Edward Edwards 1808, pp. 53–54; Alan Borg 2005, p. 119; Bromley's trade card in the British Museum Dept of P&D, 90–18.

[17] W. A. D. Englefield (1923) 1936, pp. 153, 163–167

[18] Mark Porny (1765) 1771, p. 243

[19] M. H. Heckscher and L. G. Bowman 1992, pp. 40–45, 71–114 and p. 173 fig. 116 which illustrates a white pine monument painted to resemble marble. This monument

commemorates a daughter of the Earl of Cromarty – surmounted by her coat of arms – dated 1768. Scots Presbyterian Church, Charleston, South Carolina

[20] William Dunlap (1834) 1969, Vol. II, Pt II, p. 385 footnote
[21] W. A. D. Englefield (1923) 1936, p. 57
[22] *Ibid.*, p. 57
[23] *Ibid.*, pp. 67–68
[24] British Library: Harl. Ms. 1099 fo.79 – not dated but no later than *c.* 1665
[25] *S.O.E.D.*
[26] Nicholas Cooper 1999, p. 23
[27] H. M. Colvin *et al.* 1975. Wright was Sergeant Painter to the king from 1532–1543. For Acton Court see Kirsty Rodwell and Robert Bell, *Acton Court: the Evolution of an Early Tudor Courtier's House*, London, 2004. for Holbein as a designer see Susan Foister 2006
[28] *Ibid.*, p. 71
[29] British Library: Harl. Ms. 1099.fo79
[30] This was either William Peake (*c.* 1580–1638) or Robert Peake III (*c.* 1605–1667). Both were sons of Robert Peake Jnr and grandsons of Robert Peake Snr Karen Hearn 1995, pp. 128–185
[31] W. A. D. Englefield (1923) 1936, pp. 104–108; Alan Borg 2005, p. 55
[32] W. A. D. Englefield (1923) 1936, p. 113; Alan Borg 2005, p. 60
[33] W. A. D. Englefield (1923) 1936, pp. 134–135
[34] W. A. D. Englefield (1923) 1936, pp. 134–135; Alan Borg 2005, p. 71
[35] J. S. Stalker and G. Parker (1688) 1971
[36] W. A. D. Englefield (1923) 1936, p. 153
[37] *Ibid.*, pp. 168, 169–70, 175–176 ; for Ezekiel Delight see Howard Colvin 1995
[38] *Ibid.*, pp. 191, 192–194
[39] *Ibid.*, pp. 184–185
[40] James Ayres 1998, p. 37
[41] W. A. D. Englefield (1923) 1936, pp. 181, 201, 210, 212
[42] *Ibid.*, p. 194
[43] *Ibid.*, p. 215
[44] William Dunlap (1834) 1969, Vol. I, p. 11
[45] *Ibid.*, Vol. II, p. 31
[46] *Ibid.*, Vol. ii, pp. 101–103
[47] Jessie Poesch 1983, pp. 271–262
[48] Jean Lipman (1968) 1980

Chapter 9

THE PAINTERS
Mechanic & Liberal

Before the *Stamp Act* of 1769 required every house in a city or town to have a street number an urban address took the form of what may best be described as lengthy directions. For example Joseph Emerton's address in 1744 reads as follows "Colour Man, At the Bell and Sun Over Against Norfolk Street between St Clement's and the New Church in ye Strand, London."[1] Once street numbers appeared addresses could be radically reduced. Consequently it was no coincidence that it was at this point that *Trade Directories* became commonplace. Town by town, county by county, these Directories commence with the "Nobility, Gentry and Clergy" before moving on to itemising those who were engaged in various professions and trades. Because of the hierarchical nature of these publications the painters were typically divided into two categories. There were those who are itemised as "Artists: Portrait, Landscape, Miniature" and a secondary group identified as "Painters: House, Sign &c ..." This divide became most evident after *c.* 1762 but was institutionalised by the foundation of the Royal Academy of Arts in 1768 and reinforced in various ways, which included the publication of these *Trade Directories*. Such an attitude, a prejudice even, was one that saw a pupilage and attendance at an Academy of Art as appropriate to polite society whereas an apprenticeship was adequate for "other ranks".

One example of a young gentleman who served a brief pupilage as a "liberal" painter was, as noted above, Alexander Pope (1688–1744).[2] His vision as a poet may have been enhanced during the six months he spent studying with the portrait painter Charles Jervas (1675–1739) – although as a Catholic the young Alexander Pope would have been denied entry to a University. Unlike an apprentice painter, who would have spent much of his seven years doing manual chores like grinding pigments, young Pope spent as many months indulging his vocation as a creative painter. Not that this was entirely without discomfort:

"... have you ['gentle reader'] ever fagged like Mr Alexander Pope, for ten or twelve hours at a stretch, your left-hand thumb thrust through the hole of a palette, grasping at the same time, in the said hand, a handful of *fitches, sables, hogs-hair tools, flatteners* and *sweeteners,* with the additional incumberance of a *maul-stick,* absolutely wedged in until the fingers benumbed, the arm stagnated, and the left side in a state of paralysis ...."[3]

Comparable examples of gentlemen who served a pupilage include Giles Hussey, the son of a Dorset landowner, who studied under Jonathan Richardson (1665–1745) and Sir George Chalmers of Edinburgh who was a pupil of Allan Ramsey (1713–1784).[4] This type of education was not confined to the gentry but could include the middle classes. Painters like George Kapton (1698–17778) took Thomas King and Francis Cotes RA (1726–1770) as pupils. The studio of Thomas Hudson (1701–1779) might, at times, have resembled the sort of art school with which later generations would have been familiar. His pupils included John Astley (1720/24–1787), Mason Chamberlain RA (d. 1787), Nathaniel Dance RA (1734–1811), Peter Toms RA (d. 1776), Joseph Wright RA (1734–1797) and, most famously, Sir Joshua Reynolds PRA (1723–1792). Of these Chamberlain, Dance, Toms and, of course, Reynolds were to become founder members of the Royal Academy.[5]

A pupilage in a studio was, it seems, a much less arduous education than a training as an apprentice in a painter's workshop. Articled painters do not appear to have been compelled to work as drudges. For an apprentice the seven years of servitude began at the age of fourteen, which contrasts with the four years pupilage that Reynolds commenced when he was 17.[6] In this way a student with Hudson, like an apprentice with a master craftsman, would emerge at the age of 21. Inevitably, in these rather close relationships in the painting room or workshop, conflicts could emerge. Although most contemporaries allude to Hudson's charm Edward Edwards unequivocally states that the older man's manners were not "very conciliating". For this reason John Hamilton Mortimer RA (1741–1779) "remained with him but a short time" and moved on "to the care of Mr Pine".[7] For some, a pupilage with a succession of studios could be a means of widening their experience. John Alexander Gresse (1741–1794) was first attached to the Scotin family's engraving workshops then moved on to Mortimer's painting room and completed his pupilage with John Baptist Cipriani RA (1727–1785). Like many of his contempories Gresse also benefited by studying in the Duke of Richmond's gallery of casts from the Antique and also at the St Martin's Lane Academy. This extraordinarily wide range of experience may well be atypical since Gresse's father was a rich London property developer.[8]

Eighteenth century training and education in the visual arts and associated crafts is not easily examined, not least because the terminology used at the time was interchangeable, although in some cases the historical record is more precise. For example the *Binding Book* of the Painter Stainers of London states that John Dean, son of William Dean of Berkshire was bound on 7 October 1685 to Thomas Highmore the Serjeant Painter. In contrast Highmore's nephew Joseph (1692–1780) was, as a society portrait painter, to train many artists as pupils rather than apprentices. A couple of generations later Richard Reinagle (1775–1862) recalled that his "father was [Ramsay's] *apprentice* and at the expiration of his *pupilage* ..." (my italics) remained with his master. In this case Reinagle continued to paint in Ramsay's manner for many years and went on to produce portraits for him at "fifty guineas a pair". These were passed-off as "the master's work for which Ramsay received "... two hundred guineas a pair ..." This account indicates that these were studio copies for surely, if painted from life, the sitter would have noticed that "Ramsay's portraits" were being painted by Reinagle. Nevertheless such an anecdote demonstrates the synonymous use of words like "pupilage" and "apprenticeship" and that Reinagle evidently served his master in the latter capacity. As a highly gifted journeyman portrait painter his continued employment with his master was a very profitable arrangement so far as Ramsay was concerned.[9]

In general there seems to have been a growth in the number of these pupilages during the course of the eighteenth century with a corresponding decline in apprenticeships. In provincial Britain, as in North America, this transition occurred a generation or two later. With the foundation of the Royal Academy and its Schools of Painting, Sculpture and Architecture training was to be usurped by education; a shift of emphasis made possible for painters by the availability of convenient to use manufactured paints and pre-prepared canvases. Once selected for admission to the RA Schools tuition was free so that it was in fact cheaper to become a "liberal" painter than to train in the trade.[10] This may explain why so many individuals travelled to London to become students in the Academy. One of the first was William Bell from distant Northumberland.[11] More generally students at this time graduated from a pupilage in a London studio before moving on to the Academy where they became ever more "polite" in terms of their art. Herein was a systemic danger that Gustav Waagen (1794–1868, see p. 455 and Appendix XVII) was one of the first, and one of the few, to identify in Britain. In contrast the trade painters either continued in their vernacular tradition or they realigned their position.

In general the technicalities of painting in oil were such that few amateurs emerged in pre- industrial Britain to indulge in this medium. Consequently the position of "the Lanchashire Hogarth" John Collier (1708–1786), under the alias Tim Bobbin, was anomalous – but then he was exceptional in a number of respects.[12] Towards the end of the century the ever increasing availability of ready-made paints may have increased the numbers of self–taught artists. One such was Francis Guy (1760–1820) who was born in the Lake District where he was apprenticed to a tailor, possibly an arras-tailor, in Burton-in-Kendal. In 1778, having escaped from his master, he moved to London where he was to become "dyer, callenderer and arras cleaner" to her majesty. By 1795 Guy migrated to America settling first in New York City then in Philadelphia and finally in Baltimore. This restlessness may have been driven by his need to escape his creditors, a situation caused by his tendency to indulge "at intervals in the habit of drinking, even to excess." Despite these vicissitudes art, in addition to brandy, was in Guy's veins, his maternal grandfather John Lolly of Kirkby Lonsdale having been an artist in stained glass.[13] This and his work on tapestry may have encouraged young Guy to become an easel painter. His creation of landscapes and "marine pieces" was to become an activity that Guy was to describe as his "darling pursuit". In his old age the painter Rembrandt Peale (1778–1860) recalled the methods adopted by Guy in instructing himself in his art:

> "He constructed a tent, which he could erect at pleasure, wherever a scene of interest offered itself to his fancy. A window was contrived, the size of his intended pictures – this was filled up with a frame, having stretched on it a piece of black gauze. Regulating his eyesight by a fixed notch a little distance from the gauze, he drew with chalk all the objects as seen through the medium, with perfect perspective accuracy. This drawing he conveyed to his canvas... [Thus] with a rapidly-improving eye...he produced four pictures of extraordinary merit, as rough transcripts of Nature ..."

His *Winter Scene* of 1817–1820 (Fig. 31; now in Brooklyn Museum) has all the appearance of having been worked in this way – indeed the tent in which he worked must have afforded some protection from winter temperatures (Fig. 31). In some respects this was a system of observing that related to the drawing frame described by Alberti and, much later, by Durer. Guy did not always use such a device as his view of *The Tontine Coffee House*, New York of 1797 was probably dependent upon a camera obscura (this work is now in the New York Historical Society).[14]

Despite the increasing numbers of such self-trained individuals in the nineteenth century the presence of artisan painters in the twenty-first century persists but their numbers have radically reduced. Today a trade painter capable of producing high quality wood graining or marbling will find work far and wide. Much the same is true of signwriting. In the past the *Trade Directories* that listed "Painters: House, Sign &c" left considerable scope for all manner or work in that "&c". In London, where guild regulation long held dominion, a more precise definition prevailed. Outside the capital, and especially in port cities and towns, the repertoire of these artisan painters could be very considerable. This was certainly true of Michael Edkins of Bristol (born *c.* 1742). Following his apprenticeship Edkins became free in 1756 and by 1761 had, in his turn, taken on an apprentice. His ledger books for the years 1763–1785 demonstrate the wide range of his activities which, although based on house and ship painting, extended to carriage painting and all manner of decorative work on a bewilderingly wide range of surfaces (see Fig. 41). He might paint Windsor chairs green, work on interiors and shop fronts, and produce scenery and

FIGURE 31. Francis Guy *Winter Scene in Brooklyn,* 1829–1830, oil on canvas (58 ³/₈ × 4 ⁹/₁₆ in/148.2 × 189.4 cm). For pictures such as this Guy worked in a tent in which a "window was contrived the size of his intended picture – this was filled up with a frame, having stretched on it a piece of black gauze" (*The Crayon* III (1856), 5). On this gauze Guy drew the picture from life which was then transferred to the canvas. (Brooklyn Museum, New York)

props' for the Theatre Royal, Bristol. Even more remarkably he would ornament gun barrels with a "resist" for blueing and decorate pottery, glassware, tin ware and clock dials. Rather touchingly when working for a "brother brush" he offered a ten per cent discount. His son "William Edkins: City Painter, Bristol" continued the business into the nineteenth century undertaking such work as funeral hatchments.[15] From these documents it is evident that the elder Edkins worked as both a painter and a stainer (much of the stage scenery would have been carried out employing size-bound stains and pigments on canvas). For Edkins the decoration of ceramics was just one of his activities but for Baxter this was a specialism. His son Thomas Baxter Jnr (1782–1821) trained in his father's workshop in London before moving on to the Royal Academy Schools. Despite this education the younger man returned to the family craft at No. 1

FIGURE 32. *China painters* 1810 by Thomas Baxter. Baxter's painting room was at No. 1 Goldsmith Street, Gough Square, London. The elder Baxter is shown painting with his eyes very close to the work in hand as his son stands back looking-on. Trade painters like Michael Edkins of Bristol (second half of the eighteenth century) and John Martin (1789–1854) undertook a wide range of activities – although Martin was later to make his name as an easel painter with his vast and intimidating canvases. (Victoria & Albert Museum, London)

Goldsmith Street, Gough Square, London, but he also worked for similar concerns in Swansea.[16] Perhaps even more remarkable than the careers of either John Collier (1708–1786 – see p. 153) or Edkins Snr was that of John Baskerville (1706–1775) who was born in Worcestershire. Baskerville trained as a stone cutter but later became a writing master in Birmingham. It was there, in that emerging industrial centre, that "he entered into the lucrative trade of japanning [on tin plated sheet iron]". There:

> "In the tea-tray factory semi finished sheets from Bristol were pickled, scoured, dried and primed and varnished, and then painted with birds of all kinds, some pictures and flower arrangements. Such a tray is sold at a half to 2 guineas, according to size and quality".

That account, by the Swedish traveller Angerstein of the work of such an enterprise in Birmingham in 1754, was augmented the same year by his description of the earlier centre for this type of manufacture in Pontypool. This South Wales establishment (see p. 196) was run by two brothers, Edward and Thomas Allgood, whose business made various items in tin-plate. These products were "varnished and painted in the same way as at Mr Baskerville's factory in Birmingham".[17] Evidently the Birmingham painter's reputation for such work was considerable at this time despite which, as early as 1750 "his inclination for letters [lettering] induced him to turn his thoughts to the [printing] press," ultimately designing his eponymous type-face in which he printed many books – as indeed is this one! A very comparable career path was followed by William Caslon (1692–1766) who began life in Shropshire and moved to London to become a gunsmith and chaser before he turned to the production of metal type from his business in Chiswell Street.[18]

In mid-eighteenth century London house-painting, in particular work on interiors, was confined to certain seasons, which resulted in these tradesmen being "idle at least four or five months in any one year. Their work begins in April or May and continues till the return of the Company to Town in Winter."[19] This circumstance together with the growing use of manufactured paints compelled artisan painters to seek employment by means of ever greater diversification. Inevitably some amongst them were to include easel painting as part of their repertoire.

Notes

1 Ewan Clayton, 2013, p. 255, re street numbering; Trade Card, British Museum Dept P&D, London
2 D.N.B., Pope was with Jervas, an Irishman, for six months in 1713. Following Pope's pupilage with Jervas their friendship continued; see Peter Quennell, *Alexander Pope: The Education of Genius 1688–1728*, Weidenfield & Nicholson, London, 1968
3 W. H. Pyne 1823/4. Vol. II, p. 11
4 Edward Edwards 1808, pp. 150, 178
5 Details drawn from Edward Edwards 1808 and Sidney Hutchinson 1968
6 W. T. Whitley, Vol. I, p. 147, Reynolds began his pupilage with Hudson in October, 1741
7 Edward Edwards 1808, pp. 92, 53, 124, 253
8 *Ibid.*, p. 227. Gresse's father was a Swiss-born London property developer – hence Gresse Street, Rathbone Place. The Scotin's were French in origin and practiced as engravers in London for several generations. The brothers Gerard Jean-Baptist (b. 1698) and Louis Gerard (b.c. 1690) came to England *c.* 1733; Hans Hammelmann 1975, p. 67
9 Alan Borg 2013, p. 115; W. T. Whitley 1928, Vol. II, p. 22
10 Sidney C. Hutchinson 1968, p. 50
11 Edward Edwards 1808, p. 263
12 Antonia Roberts *Enter Tim Bobbin ...*, Rochdale Art Gallery, Manchester, 1980 and James Ayres 1996, pp. 46–49. Collier was a Dutch-loom weaver, school teacher, engraver, painter and author of a number of books on and in the Lancashire dialect which he also illustrated
13 Jacob Hall Pleasants (1943) 1970, pp. 55–89
14 *Ibid.*, p. 79. Rembrandt Peale's observations on Guy are quoted at length being transcribed from *The Crayon*, vol. 3, 1856, p. 5. See also Jacob Hall Pleasants (1943) 1970, pp. 66–79
15 Edkins Snr. manuscript in Bristol Central Library B.20196. I am indebted to Sarah Richards for introducing me to these documents. For a fuller account see James Ayres 1998, pp. 225–229. Curiously Edkins is not listed in *Sketchley's Bristol Directory* of 1775. See also Louis L. Lipski 1984, cat. 605
16 Holger Hoock (2003), 2009, p. 61 and also Michael Snodin and John Styles eds 2001, pp. 169, 287
17 Torsten and Peter Berg 2001, for Birmingham see p. 33, for Pontypool p. 163. The manufactory in south Wales may, like the similar industry in Birmingham, have imported its tin plate sheet from Bristol. The name Allgood brings to mind Squire Allworthy in Henry Fielding's *Tom Jones* (1749) – and Fielding lived in the village of Weston on the western side of Bath quite close to Bristol. For Caslon see Jerry White 2012, p. 92–93.
18 W. R. (?) *A Concise History of Worcester* 1808, pp. 81–82. Baskerville invested some £600 in a type foundry but on his death these "elegant" typefaces were rejected by "the Universities" and languished unused until 1779 when they were purchased "by a literary society in Paris ... for 3,700£". See also H. H. Peach 1943, pp. 120–121 citing Henry R. Plomer *English Printing 1427–1898*, 1900; for Caslon see Ewan Clayton 2013, p. 208
19 R. Campbell 1747, p. 104

Chapter 10

EASEL PAINTING

The notion of the "liberal" painter was so widely accepted in late Georgian England that it served to differentiate "polite artists" from "mechanic tradesmen", a situation reflected in the hierarchical *Directories* that began to appear in the 1770s. As we have seen these publications list two categories of painters: "Artists: Portrait, Landscape, Miniature &c." and these are followed by "Painters: House Sign &c." On the face of it this all looks quite simple, if not simple minded – but in the arts, as in the sciences, all things are relative. In reality there was enormous diversity within a given art form, a subtle gradation of quality and qualities. Within painting the type of work that was undertaken and achieved could be as various as the functions (or non-function) that any individual product might serve. Pictures were created that would now be characterised as academic, provincial, colonial, vernacular or none of the foregoing. Such paintings may have served as overmantels, overdoors, chimney-boards, or dummy-boards. They may have provided a likeness of a person, a ship, a house, a horse or cow or they may have been painted as a framed "cabinet" or exhibition piece – an art for art's sake. These various strata of artistic endeavour and achievement imply the presence of a market for the resulting works. However patronage of the visual arts was largely confined to a very small privileged minority. Lorna Weatherill has shown that between *c.* 1675–1725 paintings and prints were only to be seen in about one third of the homes of the gentry and members of the professions and higher trades. Over the next 100 years public exhibitions and the foundation of academies of art would help to develop this market. By 1804 it was noted that "The love of pictures is not confined to persons in the higher situations in life. Do we not see in almost every, the meanest cottage, ordinary pictures and prints ... even ballads, pasted on the wall with good effect." In terms of the makers of these various works the division between the vernacular and the academic artist was not impermeable; it was always possible to move from one to the other. In most cases the direction of travel was one way; from what has been termed the "little tradition" to the "great tradition".[1] A clear example of this can be seen in the work of the American-born painter Benjamin West PRA (1738–1820). In Colonial Pennsylvania he was trained by William Williams the English, Bristol-born, vernacular painter. West's early work in America included the production of overmantel paintings and portraits within the artisan tradition. On moving to Europe in 1760 his metamorphosis from the "Colonial" to metropolitan taste, from "the little" to the "the great" tradition was startling. Furthermore transitions of this kind were not confined to Colonial immigrants to Britain. The carriage painter Charles Catton RA (1728–1798) undertook a comparable aesthetic, if not geographical, journey. This chapter will attempt a brief overview of the social history of easel painters who worked within this range of traditions. In addition some consideration will be given as to how theories of "production" and "reception" may be seen to have influenced the character of the resulting work in the age of patronage.[2]

Above the vernacular threshold a whole category of polite artists emerged who, whatever their origins in terms of training, tended to favour an aesthetic doctrine that gave less emphasis to craft values. By the early eighteenth century artists of this kind were more likely to have been articled to a successful studio in preference to serving an apprenticeship in a workshop. Studio practice was the basis on which the portrait painter Jonathan Richardson Snr (1665–1745) trained a succession of pupils. He, on the other hand had begun his career apprenticed, in c. 1679, to a scrivener, a possible explanation for his fondness for drawing on vellum in silverpoint.[3] Richardson was later passed on, in c. 1687 as a student with the painter John Riley (1646–1691).[4] Richardson's origins in the legal profession may also explain why it was that some of his students served a "pupilage" although others like George Knapton and Charles Pontien, were registered as apprentices.[5] For painters a pupilage may therefore have been a relatively new form of education and of those who were attached to Richardson one of the most significant was Thomas Hudson (1701–1779) who served a pupilage – there is no record of him being in bondage as an apprentice. Hudson was to become Richardson's son-in-law and would, as we have seen, follow his master's precedent in taking on students among them the young Joshua Reynolds. The continuity from master to pupil and onwards could be truly remarkable from Riley (b. 1646) to Reynolds (d. 1792) – some 146 years.

Despite Reynolds's belief in the pre-eminence of history painting he, like many of the artists of his generation, was primarily concerned with portraiture. In Hanoverian England such painters were sometimes known derisively as "phizmongers" and, as in previous centuries, as "face painters".[6] Late Tudor and early Stuart portraitists such as Nicholas Hilliard (1546/7–1618/9) worked in the service of the state, or to be exact, the crown.[7] In Tudor England, with its somewhat *ariviste* aristocracy, conspicuous consumption was a duty rather than a personal indulgence – a means of projecting power. This was to a great extent achieved by visual means as was certainly the case with Elizabeth I and the royal icons of her visage. These did not come into existence by chance or the whim of either the monarch or her limner. "Portraits" of this kind were a matter of public policy. Their inception was, at least in part, a direct consequence of the unflattering representations of the Virgin Queen that were produced by sign-painters. According to Sir Walter Raleigh these were by "unskilled and common painters" whose work was, on the orders of the queen, to be "knocked to pieces and cast in the fire". By a proclamation of 1563 the Queen ordained that no "pourtraict of hir Majesty should be painted" until such time as "by hir allowed" and an official image had been prepared to serve as a "patron" (model) for all future "portraits".[8] Models of this kind are preserved in the National Portrait Gallery, London (Fig. 6).[9] The model for the portrait of Elizabeth I is the sort of job that may well have been undertaken by the Queen's Sargeant Painter who, at this time, was the Frenchman Nicholas Lizard.[10] Ultimately Hilliard was to become the limner who was most regularly entrusted with representing the queen's physognomy in an acceptable manner.

At an artisan level the work of Hilliard's contemporary Sampson Strong (1558–1611) is instructive. His real name was Starke but in England he was given the surname Strong – which was presumably inspired by his Christian name. This Dutch artist painted in oil and was active in the Oxford region from *c.* 1596 to *c.* 1609. In 1596 New College paid him £6 for a conventionalised "portrait" of William of Wykeham, and he produced a second version of that subject at a reduced price, for Winchester College, Hampshire. He also painted similarly notional representations of the founders of other Oxford Colleges including Richard Foxe (Corpus Christi) Henry Chichele (All Souls) and Thomas Wolsey (Christ Church). Other works by his hand have been identified at Christ's Hospital, Abingdon. These include his spectacular *Bridge Builders* of 1607. His image of King Edward VI at Christ's Hospital cost £3-9s-9d with an additional 5s-3d for the gold leaf. In 1596 Strong was licensed to sell ale in Oxford – a trade that he evidently combined with his role as a painter. Intriguingly he was recorded as having matriculated from Magdelen College in 1598–1590 at the age of 40.[11]

In terms of the polite art of "liberal" painting portraiture is peculiarly relevant in that it raises important sociological questions. What was the degree of social separation between the sitter and the artist, and did any such divide influence the resulting work? Did such a potential gulf between the two such protagonists dwindle in the course of the seventeenth century? Any social emancipation of a minority of painters was presumably enhanced by aristocratic and even royal practitioners. Among these were Sir Nathaniel Bacon (1585–1627) who produced sophisticated oil paintings, and Prince Rupert of the Rhine (1619–1982) a fine draftsman and engraver. Knighthoods for immigrant painters like Rubens and Vandyck also played a part in raising the social standing of a select group of painters. In a highly stratified society these were matters of relevance which conditioned the attributes that a successful portrait painter was expected to possess – over and above the ability to paint. These were certainly advantages that were enjoyed by Sir Godfrey Kneller (1649?–1723) from Lübeck. He was endowed with "Health ... a good memory, pleasant conversation finely entertaining when a-painting."[12] In much the same way the Florentine born portrait painter Andrea Soldi (c. 1703–1771), when working in England was described by Hogarth as a painter who "knew how to entertain his sitters".[13] Another was Gainsborough who "was very familiar and loose in his conversation to his intimate acquaintance; *but knew his own value*, was reserved; and maintained an importance with his sitters, such as neither Beechey or Hoppner can preserve."[14]

These social skills were far from trivial for not only did they help to secure a likeness but the resulting portrait had the potential for greater vitality. It was of course this self-same social poise that enabled artists to assert their genius in the presence of their clients and sitters. Hogarth noted that Ramsay had "address [presence] enough to persuade the public that he has brought a new discovered method of colouring" into use.[15] This "method" was nothing more than the widely used and long established system of first "laying-in" the tonal values of a portrait "*en grisaille*" before adding the colour. Hogarth, with a tinge of envy, concluded that once Ramsay had painted his sitter's head he had "nothing to do but hire one of those painted tailors for an assistant." This last observation refers to the employment of "drapery painters" – a service that Hogarth generally eschewed.[16]

Many of the artists who specialised in portraiture become heavily dependent upon their drapery painters. Sir Peter Lely (1618–1680) utilised the services of Baptiste and also of John van der Eyden who, in addition to his work as a drapery painter, was also involved in the production of studio copies.[17] Sir Godfrey Kneller (1699?–1723) regularly employed the Antwerp-born John Pieters (d. 1727) who also worked for others. Indeed so successful was Pieters in ministering to various canvasses that he became known as "the Doctor". His consultations were so effective, his touches so masterly, that Pieters was said to

FIGURE 34. Sir John Baptist de Medina: *Thomas Edgar*, oil on canvas (30½ × 25½ in/77.5 × 64.3 cm) *c.* 1697. Medina was alleged to have painted a series of canvases with bodies to which he subsequently added heads. Judging by the disjuncture between the head and the torso in this portrait the anecdote seems plausible. (Royal College of Surgeons of Edinburgh)

FIGURE 33. Sir Godfrey Kneller (1649?–1723), portrait of *Richard Boyle 2nd Viscount Shannon* (36 × 28 in/91.4 × 71.1 cm). This work of *c.* 1715–20 has reached the stage at which Kneller would hand the canvas over to a drapery painter. (National Portrait Gallery, London)

be capable of bringing a dying portrait to life whilst at the same time giving it a "fictitious air of quality."[18]

Much though Kneller may have been dependent on Pieters another, probably apocryphal story, suggests that the master employed a whole team of other specialists. Of these one such assistant would create the hat, another the periwig, a third the buckle, a fourth the "glossy blue velvet coat" another the buttons, a sixth "the laced handkerchief and point ruffles" whilst yet another hand created the gold lace "which decorated the scalet waistcoat".[19] Despite the difficulties of representing passementerie this account has all the signs of being a rather libellous exaggeration. The more usual arrangement was to employ a single drapery painter.

John Elsum gives a good account of this specialism in his *Art of Painting* (1704). He describes "Drapery Garments [as being] of three sorts: Woolen,

Linen or Silk." He goes on to advise that for female portraits "Dress is no mean Circumstance and ... is best which is loose, free and neglected, and comes nearest to the Un-dress." This description tallies with many Restoration portraits of court beauties and is close to Robert Herrick's (1591–1674) "Sweet disorder in the dress/Kindles in clothes a wantonness." In great contrast male portraits established the expectation that these painters could "make a suit of Armour" (Fig. 38). This was of two types "light and Dark, its Colour is seldom proper [in the heraldic sense] but accidental according to the Colour of Neighbouring Objects; the lustre of it is hard to be imitated" – an acknowledgement of the importance of reflected light and colour. Finally Elsum considers the setting in which the subject of the portrait is placed by the painter in discussion with the client. He describes these ambient features to be represented in the picture as the "Transient View of its Scene Works and Decorations .... By-Works, or Circumstantial Ornaments."[20] These elements could extend well beyond dress to encompass a landscape background by Henry Vergazoon who, along with Pieters, was also employed by Kneller.[21] In effect Sir Godfrey Kneller was seen by some to be running a commercial enterprise to the extent that he was

FIGURE 35. Joseph Highmore (1692–1780) oil sketch on paper (10 × 7½ in/25.5 × 19 cm) of a *family group*, mid-eighteenth century (see Fig. 36). (John Harris, Badminton)

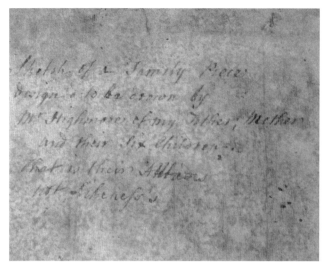

FIGURE 36. Inscription in ink on the reverse of the Highmore painting reads as follows: "Sketch of a family Pieces/design'd to be drawn by/Mr Highmore of my Father, Mother/and their Six Children/that is their Attitudes/not likeness's". Despite the somewhat confused wording of this retrospective note the sketch was presumably created as an instruction to a drapery painter. (John Harris, Badminton)

"A man lessened in his own reputation, as he chose to make it subservient to his fortune".[22] According to one eighteenth century account Kneller's "manufactory" was akin to the production of Kidderminster carpets:

> "In his hands painting became a trade ... His women [were cloathed by] one German genius [who] has the adjustment of the laced tucker, another gave the embroidered stomacher. To one he committed the care of the graceful robe ... another to paint the red and green parrot which perched on Madam's left hand and the lamb which she was stroking with the other hand was the province of the pastoral painter."[23]

This is remarkably close to the description of a group family portrait that appears in Oliver Goldsmith's *Vicar of Wakefield* (1766). The author gives an account of an itinerant artist who received precise instructions from his client:

> "My wife desired to be represented as Venus and the painter was desired not to be too frugal of his diamonds on her stomacher and hair ... Sophia was to be a shepherdess, with as many sheep as the painter could put in for nothing".[24]

Elsum's somewhat dismissive attitude towards "By-Works" in 1704 indicates a change of fashion at the turn of the century. Nevertheless many clients continued to insist that such incidentals should be retained to demonstrate their place in society as landed gentry or captains of army or navy and, at a later date, industry. Although royal portraitists generally contrived the presence of the crown, the excessive use of these props declined in metropolitan taste but remained in provincial and Colonial portraits. A good Colonial American example is Samuel King's (1748/9–1819) painting of *The Rev. Ezra Stiles* painted in 1770–71 (Fig. 37). Stiles recorded his intentions, as the client, in his diary and it was his instructions that formed the basis for the artist's work. In the background of this canvas is a bookcase containing works by Newton, Plato and Livy, whilst a column is inscribed with a diagram of the orbits of the planets. Stiles concluded his diary entry by stating that "These Emblems are more descriptive of my Mind, than the Effigies of my Face."[25] The picture of *Stiles* was more a biographical statement than a portrait as such. Much the same may be said of the parallel tradition, the other side of green baize door, for portraits of servants. These representations of retainers, menials and estate workers were similarly portrayed in association with their relevant attributes. Thus the footman is shown in livery, the housemaid with a broom and the estate carpenter with the tools of his trade. These heraldic achievements of the artisan were observed by Daniel Defoe (1724) in the village of Bloxham, Oxfordshire, where "the poor servants" at the living fairs "distinguish themselves by holding something in their hands, to imitate what labour they are particularly qualify'd to undertake; as the carters a whip, the labourers a shovel, the wood men a bill [hook], the manufacturers a wool comb and the like ..."[26]

Of all the known specialist drapery painters working in England in the earlier decades of the eighteenth century the Antwerp-born J. Van Aken was probably the best known. He was described as "an ingenious foreigner employed by old Jonathan Richardson, Jervas, Hudson and other fashionable portrait painters of the time to paint draperies, backgrounds and accessories."[27] According to George Vertue (1684–1756):

> "Mr Vanaken, having an excellent, free, genteel and fluid manner of pencilling [handling his brush in representing] silks, satins, velvets, gold lace etc., has worked hard for several painters for dressing and decorating their pictures which, without his help and skill would make but a poor figure ... They send their pictures, when they have done the face, to be dressed by him."

So formidable were Van Aken's abilities in this field that his regular clients attempted to form a monopoly over his services. In these circumstances it is all the more remarkable that Hamlet Winstanley of Lancashire (1698–1756: Stubbs's master) was able to employ Van Aken occasionally. So considerable was Van Aken's contribution to the canvases he worked on that it was said that these portraits tended to resemble one another no matter who was the sitter or who the ostensible artist. On Van Aken's death in 1751 painters such as Thomas Hudson were compelled to find alternative drapery specialists like Roth.[28]

FIGURE 37. Samuel King (1749–1819) *Portrait of the Rev. Ezra Stiles,* 1771, oil on canvas (34 × 28 in/86.4 × 71.1 cm). In his diary Stiles (1727–1795) notes that this portrait includes, in the background, emblems that characterise his learning – details which presumably formed part of his instructions to the artist. (Yale University Art Gallery, New Haven)

Work as a drapery painter offered a source of employment for those "polite" artists who, for various reasons, failed to become portrait painters in their own right – individuals who may, for example, have lacked sufficient presence or conversational skill. Alternatively such work could offer short term employment for an artist who was yet to make a name or had newly arrived in the country. When Johann Zoffany (1733–1810) reached England in 1760 he was first employed painting vignettes on musical clocks for Stephen Rimbault and as a drapery painter for the portraitist Benjamin Wilson. These were considered to be somewhat modest activities and as soon as was practical Zoffany withdrew from such employment. Attitudes towards such lowly work are reflected in a comment on a drapery painter named Rubenstein, who was dismissed as "an ingenious drudge" to portraitists. Even Hogarth in his autobiographical notes makes disparaging reference to "Jour[n]ey men call'd Back ground & Drapery painters ..." [29] Other commentators were less condescending. Edward Edwards (1808) describes Peter Toms RA (d. 1776) as a man whose: "chief excellence was in painting draperies for Reynolds, Cotes and West, especially after the death of Van Aken." According to J. H. Anderson's *Notes* from 1769 Toms was a "scholar of Hudson's [who] became Drapery Painter to Sir Joshua Reynolds [and] held some appointment in the Herald's Office." Rather dramatically Anderson adds that Toms "went to Ireland in order to practice as a Portrait painter but being unsuccessful destroyed himself in 1776."[30] Mercifully Toms's attempt to cut his throat failed and he survived to end his days back in London. It seems that despite a widely held belief in Toms's "excellence" this was a view not shared by all. According to Reynolds's pupil and biographer James Northcote RA (1746–1831) Toms's work:

> "did not exactly harmonise with the style of Sir Joshua's heads, as it was heavy and wanted freedom, so that his work had too much the appearance of having been done with a stamp as the paper hangers rooms are executed."[31]

If the drapery painter was to operate seamlessly the pose of the sitter and the idiom of the "face painter" had to synchronise. Artists such as Kneller were well aware of the importance of this. He told the one-time portrait painter Alexander Pope that it was "absolutely necessary to draw the face first, which ... can never be set right on the figure if the drapery and posture be finished before" the portrait.[32] This necessity must cast in doubt the anecdote concerning the Spanish portrait painter Sir John Medina who came to Britain in 1686. It was said of this artist that "He went carrying a large number of bodies and postures, to which he painted heads ...", a feature exemplified in some of his portraits Fig. 34.[33] No mention is made of hands which so often reflect the character in an individual portrait. In this respect one lady of fashion, who was particularly proud of the beauty of her hands, was promptly told by the artist, Godfrey Schaleken, that he always drew them from his housemaid.[34]

In early Federal America John Wesley Jarvis (1780–1840) was such a successful portrait painter that he would receive as many as six sitters a day. To achieve this level of production he was heavily dependent upon his student Henry Inman (1801–1846): "who painted upon the background and drapery under the master's directions."[35] In time Inman was to become a considerable artist in his own right demonstrating that not all these "drudges" remained in a state of perpetual subordination. In many cases the possibility of a drapery painter emerging as an independent artist was more likely to happen in the second generation of a family of artists. When Marcellus Laroon (b. 1653) first found employment in England it was as one of Kneller's drapery painters whereas his son, Marcellus Laroon the younger (1679–1772) was to emerge as an independent artist.

The production of a single painting, as the product of many hands, can be seen as a disconcerting notion to post-Freudian sensibilities which tend to assume that a work of art is the creation, or at least the reflection, of an individual psyche. And yet, as we have seen, a portrait "by" Kneller could include, in addition to draperies by John Pieters, a landscape background by Henry Vergazoon.[36] Neither should we assume that specialist painters of clothes were exclusively employed by fellow artists. In 1775 Paul Methuen paid the drapery painter Edward Francis Cunningham (known as "Calze") £26-5s-0d to bring his attire more up-to-date in an old portrait of himself.[37]

For the leisured classes, sitting for a portrait could be rather tiresome, in that it took valuable time out of the social round. For this reason, and in the interests of their clients, artists were anxious to minimise the length of time they would take over such commissions. Reynolds claimed that:

> "It requires in general three sittings [to take a portrait head and shoulders] about an hour and a half each time, but if the sitter chooses it, the face could be begun and finished in a day. It is divided into separate times for the convenience and ease of the person who sits. When the face is finished the rest is done without troubling the sitter."[38]

In painting everything but the face "without troubling the sitter" some sort of stand-in was necessary in the absence of the subject. For this purpose a life-size articulated "lay-figure", which could be dressed in the sitter's clothes, was the cheapest solution to the problem. For specialist drapery painters these mannequins must have been an essential part of their studio equipment. Peter Toms RA (d. 1776) was one such specialist who went to the trouble of making his own lay-figure. This object must have been something of a success since on his death it moved to the studio of the pastel painter John Russell RA (1744–1806). In 1771 the RA Schools commissioned a man named Addison, probably the cabinet maker Robert Addison, to make such a figure for "about eighty pounds". When it was eventually delivered to Old Somerset House he demanded £100 – a compromise £90 was eventually agreed. This high cost contrasts with the £48 that William Etty RA (1787–1849) paid a Parisian craftsman named Huot for a lay figure some 35 years later.[39]

In Hanovarian London portrait painting tended to take place between Autumn and Spring. This established a sharp divide between polite painters and house painters whose working year began in April or May and continued "till the Return of the Company to town in Winter."[40] In a fashionable city like Bath the Season in the early eighteenth century occurred in the Summer when "the roads were dry and passable." After *c.* 1730 this changed with two

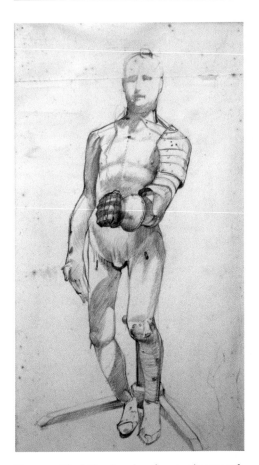

FIGURE 38. Life size *lay figure*, nineteenth century; articulated timber armature upholstered to resemble the human figure – *papier mâché* head. In general portraitists used full-size mannequins which could be dressed in the sitter's clothes – or armour. (Drawing of *c.* 1961 by the author)

seasons: September to December and April to June.[41] It was in these months that Gainsborough would have been at his busiest during the years he spent in the Spa before moving on to London.[42] These time frames, conditioned by the Season, imposed a degree of urgency on painters in the production of portraits, and consequently the employment of their sub-contractors – the drapery painters, etc. For this reason these artists were compelled to invest in their undertakings which encouraged them to ask their clients to pay half the fee in advance. By the end of the eighteenth century it was standard practice for portrait painters to display a printed or written notice to this effect in their painting rooms. This down-payment was particularly important in circumstances where the client was of the opinion that the artist had failed to secure a likeness. A situation that is known to have been experienced by painters of the stature of Gainsborough and Romney.[43] Both "liberal" and "artisan" painters expected prompt payment. Reynolds was particularly business-like in this respect as is shown by his diaries which are preserved in the Royal Academy library. For example the fly-leaf of his journal for 1765 shows that in that year his standard prices for portraits was as follows: 150 guineas for a whole length (7 ft 10 in × 4 ft 10 in/2.03 ×1.47 m); 70 guineas for a half length (4 ft 2 in × 3 ft 4 in/1.27 × 1.02 m); 50 guineas for a "kit-cat" (3 ft × 2 ft 4 in/0.91 × 0.71 m) and, for a head, 30 guineas (2 ft 5 in × 2 ft 1in/0.74 × 0.64 m). Artisan painters were inevitably no less concerned with questions of payment. This is confirmed by Daniel Defoe writing in 1727 from the point of view of the customers. In particular he advises that shop-keepers should be economical in spending on their premises adding that "the Joiners and Painters, Glaziers and Carvers, must have all ready money: the Weavers and Merchants may give credit ..."[44]

In Georgian Britain a fluid and free manner was favoured for portraiture and, to some extent, for other forms of easel painting. This freedom was an inhibiting barrier for those "liberal" artists who had begun their vocation in servitude to a trade. For example, individuals who had been apprenticed as carriage painters, where a sharp precision was appropriate, were to find the transition to the prevailing conventions difficult. This problem was also encountered by provincial and Colonial artists who were not in touch with fashionable idioms for painterly freedom. Although trans-Atlantic communication was always present it was perhaps more intermittent amongst artists for whom the ocean was generally a one-way ticket – in either direction. One such migrant artist was John Smibert (1688–1751) who famously accompanied Dean Berkeley in 1728 and painted the important *Bermuda Group Portrait* (1729) of the Dean and his family. Smibert was born in Edinburgh "and served his time with a common house painter ..." but on his move to London was compelled "to content himself, at first, with working for coach-painters." Once Smibert was established in America he received a letter from the poet Ramsey in Edinburgh concerning the latter's son – the future portrait painter Allan Ramsay (1713–1784):[45]

> "my son Allan has been pursuing his science [portrait painting] since he was a dozen years auld; was with Mr Hyssidge [Hans Hysing 1678–1752/3] in London for some time, about two years ago, has since been painting like Raphael; sets out for the seat of the Beast beyond the Alps within a month hence to be away two years. I'm sweer [loath] to part with him, but canna stem the current which flows from the advice of his patrons, and his own inclination."[46]

Ramsay's sojourn in Italy evidently had the desired effect for he went on to produce highly accomplished work which met the expectations of a sophisticated clientele. By contrast Smibert, having been apprenticed to "a common house painter" remained locked in a provincial/Colonial idiom. On the other hand his highly practical understanding of his craft enabled him to function in Boston, Massachusetts not only as a portrait painter but also as a Colourman selling pigments, brushes, prints etc.[47] Despite the rather unsophisticated nature of Smibert's work Dunlap (1834) detected his influence in the work of Copley, Trumbull and Allston.[48]

Aside from the influence, the taint, of somewhat provincial artists such as Smibert portrait painters in Colonial America were dependent upon mezzotints, imported from Britain, as their exemplars. In using these black and white images as the basis for their work, coupled with the stronger light of latitudes well to the south of the British Isles, a strong chiroscuro and sharp definition resulted. This was a distinctive North American idiom of great quality epitomised by the work of John Singleton Copley (1738–1815) in Massachusetts before he moved to Europe in 1774. His portrait of his half brother, *The Boy with the Squirrel* was sent to England from Boston in 1765 and exhibited in London in 1766. In a review in the *London Chronicle* this canvas was praised but it was felt that "the shadow of the flesh is rather dark."[49] Sadly, whilst it was acknowledged that this picture showed great skill and promise, it was of a character which was contrary to the fashionable notions that then held sway in Britain.[50] To Reynolds the work that Copley produced in distant Boston exhibited a "Hardness in the Drawing, a Coldness

FIGURE 39. Matthew Pratt (1734–1865) *The American School, London,* 1765. Benjamin West provided a home from home for his fellow artists and American compatriots in the British capital. The host, West, is shown as a Quaker wearing his hat indoors. The seated figure next to West (if he stood he would be improbably tall) is the likely author of this faintly naive picture. (Metropolotan Museum of Art)

in the Shades". Even the Pennsylvanian-born Benjamin West RA (1738–1820), after just three years in England, judged the Bostonian's work to be "too liney" and suffered from its "neatness in the lines". These characteristics in Copley's canvases probably owed much to the influence of his step-father Peter Pelham, an English engraver who, on emigrating to Boston in 1727 also worked as a painter. In particular the tonal values in Pelham's mezzotints appear to have infected Copley's American portraits. Some support for this hypothesis has recently been offered by Peter Moore's identification of a whole group of New England portraits dating to the second quarter of the eighteenth century. These are painted in imitation of engravings and some even include the familiar copper-plate inscription identifying the sitter. In view of the help that Pelham evidently gave his step-son it was unfortunate that Copley felt that he was "particularly unlucky in living in a place [Boston] into which there has not been one portrait brought that is worthy to be called a Picture."[51] With this outlook he inevitably became one of the first American painters to follow Benjamin West in settling in London. Many others would follow their example to assume European manners of painting. In London they were to find a welcome in West's studio which became, in effect, *The*

FIGURE 40. Nathaniel Emmons; *The Rev. John Lowell*, 1728, oil on panel (14½ × 10½ in /36.7 × 26.5 cm). The influence of English mezzotints on American Colonial art could extend to such prints being "quoted" in oil paint – as here. This, coupled with the light of latitudes well to the south of the mother Country, may explain the use of the strong chiaroscuro found in Copley's American work (see Fig. 20). (Harvard Art Museums, Cambridge MA)

American School celebrated in Matthew Pratt's painting of that title (Fig. 39).

Matthew Pratt (1734–1805) of Philadelphia had himself sprung from the vernacular craft tradition. At the age of fifteen he was apprenticed to his uncle James Claypole (*c.* 1720–*c.* 1796) from whom "(to use his own words) he learned all the different branches of the painting business, particularly portrait painting …" For William Dunlap, who quoted Pratt, "This allusion to 'the different branches of the painting business', shows plainly the degraded state in which the arts were, at that time, in this country [America]."[52] That observation was published in 1834. Just eight years later the young Charles Dickens found that "the different branches of the painting business" were thriving on the then frontier regions near St Louis, Missouri. The English novelist noted that the wooden houses near Belleville "had singularly bright doors of red and yellow, for the place had lately been visited by a travelling painter who 'got along', as I was told, by 'eating his way'". That night Dickens and his companions stayed in an inn at the nearby village of Lebanon. The best room in the hostelry was adorned with

> "two oil portraits of the kit-cat size [36 × 28 in/91.5 × 71 cm] representing the landlord and his infant son; both looking as bold as lions, and staring out of the canvas with an intensity that would have been cheap at any price. They were painted, I think, by the artist who had touched up the Belleville doors with red and gold paint; for I seemed to recognise his style immediately."[53]

In stylistic terms the distinction between Colonial or early Federal work in North America and provincial painting in Britain could be narrow – all part of one trans-Atlantic English speaking community. Even in eighteenth century London artisan artists remained at work and were capable of offering clients a complete package – such as a portrait, its framing and glazing. One such was "S. Morley at ye Golden Head in Salisbury Court, Fleet Street London". He announced that he could offer "Gentlemen & Ladies Pictures Drawn at their Houses in Crayons, and" that these could be "Deliver'd in a Handsome Frame & Glass at half a Guinea and a larger Size at Sixteen Shillings". He also worked "in Oil very Reasonable with Frames Compleeat".[54] Morley's prices might be contrasted with the princely fees that Reynolds imposed (see p. 169 above).

* * * *

In an age of high mortality rates portraiture was in great demand in all levels of society. It was the dominant art form. Consequently images of the current generation "proudly took possession of the drawing room" until their heirs relegated them to less visible parts of the house.[55] This desire to record appearances was extended to portraits of houses, horses, farm animals and ships – subjects that were of value, in emotional and financial terms, to the patrons. In some ways it was the portraits of houses that could be extended to form an overview that would encompass an entire estate, in effect a visual "terrier". Prominent amongst those who documented such prospects were Leonard Kniff (1650–1721) and Johannes Kipp (1653–1722) whose presence in England did much to introduce the whole notion of the Dutch "landskip". The association of this type of work with land ownership provides the link that explains how it was that Paul Sandby RA (1725–1809) evolved from his role as a surveyor to that of landscape painter.[56] In contrast the Welsh-born Richard Wilson RA (1714–1782) was apprenticed to the London portrait painter Thomas Wright "an artist of whom Mr [Horace] Walpole takes not the least notice."[57] Despite his obscure and less than relevant origins in terms of training Wilson was to emerge as "the father of English landscape painting."

From depictions of personages and their country houses this tradition quite naturally extended to thoroughbred horses and dogs etc.[58] One of the earliest of these specialist painters was Francis Barlow (1626–1704) who was "bred to the profession of painting under Sheppard a portrait painter." This case, like that of Wilson, demonstrates the dominance of the "phiz mongers".[59] Ultimately Barlow's "genius led him intirely to design after nature, birds, fish and every species of animals, which he drew with great exactness."[60] Barlow was to be followed by John Wootton (1668?–1764) who, so it was said: "was peculiarly qualified to please this country; I mean by painting horses and dogs".[61] The truth of this observation was confirmed by later artists who found similar employment, men like James Seymour (1702–1752) and Francis Sartorious (1735–1804).[62] These and others were to be eclipsed by George Stubbs RA (1724–1806) since "Previous to the emanations of this gentleman, we were so barbarised as to regard with pleasure the work of Seymour".[63]

This should not lead us to suppose that Stubbs's training in the visual arts was confined to the polite tradition of the "liberal" painter. Early in his career he developed a desire to learn engraving for the purposes of realising his anatomical drawings in printed form, without being dependant upon others. For this training he moved to Leeds where

> "he had known a house-painter who sometimes practiced that mystery and to him Stubbs went to learn its rudiments. This very rough instructor taught him to cover a half penny with etching varnish and to smoke it; afterwards, with a common sewing needle stuck in a [wooden] skewer, to etch after a fashion."[64]

Despite the emergence of this new standard of animal portraiture a more vernacular tradition persisted. One such was Richard Roper (fl. 1735–1775) "A painter of sporting pieces, race-horses, dogs and dead game … His powers as an artist were not considerable, yet sufficient to satisfy the gentlemen of the turf and stable."[65]

The more agricultural animal portraits provided some sort of visual pedigree before the general introduction of stock and flock books. As such these pictures should be read as part of the agrarian revolution that was such a necessary supplement to its industrial counterpart and an expanding population.[66] The essential feature of much of this work, even in its more elevated forms, is that it was not an "art for arts' sake" but a pictorial convention that performed a function. This was as true of a portrait of a corpulent aristocrat or a fat sheep, a square rigged sailing ship or a country house. In 1820 when H. J. Hunter visited the Rev. John Skinner he "could not but observe one thing which none but a very tasteful antiquary would have thought of: Barker of Bath (1776–1838) had painted a portrait of a great trout which he [Skinner] had taken." Of even greater antiquarian relevance were the representations of *Stonehenge* (1837) by Richard Tongue of Bath who advertised himself as a "painter and modeller of megaliths."[67]

Reynolds in his *Discourses* and Benjamin West in his conversation, as in much of his work, emphasised the importance of history painting.[68] In this respect both Reynolds and West were attempting to redress William Aglionby's (1685) regret that "we have never produced an *Historical Painter*, Native of our own *Soyl.*"[69] This was an outlook in which Aglionby was following the lead established by the French Académie Royale and promulgated in published form by André Félibien in 1669. The arts of painting were to be subject to an order of precedence according to themes adopted by artists and their clients. At the summit were placed allegorical, often classical subjects – to be followed by "history" painting, portraiture (human or animal – but, in both cases, thoroughbred) landscape and still life – a formalised series of categories.[70]

Despite all the talk of the superior nature of history painting that too was an art of record – or so it aspired to be. This was particularly true of the works of Benjamin West whose canvasses extend not only to Classical antiquity and Biblical subject matter but also to contemporary history showing the protagonists in modern dress. Curiously, and in a perverse way, the vernacular decorative painters were, in many cases, more likely to create an art that was of itself. These artisan artists were not confined to, or dependent upon, representation. Their work was not so much an objective mirror of the world as the truth of the mind's eye.

Notes

1   Lorna Weatherill (1988) 1996, tables 8.1 and 8.2; Edmund Sartell *Hints for Picturesque Improvements in Ornamental Cottages*, London, 1804, pp. 50–51; Peter Burke (1978) 1994, p. 28 citing Robert Redfield, *Peasant Society & Culture*, Chicago, 1956

2   See *Groves Dictionary of Music*, ed. Eric Blom, London, 1954 "Folk Music"

3   Carol Gibson-Wood 2000, pp. 26, 51, 123; see also Willam Kurtz Wimsatt *The Portraits of Alexander Pope*, New Haven, 1965

4   *Ibid.*, p. 27; Horace Walpole, 1786, Vol. IV, p. 32

5   *Ibid.*, p. 67

6   For Parmentier's reference to face-painters see W. T. Whitley, 1928, Vol. I, p. 53

7   Thornton and Cain eds 1981

8   W. A. D. Englefield, (1923) 1936, pp. 53–55

9   For example a "model" for portraits of Sir Henry Sidney *c.* 1573; Karen Hearn 1995, Cat. No. 102; Roy Strong 1969, p. 11

10 Howard Colvin *et al.* 1975, p. 411, HMSO

11 Note by Nigel Hammond on Sampson Strong's work at Oxford, August 2002. A detail of Strong's painting of the *Bridge Builders* (1607) is illustrated as fig. 13.6 by Stean and Ayres (2013)

12 George Vertue cited by W. T. Whitley 1928, Vol. I, p. 6

13 *Ibid.*, pp. 51, 122

14 Joseph Farington, p. 1130 6 Jan 1799

15 W. T. Whitley 1928, Vol. I, p. 58

16 Joseph Highmore (1692–1780), like Hogarth also avoided the use of drapery painters – but Fig. 35 may suggest otherwise

17 Horace Walpole 1986, Vol. III, p. 42

18 George Vertue cited by W. T. Whitley 1928, Vol. I, p. 6

19 *Ibid.*, Vol. I, p. 4–5

20 John Elsum 1704, pp. 55–60

21 Horace Walpole 1786, Vol. III, pp. 216, 219

22 *Ibid.*, Vol. III, p. 196

23 W. T. Whitley 1928, Vol. I, p. 4, 5, 22 – citing an eighteenth century newspaper

24 Oliver Goldsmith's *Vicar of Wakefield* (1766), London, 1917, pp. 84–86

25 Charles Montgomery and Patricia Kane eds 1976, p. 90 fig. 27; William Dunlap (1834), 1969, Vol. I, p. 395, fig 103. Dunlap was of the view that King lacked "that skill which would entitle him to historical notice" – but he was the first teacher of Washington Allston

26 Furbank *et al.* eds 1991, 178; Giles Waterfield *et al.* 2003

27 W. H. Pyne 1823–24, p. 411

28 W. T. Whitley 1928, Vol. I, pp. 53, 55, 56; Vol. II, p. 306. An ivory portrait relief of Winstanley dating to the 1740s is in the Victoria & Albert Museum, London: VA 96–1980. See also Horace Walpole 1786, Vol. III, pp. 36, 42, 216, 230, 275 and Vol. IV, p. 137

29 Martin Postle ed. 2011, pp. 24, 101 – see also W. T. Whitley 1928, Vol. II, p. 250; W. H. Pyne 1823–24, Vol. II, pp. 38–39. Rubenstein is also noted by Edward Edwards 1808, p. 17 who on p. 31 cites another drapery painter named Black

30 Edward Edwards 1808, pp. 17, 31; Anderson's *Notebook*, RA Library

31 James Northcote *Life of Sir Joshua Reynolds* 1813, Vol. II, p. 28; J. H. Anderson ms. *Notes* from 1769

32 Alexander Pope in a letter to Mary Wroughtley Montague – cited by W. T. Whitley, 1928, Vol. II, p. 5

[33] Horace Walpole 1786, Vol. III, p. 237. Sir John Medina was described by Walpole as the son of "Medina de L'Asturias"

[34] *Ibid.*, Vol. III, p. 245 – Godfrey Schalken worked in England

[35] William Dunlap (1834) 1969, Vol. II, Pt I, p. 81 and Vol. II, Pt II, p. 348

[36] Horace Walpole 1786, Vol. III, p. 219

[37] Susan Sloman 2002, p. 70

[38] Letter from Reynolds of 9 Sept 1777 to Daniel Daulby, a noted collector of Rembrandt etchings; W. T. Whitley 1928, Vol. I, p. 280

[39] *Ibid.*, Vol. I, p. 278–279; Ambrose Heal (1953) 1988, 3, Addison's address was in Hanover Street, London

[40] R. Campbell 1747, p. 258

[41] John Wood 1765 and Trevor Fawcett ed. 1995, p. 49

[42] Susan Sloman 2002

[43] W. T. Whitley 1928, Vol. I, p. 346

[44] Reynolds's *Journal* of 1765 – his prices are listed on the fly-leaf; Daniel Defoe 1727, p. 258

[45] William Dunlap, (1834), 1969, Vol. I, p. 27–28 citing Walpole's *Anecdotes*

[46] *Ibid.*, Vol. I, p. 27–28

[47] W. T. Whitley 1928, Vol. I, pp. 64–67

[48] *Ibid.*, p. 64 citing John Hill Morgan's *Early American Painters* which quotes Smibert's advertisement in the *Boston Gazette* of 21 Oct 1743

[49] *Ibid.*, Vol. I, p. 214

[50] For examples of slightly later portraits in this Colonial and Early Federal idiom see Nina Fletcher Little 1976

[51] Letter to the author from Peter Moore, 29 March, 2012; John W. McCoubrey 1965, pp. 11, 12, 14: Letters from London artists dated 4 August 1766 , and Boston 12 Nov. 1766

[52] William Dunlap (1834) 1969, Vol. I, p. 98

[53] Charles Dickens 1842

[54] Morley's trade label, B.M. Dept of P&D

[55] Horace Walpole 1786, Vol. IV, p. 29

[56] John Bonehill and Stephen Daniels eds 2009

[57] Edward Edwards 1808, Vol. I, p. 188

[58] John Harris 1979

[59] W. T. Whitley 1928, Vol. I, p. 53 quoting Parmentier

[60] M. Pilkington *Dictionary of Painters*, London 1769, p. 39

[61] Horace Walpole 1786, Vol. IV, p. 119

[62] Stephen Deauchar 1988, p. 9: also Arts Council of Great Britain 1974

[63] W. H. Pyne 1823–1824, p. 109

[64] Anthony Mould, ed. Ozias Humphrey and Joseph Mayer *A Memoir of George Stubbs* Pallas Athene, London 2005, p. 36

[65] Edward Edwards 1808, p. 11

[66] Christiana Payne 1993

[67] See Howard and Peter Coombs eds 1971, p. 504. Tongue's work is to be seen in the collections of the Society of Antiquaries, London, and the Victoria Art Gallery, Bath

[68] "Should begin with still life and class upwards to history" West in Joseph Farington, p. 853 9 June 1797

[69] William Aglionby *Painting Illustrated in Three Diallogues* 1685; Carol Gibson-Wood 2000, p. 10

[70] Aglionby, p. 11

Chapter 11

THE TRADE OF PAINTING
IN OIL

Amongst "liberal painters", or those who were so liberated, a whole variety of media was available to them. In contrast trade painters were perhaps more concerned with the craft distinctions between the oil media and the water-based distempers – although any one craftsman might work in both. A parallel to this situation is evident amongst provincial and Colonial wood-workers, craftsmen who might function as both carpenters and joiners whilst remaining conscious of the distinction between the two skills. In London this kind of flexibility was, in theory, prohibited by the guilds that policed the trades. By the seventeenth century some relaxation of these regulations permitted Plaisterers to apply distempers using a restricted range of pigments. At this time Plumbers and Glaziers were also authorised to work with paint – but they were confined to the use of oil-based media.

The various aspects of this trade, with its oil-based media, will therefore be considered under the following headings: *House & Decorative Painting, Sign Painting, Coach Painting* and *Marine Painting*.

House & decorative painting

Although the term "painting and decorating" remains current it is now so familiar that it evades our recognition. The locution has survived beyond its relevance. There was a time though, when house painters regularly undertook elaborate decorative work, in addition to the more hum-drum all over colour schemes. This was a tradition that was commonplace down to *c.* 1914. Certainly Robert Tressell's (*c.* 1870–1911) semi-autobiographical socialist tract of a novel offers accounts of the painting of elaborate decorative schemes for interiors.[1] Although work of this kind is not entirely extinct it certainly enjoyed a long history down to the early twentieth century. For most domestic buildings the wider introduction of chimneys in the late sixteenth century, and the associated installation of glass in windows introduced a level of cleanliness that made interior decoration both visible and viable. Because such work was possible it became significant through the sixteenth century and beyond. However, as Michael Bath (2003) has pointed out, one of the difficulties in examining these issues is caused by "the traditional neglect of the applied arts by the conventional 'fine art' historians". And yet historically the evidence points to the unity of the two disciplines. As Alan Borg has observed "Historians of British painting have traditionally focused almost exclusively on fine artists and their patrons." This was a division that scarcely began to exist until the seventeenth century. For example George Jameson, one of Scotland's most celebrated seventeenth century portrait painters, was apprenticed in 1612 to the decorative painter John Anderson.[2]

Inevitably the term decorative painting covers a multitude of activities which, in addition to the "painting and decorating" of houses included sign, coach and heraldic work. Although each will be considered separately these are somewhat arbitrary divisions since many individual craftsmen would have undertaken work in all these trades. This much is implied by Campbell (1747) who notes that "the Herald, House and Coach Painter are generally found together in the City." Outside London this diversification was commonplace. In the cathedral city of Salisbury Farr & Pike advertised their services as "House & Sign Painters in Catherine Street" from where they also undertook "Coach & Sign Painting, Gilding & Japanning in the Neatest Manner at the Most Reasonable Terms."[3]

Through most periods in history the basic "bread and butter" work for these tradesmen involved the application of all-over colour using paints, distempers and stains. Whatever the nature of their work the preparation of paints formed a significant part of their activities. This was because, especially outside London, "The Colourman buys all manner of Colours uncompounded." In a pre-mechanised context the preparation of paints, from raw pigments and media, was time consuming. In this trade "The chief secret" was the "grinding, mixing and compounding of Colours … [and] an even Hand to carry the Brush up and down according to the grain of the wood."[4] In general oil paint was applied to timber and was used both internally and externally. The distempers were most often used internally on plaster.

The range of work undertaken by house painters and decorators was conditioned by the locality in which they worked. As with all the crafts the degree of specialisation was related to the size of a population in a given district. In London the restrictive practises of the Painter Stainers were both a function and a symptom of demographics. In smaller communities, in the provinces as in the Colonies in North America, diversification was more usual. Even in a moderate sized city like Norwich Thomas Bardwell advertised his numerous services as a painter in 1738. From this we know that he undertook "History, Landskips, Signs, Shew-Boards, Window Blinds, Flower-Pots for Chimnies and House Painting."[5] A generation later Michael Edkins in Bristol (Fig. 41) was even more diverse in his activities although easel painting was not part of his oeuvre.[6] In small rural communities non-specialist painters took on a still greater variety of work. In writing about the earlier part of the nineteenth century Thomas Hardy refers to his real yet fictitious Gabriel Oak who, as a shepherd, could also: "make sun-dials, and prent [paint] folks' names upon their wagons almost like copper-plate, with beautiful flourishes, and great long tails".[7] In a port city such as Bristol the painting of ships could be as significant as the painting of houses. In the second half of the eighteenth century the port of Hull was home to John Fletcher (Fig. 72), a painter and colourman whose apprentices included Julius Caesar Ibbetson (1759–1817) who was to become the accomplished landscape painter.[8] Artisans who emerged as polite artists were the exception since most remained locked in their trade. Nevertheless some amongst them became "artisan artists" whose work retained the vernacular traditions of their craft.[9]

In measuring-up a room to be painted, in whatever fashion, account was taken of its internal architectural details. For this purpose Abraham Rees (1786) describes the use of a thread to measure with, which would allow for the undulations of mouldings, cornices, dados etc.[10] This method continued down to at least 1813 when Ilminster School, Somerset, instructed its pupils that "When the Wainscot of a Room is painted you are to measure round the room with a Line ... girting a String over all the Mouldings ..."[11] In the first half of the eighteenth century soft woods were imported in ever increasing volumes to become an important feature in internal joinery. Isaac Ware (1704–1766) noted that since fir had "superseded" all other kinds of timber "it is all one ... when ... covered with paint".

Although personal recommendation provided one means by which trade painters were offered work the so-called "houses of call" were an important form of labour exchange. In March 1769 the Painter Stainers opened "proper books ... at the Widow Minits at 2 the Sign of the Angel in Ironmonger Lane ... Cheapside," London. There "both Masters and Journeymen may [at given times] be supplied" with employees or employment. Although these tradesmen undertook numerous types of work much of the remainder of this chapter is concerned with the application of oil paint to joinery.[12]

FIGURE 41. *Bristol Delft plate* decorated in a Chinoiserie idiom by Michael Edkins. The plate carries Edkins's initials and those of his wife Elizabeth on the reverse together with the date 1760. As a trade painter in Bristol, Edkins undertook an extraordinary range of work from house painting to the ornamenting of gun barrels by the application of a "resist" for "blueing" – and the decoration of ceramics. (Victoria & Albert Museum, London)

FIGURE 42. *Sample board* of graining and marbling in oil paint – *c.* 1800. (Museum of Lakeland Life, Kendal)

Prevalent though all-over colour schemes were there was also a continuing tradition for various *trompe l'oeil* decorations like graining and marbling which, together with japanning and gilding, were deployed as a means of enlivening otherwise rather dull softwoods. For some late Georgian trade painters like William Davies of 8 Talbot Court, Gracechurch Street, London, graining and marbling was a specialism. In addition to painting "Imitations of Foreign and English Marbles Performed in a Superior Style" he concluded his trade card by adding: "NB Ceilings Clouded". Work of this kind could be achieved through close observation of nature. In the late eighteenth century the columns and piers in the Gallery at Harewood House, Yorkshire were "painted by Mr Hutchinson of London, in an imitation of the verd antique marble, and admirably transcribed from a table in the same room". Not that deception was always the intention with marbling and graining on cheap uninteresting soft woods. J. C. Loudon (1836) argued that ordinary timbers should be "grained in imitation of some natural wood, not with a view of having the imitation mistaken for the original, but rather to create an allusion to it ..." Nevertheless the work of Thomas Kershaw (b. 1819) could achieve an effect that was astonishingly close to the original as his sample boards in the Victorian and Albert Museum, London, attest. After a long apprenticeship (1831–1839) with a Bolton house-painter Kershaw moved to London where he fully established a formidable reputation in this field.[13] In general these artists based their work on exotic hardwoods like imported cedar or home-grown walnut. These timbers were imitated by painted graining which involved the judicious use of floggers, combs, megilps and varnishes. Simulated effects of this kind are known to have been carried out under the direction of John de Critz (before 1552–1642) in Queen Henrietta Maria's closet in Denmark House (later old Somerset House). This work was undertaken in 1626–1627 when de Critz was responsible for the faux graining of "wallnutree coloure" in this room. Here the panels were embellished with "antique worke the badges in the midst of them, they being guilded with fyne gold and shadowed".[14] This sounds like a description of painting and gilding in imitation of expensive carved work; a tradition that goes back to the 1530s and beyond.[15] John de Critz Snr, together with Robert Peake (*c.* 1551–1619) were joint Sergeant Painters to King James I.[16] In this role they evidently saw little, if any, distinction between the trade and the art of painting; and the royal portraiture ascribed to each man is of great distinction.[17]

Following the Restoration the post of sergeant painter was occupied by Robert Streeter. In the contract of 1665 for his work on Clarendon House, Piccadilly, London, he agreed to paint the *trompe l'oeil* roses between the modillions of the exterior cornice – a far cheaper alternative to the more usual carved flowers found in this location in a fully enriched Corinthian cornice. Remarkably the contract stipulated that this work was "not to be painted by any of his Servants, but by himself to be touched and Finished".[18] It would seem that even for decorative work the hand of the master could be seen as paramount.

This continuity between the trade and the art of painting caused some confusion amongst the aesthetes of the eighteenth century. For Horace Walpole (1717–1797) this connection between the decorative and fine arts indicated that the latter were yet to be placed "upon any respectable footing". It therefore followed that writers on the arts "had not arrived even at the common terms for its productions". By way of example Walpole cites Sir Anthony Denny's inventory of the 1530s for the palace of Westminster in which "it appears that they called a picture, *a table with a picture*, prints, *cloths stained with a picture*, and models and bas reliefs they termed *pictures of earth*".[19] These very clear craft-based descriptions were evidently beyond Walpole's comprehension.

When Celia Fiennes visited Coleshill in *c.* 1682–1696 she noted that "there was few pictures in the house only over doores and chimney".[20] Miss Fiennes clearly regarded such works as nothing more than "furnishing pictures". That was, of course, their function – almost out of sight over a door, or in a hazardous position over chimney piece where a "real" work of art would not be placed in jeopardy. John Martin's manuscript (Fig. 45; *c.* 1699–1700) belongs to this period and gives instructions on how "To cleanse old paintings done on wainscotting" using wood ashes (lye).[21] The unconscious prejudice towards such decorative paintings as expressed by Miss Fiennes was later shared by Edward Edwards RA (1738–1806) in his *Anecdotes* which was published posthumously in 1808. He prefaces his remarks on this type of work by arguing that "the Polite Arts were … little cultivated by the Natives of England in the middle of the last century". Edwards then goes on to concede that "the arts at this period were not unemployed for the painting of ceilings and staircases was much in vogue." He continues:

> "Sometimes the panels of the room, but more frequently the compartments over the chimney and doors were filled with some kind of picture, which was seldom the original work of any master, but commonly the production of some practical copyist, who subsisted by manufacturing such decorative pieces, and was glad to furnish a landscape on a half length of canvas for forty or fifty shillings. This fashion continued about half a century, but had greatly declined at the period when the Exhibitions were first established. Since when there has been a total change in the style of domestic decoration."[22]

Following this account Edwards goes on to list some of these "practical copyists" as being Vogelsang, Vandiest, Cooper and Cradock. Much of this passage is repeated by William Sandby (1862) with the additional comment that such work "tended to depreciate the demand for works of a higher character."[23]

Of the vernacular painters listed by Edwards, Horace Walpole gives a reasonably lengthy description of Luke (Marmaduke) Cradock (*c.* 1660–1717; Figs 43, 44). Cradock (or Craddock) was born in Somerton, Somerset and apprenticed to a house painter in London. This raises the possibility that he may have been related to the amateur painter the Rev John Cradock who was the father of the portrait painter Mary Beale (1633–1699). Furthermore she was related to the Rev. Dr Samuel Cradock, the prominent nonconformist who, in 1662, was ejected, for theological reasons, from his living at North Cadbury reinforcing this Somerset connection. In July 1648 Mary Beale's father John Cradock presented "a piece of painting of his own making consisting of varieties of fruit ..." to the Painter Stainers of London.[24] Some sense of the Somerset-born Luke Cradock's work can be gleaned from a surviving tea canister which he painted with birds and other decorations.[25] Disdain for this type of work, by both Edwards (1808) and Sandby (1862), was compensated for by Horace Walpole's more sanguine view that Cradock's paintings of birds were "strongly and richly coloured, and were much sought as ornaments over doors and chimney pieces".[26] Cradock's life coincided fairly exactly with the fashion for painted panels of this kind in Britain.

The tradition for such painted panels reappeared in Colonial North America where they were largely confined to overmantels for the good reason that overdoor panels were less possible in rooms with generally lower

FIGURE 43. Marmaduke (Luke) Cradock (*c.* 1660–1716) *Still Life of Dead Game c.* 1703. (The Worshipful Company of Painter Stainers, London)

FIGURE 44. Marmaduke (Luke) Cradock (*c.* 1660–1716) *A Peacock & other Birds c.* 1700. (Tate Britain, London)

ceilings. In the Colonies these paintings appeared at a time when the fashion for such works were in decline in the mother country. For example in 1737 the decorative painter Bishop Roberts advertised in Charleston, South Carolina that "Gentlemen may be supplied with Land-scapes for Chimney Pieces of all Sizes".[27] This type of ornamental painting was to persist in early Federal America where it was carried out by both native-born and immigrant tradesmen. In Massachusetts the most sophisticated work in this field was executed on canvas (rather than panel) by the Neapolitan-born Michele Felice Cornè (1751–1845) who arrived in Salem in 1799.[28] Close examination of panels and canvasses of this kind by Nina Fletcher Little has established that, in New England, most were painted *in situ*.

In contrast chimney boards, as moveable objects, were created in the workshop. These once common household artefacts were used to block a chimney piece in the summer to reduce the draughts from the wide-throated chimneys of wood burning fireplaces. Although chimney boards were once widely used in Britain the introduction of coal-burning grates with narrow throated chimneys removed their *raison d'être* – the reduction of draughts.[29] In America, by contrast, the continued use of wood as a fuel saw the maintenance of this tradition well into the nineteenth century.[30] On both sides of the Atlantic these boards were painted decoratively in a variety of ways. Curiously enough there is scant evidence that the overmantel and the chimney-board were ever painted in relationship, one to another. The more pictorial chimney boards have sometimes been framed and raised in status and position above the dado where their original function sometimes goes unrecognised.[31]

Another type of panel painting that became fashionable following the Restoration was what was known as "Dyalling" a subject to which Joseph Moxon devoted a whole segment of his *Mechanic Exercises* (issued in sections from 1678). As a member of the Royal Society Moxon was encouraged in this venture by Robert Hooke. Hooke had been apprenticed to the painter Peter Lely and for this reason Moxon's description of *Mechanick Dyalling* is an appropriate blend of arts and sciences. Here we are informed that Dyalling was "originally … a Mathematical Science, attained by the Philosophical contemplation of the Motion of the Sun."[32] These sun dials were part of the cutting edge thinking of the Age of Reason and as such were to become extraordinarily fashionable. Following this trend, wind-dials, within a building but connected to an external weather vane, were to become no less modish as did elaborately painted public clock dials. The John Martin manuscript of 1699–1700 illustrates his design (Fig. 45) for repainting the clock face on the church in Watford, Hertfordshire. For this job Martin agreed to the reuse of the existing oak panel that had been installed in 1637. This implies a recognition that the old panel was inevitably well-seasoned and had little or nothing to do with economy. Artisan painters would have had a practical understanding of well framed-up joiner-made panels. The permanence of a painter's work depended on it. In Massachusetts, John Johnson (*c.* 1752–1818) painted a sign for the Boston Dispensary in Massachusetts of *The Good Samaritan*, based on a print of Hogarth's great work in St Bartholomew's Hospital, London. The American version was painted on a panel prepared by the joiner Thomas Clements who submitted his invoice for this work in 1797: "To making a sign [-board] the moulding worked out of solid, irons and screws, putting up ditto at your shop for the Dispensatory: $7.00". From this we may conclude that this panel was framed-up with mortice and tenons but was given masons' mitres "worked out of [the] solid" in the return of the mouldings. [33]

The importance of the joiner-made support in relationship to "dialing", was stressed by William Salmon (1672). He advised that the panel was to be "shot true" with a plane to ensure that it would fit in the "Rabets of the Mouldings" of the framing-up "as a panel of Wainscot doth". He went on to explain that this would give the panel "liberty to shrink and swell without rending, whereas mouldings nailed round the edges, as the vulgar way is," would cause the panel to split.[34] These practical details, though important, were only the start, the quality of the painted work was what was of ultimate importance. One of the finest surviving examples of this type of product is the 1706 clock dial which is paired with the Arms of Queen Anne inside the Collegiate Church of St Mary, Warwick. These two spectacular works were the gift of Robert Abbott "a Painter-Steynor of London and Native of this Parish" (Fig. 46).

These are musings on the activities of trade painters who worked within the British vernacular. As such their artistry was far removed from the murals by the Italian Antonio Verrio (c. 1639–1707) or the Frenchman Louis Laguerre (1663–1734). In England the work of these two muralists was often deployed in the staircase wells of great houses: "Where sprawl the saints of Verrio and Laguerre".[35] It was their example that Sir James Thornhill (1675–1734) sought to emulate. However it seems that Thornhill, a landed gentleman from Dorset, had not entirely lost touch with his art as a trade. According to William Sandby (1862) the Painted Hall at Greenwich Hospital, one of Thornhill's most ambitious schemes, was painted at £3 per square yard.[36] As a member of the gentry Sir James was scarcely characteristic of either the trade or the profession of painting and his situation is further complicated by his role as an architect.[37] It is possible that his son-in-law William Hogarth produced his large paintings for the great stair in St Bartholomew's Hospital, London as a demonstration that he could maintain Sir James's standards. Accomplished though this work is there remains a sense that Hogarth is wearing a costume that is alien to him, a fancy dress, which stands in telling contrast to the home-grown characteristics, and characters, to be found in in his "modern moral subjects." In some ways Hogarth concedes this point. As he moved from engraving silver and the printing of trade labels and book plates he began to paint "small conversation pieces 12 to 15 inches high". He was to recollect how he graduated onto "small portraits and familiar conversations and, with a smile

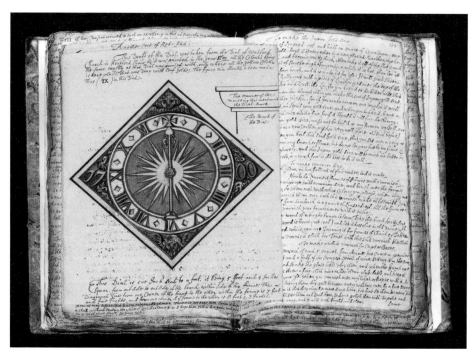

FIGURE 45. A scale drawing (1 in:1 ft) of a *Dial Board* dated 1700 which was to measure 5 ft 4 in (162.5 cm) square. This is one of only two illustrations in John Martin's manuscript manual on painting, gilding, Japanning, varnishing and "graving" (*c.* 1690–1700). The notes to this drawing indicate that the number nine was in fact represented as IX – much as four was, by this date, generally shown as IV. This is related to the clockmakers innovation, attributed to Joseph Knibb, of two tone chimes to signify differing Roman numerals (Cescinsky and Gribble, 1922, Vol. II, 301). A note in Soane's hand, on the fly-leaf of this bound manuscript, states that it was "Bought at the sale of J[ohn] Jackson RA, July 1831". (Sir John Soane's Museum, London)

at my temerity, commenced history painting". From these tentative beginnings his great canvases entitled *The Pool of Bethesda* and *The Good Samaritan* (1737) at St Bartholomew's Hospital are a triumph. On this scheme, which is both instructive and decorative, Hogarth was assisted by the theatrical scene painter George Lambert (1700–1765) whose expertise in mixing large quantities of paint and in lifting these enormous canvases (they are not true murals) into position was probably significant – a large iron staple used in this procedure remains *in situ* (Fig. 17). This great work was presented to the Hospital by the artist who, as a local man (he was born in Bartholomew Close) and a respected Governor of this medical establishment, was not above a little self promotion. Hogarth expressed the hope that this work "might serve as a specimen to show that were there an inclination in England for encouraging Historical Pictures, such a fair essay might prove the painting of them more easily attainable than is generally imagined" [38]

The ever increasing use of framed pictures was to result in a decline in mural decoration although by the early nineteenth century there was something of a revival. These late Georgian mural schemes were motivated by a desire to imitate the expensive imported French scenic wallpapers which were wood-block printed in size-bound pigments.[39] These shifts in fashion saw some trade painters turning to the polite art of easel painting whilst others moved in the opposite direction. One such was John Hakewell (d. 1791) the son of one of Thornhill's foreman. The younger Hakewell was apprenticed to Samuel Wale (1721?–1786)). In 1764, during his time with Wale, Hakewell was awarded several premiums by the Society of Arts for drawings from casts in the Duke of Richmond's gallery in London. As a painter Hakewell was considered to be: "by no means void of talents but wanted resolution … and therefore contented himself with practicing as a master house-painter in which he held considerable rank". Although, in this account, Edwards (1808) did not think that Hakewell was, "as a master house-painter", entitled to be included in his book on artists, neither did he feel he could be passed-over. It was Hakewell's "decorations in the Arabesque or Grotesque style" at Blenheim and Charlebury that persuaded Edwards to include him in his publication.[40] This was, so to speak, the "second coming" of the Grotesque reintroduced to the British Isles by William Chambers in 1759 and enthusiastically continued by Robert Adam in the 1770s as part of the Classical Revival.[41] There had been a much earlier phase in the robust guise of Elizabethan and Jacobean decorative work which, in 1611 was defined as

FIGURE 46. Robert Abbott "A Painter-Steynor of London and native of this Parish" gave the painted clock (and arms of Queen Anne) to St Mary's Church, Warwick in *c.* 1707–10.

follows: "Grotesques: Pictures wherein (as please the Painter) all kinds of odde things are represented without anie peculiar sense, or meaning, but only to feed the eye."[42] Those last five words effectively define the function of decorative painting in general.

Transitions such as those that occurred in Hakewell's career, from trade to art and back to trade, were not confined to the eighteenth century. In 1805 the Norwich drawing master, artist and theatrical scene painter Robert Dixon advertised that he now offered his services as a house-painter. This significant member of the Norwich School announced that he was prepared to undertake the painting of "Drawing rooms, vestibules, etc., ornamented in the newest and most approved stile. Clouded and Ornamental Ceilings, Transparencies, and Decorations in General."[43]

As has been noted the importance of maintaining trade secrecy, the mystery of the art, inhibited the publication of craft manuals in Stuart England. This sense of discretion persisted into the first half of the eighteenth century, a residual respect for the confidential nature of trade methods. In 1756 the East Anglian house-painter and portraitist Thomas Bardwell, referred to above, published *The Practice of Painting* in which vital details are written-in by hand on the printed page. Although Edwards (1808) repudiated Bardwell as an artist he nevertheless considered his book to be "the best that have hitherto

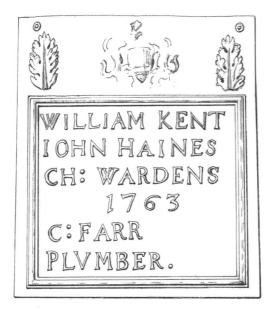

FIGURE 47. *Plumber's Tablet*, one of three located in the base of the tower of St Mary's Church, Ashbury, Oxfordshire. Similar tablets may also be seen in the nearby church of St Peter and St Paul, Church Hanborough.

FIGURE 48. *Trade Card* of the London plumber Dobie which illustrates the traditional range of their undertakings – from leadwork and glazing to both house and easel painting. (British Museum, London)

been published" on the technicalities of the craft. [44] Bardwell was not alone in combining house painting with portraiture. His contemporary George Evans practiced "chiefly as a house painter but frequently painted portraits" although in his own day his work was widely dismissed: "much cannot be said of his powers as an artist, nor will his portraits be much in request with posterity". [45]

Animal portraiture was another activity which kept these vernacular painters in employment. One example was Benjamin Barker (1725?–1793) who left his job as the foreman of the Pontypool Japanning manufactory in south Wales and moved to Bath to work as a carriage painter. It was at this time that he began to produce equine portraits. [46] This was also a speciality of a painter named Shaw who, from his address in Mortimer Street, Cavendish Square,

FIGURE 49. An easel painting by the plumber and glazier James Dunthorne showing *John Sidey and his Hounds at a Farmhouse near Hadleigh, Suffolk*, 1765 (oil on canvas 35½ × 54 in/90.2 × 137.2 cm). (Yale Centre for British Art, Paul Mellon Collection, New Haven)

FIGURE 50. *Model Windmill* (ht 24 in/61 cm) made by the plumber and painter John Dunthorne as a studio "prop" for the landscape painter John Constable RA (1776–1837). (Constable family collection)

London went so far as to build "a large painting room, with conveniences to receive the animals from which he painted." This was described as a "line of art which generally meets with encouragement from those whose chief pleasures are the sports field."[47] It seems that the contempt for some artisan painters knew no bounds. James Bunk who died in about 1780 was described as one of those "who have contributed their feeble efforts towards supporting a spirit of enrichment and decoration among the inferior virtuosi".[48]

The primary concern of this chapter has been the use of oil paint for decorative purposes. As we have seen, according to London trade regulation, this medium was seen as the preserve of the Painters, but it was not exclusive to them. For example artisan plumbers could extend their artistry within their craft in the production of rainwater heads, cisterns or leaded lights with complex patterns. They might even produce commemorative lettered mural tablets. One such was a plumber named C. Farr who in 1763 produced a large lead panel, for St Mary's Church Ashbury, Oxfordshire, which identifies the church wardens as William Kent and John Haines in relief lettering. Similar plaques, of a comparable date (1718 and 1777) survive in St Peter and St Paul, Church Hanborough, Oxfordshire. These may relate to the cast letters that form the signatures of plumbers on some lead covered roofs. By the late seventeenth century the Plumbers had established the right to apply oil paint an association largely based on their role as glaziers.[49] Numerous trade labels, Directories and manuals record this association (Fig. 48).[50] Inevitably some of these tradesmen extended their role to sign painting and sign writing. Others went still further and produced easel paintings. Among these were individuals like James Dunthorne of Suffolk (1760s) who did landscapes (Fig. 49), Desilva (1840s) who undertook ships's likenesses, and his contemporary, the animal painter & plumber, William Bagshaw of Rugby.[51]

* * * *

In early nineteenth century America the diversification in the art of these artisans was even greater. The most outstanding example of this, in relationship to house-painting, was, undoubtedly, Rufus Porter (1792–1884). In addition to his work as a decorative house painter, he embellished furniture, and created murals in distemper – not to mention his work as an inventor, a journalist and publisher (see pp. 76, 148 above).[52] Remarkable though Porter was, he was not alone in terms of diversification within his craft. For example an English emigrant to the USA established a floor-cloth manufactory assisted by his son, the future landscape painter Thomas Cole (1801–1848), young Cole's first experience of applying oil paint to canvas (Fig. 27).[53] Americans, both native-born and immigrant, were it seems, by the nineteenth century, less condescending than their British counterparts with regard to the various means of earning a living with paint. The "Fancy Painter" John Rito Penniman (born *c.* 1782) was apprenticed to an immigrant British "Ornamental Painter" and then, at the age of 21, set up in business in Towne Street, Boston. It was there that he undertook an extraordinary range of work including the ornamenting of furniture and picture frames.[54] William Dunlap (1834) was of the opinion that his work demonstrated "more talent and skill than many who aspire to higher branches of art". Dunlap went on to add that if only Penniman had possessed "the character and conduct of a gentleman [he] would have been a good artist and a respectable citizen, but he became a drunkard." According to Alvan Fisher (1792–1863) Penniman could never achieve his potential because, as an ornamental painter, "he had acquired a style which required years to shake off."[55]

This was a view that was very widely held on both sides of the Atlantic and serves to confirm an important reality, that vernacular painting conformed to standards that were all its own and distinct from the no less rigid conventions found in the fluid brushwork that characterised academic work at this time. For the latter group it was "the hardness of touch" in decorative painting that was seen to be particularly objectionable. In England it was felt that the "fancy pieces" by the immigrant Jean Pillement (1728–1808) suffered from being "finished with great care and labour". Alternatively, and by the same token, such work "… obtained much notice from those who considered neatness of execution as perfection in art."[56] A similar objection was raised with regard to the marine painter Francis Swaine (fl. 1761–1782) who "painted the face of a wind dial, with sea and ships, which he executed with great neatness" – a dubious compliment.[57]

A number of individuals who subsequently became easel painters began as tradesmen decorating tinned iron trays and other products. This material first became available as a support for the work of artisan artists following the granting of a patent in 1727 to John Cook of the Pontypool Ironworks in south Wales for an improved plate-rolling mill. As noted above painted items made of this sheet metal were decorated under the supervision of Benjamin Barker (1725?–1793) who had moved from his ancestral Nottinghamshire to South Wales. There he found employment with Edward Allgood (1681–1763) and his son Thomas as a japanner in their Pontypool manufactory which they established in 1730. The Barker family eventually moved to Bath to become a significant dynasty of easel painters.[58] A very similar trajectory was followed by

Edward Bird RA (1772–1819). He was born in Wolverhampton and, showing some disposition to draw, his father:

> "could think of nothing better than apprenticing him to a maker of tea trays – these accordingly became the boy's business to ornament and embellish … Works of this nature are produced by a kind of mechanical process, in which genius claims little share …"

On the expiration of his indenture in *c.* 1793, young Bird travelled south to Bristol. There he established a drawing school and, by 1837, was exhibiting his easel paintings in Bath. Despite this metamorphosis his earlier life came back to haunt him on at least one occasion. When visiting Boulogne with a group of friends Bird, and his companions, saw a painted tray which was clearly not made in France. In response Bird stated: "It was not made here, it was made in Birmingham, for I painted it." In this context it might be added that when the Norwich School painter John Berney Crome (1794–1842) visited France he reported back to his father that he was "not petrified by the French School" and enigmatically said "something … about the Tea Tray Painters".[59] It is very possible that Crome had seen on the Continent items that had been exported from Birmingham or South Wales, the work of British artisans. As noted above, easel painting was not always the destination for these tray painters and other such artisans. John Baskerville (1706–1775), having begun as a stone-cutter in Worcester later moved to Birmingham where he became a tray painter and, ultimately a printer (Fig. 52). At this stage in his career he devised his eponymous type face. His good friend Benjamin Franklin, as a fellow printer, took Baskerville's type with him back to America where it was adopted by the Federal Government for official documents.[60]

The extraordinary diversification possible in the work undertaken by trade painters in the early nineteenth century is very fully reflected in Pierre François Tingry's *Painter's & Colourman's* Guide of 1830 and also in Nathaniel Whittock's *The Decorative Painters' and Glaziers' Guide* of 1827. The latter publication is comprehensive in its text and in its lithographic illustrations in black & white, some of which are hand coloured. These provided tradesmen with exemplars for graining, marbling, stencilled decoration, transparencies and signs. Furthermore the authors argue that for those painters and decorators who were capable of producing such work it was but a short step to the creation of figurative and landscape murals. Surviving examples of murals by such artisans confirm that this was always a possibility. From amongst such tradesmen a few would emerge to become academic easel painters, although by no means all "liberal" painters emerged from servitude in a trade. As we

FIGURE 51. *Japanned Tray*, Pontypool – decorated with a view of old Swansea. A patent was issued in 1727 to John Cook of the Pontypool Ironworks for his rolling mill which produced plate-iron faced with tin. One of the principal decorators in the works was Benjamin Barker (*c.* 1725–1793) who later moved to Bath where he founded a dynasty of easel painters. (National Museum of Wales, Cardiff)

ABCDEFGHIJKLM
NOPQRSTUVWXY
ZÀÅÉÎabcdefghijklm
nopqrstuvwxyzàåéîõ
&1234567890($£.,!?)

FIGURE 52. John Baskerville's eponymous type face – which has been used to print this book. Baskerville was born in Wolverley, Worcestershire in 1706 and, at the traditional age of 14 years was apprenticed to a stone cutter. He later moved to Birmingham where he first worked as a Japanner of tin trays before becoming a type founder. He died in 1775.

FIGURE 53. Example of *stencilled decoration* in distemper – found in Highfield House (built *c.* 1825), Lymington, Hampshire. (Photograph: Joanna Close-Brooks)

have seen Thornhill came from a landed gentry family and a parallel situation could even be found in North America. For example John Trumbull (1756–1843) was "emphatically well-born" and a Harvard graduate. As a painter he was said to have been an autodidact although it is known that he owned a copy of Robert Dossie's *Handmaid to the Arts* (1758).[61]

Of those who emerged from a trade Charles Catton (1728–1798), the carriage painter, was one of the most remarkable English examples.[62] As a founder member of the Royal Academy he became that institutions official house-painter. Some decades earlier a parallel situation had occurred with George Vertue who was not only a Fellow of the Society of Antiquaries but was also its official engraver of archaeological subjects. On Vertue's death in 1756 the Antiquaries determined that in future their official engraver could not also be a Fellow. The Royal Academy was to follow a similar course after Catton's death in 1798. At a meeting of the Academy's Council, held on 9 February 1799, it was agreed that his old foreman Thomas Tubb should "be appointed to succeed the late Charles Catton Esq as House Painter to the Royal Academy, and that he be permitted to signify the same on his cards etc."[63] Never again would an Academician occupy that position, a connection with the trade, that had given the institution so much of its vitality at its inception, was broken. The seed of decline had been sown.

Sign painting & making

Sign painting was described by William Williams in 1787 as "the nursery and reward of painters".[64] He was not alone in that opinion. In 1831 a contributor to *the Library of Fine Arts* noted that in London, in the first half of the eighteenth century:

> "the only encouragement or rather the only means of employment, to be procured was in sign-painting, and the place of show and sale was found in Harp Alley [see Fig. 62], Shoe Lane, where, from end to end of that place, the works of the candidates for public favour and employ were to be found, – a sort of Noah's Ark, in which animals of every … kind … might be seen".

At this point, the author reins-in his enthusiasm for this type of painting only to conclude with the observation that although such work:

> "may appear contemptible in the eye of modern practice [it] was the stable traffic for the sale of art … and in those days [great sums of money were] expended on the painted sign which, with its massive carved frame and ornamented iron work, cost in many instances a hundred to a hundred and fifty pounds. It may also be observed that the style of painting required for this sort of art, a firm pencil [paint brush] and a decided touch, together with an effect which might tell at a distance – no bad foundation for skilful execution in art".[65]

Despite the prejudices of the 1830s the anonymous author of those lines was capable of recognising the value of a "decided touch". In some ways these observations are quite close to Joseph Farrington's advice to the young John Constable that it was important to "unite firmness with freedom to avoid flimsiness" in his landscapes.[66]

Street signs existed largely because street numbers had yet to be introduced. Although some attempt was made to employ street numbering in London as early as 1708 (in Prescott Street, Goodman's Fields) the identification of buildings by numerals did not become widespread until the final decades of the century.[67] In about 1698 when Celia Fiennes was visiting Bristol she noted that "in many places there are signes to many houses that are not Public Houses, just as it is in London".[68] This indicates that it was in the larger urban settlements that some sort of emblem, or a feature like a blue door, was an essential means of identifying an individual premises in a street. In a small yet vibrant ship-building town like Deptford "every House" in *c.* 1760 was "distinguished by either the sign of the ship, the Anchor, the Three Mariners, Boatswain … or something relating to the Sea".[69] For a relatively small community this was probably something of an exception, one that might be explained by the presence of numerous ship-carvers and painters in Deptford (now a London borough) at this time.

The population of Hanoverian England was widely literate and yet street signs had probably evolved before this was generally the case. In effect these devices were a form of popular heraldry in which communication was direct and visual, rather than lettered. This point was well made with regard to heraldry in 1547 by Bishop Gardiner of Winchester:

> "The pursuivent [herald] carieth not on his breast the King's names written in such letters as few can spell, but such as all can reade be they never so rude, being greate knowen letters in images of these lyons, and those floures de lice, and other beasts holding those armes".[70]

Similarly the emblematic nature of street signs was emphasised by the absence of lettered inscriptions – although some might carry initials and possibly a date (e.g. Fig. 59). When the Continental traveller François Misson visited England (1719) this was a matter of regret for "Germans and other travelling strangers" because in the absence of inscriptions on these signs, they were unable to expand their English vocabulary.[71]

In most cases street signs began with an emblem relevant to a particular trade but others were based upon a rebus on a surname; a visual pun commonly found in heraldry. Thus individuals with names like Bell, Rose or Angel would have signs based on those subjects. Of the crafts or trades a locksmith would display a Golden Key or a mercer the Golden Fleece.[72] Gilded emblems were all the more visible, glinting in the sunlight from along the street. Inns and taverns would display the generic device of a bunch of grapes of carved and painted wood (Fig. 54), together with a pictorial image to identify the particular licensed premises. This was frequently based on the heraldic achievement of a local landed family – a "retired" butler often adopting the role of "mine host" as a form of pension scheme. Once installed signs tended to remain in-situ even after a property changed hands in terms of ownership or trade. Although this frequently reduced the relevance of a given sign a device (any device) remained effective in identifying a particular property within a street. Alternatively an existing emblem was amended by an additional motif – a feature that was compared to the quartering of a coat of arms following marriage.[73]

The regular use of heraldic devices, and the ability to portray emblems with clarity, probably explains the considerable overlap between carriage and sign painting as such a facility was central to both. The ambivalent attitude towards street signs as an art form, let alone their suitability as a training for easel painters, is a recurring theme. For Edward Edwards (1808): "the universal use of signs furnished no little employment for the inferior rank of painters and sometimes even superior professors". He goes on, with regard to the latter, to describe:

> "the most celebrated practitioner in this branch …[is] a person of the name of Lamb [also cited by Larwood and Hotten], who possessed a considerable degree of ability. His pencil [brush] was bold and masterly, well adapted to the subject on which it was generally employed. At that time there was a market for signs ready prepared in Harp-alley, Shoe Lane, [off Fleet Street, London]".[74]

As late as 1862 William Sandby in his *History of the Royal Academy* described sign painting as "the greatest resource of English artists in obtaining employment". Not that this was a universally held view. Almost 100 years earlier, in September 1778, an article appeared in the *Town & Country Magazine* which sought to define a dilettanti as one of "the chosen few critics who could [discriminate between] a modern from an ancient antique, and a Carregio of Harp Alley from an original of that great master" – the condescension is palpable.[75] In general sign painting was often well received amongst artists and the wider public if not by the dilettantes.

William Williams (1787), Edward Edwards (1808) and William Sandby (1862) all wrote of the training and employment that sign-painting had once offered painters. In this respect the making of signs extended well beyond the craft of painting to include carved and gilded frames and three dimensional works in carved wood. In many instances, the whole ensemble was hung from a wrought signiron. In this way the work of the carver and gilder, the painter and decorator, were orchestrated in conjunction with that of the ironsmith's craft. For a free-standing sign the ironwork alone could assume extraordinary

FIGURE 54. *The Bunch of Grapes*, carved, gilded and painted wood; eighteenth century. A typical example of a generic sign (for an inn) of a type that was often held in-stock by sign-makers. This now vanished sign was photographed by the author in *c.* 1970 outside the *George & Dragon* public house in West Meon, Hampshire.

elaboration (Fig. 56). The numerous trades that could be involved in the production of such an emblem probably explains why many of those who were engaged in this work were gathered together in one location in the City of London – namely Harp Alley and adjacent thoroughfares.

In the early eighteenth century a sign could "cost several hundred pounds". One such, of *Shakespear*, was identified by J. T. Smith (1828) as having been painted by John Baker RA (1736–1771) in his youth for a total cost of £500 (which probably included the carved frame and signiron).[76] The impact of such works could be considerable. On the 8 January 1743 *The Spectator* (No. 744) offered the following account:

> "going down Ludgate Street several people were gaping at a very splendid sign of *Queen Elizabeth* which by far excelled all the other signs in the street, the painter had shown a masterly judgment, and the carver and gilder much pomp and splendour. It looked rather like a capital picture in a gallery than a sign in the street".[77]

FIGURE 55. Designs for two alternative frames plus a lunette – for the sign of *The Tun*. Carved wood and oil-gilt frames formed a significant component in the signs of the eighteenth century. See Figs 60 & 70 for other pages from this sketch book – probably by a member of the Harp Alley school (Ex. collection: Kenneth Clark)

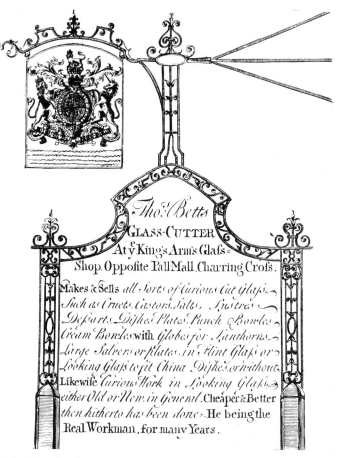

FIGURE 56. *Trade Card* for the glass cutter Thomas Betts – mid-eighteenth century. This card illustrates the degree of elaboration of some signirons. The production of signs involved the skills of smiths, carvers and painters – which probably explains the concentration of these tradesmen in Harp Alley, London. (Victoria & Albert Museum, London)

One of the best descriptions of one of these signs as an entity was given by Monsieur Grosley on his arrival at Dover in 1765 where he:

> "saw nothing remarkable but the enormous size of the public-house signs, the ridiculous magnificence of the ornaments with which they are overcharged, the height of the triumphal arches that support them, and most of which cross the streets".[78]

Although what would now be termed gantry signs were used, most signirons projected out at right angles to the street frontage. These emblems, and the bracket that sustained them, could be so large that, in two recorded cases their weight "dragged down the front of the house" to which they were attached. This certainly happened in 1701/2 to the house in Bow Street, occupied by the wood carver Grinling Gibbons. Very sadly this sign, of the *Kings Arms*, not only pulled down the frontage of the house but, in falling, killed a small girl who had been playing in the street.[79] A similar calamity occurred some years later in St Brides's Lane, Fleet Street, in the City resulting in the deaths of two young women, the king's jeweller and a cobbler.

Decades before these tragic events the hazards that signs could represent were recognised in the: "Act for rebuilding the City of London" of 1667 – the year after the Great Fire. This stipulated "that in all the streets no sign-posts shall hang across, but the signs shall be fixed against the balconies or some other convenient part of the side of the house" a regulation that followed French precedent.[80] Despite the lack of clarity in the phrasing of the Act it was taken to mean that henceforth signs would be fixed flat against the frontage of a building and would, no longer, project out over the sidewalk.[81] As early as 1667 signs were, as a consequence, carved in stone and built into the new brick facades (Fig. 57). As such they provided work for the statuaries. Twentieth century

FIGURE 57. Two carved stone signs: *The Three Crowns* and *The Three Kings* both dated 1667. The Act for rebuilding London after the Great Fire of 1666 stipulated that signs should be built into the new brick frontages – or at least fixed flat against them. (Museum of London)

FIGURE 58. Despite the legislation referred to on page 203 the more fully visible signs that projected out from the building frontage were to return. By the mid eighteenth century virtually every house on *Cheapside* in the City was equipped with such an emblem – as shown in this the detail of this print by Bowles. (Private Collection)

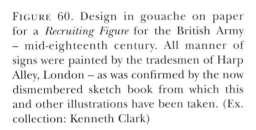

FIGURE 59. *The Sun* dated 1751. This sign would, almost certainly, have been set in a carved wood frame. With some inevitability it has been used for target practice – hence the bullet holes. (Ex. collection: Judkyn/Pratt)

FIGURE 60. Design in gouache on paper for a *Recruiting Figure* for the British Army – mid-eighteenth century. All manner of signs were painted by the tradesmen of Harp Alley, London – as was confirmed by the now dismembered sketch book from which this and other illustrations have been taken. (Ex. collection: Kenneth Clark)

FIGURE 61. Detail of a *Gunsmith's Sign*. As the head on this carved wood figure shows polychromatic treatment could be done with some subtlety – one of the advantages resulting from the sign makers working in one location. In Harp Alley these tradesmen could call on the services of a range of specialisms. (Ex. collection: Judkyn/Pratt)

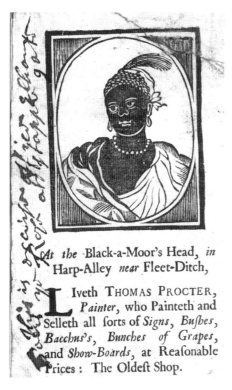

At the Black-a-Moor's Head, *in* Harp-Alley *near* Fleet-Ditch,

Liveth THOMAS PROCTER, *Painter*, who Painteth and Selleth all forts of *Signs, Bufhes, Bacchus's, Bunches of Grapes*, and *Show-Boards*, at Reafonable Prices : The Oldeft Shop.

FIGURE 62. *Trade Card* for the sign-painter Thomas Proctor, early eighteenth century. In London businesses of this kind were centred on Harp Alley off Fleet Street. The work produced in these workshops had a profound influence on William Hogarth who lived nearby. (British Museum, London)

redevelopment of much of the City has resulted in the removal of many of these stone reliefs some of which are now preserved in the collections of the Museum of London.[82] These generally range in date from *c.* 1667 to *c.* 1715. The fundamental problem with this new type of signage was that it was barely visible from down the street. For this reason the old projecting signs eventually returned to the street scene where they jostled for attention so that by *c.* 1750 the provisions of the Act of 1667 were widely flouted – as is very evident from Thomas Bowles's engraving of Cheapside at this time (Fig. 58).

New by-laws were called for. By November 1762 "the signs in Dukes' Court, St Martin's Lane [Westminster] were all taken down and affixed to the front of the houses"; a reversion to, or even a reimposition of, the measures of 1667. Similar by-laws eventually spread out across the country. It seems that inns and taverns were largely exempted from these regulations, possibly because in the past a sign on a licensed premises confirmed its legal right to sell alcohol. This is implied by the trade card of the carver William Puckeridge of 26 Hosier Lane Smithfield, London who in the 1790s, well after the introduction of these by-laws, was producing "Bacchus's, Bunches of Grapes", the generic emblems that identified inns and public houses.[83]

The artisans located in Harp Alley off Shoe Lane, Fleet Street, the undisputed centre of the London sign-making trade, probably shipped their products far and wide by means of river and sea transport. Although the by-laws of 1667 inhibited the production of such items (signs of carved stone being more difficult to transport) the business seems, as noted above, to have returned to its traditional practices early in the following century. By that time Thomas

FIGURE 63. *Trade Card* of John Fairchild and Son of London Bridge – *c.* 1757. Both Luke Cradock (*c.* 1660–1716) and Peter Monamy (1689–1749) were apprenticed to house and sign painters on London Bridge. The reverse of this card shows that Fairchild stocked no less than 131 "Signs Ready Painted" for an emerging consumerist market. (Bodleian Library, Oxford)

Proctor claimed that his was "The Oldest Shop" of this kind in Harp Alley (Fig. 62). His trade card implies that he took commissions for specific signs but he also listed generic emblems for inns and taverns. These included "Bushes, Bacchus's, Bunches of Grapes" much as Puckeridge was to offer for sale at the end of the century.[84] In taking commissions and by holding "stock" Proctor was serving both a client economy and an emerging consumerism simultaneously. By *c.* 1757 John Fairchild and Son the London Bridge "Sign & House Painters" offered a whole range of goods and services.[85] On the verso of Fairchild's trade card is a list of 131 "Signs Ready Painted" and thus in stock.

Although trade cards often illustrate the overall design of these signs, the actual character of the painting is less easily conveyed by an engraved line. Because of the legislation to discourage the use of signs, coupled with the depredations of wind, rain and snow, few eighteenth century signs survive in England. One such is the *Sign of the Ship* which once hung outside an ale house in Britford near Salisbury, Wiltshire (Fig. 64).[86] Perhaps the best overall record of the sort of work undertaken by the Harp Alley school of painters is the sketchbook that graced the collection of the art historian Kenneth Clark (Lord Clark of Saltwood). This may have served as

FIGURE 64. Sign for *The Ship* from an informal beer house in the village of Britford near Salisbury. This sign, being in the manner of Peter Monamy (1689–1749), may date from the mid-eighteenth century. The lettering on the reverse of this panel has certainly been reworked in the early part of the following century. (Salisbury & South Wiltshire Museum)

a pattern book, a catalogue of designs, to show prospective customers. The presence of the type of frames that once encompassed these designs suggests as much – samples being shown for sale as a complete package. Above all these gouache designs offer a sense of the painterly vigour that probably characterised these works.[87]

As Edward Edwards (1808), among others, indicated, signs were painted by both "inferior" and "superior professors" – by members of the "little tradition" and occasionally by those who subscribed to, or became part of, the "great tradition".[88] Inevitably, some individuals moved from one category into another. For Edwards the Harp Alley school of painters generally belonged to the artisan level of painting – despite the manifest quality of their few surviving works. But what of those who moved from the vernacular idiom of the trade painter to go on to aspire to the academic conventions of liberal painting? Many such artists are known to have painted signs as part of their artisan trade and training – among them the following:

Peter Monamy   (c. 1670–1749)
Joshua Kirby   (1716–1774)
Richard Dalton   (1720–1791)
Richard Wright of Liverpool   (1723–17??)
Charles Catton RA   (1728–1798)
John Baker RA   (1736–1771)
Julius Caesar Ibbetson   (1759–1817)
John Crome Snr   (1768–1821)

This list could be extended to include many others including Bardwell and Clarkson both of whom began as sign painters before moving on to portraiture.[89] Even where an individual undertook an apprenticeship in an entirely different craft their change of vocation may have first manifested itself in sign painting. This was true of Hogarth and also of George Romney (1734–1821).[90] Commercial art of this nature could inevitably form the basis for derision. Reynold's niece Theophila Palmer claimed to be something of an artist although Dr Samuel Johnson considered that "the best thing that she could do would be to paint checkers for ale houses".[91]

So far as Reynolds was concerned the works of a generation of artists, previous to his own, were conventionalised to the extent that they resembled "so many sign-post paintings".[92] In the next generation of Academicians a painter like John Constable (1776–1837) produced a drawing as a design for a sign of *The Mermaid*.[93] Various though the attitudes towards this commercial work were, even a partial roll-call demonstrates that many early modern artists emerged from the art and mystery of sign painting. Much later, by the late nineteenth and into the twentieth century, sign painting was to become, for polite artists, a somewhat daring expedition into alien territory.

Of all these painters the figure who stands pre-eminent in this genre is William Hogarth (1697–1764). As a Londoner he would have been fully aware of the Shoe Lane sign-makers whose work influenced his own *oeuvre*. The overlap between the trade cards he is known to have engraved, and the trade signs he would have seen, gives logic to this connection. As a one-time apprentice silver engraver Hogarth's first known essay in oil paint is his double-sided sign for a *Paviour* (c. 1725).[94] Furthermore this item adds credence to the story that he "cut out himself from pieces of cork glued together" the *Golden Head* that formed the sign to his house.[95] In this context it is no coincidence that his "modern moral subjects" abound with signs, features which often serve to develop the narrative they offer. In his engraving *Beer Street* (1751) one of these artisans is shown up a ladder hard at work painting "The Barley Mow"

FIGURE 65. William Hogarth's drawing for the engraving of *Beer Street* (1751). In the drawing the sign painter is shown participating in the general merry making – as engraved he is shown earnestly working at his art. (Pierpont Morgan Library, New York City)

whilst a group of other "workers" carouse below him – although in Hogarth's original drawing the painter is clearly participating in the general merriment.[96]

Hogarth was inclined to have his easel paintings set in frames by French wood carvers and gilders. Despite this bias he was a great believer in home-grown English talent.[97] For example his pupil Philip Daws recalled that his master described the work of sign painters as "specimens of genius emanating from a school, which he used emphatically to observe, was truly English".[98] To some extent this corresponds to Hogarth's general outlook in which he "grew so profane as to admire *Nature* beyond *Pictures*" and object "to the divinity of even Raphael, Urbin, Correggio and Michael Angelo".[99] For him nature and sign painting were more relevant to his *oeuvre* than were the "old masters" – or that was his avowed position.

Despite the vitality of sign board painting, which Hogarth was amongst the first to acknowledge, this vivid art-form was all but extinguished as a result of the by-laws that were reintroduced from 1762 onwards. In April of that year Bonnell Thornton, the manager of "The Nonsense Club", organised an exhibition in Bow Street under the auspices of an entirely fictitious Society of Sign Painters.[100] An apotheosis to a vanishing art form. The "Grand Room" in which these items were shown was "a large commodious Apartment hung round with the green Bays [*sic*] on which this collection of Wooden Originals is fixt [*sic*] flat (like the Signs at present in Paris)".[101] Green baize was a favoured background for the display of works of art at this time.[102] Colluding in the Sign Painters' enterprise with Thornton was William Hogarth who, under the transparent pseudonym of Hogarty, was one of the principal contributors to the show. Displayed prominently in the exhibition was an inscription, in gold letters on a blue ground taken from Horace's *Ars Poetica* "*Spectatum Admissi Risum Tenatis*" (Spectators who are admitted: Restrain Your Laughter).[103] This show of Classical learning (Hogarth's father aspired to Latin scholarship) was to be paralleled by the Royal Academy in its exhibition where "The Great Room" carried the inscription "ΟΥΑΕΙΣ ΑΜΟΥΣΟΣ ΕΙΣΙΤΩ" – (let no strangers to the muses enter), which was presumably an alternative way of excluding laughter.[104] Certainly the injunction in the Thornton/Hogarth exhibition seems to have resulted in a note of caution in the reviews of the exhibition that appeared in the public prints. Amongst those who lacked the wit to see with Hogarth's eye there was an apparent fear that they had seen the joke, but failed to discern the point.[105] As a popular attraction the show was a great success with stage coaches from the North of England being booked by those hastening to town to see the display.[106] The exhibition was a last hurrah for sign painting as a significant art-form in Britain. Five years later when the Rev. John Penrose was

FIGURE 66. Reconstruction of part of the Bonnell Thornton and William Hogarth exhibition of sign board art held in London in 1762. A whole variety of "wooden originals" were fixed flat on the green baize-covered walls of the gallery. The chimney board, reserved for use in the summer, was painted with a roaring fire. The curtained pictures aroused the possibility of lascivious subject-matter; a hope destined to be disappointed. Hogarth's irrepressible sense of fun may too easily have resulted in some visitors to the exhibition failing to recognise his genuine respect for this type off work. (Reconstruction by the author, Cornerhouse Arts Centre, Manchester, 1985)

visiting Bath he noted that "since last year all the signs in Bath are taken down and affixed [flat] to their respective Houses".[107] The by-laws against pendant signs were spreading out across the country. Languishing flat against street frontages signs were less visible and therefore less effective.

* * * *

The decline of sign painting in England may well have contributed to Joshua Shaw's (c. 1777–1860) decision to emigrate to America where signs continued, as they continue, to be displayed in a thoroughly uninhibited way. Shaw had been "apprenticed to a country sign painter" in his native Bellingborough, Lincolnshire. Then "at the age of manhood", presumably at the conclusion of his servitude (at 21 years), he moved to Manchester to practice this trade. He later crossed the Atlantic and in North America was to develop a reputation, not only as a portrait painter but also as "an inventor", although no further mention is made of him as a sign painter.[108]

In Colonial America, as in Britain, sign-painting was one of the many activities undertaken by the jobbing painter. In his early years as an artist in his native Pennsylvania, Benjamin West (1734–1820) painted the occasional sign and overmantel landscape.[109] In the same State, Matthew Pratt (1734–1805) was particularly well known for this branch of the art. His work was described as being "of a higher character than signs generally; [being] well coloured and well composed".[110] In early Federal America the Mount brothers of Long Island were of farming stock although all three became painters. The eldest, Henry Smith Mount (1802–1841) "was devoted to sign painting" but also "executed still lifes".[111]

In early Georgian Britain street signs were the only secular works of art that the broad mass of the population had the chance to see. This situation persisted in North America well into the following century. An example as to how this influenced an emerging artistic talent relates to Francis Alexander (1800–1880), the son of "a farmer of moderate circumstances" of Windham, Connecticut. As a youth Alexander "worked in the eight warm months on [his] father's farm, and the other four went to school". In later life he recorded the moment when the visual arts struck him as a revelation. On a visit to Providence, Rhode Island, he particularly noted "the signs there and those were the only marvels in painting that I saw till I was twenty, excepting two very ordinary portraits that I had seen at some country inn". These exemplars encouraged young Alexander to become "an ornamental or sign painter merely because I thought I would make more money than by farming". He was later to become a successful if rather conventional portrait painter – perhaps the inevitable destination for an artist whose motivation was pecuniary.[112] Alexander's near contemporary John Wood Dodge (1807–1893) followed a similar route to the fine arts in binding "himself apprentice to a sign painter at the age of seventeen".[113]

A trawl through Dunlap's *History of the Rise and Progress of the Arts of Design in the United States* (1834) demonstrates the central role that sign and coach painting played in the art education of the young Republic. Among the artists who could claim that their formative years were spent in this way were: Abraham Delanoy (1742–1795), Thomas Sully (1783–1872), Jacob Eicholtz (1776–1842), Philip Thomas Tilyard (1785–1830), Chester Harding (1792–1866), Henry Smith Snr. (1802–1841) and William Sidney Mount (1807–1868). Of these Chester Harding is known to have "opened a sign-painters shop [in Pittsburg] and continued in that branch of the useful arts until July 1817" a period of about two years, by which time he was in his mid-twenties.[114]

In his reminiscences of his childhood in Philadelphia John Wesley Jarvis

(1780–1840) referred to "old Mr Pratt" whose stock-in-trade as "an honest sign-painter" included "red lions and black bears, as well as beaux or belles". With regard to the latter he "never pretended to aspire to paint the human face divine, except to hang on the outside of a house …"[115] When work was slack he turned to painting "flags and fire buckets, [fire] engines and eagles" all of which gave Jarvis an "introduction to the 'fine arts' and their professors".[116]

* * * *

Although anecdotes of this kind offer a useful insight into the range of work undertaken by artisan painters on both sides of the Atlantic it should be added that sign-writing and lettering in general, also formed an important aspect of their work. In 1676 Joseph Moxon published his pattern book on "*the Rules of the Three Orders of Printed Letters*". This manual was intended to assist sign painters, letter cutters and type founders in the drawing of letters – both the Roman alphabet and the cursive Italic. Although this publication did not reveal trade secrets as such, it may have been seen as something of a threat to the "art & mystery" which would account for the great rarity of this book. It contains some 38 full page copperplates that were probably engraved by Moxon.[117] The ability to create letter forms offered an effective training in developing an eye for line, in short the ability to draw. In such work the skill to assess the spaces between letters is almost as important as the letters themselves. This is a matter of judgement that may not be reduced to measurement. Consequently some trade painters developed their signwriting artistry as a specialism. This was apparently true of Joseph Edwards the "House and Sign Painter of Turnagain Lane, Fleet Market, London" who advertised that he was also adept at "Arms, Escutcheons, Inscriptions on Monuments and Show Boards". His work on "Monuments" might even imply that his painted letters were later translated into cut forms. For purposes of the printing press the ability to cut letters and inscriptions back-to-front was a notably challenging skill. It is therefore no coincidence that the English caricaturist James Gillray (1757–1815) whose father was a house painter and sexton (to the Moravian burial ground in Chelsea) began his career apprenticed to Henry Ashby an engraver of letterheads, etc. Furthermore his political satires depend upon a substantial quantity of text, all of which were inevitably engraved in reverse – and that needs practice.[118]

Signwriting, in its painted form, was to become something of a specialism. In this respect, the American coach and sign-painter Edward Hicks (1780–1849), was a tradesman of great skill. As a sign writer he lettered the frames to his easel paintings and chimney boards with great expertise.[119] Outside the community of artisan artists easel painters in America remained as disdainful and inflexible with regard to vernacular work as their European counterparts. Jarvis tells us that when Gilbert Stuart (1755–1828) painted one of his numerous versions of his portrait of *George Washington* the sign writer Jeremiah Paul "thought it no disgrace to letter the 'books'" in the background of the painting.[120] Even in the idealistic, newly independent land of liberty, the reproach is self-evident.

For an Englishman like Charles Dickens visiting Lowell, Massachusetts, the proliferation of polychromatic signs in the bright light of latitudes well to the south of London was, by 1840, a revelation.

> "One would swear that every 'Bakery', 'Grocery' and 'Bookbindery' and other kind of store, took its shutters down for the first time and started business yesterday. The golden pestles and mortars fixed as signs upon the sun-blind frames outside the Druggists, appear to have been just turned out of the Unites States Mint ..."[121]

* * * *

A very late, but nevertheless instructive example of an apprentice signwriter is Robert Arthur Wilson (1884–1979).[122] In 1908, at the traditional age of 14 years, Wilson was apprenticed for seven years to George Henry Southwell a "Signwriter & Decorator of Nile Street, Sunderland".[123] At the conclusion of his time "Mr Southwell" confronted young Wilson with the following offer:

> "You are the best apprentice I have ever had so you will begin work on Monday on full pay". This offer was accepted and Wilson "continued thus as a journeyman for two years ... In those days we worked a full fifty hour week: five on Saturdays. During my early apprentice period, two remarks made to me by the shop foreman stand out clearly in my mind: 'It is not the man who works the hardest who does the most work, it is the man who plans his work'. On another occasion he said to me 'Look Bobby, never turn your back on a job you don't like or you'll never make a man of yourself'."

That last point was close to the general belief that "the first duty of an apprentice" was to learn "to like doing what you don't like doing". Wilson was to recall that:

> "Many years after leaving Sunderland, and on visiting the town, I have seen specimens of my handiwork on shop fronts and windows and have actually used hundreds of books of gold leaf on wood and glass ... the books of untransferred leaf [cost] at that time 1s 6d per book of 25 leaves".[124]

Wilson began as a signwriter but, like so many before him in previous centuries, he moved to London and built a considerable reputation as an easel painter. Yet another example of an artisan being transmogrified into a "liberal" artist.

Coach painting

In terms of capital investment, maintenance and running costs a coach was enormously expensive, and therefore only available to a very small minority – the "carriage folk".[125] For these reasons ample resources were available not only for the construction but also the decoration of these vehicles. Coach painting could be lavish. This was a trade that was divided into a series of clearly defined specialisms. So far as painting was concerned these comprised the line-painters, body painters and herald or decorative painters. It is the last category that concerns us here as it was from amongst them that some "liberal" artists emerged. Significantly there was virtually no interchange between these three categories of painter not lease because each trade employed distinctive brushes.[126]

The highly profitable nature of the coach building trade was such that few ventured beyond its confines. In this respect decorative coach painters, as distinct from either body or line painters, may have been an exception since their art and mystery held wide potential application. It is known that some might, on occasion paint a sign, but a move towards easel painting was probably a more attractive option in terms of status and income. Perhaps the most outstanding instance of such an adjustment in this vocation is that of William Kent (1685–1748). He was born, the son of a carpenter, in humble circumstances in Bridlington, Yorkshire, where he "unexpectedly demonstrated his youthful inclinations to drawing. Being apprenticed of a coach-painter and house-painter [in Hull] – from him [his master] he came to London without leave or finishing his apprenticeship". In view of the many artists who were known to have begun their careers in this way the engraver George Vertue (1684–1756) has left an account which has the ring of truth; besides they were contemporaries.[127]

Although some lumbering carriages had been available to a very small elite in late Tudor England those capable of offering a degree of comfort were a seventeenth century innovation. Consequently coach making was, in some respects, a relatively new trade in Britain and the Coachmakers and Harness Makers Company of London was not Chartered until 1677.[128] The rarity of such vehicles in the early seventeenth is shown by the figures for London. In

FIGURE 67. The *Coach Makers' Arms* painted by Peter Williamson of 2 Owen Street, Manchester in September 1826. As the yellow "cast" on this example demonstrates, coach painters used prodigious quantities of varnish. (Collection of John Gall and Rosy Allan)

1605 it was estimated that there were a mere 50 coaches, although this went up to 200 by 1652. Despite these low numbers the coaches that were built required decoration. A royal wardrobe (warehouse) account of 1634 concerns an invoice from: "John de Critz, serjeant-painter, for painting and gilding with good gold the body and carriages of two coaches and the carriage [chassis] of one chariot and other necessaries: £179-3s-4d".[129]

Horace Walpole, who quoted this lost document, goes on to express the hope that such work should not be seen to "debase the dignity of [a] serjeant painter" to the crown since other considerable artists of the past had undertaken commissions of this kind. Ultimately the importance of this "trade" was recognised by the Charter awarded to the Company of Coachmakers in 1677, an acknowledgement of the burgeoning numbers of these vehicles. By 1694 London boasted an estimated 700 carriages, and there was concern that "the too frequent use of coaches, [would result in] the hindrance of the carts and

carriages employed in the necessary provision of the city and suburbs".[130] As
a consequence the citizens became so concerned by this growth of traffic, this
"swarm" of carriages, that as early as 1635 a patent was granted to Sir Saunders
Duncombe for the introduction of Sedan chairs which, being smaller, occupied
less space on the streets. It was hoped that these conveyancies would reduce
congestion although chairmen were compelled to call out to pedestrians "to
the wall" – away from the mud of the roadway.[131] Inevitably these Sedan chairs
were to multiply in number. In London down to 1713 there were 200 licenced
for hire and from that date the figure was increased to 300 not including the
privately owned chairs.

As a coach painter William Kent was apprenticed to a trade that was yet
to fully develop.[132] On leaving his master in Hull for London, before the
expiration of his time, he aspired to evolve as a polite painter. This remained
his objective during his ten year sojourn in Italy (1709–1719) and in his first
years back in England.[133] In abandoning his obligations under the terms of the
indenture Kent had emancipated himself from servitude in the craft. This also
removed him from his obligations to the "art & mystery" to which many of his
contemporaries were subject. For Kent any sense of trade solidarity appears to
have melted away. In separating himself from such baggage he was to emerge
as a designer of prodigious scope and as such a figure who was to become the
arbiter of taste for his generation.

In the natural course of events later coach painters would follow Kent's
example and move from the trade to the art of painting, a trend which he
established and then abandoned in favour of design. Charles Catton RA
(1728–1798; Fig. 68), John Baker RA (1736–1771) and Thomas Daniell RA
(1749–1840) had all successfully been apprenticed to the London coach
painter Thomas Maxfield of Little Queen Street, Lincoln's Inn Fields. This
link across the generations was reinforced when Daniell became a journeyman
with Catton.[134] Later still Daniell again served as a journeyman for Haig, a
coach painter in Queen Anne Street East who, in his turn, was apprenticed
to Catton.[135] The earliest surviving *Binding* Book for apprentices registered
with the Painter Stainers runs from 16 August 1666 to 7 October 1795 and
shows signs of damage due to the Great Fire of London which began on
2 September 1666. This manuscript volume suggests that a training as a coach
painter with Maxfield was much sought after as he was clearly respected by
fellow craftsmen. For example the great Christopher Pinchbeck, who invented
the metal alloy that resembles gold, placed his son William with Maxfield on
6 August 1760. Another skilled tradesman to follow that example was the
carver and gilder Samuel Haworth whose son Henry was bound to Maxfield

for seven years on 4 October 1769 in "Consideration of Fifty Pounds". This high premium was also paid by John Minnett, a gardener, to Maxfield for his son's apprenticeship. These examples probably serve to explain why Richard Catton, a Norwich schoolmaster, was happy to place his son Charles, at the somewhat advanced age of seventeen, with Maxfield (5 June 1745). This training evidently served Catton well for the quality of his work was to be widely recognised. Furthermore as a Master himself he was able to attract apprentices of some social standing. On 6 July 1768 he admitted Abraham Brown, the son of a Pembrokeshire gentleman, to his workshops. Six years later, on 3 August 1774 Catton was able to take on his younger brother James for the notional premium of just 1 shilling.

Among other future artists to spring from such a background was Robert Smirke RA (1752–1845) who served his time with a coach painter and, whilst still an apprentice, was "sometimes borrowed by Catton to execute particular things". In later life, like many others, Smirke was to regret that he was unable to "eradicate those habits of painting which he had contracted during his education as a coach painter".[136] The precision of handling that carriage painting demanded could be seen as a disadvantage for those who later endeavoured to translate their craft to the art of easel painting. Richard Dalton (1720–1791) was yet another easel painter who began in this trade apprenticed in London to a coach painter in Clerkenwell. He later furthered his education in Rome and, following his return to England, was eventually appointed "Surveyor of Pictures in the [Royal] Palaces".[137] The "hardness of touch" that carriage painting demanded, and which was acknowledged by Robert Smike, may account for Dalton's move to an administrative position under the crown. In contrast to these examples John Martin (1789–1854) was first apprenticed as an heraldic painter to the Newcastle coachbuilder Leonard Wilson. Having begun his servitude in 1803, at the traditional age of 14 years, Martin abnegated his indenture well before completing his time.[138] As a consequence he was spared the precision that characterised heraldic work and which would have inhibited the scope of the vast and cataclysmic canvases that he was inspired to create as an easel painter.

Although these individuals went on to establish reputations in other fields it was Charles Catton who was to be described by W. H. Pyne (1769–1843) as "the prince of coach painters".[139] Many years later the American painter William Dunlap (1766–1839) was to argue that Catton was "… the first artist in his branch of painting in Great Britain" and that "herald painters were in his time, ranked with artists in other departments of painting …"[140] Because relatively few eighteenth century carriages survive Catton's work in this field

a

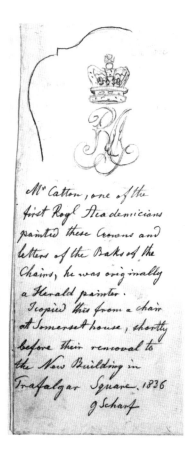

b

Figure 68. a) Hall chair of *c.* 1780–1790 painted with the Royal Academy's cypher. This series of mahogany chairs was painted by "the prince of coach painters" Charles Catton (1728–1798), a founder member of the Academy and the first and last Academician to be that institution's official house painter. (Royal Academy of Arts, London); b) George Scharf's note on Charles Catton's work on the Royal Academy's hall chairs (British Museum, London)

has proved somewhat ephemeral. Fortunately there are a few extant examples of this aspect of his work such as the group of hall chairs at the Royal Academy in London which he painted with the royal cipher surmounted by a crown (Fig. 68).[141] A further indication of his abilities in this field may be gleaned from *The English Peerage* (1790) in which the coats of arms that illustrate this folio volume were engraved by James Heath and Francis Chesham after drawings by Catton.[142]

The nexus of coach painting that formed around masters like Maxfield of Little Queen Street was also found outside the capital – although, significantly, both Dalton, a native of Cumbria, and Catton who was born in Norwich, were sent to London to learn the trade under Maxfield.[143] Others were trained within their native districts. In East Anglia John Crome the Elder (1768–1821) of Norwich was apprenticed in the city for seven years at the customary age of 14 to a coach and sign painter named Whistler.[144] Another, also from this region, was Joshua Kirby (1716–1774) who was apprenticed in the same trade in Ipswich.[145] He later moved to London where he developed a significant reputation as an architectural draftsman and architect. In these capacities he became a drawing master to the Prince of Wales (later George III) and, with his son Willliam Kirby, joint Clerk of the Works at Richmond and Kew Palaces.[146] In the north-east Robert Watson was apprenticed to a Newcastle coach painter before moving to London where he became a student at the RA Schools in 1775. In his subsequent career he worked as an engraver.[147] Thomas Collier (1746–1825) was an adopted Novocastrian who became a respected coach painter in that city. He was the son of John Collier of Rochdale (alias Tim Bobbin) a Dutch loom weaver by trade but also a teacher, painter, engraver and a writer on and in the Lancastrian dialect.[148]

FIGURE 69. John Baker (1736–1771), *Flower Piece* oil on canvas (24 × 29½ in/61 × 75 cm). This picture was presented to the Academy in 1772 by Charles Catton presumably in memory of his fellow coach painter – see Appendix V. Both men were founder members of the RA. (Royal Academy of Arts, London)

Not all carriage painters commenced their careers in that trade. As noted above Benjamin Barker Snr (1725?–1793) began as a decorative painter of tin ware in Pontypool, south Wales. In 1781 he moved to Bath where he secured employment as a herald painter with Morton Crease and Spackman the carriage builders with workshops in Monmouth Street. Charles Spackman (1748–1822) was a serious collector of paintings so that this and the fashionable clientele that visited the Spa enabled several generations of Barkers to evolve into a highly significant family of artists.[149]

As the most accomplished coach painter of his day Charles Catton was elected in 1784 as Master of the Painter Stainers Company of London. In that year, and in that capacity Catton received Sir Joshua Reynolds into the "Company as a testimony of their great esteem for his eminent abilities in the art of painting." This may have been a proud yet ironic experience for the great coach painter.[150] And yet, some 16 years earlier Catton, together with John Baker were among those former coach painters who were founder members of the Royal Academy. Men such as these were to be followed into that institution as Academicians by others who had served an apprenticeship in this trade, or had sometimes worked in that capacity. Sir William Beechey RA (1753–1839) was one such individual who had been employed by a coach-painter in Mercer Street, Long Acre, London.[151]

In Catton's day "the profession of coach-painting … [could] boast itself as holding rank among the arts, but since the opulent coach-makers have taken this branch of decoration into their own hands the herald painters are become no more than their journeymen".[152] Traditionally these coach or trade herald painters had worked as independent artists who painted various decorations, armorial achievements, crests and cyphers. By 1787, if not before, this fashion seems to have declined. Where formally "coaches were embellished with historic or fancy compositions which gave employment to genius, now those beautiful ornaments are disused, are removed to make way for the unmeaning stuff or purchased heraldry …"[153] The latter were probably ormolu mounts and crests, products "purchased" from Matthew Boulton's manufactory in Birmingham (see p. 403 below).[154]

The tendency of the "opulent coach-makers" to take all branches of the crafts "into their own hands" is paralleled by the building trades where "general contractors" were to dominate the construction industry. This reduced once proud independent specialist tradesmen to a dependant status as employees.[155] In London at this time, coach painting was to be dominated by just three companies. This triumvirate was composed of John Hatchett, John Wright and Philip Godsal.[156] This centralising trend of late Georgian industry to garner all aspects of a given trade unto itself, not only generated enormous profits for the owners of such businesses, but also resulted in absolute control of production and consequently of design. This enabled the immigrant coach designer Rudolph Ackerman to establish a "brand" image for the coach builders he worked for. Between 1788 and 1794 he designed numerous carriages for Philip Godsal (1747–1826) before becoming an independent publisher.[157] As the coach painters conceded their freedom to the large scale coach-builders these manufacturers turned increasingly to the employment of "designers". Hatchett's coach building establishment at 121 Long Acre, Westminster, was on a comparable scale employing "several hundred" artisans at the time of Sophie de la Roche's visit in 1789.[158] In these circumstances the professional coach painters lost their position as artists and therefore turned increasingly to easel painting where they rediscovered their independence. Curiously, and without any apparent sense or irony, many of the more important master coach builders collected works by "liberal" painters to hang in their own homes. This was certainly true of Spackman in Bath and of Philip Godsal in London.[159] To this end Godsal regularly attended Royal Academy exhibitions and also commissioned works from Royal Academicians.[160]

Paintshops in coach making businesses were kept immaculately clean to minimise impurities in the air that might disrupt the high gloss finish of the paint-work and varnish. According to one account the shop floor would sometimes be flooded with water so as to reduce dust levels.[161] If this was true, a fine balance would be struck since high humidity could cause paint, and more particularly varnish, to "bloom". If this was ever done it was doubtless reserved for times when the ambient humidity levels were at their lowest. In winter a workshop stove could all too easily generate dust. In mitigation of this a solid fuel heat source could be enclosed in a "sheet iron cylinder" a device which was seen as "a practical reducer of stove dirt".[162]

At Godsal's the paintshop was on the first floor above the dust of the smithy and the workshops where the carriage bodies were constructed. In this location there was evidently no possibility of flooding the floor. It was of course necessary to both lift and lower the components to be painted on this upper level. For this reason "All the main flights of stairs are broad, and so arranged that banisters may be taken down, and the finished body-work allowed to slide down on ropes".[163] An inventory of these workshops, drawn up in 1812, includes "… stools to sitt on for Painters – Grinding Stones – Potts, Brushes & all Implements for Painters's use in those lofts where they are employed".[164] This list implies that Godsal's workshop supplied its painters with their hand

tools, a feature which was not customary in most trades. It also suggests that
they ground their own pigments and prepared their own paints an activity that
had declined in London by this date.

The support, the panel, on which the carriage painter applied his art was of
fundamental importance. William Adams (1837) describes "American birch" as
being effective for this purpose. He argues that "it works easily with the plane
and yields a beautifully smooth surface, which does not show the smallest
particle of grain beneath the most delicate paint-work".[165] This timber may well
have been a relatively late introduction to carriage building. In the eighteenth
century mahogany was probably the most typical support for elaborately painted
coach panels, Adams certainly devotes much attention to the two main types
of mahogany. In describing the characteristics of these he notes the presence
of "pores [which] will be found filled with a white powder, which destroys a
cutting edge". Although specks of this white chalk-like material is present in
Cuban mahogany, it is a great exaggeration to suggest that it blunts edged tools.
It could however have disrupted painted decoration which is one of the reasons
why it was not used for coach panels.[166] Another explanation was probably the
exceptional weight of Cuban mahogany which was therefore best excluded
from a wheeled vehicle. It may have been for reasons such as these that "for
these purposes the Honduras wood is admirably adapted; as it can be procured,
if required, upwards of four feet in width and perfectly straight-grained and
free from knots and blemishes". So important were mahogany panels in this
context that the carriage painters may have introduced the notion of these
supports to the easel painting fraternity. Down to the seventeenth century panel
painting in Northern Europe was generally carried out on quarter-sawn oak.
In Georgian England painting on canvas became more significant but where
a panel was used it was, more often than not, of mahogany.

In view of the care taken in building coaches, and the scrupulous attention
to the details of their painted surfaces, they were handled with great care on
the road as in the carriage house. This was emphasised by William Adams
(1837): "The materials of a carriage are delicate and require as much care as
the furniture in a drawing room; and therefore they should be as carefully
preserved from the stable [as was practical]";[167] a curious, if understandable,
injunction for vehicles that were dependent upon horse power.

According to a *Book of English Trades* (1818) a coachbuilder's employees
were paid "in proportion to the nicety of the work". This hierarchy resulted
in "body makers" receiving £2 or £3 a week and "trimmers", the upholders
of the carriage building business, "about two guineas". For painters in such
a manufactory a separate scale of remuneration seems to have applied. Here

the herald painters, who embellished the vehicles with coats of arms and other devices, were paid between £3 and £4 per week and for special jobs considerably more. Line painters were paid about £2 as were body painters – their journeymen between 20 and 30 shillings.[168] Furthermore, work of this kind was not confined to carriages for Sedan chairs were similarly decorated to the extent that they became "walking picture galleries, the panels being painted with all sorts of subjects".[169] The pay scales outlined above go some way to explaining why the Painter Stainers of London fought the College of Heralds so tenaciously for the right to paint heraldry (see p. 137 above).

Aside from the large capitalist enterprises smaller establishments could be so dependent on out-workers ("piece-masters" as they were known) that some so-called carriage builders were little more than "retail shop-keeper[s]". In such circumstances the ostensible "carriage-builder" did not possess "a control over his tradesmen" and was therefore unable to ensure "the quality of the work [because] no control is so effectual as that of paying them ready money". Many of these "piece-masters" remained in a state of perpetual "thraldom" from which it was "difficult for a man to free himself". Despite the extensive elements of "drudgery" involved in the construction of carriages the trade remained, in the 1830s "aloof from the innovations of steam" power used for the mechanisation of workshops. For this reason it was believed that carriage building remained: "to a certain extent, an art, like that of statuary".[170]

If a carriage, as an entity, could be seen as a work of art what was the relationship of these objects to those who purchased or commissioned them – the patrons? In 1756 Stephen Fox (Lord Ilchester) acquired from Budworth the London coachmaker a "double chaise" with a pair of "bellows roofs" – an early and therefore somewhat clumsy description of what was probably a landau with a pair of calash hoods. Externally the vehicle was given a "light ground colour [with] arms and crests in the panels [and] very handsome shields adorned with eagles and palm branches heightened with gold". This new vehicle cost £85-8s which included £8 "for the search in the Herald's Office" to ensure the accuracy of these achievements and their constituent parts like crests (see p. 136 above). This demonstrates that the College of Heralds in London was maintaining its authority over such matters and gaining an income from their research in the process. Seventeen years later the Earl of Ilchester (as he was by then) acquired a new four-wheeled post chaise for £90 the body of which was painted with "mosaic shells and cyphers in flowers, and coronets heightened with gold". It seems from this that, by then, the decline in the use of armorial bearings had begun. Nevertheless the newly created Earl insisted on the coronets if not on a full coat of arms. The repair and repainting of

DUKE

EARL

LORDS

MARQUIS

FIGURE 70. Four coronets (signifying the four degrees of the peerage) – such as would be painted on carriages. These designs appear in the sketchbook by a probable member of the Harp Alley school of sign painters – many of whom would have also worked as carriage painters. The association between heraldic and coach painting is confirmed by an edition of *The English Peerage* (1790) which was illustrated by Charles Catton (National Art Library London 44.F.17–19). (Ex. collection: Kenneth Clarke)

an existing vehicle can offer some insight into the cost of such work. In 1771 Lord Digby of Sherborne Castle paid £10-10s for "painting and gilding a Town chariot" the guineas denoting the professional status of such a commission. In 1792 Thomas Talbot, a kinsman of Lord Ilchester's, paid 50 guineas for a "socialette", a vehicle which was supplied by Thomas Garland of Monmouth Street, Bath where Spackman's workshops were also located.[171] This was clearly the centre of the coachmaking trade in the Spa and, even today, a specialist paint retailer may be found there.

So expensive could coaches be that it was apparently no shame to purchase a reconditioned vehicle. The care and maintenance of carriages was an important aspect of the trade. Sir Joshua Reynolds's coach was "an old chariot of a Sheriff of London newly done up". Northcote described it as "particularly splendid, the wheels were partly carved and gilt; and on the pannels were painted the four seasons of the year, very well executed by Charles Catton RA, the most eminent coach-painter of his day".[172] This was by no means the only example on record of an old vehicle being rehabilitated. Thomas Talbot purchased an old coach in January 1794 which was to be repainted in a colour chosen by his fiancée. For this Mary Strangeways selected a dark green ground which she believed to be "one of the prettyest colours under the sun, in the rainbow, on earth, etc., etc.".[173] As a general rule the prices for post chaises at this time ranged from £93 to £108. An elaborately decorated coach, embellished with family crests, would cost in the region of £189 which demonstrates the high value attached to such painted work, which could account for almost half the cost of the vehicle.[174]

At the opposite end of the scale to such revamped second hand vehicles were the great state coaches that were statements of power as much as a means of transport. Truly enormous sums of money were expended on these emblems of prestige which were decorated accordingly. The architect Sir William Chambers designed George III's great state coach but its sculptural elements were contrived by Wilton and its painted decoration the work of Cipriani.[175] In this way no less than three of the founder members of the Royal Academy were involved in this commission. Exceptional though this coach was it was not an isolated example of conspicuous consumption by the state. Private individuals at home and abroad could also become caught up in excessive expenditure of this kind. In these circumstances it was probably inevitable that Howard of Wardour Street, London, who "made coaches for members of the French aristocracy" was bankrupted as a direct consequence of the Revolution of 1789.[176]

In that very year Lord (John) Fitzgibbon of Dublin ordered a state coach from Godsals of London rather than awarding the contract, more diplomatically, to the trade in Ireland's "fair city". Perhaps in mitigation this London-made coach was decorated with shamrocks and harps. The painted embellishment was undertaken by Charles Ackroyd whom Philip Godsal (1747–1826) believed to be the best coach painter in practice in 1789 – the year of Catton's death. Even so the coach was also adorned with panels illustrating allegorical figures painted by William Hamilton RA (1751–1801) at a cost of 500 guineas. The carved wood decoration was supervised by the sculptor Richard Westmacot Snr (1746/7–1798) whose studio also superintended the production of the ormolu mounts. This ensemble, which was designed by Ackerman, was said to have cost £7,000. So important was this commission that Godsal exhibited the completed work in his Long Acre manufactory in 1790 prior to its being shipped to Dublin. In November of that year it made its first ceremonial appearance in the Irish capital.[177] This splendid if cumbersome conveyance evidently produced the desired effect in London if not in Dublin. When ordered the client was Baron Fitzgibbon, by the time it was delivered he was Lord Chancellor of Ireland with further honours to come.[178]

The improvement of the road system in England saw an increase in the number of carriages. By 1787 there were some 16,000 four and two-wheeled vehicles paying duty.[179] In addition to the heavy public stage coaches, and the state coaches of the ruling elite, lighter weight vehicles, drawn by fewer horses, were appearing. These included the half-landau, chariot, socialette and the "sporty" curricles. With better roads these lightweight vehicles evolved into spare designs with an almost anorexic elegance that left less room for decoration. A form of Georgian minimalism had evolved which was often complemented by startling colour schemes.

* * * *

As outlined above, the rise of the large capitalist coach builders, and the simultaneous decline in painted decoration, caused some of these herald painters to seek alternative employment. This situation may have accelerated the drift to easel painting following the example of Charles Catton, John Baker and others. An alternative was to emigrate to North America where smaller independent carriage builders continued to thrive. One such migrant was Charles Catton Jnr (1756–1819) who arrived in New York in 1804 – although by this date he had abandoned his father's trade as a carriage painter.[180] Another such individual was Thomas Barrow. Having begun his working life as a coach painter in England he moved to New York sometime before 1792 where he was to practice as an easel painter and as a print dealer. During his residence on Manhattan he was respected as "a gentleman of cultivated taste in the arts".[181]

Following the opening of the Royal Academy Schools in 1769 an increasing number of aspiring artists were to attend such establishments in preference to being placed in servitude to a relevant craft. By contrast more informal apprenticeships persisted in North America although the foundation of the Pennsylvania Academy in Philadelphia in 1805 was to result in a decline in craft training in the visual arts comparable to that which had been seen in Britain decades before. Nevertheless large numbers of American easel painters owed their initial training to the coach-painting trade. Among these were Bass Otis (1784–1861), Willliam Jewett (1789/90–1874), John Neagle (1796–1865) and George Washington Tyler (1803–1833).[182] Of these John Neagle was apprenticed for five years and five months to "Thomas Wilson a coach and ornamental painter". During Neagle's apprenticeship his master began to study easel painting with the former coach-painter Bass Otis. Wilson encouraged Neagle to become a portrait painter in which field one of his finest works is his image of the blacksmith *Pat Lyon at his Forge* (1826–1827). This particular canvas has an empathy born of the trade origins that the artist shared with his subject.

One of the few American artists to experience a craft training comparable to that which had once been typical in Britain was the short-lived George Washington Tyler who "at the age of fourteen was put apprentice to a coach-painter". Formal training of this kind was not always available in Colonial and Early Federal America. The experience of James Frothingham (1786–1864), who later became a prominent Massachusetts portrait painter, was more typical. His father was a builder of chaise bodies and young Frothingham inevitable joined the family business – in his case as a painter. As a craft coach painting:

> "was at the time, one of the mysteries only imparted by masters to their apprentices under the seal of secrecy, and the youth had to devise means by which to compel the colours to adhere to the wood, and make one layer of paint keep its place over another ... He had found that coach-painters had secrets, which could only be obtained by a long service as an apprentice".[183]

At a slightly later date, William Jewett (1789/90–1874) "was placed with a relative who was a coach maker in New London ... and there, for more than two years, his employment was preparing and assisting in colouring carriages". Jewett was then invited by the portrait painter Samuel Waldo (1783–1861) to work in his New York studio. However although Jewett was not formally bound, his master was reluctant to release him. Eventually Jewett received his freedom on the basis of a promissory note in which the young painter agreed to reimburse his master, for the lost years of apprenticeship, at some point in the future. Some years later, as a successful portrait painter, Jewett was able to meet this ostensibly unreasonable obligation.[184]

Men such as Otis, Neagle or Jewett were trade painters who emerged to establish reputations at a "polite" level, artists who would be fully recognised as such in *The Rise and Progress of the Arts of Design in the United States* (1834) by the American painter William Dunlap (1766–1839). Despite the faint prejudice that one encounters in this three volume work, Dunlap's first teacher of painting was Abraham Delanoy (1742–1795) of New York whose "occupation, at this time, was sign painting".[185]

For others it was possible to remain loyal to the values and craft traditions of their origins. Of these one of the most remarkable was the carriage painter Edward Hicks (1780–1849) of Pennsylvania. This loyalty to his "art and mystery" was the cause of a serious crisis of conscience due to his tenets as a convinced Quaker.[186] His autobiography (1851) certainly indicates the difficulties that he encountered in reconciling what he saw as his trivial pursuit of easel painting with his spiritual convictions. As a carriage and ornamental painter Hicks was able to deploy many of the skills of his trade in his pictorial works – lettering for example. Perhaps too, his Quakerism was the inhibiting factor that encouraged him to base most of his easel paintings on existing engravings.[187] The mystery of his art is that despite these very direct quotations from other sources his work achieves great originality.

The situation of carriage building in England by the 1830s is reflected in William Adam's *English Pleasure Carriages* (1837). Adams (1797–1872) lived through an age of great change in terms of transport. This is demonstrated by the four sources of energy that he lists: Animal, Wind, Water and Steam Power.[188] Consequently he includes in his book a whole section on the painting of carriages for steam trains. On both sides of the Atlantic the tradition for coach painting continued and overlapped not only with the age of steam, but also the emergence of the internal combustion engine. Nevertheless two later books, both published in North America are *The Coach Makers' Illustrated Hand-Book* (no author given, 2nd edition 1875) and Hillick's *Practical Carriages & Wagon Painting* (1898). These two highly technical volumes draw on long established experience with regard to paints, varnishes and the care and maintenance of brushes.[189] Like Adam's *Pleasure Carriages* (1837) the *Hand-Book* (1875, p. 366) emphasises the importance of a *"dry, clean carriage-house, entirely separated from the stable or stable manure ..."*

Of even greater significance in relationship to the visual arts is chapter xiv in Adam's book which is devoted to questions of aesthetics in relationship to the carriage building trade. His opening sentence in this chapter reads as follows: "There is a notion prevalent amongst uninstructed people that the quality called 'Taste' is a peculiar 'gift' which an individual is endowed with at birth, and which cannot be acquired by any amount of application".[190]

The whole burden of Adam's narrative demonstrates that some trades, or aspects within them, enabled a few practitioners to develop a visual "taste".

Marine painting

The arts of the seafarer in the West were, to some extent, independent of the cultural attitudes of their home ports. They were therefore partially free of nationally-based academic convention and regional vernacular tradition. On the other hand contact was maintained with received opinion through the "top brass" of the Royal Navy and via ship builders and ship owners. In addition, craft values remained persistent in the shipyards. With regard to painting the vernacular tradition was maintained in most ports where these tradesmen's work on houses was inextricably linked with the painting of ships and ship painting. This feature was reflected in chandlers stores across the globe, emporia that were not confined to the maintenance of ships but also offered supplies for their decoration. Joseph Conrad describes just such a store in the Far East "where you can get everything to make her [a ship] seaworthy and beautiful, from a set of chain-hooks for her cable, to a book of gold-leaf for the carvings of her stern".[191]

For the age of sail beauty was evidently considered to be almost as important as seaworthiness. In this respect William Sutherland's *The Ship-Builders Assistant* (1771) includes an important chapter under the title "Of Beauty". Rather remarkably he argues that: "This branch teaches to deck or adorn a Ship or Such like Machine, with the symmetry of the Parts, as to render it agreeable to every spectator" provided that "The Beautifying may be no Detriment to the other good Properties". This strong aesthetic sense among mariners was not always balanced by such practical concerns to the extent that the British Admiralty was compelled to place a limit on the expenditure on adornments with regards to Royal Naval vessels. These measures were first imposed in 1703 but by 1796 it became necessary to reassert them.[192] This was to have an effect on the quantity of wood carving but painted and gilded decoration persisted. Much of this work was done by outside contractors and this resulted in some exchange between the traditions of the Royal and Merchant Navies. Nevertheless with the decline in carved decoration there was a corresponding reduction in the painting of ships which may have caused an increase in ship portraiture. As a consequence whole schools of "pierhead painters" emerged who worked within a vernacular tradition. One such was Messrs. "Bowen and Fuss, Painters and Glaziers in General [of] 29 Artichoke Lane, near Sampson's Gardens, Wapping" East of London whose trade card of *c.* 1800 concludes "N B Ship's Likeness's taken".[193]

On taking a portrait of a vessel these dockyard painters understood both the anatomy of their subjects and also the properties of the paints and varnishes they used. Not that they were necessarily confined to oil paint since watercolour and gouache were also used to create such images. Christopher Thomson (1847) recalled a fugitive seaman-artist who hid in his family home in Hull in *c.* 1810. This man had been "flogged through the fleet" so that the back of his torso was "all cicatriced and many coloured." During his stay with the Thomson family:

FIGURE 71. William Morrison *A Beam View of His Majesty's Frigate Hussar, 44 Guns, Lost on the Saint Rocks, Feby the 8th 1804*, watercolour on paper (22 × 27 in/53 × 65 cm). For work of this kind one such marine artist was described as using a "sailor-like composition – a solution of tobacco water". (Collection of John Gall and Rosy Allan)

> "his favourite amusement was the drawing of ships; in which he used to give me lessons, describing the masts and the various ropes, and explaining to me their uses; he also prided himself upon a rare colour for the tinting of ships' sails – it was a sailor-like composition – a solution of tobacco water; this with Indian ink, gamboge and vermilion constituted his palette for ship painting".[194]

Outside the seventeenth century Dutch tradition for ship portraiture it seems likely that many of the English painters who specialised in marine subjects began their careers as apprentices in the dockyards or at sea. There were important exceptions. Peter or Pierre Monamy (*c.* 1682–1774), though born in the Channel Islands, was apprenticed on 3 September 1696, to William Clarke a house painter with workshops on London Bridge. In his native Jersey ship-building was an important trade whilst from Monamy's eyrie on London

Bridge he would have been able to observe all manner of ships. As Horace Walpole was to remark in his inimitable fashion "the shallow waters which rolled under his window taught him what his Master could not, fitted him to imitate the turbulence of the ocean".[195] Not that Monamy was confined to painting the sea and ships for he also painted portraits. He is known to have decorated a carriage for the doomed Admiral Byng and painted a portrait of Admiral Vernon's ship as a sign for the Porto Bello, a public house in St Martin's Lane, Westminster.[196] In 1726, some 35 years after Monamy would have completed his apprenticeship, he was admitted to the livery of the Painter Stainers Company of London "in consideration of his presentation of a valuable sea piece of his own painting".[197] In some ways this may be seen as an extension of the whole notion of a proof piece or master piece (in the original sense of the word).

In addition to London other major ports were centres for ship painting. On the west coast of England the Atlantic trade was dominated by Bristol and Liverpool. On the east coast, in the North Sea port of Kingston upon Hull, the Fletcher family were dominant in the eighteenth century as shipwrights, carvers and painters. Christopher Fletcher, the probable founder of this dynasty, was a Hessle shipbuilder and his son John Fletcher was apprenticed to the Hull carver and compass maker John Campsall.[198] John Fletcher advertised himself as a painter, but from his shop on the High Street in Hull, his trade card of *c.* 1730–40 shows that he sold "all sorts of Oil & Colours ... Prepared" together with other "Shipchandlery Ware", (Fig. 72). John Fletcher's son Thomas was admitted as a freeman of Hull on 30 April 1747 having successfully completed his apprenticeship with his father. In his turn Thomas was to be the head of a whole line of Hull-based marine painters including Thomas II (b. 1759), Rouncival (b. 1764), John II (bapt. 1767) and, in the next generation Rouncival Fletcher II. By 1834 a Miss Fletcher was advertising drawing lessons at No 3 New Dock Wall, Hull.[199] This demonstrates that a single family, over several generations, could establish a whole school of painting spanning a century or more. Via their apprentices their reach could be even greater. From 1772 to 1777 Julius Caesar Ibbetson (1759–1817) was apprenticed to Thomas Fletcher. This involved working:

> "from daylight [daybreak] to night [painting] the inside and outside [of] ships in the port of that town [Hull]. His remonstrances against this were ridiculed by his master and he could only practice drawing and other painting at stolen hours. He did, notwithstanding, so far advance in the art as to paint several signs which were much admired".[200]

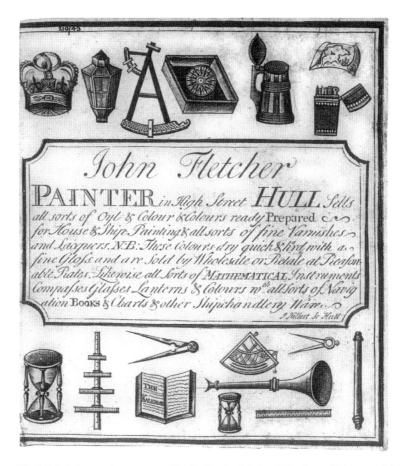

FIGURE 72. Mid-eighteenth century *Trade Card* of John Fletcher, Painter of Hull. In addition to being a practicing painter and supplier of paints Fletcher retailed all manner of "Shipchandlery". (Castle Museum, York)

Ibbetson also undertook scene painting for the theatre and, on moving to London worked as a picture cleaner before becoming a recognised landscape painter. One curiosity, noted above, is that John Fletcher Snr was apprenticed to the Hull carver and ships' compass maker John Campsall before establishing himself as a painter and ship's chandler. This rather strange combination of trades may have been unusual but it was not exceptional. No less a figure than the American "scholar and gentleman", the artist Washington Allston (1779–1843) received some "instruction from a very worthy and amiable man, a Mr King of Newport [Rhode Island] who made quadrants and compasses, and occasionally painted portraits". Yet another example is Ephraim Byram

(1809–1881) of Sag Harbor, New York; whose many skills included clock and globe making as well as portraiture.[201]

In writing about the Hull ship painters Arthur Credland has noted that "the skills of all native marine painters of this period were generally based on apprenticeship with a house or ship painter, the two trades often being combined" in port cities and towns. Another example of this type of individual was the Hull-based Robert Willoughby (1768–1843) who advertised himself as a "House, Ship and Sign Painter" who also produced marine paintings in a seamanlike manner.[202] Although some of his canvasses demonstrate a somewhat conventionalised sophistication he evidently had trouble representing the human figure. At least one of his paintings carries the inscription "Figures by Brookes". This was probably Thomas Brookes (c. 1780–1850) a house and ship-carver who also worked as a gilder, mirror and picture frame maker. As a carver Brooks must have had a trade training, probably in the shipyards but, as a figure painter, he is known to have received some instruction from Henry Perronet Briggs RA (1791–1844).

Although the Fletchers dominated trade painting in Hull in the eighteenth century they were to be eclipsed from c. 1799 to 1860 by the Meggitts. Their trade card lists the extraordinarily wide range of work that they undertook. From their headquarters in George Yard, Hull they offered their skills as decorative painters, japanners and gilders and many other services like "Room Floors Chalked for Balls, etc".[203] From such utilitarian, even prosaic, origins easel painters continued to emerge. The artist John Ward (1798–1849), as the son of a master mariner, was apprenticed to the Meggitts. He also had direct experience of the sea, in his youth sailing to the Arctic on a Hull whaler.[204] Through both training and experience many of the best marine artists painted what they knew.

The Port of London, despite its importance, and the presence of naval ship-building yards at Deptford, does not seem to have inspired many pierhead painters at this time – particularly when compared with Hull and Liverpool between c. 1780–1840. Nevertheless in earlier generations marine painters like Monamy were largely centred on London. The artist Charles Brooking (1723–1759) is known to have "been bred in some department in the Dockyard at Deptford but [later] practiced as a ship painter in which he certainly excelled all his countrymen". Many of his canvases were sold by an unscrupulous dealer in Castle Street, Leicester Square, London, who removed Brooking's signature from his works.[205]

A contemporary of Brooking's in Deptford was John Cleveley Snr (c. 1712–1777). He is a classic case of a tradesman turned artist. His father was a joiner

FIGURE 73. Robert Willoughby (*c.* 1768–1843), *William Westerdale's House*, *c.* 1816, Oil on Canvas (24 × 32½ in / 61 × 87.6 cm) – the artist consistently used canvases measuring 24 × 36 in. Willoughby practiced as a house, ship and sign painter in the High Street, Hull before moving, in 1807, to Savile Street close to Westerdale's mast, block and pump making yard. From that address Willoughby seems to have worked primarily as an easel painter for Westerdale who was his chief patron. (Ferens Art Gallery, Hull)

of the north London suburb of Newington Butts but had died by the time his son was apprenticed on 3 November 1726 to Thomas Miller, also a joiner. Later young Cleveley was turned over to John Hall, a shipwright of Deptford south of the River Thames, eventually being made free of the Shipwrights Company of London on 9 June 1743. From 1747, if not before, he lived at Kings Yard Row, Dogg Street, Deptford, although many, if not all these houses were redeveloped in 1770–1772.[206] John Cleveley Snr was to specialise in paintings which can be seen as thoroughly autobiographical – they illustrate ship building and launching. Of his sons, who were all born at Deptford, John Cleveley Jnr (1747–1786) was to become best known. It was he who joined an expedition to Iceland in 1772 as the official artist. Nevertheless Clevely Jnr like his father, began work in the shipyards, in his case as a caulker. This was a very highly paid job which, by 1795, attracted pay of "20 shillings a day" (£1). Despite this level of remuneration Cleveley abandoned the trade because his fellow workers laughed at him for wearing gloves. He promptly turned to his father's vocation becoming, in due course, "marine painter" to the Prince of Wales.[207] Young Cleveley had, presumably, received instruction in oil painting from his father and it is known that Paul Sandby (1725–1809) introduced him to watercolour. John Jnr's twin brother Robert Cleveley (1725–1809) was also an easel painter. The third brother James, a ship's carpenter by trade, was not wholly devoid of artistic talent. It was he who sailed with Capt. James Cook on his third and final voyage (1776–1780) aboard the *Resolution* and returned with sketches which his brother John worked-up as pictures.[208]

Others who worked in this way include the Bristol born Nicholas Pocock (1740–1821) who was to captain merchant vessels before settling in London as a marine painter in 1789. Similarly Thomas Luny (1759–1837), though born in the capital, served in the navy before his training with the Cornish-born Thames-side shipping painter Francis Holman (active 1760–1790) who lived and worked at Shadwell and Wapping. In effect whole flotillas of such artists had developed an eye for the sea and ships via practical experience – a tradition that extended from the eighteenth to the twentieth centuries. In addition to those touched on above mention should be made of the Scottish artist William Anderson (1757–1837) who first trained as a shipwright. Others who served before the mast included men such as Samuel Atkins (exhibited 1787–1808), James Carmichael (1800–1868), George Chambers (1803–1840), William Huggins (1781–1845) and Charles Raleigh (1831–1925).[209]

The first decades of the nineteenth century seem to have been particularly rich in marine painting, not only in Hull but elsewhere. In this respect the seaman-like qualities of the Newcastle-born John Wilson Carmichael (1800–1868) are typical of the *genre*. He was the son of a ship's carpenter, was apprenticed to a ship-builder and may have gone to sea. Appropriately, examples of Carmichael's work adorn the walls of Trinity House, Newcastle. From the north-east coast of England trade across the North Sea is exemplified by the work of the Danish marine artist Jacob Petersen (1774–1855) whose ship portraits include vessels built in Sunderland just a few miles to the south of Newcastle.[210]

Like Hull, Newcastle and Sunderland east coast Scottish ports such as Aberdeen and Leith were also heavily involved in the North Sea trade. In these ports painters like Arthur Smith (fl. 1830–1860) and B. M. Dowinar (fl. 1850–1880) continued this vernacular tradition for taking ships' likenesses well into the Victorian age.[211] Similarly the Scottish Atlantic trade, especially for Virginia tobacco, was met in Glasgow and also in Greenock further down-stream in the deeper waters of the Clyde. It was in Greenock that William Clark (1803–1883) spent his entire working life. As with so many artists of this kind Clark was the son of a seaman but apprenticed to a house painter before becoming a marine artist.[212]

In England, merchants based in Bristol and Liverpool dominated commerce across the Atlantic. Curiously Bristol, despite its importance in the "triangular trade", fostered relatively few pierhead painters. Of those that did emerge there Joseph Walters (1783–1856) was the most important. A native of Bristol he spent his entire working life in the city where other members of the family practiced as house and decorative painters. A Thomas Walters (Fig. 84 below) is listed in the *Trade Directories* at various addresses as a "Sign & Furniture Painter" from 1819 to 1847.[213] A ship portrait dated 1827 and signed "Walters", is presumably by Thomas (Bristol City Art Gallery). This portrays *The William Miles of Bristol* which raises the possibility that there may have been some relationship between the Walters of Bristol and Miles Walters (1774–*c.* 1849) of Liverpool. The latter had been apprenticed to a shipwright in his native Ilfracombe, Devon and later became the master of a coasting vessel. In 1805 he was living in London before settling in Liverpool in 1811. There he started a framing and gilding business and also produced ship portraits. His son Samuel Walters (1811–1882) was born on a coaster sailing between Bideford, Devon and London and was to work with his father as a ship portraitist. Other Liverpudlian artists of this kind appeared at a fairly early date. Richard Wright (1723–1775) "practiced as a painter of sea pieces and acquired his art by his own industry having been bred to the humble department of a house and ship painter, [He] was of rough manners and warm temper".[214] Another such Liverpool tradesman in this *milieu* was Joseph Desilva (1816–1875) a "Painter, Plumber & Glazier" who undertook "Portraits of Ships taken in any situation – Specimens always in hand".[215]

Of the trade training that did so much to inform the work of these painters mention should be made of the mould lofts. This was where the full size setting-out for ships's timbers was done, comparable to the tracing floors of the mason (which were also located on upper floors).[216] It was in those setting-out workshops that the final design work was resolved – as relevant a training for marine painters as the mason's tracing floor was for those who later became, in effect, architects. Samuel Walters is known to have worked in the mould-lofts of Liverpool and in Hull Christopher Thomson was similarly employed before becoming an itinerant house painter.[217]

In this context Philip John Ouless (1817–1885), a native of Jersey, Channel Islands, is something of an enigma. Despite some academic training in Paris his work remained within the vernacular idiom of the pierhead painters. Moreover, because of the island's long established links with Canada, many of his subjects are set in that Dominion giving him a trans-Atlantic place in art history.[218]

* * * *

A parallel tradition developed in North America, one that was regularly reinforced, especially in the nineteenth century, by emigrants from other European countries. Of these one of the finest was Michele-Felice Cornè (1762–1832) who was born on Elba and arrived in Salem in 1799. His work is rather too sophisticated to be seen as part of the tradition for pierhead painting although shipping scenes were part of his *ouvre*. Later emigrant Continental ship portraitists maintained the artisan tradition into the early twentieth century. These included the Dane; Antonio Nicola Gasparo Jacobsen (1850–1921) and the German-born Fred Pansing (1844–1926).[219]

Of the English-born marine painters one of the first to move to America was Robert Salmon (1775–*c*. 1844). He was born in Whithaven, Cumbria and, after travelling and working in various parts of Britain lived and practiced his craft in Boston between 1829 and 1840 returning to Europe in 1842. A similar trajectory was followed by the Yorkshireman Thomas Chambers (1808–1869) who moved to the USA in *c*. 1832 but ended his days back in England.[220] Chambers was born in the small port of Whitby which serviced the colliers that sailed between Newcastle and London. Leaving school for work at the age of eight, he was, by his tenth year at sea on an uncle's timber trading vessel. He presumably had completed his apprenticeship as a mariner by the time he found work at the age of eighteen with a Whitby house and ship painter. As with so many of these artists the training was, in effect, both at sea and on land – an amphibious art.[221]

Most individuals whose art began in the shipbuilding yards remained locked within the artisan tradition, but this was not true of all such painters. Henry Sargent (1770–1845) was born in Gloucester, Massachusetts, the son of a wealthy merchant whose home was graced with canvases by Smibert and Copley. Despite such a background and a Classical education at "the celebrated Dummer Academy" it was the sight of "a house and ship painter … employed to decorate one of his father's ships" that determined the direction of his career. Eventually Sargent moved to London for four years where he fell under the spell of Benjamin West's "American School" (see Fig. 39).[222] More typical was Clement Drew (1806–1889) who was born in Kingston, Massachusetts. He worked in Boston and later in Gloucester where he gained a reputation as a carver of ship's figureheads. Wood carving is such an extraordinarily difficult and specialist craft that he must have been apprenticed to that trade, perhaps in Boston, before becoming a marine painter.[223]

Of all these American artisan artists the most distinctive, and for whom there is no British equivalent, are the Bards, twin brothers who specialised in representations of the Hudson River boats in the early days of steam. Perhaps the riverine setting, so different to the marine subjects of the pierhead painters, accounts for the originality of much of their work – although they also produced some portraits of seagoing vessels. From their base on Manhattan James Bard (1815–1897) and John Bard (1815–1856) worked together creating what are, in effect, architectural drawings, elevations of steam powered boats shown in a naturalistic setting.[224] The port of New York was, like Liverpool, an attractive location for pierhead painters. It has been estimated that between 1798 and 1920 no less than "seventeen major maritime artists [were] plying their trade in New York" including Jacobsen, Buttersworth, Pansing, Cozzens and Samuel Ward Stanton.[225] Among these James Edward Buttersworth (1817–1894) might be singled out. His father Thomas Buttersworth (1768–1842) was born on the Isle of Wight and, after a career in the Royal Navy became a marine artist of some distinction exhibiting at the Royal Academy. His son James trained with him before emigrating to America in 1845 settling at West Hoboken near New York City.[226]

* * * *

For the most part ship portraiture was far from being an art for art's sake it was therefore quite unlike "fine art" with its "patrons". On the contrary most of the "customers" for this type of work were ship owners or seamen with a knowledge of ships and a corresponding desire for accurate representations. It is known that those who purchased pictures from the Bard brothers were almost exclusively ship builders or owners. To provide for this demand those who had been trained in the shipyards were best qualified to meet these expectations for portraits of ships – canvases which demonstrated an understanding of the anatomy of these vessels. If, in addition, such artisan artists had also sailed before the mast so much the better.

Fidelity to their subject matter was the primary concern of marine painters and those who purchased their work. The tenets of "production" and "reception" coincided. In common with other pictures of record, like botanical illustration, the artists who made them were emancipated from the obligation to produce "Art" or the expectation to be "original". As a consequence some of the works created by painters of this kind, may have great aesthetic value. The emphasis on verisimilitude is characterised by the canvases of Robert Woodcock (c. 1691–1728). He was described by Horace Walpole as being "Of a gentleman's family [and] became a painter by genius and inclination". He specialised in "sea pieces" which were greatly influenced by the work of the Van de Veldes, father and son. Significantly he "studied the technical part of

ships with so much attention that he could cut out a ship, with all the masts
and rigging to the utmost exactness".[227] Such an approach to taking ships'
likenesses persisted, like animal portraiture, into the early twentieth century
simply because photography was unable to compete. This is explained by the
slow film and shutter speeds used in cameras down to this time – a moving
target was beyond the capabilities of the available photographic equipment.

Notes

[1] Tressell was the pseudonym of the Hastings-based house painter Robert Noonan
(*c.* 1870–1911). See Workers Educational Association (WEA) publication *Robert Tressell
Papers*, Rochester, Kent, 1982, pp. 25–27; also Robert Tressell (1914) 1993

[2] Michael Bath 2003, pp. 2, 4, 10; The most comprehensive overview of this theme is
Edward Croft-Murray's two volume work of 1962; Alan Borg 2005, p. 103

[3] R. Campbell 1747, p. 102. Farr & Pike trade label in the British Museum Dept of P&D.
90.40

[4] R. Campbell 1747, p. 105, p. 101

[5] *The Norwich Gazette* 10 June 1738 cited by John Harris 1979, p. 307

[6] Michael Edkins manuscript Day-books 1771–1784, Bristol Central Library B20196

[7] Thomas Hardy *Far from the Madding Crowd* (1874), chapter 15

[8] Arthur G. Credland 1993, pp. 8, 31

[9] A. S. Davidson 1986 and Roger Finch 1983

[10] Abraham Rees, *Encyclopaedia*, 1786, see Painting

[11] Simeon Bullen's *Exercise book* 1813, manuscript in author's collection

[12] Isaac Ware 1756 cited by James Ayres 1998, p. 212; Alan Borg 2005, p. 123

[13] Davies' trade label: British Museum Dept of P&D: 90.35, Gervase Jackson-Stops "Harewood
Rehung", *Country Life* 26 July 1990, citing a guidebook of 1822; J. C. Loudon 1836,
p. 277; Kershaw's sample boards are on loan to the Victoria & Albert Museum from
Bolton College of Art & Design

[14] Peter Thornton (1978) 1979, p. 298. This work was probably supervised by Inigo Jones
who is known to have worked with de Critz on other royal commissions

[15] For example a panel of *c.* 1530–1540 painted to resemble carved linen-fold – James
Ayres 2003, fig. 82

[16] Howard Colvin ed. 1975, p. 411

[17] Examples illustrated by Karen Hearn 1995

[18] Ian Bristow 1996, p. 206

[19] Horace Walpole 1762, Vol. I, p. 58 – see also Howard Colvin ed 1975, p. 12

[20] Christopher Morris ed. of Celia Fiennes (diaries, 1685–1712) 1982, p. 47

[21] John Martin manuscript AL/41c: Sir John Soane Museum, London

[22] Edward Edwards 1808, pp. vii, viii

[23] *Ibid.*, p. ix; William Sandby 1862, p. 13

[24] Tabitha Barber 1999, 13; W. A. D. Englefield (1923) 1936, p. 113; Alan Borg 2005, p. 53

[25] Victoria & Albert Museum, London, M.70-1919. See also Horace Walpole 1786, Vol. IV,
p. 19

[26] Horace Walpole 1786, Vol. IV, pp. 19–20. Walpole also describes another artist of this kind named John Stephens (d. 1722)

[27] Nina Fletcher Little (1952) 1972, p. 17 citing the *South Carolina Gazette* 23 July 1737

[28] *Ibid.*, pp. 18, 42

[29] English examples illustrated in James Ayres 2003, pp. 32–35

[30] Nina Fletcher Little (1952) 1972, chapter v

[31] A number of works by the American vernacular painter Edward Hicks (1780–1849) were painted as chimney boards

[32] Joseph Moxon (1703)1994, pp. 307–352

[33] John Martin manuscript in the Sir John Soane Museum, London Ms. AL/41c, p. 135. For the Dispensary sign see Nina Fletcher Little 1976, Cat. 60. Johnson, who had been apprenticed in 1767 to the ornamental painter John Gore, based his design on a print after a detail in Hogarth's 1737 large canvas of this subject in St Bartholomew's Hospital, London; see Paulson 1992, Vol. II pp. 83–84; John Gooddy in Medvei and Thornton 1974, pp. 335–357

[34] William Salmon (1672) 1701, Vol. II, chapter 17

[35] Geoffrey Beard – Verrio arrived in England in *c.* 1672 and Laguerre in 1684. The line by Alexander Pope was cited by Horace Walpole 1786, Vol. IV, p. 6

[36] William Sandby 1862, p. 13

[37] Howard Colvin 1995; Jerry White 2012, p. 121

[38] John Gooddy (who wrongly gives Lambert's first name as "John") in Medvei and Thornton 1974, pp. 333–335. The scaffolding in the great stair was struck on 14 July 1737 – *Grub Street Journal*. In the same month the Board of the Hospital "Resolved that our thanks ... be given to William Hogarth Esq, one of the governers, for his generous and fine gift of the painting[s] on the great staircase, performed by his own skilful hand ..."; Jerry White 2012, p. 100.

[39] James Ayres 2003, pp. 157–159

[40] Edward Edwards 1808, Vol. I, p. 183

[41] The fashion began in Italy in the sixteenth century following the excavation in *c.* 1500 of the Domus Aurea of Nero. The French termed this style *Arabesques* and for Robert Adam it became the "Etruscan style". Peter Thornton 1984, pp. 140–141

[42] Michael Bath 2003, p. 109, citing Cotgrave's definition in his *Dictionarie of the French and English Tongues* (1611)

[43] Trevor Fawcett 1974, p. 17; quoting the *Norwich Mercury* 7 Oct 1815 – see also Josephine Walpole 1997, pp. 150–153 who makes reference to his role as a house painter

[44] Edward Edwards 1808, Vol. II, p. 7

[45] *Ibid.*, p. 31

[46] Iain McCallum 2003, pp. 8, 9, 10, 11, 12

[47] Edward Edwards 1808, Vol. I, p. 39. Shaw died in *c.* 1772

[48] *Ibid.*, p. 32

[49] Kurt Wehlte (1967) 1982, pp. 70, 91, 103, where reference to lead-based paints, etc may be found. This trio of lead tablets each measure some 2 ft 6 in by 4 ft (76 × 122 cm). The first in this series is dated 1704 and is signed "G.F.", presumably C. Farr's father. For cast lead plumber's signatures see Warwick Rodwell 2012, 223.

[50] A. S. Davidson 1986, p. 86 cites the plumber and glaziers Joseph Desilva (1816–*c.* 1875) of Liverpool

[51] For Dunthorne see Stephen Deauchur 1988, fig. 101 and for Bagshaw, James Ayres 1980, figs 111, 112

52 Jean Lipman (1968) 1980
53 William Dunlap (1834) 1969, Vol. II, Pt II, p. 356. For floor cloths see James Ayres 2003, pp. 98–100
54 Sumpter Priddy 2004, pp. 68–69
55 William Dunlap (1834) 1969, Vol. II, Pt I, pp. 260, 264
56 Edward Edwards 1808, p. 11
57 *Ibid.*, Vol. I, p. 76
58 Iain McCallum 2003, pp. 9, 10. For the "Skill of the Pontypool Japanners" see G. Bernard Hughes in *Country Life Annual* 1968. The factories for this work in the West Midlands were, in effect an off-shoot of the south Welsh enterprises at Pontypool and Usk
59 Allan Cunningham 1830, Vol. II, pp. 242–244. For further details on Bird see Trevor Fawcett 1974, pp. 67, 68 and p. 204n. For J. B. Crome see Josephine Walpole 1997, pp. 35–36
60 Anon; *A Concise History of Worcester* 1808, pp. 81–82. Shena Mason 2009, pp. 129 Cat. 37. The type founder William Caslon (1692–1766) was also born in Worcestershire – see Jerry White 2012, pp. 92–93
61 William Dunlap (1834) 1969, Vol. I, p. 340
62 W. H. Pyne 1823–24, Vol. II, p. 38
63 Martin Myrone "The Society of Antiquaries and the Graphic Arts: George Vertue and His Legacy" in Susan Pearce *Visions of Antiquity*, London 2007, p. 108; W. T. Whitley 1928, Vol. II, p. 219
64 William Williams 1787, pp. 10–11
65 "Paul Sandby and His Times", *The Library of Fine Arts* Vol. II, No. 11, 1831
66 Joseph Farrington p. 1553 25 May 1801
67 Jacob Larwood and John Camden Hotten 1866, p. 30
68 Christopher Morris ed. 1982, p. 193
69 Ned Ward *c.* 1700 – quoted by Peter Guillery *The Small House in Eighteenth Century London*, New Haven and London 2004, p. 194
70 Phillip Lindley 2007, p. 21
71 Francois Maximilian Misson (*c.* 1650–1722) quoted by Larwood and Hotten 1866, p. 26
72 Bodleian Library exhibition catalogue *A Nation of Shopkeepers*, Oxford, 2001, p. 1
73 Joseph Addison in *The Spectator* No. xxviii of Monday 2 April 1710/11 which states that "it is usual for a young tradesman at his first setting-up, to add his sign to that of the master he served; as a husband, after marriage, gives a place to his mistress's arms in his own coat"
74 Edward Edwards 1808, Vol. I, pp. 117–118
75 Jason M. Kelly 2009, p. 9 citing *Town & Country Magazine* No. lxxii, Sept 1778, p. 478
76 J. T. Smith (1828) 1949, John Bucker's sign costing £500
77 Joseph Addison *The Spectator* No. 744, 8 January 1743, citied by Larwood and Hotten 1866, pp. 37, 38, 39
78 Larwood and Hotten 1866, p. 26
79 *Ibid.*, p. 106
80 C. C. Knowles *The History of Building Regulation in London 1189–1972*, London, 1972, p. 33 on this measure London was following French precedent
81 Adrian Tinniswood *By Permission of Heaven: The Story of the Great Fire of London*, London 2003, p. 229; citing not only the Act for rebuilding but also the Order of Common Council 8 May 1667
82 Museum of London: for example one dated 1715 accession number: B664

[83] *Daily News* (November 1762) quoted by Larwood and Hotton 1866, p. 28. The Act regarding signs in Westminster 2 Geo III c 21. Puckeridge is listed in the *Directories* in 1790, 1793, 1802, 1809. According to his trade card (B.M. Dept of P&D 33.46) he made "all sorts of signs in Elm or Mahogany Plain or carved" as well as furnishing "all Manner of Carved work at reasonable rates". See also Ambrose Heal (1953) 1988, pp. 140, 146

[84] Trade label in British Museum, Dept of P&D

[85] Bodleian Library Catalogue 2001, pp. 6, 7. The goods and services included the painting, repair and repainting of floor cloths

[86] Salisbury & South Wiltshire Museum – the lettered verso of this sign is later being of early nineteenth century date

[87] The sketchbook was sold at auction in London in the 1990s and the individual pages have since been dispersed

[88] Peter Burke (1978) 1994, p. 28

[89] J. T. Smith (1828) 1949, p. 13

[90] Allan Cunningham 1830, Vol. V, p. 61

[91] Richard Wendorf 1996, pp. 66–67. The chequers were painted externally by the ale house door – probably to denote that credit was offered. This feature is recorded in topographical pictures as in Hogarth's engraving of *The Invasion* Plate 2 of 8 March 1756 (first state) – see Tate Britain, Catalogue 115, London, 2006

[92] Richard Wendorf 1996, p. 19

[93] In the collection of a descendant of the artist. The Harp Alley school sketchbook includes a similar design and *The Mermaid* was the sign of the Colourman: Owen Marlow – both illustrated by James Ayres 1985, p. 25

[94] The sign measures 22 × 22 in (56 × 56 cm). Although once double-sided the reverse is now only recorded by an engraving

[95] J. T. Smith (1828) 1919, Vol. II, pp. 145, 293. The Golden Head was a device often used by artists as their sign

[96] Both the drawing and the engraving of *Beer Street* are illustrated in James Ayres *British Folk Art*, Woodstock, 1976

[97] Hogarth's frame-makers included the Hugenot carver and gilder Isaac Gosset (1713–1799) – Gosset also worked as a wax modeller. Tessa Murdoch ed. 1985, p. 214; Jacob Simon 1996, pp. 88, 132

[98] Ronald Paulson 1979, p. 35

[99] Ronald Paulson ed. 1997, p.xxxvi

[100] William Sandby 1862, p. 15

[101] Larwood and Hotten 1868, pp. 512 and 521 quoting *The London Register* April 1762

[102] When Scheemakers' effects were sold by auction over two days in 1756 his sculptures were displayed "upon tables, stands and shelves covered in green baize", J. T. Smith (1828) 1919, Vol. II, p. 41

[103] In this respect it should be noted that Hogarth's father was something of a Latin scholar. *Ars Poetica* satarises animal assemblages like centaurs – see also Michael Bath 2003, p. 24

[104] Holger Hoock (2003) 2009, pp. 206–207

[105] Larwood and Hotten 1866, pp. 512–526 which quotes a number of these newspaper reviews and reprints the itemised catalogue

[106] W. T. Whitley 1928, Vol. I, p. 181

[107] Brigitte Mitchell and Hubert Penrose eds *Letters from Bath: 1766–1767 by the Rev. John Penrose*, Gloucester, (1983) 1990, p. 170

[108] William Dunlap (1864), 1969, Vol. II, Pt 2, p. 320

[109] Robert C. Alberts 1978, chapter ii

[110] William Dunlap (1834) 1969, Vol. I, pp. 98–103

[111] *Ibid.*, Vol. II, Pt 2, p. 408. The other brothers being Shepard Alonzo Mount (1804–1868) and the best known, William Sidney Mount (1807–1868)

[112] *Ibid.*, Vol. II, Pt 2, pp. 426–428. We are told nothing more about Alexander's work as an "ornamental painter"

[113] *Ibid.*, Vol. II, Pt 2, pp. 444–445

[114] *Ibid.*, Vol. II Pt 2, see Index

[115] Ibid., Vol. II, Pt 1, p. 75. In addition to "old Mr Pratt" Jarvis lists Jeremiah Paul (?–1820), Clark (a miniature painter) and Retter (another sign-painter) all of whom worked in Philadelphia

[116] *Ibid.*, Vol. II, Pt 1, p. 75 under Jarvis

[117] Joseph Moxon *Regulae Trium Ordinum Literarum Typographicarum: or the Rules of the Three Orders of Print Letters*, London, 1676. Despite its title this book was not primarily concerned with printing for that was the subject of a book that Moxon published seven years later. Cited by Carey S. Bliss 1965, p. 17; Ewan Clayton 2013, p. 191

[118] Edwards's trade card is in the British Mueum Dept of P&D, 90.38. Richard Godfrey; *James Gillray: The Art of Caricature* , London, 2001, p. 45

[119] For examples of lettered frames see James Ayres 1976, p. 367; also Carolyn J. Weekley *The Kingdoms of Edward Hicks*, New York, 1999, figs 86–97

[120] William Dunlap (1834) 1969, Vol. I, p. 417

[121] Charles Dickens (1842) n.d./*c.* 1910, p. 38

[122] Information from his son Arnold Wilson a former Director of Bristol City Art Gallery

[123] I am indebted to John Gall for some information on Southwell

[124] Autobiographical notes by Robert A. Wilson kindly lent to me by Arnold Wilson. For the first duty of an apprentice see Seamus Murphy (2005) 2010, p. 153

[125] These costs might today be comparable with owning and running a helicopter

[126] John Ford 2005, p. 24. The broad brushes of the body painters might be contrasted with the long-haired stripers of the liners

[127] J. Wilton-Ely *A Tercentenary tribute to William Kent*, Hull, 1985

[128] Jennifer Lang 1975, p. 11; for late sixteenth century coaches in England see Julian Munby "The Moscow Coach ..." in Olga Dmitrieva and Tessa Murdoch *Tudors, Stuarts & the Russian Tsars*, London, 2013

[129] Horace Walpole 1786, Vol. II, p. 210

[130] The coachpainter/artist cited by Walpole was Solimeni who did such work for the King of Spain. See also W. B. Adams 1837, p. 48

[131] Taylor the Water Poet argued that coaches "swarmed ... to pester the streets as they do now" – 1605; W. B. Adams 1837, pp. 43, 46; Jerry White 2012, p. 10

[132] Chambers *Encyclopaedia* 1862

[133] Geoffrey Beard 1981, p.xxi

[134] Edward Edwards 1808, for Baker, p. 181 for Catton, pp. 259–260. For Daniell see Joseph Farington p. 62 29 July 1796 who gives the master's name as "Mansfield"

[135] Joseph Farington p. 612 20 July 1796

[136] *Ibid.*, p. 623 29 July 1796. Farington also names a man named Wilder as having been "brought up to Coach Painting" and who later became an actor

[137] Edward Edwards, 1808, p. 181. He was appointed surveyor of pictures following the death of the previous incumbent George Knapton (1698–1778)

[138] Trevor Fawcett 1974, p. 50 and Martin Myrone ed. 2011, p. 13

[139] W. H. Pyne 1823–24, Vol. II, p. 3

[140] William Dunlap (1834) 1969, p. 208

[141] Inscription on a drawing of this cypher by George Scharf, British Museum Dept of P&D

[142] A copy of this publication is in the National Art Library 44.F.17–19 in the Victoria & Albert Museum, London

[143] Edward Edwards 1808, p. 181

[144] Josaphine Walpole 1997, pp. 15–16. Before his apprenticeship to Whistler, Crome worked from the age of 12 for Dr Rigby a prominent Norwich physician

[145] Edward Edwards 1808, pp. 31, 34

[146] Howard Colvin 1995; Anthony Gerbino and Stephen Johnson 2009, pp. 136–142, 145–146

[147] W. T. Whitley 1929, Vol. I, p. 344

[148] Antonia Roberts *Enter Tim Bobbin …* Rochdale Art Gallery, 1980. The younger Collier joined the Newcastle Philosophical Society when it was founded in 1775; Jenny Uglow 2006, pp. 87, 126

[149] Iain McCallum 2003, pp. 11–14

[150] Edward Edwards 1808, pp. 259–260; Alan Borg 2005, p. 126

[151] Joseph Farington, p. 984 18 Feb 1798

[152] Edward Edwards 1808, pp. 259–260

[153] William Williams 1787, pp. 10–11

[154] Nicholas Goodison (1974) 2002

[155] See, for example, Hermione Hobhouse 1971

[156] John Ford 2005, pp. 18–19. All these were to become wealthy men enabling their sons to have academic educations and become gentlemen of independent means. John Hatchett's son Charles Hatchett was to become the distinguished chemist

[157] John Ford 2005, p. 24

[158] Jerry White 2012, 215; John Ford 2005, pp. 22–23

[159] Iain McCallum 2003, p. 15

[160] John Ford 2005, p. 10

[161] Kurt Wehlte (1967) 1982, p. 405. Although first published in Germany Wehlte states that this was an English practice. For an account of the varnishes used by coach builders see P. F. Tingry (1803) 1816 – e.g. p. 52

[162] M. C. Hillick (1898) 1997, p. 7

[163] John Ford 2005, p. 23

[164] *Ibid.*, p. 22

[165] W. B. Adams 1837, pp. 77–78

[166] The author has worked Cuban mahogany and can vouch for the presence of this "white powder" but this is the first published account of this feature that he is aware of

[167] W. B. Adams 1837 – cited by John Ford 2005, p. 23

[168] Cited by E. P. Thompson (1963) 1991, pp. 261, 262

[169] Larwood and Hotton 1866, p. 38

[170] W. B. Adams 1837, chapter xii, pp. 172–174

[171] Joanna Martin 2004, pp. 295–296

[172] Richard Wendorf 1996, pp. 104–105. On the theme of the seasons Reynolds had a seal of winter cut by Pierre Etienne Falconet – see Wendorf p. 108

[173] Created Lord Ilchester 11 May 1741 and advanced as Earl of Ilchester 5 June 1756 – see John Collinson 1791, 305; Joanna Martin 2004, p. 298

[174] John Ford 2005, p. 40

[175] Geoffrey Beard 1981, p. 212.; Sidney C. Hutchinson 1968, p. 29

[176] Joseph Farington, p. 91 9 November 1793. Howard's son became a pupil of the painter Philip Reinagle RA (1749–1833)

[177] John Ford 2005, chapter 4. Knight of Glin and James Peill 2007, pp. 179–181

[178] In Ireland the Lord Chancellor's coach was less well received. Nevertheless, and in response, the city fathers in Dublin ordered a coach from a Dublin coach builder for their Lord Mayor which, in 1792, cost £2,690 13s 9d. Knight of Glin and James Peill 2007, p. 179

[179] John Ford 2005, p. 21. The figure of 16,000 coaches in England in 1787 contrasts with the 700 in London and Westminster in 1694

[180] William Dunlap (1834) 1969, Vol. II, Pt I, pp. 208–21

[181] *Ibid.*, Vol. II, Pt I, p. 31 under John Vanderlyn (1775–1852)

[182] *Ibid.*, Vol. II, Pt I for Otis p. 227, Jewett p. 256, Vol. II, Pt II Neagle pp. 372–373 and Tyler p. 434

[183] It seems that Frothingham did not enter into a formal apprenticeship with his father whose premises may not have included a paint shop. Frothingham later became a pupil of Gilbert Stuart (1755–1828). William Dunlap (1834) 1969, Vol. II, Pt I, pp. 213, 215

[184] William Dunlap (1834) 1969, Vol. II, Pt 1, pp. 256–25

[185] *Ibid.*, Vol. I, pp. 161, 250

[186] *Memoirs of the Life and Religious Labours of Edward Hicks of Newtown, Bucks County, Pennsylvania,* Philadelphia 1851

[187] Carolyn J. Weekley, *The Kingdoms of Edward Hicks,* Colonial Williamsburg, Virginia, 1999; James Ayres 1976

[188] W. B. Adams 1837, p. 5

[189] M. C. Hillick (1898) 1997 and *The Coach-Makers Illustrated Hand Book Hand-Book* (1875), 1995, both reprinted by the Astragal Press, Mendham NJ.

[190] W. B. Adams 1837, chapter xiv, p. 205

[191] Joseph Conrad *Lord Jim,* 1900, chapter 1

[192] Lt Cdr P. K. Kemp RN "Sailing Ships of the Atlantic Seas" in Gervis Frere-Cook 1974, p. 46

[193] Ambrose Heal Collection, 90.5, British Museum Dept of P&D

[194] Christopher Thomson 1847, pp. 48–49. Thomson worked in the mould lofts of the shipyards at Hull before moving on to become a sawyer and, later, a house painter

[195] Quoted by William Gaunt 1975, pp. 69, 253 and by John Wood "Seascapes worthy of Greater Fame", *Country Life,* 28 May 1959

[196] J. T. Smith (1828) 1949, p. 13. This may have resembled the sign of the ship from an ale house in Britford now in Salisbury and South Wiltshire Museum. Monamy, along with Hayman, also decorated some of the boxes at Vauxhall Gardens

[197] W. A. D. Englefield (1923) 1936, p. 163. This painting was probably either *A Calm at Sea* or *A Sea Storm*; the Company still owns two works by the artist including *A Calm at Sea*; Alan Borg 2005, p117

[198] Hessle is now in the western suburbs of Hull

[199] Arthur G. Credland 1983, pp. 29–32. Rouncival Fletcher 1st also worked as a carver and gilder

[200] *Ibid.*, p. 7, quoting Joseph Farington

[201] William Dunlap (1834) 1969, Vol. II, Pt 1, pp. 153, 154. In some ways this calls to mind the S*elf-Portrait* by Capt. Thomas Smith: Mariner, painted in Colonial America as early as *c.* 1690; James Monroe Perkins "Ephraim Byram: versatile nineteenth-century craftsman", *Antiques,* New York, May 1970

[202] Arthur G. Credland 1993, pp. 7, 33–38

[203] Trade card reproduced: James Ayres 1998, p. 213, fig. 318

[204] Arthur G. Credland 1993, p. 8; Roger Finch 1983, p. 153; James Ayres 1998, p. 21

[205] Edward Edwards 1808, p. 5

[206] *Dictionary of National Biography.* For Kings Yard Row see Peter Guillery 2004, p. 208 and for a 1946 photograph of the Row before demolition – then described as Kings Yard Row, Prince Street

[207] Joseph Farington, p. 308 22 Feb 1795; William Gaunt 1975, p. 247

[208] Stephen Deauchur and James Taylor, *DNB*. James Ayres "The Death of Captain Cook; two views", *Antiques*, New York, May 1970, pp. 724–727

[209] William Gaunt *Marine Painting* (1975) Biographical Notes, pp. 244–261

[210] Roger Finch 1983, pp. 66, 128

[211] *Ibid.*, p. 48

[212] *Ibid.*, p. 48

[213] For the full list of the Walters family of Bristol painters see James Ayres 1980, p. 17 and fig. 122 for the ship portrait

[214] Edward Edwards 1808, pp. 48–49, A. S. Davidson 1986, pp. 16–17

[215] *Ibid.*, pp. 84–86

[216] The masons' plaster tracing floor at Wells Cathedral is in the upper room of the north porch

[217] Christopher Thomson 1847, p. 40

[218] Roger Finch 1983, p. 150

[219] *Ibid.*, pp. 145–154 "Biographical Notes …" For information on Cornè see Nina Fletcher Little (1952) 1972, pp. 18, 42

[220] Kathleen Foster 2008, pp. 1, 2, 3

[221] Christopher Thomson 1847, p. 48–50

[222] William Dunlap (1834) 1969, Vol. II, Pt II, pp. 58–63

[223] Roger Finch 1983, p. 147

[224] Robert Morton ed. 1997, pp. 16, 19, 36, 40

[225] *Ibid.*, pp. 16, 19, 36, 40

[226] Roger Finch 1983, p. 146

[227] Horace Walpole 1786, Vol. IV, p. 75, and William Gaunt 1975, p. 70

Chapter 12

SIZE PAINTING

Most stains and distempers used water as the vehicle and a size as the binder which together formed the medium. Size was generally derived from animal sources. Of the trades that used this medium the Stainers of London had claim to the longest pedigree as a formally constituted guild – but others had for long used this group of media. The following pages will therefore include sections on the work of Stainers: their Hangings, Transparencies and Scene Painting, together with the work of the Plaisterers.

Stained hangings

The Stainers were an independent guild in London and their early autonomy demonstrates the importance of the craft. Once the Stainers were united with the Painters in 1502 the two crafts maintained their distinctiveness within the combined Company.[1] The constitution of the united guild (see p. 134), made provision for an equal number of brethren representing each trade, thus demonstrating the individual nature of each craft, at least within the orbit of London and Westminster. This may be compared with the clearly defined demarcation between Carpenters and Joiners in the capital as compared with a more flexible attitude found in smaller communities elsewhere. For example in Edinburgh the Stainers belonged to the same guild as the Wrights and Masons.[2] In sharp contrast to London demarcations between the crafts were often absent or not observed in the constituent parts of the British Isles or the regions within them. This is evident in the 1665 notebook of John Abbot in which the Devon plasterer casually includes recipes for both oil and size painting together with information on making stained hangings.[3]

Stained hangings were widely used in pre-Reformation England and this fashion persisted in the domestic interiors of the Tudors.[4] The inventories

249

of the day give some suggestion that in Devon these textiles may have been a largely urban feature but nationally they were found in homes of all social levels.[5] Part of the reason for this is that, whilst very superior stained hangings were made for the elite, they remained less expensive than dyed-in-the-wool tapestries.[6] Following the Reformation the increasing use of panelling and framed pictures led to a very gradual decline in the use of wall hangings in general – including stained cloths.

It is not our purpose here to discuss craft methods in any detail but, because stained hangings are now virtually extinct, it seems reasonable to give some account of these textiles and the methods used to decorate them. In general these hangings are often referred to in inventories as "painted cloths" but as they were the product of the Stainers it is as "stained hangings" that they will be described here.[7] The lightweight yet coarse linen canvases used for this purpose were variously known as "hurds" or "osnaburgs" (from Osnabrück in Germany).[8] In England chapmen continued to sell brown osnaburgs for "ordinary painting" down to the eighteenth century.[9] The dyes and stains applied to these textiles were used in liquid form so that the weave of the canvas remained visible. This resulted in a hanging that would more closely resemble the highly expensive woven tapestries. There can be little doubt that this was the intention because the Scottish painter and stainer John Melville (or Mellin – fl. 1587–1604) was well known for his "imitation tapestry".[10] The fluid nature of the stain used for this work is emphasised by William Shakespeare in his reference to such a hanging as "a German … water work", a phrase that shows that many were then imported.[11] This though was once an English art form as is demonstrated by the earliest known description of the making of these hangings; an account that was transcribed in 1410 by Theodoric of Flanders then working in Bologna:

> "… in England the painters work with these waters upon closely woven cloths wetted with gum-water [size and water] made with gum-arabic and then dried, and afterwards stretched out upon the floor of the solar upon thick woollen and frieze cloths; and the painters walking with their clean feet over the said cloths, work and paint upon them figurines, stories and other things. And because these cloths lie stretched upon a flat surface, the coloured waters do not flow and spread in painting upon them but remain where they are placed, and the watery moisture sinks into the woollen cloth which absorbs it …"

As a transcript by Theodoric the mystery of this art was preserved simply because such a manuscript would have had very limited circulation, his reference to this work being done "upon the floor of the solar" is significant. The word *solar* derives from the French *sol*: floor and *solive* beam or joist.[12] In other words stained hangings were made in an upper floor workshop – a boarded floor supported by joists being preferable to working on the ground of a ground floor or even one that was paved with stone or tiles. This upper floor location is confirmed, at a much later date, in Joseph Highmore's (1692–1780) reminiscence of visiting a Dutch artist in his London garret workshop [in *c.* 1714] where he described Vandestraeten as "one of the most expeditious painters who ever lived":

> "He worked with large pans filled with ready mixed paints [stains] standing on the [floor][13] near his easel, some of which contained what he called cloud colour and different shades of blues and whites for the skies and other various tones of greens, reds and browns. With the aid of a boy to remove the canvases in turn and replace them by others he went over them in regular stages, first painting all the skies, then the middle portions [middle distance], and finally the foregrounds.
>
> He lived in a garret, where he painted cloths many feet in length, as long as they were woven, and painted the whole at once, continuing the sky in the manner above described from one end to the other, and then the several grounds, etc. until the whole was one long landscape. This he then cut and sold by parcels as demanded to fit chimneys, etc. and those who dealt in this way would go to his house and buy three or four of them, or any number of feet of landscapes. One day when Vanderstraeten's wife called him to dinner he cried out, 'I will come presently; I have done our Saviour, I have only one of the Twelve Apostles to do ...' And notwithstanding they were so slight even these pictures were not altogether devoid of merit, for he had something like genius and taste".[14]

The bulk and weight of woven tapestries is such that they may be hung against a wall and remain relatively static. The rather flimsy nature of stained canvas means that it has to be fixed in position in one of two ways. Either the canvas was stretched and incorporated into a scheme of panelling or it was nailed to the wall, with or without battens, by means of upholstery tacks and strips of leather or Dutch loom tape serving as a gimp. The deployment of stained hangings set in a scheme of panelling has been recorded in Munslow Farm, Shropshire and in The Lockers, Hemel Hempstead, Hertfordshire. The use of upholstery tacks and strips of leather for this purpose were adopted as a method of fixing in Yarde Farm, Malborough, South Devon (Fig. 74) whereas textile tapes were used in Le Mariuel on Jersey (see below and Fig. 76).[15] Leather hangings, decorated with oil paint (and sometimes oil gilding), such as the examples of *c.* 1690 in Dunster Castle, Somerset, belong to a distinct Spanish, or Spanish Netherlands, tradition.

FIGURE 74. Early eigh-
teenth century *stained
hanging*, overall height
7 ft 4 in (223.6 cm), in
Yarde Farm, Malborough,
South Devon. This is one
of a whole group of such
verdure hangings, which
appear to be from the
same workshop, examples
of which have been found
in houses across the
south of England. (Exeter
Archaeology)

As mentioned above these stained canvases are often referred to in
inventories as "painted cloths". Some were in fact executed in oil paint and
designed to resemble panelling – the solid paint resulting in a similar surface
texture to that of wainscot. It is also probable that the underlying drawing in
these pictorial schemes was carried out in a solid colour. This is evident from
the employment of stencils, although the guild did not officially permit their
use. The *Book of Ordinances* drawn up by the Painter Stainers in 1581/2 states
in Article 10 that it was forbidden: "to make false and deceitful work wrought
with stencil pattern or otherwise as painted and printed sleight upon cloth,
silk, leather or other things ... with work of sundry colours or with gold foil or

FIGURE 75. Detail of a *stained hanging* of *c.* 1700 at Owlpen Manor, Gloucestershire. (Sir Nicholas Mander, Gloucestershire)

FIGURE 76. Early eighteenth century *stained hangings* in a ruined house known as Le Marinel in the parish of St John, Jersey, Channel Islands. (Photograph: the author, 2009)

silver foil that is deceitful" – for which the penalty was £3-6s-8d. So significant was this "deceit" that most of these regulations were repeated in Article 14.

Following the Restoration, but before 1665, a similar set of rules was drawn up. Clause 7 of this document insisted "That all Painters, free and foreign, be prohibited from using deceitful work of stencilling or tillet printing".[16] Despite these requirements, the use of stencils for this type of work evidently persisted. In a whole group of stained hangings, dating to about 1700, the same motifs recur all deriving from a common set of stencils. This group of half a dozen examples, all of which include a hunting scene in a wooded landscape, has been found in various houses across the country from Owlpen Manor, Gloucestershire to Chichester, West Sussex. The use of the same stencils suggests that all were made in a single workshop (Figs 74, 75). Certain details stained into this group of canvases, such as buildings with crow-stepped gables, suggest a Dutch artist, possibly working in London – perhaps Vanderstraeten.[17]

Outside this group, and a generation later, are the stained hangings that cling to survival in a bedroom of a ruined house known as Le Mariuel, in the parish if St John on Jersey in the Channel Islands. Despite the French traditions of Jersey this room, with its panelled chimney breast of *c.* 1725–1730, has a thoroughly English character. However it should be conceded that their faintly Chinoiserie appearance may suggest that these stained cloths are somewhat later than the room that they decorate. It should though be acknowledged that this rather modish aesthetic was introduced to the British Isles by Robert Robinson (fl. 1674–1706) in the late seventeenth century. Alternatively the orientilism reminiscent of Jean-Antoine Watteau's *Figures chinoises et tartares* (*c.* 1709) may indicate that these decorations were imported from France.

Native or foreign only three or four examples (including these) of hangings of this type are known to remain in their original context – and those at Le Mariuel are unlikely to survive. Of the existing group of *verdure* stained hangings to have been identified in Britain most date from a couple of decades either side of the year 1700. This rather neatly coincides with a revival of interest in this art form. William Dix was to claim the credit for this renewed interest. Dix was a Haberdasher by affiliation but his work as a Stainer was to result in his being admitted to the Painter Stainers on 30 Oct 1676.[18]

The decline in the production of stained hangings in England pre-dates the Reformation. As early as 1483 attempts were made to stem the tide of imports and by 1598 John Stow was of the view that "the workmanship of staining is departed out of use in England". As we know from surviving inventories hangings of this type were widely deployed in English interiors at this time – this suggests that Stow is referring to a rapid decline in their manufacture rather than their use in England. By 1601 the Painter Stainers lamented that "not an hundred yards of new Painted Cloth [has been] made in a Year here".[19] The early demise in the practice of this craft in England may explain why little or no evidence has so far come to light concerning Stainers as apprentices.

Following the merger in London between the Painters and the Stainers in 1502 the latter were to lose status. This occurred despite the theoretical equality between the two trades that the constitution of the united guild was designed to maintain. This rather secondary position for Stainers was also found in Continental medieval Europe where those who created stained work were regarded as subordinate to the painters. Such a position was reflected both in the terminology used, and in the shorter apprenticeships undertaken by stainers.[20] There is even a possibility that this somewhat condescending view of works on canvas may have accounted for the persistence of panel painting. As paintings grew inexorably in size the technical problems of glueing-up quarter-sawn panels into large dimensions was an ever greater problem, one that extended to transport and hanging. Easel painting on canvas was simpler in all these respects.[21]

With the rise of framed, moveable and "polite" paintings on canvas there was a corresponding decline in the use of stained hangings. Although this form of mural decoration persisted into the first decade, or so, of the eighteenth century at a gentry level they were probably considered somewhat *retardataire* by the aristocracy. In 1727 when the inventory for Thorp Salvin (one of the Yorkshire seats of the Marquess of Carmathen) was drawn up, two small closets were listed both of which were "Hung with Stain'd Linen". These adorned the small servants' bed chambers which adjoined the principal bedrooms. In such a location stained hangings would have been considered adequate for staff at this date.[22] One of the last allusions to these textiles appears as a passing reference in Robert Dossie's *Handmaid to the Arts* (1764) in which he describes a distinct category of pictorial art as "the kind called painting in distemper, being for scenes, canvas hangings ... and other coarser work". It is possible that hangings of this kind persisted longer in Colonial America than in the mother country. In 1766 John Adams was astonished at the furnishing of Nick Boylston's house in Boston with its "Turkey Carpets, the painted Hangings, the Marble Tables" and much else besides which, collectively were "the most magnificent of any Thing I have ever seen."[23]

Back in England stained hangings were, by the 1760s, decades out of fashion and had always been viewed as of secondary importance to woven tapestry. Despite which the work of the Stainers, if not always undertaken by such tradesmen, was to have an after-life as stage scenery and in "transparencies" for windows.

Stained transparencies

Although the stained hanging as a fashionable art-form declined in Stuart England, and was all but extinct by *c.* 1725, the technique survived in other guises. These alternative uses to which the art of the stainer was applied had, in many cases, a long history.

Before the widespread introduction of glass, late in the reign of Elizabeth I, windows were often equipped with fenestrals of parchment or oiled paper. Although these fenestrals admitted some light, kept out the weather and maintained a degree of warmth in a building, they also blocked the view. For this reason they were customarily decorated, a feature described by Sir High Platt (1594). For these he advised that "the finest, thinnest parchment" should be used, skiveings that could be given some translucence by the application of "oil of sweet almonds". This parchment could also be decorated with "anie personage, beast, tree, flower or cote armour".[24] For Platt any lack of clarity in these windows was compensated for by the privacy that they offered from "overlookers". Nearly a century later, despite the dramatic increase in the use of glass in windows, John Smith (1687) describes "sashes", frames or fenestrals, of "Painted Cloth or Sarsnet" (a thin silk fabric). These textiles could be washed with "distilled Verdigrease" a green colour that appealed to those who "cannot indure bright light". Alternatively Smith suggests that they could be decorated with "whatever fancy you please".[25] The translucent nature of the stains used to embellish these "sashes" were well within the scope of the stainers.

By the eighteenth century, with glass very widely available in as many as six qualities, "transparencies" as the ornamental textile fenestrals became known, found a new use as blinds or window shades. When back-lit within buildings these could also be visible externally at night as decorations for national or private celebrations. On 19 May 1723 one grandee sought to enliven the social season in Bath with "illuminations..." [26] A couple of decades later a national event took place in St James's Park in London to applaud the Peace of Aix la Chapelle of 1748. The fireworks for this occasion were accompanied by music "composed by Mr Handel" – his "Firework Music". In addition there was a backdrop – an outdoor stage set – with transparencies painted by Andrew Casali which were backlit by "a great number of lampions" (Fig. 77).[27] A very similar "Thanksgiving" for this peace treaty, with its own set of "illuminations", was held in Spalding, Lincolnshire. This was created in direct imitation of the London celebration except that in Lincolnshire the scheme was designed by the local mason and architect William Sands (d. 1751).[28] A decade later, in 1759, the frontage of the *Turk's Head* tavern in Gerrard Street, London was adorned

FIGURE 77. Engraving of *The Great Fire Works* held in Hyde Park London in 1748 to celebrate the Treaty of Aix la Chapelle. This "stage set" was furnished with transparencies, by Andrew Casali, which were back-lit by "lampions" the whole event being accompanied by the music of "Mr Handel". (Museum of London)

with illuminations of this kind to mark the coming of age of Prince George, who became King George III the following year.[29] As this hostelry was a haunt of artists these transparencies were the work of Samuel Wale (1721?–1786) who, presumably, used his past experience as a coach painter to give them a suitably heraldic power. Following George III's foundation of the Academy in December 1768 this institution celebrated the royal birthdays between 1769 and 1771 with illuminations, designed by Giovanni Cipriani RA (1727–1785), which were placed on the façade of its Somerset House headquarters. In 1789 the Academy again expressed its loyalty to its founder with similar illuminations in the Strand to celebrate the king's recovery from porphyria. On this occasion decorations of this kind were installed in Soho Square and later moved to the Bank of England; these transparencies were designed by William Hamilton ARA – later RA (1752–1845), to mark the monarch's return to good health. For transparencies of a politically charged nature their deployment could be close to compulsory. In 1779 a crowd enforced the display of illuminations to celebrate the acquittal of Admiral Keppel at a Portsmouth court martial – householders who did not conform had their windows broken. Many transparencies were designed as a reiteration of the façades that they both masked and decorated. This was certainly true of the scheme used to provide festive lighting for Matthew Boulton's Soho Manufactory in Birmingham as a celebration of the Peace of Amiens in 1802.[30] These temporary decorations were inevitably ephemeral. Remarkably one such object, and its design drawing by the mason-turned-architect John Carr of York (1723–1807), is preserved at Raby Castle, Durham. This transparency was made to mark the coming of age, in 1787, of William Harry, Baron Barnard.[31]

FIGURE 78. Drawing showing Matthew Boulton's manufactory in Birmingham hung with transparencies and illuminated by hundreds of oil lamps to celebrate the Peace of Amiens, 1802. (Birmingham Archives & Heritage)

These celebratory transparencies were mostly made for public events and as such were in vogue throughout Georgian England. In Norwich they have been recorded in 1798 and again in 1814.[32] On 12 October 1802 they were deployed in Newcastle to celebrate The Treaty of Amiens. This occasion must have been almost as noisy as the London event of 1749. The church bells of Newcastle rang out, guns were fired in salute, the ships in the harbour were "dressed overall" and the populace emerged from their houses to see the transparencies in the windows backlit by candles. Again Newcastle saw similar illuminations on 30 May 1814 to mark the Treaty of Paris. Once again transparencies were placed in windows and the most popular of these showed John Bull drinking beer and, in the background, Bonaparte hanging from a gibbet and the inscription "Good Old Times Revived".[33]

All these transparencies were backlit, temporary, ephemeral and designed to be seen in hours of darkness. In contrast window blinds were intended to be drawn down during the day to protect furniture, rugs and carpets from fading in sunlight. Day or night, transparencies or window blinds also served to provide privacy. In 1796 it was observed that when the Prince of Wales visited Lady Jersey "she was accustomed to drop the linen blinds of the windows".[34] With stained blinds their transparent nature inspired designs which resembled stained glass windows. Although, in origin, transparencies were within the scope of stainers, by the mid-eighteenth century this was work for jobbing painters. One such was John White at the *Golden Head*, Shoe Lane, Fleet Street, London. His trade label lists the range of his goods and services: "Pictures Painted, Mended, Cleaned and Framed, Blinds for Windows Painted on Canvas or Wire".[35] In contrast to decorated transparent window blinds, designed to be seen internally, the wire gauze window screens, when decorated, were also intended to be visible during the day but they were intended to be viewed externally. By the nineteenth century these wire gauze screens were often used to identify a lawyer's office or a business premises by means of a lettered inscription.[36]

* * * *

Roller window blinds may have been in use by the late seventeenth century but by 1729 they seem to have been a standard element in interiors.[37] In that year a supplier in London advertised that he

> "made and sold Window Blinds of all sorts, painted in Wier Canvas, Cloth and Sassenet, after the best and most lasting manner ever yet done so that if ever so dull and dirty they will clean with sope and sand and be like new, where may be seen great choice of the same being always about them".[38]

The reference to items being held in stock is yet another indication of an emerging consumerism at a comparatively early date.

In 1771 the decorative and landscape painter Edmund Garvey (d. 1813) produced a series of transparent blinds, embellished with Neo-Classical motifs, for the new Assembly Rooms in Bath. In this case a visitor to the Upper Rooms in 1794 noted how effectively the internal architraves to the windows acted as frames for the transparencies as pictures. Gainsborough's friendship with Garvey may have encouraged the portrait painter to decorate the transparencies for the Hanover Square concert room in London in 1774–1775.[39] By 1807 Edward Orme had published his "essay on transparent prints, and on transparencies in general". In this book Orme gives detailed instructions on the making of these transparent prints – a process he claims to have invented.[40]

The transparent nature of all these products was dependent on the translucence of the material on which they were painted. For this purpose Nathaniel Whittock (1827) recommended Scotch cambric and added that the dyes, stains and pigments used to decorate this material should be suspended in a size of isinglass – derived from freshwater fish. This medium has a long history and was described by William Salmon (1701) as follows: *"Ising-glass or Ichthyocolla:* That which is dearest, whitest [clearest] and freest from Yellow, is the best. It is of use for making size and may be had for about 4s a pound or less".[41] Whittock illustrates a number of designs for transparent blinds as exemplars. He was certainly of the opinion that the production of these items was well within the capabilities of the better trade painters and glaziers.

As late as 1764 Robert Dossie argued that the work of the Stainers was "a distinct method of painting". It seems that the contradiction inherent in referring to "painting" stands as a silent acknowledgement that, contrary to protestations to the contrary, the work of the Stainers was ceasing to be "distinct".[42] The involvement of "liberal" painters (or newly liberated ones like Wale) in the production of transparencies demonstrates that the craft of the Stainers, as an independent trade, was drawing to a close.

* * * *

In Colonial and Early Federal America these distinctions had always been more fluid. In 1784 the painter and polymath Charles Wilson Peale (1741–1827) produced a series of transparencies that were incorporated into an outdoor "triumphal arch" to celebrate the Treaty of Paris. Almost 20 years later in 1813, James Barton Longacre (1794–1869), who was then apprenticed to the engraver George Murray (d. 1822), was "lent" to the Philadelphia studio of

John Barralett (*c.* 1747–1815). This temporary arrangement was made so that Longacre could assist "in painting a transparency which Murray was preparing to display in honour of Perry's victory on Lake Erie" in the war against the British of 1812.[43]

As for the use of decorated window shades and wire gauze screens in North America, climatic considerations were such that, these were always in greater demand there than in the British Isles. In 1796 Hugh Barkley and Patrick O'Meara of Baltimore advertised "transparent blinds for windows". At this time William Matthews the Philadelphia "House, Sign and Ship Painters" were also offering "transparencies, silks for windows".[44] The extent to which these items were a feature of American, as distinct from British, interiors is characterised by Mrs Francis Trollope. In 1828 this English visitor to America, infamous for her caustic observations on the young Republic, objected to the "same uncomfortable blinds" that she encountered "in every part of America". The ubiquity of window "shades" in North America was confirmed by Oscar Hammerstein's libretto in *Oklahoma* of 1943 in which "The Surrey with the Fringe on Top [had] isinglass curtains y'can roll right down".[45]

Scene painting for the theatre

To the limited extent that the Elizabethan and Jacobean theatre used scenery this frequently took the form of stained hangings.[46] As the stage set evolved, and as "the scene" came to be framed by a proscenium arch, sets were frequently painted in distemper – but size remained the common denominator.

Amongst eighteenth century scene painters Joseph Goupy (b. London 1689) may be numbered – although he also worked on an altogether different

FIGURE 79. *Set Model* by P. J. de Loutherbourg for the production of the play *Omai* – this scene showing Kensington Gardens. The voyages of Captain James Cook were the inspiration for this production. Many of the features found in stained hangings and transparencies were deployed in set design. (Victoria & Albert Museum, London)

scale as a painter of miniatures. Once again a gum or a size based medium, was central to both activities despite the differing dimensions. Goupy's ability to work on both scales must have been considerable for he is known to have assisted Peter Tillemans (d.1734) on a much admired set for the Opera House in the Haymarket, Westminster.[47] That Goupy was prepared to work in these various ways, and that he could find employment in London by so doing, suggests that there were, at this time, few trade demarcations between these two activities. This implies that, in the absence of regulation, there were few if any formal apprenticeships or studentships available in this field at that time.

The importance attached to this type of work is signified by the very high salary that David Garrick (1717–1779) paid some scene painters. When Philippe de Louterbourg (1740–1812) moved to England in 1771 the theatrical impresario offered the painter £500 a year for the production of sets for the Drury Lane Theatre. Although primarily an easel painter de Louterbourg's innovative approach in his work for the stage was highly thought of. This included the use of "flats" to the foreground (down stage) such as "cottages or broken stiles" which gave "a stronger resemblance of nature". Of even greater importance was his introduction of transparent gauzes to the theatre. These may have been inspired by the "transparencies" of the type described above and which, of necessity, involved the use of the dyes of the stainers (see pp. 250, 251).[48] De Louterbourg was one of the last in a whole series of scene painters to benefit from Garrick's patronage. Others included the Irish-born Robert Carver (d. 1791) and more importantly, Francis Hayman (1706–1776).[49] Lord Radnor argued that had Hayman "not fooled away many years at the beginning of his life painting harlequins, trap-doors, etc. for the playhouse, he would certainly, by this time, be the greatest man of his age, as he is now of this country".[50] For Lord Radnor the theatre was a corrupting influence on a painter's potential as an artist. Gainsborough in contrast believed that scene painting could broaden an artist's horizons – but then his "showbox" demonstrates some of the features of a *maquette* for a stage design.[51] Certainly the ability to work at speed on large canvases must have done much to develop artistic flair and breadth of handling. Some of these scene painters achieved a relaxed accomplishment in both their work and their demeanour. George Lambert (1700–1765) "for many years principal scene painter to the theatre at Covent Garden", where he had a painting loft, was even known to "hold court" there while painting. It seems that he was "a person of great respectability in character and profession [who] was often visited while at work in the theatre by persons of the first consideration both in rank and talents".[52] Of the many foreign artists working in England at this time Michael Novosielski (1750–1795) though born in Rome was of Polish descent. In London Novosielski was not only a scene painter but also practiced as an architect and property developer.[53]

For the most part these artists and artisans were working as both painters using an oil medium and as stainers using dyes and distempers. This was certainly true of the jobbing Bristol house painter Michael Edkins whose letter books for the years 1756 to 1761 show an extraordinarily wide range of work from house and carriage painting to props for the stage and other undertakings for the Bath-based impresario John Palmer Jnr.[54] In Bath Thomas French (d. 1803) and the Irish-born Walmsley (d. 1805) found employment in the Spa's theatres.

* * * *

At the end of the eighteenth century more formal training in this work seems to have become available in England. In London John Joseph Holland (c. 1776–1820) was "apprenticed to Marinelli the scene painter" at the exceptionally early age of nine years. This was said to have taught him both "theory and practice", a feature that is characteristic of such an empirical system of training. The influence of English scene painting was probably conveyed to early Federal America by means of migration. In 1796 John Holland moved to North America where he found employment in the theatres of Philadelphia and later in New York. On Manhattan he became the master of John Evers (1797–1884) who also developed as a scene painter. Holland's knowledge of size painting enabled him to become "a good watercolour draftsman and architect".[55] His works on paper are locked in a theatrical idiom for landscape and, significantly, he never ventured into the use of oil paint. Despite these limitations his work for the theatre won the plaudits of William Dunlap (1834):

> "When he entered the workshop he uniformly changed his dress; and by both precept and example, forwarded the business of his employers with wonderful dispatch. Streets, chambers, temples or forests, grew under his hand as if by magic".[56]

The transition from size painting to working in an oil medium may have been a barrier for some who began as scene painters – but not all. Evers, in contrast to his master Holland, went on to "exhibit landscapes in oil of decided merit".[57] Despite his short life this was a Rubicon that was also crossed by Edward G. Malbone (1777–1807) of Rhode Island and later by William Strickland (1788–1854) in Philadelphia.[58] In terms of subject matter, scene painting tended to anchor these artists within the landscape tradition when they advanced to easel painting. Despite which Christian Gullager (1759–1826) was to establish a reputation as a portrait painter in Boston after a career as a scene painter in the theatres of Philadelphia and New York.[59] Gullager like Holland was an immigrant to the United States.

In moving from large scale size painting on canvas sets for the theatre, to watercolours on paper of small dimensions, these artists seem to have been following a well-trodden path – one that could even establish a link with architectural drawing – as was certainly the case with Novosielski and Holland. These trade size-painters regularly established an abiding craft tradition that extended well beyond an individual life-time or nationality. For example the Italian Marinelli in London was the master of John Holland. On migrating to North America Holland was to become the master of a number of individuals including John Evers. This continuity down the generations established a direct line of artistic and technical innovation from Europe across the Atlantic to North America.

The plasterers

The relationship between lime plasters and lime-wash was close and thus the application of the latter to the former became central to the craft. Not that this progression from one trade to the other had always gone unchallenged. In 1575 the Painters Stainers of London petitioned Queen Elizabeth with the objection that "now for lack of good orders both Plasterers and others [e.g. plumbers] doth entermeddle in the same science".[60] Implicit in the petition is some acknowledgement that plasterers would inevitably be involved in "washing and stopping". The "washing" referred to the application of limewash or distemper; the "stopping" to making good the plasterwork. This situation is mentioned by both Gerbier (1663) and Campbell (1747) the latter being categorical in stating that "The Plaisterer is always White-Washer".[61] As an extension of lime plastering, white was the predominant colour, a feature confirmed by many seventeenth century paintings of interiors in the Low Countries – just across the North Sea. In Britain this emphasis on white-wash may have been connected with the restricted pallet to which plasterers were confined. An Act of 1606 (4 Jac.I.c20) permitted Plaisterers to apply distempers but they were confined to "whiting, blacking, redlead, redoker, yellow oker and russet mingled with size only".[62] The size was derived from various animal sources including animal bones and skins, fish, cheese or milk. The problems with the use of caseins, especially milk, was that it could turn sour and result in an unpleasant smell.

This tendency could be reduced by the addition of ammonia – in the convenient form of urine. Many of these features have been identified in the recently conserved mural schemes in the Merchants House, Marlborough (Fig. 81a,b). The plasterer in this Wiltshire town house in 1656 was William Brunson so it is reasonable to attribute this work in distemper to him. Recent analysis has shown that the pigments are bound in casein which was most probably milk owing to the presence of urine in the mix. In addition, although the colours used do not fully conform to those that plasterers were permitted to apply in London, the palette is restricted to just three colours: indigo, red and yellow on a white ground (plus combinations of these).[63] This association between plastering and size painting is evident in John Abbott's (1640–1727) *Notebook* (1662–1663) which describes "glews" for this purpose – although Abbott later confined himself to decorative Baroque plasterwork.[64]

A further indication of the sort of restrictions that plasterers were placed under by the Painter Stainers concerns the use of sgraffito plaster decoration using two or more tones (often black and white) or colours of plaster. In England sgriffito work goes back at least to the early sixteenth century and may be an Italianate influence.[65] In about 1546 the outside walls of Beckingham Hall, Tolleshunt Major, Essex, were decorated in this way. This craft tradition is known to have persisted until 1719 when a mural scheme was applied to the external face of Calico House, Newnham, Kent.[66]

FIGURE 80. Sgraffito decoration in the reveal of a window in St Nicholas Priory, Exeter. In 1579, some decades after the Dissolution of the Monasteries this building was converted into a private house – the likely period of this decoration. A postcard of the 1920s has been reproduced here since the work is now in less good condition. (Postcard: Author's Collection)

These external decorations are very vulnerable and the Newnham example has been seriously corrupted by "restoration". Even when protected from the elements these decorations were ephemeral. The sgraffito work of *c.* 1570–1590 in the internal reveal of a window in St Nicholas Priory, Exeter is now in a far worse condition than when it was recorded in a postcard of the 1920s (Fig. 80).

In these locations this type of work may never have been particularly common in England. There was though another zone within the house where sgraffito work was probably once widely deployed in the seventeenth century – namely the lining within a fireplace. The shaft of chimneys, below the roof-line, were customarily pargeted both internally and externally.[67] This was done to limit the likelihood of smoke escaping, through the masonry or brickwork, into the adjacent rooms. Inevitably this plasterwork ran down within the flue to be visible within the fireplace – until coal burning grates were introduced. These were the surfaces that the plasterers customarily decorated with their sgraffito technique in two or more layers of plaster. A fragment of a distempered version of one of these survives in the dining room of the Marlborough Merchants House – further evidence for this decorative work being by the plasterer Brunson (Fig. 81). In this location such embellishment inevitably became discoloured and in some examples one layer of decoration was eventually covered by another. This may have occurred at ten or twenty year intervals. With work of this kind plasterers were able to indulge their artistic inclinations without in any way impinging on the preserves of the Painter Stainers.[68]

As for the restricted palette, to which plasterers in London were in theory confined, the Jacobean fashion for "Blackwork" decoration was fortuitous. This was a fad that was applied to all manner of surfaces – from embroidery on cloths to size painting on plaster. One exponent of blackwork in distemper was John Bossam who was singled out by the goldsmith and miniature painter Nicholas Hilliard (1546/7–1618/9) as "the most rare *English Drawer* of Story Works in black and white".[69] This raises the possibility that the blackwork decoration shown in the background of Hilliard's portrait miniature of the Earl of Leicester illustrates work by Bossam (Figs 85 & 86).[70] Another exponent of this type of decoration was Thomas Trevelyn who produced manuscript pattern books for blackwork in 1608 and 1616.[71]

Work of this black and white kind was well within the scope of the plasterers craft, but what of the size painting which used a limited range of colours of the type that plasterers were officially permitted to employ after 1606 if not before? Much of this work was of a fairly simple nature. For example the herald painter Randle Holme writing in 1648/1649 describes distempered decoration on plaster walls "made to look like Wainscot or outlandish Timber".[72] A few decades later the Merchants House murals in Marlborough would certainly qualify as "outlandish" although these were made to resemble textile hangings rather than "Wainscot" (oak panelling). More elaborate schemes might take the form of landscape overmantels. Examples discovered in No. 2 Wardrobe Place in the City of London were painted in distemper on plaster in *c.* 1689 and, together with their *trompe l'oeil* representations of carved wood frames, have a distinctly Anglo-Dutch character.[73]

Although figurative mural decoration on plaster using size-based distemper, does appear in the eighteenth century at the vernacular level, the rising fashion for moveable pictures and panelling discouraged such work. In these circumstances it is perhaps no accident that one mural scheme in Cheshire of *c.* 1770–1780 takes the form of a gallery showing a series of landscapes in fictive frames, hung on illusory hooks over a notional wood grained panelled dado, all represented in distemper.[74] In the closing decades of the eighteenth century the Classical Revival brought with it a renewed interest in polychromatic decorative work. In the first quarter of the following century landscape murals became a significant feature. These imitate the more expensive imported, and taxed, French scenic wallpapers by Jacquemart & Bérnard or Dufour of Paris.[75] As these were printed with wood blocks using size bound pigments their effect could be imitated effectively in distemper direct on plaster. In England scenic murals in distemper with oil-based highlights were produced by Thomas Walters of Upper Maudlin Street, Bristol – a landscape scheme worked in a *grisaille* of blue over a pink ground (Fig. 84). A somewhat comparable early nineteenth century mural scheme, although in full colour, has recently been rediscovered in a first floor room in a house in Ashbourne, Derbyshire. This shows the Meynell hunt in full cry in a landscape furnished with local landmarks like Kedleston Hall. The mural is by a local housepainter, Thomas Ravensdale (bapt. 1811–d. 1872) who sadly ended his days in a workhouse.[76]

In America, where early nineteenth century French scenic wallpapers were probably more widely used than in Britain, landscape murals became something of a speciality for Rufus Porter.[77] Both Walters in England and Porter in New England were general painters and decorators. Size painted murals on plaster of this kind were also well within the scope of some plasterers. This may explain why English examples of plasterers straying into the production of oil paintings on canvas or panel are rare – their creative instincts being fulfilled by the creation of murals. The linkage between ornamental plasterwork and size painting remained constant and was well established. A clear early nineteenth century instance of an exponent of these twin trades is P. Summers of 3 Batholomew Street, Birmingham who advertised himself as a "Stucco Colourer

a

FIGURE 81. a) Sgraffito fireplace lining and mural decoration of *c.* 1656–1670 in the Merchant's House, Marlborough, Wiltshire. This work may be attributed to the plasterer William Brunson; b) Brunson's signature and the date 1656 on the interior face of the east gable.

b

FIGURE 82. Faux sgraffito dis-tempered fireplace lining, *c.* 1648, Netherstead, Morton Bagot, Warwickshire. (Photograph: N. W. Alcock)

FIGURE 83. *Mural Decoration* in distemper by the house painter Thomas Ravensdale (bapt. 1811–1872). This landscape scheme of *c.* 1835 includes a number of local features and the Meynell Hunt in full cry. The mural is located in a house in St John's Street, Ashbourne, Derbyshire. (Photograph: Melissa Thompson, English Heritage)

FIGURE 84. Detail of a *landscape mural* by Thomas Walters of Bristol in a first floor chamber in Phippens Farm, Butcombe, north Somerset. This mural of *c.* 1835–1840 is in distemper with highlights picked-out in oil paint. (Photograph: Delmar Studios)

and Ornamental Plasterer". At about the same date Brown & New of 38 Poultry, London, advertised themselves as "Ornamental Painters in Distemper".[78]

* * * *

In much of Northern Europe where true fresco (*fresco buono*) is virtually unknown, murals were generally applied to dry plaster (*fresco secco*) rather than being compounded within it when wet. The Northern tradition was for the use of distemper and limewash, media that was less likely to trap moisture than the oil-based paints. The *kalkmalerier* of medieval and early modern Denmark or the simple domestic murals found on plaster walls in Britain and North America down to the 1840s, are characteristic.[79]

Rather unusually, John Martin's *Notebook* of *c.* 1690–1700 (Fig. 45) includes instructions for true fresco from which the importance of the plasterers trade in relationship to such murals is self-evident. He advises that the first coat of plaster should incorporate ox hair, be "a pretty thickness" and that it should be allowed to "dry [nb. cure] for a day". It was then to be scratched with "the point of a trouell, longways and crossways" to provide a good key for the next coat of plaster which should be "about the thickness of half a barley corn". The final coat of plaster was to receive the pigments: "So will your painting unite and joyn fast to the Plaister".[80] Much of Martin's manuscript derives from earlier sources, notably William Salmon (1672) which in turn owes much to Lomazzo as "Englished" by Haydocke (1598). Despite the possible use of earlier accounts Martin's instructions do suggest some hands-on experience – as in his reference to "half a barley corn".[81]

Although true fresco was never fully part of the British tradition, on either side of the Atlantic, there were a few exceptions. One example is an overmantel landscape of 1775 in Sundial House, Corton, Wiltshire.[82] Another is Thomas Barker's (1767–1847) experimental *fresco buono* in his studio at Doric House, Bath.[83] Certainly at an exalted social level architectural mural paintings, often in oil, appear in palatial interiors by Italians working in England – men such as Antonio Verrio (*c.* 1639–1707). These though are the work of immigrants and as such are alien albeit within an English context. Artists working in this idiom were accused by Cunningham (1830) of covering walls and ceilings:

> "with mobs of old divinities – nymphs who represented cities – crowned beldames for nations – and figures ready ticketed and labelled, answering to the names of virtues .. the chief apostles of this dark faith were two foreigners and one Englishman – Verrio, La Guerre and Sir James Thornhill".[84]

Certainly this "dark faith" was to be briefly adopted by Thornhill's son-in-law William Hogarth but it never became fully part of the aesthetic tenets of the British tradition – in fact Hogarth painted on large canvasses rather than the wall. The Italian approach to mural painting was very far removed from the art of the plasterer. The scenic murals by tradesmen of the late eighteenth and early nineteenth century, of the type mentioned above, belong to an altogether distinct tradition. Some of the later examples of this work may have been inspired by French scenic wallpapers but generally these murals were thoroughly Anglicised in the hands of English and, it may be added, American artisans.

✳ ✳ ✳ ✳

Unlike the oil media size painting is far less likely to darken with age; although some pigments may fade. For William Blake (1757–1827) the advantages of painting with size-bound pigments were decisive:

> "Oil has been falsely supposed to give strength to colours, but a little consideration must show the fallacy of the position. Oil will not drink or absorb colour enough to stand the test of any little time in the air. Let the works of artists since Ruben's time witness to the villainy of those who first brought oil painting into general opinion and practice, since when we have never had a picture painted that would show itself by the side of an earlier composition. This is an awful thing to say to oil painters: they may call it madness but it is true. All the genuine old little pictures are in fresco and not in oil".[85]

In using the word fresco Blake undoubtedly meant egg tempera, or one of the other sizes, animal in origin. In the age-old tradition of the "mystery" Blake kept his methods of painting a secret that he only divulged to his wife arguing that the procedures he employed had come to him in a vision – he had certainly not learnt them in his apprenticeship to an engraver. Despite this J. T. Smith has left us an account of Blake's painting methods:

> "His modes of preparing his grounds and laying them over his panels for painting, mixing his colours, and manner of working, were those which he considered to have been practiced by the early fresco [tempera] painters whose productions still remain in many instances vividly and permanently fresh. His ground was a mixture of whiting and carpenter's glue, which he passed over several times in the [priming] coatings; his colours he ground himself, and also united with them the same sort of glue, but in a much weaker state.[86]

This ground was, in effect, a gesso, a material which had long been used as a preparation along with Armenian bole (a clay) for carved and water-gilt frames in Britain. A revival of interest in this preparation amongst easel painters seems to have occurred at this time. In 1799 Sir Abraham Hume, advised the use of "Honey and water [which] prevents colour from absorbing too fast, or sugar and water will do, washed over the Jess [gesso] ground".[87]

In Blake's use of the word "fresco", and his employment of carpenter's glue rather than rabbit-skin or parchment size, it is evident that the artist is attempting to re-invent a surviving technique.[88] Blake's problem was that he had been apprenticed to the particularities of engraving rather than painting. In 1771 at the traditional age of 14 years he was bound to the engraver James Basire (1730–1802) of Green Street, Lincoln's Inn Fields, London. Basire used his apprentice to draw medieval antiquities around town, especially in Westminster Abbey.[89] This work introduced Blake to medieval tempera paintings on gesso: but his master would have been unlikely to have been capable of demonstrating this technique for his apprentice. The young William Blake, probably in common with others who sought to move beyond the confines of their craft, faced technical challenges. His understanding of painting in tempera on a gesso ground may have been deficient but its advantages were manifest; colours that remained "vivid and permanently fresh".

Size painting is a broad category which involved a medium based on various animal sources (glair, isinglass, casein, parchment) and also gums derived from vegetable materials. In addition to the Stainers these media were used by plasterers, by scene painters for the theatre or by those who produced transparent blinds. The dyes and pigments used by the Stainers were similarly bound in size. The various animal based sizes and vegetable gums were used by the limners (who worked in solid *gouache*) and also the watercolourists (who used mostly translucent colour) who worked on vellum or paper – the subject of the next chapter. Size was the common denominator, the medium used by all these individuals – both artists and artisans.

Notes

[1] The petition for the united Company of Painter Stainers was submitted to the Lord Mayor of London on 19 October 1502 with a constitution that gave equal rights to men from each craft. W. A. D. Englefield (1923) 1936, pp. 46–47
[2] Michael Bath 2003, p. 10; John Harvey 1975, pp. 118–119, 162, 166, demonstrates the pre-Reformation association between painting and masonry, etc
[3] John Abbott *Notebook*, Devon Record Office, Exeter
[4] One of the earliest surviving English hangings of this kind is a banner known as The Buxton Achievement of *c.* 1470 – Norfolk Museums, Stranger's Hall – see Richard Monks and Bruce Williamson, *Gothic*, Victoria & Albert Museum, London, 2003, Cat. 155
[5] James Ayres 2009
[6] One of the most sophisticated sets of stained hangings in England is that at Hardwick Hall; attributed to Jehan Balechon, *c.* 1600; Anthony Wells-Cole 1997, p. 276
[7] For example Jannine Crocker's transcripts of the late sixteenth century: Exeter Orphans' Court documents
[8] For "hurds" see Christopher Hussey "Owlpen Manor" *Country Life* 9 Nov 1952. For "osnaburgs" see Nicholas Mander *Owlpen Manor*, Uley, 2006, p. 139
[9] Tessa Watt 1996, p. 199
[10] D. Thomson 1975, p. 38; Melville is known to have worked mainly in Aberdeen – see also Michael Bath 2003, p. 10
[11] 2 Henry IV, II, 1, "*Mistress Quickly*: … and for thy walls, a pretty slight drollery, or a story of the Prodigal, or a German hunting in water-work …"
[12] For Theodoric see Charles Lock Eastlake (1847) 1960, Vol. I, pp. 95–97. For "solar" see Margaret Wood *The English Medieval House*, London, 1965, glossary, p. 414
[13] The text here states that this was on the "ground" but the workshop was in an attic – so "floor" has been substituted
[14] W. T. Whitley 1928, Vol. I, pp. 23–24
[15] James Ayres 2003, pp. 130–137
[16] W. A. D. Englefield (1923) 1936, pp. 68, 69, 96. A "tillet" was probably a toilette, a small cloth from which stencils were cut – or it refers to printing on cloth – Alan Borg 2005, p. 71
[17] James Ayres 2009
[18] Visited and photographed by the author in 2009 – for Chinoiserie in England in the late seventeenth century see Alan Borg 2013, pp. 112–114. An alternative source for orientilism was Antoine Watteau's *Figures chinoises et tartars* (*c.* 1709) which could indicate that these hangings were imported from France. For the reference to William Dix see Borg, 2005, p. 85
[19] Nicholas Mander 1997, pp. 131, 132, 137

[20]   C. Villiers *The Fabric of Images*, London, 2000

[21]   A recent small exhibition of Marcus Gheerart's Jnr (1561–1635) work in England comprised six small panel paintings and four large works on canvas; Karen Hearn 2002, p. 63

[22]   Tessa Murdoch ed. 2006, p. 266

[23]   Robert Dossie 1764, p. 266; Colin Platt 2005, p. 177, citing Butterfield *Diary of John Adams* Vol. I p. 294. The Collections of New England Heritage in the Harrison Gray Otis House in Boston include a fragment of a stained hanging with an American provenance; pers. comm. Abbott Lowell Cummings

[24]   Sir Hugh Platt *The Jewel House of Art and Nature*, 1594, pp. 76–77, quoted more fully in James Ayres 2003, p. 74. See also John McCann "A Vernacular Window of 1618" which discusses oiled linen, fenestrals, *Vernacular Architecture* 41, 2010, pp. 81–83

[25]   John Smith 1676, pp. 90–91; Peter Thornton 1978, p. 41

[26]   William Connely *Beau Nash: Monarch of Bath and Tunbridge Wells*, London, 1955, pp. 72–73 quoting the Countess of Bristol

[27]   Edward Edwards 1808, Vol. I, pp. 22–23 who states that "for many years" these transparencies "were to be seen in the Ordinance Office at the Tower of London"

[28]   The link between the two events is established by the correspondence between Frederick Johnson in Berkeley Square, London and Maurice Johnson in Spalding; Diana and Michael Honeybone ed. 2010, pp. 178–179, March 1749. For Sands see Howard Colvin 1995

[29]   W. T. Whitley 1928, Vol. I, p. 158

[30]   Holger Hoock (2003) 2009, pp. 137–138 and fig. 5.1 and pp. 178–179; Hans Hammelmann 1975, p. 68. Smirke's design is in the Sir John Soane Museum, London; Shena Mason ed. 2009, p. 204, Cat. 241; Jerry White 2012, 533

[31]   James Ayres 1998, p. 225 illustrates both the drawing and the transparency

[32]   Trevor Fawcett *Norfolk Archaeology* 1968, pp. 245–252

[33]   Jenny Uglow 2006, pp. 280, 338

[34]   Joseph Farington, p. 627 1 August 1796

[35]   British Museum, Dept of P&D, Collection of Trade Labels

[36]   The author knows of no such wire screens surviving from the eighteenth century – James Ayres 2003, pp. 80–82

[37]   Between 1682 and 1692 the Uphoder John Hibbert supplied "umbrellas" to the Earl of Bedford to shield the room from the sun at Wooburn; Geoffrey Beard 1997, pp. 107–108

[38]   Heal Collection of Trade Labels, British Museum Dept of P&D

[39]   Susan Sloman 2002, pp. 126–127

[40]   Edward Orme *An Essay on Transparency Prints* ... London, 1807 – the illustrations are hand coloured

[41]   William Salmon (1672) 1701, Vol. II, p. 857

[42]   Robert Dossie 1764, p. 178

[43]   William Dunlap (1834) 1969, Vol. II, Pt I, pp. 143–144 for Murray and Vol. II, Pt I, p. 43 for this episode. The naval battle on Lake Erie against the British was part of the War of 1812; Oliver Hazard Perry (1785–1819) was in command of American vessels

[44]   Sumpter Priddy 2004, pp. 128–130; see also: William Jedlick "Landscape Window Shades of the Nineteenth Century in New York and New England" MA Thesis, State University of New York, at Oneonta, 1967

[45]   Richard Rogers and Oscar Hammerstein II's *Oklahoma* was based on Lynn Rigg's 1931 play *Green Grow the Lilacs*. The original Broadway production of *Oklahoma* opened on 31 March 1943

[46] In this respect it is possibly not without significance that Shakespeare regularly makes reference to stained hangings or painted cloths in his plays. His grandfather, Robert Arden, left no less than 11 sets of stained hangings in his Will. J. R. Mulnyne and N. Margaret Shewring eds *Shakespeare's Globe Rebuilt*, Cambridge, 1997, pp. 136–137, 152–154

[47] W. T. Whitley 1928, Vol. I, p. 72

[48] W. H. Pyne, 1823–24, Vol. II, p. 172

[49] Edward Edwards, 1808, Vol. II, p. 179; W. H. Pyne 1823–24, Vol. II, p. 91

[50] W. T. Whitley 1928, Vol. I, p. 81

[51] *Library of Fine Arts*, Vol. I, p. 326. Gainsborough's "showbox" is in the Victoria & Albert Museum – see James Ayres 1985, p. 161, figs 83–84

[52] Edward Edwards 1808, Vol. II, p. 1; Alan Borg 2013, p. 117

[53] Howard Colvin 1995. Novosielski's property venture centred on the south side of the Brompton Road, in London

[54] Edkin's letter books, Bristol Central Library B20196 cited by James Ayres 1998, pp. 225–227

[55] William Dunlap (1834) 1969, Vol. II, Pt I, p. 64

[56] *Ibid.*, Vol. II, Pt I, pp. 64–65

[57] *Ibid.*, Vol. II, Pt I, pp. 307–308

[58] *Ibid.*, Vol. II, Pt I, p. 14, Vol. II, Pt II, pp. 378–379

[59] Gullager's portraits have a strong immediacy that falls outside academic conventions. See Nina Fletcher Little 1976, cat. 47

[60] W. A. D. Englefield (1923), 1936, p. 57

[61] Ian Bristow 1996, p. 111; James Ayres 1998, p. 208

[62] W. A. D. Englefield (1923) 1936, p. 75

[63] James Ayres 2003, pp. 146–149

[64] John Abbott: Sketchbook 2 Notebook, Devon Record Office, Exeter, 404, MB1 B2 Abbott also mentions "linseed oyle" which, in London, plasterers were not permitted to use

[65] The technique was certainly described by Vasari, Louisa S. Maclehose 1907, chapters xii and xiii

[66] Nathaniel Lloyd 1931, figs 306–307 and S. O. Addy (1898) 1933, following p. 136 for illustration. The Calico House sgraffito work has since been so damaged that the date on this scheme now reads "1710". For its appearance prior to mutilation when it was dated 1719 see Addy (edition of 1933) black and white photographic illustration between pp. 136 and 137

[67] An example of this has been identified in No. 36 Craven Street, London, a street first built *c.* 1720–1730 in which Benjamin Franklin lived for ten years. The chimney was found to be plastered within the flue and externally (as became visible when the panelling was removed). See also Wilfred Kemp *The Practical Plasterer* (1893), London, 1926, chapter xvi "Sgraffito"

[68] For a fuller discussion of this type of work see James Ayres 2003, pp. 26–28

[69] Thornton and Cain eds 1981, p. 66

[70] Victoria & Albert Museum, London, E.1174–1988

[71] James Ayres 2003, pp. 144–145, figs 207–209; Kathryn Davies 2008

[72] Randle Holme *Academy of Armory* 1648/49, Vol. I, 1701 edition, p. 149

[73] James Ayres 2003, fig. 215

[74] *Ibid.*, fig. 223. Michael Bath 2003, p. 101 cites an early seventeenth century example

[75] E. A. Entwistle *The Book of Wallpaper*, Bath, 1970, pls 46, 47

76 James Ayres 2003, pp. 158, 159 fig. 227. Pers. comm. Melissa Thompson, English Heritage, East of England Region – Sept 2012 (the mural was first rediscovered in 1914)

77 Jean Lipman (1968) 1980

78 Illustrated in *Country Life* 17 March 1960 and B.M. collection of Trade Labels 90.19 in the Dept of P&D. Other services offered by Brown and New included carving and gilding – but at this late date it was probably sub-contracted. In addition "Mr Brown" taught drawing and lent drawings to copy from

79 R. Broby-Johansen *Kalkmalerier* ... Copenhagen, 1948 – for American examples see Nina Fletcher Little 1972 and for English murals see James Ayres 2003; for Scottish examples Michael Bath 2003

80 John Martin manuscript, 1690–1700, p. 4, Sir John Soane Museum, London

81 Giovanni Paolo Lomazzo (1538–1600) Italian painter and author of *Tratto dell'arte della pittura* ..., Milan, 1584: Richard Haydock transl., Oxford, 1598

82 James Ayres 2003, fig. 216

83 Iain McCallum 2003, p. 104, fig. 38

84 Allan Cunningham 1830, Vol. I, p. 51

85 *Ibid.*, Vol II, pp. 162–3 – quoting William Blake

86 J. T. Smith (1828) quoted by Allan Cunningham (1830), Vol. II, p. 178

87 Joseph Farington, p. 160 17 Feb 1799

88 Carpenter's or "Scotch glue" was derived from boiled animal bones

89 Hans Hammelman 1975, p. 17

Chapter 13

LIMNING & WATERCOLOUR PAINTING

Liming is a transliteration of the verb to illuminate, as in an illuminated manuscript. Consequently the craft has a far longer history than is our central concern here. For our purposes this art may be seen to be bracketed by the careers of the goldsmith and limner Nicholas Hilliard (1546/47–1618/19),[1] who worked chiefly as a portraitist, and Thomas Robins (1716–1770),[2] who is primarily known for his decorative topographical landscapes. In the interests of brevity this account will omit reference to the continuing use of this technique, into the nineteenth century, by portraitists working in miniature. In its essentials limning was an art-form in which pigments are bound by gums, etc and used as solid watercolour or *gouache*. The use of translucent watercolour by artists like Paul Sandby (1725–1809) and J. M. W. Turner (1775–1851) was generally a later development of this art which was based on the watercolour cakes devised by the Reeves brothers in the 1770s.

Limning

An unequivocal definition of limning was offered in 1672 by William Salmon who described it as: "… an Art whereby, in water Colours, we strive to resemble Nature in everything to the life".[3] Despite Salmon's precision the word was to be corrupted to signify naïve, provincial or Colonial painting. As early as 1766 limning is referred to in this inexact sense in Oliver Goldsmith's *The Vicar of Wakefield*. This novel includes a lengthy description of an itinerant "limner" who evidently painted in oil on canvas and was thus, by definition, not a limner.[4] Goldsmith was not alone in this flexible usage. In the same year (1766) John Penrose, on a visit to Bath, refers to the prices charged by a "limner" for a

277

quarter, half and full-length portrait in what is a clear reference to work in oil on canvas.[5] Even James Boswell, the biographer of the great lexicographer Samuel Johnson, misuses the word in his comment on the way in which Reynolds "limned" his last self-portrait of 1788.[6] Despite such casual usage Mrs Phelps in her *The Female Student* (1836) refers to "Painting in water-colours … often called Limning".[7] Whatever definition is accepted it is certain that the Painter-Stainers of London regarded limning as one aspect of their trade. Article 5 of their Charter of 1581/82 concerns "lymming" and staining upon numerous supports including: "paper, parchment, vellum or other thing".[8] The legal nature of this Charter is indicated by its precision for parchment was made from a whole variety of animal sources whereas vellum, a word having the same route as veal, was exclusively calf skin. The range of supports on which limners worked would, at a later date include ivory. In terms of the media (the carrier and the binder) William Salmon (1672) identifies "Rectified Spirits (from wine, sugar, Cyder or Perry), Gum Arabic [and] Ising-glass".[9]

The small dimensions at which limners generally worked involved great care in the grinding of pigments and the preparation of the media, all of which demanded an almost surgical precision. For Nicholas Hilliard limning was "fittest for gentlemen … presizly" because it was "klenly … as in grinding his coulers in [a] place wher ther is neither dust nor smoke, the watter wel chosen or distilled most pure".[10] As Hilliard predicted, the cleanliness of this art encouraged a number of amateurs (in the modern sense of the word) to engage in this activity and some, like Thomas Flatman (1635–1688), achieved

FIGURE 85. Nicholas Hilliard (*c.* 1547–1619) portrait miniature of *Robert Dudley Earl of Leicester* gouache on vellum (diam. 1¾ in/4.4 cm). The background shows a wall the decoration of which was possibly by John Bossam who was described by Hilliard as "the most rare *English Drawer* of Story Works"; see Fig. 86. (Victoria & Albert Museum, London)

a professional standard.[11] The immaculate cleanliness and tidiness of this art may be at the root of John Aubrey's (1626–1697) objection that "limning is too effeminate; Painting [in oil being] more masculine and useful".[12] The supremacy of the oil media in terms of its prestige had begun.

For earlier centuries a greater equality between the various media seems to have prevailed. In Elizabethan and early Jacobean England the limners served the elite whereas the Serjeant Painters to the Crown, working primarily in oil paint, were gradually being reduced to the role of jobbing artisans.[13] So how was it that a craftsman like Hilliard emerged from provincial Devon to work in the courtly *milieu* of London and Westminster? What were his origins geographically, socially and in terms of his craft? Hilliard was born in Exeter, Devon in 1546 or 1547, the son and grandson of prosperous goldsmiths. As a Protestant, during Queen Mary's reign, the young Hilliard seems to have sought refuge on the Continent in the service of John Bodley's family who also came from Exeter.[14] This would have given young Hilliard a sense of a far wider world and probably made something of a gentleman of him. As the son and grandson of goldsmiths he already belonged to the mercantile elite of Exeter.[15] In their role as bankers, goldsmiths were potentially a cut above the many other tradesmen in financial, if not always social terms.

Although Hilliard would have imbibed an understanding of the goldsmith's craft from members of his family, he was not apprenticed to the Queen's goldsmith Robert Brandon until 1562 at the somewhat advanced age of fifteen or sixteen years. By 1569, at the age of 23, he had become a Freeman of the

FIGURE 86. Detail of "Blackwork" decoration of *c.* 1578 of the kind that Bossam created. This example is in a chamber in the Long House, Strand Street, Sandwich, Kent. The town was one of the Cinque Ports and as such was in touch with the Court, members of which passed through these harbours en-route to the Continent. Consequently this mural scheme is highly sophisticated. (See Fig. 85)

Goldsmith's Company of London and so it is likely that he served a delayed yet full seven year apprenticeship. As surviving examples of his goldsmithing attest he was to become, as he was to remain throughout his years as a limner, a very accomplished artist in precious metals. His magnificent Amada Jewel (*c.* 1600) manifests these twin aspects of his achievement. The linkage of these two art forms was to take practical effect in 1592 when Hilliard, as a Goldsmith, found his name attached to the Painter Stainers petition to Lord Burghley concerning their on-going conflict with the College of Arms.[16]

The connection between the goldsmith's craft and limning, improbable though it may seem, has a long history reaching back to Renaissance Italy and forward to early Federal America. Hilliard's contemporary Robert Peake (*c.* 1551–1619) was also apprenticed to a London goldsmith before developing as a portrait painter.[17] One hundred and fifty years later the young Henry Raeburn (1756–1823) was apprenticed to an Edinburgh goldsmith before he emerged as the Scottish portraitist.[18] In early Federal America a young Joseph Wood (*c.* 1778–1830), on a visit to New York City "was attracted by some miniature pictures in the window of a silversmith's shop". As a result of this chance sighting "He offered himself to this silversmith as an apprentice and was received". Wood was to become a fine silversmith and, like Hilliard two centuries earlier, also worked as a limner creating highly refined portrait miniatures.[19]

Hilliard is known to have painted in oil "a fair picture of her Majestie [Queen Elizabeth] to remain in the House [the Hall of the Goldsmith's Company] for an ornam't and remembrance"; but he worked in this medium under sufferance.[20] The phrase "an ornam't and remembrance" could have been designed to describe what are now sometimes referred to as "Elizabethan Icons".[21] In the last years of the Virgin Queen's reign her visage was awful to behold with her white face and black teeth. For his later portraits of the monarch Hilliard probably relied on earlier representations which had been taken by him, at the Queen's request, in the most flattering light.[22]

It seems that Queen Elizabeth was intent on sponsoring an official image of the royal personage, one that would portray her, the personification of the crown, in as favourable a way as possible. To achieve this she was, as noted in Chapter 10, prepared to take drastic action against unauthorised versions. In the Preface to his unfinished *History of the World* Sir Walter Raleigh states that such images of Her Majesty made by "unskilled and common painters" were, by the Queen's command "knocked to pieces and cast into the fire".[23] Of particular concern were the less than flattering representations of the Queen by sign painters.[24] As early as 1563 a Proclamation was issued with a view to commissioning official portraits of her majesty which would meet "the contynuall requests of so many of hir Nobility and Lords". For this purpose "some coning persons ... therefor shall shortly make a portrait of her person or visage to be participated to others". In the "meantime", artists were "to forbear from paynting, graving, printing and making of any portrait of hir Majesty until some speciall person that shall by hir allowed shall have first finished a pourtraiture thereof after which hir Majestie will be content".[25] The repetition of an official image, based upon a standard pattern, was not new. Patterns or "patrons", pricked for pouncing, survive and demonstrate that they were used for the production of repeat "portraits" (Fig. 6). Examples, in oil, include the heads of Bishop John Fisher after a 1532–4 drawing by Holbein and a later portrait of Sir Henry Sidney of *c.* 1573.[26] Patterns of this kind are known to have belonged to the Elizabethan goldsmith Myles Bygland and also to Hilliard.[27] Hilliard's reputation for making the image of the Queen to her liking offers some circumstantial evidence that he made such a pattern "portrait" for others to follow – "to be participated" in.

In 1586 Isaac Oliver (before 1568–1617), a journeyman goldsmith in his late 20s, entered Hilliard's workshop presumably with the intention of acquiring the art of limning. According to Richard Haydocke, he was to become Hilliard's "well profitting scholar" to the extent that in the course of time Oliver was to eclipse his master. He was also to pre-decease him. As a foreigner Oliver (Olivier), who was related by marriage to the painter Gheeraerts the Younger,[28] was not listed either as a Goldsmith or as a Painter-Stainer in the records held by these Companies. Like other foreign artists and artisans, he lived at Blackfriars, one of the "peculiars" in London that fell outside the jurisdiction of the City's guilds.[29]

By the early seventeenth century, possibly under the influence of Continental artists like Oliver, this once quintessentially English art form began to adopt alien characteristics. Where Hilliard had happily worked on vellum backed by card (often a playing card) new supports were to be adopted. In this respect Isaac Oliver's son Peter, with the encouragement of Sir Balthazar Gerbier (b. Middleburg 1592–d. 1663) introduced a more lavish use of a gesso ground for limning.[30] Furthermore Isaac Oliver experimented with a miniature in 1615 which was stained on cambric and may have been intended to hang in a window as a transparency.[31] Of more long-term significance to limning, as a distinct craft, was the tendency, begun by Hilliard, for its practitioners to work in oil paint. Isaac Oliver may have employed this medium at times and Hilliard's apprentice Rowland Lockey is known to have done so later in life. The confusion between limning and oil painting had begun. A writer in

1706, looking back on the work of John Hoskins (*c.* 1595–1665) referred to him as "a very eminent limner … bred a face-painter in Oil".[32] Experience of working in oil paint may have encouraged a progressively greater use of bold brush strokes, even when using size or gum bound pigments. Some have attributed this stylistic change to Samuel Cooper (1608–1672) who, according to Horace Walpole, "gave the strength and freedom of oil to miniature."[33] The employment of ever greater chiaroscuro was also part of this trend, an effect that would have been anathema to both Hilliard and his principal patron, the Queen. With regard to Rowland Lockey his brother Nicholas, like their father, was an Armourer by trade. Nicholas Lockey may also have been an Armourer by patrimony which would explain why he was careful to describe himself as "useinge and professinge for his livinge … the art of lymeinge … pictures".[34] Be that as it may Lockey is yet another possible example of the association between metal working and limning.

The aesthetic contamination of English limning, by Continental values in oil painting, became particularly evident following Van Dyck's arrival in London in 1632. Appropriately, for an alien, the King provided the painter with a house overlooking Blackfriars. Van Dyck's fondness for dramatic skies and the general flamboyance of his approach was continued by Sir Peter Lely (1618–1680) also working in oil. Confirmation of these trends, within the British tradition was reinforced by the limners Charles Beale Jnr and Richard Gibson who are both believed to have worked in Lely's studio. According to Horace Walpole, Gibson was a "Dwarf [who] being page to a lady at Mortlake" was placed by her "for his training as a painter" with "Francesco Clyne".[35] Gibson used a particularly strong impasto in his miniatures, another feature that is more characteristic of oil painting.[36] This drift towards the use of oil-based media was to have some practical benefits. According to Claude Boutet's manual of 1684 "*Painting in Oil* has its advantages" in that "it takes up less time". In the next paragraph the author reverses his position and goes on to say that "*Miniature* like wise has its Advantages" not least the portable nature of the implements which may be carried "in your Pockets".[37]

Boutet's *Traité de mignature* … (Fig. 87) was later published in English (2nd edition of 1730), but because the original was "written in the Romish Communion" some features were omitted in the translation on the grounds that certain phrases in the original French would not "appear very gracefully in the Language of a Protestant Country". As with so many manuals published at this time the author expresses the hope that it shall not offend "the masters of the mystery" regarding trade secrecy. Consequently the title page claims that the book was intended for "young Persons of Quality" and that miniature painting was a "charming Accomplishment". By implication, artisans were to have no cause for concern with regard to this publication. In contrast to the title page the Preface attempts to play these issues in both ways. On the one hand every effort had been taken to "guard against any Offence which Skilfull Painters" might take against "this little Assemblage of Instructions". Alternatively the manual could be useful "to such as cannot easily be provided with a Master to qualifie them for this charming Employment" – in the circumstances "accomplishment" would have been a more diplomatic choice of words. Despite this contradictory stance Boutet's book declares that ultimately it was designed for the "Tyro" whatever their social position or professional intentions.

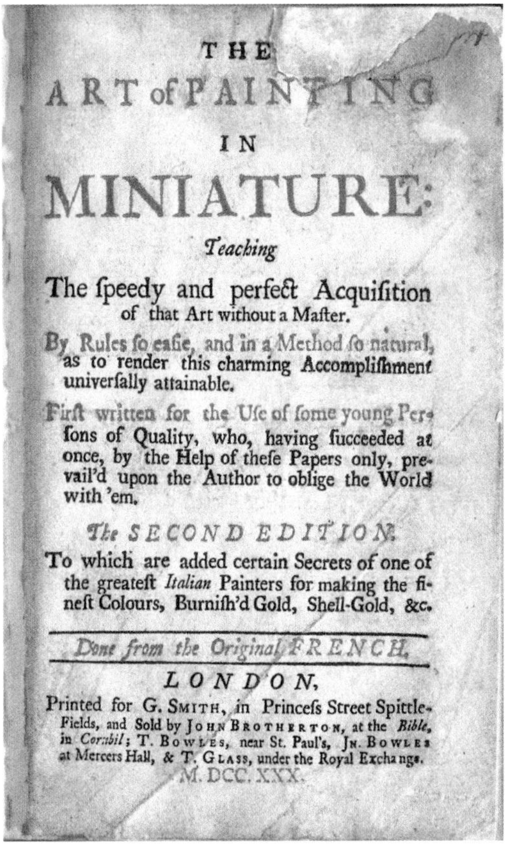
THE
ART of PAINTING
IN
MINIATURE:
Teaching
The ſpeedy and perfect Acquiſition of that Art without a Maſter.
By Rules ſo eaſie, and in a Method ſo natural, as to render this charming Accompliſhment univerſally attainable.
Firſt written for the Uſe of ſome young Perſons of Quality, who, having ſucceeded at once, by the Help of theſe Papers only, prevail'd upon the Author to oblige the World with 'em.
The SECOND EDITION.
To which are added certain Secrets of one of the greateſt *Italian* Painters for making the fineſt Colours, Burniſh'd Gold, Shell-Gold, &c.
Done from the Original FRENCH.
LONDON,
Printed for G. Smith, in Princeſs Street Spittle-Fields, and Sold by John Brotherton, at the *Bible*, in *Cornhil*; T. Bowles, near St. Paul's, Jn. Bowles at Mercers Hall, & T. Glass, under the Royal Exchange.
M.DCC.XXX.

FIGURE 87. *The Art of Painting in Miniature,* London, 1730. Claude Boutet's manual was first published in French in 1684. (Author's Collection)

Although this publication may have addressed conflicting markets it certainly included much information of a practical nature whoever it was intended for. Lurking within these pages are a number of trade secrets that must have been of concern to professional limners. For example, he recommends the use "of the Gall of an Ox, a Carp, or an Eel, particularly of the last; in green, black, gray, yellow and brown Colours, it will not only take away their greasy Nature, but also give them a Lustre and Brightness". The animal gall was to be mixed with brandy, ingredients which, when combined, were believed to make "the Colour stick better to the Velom". Boutet also advisd that "Your Velom must be pasted upon a little Plate of Brass or Wood", although card was more usual.[38]

In 1705 Rosalba Carriera submitted a miniature painted on a thin sheet of ivory to the Academy of St Luke in Rome as her diploma piece (masterpiece?).

Two years later Bernard Lens (1682–1740) painted what is believed to be the first miniature executed on ivory in England.[39] In some ways a new age of painting in miniature had arrived which may be seen as somewhat distinct to that of the earlier limners. In effect the victory of the easel painters was conceded and the limners sought to emulate the painterly effects more typical of the oil-based media. In contrast an art predicated on the use of pigments suspended in a medium of gum Arabic and applied as solid colour to paper or vellum was limning in its historic sense. This was the theme of Henry Gyles's *The Art of Limning...* written before 1660. His account makes reference to John Gwillims' *The way how to lymme & thou shalt lay colours & make syse for Lymminge or to cowche thy gold upon velome or parchment* a text which was "taken out of a booke ..." written before 1582. From references such as these it is evident that limning was understood as a distinct art and craft. As such this was an art that Hilliard (*c.* 1598) described as "a thing apart ... [which] excelleth all other painting whatsoever".[40]

The artistic community in Elizabethan London and Westminster, of which Hilliard was a member, was centred on serving the court. In portraiture many of these artists placed their more regal sitters against a blue background. This was certainly Holbein's practice and one that was conscientiously followed by Hilliard.[41] The choice of this colour was probably as much to do with questions of status as with issues of aesthetics for ultramarine was made from ground lapis lazuli from distant Afghanistan and was so expensive that it came to be seen, in effect, as the "Imperial Purple" of Tudor England.[42] Consequently the "Royal Blue" of the sixteenth century was reserved for the elite partly on the basis of cost but also out of some residual sense of the sumptuary laws of the past. In this way certain pigments, together with gold and gilding, were not purely a question of artistic choice but examples of conspicuous consumption – emblems of power and status. In this sense the monarchy and aristocracy of Tudor and early Stuart England were meeting an obligation to demonstrate the strength of the realm rather than acting as self-indulgent individuals. The miniatures by Hilliard and his generation both mirror and embody these features.

* * * *

In Hanovarian England status remained significant but the "Divine Right of Kings" was firmly in the past. Perhaps for this reason a less centralised culture emerged. In the provinces fashion was sometimes followed in unfashionable ways. A limner might represent the latest fad in terms of dress, architecture or gardening, but could do so in a less than up-to-date idiom. For example

Alexander Marshall painted "in water-colours...on vellum a book of Mr Tradescants [Jnr 1608–1662] choicest flowers and plants", a late example of the medieval tradition for a herbal.[43] This may have established a renewal of the limner's craft which Thomas Robins the Elder (1715/16–1770), among others, was to exemplify in his work. In the early 1750s Robins painted the ultra-fashionable Rococo gardens at Painswick House, Gloucestershire, but he did so as a traditional provincial limner, applying his size-bound pigments to vellum. Robins was born near Cheltenham and apprenticed to Jacob Portret, a local fan and ceramic painter. By October 1742 Robins is known to have been associated with the fan painter George Speren whose toy shop (in the sense of *etui*) was in Orange Grove, Bath. Lady Mary Somerset at nearby Badminton House was to be taught drawing by these limners.[44] Spas were important centres for artists of all kinds in that they attracted the fashionable society which visited such resorts to take the waters – where they became potential patrons of the arts. It was presumably for this reason that Thomas Gainsborough spent some years in Bath.[45] Another limner, and a contemporary of Robins, was Thomas Loggon who, like Richard Gibson before him (see p. 282 above) had previously been a court dwarf. Loggan worked in both Bath and Tunbridge Wells as a fan and miniature painter. His view of Tunbridge Wells (1748) was engraved much later by Richard Phillips and published in 1804 (Fig. 88). This print is equipped with numbered identifications of the individuals portrayed in this general view of the spa. These include William Pitt the Elder, Samuel Johnson, Colley Cibber, and Beau Nash who spent part of each year at his "colony" Tunbridge Wells when not presiding over the Assembly Rooms in Bath. At No. 22 on the far right is "Mr Loggan " the artist. The following year in 1749 Loggan also created a *View of North Parade, Bath* suggesting that he may have accompanied Beau Nash in his journeys between the two spas. His engraved view of *North Parade* is printed on a fan which is hand painted in gouache.[46] The work of Speren, Robins and Loggan was somewhat towards the artisan spectrum of the limners art and as such has considerable charm, and as historical topographical works possess great verisimilitude. At this time liming in general, and fan painting in particular, were seen as secondary, if not exactly second rate, artistic activities. It was an attitude that expressed itself, as prejudices so often do, in oblique ways. This is reflected in Horace Walpole's assessment of Charles Jervas's canvases which he saw as "a light flimsy kind of fan painting, but as large as life."[47] Despite the perceived secondary nature of this kind of painting the architect James "Athenian" Stuart (1713–1788) worked, in his youth, as a fan painter for Lewis Goupy. A generation later Ozias Humphrey RA (1742–1810) studied under Collins, a Bath limner, before

FIGURE 88. Thomas Loggon *The Walks, Tunbridge Wells*, Kent; gouache, *c.* 1748. Loggon also worked in Bath, and may have accompanied "the king" of the Somerset Spa when he was visiting his "colony" in Kent (Willard Connely, 1955). (Tunbridge Wells Museum)

emerging as a painter in oils in London.[48] There were exceptions to this less than whole-hearted endorsement of fan painting, which characterised attitudes at this time. For example, Anthony Poggi's work was seen as representing the more "polite" values that were possible in this art form. In 1781 Reynolds wrote the promotional blurb for one of Poggi's exhibitions of fan painting, in which he argued that: "… none of the inferior arts are ever likely to be improved unless undertaken by men who may be said to be above them …"[49] Clearly the President of the Royal Academy saw fan painting as one "of the inferior arts" whilst acknowledging that Poggi was one of its finest exponents.

Watercolour painting

Pigments mixed with a medium composed of water bound by a size or gum and used in translucent washes shall here, for reasons of concision, be termed "watercolour". In this sense watercolour was generally distinct from liming which deployed solid *gouache*. Both these methods were, until the

FIGURE 89. Richard Jones and Dormant Newman *The Excellency of the Pen and Pencil* 1668. This manual was evidently a later version of Jenner's book on "....Washing or Colouring of Mapps and Prints..." published by the Moxons in 1647. The gentleman shown colouring the two hemispheres of the globe is evidently using translucent colour so as not to obscure the printed line. Liquid watercolours of this kind were held in shells as shown here on the artist's table. (H. F. duPont Museum Delaware)

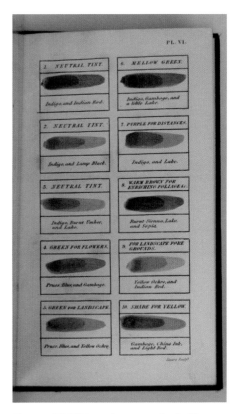

FIGURE 90. Watercolour samples in George Marshall Mather's *Elements of Drawing*, Edinburgh, 1830. (Author's Collection)

1770s, sufficiently complex to have been largely confined to trained practitioners. The distinction, such as it was, between the two systems may have begun to emerge in the fifteenth century. This was probably a response to the rising importance of blockbooks, woodcut illustrations and text cut into a single block of wood (the precursors of printing with woodcuts and moveable type). In the polychromatic age of the illuminated manuscript these printed books were inevitably hand coloured. For this purpose translucent washes of colour were required that would not obliterate the underlying printed line.[50]

Some authorities have argued that there was a continuum between the craft of the limners (illuminators) and that of the watercolourists who decorated woodcut illustrations. The evidence would suggest that the opposite was true for although manuscript and printed books were clearly related, the distinction between limning and painting in watercolour was such that the latter was dependent upon the burgeoning use of "clothlets". These were small pieces of cloth that had been soaked in a colour and then dried as a means of "locking up" small quantities of pre-prepared watercolour. Eastlake (1847) makes reference to a fifteenth century Venetian document which states that when artists wish to use such colours they should "cut off a small portion [of cloth] and place it in a shell with a little water, the evening before. In the morning the tint will be ready, the colour being extracted from the linen". This was, very evidently, a source of translucent watercolour, a "tint", rather than opaque *gouache*. In Italy Cennino Cennini refers to clothlets as a source of colours for glazes: "to shade with colours" which further emphasises their translucence.[51] In fifteenth century Germany, where clothlets were used to colour blockbooks, they were known as *"tuchlein varwen"* (literally "clothlet colours").[52]

With the development of moveable type in the late fifteenth century, and the expansion of publishing in the following decades, the use of translucent washes became essential if black and white images were to be given polychromatic treatment. This was of vital importance in relationship to printed maps. Consequently this art-form may, to some extent, be associated with the Age of Discovery. There is therefore a certain historical logic in the position of John White (fl. 1585–1593) as one of the first English exponents of watercolour painting. As an explorer his eye witness portrayals of Elizabethan Virginia [South Carolina], her indigenous people, flora and fauna are such an important historical record that they have eclipsed White's importance as an artist.[53]

Eventually this new form of watercolour painting was to inspire the publication of instruction manuals. One of the first of these was Thomas Jenner's *Book of Drawings, Limning, Washing or Colouring of Maps and Prints* which was published by the brothers James and Joseph Moxon in 1647. The title of that book makes an effortless distinction between "Limning" and "Washing" and the primary purpose of the latter. The hand colouring of maps and prints was to become something of a subsidiary industry that straddled publishing and the visual arts, an activity that persisted into the first decade of the twentieth century (Fig. 89).[54] In 1796 such work could be well paid, for in that year a young man named J. Barron was employed by Green of Manchester "in colouring prints". He was to receive 15 shillings a week in his first year rising to 18 shillings in the following year and I guinea a week in the third year.[55]

Up to the last decades of the eighteenth century the most widely available watercolour wash was either bistre or Chinese ink (also known as Indian ink). These were mainly used monochromatically as a means of providing tonal values for works on paper. For polychromatic effects watercolour paints could be prepared using pigments carried by water and "bound" by various gums or sizes. Because of the relatively complex nature of these procedures polychromatic watercolour painting was long confined to its full-time practitioners. This is demonstrated by the fact that very few architectural drawings were embellished with colour until the late eighteenth century – although details like window openings on an elevation might be picked out with a monochromatic bistre wash.

Before the 1770s this basic lack of access to watercolour and other paints probably explains the enthusiasm, amongst the leisured classes, for making pictures out of all manner of materials like cut paper (Fig. 16), micre, human hair, shells, straw and much else besides. Consequently the use of such materials were seen to typify the amateur in contrast to the trained artist. On the basis of that outlook the Royal Academy, with its emphasis on the new "professionalism" of artists decided, in 1769, to exclude such "baubles" from their exhibitions.[56]

Despite the limitations placed upon the creative impulses of the leisured classes drawing remained one of their accomplishments. According to John Evelyn (1662) Lord Arundel was of the opinion that "one who could not design a little, would never make an honest man".[57] There were various reasons why such activities were to become far more than a polished skill in polite society. In 1693 penmanship was introduced to Christ's Hospital School in the City of London. In 1703 John Lens was recruited to teach drawing and designing at Trinity House in the City where mathematics and navigation were a central part of the curriculum. Significantly Lens was described in 1708 as a gunner who had been poached from Major John Ayres's school at the Hand and Pen near St Paul's. It was there that Ayres included "navigation, surveying, dialling, gauging, perspective, gunnery, algebra and geometry" among other subjects that he taught.[58] Such a list of ostensibly unrelated activities obscures a certain logic. This was a time when an army officer would draw a panoramic view ("perspective") on which, by means of trigonometry, calculations were written down so that a gunner could establish the range of his target (see Fig. 15a). In much the same way a naval officer would, by triangulation, produce a drawing of a coastline in the preparation of a chart.

For the officer class landscape drawing was central to their education and their careers. One example of this concerned the son of the painter Joseph Farington RA who, as a naval cadet with an artistic background, was in full possession of these graphic skills as compared with most of his fellow students. On 7 August 1799 young William Farington was interviewed by the examining "Captains [who] told him they should not trouble him with questions" so impressed were they with his watercolour drawings of "substitute rudders" and of "Coasts".[59] Needless to say, he was granted a commission.

It was in this context that Paul Sandby RA (1725/6–1809) taught watercolour painting at Woolwich Military Academy. This Academy was divided into an "upper, middle and lower school" with Sandby being engaged to teach in the "upper school".[60] One of the greatest military exponents of the art of watercolour painting at this time was Maj. Gen. John Gaspard le Marchant (1766–1812), the founder of the Royal Military Academy, Sandhurst. Another officer and gentleman who achieved a professional standard as a painter in watercolours was Coplestone Warre Bampfylde (1720–1791) of Hestercombe Park near Taunton. As a friend of Henry Hoare it was Bampfylde who produced an important series of watercolours of Stourhead – he also exhibited at the Royal Academy in the 1770s and 1780s.[61] At the other end of the social scale there emerged a vernacular tradition for watercolour images – they are less than portraits – of "other ranks" and N.C.Os. These were generally taken of soldiers about to be sent overseas to outposts of Empire and the hazards that implied – hence the dedicatory inscriptions to loved ones that these images often include. Dickens describes an artist who specialised in such work, a Miss La Creevy, in *Nicholas Nickleby* (1839). Samples of her work included "naval

FIGURE 91. Isabella Avis of Twickenham *James Ayres, 18th Hussars, c.* 1811. In that year the regiment moved from Wiltshire to Hounslow, Middlesex when this watercolour was probably painted. The introduction of watercolour cakes by the Reeves brothers in *c.* 1770 increased the use of this medium by all manner of artists of varying degrees of proficiency and professionalism. (Private Collection)

FIGURE 92. Thomas Rowlandson "Exhibition ... by the Society of Painters in Watercolours" from J. C. Stadler's aquatint in *The Microcosm of London* (1808). As can be seen here watercolours were, at this time, presented like oil paintings – carved or "compo" frames without visible mounts. The close-hanging of such exhibitions would later encourage the use of wide mounts (or mats) so that pictures were furnished with the built-in ability to be separated from their neighbours. It should be added that in the earlier system, mounts were inserted beneath the rebate of the frame to separate the glass from the surface of the watercolour. In addition it was considered good practice to line this rebate with a dark toned paper to minimise any tendency of the light from the cut edge of the glass from being refracted into the picture. (Bridgeman Art Library)

dress coats with faces looking out of them and telescopes attached; one of a young gentleman in a very vermilion uniform flourishing a sabre ..." From this description it is evident that La Creevy lacked a thorough training and was dependent upon the newly invented watercolour cakes by the Reeves brothers (see below). It is just possible that Dickens, in his description of Miss La Creevy, was mindful of a watercolourist like Isabella Avis who is known to have worked in Twickenham west of London in 1811–1812. [62]

Appropriately Paul Sandby, like his elder brother Thomas (1721–1798), had begun his career as a surveyor. In 1747 he was appointed draughtsman to the "Military Survey of North Britain" (Scotland). In this capacity he produced maps and plans of fortifications tinted with translucent watercolour.[63] This association between surveying and watercolour painting goes back to Ralph Treswell (*c.* 1540–1616) if not before. His pictorial surveys of Tudor London are reinforced by translucent watercolour. Treswell was a Painter Stainer who is known to have painted heraldic banners. This suggests that he was very much a Stainer as this would be consistent with his use of watercolour on his topographical surveys. A couple of centuries later the Sandby brothers were following in this tradition. From such origins Paul Sandby emerged as a painter who was just as likely to use solid watercolour in combination with translucent washes – he was more the artist than the purist. Examples of this flexible approach include his *Magic Lantern* (1753) and *Windsor on Rejoicing Night* (1768).[64]

For much of his work in Scotland it is likely that Sandby prepared his own watercolours. An insight into what this entailed may be gleaned from an account which, unusually, was written by a member of the leisured classes: "We have been very busy grinding paints today. I bought the colours in powder and mixed them with gum-water and white sugar until they were like paste, and then put them in little saucers … We made eighteen sorts … it was such nice dirty work".[65] This description by the aristocratic Mary Talbot, writing from Penrice Castle, Glamorgan in 1812 is unusual as by this date commercially produced watercolours had been available for some decades.

On Sandby's move to London from Scotland he probably had access to manufactured watercolours sold by colourmen. At this juncture he stood on the threshold of a revolution in watercolour painting, a situation that was well described in 1811 as follows:

> "For many years after Mr Sandby commenced landscape drawing, no colours were in general use except such as were peculiarly adapted for the staining of maps and plans, and it was himself [Sandby] who set Middleton the colour maker to prepare them in somewhat like their present state, and which is now brought to so great a perfection by Reeves, Newman and others".[66]

Of these colourmen the Reeves brothers were the most significant in this respect. It was they who most fully developed the manufacture of these easily soluble watercolour cakes. In 1766 they submitted samples of this product to the Chemistry Committee of the [Royal] Society of Arts. These samples were then forwarded for practical trials to be undertaken by the painters Mary Black, Hendrik de Meyer and Thomas Hearne. Of these three de Meyer was to reflect on the "usefulness on travels and voyages" of these highly portable watercolours. This was prophetic. A couple of years later Isaac Smith sailed as a midshipman on Captain James Cook's first circumnavigation of the globe and took with him a box of Reeves's watercolour cakes.[67] The impact of this innovation was magnified by the improvements in paper-making technology at this time, when "laid" paper was joined by the innovation of the "wove" variety. When held to the light the latter reveals what is, in effect, a watermark of lines whereas the laid paper is plain.[68] In 1768 the painter Thomas Gainsborough was one of the first to recognise the potential of this innovative "wove" paper that the *New Bath Guide* was printed on in that year.[69]

As a direct consequence of these developments a flood of watercolours would pour forth from amateurs and professionals, men and women. Of still greater consequence was the way in which these innovations enabled *plein air* painting to become more possible. For the amateurs numerous instruction manuals appeared, a market which the German-born Rudolph Ackemann (1764–1834) was to exploit. Having trained as a coach designer, and following his role in that capacity working for the coach-builder Antoine Cavassi in Paris, Ackemann settled in London in the late 1780s. in Britain he continued his work as a designer of such vehicles (see p. 233 above). By 1791 his *Imitation of Drawings of Fashionable Carriages* was published by J. C. Stadler. This was followed by later volumes which Ackemann published himself and it is as a publisher that he is now chiefly known. By 1794 at his showroom on the Strand (No. 96, later moving to No. 101) he sold his numerous publications together with his "own label" watercolours which were also available "at all Booksellers, Printsellers and Stationers in Great Britain". In connection with these watercolours he set up a drawing school which taught upwards of 80 pupils – an establishment that closed in 1806. The numerous primers on watercolour painting that Ackemann published at this time exploited the market that he helped to develop.[70] With such an entrepreneur the overlap between art and artistry, between manufacture and commerce, could be exploited to great effect. In terms of instruction manuals this was a demand that was met by numerous authors and publishers. Among the former was Charles Hayter and his *Introduction to Perpective, Practical Geometry, Drawing and Painting* (1813). The 1832 edition includes on its title page the recommendation that it was "properly adapted for the instruction of females".

In Regency England, as in early Federal America, it seems that everyone, the trained and the untrained, were indulging in watercolour painting. As an art, the work of the limner was in decline, painting in watercolour was in the ascendant.

Notes

[1]   Thornton and Cain eds 1981

[2]   The rediscovery of Thomas Robins is entirely due to research on this artist by John Harris, 1976

[3]   William Salmon 1672, Vol. II, chapter xv

[4]   Oliver Goldsmith *The Vicar of Wakefield* (1766), London, 1917, pp. 84–86. *The Shorter Oxford Dictionary*, 2002 defines Limner as follows: 1. Hist: An illuminator of manuscripts M E; 2. A painter, esp. a portrait painter, Now literary

[5]   Brigitte Mitchell and Hubert Penrose 1990, p. 4,1 April 1766. The charges were £20, £40 and £60

[6]   Richard Wendorf1 996, p. 45

[7]   Although Mrs Phelps ran a female seminary in New England this book was published in London

[8]   W. A. D. Englefield (1923) 1936, p. 67

[9]   William Salmon 1672, Vol. II, chapter II, p. 857

[10] Thornton and Cain eds 1981, p. 72

[11] Katherine Coombs 1998, pp. 71–72

[12] Kim Sloan 2000, p. 43

[13] Thornton and Cain eds 1981, Introduction, p. 23

[14] *Ibid.*, Introduction, pp. 20–21. John Bodley's son Sir Thomas Bodley was to found the Bodleian Library, Oxford

[15] Early modern goldsmiths often functioned as bankers

[16] Thornton and Cain eds 1981, pp. 20, 21, 26; Alan Borg 2005, p. 38

[17] Karen Hearn 1995, pp. 185–186

[18] Allan Cunningham 1830, Vol. V, pp. 204–207

[19] William Dunlap (1834) 1969, Vol. II, Pt I, p. 97

[20] Thornton and Cain eds 1981, pp. 31–32

[21] Roy Strong 1969

[22] The description of Queen Elizabeth I's white face and black teeth was recorded at Greenwich by the German traveller Paul Hentzner; Thornton and Cain eds 1981, p. 86 – quoted in full in Chapter 1. See also p. 160 here

[23] Raleigh's *History* … was written while he was imprisoned in the Tower of London and left incomplete on his release in 1616

[24] In Hanovarian England street signs of Queen Elizabeth remained popular. On 8 January 1743 *The Spectator* (No. 744) reported that on Ludgate Street in the City of London "several people were gaping at a very splendid sign of Queen Elizabeth which far exceeded all the other signs in the street, the painter having shown a masterful judgement and the carver and gilder much pomp and splendour. It looked rather like a capital picture in a gallery then a sign in the street"

[25] W. A. D. Englefield (1923) 1936, pp. 53–54

[26] Susan Foister *Holbein in England*, London, 2006, Cat. 132, 133 – also Karen Hearn 1995, Cat 98, 102

[27] On 23 February 1571 the wife of the engraver John Rutlingen, who worked closely with Hilliard, promised to send "unto Thomas Clerke a booke of portraitures within this sennygt [signet seal] wholle and perfett, wch is now in the hands of Nichas Helliard" Karen Hearn 2002, Cat. 102

[28] Karen Hearn 1995, p. 171

[29] Katherine Coombs 1998, pp. 34–54. Isaac Oliver was the son of Pierre Olivier, a Rouen goldsmith who, as a Protestant, sought refuge in London. The family is known to have visited England in 1568 and may well have settled in their adopted country by 1577

[30] *Ibid.*, p. 61. Gesso was used by medieval limners in relationship to gilding on illuminated manuscripts

[31] *Ibid.*, pl. 26 *The Goddess Diana* this possible transparency is now laid on a thin panel of lime tree

[32] *Ibid.*, pp. 58, 62 quoting Bainbrigge Buckeridge

[33] Horace Walpole 1786, Vol. III, p. 110

[34] Katherine Coombs 1998, p. 60

[35] Horace Walpole 1786, Vol. II, p. 226

[36] Katherine Coombs 1998, pl. 45

[37] Claude Boutet, English edition of 1730, p. 96

[38] *Ibid.*, pp. 9, 13

[39] Katherine Coombs 1998, p. 76

[40] Thornton and Cain 1981, p. 24

[41] *Ibid.*, p. 22

[42] Imperial or Tyrian Purple was extracted, in minute quantities from *Murex trunculus*, a Mediterranean mollusc, and used for dyeing textiles. For sculpture purple porphrey from Egypt enjoyed similar status

[43] Horace Walpole 1786, Vol. II, p. 120; Jennifer Potter 2006, pp. 9, 288, 335

[44] John Harris 1976, also Cathryn Spence "Thomas Robins: Back In Bath" *The Bath Magazine* November 2007. Portret looks very much like a surname based on his trade? Tim Richardson (2007) 2008, 430.

[45] Susan Sloman 2002. In the early nineteenth century George Smart sold his "Cloth & Velvet" pictures in Tunbridge Wells using the off-cuts from his trade as a tailor to make them

[46] Examples of Loggan's work are in Tunbridge Wells Museum and a fan by him a *View of North Parade, Bath* is in the Holburne Museum, Bath. See also Willard Connely *Beau Nash: Monarch of Bath and Tunbridge Wells*, London 1955

[47] Horace Walpole 1786, Vol. IV, p. 24

[48] J. T. Smith (1828) 1919, Vol II, p. 290

[49] Richard Wendorf 1996, p. 111

[50] Shelley Fisher, Lisha Glinsman and Doris Oltrogge "The Pigments of Hand-Coloured Fifteenth Century Relief Prints …" in Peter Parshall ed. 2009, p. 277

[51] Sir Charles Lock Eastlake (1847) 1960, Vol. I, p. 127. Cennini (b. 1310) translated by Daniel Thompson 1933, chapter x

[52] Christopher Thompson 1847, pp. 126–127

[53] Kim Sloan 2007, p. 234

[54] For the Moxon brothers see Derek A Long 2013, pp. 8–9. The author's grandfather Henrik Grönvold (1858–1940), the Danish-born ornithologist and artist, regularly travelled from England to Germany to supervise such work

[55] Joseph Farington, pp. 730–731 27 December 1796

[56] Cited by Robert C. Alberts 1978, p. 96

[57] John Evelyn 1662, p. 103

[58] Kim Sloan 2000, p. 105; see also John Ayres 1700; Ewan Clayton 2013, p. 164–165

[59] Joseph Farington, p. 1264 7 August 1799

[60] *Ibid.*, p. 951 20 December 1979

[61] Many of le Marchant's watercolours remain with his descendants including his final work, a prospect of the battlefield at Salamanca painted on the eve of the battle in which he was killed. For Bampfylde see Tim Richardson (2007) 2008, 414, and also Kim Sloan 2000, Cat. 64 and 65

[62] Charles Dickens *Nicholas Nickleby* 1839, chapter 3. Watercolour portraits of this type were to be displaced by the introduction of photography. See also James Ayres 1996, pp. 44–45 which illustrates Isabella Avis's portrait of *James Ayres, 18th Hussars*

[63] For example Sandby's *Plan of Castle Duirt* (1748); John Bonehill and Stephen Daniels eds 2009, pp. 92–93

[64] *Ibid.*, p. 163; for an example of Treswell's work see Anthony Quiney *Town Houses...* Yale, 2003, fig. 308; also Alan Borg 2005, p. 40 and James Ayres 1985, p. 64

[65] Joanna Martin, 2004, p. 232

[66] W. T. Whitley 1928, Vol. II, pp. 360–361

[67] James Ayres 1985, pp. 130–131, 105–107

[68] John Krill 1987; Joyce Townsend, *Watercolour* (glossary to booklet), London 2011. "Laid" paper was made by suspending rag fibres in a shallow tray with water and the draining off the water to allow the resulting paper to be dried and pressed. Wove paper is made in much the same way except that the base of the tray is made of woven wire to enable the water to drain off. The lines in this sieve remain visible as a watermark in the resulting paper – especially when it is held to the light.

[69] James Ayres 1985, p. 87, fig 123

[70] Simon Jervis 1992, pp. 100–102

Part 3

SCULPTORS

Chapter 14

SCULPTURE

For well over a century the word "sculpture" has come to be used so promiscuously that it all but defies definition.[1] It would therefore seem reasonable to consider briefly, how this word was understood in the early modern past amongst English speaking peoples. Take, for example, Lomazzo's *Tracte Containing the Arts of Curious Paintinge, Carving and Building* as "Englished" by Richard Haydocke (Oxford, 1598). In that title the word "sculpture" is scrupulously avoided and care is taken to make reference exclusively to "Painting" and "Carving".[2] Over 60 years later John Evelyn was unequivocal. For him only those arts that involve "cutting [may] in Propriety of Speech" be called *Sculpture.* This observation is to be found in his book *Sculptura: or the History and Art of Chalcography and Engraving in Copper (1652).*[3] It is in this sense that a published print will credit the engraver as *"Sculp[t]."* along with the draftsman or designer as *"Delin[t]."*.

The emphasis that Evelyn and others accords to "cutting" as the defining characteristic of "sculpture" naturally encompassed, in addition to engraving, carving in wood, stone and marble as well as gem cutting in intaglio and die-sinking. With regard to the latter some aspects of chasing were also included. By omission modelling in clay or casting in plaster, bronze, lead, iron or some other material, were excluded by Evelyn as examples of sculpture. In the following century a more permissive notion of "sculpture" developed so that the art now comprised both "Carving and Plasticke". For example, the glossary or "Builder's Dictionary" in *The Rudiments of Architecture* (1778) offered the following:

> "'*Plastique or plastic art*' is a branch of architecture that is not only comprehended under sculpture but is indeed [the] very sculpture itself; but with this difference, that the plasterer [or modeller], by his plastic art, makes figures by addition but the carver by subtraction".[4]

Sculpture, in its original or exact sense involved the cutting of a material that derived from animal, vegetable or mineral sources. This work could take either three dimensional or relief form. It was an expensive process not only because of its high level of skill, but also due to the often high cost of the materials. This was time-consuming work that resulted in a one-off product. In contrast, modelling was often quicker and casts could be produced as multiples – although a cast bronze, if elaborately chased, has the potential to become a unique object.[5]

A further issue of importance, and one that relates to sculpture both plastic and carved, concerns what might be termed "the discipline of form". This is a principle in which only that which is present as *form* might be given sculptural expression. On this basis a sculptured portrait head of an individual person would sometimes be created to imply a dark-haired subject by emphasising the hair line. Alternatively fair hair could be indicated by suppressing this junction. This was a sculptural trick which suggested "local colour" without offending the basic tenets of the art whilst enabling a likeness to be more plausible. One important challenge to these essential principles concerned the treatment of eyes in such a portrait head. This may be but a detail but one that emphasises the fundamental characteristics of sculpture – the treatment of form. In those terms the eye is the visible part of a sphere; the pupil within it being present only as "local colour". In Classical antiquity this conundrum was resolved by the sculptor leaving the eye sightless, or by painting in the pupil, or by inlaying a material of a different colour. The painter Jonathan Richardson Jnr (1694–1771) observed these important details in a group of Greek and Roman marble sculptures that he saw in the Villa Medici in Rome. In particular he describes what he believed to be a Greek figure of an old man in marble. In this he noted the head had "the Eye-balls mark'd which the Greeks never did nor is this done in any of the other Figures in the gallery".[6] On the basis of this evidence Richardson concluded that this was a Roman head that had been added to a Greek sculpture in a "restoration".

Of the truly sculptural materials wood, when carved with the sort of elaborate virtuosity that exploits its fibrous nature, is extraordinarily difficult. A lime tree carving of the school of Grinling Gibbons utilises these characteristics to the full. In contrast a reclining figure in elm by Henry Moore reveals the grain of the wood but is otherwise handled in a manner akin to stone. Generally speaking, and from a strictly technical standpoint, wood carving is far more of a challenge than working either stone or marble. The evidence for this, possibly disconcerting observation, will be examined further in the chapter on carving. For the moment, suffice to say, that there are numerous examples through history of sculptors who trained as woodcarvers but subsequently added stone and marble to their repertoire. The reverse was seldom, if ever, true.[7] In some ways this constituted what was, so to speak, a one-way valve between the two skills. The list of those who began working in wood, and later turned to stone and marble is long and distinguished (see Appendix XI). Such a roll-call would include Thomas Ventris of York (active 1620–1630),[8] Grinling Gibbons (1648–1721), William Barlow II (fl. 1740–1752), Sir Francis Chantrey RA (1781–1841) and John Gibson RA (1790–1866). Another example of this extension of skill was also true of the Dublin-born, London-trained American sculptor John Dixey (*c.* 1762–1820) who was to become Vice President of the Pennsylvania Academy in Philadelphia.[9] Thomas Banks RA (1735–1805), who began as a woodcarver apprenticed to William Barlow II underwent a similar metamorphosis. In Banks's case the transition from wood and stone to marble was not seamless (see p. 410 below). J. T. Smith (1828) stated that Banks "commenced carving in marble in 1763" and the sculptor certainly acknowledged that it was while he was in Rome in 1774 that Capizzoldi was "truly kind to me … by the instruction he has given me in cutting marble in which the Italians beat us hollow".[10]

In terms of working stone and marble the geological characteristics of a given region will inevitably result in carvers and masons becoming most proficient in their local materials. Thus the Italians were seen to "beat us hollow" in working marble. Similarly the so-called "marble" found in the Isle of Purbeck in Dorset was particularly difficult to work largely because it is composed of hard fossilised shells set in a relatively soft matrix of silica. This "marble", and related materials, was fashionable in England from *c.* 1170 to *c.* 1350.[11] Despite its widespread use at this time the limestone was so difficult to work that only those masons and carvers who were trained in the small Dorset town of Corfe on Purbeck were capable of working it – a situation reflected in surnames like de Corfe that identify these specialists.[12]

From the fourteenth century a comparable expertise developed in the Midlands where the carving of the local alabaster, a soft yet tenacious material, became a specialism. This was recognised in Nottingham and Chellaston to the extent that those who worked this mineral came to be known, in those locations, as "alabasterers".[13] Their work appears to have been carried out using marble carving implements but much of the detail was achieved with edge tools of the kind used by wood carvers. This explains certain features such as long ribbons of undercut alabaster, details more commonly found in fibrous materials like wood. Furthermore Nottingham alabaster panels in high relief were often set in elaborately carved wood retables and altar pieces

– an integration of both materials and skills. Possible confirmation for this hypothesis is offered by some of the oak panels dated 1541 in the west wall of the hall at Magdalen College, Oxford which have a strong resemblance to these alabaster panels.[14] Furthermore the edge tools used for wood carving were also employed for working ivory and hard white woods like holly which demands similar techniques. These associations between materials of vegetable, animal and mineral origin (wood, ivory, alabaster) have implications for an understanding of works in these substances. In this respect Lawrence Stone (1955) argued that "some of the [medieval] ivory carvers in England may also have worked "in alabaster".[15] He advances this hypothesis on stylistic grounds but this is surely but a symptom of the close relationship between these materials in craft terms.

Although the transition from carving wood to working stone or marble was always possible (if only in that one direction), each material required the development of tools that were peculiar to their respective characteristics – with some exceptions cited above. This basic principle extended to the care and maintenance of edged tools – see p. 344 below. These practical realities demonstrate that stone and marble are as distinct in craft terms, as they are by geological definition, and should not be referred to as if they are synonymous. True marble has been subjected to volcanic heat whereas stone has not. Consequently stone often retains the fossils that were present when the material was laid down by sedimentary deposit – which established the "bed". In the general absence of true marble in England masons and sculptors turned to the use of hard limestones that were capable of taking a friction polish – Purbeck "marble" being just one example.[16] This material does not survive frost and so was used internally, or at least under cover, in medieval England for columns, tombs and fonts. It was also employed for paving and as a matrix for memorial brasses which were set into the floor. The demise of the Marblers Company in 1585 may be associated with the decline in the fashion for memorial brasses. In that year the Marblers Company of London merged with the Masons guild. This linkage between memorial brasses and commemorative sculpture in marble is evident in the work undertaken by Edward Marshall (1597/98–1675) and his apprentice Thomas Burman (1617/18–1674). Both statuaries worked in black and white marble and each engraved memorial brasses and also coffin plates – a very complete funeral service.[17]

As noted above those who worked Purbeck "marble" generally came from Corfe adjacent to the quarries where this difficult material was extracted. Much the same was true for the marble of the Mediterranean at which the Italians and Greeks were adept at working. A corresponding expertise was developed amongst sculptors and masons in the Tournai region of the Low Countries with respect to working the black "marbles" found there. As early *c.* 1160–*c.* 1180 fully worked fonts and column shafts were imported to England direct from Tounai.[18]

Rather curiously, it seems that in the sixteenth century, white Italian marble was introduced to England by immigrants from Flanders. This was frequently used by them in association with the Tournai marble of their native region – a strangely black and white aesthetic in an age that otherwise remained remarkably polychromatic.[19] The reintroduction of black marble from the Low Countries may have begun with the tomb of Lady Margaret Beaufort (d. 1509) in Henry VII's chapel at Westminster. For this work "good clene and hable touche stone" was specified – touchstone being from the old French *touche Pierre*, from Tournai which is a form of jasper also used for testing gold.[20] Amongst the first of these sixteenth century sculptors from the Netherlands to settle in England was William Cure the Elder (or Cuer, d. 1579). In a Return of Aliens made in 1571 he was living in Southwark opposite the City of London across the River Thames. At that time he was recorded as having been in England for some 35 years (since *c.* 1540) – having been "sent for hither when the King did byulde Nonesutche".[21] Working by Royal command in Surrey, on that long since destroyed palace, Cure though an alien, was to emerge as Master Mason to the Crown, in which role he was to be joined and succeeded by his English-born son, William Cure II.[22] Having been established in the London area since *c.* 1540 the elder Cure may well have provided a bridge-head for subsequent immigrant sculptors from the Low Countries – many of whom were to Anglicise their names. These immigrants specialised in working stone and marble but there was also a well-established tradition for woodcarvers from the Low Countries settling in England.[23]

These later immigrant stone and marble workers included Garret Jansen (Gerard Johnson) from Amsterdam and Richard Stevens (1542–1592) who arrived in England from Brabant in 1567. Among Steven's apprentices was Isaac James (or Harrer) who came from the same region. In his turn James was to become the master of the Devon-born Nicholas Stone (*c.* 1587–1647).[24] These connections almost certainly resulted in Stevens introducing young Stone to the Amsterdam sculptor and architect Hendrik de Keyser (1565–1621) who is known to have visited London in 1606. Stone was to cross the North Sea to join de Keyser's workshops as a journeyman in *c.* 1613. In marrying de Keyser's daughter this trans-national connection was to be continued into the next generation, most notably by John Stone (1620–1667) who followed the family vocation.[25] In this way a continuity of skill and understanding was to be maintained for a century via apprenticeships and family connections – from Stevens in London in 1567 to John Stone's death in 1667. In later life Nicholas Stone was to recognise his debt to his master Isaac James – the pupil (Stone) bringing his old master (James) into partnership "in cortisy" for the work on the 1615 tomb of Henry Howard Earl of Northampton (relocated from Dover to Trinity Hospital, Greenwich, in 1696). In the same year Stone's West Country origins and connections may well have helped him to secure the commission to undertake the monument to his fellow Devonian Thomas Bodley (Merton College, Oxford) the founder of the Bodleian Library and son of Hilliard's patron John Bodley.[26] Despite the continuities that were possible through the alternating generations of masters and apprentices this was an age of high mortality. Of Stone's sons only John outlived him. Of Stone's siblings Nicholas Jnr (1618–1647) became a sculptor and Henry (1620–1667) a painter. In 1638 these two brothers embarked on a four year Grand Tour visiting France and Italy. Although Inigo Jones, almost certainly a joiner by trade before becoming a painter, masque designer and architect, had undertaken similar journeys, such ventures were unusual for English artists and artisans at this time. Fortunately Stone's elder son Nicholas Stone Jnr, maintained a diary of their travels which miraculously survives. Among the many details that this journal offers we learn that Italian masons were using sheet iron moulds (templates) at this time when in Britain thin sheets of wood remained in use for this purpose.[27]

Such a knowledge of "abroad" was to become almost compulsory as a consequence of the Renaissance – and a great advantage for foreign-born artists and other craftsmen working in England. William Cecil, first Baron Burghley, was of the opinion that William Cure's (d. 1579) chief value as a sculptor was that, as an immigrant, he "hath sen much work in forrein places".[28] Quite how "forrein" these "places" were is a matter of conjecture but Cure, like other sculptors from the Low Countries, worked in a northern European interpretation of Italianate work. Through such individuals Mediterranean influences were mediated in England by means of Flemish eyes. As noted above these foreign sculptors were located in Southwark and certain London "peculiars". This was a situation that could very easily have resulted in ghettos that were not simply geographical but cultural. That this did not happen was largely due to these immigrant masters taking on both native and alien apprentices. For example, the Brabant-born Richard Stevens was not only the master of his compatriot Isaac Harrer (alias James) but also of the Herefordshire-born Epiphanius Evesham (1570–after 1632).[29] This raises the question as to how such apprentices could have been registered with the Masons Company? Evesham was the son of a Gentleman and may have purchased his freedom, but what of Harrer (James)? The implication is that Stevens may have been "made Denizen" as was permitted for masonry and other building trades by an Act of 1548. In whatever way these problems were overcome, overcome they were, resulting in multi-cultural workshops which fostered a merging of traditions. One manifestation of this may be the late sixteenth century chimneypieces, of monumental proportions, at Hardwick Hall and at Wollaton – in both locations these are the work of Thomas Accres.[30]

The influence of the Low Countries on English sculpture was to persist for some two hundred and fifty years, although not all who crossed the North Sea were to settle. In addition to William Cure Snr, Garret Jansen, Richard Stevens and Isaac Harrer (alias James) many were to follow. Among these were Maximillian Poultrain (alias Colt, from Arras), John van Nost (from Malines, d. 1710), Laurence van der Meulen (from Malines, 1645–1719), Arnold Quellin (from Antwerp, 1633–1686) Peter Scheemakers (from Antwerp, 1691–1781), Peter Mathias van Gelder (from Amsterdam, 1739–1809) and Philip Regnart (from Flanders via the West Indies and probably a Huguenot b. 1745). It was in respect to foreigners such as these, working in England, that Christopher Wren was to observe that "our English artists are dull enough of invention" although he went on to concede that "when once a foreign patterne is sett, they imitate soe well that commonly they exceed the original". These immigrants introduced English sculptors to new ideas, techniques and materials.

With reference to immigrants from the Low Countries to England Margaret Whinney (1964) has identified "the workshop tradition established by the Netherlandish sculptors settled in Southwark".[31] It would though be a mistake to see this as an exclusively Anglo-Netherlandish school without reference to the role of Denmark as a centre of patronage. Under Christian IV (reigned 1588–1648) this Scandinavian nation remained, until the latter part of his reign, one of the most formidable powers in Europe. At this time Denmark, Southern Sweden, Norway and Iceland all came under the Danish crown whilst Schleswig-Holstein was a joint Danish/German province.[32] Strategically dominion over the Kattegat and the Sound between Zealand and Scania gave Denmark control of the Baltic and the income from the tolls on the shipping that passed through the Sound.[33] So significant was this Nordic power that the astronomer and Danish nobleman Tycho Brahe (b. Scania 1546–d. 1601) left Prague with his assistant Johannes Kepler (1571–1630) to return to Denmark and the patronage of Christian IV.[34] Back in his native country Brahe was furnished with a salary of 3,000 crowns a year and an observatory was built for him on the Island of Hveen.

Patronage on such a scale not only attracted scientists but others, including artists and artisans from the Low Countries. As a result a Dutch/Danish tradition for sculpture and architecture emerged under Christian IV which probably exceeded anything being done in England at this time. In 1589 Anne of Denmark (1573–1652) Christian IV's sister, married James VI of Scotland. This may account for the resemblance, that some have seen, between the design of Frederiksborg Castle, north Zealand and Heriot's Hospital, Edinburgh. George Heriot (1563–1623) was a jeweller in the Scottish capital where he became goldsmith to Queen Anne – "never, truely, did tradesmen get a better customer" and it was his fortune of £24,000 that endowed the Hospital. When the Scottish king (James VI) assumed the English crown as James I his consort continued her interests in architecture together with the production of masques – two fields of endeavour for which Inigo Jones (1573–1652) was to become the leading designer. Consequently Jones's visit to Copenhagen in 1603 may have been influenced, or even sponsored, by Anne of Denmark. For many reasons it is probably more helpful to think in terms of a North Sea culture as an entity.[35] And it was by sea that these cultural links developed and were maintained. Not so much a bilateral relationship as a tripartite one.

In this nexus of aesthetic influences one of the most significant figures was Hendrik de Keyser. As we have seen his contacts with England ran deep but so too did his association with Denmark. Both Hans van Steenwinckel the Younger (1587–1639) and his brother Laurens (c. 1585–1619) worked for de Keyser in Holland and Denmark. Hans van Steenwinckel was to succeed Casper Boegart as master mason to Christian IV at Frederiksborg Castle, a thoroughly Dutch edifice. The sculpture on that castle was mainly carved by Geraert Lambertsz, one of de Keyser's most accomplished assistants.[36] As an architect and sculptor de Keyser was recognised as a figure of significance across Northern Europe. His renown was such that the artists' Guild of St Luke in Delft made no objection when he, an Amsterdammer, undertook a major commission in "their" city.[37]

Some of this travel and/or migration by artisans and artists was motivated either by religious or political upheaval, or as a matter of personal choice, or the opportunities offered by a foreign patron. De Keyser visited England in 1606 specifically to see the design of the Royal Exchange in London. Similarly Inigo Jones's visit to Copenhagen took place in 1603 when he may have designed the Rosenborg gateway there.[38] These journeys across Northern Europe continued in subsequent generations. The woodcarver Grinling Gibbons (1648–1721) was born to English parents in Rotterdam. The reverse of this was the case with the sculptor Francis Bird (1667–1731) who was born in Westminster to a recusant family. For this reason he was sent to Flanders at the early age of eleven years as apprentice to the sculptor Cozins (or Cosyns). On his return to England in 1689 he worked for both Gibbons and the Danish-born Caius Gabriel Cibber (1630–1700).[39] Gibbons, Bird and Cibber all worked in both wood and stone but, in the early seventeenth century, many in this community of North Sea sculptors tended to confine their activities to stone and marble. Such an emphasis on glyptic materials enabled practitioners to function as mason-contractors and thus, by extension, as architects. This was certainly the case with de Keyser in both the Netherlands and in Denmark and was also true of Hans van Steenwinckel of Antwerp who was also active in Denmark and Nicholas Stone the Elder in England and the Netherlands.[40]

The peripatetic lives of these sculptors seem to have established a tradition that was to be continued by later generations. The Antwerp-born Arnold Quellin (1653–1686) worked both in his birthplace and in England whilst his younger brother Thomas (1661–1709) practiced in both these countries before settling in Copenhagen.[41] This trans-national cultural exchange inevitably resulted in Danish artists and artisans joining these migratory patterns. The most important of these was probably Caius Gabriel Cibber (1630–1700). He was the son of the cabinet maker to Christian IV and therefore his earliest training almost certainly involved working in wood. Christian IV died in 1648 and his successor, Frederick III, promptly sent the eighteen year old Cibber to Rome to further his sculptural education. The young Cibber eventually returned north via the Netherlands where he probably encountered the de Keyser brothers. He eventually reached London in *c.* 1655 and found work with the younger de Keysers's cousin John Stone (1620–1667). Cibber was to settle in England where the Michelangelesque character of his stone figures of *Raving* and *Melancholy Madness* (*c.* 1676) for the Bethlem Hospital, London are evidence of his sojourn in Italy (see p. 335).[42]

In the following century the Danish-born Lawrence Holm (or Holme – fl. 1759–1774) arrived in England before 1760 where he was to become the master of Charles Banks (*c.* 1745–1792). Another was Michael Henrik Spang (d.1762) who left his native Denmark for London in *c.* 1756 and by 6 May 1761 was a member of the Society of Arts.[43] In contrast to these Danes who came to England Simon Carl Stanley (1703–1761) was born in Copenhagen to a Danish mother and an English father. In 1718 he was apprenticed, in the Danish capital, at a reasonably traditional age, to Johann Adam Sturmberg (1683–1741) the sculptor to the court of Frederick IV. Sturmberg put Stanley under the supervision of his assistant Peter Scheemakers of Antwerp (1691–1781) who was then working (for some three years) in Denmark, before settling in England in about 1720. When Stanley moved to London in 1727 he, with some inevitability, found work with Scheemakers although, by *c.* 1730, he was working as an independent decorative plasterer and sculptor. By the summer of 1746 he accepted an invitation to return to his native country to become the court sculptor to Frederick V, a post he retained until his death in 1761. One of Stanley's apprentices, while he was court sculptor in Denmark, was Christian Carlesen Seest (fl. 1734–1757).[44] For many of these sculptors travel had become a way of life. In 1734 young Seest crossed northern Europe visiting Germany, Holland and France. By 1748 he followed his master as court sculptor to Frederick V of Denmark (ruled 1746–1766) a post he held until 1768 (into the reign of Christian VII). Not that this role seems to have prevented him making working visits to England where he was employed as an assistant to Louis François Roubiliac (1705?–1762).[45] Another of these Danish-born sculptors to work in England was Sefferin Alken (1717–1782) the wood carver and gilder who also worked in stone. He is known to have settled in England by 1744 when he undertook decorative carving at Stourhead.[46]

The continuity of experience offered by generations of masters and apprentices has been noted in relationship to the Netherlandish sculptors Stevens and James who transmitted their expertise to two generations of the Stone family. The communication of skill down the generations may also be traced backwards in time. One example is that of the stone carver John Bushnell (1636–1701). This sculptor appears to have suffered from some mental instability resulting in what Horace Walpole described as "a capricious character". At one stage "his next whim [was to build] a Trojan Horse" a project which cost him £500. His father Richard Bushnell was a plumber which raises the possibility that the statuary was subject to a genetic susceptibility to lead poisoning. Certainly the surliness of the sculptor Andrew Charpentière (or Carpenter 1676–1737) was attributed to his production of lead statuary.[47] So far as John Bushnell was concerned he was, in some ways, fortunate to be apprenticed to Thomas Burman (1617/18–1674) who, in his turn was bound to Edward Marshall (1597/8–1675) who did his time with the mason John Clarke (c. 1585–1624).[48] The weight of several generations of sculptural experience would, in theory, have provided Bushnell with a thorough training. His apprenticeship had probably begun in about 1650 but just before his seven years were completed his master seduced a servant "maid" and expected his apprentice (Bushnell) to accept responsibility for the resulting pregnancy. In 1656 or 1657 Bushnell fled to the Continent and remained abroad for a decade.[49] This was not an isolated case. A pregnancy had compelled the wood carver Thomas Johnson (1725–1799) to abandon London for Liverpool and Ireland.[50] Situations such as these brought about a form of involuntary transmission of technical and aesthetic ideas. Bushel headed south and brought an Italianate idiom back to Britain whereas Johnson travelled west and did much to introduce Rococo ornament to Liverpool and Dublin. Perhaps, more often than not, an apprentice sculptor was happily adopted into his master's family. A case in point concerned the sculptor Joseph Nollekens (1737–1823) who was apprenticed to Peter Scheemakers in 1750. The closeness of this familiar situation is reflected in Mrs Scheemakers' domestic reminiscence of the young apprentice helping in the kitchen: "Joey [Nollekens] was so honest she could always trust him to stone the raisins consciously".[51]

Even where an apprentice sculptor joined the workshop of a well-established statuary he did not always continue in that vocation. Robert Taylor II (1714–1788) was the son of Robert Taylor I, a master mason and sculptor. The younger Robert would have been given a grounding in his craft by his father which would explain why he began his apprenticeship with Henry Cheere (1703–1781) in 1732 at the somewhat advanced age of 18. In agreeing to take on young Taylor the premium that Cheere received was £105. As with many artists and artisans, Cheere was part of a long chain of skill going back through the generations. In his youth he had been apprenticed to a member of the Hartshorne family of statuaries (probably Robert) who in his turn had served his time with Edward Stanton (1681–1734) who had been bound to his father William Stanton (1639–1705). Taylor continued working for Cheere until 1757 and later established his reputation as an independent sculptor. By 1764 Taylor became surveyor to the Bank of England with a burgeoning architectural practice. Today he is almost exclusively known as the architect Sir Robert Taylor whose wealth made possible the foundation of the Taylorian Institute at Oxford University.[52]

The rise in the cult of the individual in relationship to sculpture in England may have occurred at a later date than was typical for painting and painters. In this respect Torrigiano's work for the English crown (1512–1518) marks a shift in attitude but one that was very slow to take effect. Over half a century later the Herefordshire sculptor John Guldon inscribed his name and the date 1573 on the tomb of John Harford in Bosbury Church – the earliest known signature in English sculpture.[53] Perhaps there was a particularly strong tradition for sculpture in Elizabethan Herefordshire and Worcestershire. This was certainly the region that gave birth to other statuaries like Anthony Tolly (1546–1594). Even more significant was Epiphanius Evesham (1570–after 1633) the son of a Herefordshire squire who, as we have seen, was sent to London to serve his apprenticeship where he eventually became one of the finest statuaries of the age.[54] These sculptors were primarily engaged in the production of memorials in ecclesiastical settings and chimney pieces in domestic environments. As long ago as 1755 William Hogarth's friend and fellow painter Jean André Rouquet noted that English sculpture "has hitherto been almost wholly monumental [*funéraire*], but is now beginning to be used for other purposes".[55] As Phillip Lindley (2007) has pointed out, the practical purposes to which much of this work was put has resulted in a distorted overview of the history of English sculpture because of the general tendency amongst art historians to omit monumental sculpture, ornamental carving or decorative plasterwork as part of the history of English art; a long-standing prejudice.[56]

The first sculptor to have been credited by his contemporaries, with the introduction of Neo-Classicism to statuary in England was Thomas Banks (1735–1805). Although born in London he spent his childhood

FIGURE 93. Sir Henry Cheere (1703–1781) *Portrait bust of Colley Cibber* plaster, *c.* 1740. This portrait was described by a contemporary as "coloured from the life and extremely like" (Snodin 2012). (National Portrait Gallery, London)

in Gloucestershire where his father was gardener to the Duke of Beaufort at Badminton. From there young Banks was sent in *c.* 1749 to London to serve a full seven year apprenticeship with William Barlow II, the ornamental carver who worked in both wood and stone. This training was supplemented by drawing in the evenings in both Scheemaker's studio and at the St Martin's Lane Academy. By 1769 he was among the first intake of students at the Royal Academy Schools. From there, in 1772, he won a scholarship to Rome remaining in the "Eternal City" for seven years. His training with a carver suggests that Banks was proficient in this skill although, while in Rome, he received additional instruction in working in marble from Capizzoldi (see above) on which Neo-Classical sculpture is peculiarly dependent. As with many of his generation, including those who were capable carvers, Banks employed assistants to help translate his work into marble. This is most evident in his high reliefs some parts of which fail to maintain the elliptical forms of this convention and spring fully into the round – a feature suggesting that they were conceived in clay. This is most evident in Banks's oval "relief" in marble of *Thetis and her nymphs rising from the sea to console Achilles* (1778 – in the Victoria & Albert Museum). As for Banks's probable use of an amanuensis the most obvious example is "his" marble bust of Alderman Boydell (1791; St Margaret's Church Lothbury, City of London) which is inscribed: "Banks del. F. Smith sc." The failure of many sculptors to conform to the conventions of relief work was a widespread problem, particularly amongst modellers. Isaac Ware (1756) objected to seeing "boys [cherubs] hung up whole by the back in some coarse old ceilings". [57] Such features in decorative plasterwork would have first been modelled in clay.

As indicated above, those who had been trained to carve wood were well placed to work in a very wide range of materials, irrespective of any claim they may have had to be termed sculptors. In the early 1790s Charles Francis le Grand of Dublin emigrated with his three sons to Philadelphia. By 30 November 1797 "Legrand & Sons" advertised in the Philadelphia *Aurora* that, together with much else, they could provide or accept commissions for ornamental work in wood, marble, stone and models in clay, terracotta and plaster, portraits modelled in four sittings and, as if all that was insufficiently comprehensive, they also provided "Patterns for [cast iron] stove furnaces".[58] These would have been carved wood patterns for impressing into sand for the sandcast plates of American or Franklin stoves. Not that versatility was the exclusive preserve of wood carvers. The trade card of the "masons and carvers" James and Elizabeth Annis announced that they, or more probably he, did work:

> "In the most Modern and Curious manner, consisting of marble Monuments, Tombs, Chimneypieces, etc. also performs All sorts of Mason's works whatsoever necessary to Building and are well acquainted by great Experience in [the needs of] all sorts of Brewers, Chemists, Dyers, Soap Boilers & Sugar Bakers works …"[59]

Possibly even more remarkable was John Harvey II (d. 1742) who was described by John Wood the Elder (1704–1754) as "a Painter Stainer and Stone Cutter of Bath" and the likely designer of "St Michaels-extra-Muros" in the Spa.[60] It is possible that Harvey, like Edward Pearce before him, was a Painter Stainer simply by patrimony. Nevertheless in 1726 Harvey was listed as an "Architect & Painter" in his capacity as a Steward of the Society of Virtuosi of St Luke in London.[61]

The multitude of skills, the dust and dirt and the physical nature of the work all form part of a sculptor's life and discouraged amateurs from participating in this art. This contrasts with painting, where the Industrial Revolution brought in its train various types of easily used manufactured paints which opened the art to those who lacked the relevant craft training. Furthermore a painter's studio could resemble a drawing room. No such surroundings or innovations were available for sculpture which generally remained the preserve of its full-time practitioners. Inevitably there were some who claimed to be amateurs (in both senses) in and of this art. Take, for example, the case of the actress Sarah Siddons (1755–1831). It was said that she turned to modelling self-portraits because she believed that those by professional sculptors were insufficiently accurate – if accuracy was what she truly sought? She may have been influenced in this venture by her great friend, the sculptress Mrs Damer (1748–1828). The aristocratic Anne Seymour Damer was the niece of Horace Walpole and a beneficiary of his will – she inherited a lifetime interest in his idiosyncratic country house, Strawberry Hill. Allan Cunningham (1830), himself a highly skilled sculptor, noted that some of Mrs Damer's works in marble were "wrought by a skilful hand" implying that the "hand" was not her own. With some tact he added that "her sex and situation render it difficult to estimate her real merits as an artist ... the marble bust of Nelson (1803), which she gave to the Common Council [of London], is very rudely carved" in white marble. The deficiencies in this work might suggest that it is indeed the work of the sculptress and if so was something of an achievement. According to Walpole she had only received six lessons from John Bacon the Elder (1740–1799) and four or five from Guiseppe Caracchi (1751–1801). Cunningham's circumspection and Walpole's praise of his niece may be contrasted with the outspoken comments on this lady by the sculptor Nathaniel Smith (c. 1741/3–after 1800): "She be hanged! She could carve little or none; I carved most of her busts". On one occasion Mrs Damer asked Smith for a hammer and a complete set of tools "to be added to the stipulated payment" for his assistance on one of "her" carvings – suggesting that she purchased the tools after the work was completed. According to Cunningham she was assisted "in both modelling and carving" by Ceracchi which left her with little to do other than to sign the work.[62]

Perhaps one of the most spectacular examples of a "ghosted" sculpture is the marble figure of Queen Victoria in Kensington Gardens. This over twice life size figure of the seated monarch in her coronation robes was allegedly the work of the Queen's daughter HRH Princess Louise (1848–1939). Although the Princess may have been the been the author of a maquette for this figure the production of a full-size model in clay, its casting in plaster for "pointing up" and carving in marble would have been beyond her capabilities. The work in marble is known to have been carved by very highly trained Italians. A related maquette cast in bronze for a similar seated figure of the Queen may have been, in part, created by the Princess assisted by her very close friend the sculptor Sir Joseph Edgar Boehm RA (1834–1890).[63] Although Princess Louise's claims as a sculptress may have been exaggerated her role in the foundation of the South Kensington School of Art Woodcarving was a real achievement (Fig. 116).

Aside from the employment of assistants for much, or even all, of a given work there was a further situation which complicates questions on the authorship of sculpture. As early as 1397 the great mason-architect Henry Yevele (c. 1320–1400) designed a tomb for Richard II and his Queen Anne of Bohemia. The two effigies, 12 weepers and eight angels were all to be in bronze, the work of Nicholas Broker and Godfrey Prest.[64] As this example demonstrates the situation in which a designer sub-contracts the work for others to bring into being has a long history. By the early eighteenth century an arbiter of taste like William Kent would take much of the credit for the monument to Sir Isaac Newton in Westminster Abbey – a commission that was executed in 1727 by John Michael Rysbrack (1694–1770).[65] As Horace Walpole adroitly observed, this figure "besides its merits had the additional recommendation of Mr Kent's fashionable name".[66] Much the same situation was experienced by Scheemakers with his sculpture of Shakespeare – also in the Abbey. In 1830 Cunningham (1784–1842) condemned the way in which architects had a "long established tyranny" over sculptors, a situation that is "not readily got rid of". He goes on to list:

> "the names of Kent and Gibbs and Chambers [which] appear on public monuments as inventors of designs, while the artists who executed them are mentioned as mere modelling tools or chisels which moved as if they were directed by the architectural Lords Paramount".[67]

This whole sorry business, although lacking Cunningham's observations on the matter, was reflected in Tim Knox's 1994 exhibition *Architects' Designs for Sculpture 1660–1951.*[68] Interventions of this kind by designers were made all the more possible by the ever increasing reliance on plaster casts of modelled works being translated into marble or stone by means of the "pointing machine" (see Chapter 16). Much of this work could be carried out by apprentices, journeymen and other assistants. As a consequence some sculptors developed a dependence, not simply on a single amanuensis, but on a whole team of supporting staff. An example of this type of "sculptor" was Frederick Thrupp (1812–1895). He was the son of Joseph Thrupp the successful London coach builder who, on his death in 1821 left a fortune of £60,000. In an article on Thrupp published in the *Hampshire Chronicle* (10 Nov 1894) the sculptor was described as a "gentleman of independent means [who was able to pursue] his art more for arts sake than for purposes of gain". The collection of his works at Torre Abbey, Torquay consists entirely of plaster casts – their conversion into marble would have been sub-contracted.[69] In these circumstances it is likely that some leading "sculptors" never learnt to carve. For very obvious reasons few such individuals would admit to being deficient in this skill so the documentation is largely absent leaving us dependent on circumstantial evidence. One surviving anecdote indicates how this lack of skill might be obscured. In his youth Joseph Nollekens RA (1737–1823) carved his own works but so successful was his practice as a statuary, that this was to distance him from the hammer and chisel. Nathaniel Smith (*c.* 1741–3–after 1800) who was one of Nollekens' principal assistants, recalled how his master would sometimes fake the carving action in the presence of a client who sought an amendment in the work. If Nollekens was resistant to such a change he would give the appearance of reworking the marble whilst making no changes whatsoever: "the deception of cutting away [was] effected by the help of a little stone dust which the sculptor allows to fall gradually from his hand every time he strikes his chisel or moves his rasp".[70] In contrast to such dissembling there were occasions when Nollekens wished to revise his statuary, as was the case with the drapery on his figure of William Pitt (1812) after it was installed in the Senate House, Cambridge.[71] In these circumstances his skill as a carver was very evident.

By the nineteenth century large numbers of Italian carvers were employed to work for British "sculptors". A probable example of a man who was dependent upon such imported skill was Patrick Macdowell (1799–1870) who was sometimes described as self-taught. This is a highly unlikely proposition if he was to have functioned as a carver to the very high technical standards expected in nineteenth century Britain. So what was his background? He was first introduced to the visual arts at his school in Belfast which, not only taught drawing but also (unusually) engraving. On moving to England he was apprenticed to a coachbuilder in Long Acre, London. After just four and a half years his master became bankrupt and Macdowell was transferred to the wax modeller Peter Chenu (1760–1834). This training was supplemented by attendance at the RA Schools. Everything that is known about Macdowell suggests he was a modeller and that the marble works that carry his name were pointed up and carved by assistants or they were sub-contracted.

The subordination of carving would inevitable lead to a reaction. For sculptors of the generation of Eric Gill (1882–1940) and Henri Gaudier-Brzeska (1891–1915) the response took the form of a rather self-conscious return to "direct carving" in stone. Woodcarving was to decline during World War I largely because it utilised skills that were ideal for pattern making in wood

from which metal castings could be made as part of the war effort. This was
the context in which the carvers at H. H. Montyn & Co came to establish the
Gloucester Aircraft Co.[72]

* * * *

For modellers and carvers working in three dimensions, or even in relief,
the relationship between drawing and sculpture was oblique. Although some
individuals working in clay deployed a formal technique, based on a series of
cross sections, known as "sectional modelling", most thought in terms of the
silhouette as seen from every angle on elevation, without losing sight of the axis
and cross-section of forms.[73] As a system of seeing an approach based on a series
of silhouettes was comparable to drawing on parchment or paper. For painters
the association of drawing with their ultimate work could be so close that lines
on paper could be pricked through and pounced with charcoal dust onto a
support, such as a panel, as a guide for the picture.[74] In addition a painter's
drawings may include such incidentals as cast shadow or represent "local colour"
tonally – features which had little relevance for sculptors. It should be added
that there were some fundamentals in drawing that were equally applicable to
both painters and sculptors. With some eccentricity the illustrator and writer
Mervyn Peake (1911–1968) valued drawing as "a craft – not an art" although,
as he goes onto say, "Without the former the latter cannot exist. This in reverse
is, of course, painfully untrue". Drawing, in all its forms, provided the basis
on which the visual arts were, historically, constructed. For Peake all the arts
were reliant upon some such foundation. Thus "For the pianist his keyboard.
For the writer his vocabulary. For the draughtsman a stick of graphite …"[75]

Because the relationships between a three-dimensional work and a design
drawing is somewhat remote any connection between the two was often best
made diagrammatically. Most obviously this is true of an architect's plans
and elevations. Even so, many architects considered drawing to be such
an approximate means to their ends that, with understandable humility,
they commissioned the construction of full-size segments of their schemes
in ephemeral materials like wood or plaster. From these a more reasoned
conclusion could be arrived at concerning the proposed design.[76]

So problematic were some of these issues that the sculptor John Flaxman RA
(1755–1826) warned that "drawings shd. never be recd. *as designs for sculpture* for
it cannot be ascertained from them what degree of relief is to be given to any
figures. *Models* should always be made."[77] For John Bacon RA (1740–1799) even
three-dimensional maquettes were of very limited value since: "an ingenious

young man might ... produce a Captivating sketch in Clay who wd. by no means be equal to finish the statue in marble. He knows striking instances to justify such a probability".

The problem of translating a two-dimensional drawing, or series of drawings, into three dimensions could prompt caustic observations. An Irish stonemason recalled that he had "seen many damn clever fellas about drawings and plans and they weren't worth a chew of tobacco at the banker [bench]."[78]

In summary "a marble statue is of slow growth, it has to be conceived, sketched, modelled and cast in plaster, rough hewn and carved".[79] These various stages will now be considered in the following pages together with processes such as casting in metal, chasing, pointing and also die and intaglio cutting.

Notes

[1]   A problem that is evident in *The Shorter Oxford Dictionary* (2002)
[2]   Lomazzo, transl. Haydocke 1598, p. 7. A 1640 edition of Horace's poetry was similarly "Englished" in this case by Ben Jonson
[3]   John Evelyn 1662, p. 187
[4]   Anon *The Rudiments of Architecture*, Edinburgh (1773) 1778, Reprint, 1992. This work derives from other sources – for example, all the stones that it cites derive, not from Scotland but the south of England, e.g. Portland stone. A similar definition of sculpture may be found in John Barrow's *Dictionary of Arts and Sciences*, London, 1754
[5]   For an example of a bronze figure almost entirely created by chasing see *Arione with his Violin* (late fifteenth century), Museo Nazionale, Florence – reproduced as fig. 236 in James Ayres 1985. See also Rudolf Wittkoer 1979, pp. 184–185
[6]   Carol Gibson-Wood 2000, p. 215
[7]   This extension of skill from wood-carving to stone and marble was once commonplace. The author's father, Arthur J. J. Ayres (1902–1985) trained at the South Kensington School of Art Woodcarving in London (between 1916–1919) before moving on to work in stone and marble at the RA Schools and later at the British School, Rome. See *An Architectural Sculptor* RIBA Heinz Gallery/RIBA Drawings Collection Victoria & Albert Museum, London, 1986
[8]   David Jones ed. Christopher Gilbert *Selected writings on Vernacular Furniture*, Leeds 2001, p. 2. From his workshops in Coney Street, York, Ventris worked in both wood and stone producing both architectural ornament and garden statuary. His principal patron was Sir Arthur Ingram of Temple Newsam near Leeds but he also worked in the chapel at Peterhouse, Cambridge. His son's work extended to decorative painting
[9]   William Dunlap (1834) 1969, Vol. I, p. 329
[10] J. T. Smith (1828) 1919, Vol. II, p. 90; Allan Cunningham 1830, Vol. III, p. 91; Ingrid Roscoe *et al.* eds 2009. Capizzoldi may be identified as Giiovanni Battista Capizzoldi who was working in Florence in about 1760. In that year he visited England and may have visited again in 1774. He was presumably in London when he produced the bronze relief in 1772 of Wolfe's conquest of the Heights of Abraham, Canada, on the general's

monument by Sir Joseph Wilton in Westminster Abbey; Katherine A. Esdaile 1946, p. 68

[11] These include Sussex "marble" (also known as "winkle stone"), Frosterley "marble", and Alwalton "marble" Alec Clifton-Taylor and A. S. Ireson 1983

[12] Knoop and Jones (1933) 1967, pp. 12, 67–68,132. In 1292 some of the masons and carvers, then working at Westminster included: Edmund de Corfe, John de Corfe, Hugo de Corfe and Peter de Corfe

[13] Knoop and Jones (1933) 1967, pp. 71 and 75. The word "alabasterer" is recorded in 1479 and "alabasterman" in 1495

[14] RCHM *Inventory of Historical Monuments in the City of Oxford*, 1939, pl. 137

[15] Lawrence Stone 1955, p. 188

[16] Alec Clifton-Taylor and A. S. Ireson 1983, pp. 46–50

[17] Knoop and Jones (1933) 1967, pp. 200–201 footnote 6 and Margaret Whinney 1964, p. 16 – by 1585 the Marblers Company had dwindled to a dozen brethren when it merged with Mason's Company in that year. S. Badham and M. Norris, Early "Incised Slabs and Brasses from the London Marblers" *Antiquaries Journal* 1999. Ingrid Roscoe *et al.* eds 2009. The bill for Thomas Burman's monument to the 3rd Earl of Essex and for the Earl's coffin in plate is in the British Museum BM Add Mss.46189, fol.113

[18] Lawrence Stone 1955, p. 188. Seven such fonts survive in England, the best known at Winchester Cathedral. The internal column shafts in Iffley Church (1170–1180), Oxfordshire are of Tournai – not Purbeck as described by Jennifer Sherwood and Nikolaus Pevsner, *Oxfordshire*, 2002

[19] White marble from Italy was used in Roman Britain. The fashion for black and white work (murals, embroidery, etc) began in the late sixteenth century but was largely an early seventeenth century enthusiasm

[20] John Physick 1969, pp. 2–4. Curiously the merchants who imported Tournai marble for this tomb were from Florence

[21] Margaret Whinney 1964, p. 16

[22] Howard Colvin ed. 1975, p. 408

[23] L. F. Salzman (1952) 1992, p. 259. In 1251 Master John of Flanders was recorded as "the king's carver" working at St Alban's and on a great lectern for Westminster Abbey. In 1411 John Van de Nym was employed as a woodcarver on London Bridge. At St George's Chapel, Windsor, Dirick Vangrove and Goles Vomcastell undertook the more significant parts of the woodcarving in the stalls and rood screen in 1477

[24] Margaret Whinney 1964, p. 17. Nicholas Stone spent the first years of his apprenticeship in Devon before moving to Steven's London workshops

[25] *Ibid.*, pp. 24, 29

[26] Margaret Whinney 1964, p. 25

[27] The diary by Nicholas Stone Jnr is in the British Library (Harl.MS.4099) reprint *Walpole Society* VII, 1919, 158f. Nicholas Stone saw these moulds on 12 June 1638

[28] Howard Colvin ed. 1975, p. 101

[29] Margaret Whinney 1964, pp. 17–19

[30] Mark Girouard, *Robert Smythson* ... New Haven and London, 1983, p. 147

[31] *Ibid.*, p. 23

[32] Klaus Randsborg *The Anatomy of Denmark*, London, 2009, pp. 72–74

[33] *Ibid.*; Palle Lauring *A History of Denmark*, Copenhagen, 1960

[34] Lauring 1960 p. 149; Joakim Skovgaard 1973, pp. 118–121

[35] This North Sea Culture may be seen to have emerged on the basis of the Hanseatic League for despite England's somewhat semi-detached position in relationship to that

trading group the Hansa maintained a presence in the Steelyard in London. See also Thomas R. Liszka and Lorna E. M. Walker eds 2001. Joakim Skovgaard (1973 p. 135) has compared Frederiksborg Castle with Heriot's Hospital. Klaus Randsborg *The Anatomy of Denmark*, London, 2009, pp. 132–133 notes Inigo Jones's visit to Copenhagen in 1603 and Christian IV's visit to Anne of Denmark in England in 1606. A. J. Youngson *The Making of Classical Edinburgh*, Edinburgh (1966) 1993, p. 306 endnote 22 gives details on George Heriot citing W. Steven

[36] Joakim Skovgaard 1973, pp. 131–132

[37] This commission was for a Figure of Justice (1620) for the Town Hall in Delft for which de Keyser was paid 200 guilden; John Michael Montias 1982, p. 185

[38] Klaus Randsborg *The Anatomy of Denmark*, London, 2009, pp. 132–135

[39] Ingrid Roscoe *et al.* eds 2009

[40] Joakim Skovgaard 1973, p. 131 – van Steenwinckel (1545–1601) and van Steenwinckel Jnr (1587–1639)

[41] Ingrid Roscoe *et al.* eds 2009

[42] Margaret Whinney 1964, pp. 48–51

[43] Allan and Abbott 1992, pp. 62, 118. Spang's terracotta figure of Hogarth is in the Victoria & Albert Museum, London and his *L'Ecorché* of a horse was repaired by Michael Moser

[44] Ingrid Roscoe *et al.* eds 2009

[45] *Ibid.*

[46] Alken's English-born son Samuel Alken (1756–1815) was a sporting painter and he was followed in that field by Henry Alken (1785–1815) whose son Sefferin Alken (1821–1873) continued the family tradition. Arts Council Ex. *British Sporting Painting*, London, 1974, pp. 65, 93, 154

[47] Margaret Whinney 1964, p. 41; Ingrid Roscoe *et al.* eds 2009; J. T. Smith (1828) 1919, Vol II. p. 259; Ava O. Onalaja and Luz Claudio "Genetic Susceptibility to Lead Poisoning" *Environmental Health Perspectives* 108 Suppl. I, March 2000; for Carpentière see Tim Richardson (2007) 2008, 300.

[48] Margaret Whinney 1964, p. 31 and Howard Colvin 1995

[49] Ingrid Roscoe *et al.* eds 2009

[50] In Johnson's case it was he who caused the pregnancy having been seduced by a much older woman servant; see Jacob Simon 2003, pp. 1–21

[51] J. T. Smith (1828) 1949, p. 2

[52] Howard Colvin 1995, Taylor's designs for houses are well known for their compact plans – exemplified by Asgil House (1761–1764), Richmond, Surrey

[53] Guldon also signed a tomb to Richard Willison (dated 1574/5) in Madley church. Another Worcester statuary Anthony Tolly (1546–1594) was to sign the monument of *c.* 1591–1594 to Bishop Edmund Freake (1516–1591) in Worcester Cathedral

[54] Margaret Whinney 1964, p. 18

[55] Katharine A. Esdaile 1946, p. 44, citing Rouquet's *The Present State of the Arts in England* (1755) – see also Hans Hammelmann 1975, p. 49

[56] Phillip Lindley 2007, p. 32. Lindley was here concerned with the period from Elizabeth I to Charles I – but much the same was true for later periods

[57] Margaret Whinney 1964, pp. 175–176 citing Allan Cunningham 1830, Vol. III, p. 86. See also Joseph Farington's *Diary* 14 Nov 1795. Banks's *Death of Germanicus* in high relief (1774 Holkham Hall, Norfolk) is regularly cited as the first English Neo-Classical sculpture – an opinion shared by both Flaxman and Westmacott – who both died after Banks. Isaac Ware *Complete Body of Architecture* London, 1756, p. 496

58 Knight of Glin and James Peill 2007, p. 181

59 Label in Heal Collection 32.1, British Museum, Dept of P&D

60 John Wood (1765) 1969, pp. 231, 307; Harvey's St Michael's was the second in a series of three churches on that site

61 Ingrid Roscoe *et al.* eds 2009; W. T. Whitley 1928, Vol. II, p. 343

62 Allan Cunningham 1830, Vol. II, pp. 245–272, Walpole may have compared Mrs Damer's work to that of Praxitiles but her modelling could be dire – if her *Two Sleeping Dogs* (1782) is anything to go by; Michael Snodin ed. 2009, p. 164, fig. 178

63 I am indebted to Lee Prosser of Historic Royal Palaces for information on this maquette and on the Italian carvers, pers. comm. 15 Jan 2014. The carving of the sculpture of Queen Victoria was sub-contracted to A. Castioni of Oakley Cottage Studio, Upper Cheyne Row, Chelsea. Years later his assistant J. Lomaini wrote to the Office of Works in June 1898 requesting permission to examine the border of the Queen's dress so that he could copy it (he had carved it himself but had forgotten the details). Significantly, Princess Louise instructed the Office of Works to refuse permission. See also Lucinda Hawksley 2013

64 Lawrence Stone 1955, p. 193 – Messrs Broker and Prest were "Citeins & Copersmythes de Londres"

65 John Physick 1969, pp. 80–81

66 Horace Walpole 1786, Vol. IV, p. 209

67 Allan Cunningham 1830, Vol. III, pp. 71–72

68 Tim Knox *Architects Designs for Sculpture 1660–1951*, RIBA Heinz Gallery, London, 1994 – see also John Physick 1969, eg pp. 80–81

69 The author was "pointing up" work for sculptors from the age of 13. For Thrupp see Martin Greenwood *c.* 2008

70 J. T. Smith (1828) 1919, Vol. I, p. 290

71 *Ibid.*, Vol. I, p. 231

72 Ingrid Roscoe *et al.* eds 2009; John Whitaker 1998

73 James Ayres 1985, pp. 151–153. One of the last exponents of sectional modelling in Britain was (James) Harvard Thomas (1854–1921) – as in his work on the Guards Memorial, Horse Guards Parade, London

74 *Ibid.*, p. 62

75 Mervin Peake 1939, pp. 1–2

76 In 1902 the architects for the New York Public Library: John Carrère and Thomas Hastings ordered a full-size plaster model of two bays of the proposed building: Henry Hope Reed *New York Public Library*, Norton, NY, 1986. Sir Christopher Wren ordered a carved wood model of a weather vane for similar reasons – see p. 347

77 Joseph Farington, p. 1331 25 December 1799 regarding the Academy's advice on Monuments in St Paul's Cathedral

78 *Ibid.*, p. 367 16 July 1795, pp. 368 and 369; Seamus Murphy (2005) 2010, p. 122

79 Allan Cunningham 1830, Vol. III, p. 136

Chapter 15

MODELLING IN CLAY & CASTING IN PLASTER

Modelling

Within the British tradition modelling in clay was, generally speaking, little more than a means to an end. This was because terra cotta will not easily survive the rigours of northern latitudes although stoneware, the basis of "Mrs" Coade's "stone", is more resilient. The terra cotta selected by Giovanni de Maiano for the commission of 1521 to adorn the external elevations of Hampton Court with his tondos of emperors were securely let into the brickwork to resist the English winter.[1] Much the same precaution was taken with the terra cotta enrichment of *c.* 1525 on Layer Marney Hall, Essex and Sutton Place, Surrey. More often these Italian or Italianate works of art in Britain were intended for display in interiors – as for example the "picture of Moses made of earth and set in a box of wood" that was stored in the royal "wardrobe" or warehouse in early Tudor London.[2] Fully three-dimensional terra cotta works were destined for the interiors of churches as, for example, the Italianate tomb of *c.* 1530 which commemorates Lord Marney at Layer Marney, Essex, his tomb being an echo of his house.[3] More usually terracotta was used by English sculptors for the preparation of maquettes for large scale works or portrait busts that might subsequently be translated into marble or used as the basis for a full-sized figure.[4] Alternatively a preliminary sketch or full-size work was modelled in clay and cast in Plaster of Paris as the first step towards its metamorphosis into wood, stone, marble, bronze or lead.

A remarkable exception to this notion of fired earth as little more than a

FIGURE 94. Francis Hayman RA (1708–1776), *Joseph Wilton and His Family*, 1760, oil on canvas (34 ⁵/₈ × 42 ⁵/₈ in/80.8 × 106.7 cm). On the easel is a clay *modello* for a marble overmantel relief destined for Northumberland House (dem. 1874) Westminster. The clay model was believed to have been translated into marble by Benjamin Carter. A sculptor of Wilton's kind was the supervisor rather than the executant of much of "his" work. This was a situation that made possible the fine clothes and drawing-room setting shown here. (Victoria & Albert Museum, London)

preliminary is the work carried out in John Dwight's (1633/6–1703) "Potthouse" in Fulham. In terms of his background Dwight falls well outside the craft traditions of his day. Following his graduation from Christchurch, Oxford, where he read Civil Law and "Physick", he spent a decade (*c.* 1660–1670) as an ecclesiastical lawyer. While still at Oxford he began experiments with ceramics and, by 1672, had established his pottery near his house in Fulham, immediately to the west of London on the north bank of the River Thames. At Oxford Dwight became acquainted with Robert Boyle and Robert Hooke and through them the emerging Age of Enlightenment. These connections show that, with regard to his ceramics business, Dwight was more the chemist and entrepreneur than the working craftsman.[5] Robert Plott (1677) implied as much by stating that Dwight "hath ... caused to be modelled Statues of Figures" and that these were created in such a durable material that they were "capable of more curious work than *stones* that are wrought with *chisels* or *metals* that are cast. In short he has advanced the *Art Plastick* that 'tis dubious whether any man since *Prometheus* have excelled him ..."[6] Dwight's products were cast in multiples and fired (hence the reference to Prometheus) to become stoneware. They were therefore more robust than terra cotta. Less certain is the identity of the sculptors that Dwight "caused" to make his products (Fig. 97). The known connections between the Fulham potteries and those down river at Southwark and Lambeth could point to a member of the Anglo-Netherlandish school of sculptors. Despite this possibility Chris Green (1999), the authority on Dwight and his "Potthouse", suggests that Edward Pearce (*c.* 1635–1695) was the author of many of the surviving pieces of this ware. Dwight patented his processes in April 1672 and in June 1684. These rights extended to the "Mistery & Invencon of making transparent Earthenware ...

And also the Mystery & Invention of making the Stone Ware vulgarly called Collogne Ware".[7] The stoneware *"Statues or Figures"* were discontinued but hollow earthenwares continued to be made at the Fulham pottery down to the late 1960s.[8]

If modelling in clay was generally regarded as a preliminary towards a more permanent material what was the next stage in this ongoing process? A good example concerns a closed

FIGURE 95. John Bacon RA (1740–1799) *The Marquis Cornwallis*, 1791. The extent to which Bacon was able to work marble is uncertain. This is clearly a highly accomplished work which was probably carved by an assistant. For structural reasons, the cloak and the cornucopia of fruit help to sustain the figure at the legs and ankles. Similarly the sword and olive branch support the wrists and hands by which they are ostensibly held. (Foreign & Commonwealth Office, London; Photograph: Courtauld Institute of Art)

competition in 1795 for a statue of Lord Cornwallis to be erected in Madras, India.[9] In connection with this venture the Royal Academy held its first meeting on 16 July that year and it was eventually agreed that Thomas Banks RA (1735–1805) and Joseph Wilton RA (1722–1803) would compete for this commission. Of these two men much the most accomplished as a carver was Banks and, probably for this reason, Wilton quietly withdrew as a contestant. By 25 May 1796, less than a year after the initial discussions, Banks invited members of the RA Council to see the figure. By this date it had been modelled half size (n.b. one-eighth volume (Fig. 107)) in clay and cast in plaster so the sculptor sought the imprimateur of the Academicians "before he [began] work on the marble [which] he thought he should compleat ... by next Christmas twelve months" – a year and a half to carve the figure. It was anticipated that Banks would make a profit on this job of "12 or £1300" since the marble "including the Pedestal" was unlikely to cost more than £200. The figure was then transported to India and unveiled on 15 May 1800.[10]

As usual this progression from clay to plaster to marble was typical and serves to demonstrate the importance of modelling in clay as the first step to realising the work in marble. The place of clay in the sculptor's studio was paralleled in the decorative plasterer's workshop where the components of a given scheme were often modelled before being cast and offered up and fixed in their final position – although mouldings were frequently "run" *in situ*.

The sculptor Sir Joseph Wilton RA emerged from just such a plasterers workshop. His father William Wilton (d. 1768):

> "though a common plasterer, acquired a fair fortune ... in his workshops in Hedge Lane, Charing Cross and in Edward Street, Cavendish Square, he employed several hundreds of men and boys in this profitable manufacture. These premises were afterwards occupied by his more eminent son."[11]

With such a background, and equipped with such studio space it was perhaps inevitable that this son, Sir Joseph Wilton, was principally a modeller. He employed others to transfer his work into marble.

Although the association between plastic and wrought sculpture was close most large studios were organised so as to separate the activities which involved modelling, plaster casting and carving. This division was an important way of maintaining the purity of the clay and ensured that it was not contaminated by plaster, stone dust, wood chips or marble gallets. This separation of the crafts led to specialisms in modelling, casting and carving. With regard to casting in plaster one such specialist was Thomas Collins (born *c.* 1740–d. after 1796) who was "bred to the Plaistering business by his uncle" William Wilton.[12]

In addition to its sculptural potential modelling in clay was far from devoid of craft skills for, like any other trade, it involved the deployment of its own highly specialist range of tools. These were of two basic types. They would include the spatulas of steel, wood or ivory for purposes of addition, and a range of wire tools to remove clay. In essence modelling was, as it remains, a process of both addition and subtraction. The flexible nature of clay offered, and continues to offer, the potential for a change of mind; the perfect material for rehearsing a whole series of ideas. For this reason modelling performed an important role in the training of carvers. When Thomas Banks (1735–1805) was serving his apprenticeship with the wood carver William Barlow II (fl. 1740–1752) the

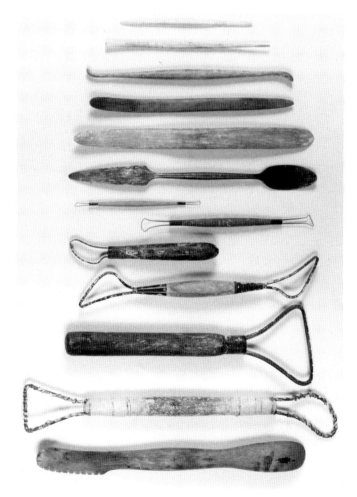

FIGURE 96. Modelling tools of various sizes and materials: ivory, wood and metal. Some of these implements are designed to apply clay, others to remove it. (Author's Collection)

working day, at least in summer, was from 6
in the morning to 8 in the evening. Despite
these long hours young Banks then "drew
or modelled in Mr Scheemaker's study every
evening from 8 till 10 or 11" at night.[13] A close
parallel with this concerns the wood carver
Thomas Johnson (1723–1799). Fairly early
into his career he secured employment with
James Whittle (d. 1759) the London furniture
maker who employed "upwards of thirty men
amongst which was the famous Matthias Lock
[c. 1710–1765] a most excellent Carver". As
Johnson wished to emulate Lock's work, the
younger man accustomed himself "to set up
three nights in the week modelling, etc".[14]
By 1763 Johnson was advertising himself as a
"Carver; teacher of drawing and modelling".
The connections between modelling and
carving are also exemplified in the work of
Matthew Gosset (1683–1744) the Huguenot
wax modeller and frame carver.[15] His nephew
Isaac Gosset (1713–1787) was similarly
versatile, although now better known for his
small wax relief portraits, he remained, as
a wood carver, the official frame maker to
the King from 1774 to 1785.[16] This tradition
amongst wood carvers for modelling in clay
persisted into the early twentieth century at
the South Kensington School of Woodcarving
as photographs taken in that institution attest
(Fig. 116).

FIGURE 97. *Lydia Dwight Resurrected,*
c. 1674 (she died age 6) modeller
unknown. John Dwight's Fulham
pottery was on the Thames
a short distance to the West of
London, where this entrepreneur's
employees produced stoneware.
(Victoria & Albert Museum,
London)

Work in terra cotta, if destined for the kiln,
was not given a permanent armature. On the contrary large three-dimensional
works in fire clay were dissected when leather hard and hollowed out to a
fairly consistent thickness so as to survive their baptism of fire in the kiln.
Where a clay model was to be cast in plaster an armature of wood, iron and
wire was possible and often necessary – the ferrous metals being treated with
Brunswick black to minimise rusting which would stain the clay. Cunningham
(1830) argues that "little labour and little thought go to construct a skeleton

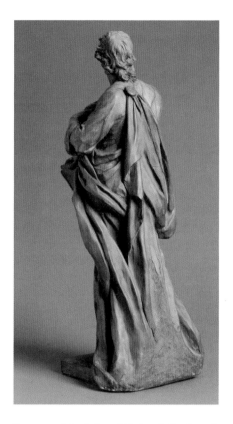

FIGURE 98. John Michael Rysbrack (1694–1770) *John Locke*, rear of the terra cotta sketch for the full size posthumous marble figure of 1755. At about this time John Bacon was inspired to become a sculptor on seeing the clay maquettes that men such as Rysbrack had taken to the Bow porcelain works to be fired in a kiln. This is known to have encouraged Bacon to extend his horizons from small scale porcelain to full size sculpture. (Victoria & Albert Museum, London)

FIGURE 99. *Bow Porcelain figure c.* 1754. John Bacon RA (1740–1799) began his career apprenticed to Nicholas Crisp at his Bow manufactory. It was there that he learnt to model, among other subjects, the shepherd and the shepherdess (see Fig. 95). (Victoria & Albert Museum, London)

of wood in the shape of a figure to be made, round which the modelling clay is wrought". The lengthy description that follows that somewhat dismissive observation rather contradicts this assertion (see Appendix XII). He does however emphasise that the clay should be "nicely beat up till it is pliable as the softest dough".[17] Even in a studio that was limited to modelling in clay and casting in plaster there were many potential jobs for apprentices, journeymen and labourers. In April 1788 the elder John Flaxman Snr (1726–1803) was able to take in Isaac Dell of Berkhamstead, Hertfordshire as an apprentice to train him as a "Moulder and Caster of Plaister Figures" (see Appendix I).[18]

With the benefit of hindsight John Dwight may be seen as one of the first ceramic entrepreneurs who recognised the potential of his industry – the possibility of producing sculpture in multiples at a low cost. To meet these objectives capitalists such as Dwight were to become reliant on highly trained modellers. Dwight's stoneware was to inspire a whole industry for artificial stone – which was closely related to stoneware. These fired clay products were sold as a substitute for carved and masoned stone and were therefore first known as "Lithodepyra". A patent for this material was granted to Thomas Ripley and Richard Holt as early as 1722.[19] Another pioneer manufacturer of this artificial stone was Daniel Pincot (d. 1797) of Paternoster Row, Spitalfields in the City of London. By 1765 the sculptor John Bacon RA (1740–1799) was working for Pincot as a "Stone Carver and Modeller" preparing patterns for this production line at the manufactory in Goulston Square, Whitechapel.[20]

Bacon's understanding of fired clay began in his childhood south of the River Thames close to the Lambeth potteries. More importantly his apprenticeship began on 7 June 1755 with Nicholas Crisp the Jeweller and owner of the Bow porcelain manufactory. In the second quarter of the eighteenth century this business was located on the Essex bank of the River Lea and employed some 300 hands of whom 90 were painters. For obvious reasons Crisp was to name the site of his porcelain works *New Canton*, an example followed by Josiah Wedgwood whose workers and pottery were, from 1769 to be housed at Etruria, Staffordshire. Unlike Wedgwood Crisp was not himself a ceramicist for he began his training on 3 July 1719 with John Michael Harnigh of Foster Lane, London, a jeweller by trade but a Haberdasher by affiliation but his apprentice did not become free for some 13 years – in 1732. An inheritance enabled Crisp to establish his business.[21] During Bacon's apprenticeship with Crisp he developed at the Bow porcelain manufactory (Fig. 99) "the art of modelling the deer and holly-tree, the bird and bush, the shepherd and shepherdess, and birds of all shapes and beasts of every kind". In addition the young apprentice discovered that it was "the practice of sculptors in those days to send their sketches, and small scale models, to the pottery furnace to be burnt" (Fig. 98). In this way Bacon's eyes were opened to the possibilities of sculpture and it was there that he was "said to have first formed the idea of making figures in artificial stone ..."[22]

This must have been the point at which Bacon, then in his mid-20s, got to know Pincot and his artificial stone. Not that Pincot was alone in developing such a material for Horace Walpole credits Batty Langley (1696–1751) with inventing "an artificial stone of which he made figures; an art lately brought to great perfection."[23] As these last words indicate the full development of this alternative material was to be in the hands of others. Pincot's premises in Goulston Square were to be taken over by George Davy (fl. 1767–1773).[24] Then at about this time Eleanor Coade (1733–1821) took over a premises in Lambeth that had previously belonged to Pincot. She was to date the foundation of her business to 1769 which was presumably the year she acquired Pincot's old premises. This enterprise was to dominate the trade in the production of her eponymous "stone" which was to be used for both sculpture and architectural ornament. By 1771 Pincot was working for her. With some inevitability one of the principal sculptors she employed, to produce the master patterns for her products, was John Bacon. He was to be joined and followed by many others including Thomas Banks RA (1735–1805), John Flaxman RA (1755–1826), John Rossi RA (1762–1839) and Joseph Panzetta (fl. 1789–1830). On Mrs Coade's death in 1821 at the age of 88, she was succeeded, in succession, by John Sealy, William Croggan and, by 1836, Croggan's son, John. Perhaps one of the last works to be made in this material was the great lion created in 1837 by William Frederick Woodington (1806–1893) which still stands by Waterloo Bridge on the south side of the Thames – appropriately in Lambeth.[25]

An account of Coade's business, under William Croggan's management, appeared in 1824. This describes the "shew rooms [which] contained a great variety of ornamental figures, enriched vases, baptismal fonts, garden fountains, and capitals of pillars of the different orders". In this "art & mystery" secrecy was vital: "the materials of the composition of this artificial stone, but chiefly the proportion of the ingredients" was highly confidential.[26] In terms of production some "particular enrichments [were] prepared in *matrices* [probably carved wood moulds; Fig. 112] and added later".[27] The production of notably large Coade stone works, such as Bacon's *River God* (1784) at Ham House, Surrey, demanded special procedures, described by Pyne (1824) as follows: "After the figure is completed in all its parts it is cut into separate pieces for the conveniency of introducing it to the oven, and it is afterwards put together, firmly cemented, and iron rods introduced into the arms [etc]".[28]

This was the system that Bacon later used for his large bronzes which were cast in segments in his own foundry and then bolted and welded together – despite the very considerable technical difficulties in welding bronze (Fig. 125).[29]

Of these manufacturers of ceramic-based products Dwight was followed not

FIGURE 100. Watercolour illustrating "Mrs" Eleanor Coade's "stone" manufactory, Lambeth, in the late eighteenth century. The figure of the *River God*, by Bacon is now at Ham house. Such a large sculpture would have been divided into segments to fit into the kiln and subsequently reassembled. Bacon incorporated a very similar figure in his bronze group of *George III and Father Thames* in the courtyard of Somerset House, London. (London Metropolitan Archives)

only by Coade but also by the great potter and capitalist Josiah Wedgwood (1730–1795). Unlike John Dwight, who was a gentleman and scholar, Wedgwood had the distinction of having emerged from his trade as a potter – in which craft he followed his father – to become an entrepreneur. For this reason, and unlike Dwight or "Mrs" Coade, he had an empirical knowledge of ceramics; its clays, its grogs, its glazes and the firing. Eventually, through experimentation, he was to develop an understanding of the chemistry of his *metier*. Dwight, Coade and Wedgwood were all, however various their backgrounds, entrepreneurs. Of these three, Wedgewood was probably the greatest in that the emergence of the "consumer society" owed more to him than either Dwight or Coade.[30] However all three demanded master-patterns for their products with the consequence that they became, almost involuntary, patrons of sculptors. Modelling and casting were now part of the Industrial Revolution. The employment of these artists by industry established a built-in tendency towards the development of a "house style". In Wedgwood's case this can be seen to have been inspired by the Portland vase as interpreted by John Flaxman II (1755–1826). Not that Flaxman was, by any means, the only sculptor employed by the Staffordshire potter. For example, John Voyez (b. 1740–?) and William Hackwood (1753–1839), were under contract to Wedgwood for three and four years respectively. These men seem to have worked in London rather than at the manufactory in Etruria, Burslem. The use of contracted sculptors by Wedgwood extended well into the next century with individuals like Edward William Wyon (1811–1885). As with other members of that dynasty of sculptors, Wyon is now known principally as a die-sinker, producing intaglios for the production of low reliefs for coins and medals – products that were not dissimilar to the reliefs found on many of Wedgwood's products. As with coinage the question of miniaturisation was no less important for Wedgwood's familiar jasper wares. In the potteries this problem was solved in a way that was quite distinct to that employed by a mint. For ceramic wares a relief was reduced by being modelled in clay and by allowing that clay to dry and shrink before casting a plaster mould. This mould was then used to produce a further clay positive and the process was then repeated until the relief was reduced, by successive shrinkages, to the desired dimensions.

Central to the business plans of these commercial potters was the casting of multiples – a system of production that was inevitably cheaper than the one-off products that typified the client economies of the past. So inexpensive was Coade stone that, in 1784, Eleanor Coade issued what was, in effect, a mail order catalogue. Not that her business ignored individual commissions. In 1799 John C. F. Rossi RA (1762–1839) estimated that an eight foot portrait figure of Sir Edward Coke in Coade stone would cost a mere £100.[31]

The exploitation of the modellers' skill for commercial and other purposes has a long history. In 1671 Allain Manesson Mallet illustrated a three-dimensional scale model for military fortifications being modelled in clay.[32] Modellers were also employed by goldsmiths. In the late 1760s the London goldsmith Germain advertised for "two Modellers of Figures and three of Ornaments [to execute] Sculpture, Bronzes, Gold and Silversmith's Works".[33] This distinction between the two categories of modeller is of some significance. A very special training was necessary to understand the conventions of ornament as distinct from a knowledge of anatomy, human or animal. For example, an understanding of ornament and an ignorance of the human form is evident in many of the late eighteenth century drawings by members of the Rose family of ornamental plasterers. In this respect Borguis & Son of 15 Titchfield Street, London were an exception in advertising themselves in 1799 as "Figure" and "Ornament" painters who were thus uniting what were generally distinct vocations in either two or three dimensions or in relief work.[34] The employment of modellers by commercial organisations probably contributed towards a shift in the relevance of the plastic, as distinct from works cut out of wood, stone or marble. Although carved sculpture was to retain its status as a one-off luxury product, it was the modellers who could most easily meet the demands of industry, mass production and consumerism.

In working for manufacturers as modellers, many sculptors became central to some aspects of the Industrial Revolution. From his workshop in Newman Street, London, John Bacon was to work simultaneously for Coade, Wedgwood and Matthew Boulton. In contrast to cast work a carved item could be repeated but not replicated. Manufacturers of products derived (cast) from cheaply produced modelled master patterns were able to mass produce their merchandise with relative ease. This not only enabled a "house style" to emerge but also brought unit costs down dramatically. Indeed to maintain the desirability of his wares Wedgwood inflated his prices – and his profits.[35] In the long run, cheap luxury goods would be seen as a fundamental contradiction – to the extent that demand would decline.

Casting in plaster

In the *London Tradesman* (1745) Campbell makes reference to one branch of "Statuary" as follows:

> "There are others who make figures in clay, wax and plaster of Paris. The taste of busts and figures in these materials prevails much of late years, and in some measure interferes with portrait painting. The Nobility now affect to have their busts Done in that way rather than sit for their pictures and the fashion is to have their apartments adorned with bronzes and figures in plaster and wax".

These busts were often based upon plaster masks taken direct from the living or the dead. In his trade card of 1738 the statuary Benjamin Rackstrow (d. 1772) stated that he "takes off Faces from the Life and forms them into Busts to an exact likeness & with as little trouble as sitting to be shaved" (Fig. 102).[36] For posthumous portraits Joseph Nollekens RA (1737–1823) was said to ask his studio assistants to prepare plaster and tools as soon as he read an obituary to an important personage in the public prints. Thus equipped he would

FIGURE 101. A clay wall being used to divide a portrait head, itself modelled in clay, into two. To make a mould plaster would be applied to one half, the clay wall removed, and then plaster applied to the other half. Thus by applying a barrier (*e.g.* a wash of slurry) each half would then separate providing the pair of moulds for the production of a positive cast. (Photograph: Author's Collection)

rush off to take the mask of the deceased, seemingly with or without, the invitation of the bereaved family.[37] In this way Nollekens positioned himself to carry out the commission for a memorial.

As its name implies, a plaster mask taken from the human face is a frontal object. To create a negative cast, of a fully three-dimensional clay original, a piece mould was necessary. This was achieved by dividing the cast into a series of segments by means of clay walls and applying plaster zone by zone.[38] These segments could then be removed and separated, cleaned and reassembled and the void filled or skimmed with plaster. Once the mould was separated or chipped away the positive cast was revealed. As Rackstrow (1738) and Campbell (1747) make clear, plaster casts were sometimes considered acceptable as the finished product (Fig. 93). If however a more permanent material was commissioned a wax positive might become a route to *cire-perdu* bronze casting. There is a possibility that this procedure deprived wax of its status as a material in its own right. Certainly the Royal Academy was to exclude polychromatic waxes from its exhibitions.[39] Despite the secondary status of this art the Irish sculptor Eley George Mountsteven (fl. 1782–1792) was said to have brought such work "to a higher degree of perfection than ever it had attained before".[40]

The production of a metal cast was dependent upon a master pattern for which founders might employ a carved wood original that could be impressed into sand – for sand casting. An example of this concerned a proposed, but not realised, scheme for a tomb for Henry VII. This earlier design was well within the late medieval tradition and included

FIGURE 102. Benjamin Rackstrow's *trade label* engraved by Henry Copland in 1738, an unusually early date for the Rococo idiom in England. Among his many skills Rackstrow states that he "takes off Faces from the Life & forms them into Busts". (Victoria & Albert Museum, London)

a series of small figures of weepers to surround the tomb chest. These were to be created by "Lawrence Ymber, Karver" who was to produce the wood patterns for these figures which were to be sand cast by "Humfray Walker, Founder".[41]

The alternative to a wood pattern was the production of a plaster positive for sand casting or a plaster piece mould for casting a wax positive for the so-called "lost-wax" method. Wood, plaster and wax were the master patterns that were most often produced in the studio as a preliminary to casting in metal – a subject that will be examined in greater depth in Chapter 18.

Notes

[1] Lawrence Stone 1955, p. 212; F. Saxl and R. Wittkower 1948, pp. 38–39; Howard Colvin ed. 1975, p. 43

[2] Horace Walpole 1786, Vol. I, p. 58 – Sir Anthony Denny was then Keeper of the Wardrobe

[3] Margaret Whinney 1964, fig. 4 and pp. 6, 232/12

[4] One example of a terra cotta sketch for a full-size work is Roubiliac's 1745 model for the *Monument to John 2nd Duke of Argyll*, Victoria & Albert Museum, E.21-1888. Rysbrack's terra cotta bust of Sir Hans Sloane appears to have been used as the basis for the carved figure of Sloane of 1737 in the Chelsea Physic Garden

[5] Chris Green 1999, p. 1–4 which quotes Hookes's *Diary* 17 Feb 1674 "Saw Mr Dwight's English China" … in Boyle's laboratory "at Oxford in 1650"

[6] *Ibid.*, p. 332

[7] *Ibid.*, pp. 82, 90, 330, 332. For "Collogne Ware" see David Gaimster *German Stoneware 1200–1900*, London, 1997

[8] The author purchased clay from this establishment in the 1960s

[9] Joseph Farington *Diary* p. 367 16 July 1795, p. 556 25 May 1796

[10] Holger Hoock (2003) 2009, pp. 238–239

[11] Allan Cunningham 1830, Vol. III, pp. 68–69

[12] Joseph Farington, p. 703 27 November 1796 – who also noted that "Mr Collins of Berners Street is Sir Wm [Chambers's] principal Executor"

[13] Allan Cunningham 1830, Vol. III, p. 200–207

[14] Jacob Simon 2003, pp. 36–37

[15] The frame to Hogarth's *Beggar's Opera: Prison Scene* 1731 (Tate Britain 1909) may be by Gosset for it incorporates a relief portrait of the painter – possible by Isaac

[16] *The Quiet Conquest: The Huguenots 1685–1985* Museum of London, Cat. No. 313. Also Jacob Simon 1996, p. 144. Gosset is not listed in the index but reference is made to him on pp. 63, 68, 92, 131, 132, 144

[17] Allan Cunningham 1830, Vol. III, pp. 327–328

[18] See Fig. 11 and Appendix I

[19] John Bacon's trade label, Banks Collection 106.2 British Museum Dept of P&D, London

[20] Allan and Abbott eds 1992, pp. 56–59

[21] Jerry White 2012, 219; Allan Cunningham 1830, Vol. III, pp. 158–9, 201–3

[22] *Ibid.*

[23] Ingrid Roscoe *et al.* eds 2009

[24] *Ibid.*

[25] Alison Kelly 1990; Eleanor Coade lived from 1733 to 1821

[26] W. H. Pyne, 1824, Vol. II, p. 381–382

[27] Alison Kelly 1990, chapter 4 "The Making of Coade Stone"

[28] W. H. Pyne 1824, Vol. II, p. 382

[29] Allan Cunningham 1830, Vol. III, pp. 240–241
[30] Neil McKendrick *et al.* 1983
[31] Joseph Farington, p. 1284 6 Oct 1799
[32] A. M. Mallet *Les Traveaux de Mars on L'Art De la Guerre*, The Hague, 1671 (later edition 1696), Vol. I, p. 175. This illustration is reproduced as 11.1 in Andrew Saunders's *Fortress Builder: Bernard de Gomme: Charles II's Military Engineer*, Exeter, 2004
[33] Joseph Farington, p. 1384 6 Oct 1799
[34] The drawings by Joseph Rose and other members of his family are in the RIBA Drawings Collection in the Victoria & Albert Museum, London. An example is reproduced as fig. 309 in James Ayres 1998. Borguis trade label in British Museum, Dept of P&D. This business also operated as house painters and gilders
[35] Neil McKendrick *et al.* 1983
[36] Trade Card, Victoria & Albert Museum, London: E16-46-1907
[37] J. T. Smith (1828) 1919, Vol. I, p. 229. In some cases Nollekens was able to take the death mask of an individual who was not prepared to sit for the sculptor in his lifetime
[38] From the twentieth century onwards brass "shim" has been used for this purpose – see James Ayres 1985, pp. 161–162
[39] Holger Hoock (2003) 2009, p. 162
[40] R. Walsh's *History of Dublin*, 1818, p. 1187
[41] John Physick 1969, p. 7

Chapter 16

THE POINTING MACHINE

B y the late eighteenth century "the classic sculptor of high fame, whose mind must necessarily be engaged upon his designs" in clay or wax, employed assistants to give permanence to his *ouvre*.[1] Sculptors of this type were so persuaded of their genius that they expressed some condescension towards those craftsmen upon whom they were now dependent. In Hanoverian Britain marble assumed a dominance over other possible sculptural materials, a supremacy which conformed well with the prevailing taste for the Classical and Greek Revivals. In converting a plaster cast into marble, or some other material, a "pointing machine" was used – in effect a three-dimensional pantograph.[2] This established a series of measurements at given "points" in three dimensional space. By this means a plaster "original" could be transferred to another material at the same size, or be enlarged or reduced. For this purpose it was important that the "original" should be prepared in such a way that it conformed to the possibilities of the ultimate material. For example Roubiliac's practice of creating drapery on a plaster model by means of linen "dipped into warm starch water" would have presented a marble carver with serious problems unless necessary adaptations were made.[3]

On the evidence of surviving work it seems that sculptors in seventeenth century England were less reliant on such measuring devices – hence the vitality of their work. Cibber was said to have carved his figures of *Raving* and *Melancholy Madness* (*c.* 1676) "at once from the block, without any previous drawing or model whatever".[4] This anecdote is recorded in J. T. Smith's book on *Nollekens* (1828) and probably derives from the reminiscences of the author's father – the sculptor Nathaniel Smith (*c.* 1741/3 – after 1800). This story, seen from the vantage point of late Georgian London, appears to retain a relative rather than an absolute truth. In reality it is known that Cibber produced small maquettes for these figures. One such terracotta sketch for the figure of "Raving Madness" survives in the Staatliche Museen in Berlin and measures

FIGURE 103. *Pointing Machine* of the type known as "The Cage" – shown here with the plaster *maquette* and the "roughing-out" of the full-size woodcarving; at a ratio of 1:2. Note the graduated rails at the top of each "cage". The T- squares that hang from these rails are also graduated down their length to establish the location of the "box" which carries the pointer which is also graduated. This type of preliminary work was well within the capabilities of a 14-year-old apprentice (in this case the author).

$9\frac{5}{8} \times 11\frac{5}{8}$ in (24.5 × 29.5 cm). A terra cotta such as this would have been used to transfer the sketch into the full-size work by means of proportional dividers and callipers. These instruments were hinged by moveable wing-nuts which could be moved to establish the appropriate ratio (Figs 105 & 106).[5] This rather approximate method would account for the variations between the sketch and the resulting work which consequently maintains the vitality of being fully realised in its ultimate material – Portland stone. In this way Cibber's works escaped the more restrictive features that tend to result from the excessive use of the pointing machine.

In Hanoverian England, sculptors were so familiar with these various devices that it is very likely that painters, in addition to sculptors, were aware of these methods. In this respect Hogarth, in his *Analysis of Beauty* (1753), offers what appears to be, a very confusing account of a pointing machine being used on a wax bozzetto. He concludes this account as follows:

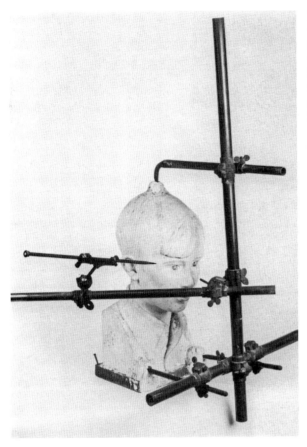

FIGURE 104. A tubular *pointing machine* articulated on ball and socket joints, probably early twentieth century. John Bacon RA (1740–1799) claimed to have invented a device of this kind – and gave one to Jean-Antoine Houdon. Some decades later Chantrey developed this type of instrument still further sending drawings of it to Antonio Canova in Rome. (Author's Collection)

"where the wires have pierced the wax, remaining on its surface, will mark out the corresponding opposite points in the external muscles of the body; as well as guide us to a readier conception of all the intervening parts. These points may be mark'd upon a marble figure with callipers properly used".[6]

Inevitably some sculptors were more dependent on these various measuring devices than others. John Bacon, having begun his career working on a small scale as a modeller in a porcelain manufactory, was probably more reliant than many on pointing machines when carving large scale marble statuary (Figs 95, 99). This probability is confirmed by the report that in the last decades of his life, Bacon employed some twenty assistants.[7] Such a dependence on this contrivance would account for the importance attached to these "machines" in biographies of Bacon and would explain the sculptor's incentive to develop improvements in these mechanisms.

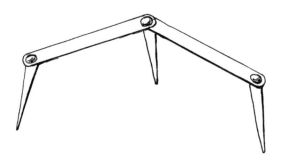

FIGURE 105 .Three leg dividers; bronze with copper rivets.

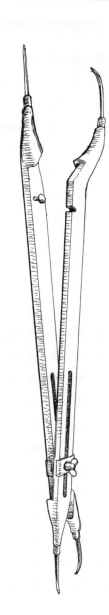

There are three basic types of pointing machine – namely "the cage" (Fig. 103), "the long arm" and a device made of brass that relies on a ball and socket joint to articulate a pointer which may reach out and round a three-dimensional work (Fig. 104).[8] Early in his career it seems that Bacon used a very simple version of "the cage", which he termed "the gallows". He later claimed to have "invented an instrument of a very superior kind ... which takes measurements, reaches all round and, by means of a ball and socket joint, the measuring pen [the pointer] can be directed according as the model requires". This was clearly the third type of mechanism listed above. It seems that the French sculptor Jean Antoine Houdon (1741–1828) saw this device in Bacon's studio and was promptly presented with one. At a later date Sir Francis Chantrey (1781–1841) developed this mechanism still further sending working drawings for it to Antonio Canova (1757–1822), following a visit to London by the Italian sculptor in November 1816.[9]

The use of the pointing machine was described by the sculptor and writer Allan Cunningham (1830) as "a subordinate art, that of transferring the express[ed] image of the model to marble" –

FIGURE 106 (above). Proportional dividers set by means of the wing nut to a ratio of 1:3. American walnut, steel and brass. Overall length 34½ in (87.6 cm).

to which should be added stone or wood. As a subsidiary activity much of this work was deputed to apprentices and journeymen. Generally speaking each "point" in the ultimate material was established some distance in advance of the likely final surface (say ½ in or 12 mm). In theory this gave the true sculptor (the carver) some latitude and even some spontaneity in finalising the work.[10] Pointing machines of various sizes could be used in a pre-mechanised situation to repeat, enlarge or reduce the dimensions of the "original". This explains the "editions" of some works at various sizes.

In his earlier works it was John Flaxman's (1755–1826) practice "to work his marbles from half-size models – a system injurious to true proportion. The defects of the small models were aggravated at the rate of eight to one".[11] The apparent mathematical anomaly here is easily explained: twice in two dimensions being four times area, whereas twice in three dimensions is an eight-fold enlargement in volume (Fig. 107). As Flaxman was primarily, and possibly exclusively, a modeller it seems that the necessary amendments were not made in his earlier work. With his burgeoning reputation the sculptor was able, in later life, to employ a greater number of assistants and this enabled him to produce full-size *bozzettos* so that the "defects" in his work became less numerous – and his sculpture less spontaneous. A frigid art.

Cunningham (1830) makes a fairly good case for full-size maquettes although the contrary view was well made by the sculptor Eric Gill (1929): "It is not desirable to make exact models in clay, because the sort of thing which can easily and suitably [be] constructed in clay may not be suitable for carving in stone".[12]

Gill doubtless had many reasons for arguing in favour of simple small scale models, and therefore eschewed the pointing machine. For his purposes three (or four) legged calipers (Fig. 105) offered an effective means of establishing a third point in space between two pre-existing and fixed points. As an advocate of "direct carving" Gill was attempting to turn back the clock to an age when sculptors regularly carved their own work.

From the eighteenth century the rising influence of sculptors like

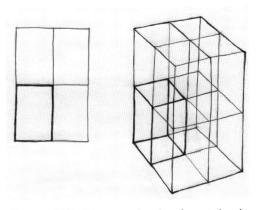

FIGURE 107. Diagram showing how twice in two dimensions amounts to four times area whereas twice in three dimensions results in eight times volume.

Wilton and Flaxman probably marks the beginning of this reliance on carvers as sub-contractors rather than as originators. Joseph Wiltons's (1722–1803) father William may have been dismissed as a "common plaisterer" but it was the elder man's wealth that enabled young Joseph to go to Paris to study under the French sculptor J. B. Pigalle (1714–1785).[13] Although this spell on the Continent doubtless widened the young sculptor's horizons the fact remains that his background was rooted in modelling, in clay and casting in plaster.

Although John Flaxman's (1755–1826) *milieu* was similar to Wilton's his was far less affluent although the elder John Flaxman (1726–1795) was described as "a worthy man of diligence and skill".[14] Flaxman *père* had worked for Roubiliac, Scheemakers and Wedgwood as a modeller but had begun in business making and selling plaster casts (see Indenture, Appendix I). It was this background that provided the introduction for young Flaxman to work for his father's old employers Roubiliac and Wedgwood. Employment in the family business enabled Flaxman Jnr to model and draw "most assiduously [for] his father's shop was his academy". There is, however, no record of his learning to carve.[15] When Richard Payne Knight commissioned Flaxman "to make a statue of Alexander the Great in marble", the sculptor was "at this time no skilful worker in that material, if indeed he ever became such, [so he] employed [Nathaniel] Smith in executing it".[16] This reaffirms the Roubiliac connection for whom Smith had previously worked.

A close contemporary of Flaxman's was John Rossi RA (1761–1839) who had been apprenticed to Giovanni Locatelli (1734–1805). When Locatelli first arrived in England he lodged in The Haymarket, Westminster, with Rossi's father, a fellow Italian. In general parents would seek to apprentice a son to a master who was known to them. In addition to his training in Locatelli's workshop, young Rossi was to gain an education at the RA Schools into which he was enrolled in 1781. From there he, and his contemporary John Deare, were to win the travelling scholarship to Rome in 1785. Whilst there he claimed to have carved a marble relief (probably pointed-up for him) which he sent back to England for exhibition at the RA. In response the Academy's Council sent him a letter advising that his time [in Rome] would be more properly employed in Modelling than in working Marble," and that in future he should send "only models".[17] This may well have been an oblique comment on Rossi's proficiency as a carver, or on the quicker results possible in modelling in clay, or on the lower costs involved in sending a plaster cast back to England. As the Academy met Rossi's expenses this last possibility may well have been significant.

For John Flaxman "craft" was very evidently trumped by "art", practice was dominated by theory to the extent that in 1810 he was appointed the first

Professor of Sculpture at Royal Academy Schools – as commemorated by his published *Lectures on Sculpture*. Under the terms of the appointment Flaxman was to deliver six lectures; later increased to ten and published in the edition of 1865 with the addition of eulogies following the deaths of Thomas Banks, Canova and Flaxman himself.

The best contemporary account of Flaxman's technical abilities is provided by Allan Cunningham (1830). Cunningham (1784–1842) had been apprenticed at the early age of 11 years to his elder brother James, a Dumfriesshire stonemason. On moving to London in 1810 the younger man secured employment with the sculptor J. G. Bubb (1781?–1853) at 26s a week, later increased to 32s. From there, in 1814, he moved on to work as a pointing assistant to Chantrey whose foreman and confidant he became. In addition, Cunningham was to establish a reputation as a poet and biographer of artists. In that last capacity he came to know Flaxman in the final year of his life. For all these reasons Cunningham's verdict on Flaxman may be considered definitive: "Had his skill with the chisel equalled his talents with the modelling tool and pencil, Flaxman would have obtained a more universal admiration".[18]

* * * *

A number of American sculptors of the nineteenth century followed this arms-length approach to their art by means of the pointing machine. Among these was Horatio Greenough (1805–1852) on whom Fenimore Cooper has left a valuable insight.

> "Most of our people who come to Italy employ the artists of the country to make copies, under the impression that they will be both cheaper and better than those done by Americans studying there ... The very occupation of the copyist infers some want of that original capacity ... However exact it may be in its mechanical details ... In the case of Mr Greenough I was led even to try the experiment of an original. The difference in value between an original and a copy, is so greatly in favour of the former".

Fenimore Coper had selected a maquette of a group of two little cherubs by Greenough. Sadly, and despite his views on originality he "left Florence for Naples before the work commenced in marble, and I can only speak of it, as I saw it in plaster ... the first work of its kind which has come from an American chisel".[19]

Despite Cooper's best intentions the probability is that on his departure for Naples the plaster was handed to an Italian to be pointed up in marble. The evidence for such a likelihood is that in 1827 Greenough "proceeded directly to Carrara [via Rome] where he remained three months or more during which time he finished two busts and saw others prepared". A time frame of months would be insufficient to achieve so much which implies that Greenough was little more than a spectator. On the other hand this account does emphasise that Carrara was more than a quarry with quarrymen and masons but was also "the grand workshop of Italian sculptors".[20]

Notes

[1] J. T. Smith (1828) 1919, Vol. II, p. 353
[2] James Ayres 1985, pp. 148–153
[3] Allan Cunningham 1830, Vol. III, p. 64
[4] J. T. Smith (1828) 1919, Vol. I, p. 199
[5] For various types of dividers and callipers see James Ayres 1985, p. 148, figs 210, 211
[6] Ronald Paulson 1997, p. 23. It is just possible that this was a mechanism devised by Hogarth but inspired by a pointing machine, for analysing sculptural beauty
[7] Ingrid Roscoe *et al.* eds 2009
[8] James Ayres 1985, pp. 148–153
[9] Allan Cunningham 1830, Vol. III, pp. 209–210
[10] A large number of nineteenth century marble sculptures remain shackled to their clay "originals" – with the incidentals of modelling in clay still evident. This is true of works in marble to which the name of the great modeller Rodin has been attached
[11] Allan Cunningham 1830, Vol. II, pp. 326–327
[12] Eric Gill (1929) 1934, pp. 85–86
[13] Allan Cunningham 1830, Vol. III, pp. 61–69
[14] *Ibid.*, Vol. III, p. 274
[15] *Ibid.*, Vol, III, p. 279. The Victoria & Albert Museum has in its collections a portrait medallion by John Flaxman II of his father – Ingrid Roscoe *et al.* eds 2009
[16] Allan Cunningham 1830, Vol. III, p. 288; Nathaniel Smith *c.* 1741/3–after 1800 worked chiefly for Nollekens
[17] Ingrid Roscoe *et al* eds 2009; Holger Hoock (2003) 2009, p. 112
[18] Ingrid Roscoe *et al.* eds 2009; Allan Cunningham 1830, Vol. III, p. 366
[19] William Dunlap (1834) 1969, Vol. II, Pt II, pp. 419–420 footnote which gives the extract from a letter from J. Fenimore Cooper published in the *New York American* 30 April 1831
[20] *Ibid.*, Vol. II, Pt II, p. 416–417

Chapter 17

CARVING

In its exact or historical sense, the word "sculpture" was synonymous with cutting. From its Latin root in the *scalpellum* (a cutting tool) to the *scalpel* of the surgeon, or the *scalper* of the engraver – the true sculptor's craft was centred on cutting.

From a strictly technical point of view carving in wood is more difficult than working in stone or marble. For this reason many woodcarvers were capable of adapting their skills from the ligneous to petrean materials (see Appendix X). In contrast those who were apprenticed to working in stone or marble were not destined to become adequate carvers of wood.

Woodcarving

Rarely is it possible to form an impression of workshop experience as it was lived in the eighteenth century. An exception to that generalisation is found in the pages of Thomas Johnson's (1723–1799) autobiography. Johnson was, by trade, a woodcarver, but his account (reprinted by Jacob Simon, 2003) offers a wide insight into the lives of the craftsmen of his generation.[1]

As the son of a highly successful bricklayer and property developer Johnson had the advantage of a "liberal" education at the Soho Academy in London. His premature departure from that school in 1731 was caused by his father's early death which depleted family resources. His father's success in the building trade probably explains why young Johnson was sent, at the early age of almost 13 years, to gain work experience with G. Hoare, a bricklayer of Cannon Street in The City. In that employment young Johnson proved accident prone and so, in the interests of self-preservation, he moved on to a physically safer alternative career. On 29 August 1737, at the age of fourteen years, he was bound apprentice to his cousin Robert Johnson. Later in life he was to describe this relative as "the worst carver I ever saw that had any title to that profession [so that] for want of proper instruction [young Johnson] made very slow progress towards becoming an artist". This may have been more a conflict of personalities than differing views on their art. At one point the apprentices in this workshop came to blows with their master and his wife, although at the conclusion of their time these youths parted with their master on amicable terms. The decorative details in Robert Johnson's trade card of *c.* 1760 certainly suggests that he produced sophisticated work.[2] So what skills and processes would a youth such as young Johnson have acquired as an apprentice wood carver; that most demanding of all the sculptural skills?

Some species of timber are notably tough. This is particularly true of English oak but for this reason it inspires character. In contrast another hardwood (deciduous) like lime-tree is more demanding by virtue of its relative blandness. Also, and contrary to expectations, softwoods (coniferous) such as pine or fir require very well-sharpened carving tools – edge tools used on oak demand far less sharpening. For this reason, in "trying" a tool for sharpness, sample cuts are made across the grain in a piece of best yellow pine. Learning to give an edge to the variously shaped cutting implements used for wood carving was the primary skill to be developed by an apprentice. These tools were sharpened on their backs with a flat oil-stone so that for a gouge it was necessary to do this with a rocking motion that corresponded to its curvature. Internal curves were sharpened with shaped oil stones known as "slips". In most European traditions these tools were given both an external and an internal bevel before being "stropped" on a leather.[3] It seems that various local sources of suitable stones for this purpose became available. For example Edmund Rack, writing in the 1780s, noted that Crowcombe in Somerset was a source of "Whet-stones pretty much like those of Devon ... and are used and sold for sharpening edge tools". Eventually slips known as "Turkey stone" from Smyrna in Asia Minor became available. According to the wood engraver Thomas Bewick (1755–1828) oil stones of this type could "be got at any of the Hardware Shops [in Newcastle] but I fear it will require a good deal of practice before you are able to sharpen your tools properly".[4] The acknowledgement of the difficulty of sharpening burins may be contrasted with the still greater challenge of creating a clean cutting edge in woodcarving tools.

The subsidiary internal bevel on woodcarvers' tools was significant in itself but it also drew a clear distinction between their edge tools and those of the makers – the latter included joiners and cabinet makers. For purposes of geometrical precision makers tools have a single bevel in contrast to those used by carvers for whom the major and minor bevel offers greater freedom.

FIGURE 108. Woodcarving tools were traditionally fitted with handles that were distinctive one from another. This enabled them to be picked up off the bench by the carver at speed as and when needed. These tools were ranged on the work surface with their sharp edges pointing towards the carver. (Author's Collection)

According to Joseph Moxon (1703 edition) the edged tools used by turners were sharpened in the manner of those employed by carvers including: "Flat Chissels which are not ground to such a Basil as the Joyners Chissels are, which are made on one of the Flat sides of the Chissels, but are Basil'd away on both" sides.[5] Today turners give their cutting tools a bevel on just one side but quite when this fundamental transition occurred has yet to be established. Because of this essential distinction between the two ways of sharpening edged tools it was traditionally considered inadvisable to employ carvers as either joiners or cabinet makers – although in small communities this often happened.[6] This divide between woodcarvers and furniture makers raises important questions regarding a figure like William Linnell (c. 1703–1764).[7] Linnell was by trade a woodcarver and set up in business as such in c. 1730. His workshops later undertook furniture-making and upholstery but in view of the near impermeable distinction between these trades Linnell himself, rather than his business, should probably be viewed as a carver and designer – and not as a furniture maker. The business was developed still further by his son John Linnell (1729–1796) from their premises at 28 Berkeley Square, London.[8] From this address the younger man not only designed chimney pieces, furniture and upholstery but also silver.[9] In 1760 John Linnell, in conjunction with his uncle the coach-builder Samuel Butler, submitted designs for a new state coach. Although their proposal was not accepted Butler went on to build Sir William Chambers's design for this important Royal commission.[10]

The demarcation between the practice of woodcarving as distinct from other wood-working trades, is all the more remarkable when one considers that in London and Salisbury carvers were incorporated into the Joyners Company in each city where:[11] "All carved workes either raised or cutt through or sunck-in, with the Grounde taken out being wrought with carving Tooles without use of Plaines".[12]

Shallow relief work of this type was well within the capabilities of joiners, being based on largely geometric forms, in contrast to the high relief and fluid form that typifies carving by specialists. In 1617 the Joiners Company of Salisbury was explicit on this point in stating that the brethren were only permitted to do carving such "as joyners do use".[13] By way of illustration one member of that guild, Humphrey Beckham was paid in 1634 for his work on the Council House in Salisbury where "he hath artificiallye set up ye waynscotte and carved workes" – of the type that was within the scope of a joiner.[14] In Benno Forman's (1971) survey of Continental woodcarvers active in the London area in the sixteenth century, comparable evidence may be found for the modest role of joiners as carvers. Forman's listing included only three joiner-carvers but other such foreign tradesmen were probably working discreetly in Southwark and various peculiars beyond the jurisdiction of the guilds. Among those identified by Forman was Diricke Cornelys from Amsterdam who was active in the London area by 1568 – specifically as a "carver for joiners' work".[15] In contrast to these specialists the Joyners Company of London included men who were active as carvers in a far wider sense. In 1632 the Court of Aldermen of the City drew up an 18 paragraph list of those activities that were confined to members of the Company of Joyners and Ceilers – (as distinct from the Carpenters – "ceilers" made panelling). Paragraph 14 lists picture frames, "Latesses for Scrivenors, or the like" and Item 15: "All signboards of wainscot or carved" and Paragraph 17: "All carved works using carving tools and not planes".[16]

In the second half of the seventeenth century a vigorous sculptural tradition for working in wood was maintained by Edward Pierce (or Pearce, c. 1630–1695). This man also worked in stone and marble and developed a considerable reputation as a mason-contractor and architect. Moreover in addition to his work as a statuary he was also a capable ornamental carver.[17] The Painters' Hall in London possesses works by Pierce which reflect his considerable and various abilities. These include the ornamental woodcarving from a doorcase to the Old Hall and a portrait bust in marble of the Master Thomas Evans (1667) which has something of the panache of a Bernini. As has been noted by Margaret Whinney (1964) this "artist's technical accomplishment" as a woodcarver is very well exemplified in the "lively and vigorous cutting of the head" in his figure of *Sir William Walworth* (1684) (Fig. 110).[18] Unfortunately little is known of Pierce's training but the quality of this particular work provides compelling internal evidence that woodcarving was his primary training. It is known that his father was a decorative painter of London and that the sculptor was "made free by patrimony" of the Painter Stainers on 16 January 1656 and was "chosen of the Livery" on 20 February 1668. By 1683 Pierce himself was Warden of the Company. As a woodcarver he was employed by Wren in 1680 to carve the pattern for the weathervane for the church of St Mary Le Bow: "for a carving of the wooden dragon for a moddell for the Vane of Copper upon the top of the Steeple for cutting a relieve in board to be proffered up to dycerne the right bignesse".[19] This "modell" was later used as the basis for the coppersmith's work.

The timber selected for a particular job inevitably influences the nature of the resulting work. In much of Northern Europe oak long remained the material of choice for many purposes but in South Germany and Austria lime-tree was favoured rather as poplar was often used for preference in Italy.[20] Distinctive though these traditions were, the River Rhine probably kept the Low Countries in touch with materials that were more typical of regions to the south. Certainly Grinling Gibbons (1648–1721), who was born to English parents in Rotterdam, favoured lime-tree for his woodcarving. As he did not come to England until about 1667 when he was 19 or 20 years of age we may conclude that much of his training was received in the country of his birth. The idioms from which his reputation as a carver emerged derived from a Netherlandish tradition for "swags" and "drops" of fruit and flowers carved in low relief (Fig. 109). Gibbons was to build on that idiom by carving in such high relief that his confections became fully three-dimensional cornucopia of nature – although remaining firmly attached to an oak backboard. For these works the mild yet fibrous tenacity of a hardwood like lime-tree was the perfect choice of material. His achievement was well summarised by Horace Walpole who observed that: "there is no instance of a man before Gibbons who gave to wood the loose and airy lightness of flowers … and chained together the various productions of the elements with a free disorder natural to each species".[21]

To achieve this effect the carvers of this school layered their work so that the lower strata could be finished before later ones were added. These carvings are carved and laminated layer by layer (Fig. 111).[22]

As a master carver Gibbons was to pass his skills and methods on to his apprentices, individuals such as John Seldon who was to work at Petworth House from 1687.[23] Two of his other trainees were named Hunt, one of whom began his time in 1675, the other in 1676. One of these was John Hunt of Northampton (d. 1754) (see Fig. 12). Important though training under Gibbons was, the Anglo-Dutch master's influence was wider than those whom he taught directly. For example, Samuel Watson of Derbyshire (1662–1715) though apprenticed

to Charles Oakey of Westminster was to emulate
Gibbons's manner at Chatsworth House in his native
county.[24] Something of the Gibbons tradition was to
persist in the next generation of carvers, notably in
the hands of John Boson (*c.* 1696–1743) who, like
Gibbons, was adept in both wood and marble. Boson
appears to have been born in Witham, Suffolk and
yet, like Watson, was apprenticed in the London
area. Again and again provincial youths were sent
to the capital to serve their apprenticeships. Boson's
master in London was Jarvis Smith, who belonged
to the Joyners Company and was himself almost
certainly a specialist woodcarver. Boson worked
for Hawksmoor and his yard at Greenwich would
have brought him into the orbit of craftsmen
and artists who worked for Burlington & Kent.
This carver therefore became conversant with
the prevailing architectural fashions; from the
Baroque of Hawksmoor to the second coming of
Palladianism.[25]

FIGURE 109. Detail of a carved oak Anglo-Dutch overmantel,
third quarter of the seventeenth century. Such work may be
seen as the precursor to the free and high reliefs carved in
lime-tree by Grinling Gibbons (1648–1721) and his school.
(Author's Collection)

FIGURE 110. Edward Pierce (*c.* 1630–1695)
carved wood figure of *Sir William Walworth*,
1684. Pierce was a sculptor of genius in
one exact meaning of the word – he was
adept at two very distinct skills – for he
carved in both wood and stone and worked
as a statuary and as an ornamental carver.
At a technical level wood carving is more
difficult than working in stone or marble,
indicating that Pierce was trained as a
woodcarver. He also operated as a mason
– contractor and architect. His father
was a prominent Painter Stainer – the
Company to which his son was admitted
by patrimony in 1656. (Fishmonger's Hall,
London)

FIGURE 111. Three photographs of a Gibbons school picture frame carved in lime-tree in the late seventeenth century. This demonstrates how the high relief and attached three dimensional elements were worked in layers and later combined to achieve the desired effect. (Ex. collection: Jeanne Courtauld)

In acquiring a craft skill a youth was put through an almost military discipline. After one or two years engaged in menial tasks: fetching and carrying, sweeping the workshop floor or lighting the stove, an apprentice woodcarver might be granted the privilege of learning to sharpen tools. This, as we have seen, was a difficult procedure, particularly with "V" tools or veiners.[26] It was also a very time consuming chore, particularly with tools where the shank was bent. A woodcarver's kit would comprise some 300 edged tools although perhaps only 30 of these would be on the bench at any given time; selected according to the nature of the job and the stage that it had reached. Once an apprentice had demonstrated his usefulness in sharpening tools he might then be permitted to begin carving wood in a simple two-dimensional way – like working back the ground for a relief. Sometimes this ground was given a punched texture, another activity suitable for an apprentice. Only later might the best trainees gradually become capable of seeing and therefore working in a fluid three-dimensional way. For all these reasons the skills that a young woodcarver hoped to develop during his seven years of servitude were formidable. These were circumstances in which there was barely time for artistry, still less art, to emerge. In the first couple of decades of the twentieth century, when these skills survived as part of a living tradition, it was believed that only one in ten apprentice

FIGURE 112. *Mould* carved in lime-tree for the production of composition ornament (15 × 11 × 2¼ in/38.1 × 28 × 5.8 cm) – late eighteenth century. Towards the end of his life Thomas Johnson (1723–1799) attributed the decline in the demand for woodcarving to the ever increased use of "compo" (see pp. 363 & 366). (Author's Collection)

woodcarvers would fully reach the expected standard of work.[27] Those who failed in that endeavour either moved to alternative employment or spent their working lives carving miles of repetitive enrichments on mouldings – such as egg and dart or a guilloche. Others became employers and in financial terms, could become quite successful. For example it is likely that on the back of his employees "Mr Doggett", of Boston, Massachusetts, was able to become, in the first decades of the nineteenth century "a wealthy and worthy frame-maker".[28]

It might be objected that these various purposes to which woodcarving was put, were of a commercial nature, an "applied" or "decorative art", that was of little relevance to the "fine art" of sculpture. These though were the very skills, on the basis of which, some individuals emerged as statuaries (see p. 366). Moreover many of the distinctions that the modern world has seen fit to impose on the visual arts are ones of which pre-industrial economies were innocent. The emphasis was on the quality of the artistry rather than its designation as "art". In many ways the work of Grinling Gibbons, and his school, demonstrates how meaningless these distinctions can be.

Much the same could be said of the carvings of Thomas Johnson – referred to at the start of this chapter. On 19 July 1744 stamp duty was paid on Johnson completing his apprenticeship and he began working for the master carver James Whittle (d. 1759) of Great Andrews Street, Soho, London. As a journeyman Johnson described himself modestly as "a very indifferent hand" and so he was paid just 15 shillings a week.[29] At that time Whittle employed "upwards of thirty men, amongst whom was the famous Matthias Lock [fl. 1710–1765] a most excellent carver and reputed to be the best Ornament draughtsman in Europe". The young journeyman intended to be "emulous" of Locke's carving as a consequence of which Johnson's work and pay improved – to 26 shillings a week.[30] After a couple of years in Whittle's workshop the young journeyman, and two companions, set off on 30 March 1746 to walk to Liverpool. They carried with them their tools and "leather aprons" bundled up and born over their shoulders on a traditional pedlar's "hook stick".[31] Walking considerable distances from job to job remained common practice amongst tradesmen down to the first decades of the twentieth century.[32] Not even the coming of the railways changed this situation. The stone-mason Henry Broadhurst (b. 1840) recalled that "most working men" walked from job to job, any other mode of travel being confined to "the lazy and foolish".[33] Before and after the coming of the railways economy was only part of the reason that persuaded artisans to walk "from job to job". The route selected by Johnson and his companions took them via Coventry and Chester presumably for the good reason that cathedral cities were well recognised as centres of employment for

Figure 113. Detail of a *carved mirror* in the chinoiserie taste of *c.* 1758–1760 – school of
Thomas Johnson (1723–1799). (Victoria & Albert Museum, London)

such tradesmen. In the event Johnson found employment in Liverpool with
the ship-carver Richard Prescott (active from *c.* 1702 to his death in 1747).
The Lord Street workshop that Prescott occupied was one where "the window
had no sash [but] was open to the street" as was then common practice for
workshops.[34]

When a craftsman sought employment in a location where he was unknown
qualifications (apprenticeships, etc) were irrelevant – the prospective employer
needed to see what the applicant could do. Accordingly the Liverpudlian
offered Johnson the Londoner, a piece of wood in his workshop saying "thou
may'st take it, and do what thou wilt; do something in the tross [truss/console?]
way, if its worth anything I'll buy it of thee …". Once carved the work was duly
purchased but Prescott only paid a guinea for it, and it had taken six days to
carve. This exemplified pay differentials between London and the provinces,
rather than meanness on Prescott's part, since the standard pay for a carver in
Liverpool at this time was two shillings a day. After a year or so in Liverpool,

Johnson crossed the Irish Sea to Dublin for what proved to be an eight month stay. On this occasion his reputation seems to have preceded him for he was received "very politely" by John Houghton (fl. 1739–1748) who was probably the best carver in Ireland at that time.[35] In these circumstances there was no question of Johnson producing a sample of his artistry for Houghton, "a wood statuary" with particular expertise in "basso-relievo figures". Under this master – craftsman's tutelage Johnson "made great improvements ... and his apprentices from me". Art education in a craft workshop was both vertical down the generations and across from one journeyman or apprentice to another. Even more to the point these high skills were a matter of lifelong learning.

Following a brief sojourn in the Irish capital Johnson returned, on impulse, to Liverpool. There he found work carving a doorcase for Mr T. Ball, a merchant whose niece, Mary Bell, Johnson was to marry in 1750.[36] One of this carver's last jobs in the port was to work on the interiors of the Liverpool Exchange designed by John Wood the elder (1704–1754) of Bath.[37] Then, in 1753, Johnson and his wife set off for Dublin where he and his three apprentices and four journeymen found employment with William Partridge of Blind Quay, a carver who specialised in mirror frames.[38] From this it is evident that a master carver, working as a sub-contractor for another business, was sometimes accompanied by his own team.

Johnson's career demonstrates that he worked on large-scale architectural work and on small-scale furniture carving. A range of undertakings of this kind were also well within the scope of Simon Hennekin in mid-eighteenth century London. From his address in Edward Street Hennekin advertised that he was capable of: "Carving and Gilding either in the Building, Ship, Sign or Furniture way executed with the utmost expedition at Reasonable prices". As if this range of activities was insufficiently comprehensive he added that he also made "Frames of all sorts ... in the neatest taste" and was furthermore "Eminent for making laymen for painters" (see p. 168, Fig. 38). This level of diversification may have been unusual but, in the 1790s, Thomas Hartley of Newgate Street, London stated on his trade card that he performed "all manner of house and furniture carving".[39] In Colonial North America diversification of this kind may have been even greater. The woodcarver Stephen Dwight advertised on 22 September 1755 that having been of "late an apprentice to Henry Hardcastle" was about to "set up his business between Ferry Stairs and Burling Slip" in New York City. From that location Dwight undertook to carve "all sorts of ship and house work and also tables, chairs and looking-glass frames, and all kinds of work for cabinet makers in the best manner and on reasonable terms".[40]

The English carver Thomas Johnson, his family, apprentices and journeymen

sailed by "yacht" from Dublin for England, travelling via Chester where his wife
Mary had inherited some property. From there Mary and the luggage travelled
to London in the wagon and Johnson and the eldest apprentice walked to the
capital "arriving there in 1755". Back in London Johnson approached his old
employer Whittle for work. Rather surprisingly he was asked, once again, to
demonstrate his skill and artistry. This challenge prompted him to create a
Rococo girandole "in a taste never before thought on" which incorporated "a
ruinated building with cattle, etc".[41] This was "so greatly esteemed, that many
of the men took moulds" of the details in it (Fig. 113). Johnson's influence was
further extended by the publication, in 1755 and 1756–57, of his two books of
designs.[42] He later found work with Thomas Vialls doing "the principal part"
of his (Vialls's) work assisted by four apprentices and 25 journeymen.[43] This
number of apprentices probably exceeded what was authorised by the guild
which was generally a maximum of three. However with such a large workforce,
including more than one master carver, this regulation may have been met –
although it was not easily enforced. By 1757, apparently concurrently with his
work for Vialls, Johnson became the foreman of Whittle's business which was
now run by the owner's son-in-law, Samuel Norman.

As an ornamental carver and gilder, Johnson worked primarily in soft woods
at various scales and dimensions on consoles, table frames and architectural
carving for interiors. In working in a variety of woods and at different scales, an
ever evolving tool kit would have been necessary. In his youth Johnson's tools
were probably narrowly focused on the needs of small-scale decorative work
in pine. On his arrival in the north-east he found that "Liverpool was then not
so polite as it now is" so that the type of refined decorative work, for which his
training had equipped him, was not in much demand. Inevitably the principal
employment for such tradesmen in this port city was ship carving. Prescott,
his first employer in Liverpool, was himself a specialist in work of this type,
although he is known to have carved a series of picture frames for Knowsley
Hall, the Lancashire seat of the Earl of Derby. Johnson's "chief motive" for his
employment with Prescott was "to get an insight into their manner of ship work".
His employer was doubtful that the young journeyman would have sufficient
strength for such an activity "which would soon break [his] catstick arms".[44]
Furthermore carving on this scale, particularly where hardwoods were used,
was likely to break Johnson's delicate edged tools. These issues demonstrate
that he evidently adapted to the very different demands of ship-carving with
an enlarged range of tools. In 1746 he was commissioned by the Liverpool
ship owner Thomas Seel to carve "a figure of Miss Jenny with a white rose at
her breast; and a deal of ornament for her stern".[45]

FIGURE 114. *The Shipbreakers Yard* of Henry Castle & Son, Baltic Wharf, Millbank, Westminster – photographed 25 March, 1909. The decline of timber-built sailing vessels resulted in the loss of this great sculptural tradition. (London Metropolitan Archives)

In accordance with Johnson's wish to gain an understanding of "ship work" this type of carving certainly offered a basis for other species of sculpture. Among those who doubtless owed much to such a background was Edward Hodges Baily RA (1788–1867) whose father was a gifted Bristol ship-carver.[46] Many port-based woodcarvers were involved in a whole range of domestic and ship-carving as for example in the east coast port of Hull – where both Thomas Ward (1782–1850) and Thomas Banks (1778–1850) undertook such work although, by the nineteenth century, there was less demand for woodcarving. According to Thomas Wilkinson (1821–1903), who had been apprenticed to Ward, ship carving was regarded by his day as a lowly type of work only to be undertaken when carvers were otherwise unemployed, a situation that may be compared with the out of work stone-carvers who turned to "field ranging" (see p. 382).[47]

Decoration of merchant vessels had for long been exceeded by the even greater enrichment accorded to the ships of the Royal Navy, a means of projecting state power. In the France of Louis XIV the chief minister Jean Baptiste Colbert (1619–1683) declared that the "Sun King's" vessels were to serve as an arm of diplomacy "to carry to foreign shores magnificent testimony to the grandeur of the King of France".[48] A similar position was adopted by the English crown which, until 1726, required all Royal Naval vessels to carry a lion as their figurehead. As the naval budgets were reduced, and as the insistence on a lion figurehead was abolished, redundant examples found alternative uses as when "the head of an old ship [was] fixed at the door, as is commonly seen at public houses" – the Royal Navy's lion spent its retirement as a pub sign.[49] In place of the English lion, ships of the Navy now generally adopted the name of the vessel as their emblem for the prow. By 1754 Mungo Murray objected to:

> "The barbarous and unnatural mixture of Gothic and Chinese ornaments, clumsy heroes and fat-headed gods on the same ship, the monstrous issue of a savage conception and wayward genius as deformed and perverse as their own cant timbers".[50]

"Savage" though some of this work may have been its cost could be substantial. In 1703 and again in 1796 attempts were made to economise in this work in Royal Naval yards.[51] Despite these measures, elaborate carving continued to be applied to these vessels. In 1797 Joseph Farington was given a list by White the shipbuilder of Lysons and White of Deptford, which itemised the cost of ship carving in relation to tonnage. This in turn was based on the "rates" of ships in the King's Navy; indicating that a first rate ship of the line would have more lavish decoration than a lesser vessel in the fleet. On this basis "Victory of 100 guns – 2162 tons [carried] carving at 3s a ton", a total of £324-6s-0d in carved work. In contrast the "Kingfisher … of 18 guns … 300 tons at 1s-6d" per ton resulted in a total of just £22-10s-0d. This informant stated that such a relative economy "by not allowing ships to be carved as formally, does not amount in all [as a saving for the Treasury] to £6,000 a year" – see Appendix XIII.[52]

* * * *

The international nature of marine art is reflected in the work of Benjamin Rush (1756–1833) who was possibly the finest of all American ship-carvers. For his larger works he was said to "hire a wood chopper, and stand by and give directions where to chop".[53] "Roughing out" work of this kind was executed using a short-handled carving axe which offered far more precision than that account implies.[54] William Dunlap's (1834) ignorance of Rush's *metier* resulted in strangely contradictory remarks. He bemoaned the fact that Rush "never worked in marble" and went on to observe that "Mr Rush ... though by trade a carver of ship's heads was, by talent and study, an artist"[55] – as if the two were contradictory or even mutually exclusive.

Rush was apprenticed in about 1771 at the traditional age of 14, to the English trained ship-carver Edward Catbush, although his apprenticeship was brought to a slightly premature end by the outbreak of the War of Independence (1776).[56] Despite this somewhat abbreviated training Rush's natural ability evidently carried him through to become a supreme artist. He was also well aware of contemporary developments in "polite" sculpture. His figurehead for the *Benjamin Franklin* was clearly influenced by Houdon's bust of the "Doctor". Despite the very evident qualities of his work academic sculptors, in addition to painters like Dunlap, regretted that Rush's art was chiefly applied to ships and that he worked in wood rather than marble. Prejudice of this kind did not prevent his fellow ship-carvers respecting his achievement. When the ship William Penn, carrying his figurehead of the *Indian Trader* docked in the Port of London the British ship-carvers "would come in boats and lay near the ship and sketch the designs from it. They even came to take casts of Plaster of Paris from the head".[57]

In keeping with tradition Rush's shipyard work was given polychromatic and oil gilt embellishment. In the long sweep of history

FIGURE 115. William Rush (1756– 1833), *Comedy*, 1808, pine, originally painted (ht. 90½ in/232.4 cm). Rush occasionally ventured into the creation of classsical statuary but this did nothing to emasculate the vigour of the shipyard tradition within which he prospered. (Philadelphia Art Museum)

most sculpture, in marble, stone or wood, was treated in this way; but for a generation whose taste was based on the Renaissance, painted sculpture was heresy. The Classical Revival, which was founded on a somewhat more sophisticated archaeology, saw the reintroduction of polychromatic interiors and furniture in deference to Antiquity. Rather strangely this had little impact on sculpture which remained loyal to the virgin whiteness of marble. In relationship to Rush's role in 1794 as one of the founders of the Columbian (the forerunner of the Pennsylvania Academy of Fine Arts), he painted some of his carved wood sculptures white; presumably an attempt to conform to the prevailing taste.[58] Fortunately this superficial measure did nothing to emasculate the vigour of his work which owed everything to the rigours of the sea and the transatlantic traditions of the shipyards.

Benjamin Rush was the leader of the Philadelphia school of ship-carvers and was to pass his skills on to his son John Rush (1782–1853). The transmission

FIGURE 116. Modelling in clay has always provided a means of rehearsing a carved work – as shown in this photograph of *c.* 1917. In translating from one material to the other three legged dividers are particularly useful in that they establish the distance between two points and the depth/height in the intervening points. Here we see a 15-year-old student (Arthur Ayres, 1902–1985) at the South Kensington School of Woodcarving. (Author's Collection)

of his art and mystery was also to be carried to other ports on the Eastern Seaboard by his apprentices and journeymen. Among these were John Brown, who moved south to Baltimore, and Daniel N. Train, who migrated north to New York City. A very direct example of Rush's vision being adopted elsewhere were his designs for ship-carvings destined for the US Naval vessel Constitution of 1799, carvings which were realised by John Skillin of Boston.[59] These carvers generally occupied workshops adjacent to the mould lofts which enabled them to align their work with the vessels they were to embellish.[60] Work of this type was generally carried out in fir.[61] From a twentieth century standpoint the burden of ornament borne by the ships of the age of sail looks excessive. As early as 1711 William Sutherland seemed to share these concerns warning that when a naval architect is about "to deck or adorn a ship" it was essential to ensure "that the Beautifying may be no Detriment to the other good Properties" of the vessel.[62]

* * * *

Similar considerations were presumably involved in the carved decoration applied to carriages. On the other hand this was not the case with some of the massive state coaches of the eighteenth century where ostentation rather than mobility appears to have been the primary objective. The most obvious example of such a ponderous wheeled edifice is George III's State Coach of 1760–1761.[63] This vehicle was conceived by Sir William Chambers who, in this respect, was following the precedent established by William Kent – who designed practically everything including the 1732 State Barge. As with so much of Kent's *œuvre* the quality that was necessary to translate these schemes into reality was achieved by others. In this case the river barge was built by Hercules Taylor and decorated by James Richards (1671–1759) the carver in wood, marble and stone to the King and as such successor to Grinling Gibbons. A generation later the link between the ostensible designer and the executants was at one remove. For the embellishment of the State Coach its architect Sir William Chambers turned to the fashionable sculptor Sir Joseph Wilton who, notionally, served as the King's State Coach carver. Despite this office there is no evidence that Wilton possessed any capabilities as a carver of any kind, still less as a woodcarver. For this reason he seems to have been dependent, for realising this work,on the Danish-born Sefferin Alken (1717–1782) of St James's, Westminster.

Wilton may have established something of a precedent as the executive "sculptor" rather than the executant carver of a coach. In 1790 Richard

Westmacot created four bronze allegorical figures for the State Coach that was built for "Black Jack" Fitzgibbon, first Earl of Clare (1749–1802), Lord chancellor of Ireland. This vehicle also carried much carved decoration which Westmacot simply supervised. Godsals of Long Acre, London built this coach but they sub-contracted specialist carvers for this particular job. These men evidently needed encouragement. Philip Godsal's *Diary* notes that he paid "Dan Reeves, publican, in full of all their demands for carvers men's dinners during the time Lord Fitzgibbon's State Coach was in hand".[64] Not to be outdone by English coach builders the Lord Mayor of Dublin was quick to order an Irish-built vehicle from William Whitton of Dominick Street, Dublin. The carving on this coach was by Charles Francis le Grande, also of Dublin.[65]

By the early nineteenth century improved roads and a chaste aesthetic conspired to establish a more minimalist effect in carriage design. Not that carvers were totally displaced. In 1837 William Adams described carvers as "the workmen who execute the ornamental woodwork of carriages". He goes on to argue that "some of them are artists, furnishing designs as well as executing them, and of course are, in such cases, highly paid … The earnings of carvers are from thirty shillings up to four and five pounds per week according to their skill".[66]

Coach- and ship-carving was lavishly painted and gilded and, like street signs, maintained the medieval tradition for polychromatic decoration into a somewhat anaemic age of white stone, marble and unpainted wood. The Civil War and the following inter-regnum seems to have seen a suspension of aesthetic development. At that time "William Byrd of Hollywell [1624–1690? – in the, then, suburbs of [Oxford] Stone cutter [found] out the paynting or stayning of Marble A specimen of which he presented to the King [Charles II] after his restoration …" A possible example of this type of work survives in the form of an altar frontal stained on marble in St Helen's church in the City of London (p. 382). In general though the whole notion of polychrome sculpture was in decline in the late seventeenth century. Despite this new outlook there was a persistent expectation, as late as *c.* 1698, that architectural works of sculpture in wood were given polychromatic treatment. In that year Celia Fiennes visited Durham Cathedral where she admired the font cover "of fine carving of wood very high and terminates in a point, and resembles the picture of the Building [the tower] of Babel – its not painted".[67] The transition in outlook with regard to painted sculpture, in stone as in wood, is discernable in a letter that the limner and goldsmith Nicholas Hilliard (*c.* 1547–1619) sent to Robert Cecil in 1606 advising on the treatment of the stone and alabaster tomb for Elizabeth I in Westminster Abbey:

"I requested to haue the trymyng of the sayde Toumbe, because as a Goldsmith I understand howe to set foorthe & garnishe a peece of stone woork not with muche gylding to hyde the beawty of the stone, but where it may grace the same, and no more. And having scill to make more radient cullors like vnto Ammells [enamels], then yet is to Paynters knowne, I would have taught sum one which woulde not have made it common".[68]

This was the monument by Maximilian Poultrain (alias Colt) for which the sculptor received, by 1607, a total of £720. In the event the painted work was carried out by John de Critz the Sergeant Painter who received £600 and was thus, in relationship to the relative amount of work involved, far more highly rewarded than the sculptor.[69]

The trend which began to favour unpainted external architectural elevations, and similarly treated sculpture, was probably based upon a primitive archaeology that failed to identify polychromatic decoration of this kind on the works of antiquity. Furthermore in relationship to expensive imported marble and exotic hardwoods there was every incentive to leave these luxury materials visible and unpainted. For cheaper, and therefore less prestigious purposes, native alabaster and the use of yew tree, as an alternative to imported cedar, were available. Further economies could be made by painting less valuable materials to counterfeit expensive carving.

With the Restoration (1660) a whole new aesthetic outlook was introduced from the Continent, a reflection of the years of exile of Charles II and his court. This reinforced the taste for unpainted sculpture and architecture. The lime-tree carvings of the Gibbons school were left in their natural condition and are but one manifestation of this change in taste. Carvings in this idiom are generally attached to quarter-sawn English oak panels and framed by bolection mouldings – also of oak. With the passage of time the oak has darkened whilst the lime-tree has remained relatively pale in tone. This has resulted in a cameo-like effect that does not relate to their appearance, when first made.

Although the ancient tradition for the uninhibited use of colour declined amongst the elite it nevertheless persisted for their carriages and for the ships of the King's Navy. Ship-carving, carriages and trade signs with their polychromatic decoration addressed, and were enjoyed by, all classes on the open seas and in the High Street. It would be a mistake to assume that these gaudy effects were lacking in subtlety. Certainly the application of colour to sculpture demanded a sophistication that specialists were best equipped to provide. As we have seen John de Critz undertook this work on the tomb of Queen Elizabeth I in Westminster Abbey – for which he may have received probably unwanted advice from Hilliard. With some inevitability polychromatic sculpture continued to remain "popular" in provincial Britain and in Colonial circumstances. In 1673 a quantity of elm comprised of seasoned "ould peeces" and newly cut timber was purchased in the Wrexham area of Wales. This well-seasoned timber was to be carved by a travelling sculptor from Shropshire named Needham, work that was to include the figures of a "Turke and blackmore". Needham and his two assistants (probably apprentices) were to be paid a total of 4s-6d a day. Once the carving was complete it was to be coloured by Thomas ffrancis of Montgomery "the Herald Painter" who was also to decorate some panelling "walnutt color" for £32-9s-6d.[70] For his work on the figures ffrancis was to be paid piece rate but for painting the panelling he was remunerated by the square yard – a distinction that indicates a differential in status between the two categories of work.

Polychromatic decoration of carving within the British tradition was nowhere more evident in the eighteenth century than in the three-dimensional street signs and some related charity figures.[71] This was a truly "popular art". Sculptural works of this kind were amongst the stock-in-trade of the Harp Alley signmakers in the city of London. Their products could have a very wide distribution as is possibly demonstrated by one rather well documented example (Fig. 117). In 1712, the regulations for the Oliver Whitby School in Chichester, Sussex, stipulated: "that a box [was to] be set up in ye Hall [of the school] with a Blew Coat Boy painted over it to receive the Benevolence of Strangers and Visitors". In 1725 one of the school's trustees, a "Mr Watts" was reimbursed for the sum of £1-4s-0d in connection with a "Carv'd Boy". This modest payment would have been insufficient to create such a figure and may well relate to transport costs – perhaps from Harp Alley in London. Attitudes to the painting of such carved work at this time are reflected in the annual accounts of the school. Apparently a payment of five shillings was made each year for the repainting of this figure before the annual founders day service in the Cathedral. Similar provision was made in Coventry for the carved figure of Lady Godiva's infamous peeping Tom which was placed in the window from which he observed the Lady. In this case "whoever lives in that house, is obliged to new paint the statue every year, and to provide him with a periwig and a hat".[72] If bright new paint was the expectation for an almost military inspection, sculpture could also be given "proper"[73] colours of great sensitivity through the close observation of nature. The painted plaster bust of Colley Cibber of *c.* 1740 was described in 1774 as a portrait of the poet taken "when old, coloured from the life, and extremely like" (Fig. 93).[74]

The rising status of marble statuary was matched by a corresponding decline in the demand for woodcarving. For practical reasons wood inevitably remained the only suitable material for some purposes like picture and mirror frames. Consequently work of this kind continued as a source of employment until the widespread introduction of a cast composition material known as "compo". William Salmon (1701) gives instructions for making this which he describes as being a preparation of: "Glew-water stronger than any size, yet weaker than the joiners melted glew: mix Whiting [chalk] in a fine powder therewith till it is as thick as Paste or Dough: kneed it very well wrapping it up in a double cloth [and leave it to cure in a warm room]".[75]

In other words "compo" was a form of strong gesso. This was usually cast in carved wood matrices. Consequently the carvers who made these moulds were, in effect, conniving at their own demise (Fig. 112). The decline in wood carving and the reciprocal rise in the use of "compo" is evident in advice that the Norwich frame maker Benjamin Jagger sent in a letter in 1799 to John Thirtle (1777–1839), who was then working as a carver and gilder for Attwood, the London frame maker:

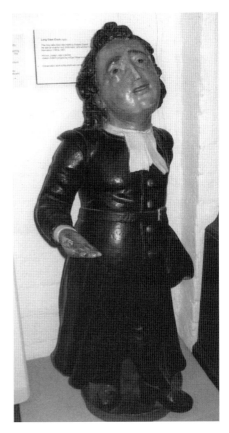

FIGURE 117. *Blue Coat Boy* (*c.* 1725) of the Oliver Whitby School, Chichester. Carved and polychromed wood – a possible work by a Harp Alley tradesman since these London workshops distributed their products widely. The accounts for the school show that this figure was repainted annually for the founders day service in the Cathedral. (Chichester Museum)

"Am glad to hear you are at Mr Attwood's – take care to continue there for 2–3 months and part of these as [a] carver – tho' you will, if in the gilding Shop, see their Methods of Working and thereby practice on evenings – that alone will not be sufficient, you must enquire about the shops and where the best work is done, you sh'd also see the Methods of the City, for they work quick, cheap and skewy [waste gold leaf used as an economy]. This method you must also learn – don't forget the putty [compo]. Work – your time is at best very short".[76]

His time was indeed short and "2–3 months" suggests that this good advice is addressed to a journeymen who knew the basics but, in that time, could have picked up a few tricks of the trade from various workshops. Three details suggest themselves in that passage. The "Gilding Shop" was evidently segregated, and the "putty" is possibly a reference to "compo", whilst "skewy" could denote the skewings or fragments of gold leaf that were applied to less significant zones on a frame or applied to second rate work. The whole emphasis of this letter concerns the economy of production – a sure sign of decline in the quality of wood carving at this time.

On Thirtle's return to his native Norwich in 1800 he developed his business as a frame maker working for a wide range of Norwich School painters including Cotman, Crome (Snr & Jnr), Clover, Dixon, Leman, Stark and Vincent. In addition Thirtle himself established a fine reputation as a landscape painter.[77] The relationship between the painting of pictures and the carving of frames was not unknown in Norwich. The son of the Norwich painter Robert Ladbroke Snr became a carver and gilder who produced picture frames.[78] The situation in which one individual was involved in two such activities seems to have occurred in earlier centuries despite the restrictions of the guilds. The engraver George Vertue (1684–1756) cites a seventeenth century frame maker named Flesshier who was also an easel painter whose work was in the collections of Charles I and Peter Lely. At Ham House in Surrey Lord Dysart owned "two pretty small sea-pieces by Flesshier".[79]

In addition to "compo" another threat to the carvers' trade was *papier mâché* which had been used in France from at least the seventeenth century.[80] Curiously it does not seem to have been much employed in England until *c.* 1750 when the carver and gilder Joseph Duffour advertised in London as the "Original Maker of Papier Mâché" from his premises at the Golden Head, Berwick Street, Soho. The uses of papier mâché were many and various and it was sometimes employed as a lighter weight, and therefore safer, alternative for decorative plaster ceilings. Duffour was succeeded in 1772 at the same address in London by René Stone (Pierre?).[81] The French origins of *carton Pierre* probably explains one of J. T. Smith's (1829) more unlikely anecdotes in which he refers to the "two old French women" who were employed "to chew for the papier maché" manufacturers.[82]

As noted above frame carving and gilding remained a source of employment for these tradesmen into the nineteenth century. This was a specialist skill the later stages in which involved "cut-in-the-white" gesso followed by the application of Armenian bole (the gold size) for water gilding. The manipulation of loose leaf gold was, as it remains, more of a knack than a skill, but demanded a lot of practice to avoid a profligate use of this precious material. For this reason water-gilding became something of a specialist activity. The organisation of a carver and gilders workshop was, as indicated by Duffour, of some significance. It was, for example, advisable for gilding to be done in a separate workshop away from the dust and wood chips of the carver. In Jacobean London George Geldorp, a native of Cologne who came to England in *c.* 1623, was one of the more important frame carvers in the capital. His business was conducted in "Franglais" and its documentation shows that his wife did much of the gilding. In 1626 she worked on a group of frames for Lord Salisbury as shown in her husband's invoice: *"pour le dorure de 7 bordures que ma femme a dorée pour l'or et ouvrage"*.[83] Over a century later Thomas Johnson similarly employed his wife "whom he had learned to gild" for this aspect of his work.[84]

Johnson was probably locked into the Rococo idiom of his youth and so his work was destined to be outmoded in his old age. Indeed so short-lived was this fashion that it was repudiated by some, of an earlier generation, whose lives overlapped Johnson's. Isaac Ware (1756) objected to the "very childish taste in sculpture" that we had "of late fallen into". The work that he rejected extended:

> "from the frames of looking-glasses to the entablatures of the orders. This is called the French taste, a frivolous people whom we are apt to imitate. It consists in crooked lines like Cs and ƆCs, the Gothick is hardly more contemptible." [85]

In contrast to Johnson, a slightly later generation of carvers, men like Edward Wyatt (1757–1833) of 360 Oxford Street, London, were able to accept the restraint of Neo-Classicism. Much of his carving was done in conjunction with his architect kinsmen despite which Wyatt worked to his own designs in both wood and stone. Wyatt's contemporary Robert Carpenter (1750/51 – after 1817) was similarly able to survive the declining importance of woodcarving by diversification. On 25 October 1798 he advertised his services in the *Bath Chronicle* as follows: "R. Carpenter (from London) carries on business at the mirror and looking-glass manufactory: 3 Bridge-street, Bath. Gentlemen's coats of arms carved in wood, stone; single figures from 1 inch to 6 feet high".

Significantly he emphasised that he came from the capital and could work to very different scales and dimensions in both wood and stone.[86] Among the many provincial carvers and gilders who trained and worked in London was Robert Davy from distant Penzance. In 1782 he inherited a 97 acre (*c.* 40 ha) farm in Cornwall and, as a consequence, moved back to his native county at a time when woodcarving was showing some signs of decline, he was no longer dependent on his craft. When his son, the great scientist Sir Humphry Davy, was in Paris in 1813 he and his wife visited the Louvre. In looking at the works of art exhibited there Davy enthused about the quality of the "Splendid picture frames", a poignant moment recalling his father's craft.[87]

The severe aesthetic discipline of Neo-Classicism may be seen as a reaction to the frivolous yet accomplished nature of the Rococo. The latter, under the leadership of highly skilled carvers such as Luke Lightfoot (*c.* 1722–1789), was a French Idiom that took root in England, with branches in Colonial North America, for a couple of decades in the third quarter of the eighteenth century.[88] Even more influential than Lightfoot was Matthias Lock (*c.* 1710–1765) who published his designs for *Six Sconces* in 1744 the first English Rococo pattern book. Lock, as we have seen, was a great influence on Thomas Johnson and, by extension, on Johnson's two pattern books.[89] Johnson's *Designs for Picture Frames, Candelabra, Ceilings etc. w*as first published in parts from 1758 (as a book in 1768) when it was dedicated to Lord Blakeney as president of the Antigallican Association. It seems that Johnson, like Hogarth, rejected the source if not the idiom of the French Rococo. At a more practical level the publication of 1758/1768 was more than a collection of pretty pictures. In the preface the author asserts that "the designs may all be performed by a Master of his art ... as I am well satisfied they can be executed by myself."

These woodcarvers were able to rise to the very considerable technical challenges of the Rococo. Eventually this fashion fell from favour and so too did the demand for the work of these carvers. The rising use of substitute materials like "compo" and papier maché further reduced demand. Writing in the 1820s W. H. Pyne referred back to John Linnell (1729–1796) whom he described as "an excellent carver in wood, a branch now almost obsolete".[90] By 1830 Allan Cunningham described how the sculptor Thomas Banks (*c.* 1745–1792), who had been apprenticed to the ornamental carver William Barlow II (fl. 1740–1752) had, in his early days, "pursued ... the profession of a wood carver, then a matter of higher moment than now, for it was closely interwoven with sculpture" (p. 351).[91] Decades earlier this decline did not pass by unrecorded. Thomas Johnson (1793) referred, with some despair, to the dwindling position of "the carving business" which had been "ruined by the invention of composition, etc" which, as a material cast in quantity, was inevitably cheaper than a "one-off" carving.[92]

Stone & marble carving

The surgeon J. R. Kirkup (1982) has usefully divided the instruments of his vocation into three categories, and these classifications are of equal relevance to the sculptor's craft. These designations comprise those implements involving unimanual control (e.g. a screw driver), double unimanual control (e.g. mallet and chisel) and bimanual control (e.g. a bow and drill).[93] With double unimanual control it can be advantageous for a sculptor to be ambidextrous.[94] For example when working on scaffolding the "standards" (vertical poles) may inhibit hammer-room so that the angle of attack must be reversed. This manual duality could also be an advantage in other crafts. For example the engraver John Keyse had "an extraordinary command over the use of both hands" so that when engraving a copper plate he did not need to turn it.[95] For the bimanual control of a bow and its drill the sculptor's command of this implement is such that it is possible to drill a channel with almost as much ease as a hole (Fig. 119). For the sculptors of Classical Antiquity, as for their Neo-classical followers, this was an invaluable device for the representation of drapery and hair.[96]

* * * *

The working of stone and marble required edged tools that were very distinct from those used on wood. For the latter the tools are given a cutting edge by means of fine grained stones using oil as a lubricant. For stone and marble a fairly course whetstone (using water) is used and this is a much simpler and less skilful procedure than the sharpening of the edged tools used to work wood. Inevitably, in sharpening stone-working tools by rubbing their cutting edge on a York-stone flag, metal is removed to the extent that the implement is eventually worn down past its temper. This was the stage at which the tool was sent to the smith to be "drawn-out", which is why they were known as "fire sharps". In England this work was carried out by specialists but in Ireland an alternative tradition prevailed. According to Seamus Murphy[97] such work was best undertaken by the masons and carvers themselves. This was because smiths tended to temper the tools to the extent of making them brittle. In heating the tools in the forge Murphy allowed "hard steel" to become "purple and with mild steel as far as straw colour" at which point the chisel could be drawn-out on the anvil. For these all-important colours to be visible a dark workshop was essential.

An important sub-division existed between those tools intended for hewing

stone as distinct from those used in working marble. For the latter the tools
were drawn-out by the smith to a more delicate refinement than was the case
with the implements used on stone. For example, a marble "point" is just that
whereas a stone "punch" is, in effect, a very narrow chisel (about $1/8$ in/4 mm).
These edged tools were given kinetic energy by means of hammers or mallets.
For "roughing out" stone and marble, steel headed hammers offered a more
staccato action, but for more refined work hammers of wrought-iron, or even
bronze, were favoured. Masons' mallets (diminutive of mall) were generally of
elm. The use of these implements resulted in edged tools being either hammer
headed or mallet headed. Woodcarvers did not use hammers and their mallets
were made of various hardwoods, available in numerous sizes. All these mallets
were of turned wood – and occasionally small "dollys" were used with heads
of a soft metal like lead. Cuboid mallets were confined to the more geometric
precision demanded by carpenters, joiners and furniture makers.

This, in very broad terms, demonstrates the adjustments that were made
in response to the characteristics of individual materials which conditioned
the tools used to work them. Inevitably there were more subtle graduations
between these fundamental categories. This brings us to a brief overview of
the numerous types of stone to be found in the British Isles in contrast to the
paucity of marble.

In general the sedimentary rocks constitute the stones whilst materials like
marble and granite were formed by volcanic activity. The granites of Scotland,
south-west England and New England were so intractable that they were
little used, except for walling and in boulder form, until the introduction
of mechanisation. For this reason medieval stonemasons and sculptors in
south-west England used the more tractable white elvan of Devon or the blue
elvan of Cornwall for dressed or carved work where it blends well, in colour
and texture, with granite walling.[98] Slate, in its various types (e.g. Delabole,
Westmoreland and Welsh) was ideal for cladding a roof, or even wall building,
but was otherwise reserved for the tablets that carried incised inscriptions on
monuments, etc.[99]

A number of limestones will accept a friction polish and, for this reason, are
traditionally known as "marbles". Purbeck "marble" from Dorset is an example
and is closely related geologically to Sussex "winkle stone". Other materials of
this type include the Alwalton "marble" of Cambridgeshire, "Derbyshire fossil"
and the Frosterley "marble" of Durham. In effect these are conglomerates
in which fossilised shells are held in a relatively soft matrix. In cutting these
materials with a hammer and chisel these fossils may all too easily be "plucked"
out, contrary to the intensions of the mason or carver. Consequently the

FIGURE 118. *Stone working tools*: left to right: stone punch, bolster and claw bolster (both mallet headed), claw tool and chisel. The last three tools are "drawn-out" to a more delicate refinement for working marble – namely two "points" and a claw. (Author's Collection)

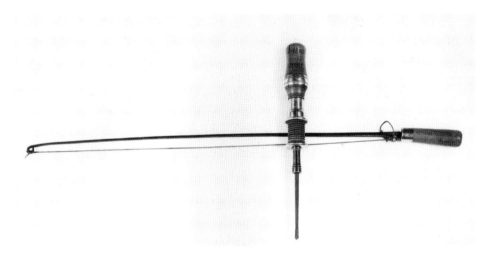

FIGURE 119. *Bow-drill*; steel, brass and box-wood *c.* 1810–1820 – overall length of the bow 2ft 6 in/77.3 cm. The control is absolute as the bow may be moved at any speed and may as easily cut a channel as a hole. The chuck inevitable revolves clockwise and then anti-clockwise so that the resulting cut clears itself with each reversal. (Author's Collection)

working of these materials became a specialist activity within the region where they were quarried. Much the same was true for the alabaster found in the Midlands the working of which became centred on Nottingham and Chellaston. In this case the cloying softness of alabaster probably inspired the extensive use of woodcarving tools. This interpretation of the likely methods employed seems to be confirmed by the undercutting and various details such as long ribbons of alabaster – features that are otherwise more characteristic of woodcarving.[100]

These material considerations are of great relevance when considering the complex range of geological specimens often found in the more opulent Elizabethan and Jacobean monuments. For these confections alabaster, both painted and unpainted, regularly formed an important component in such edifaces. A good example was the 1628 monument to Sir John Doderidge in Exeter Cathedral in which "his Effigies is lively Pourtrayed in Alabaster in his scarlet Gown and Robes, and a Court Roll in his hand".[101] The importance of alabaster for these purposes is emphasised by the presence in Burton-on-Trent, close to the quarries, of Jasper Hollemans, a late sixteenth century immigrant from the Low Countries.[102] From his base in the Midlands he was well placed to supply his fellow Flemmings in Southwark with this translucent gypsum.[103] This was a trade that the sculptor Nicholas Stone (1586/7–1647) would later become engaged in, exporting English alabaster to Flanders in exchange for black Tournai marble.[104]

In contrast to the soft yet tenacious alabaster the working of the hard brittle and glass-like Tournai marble was an altogether more challenging proposition. In common with so many other materials with a difficult and distinctive character Tournai marble was best worked by those craftsmen who came from areas near its source. As a consequence this obdurate black jasper forms a significant element in the work of the Anglo-Dutch-Danish school of sculptors of the mid-sixteenth to early seventeenth centuries. The men that hewed stone had a practical understanding of geology much as painters, working in a pre-industrial context, had an empirical appreciation of their pigments and media. This was a circumstance that was fully understood by the Irish sculptor Seamus Murphy (1907–1975) – a man who had been apprenticed as a stone-carver at the traditional age of 14:

> "'Tis all in the method. I remember seeing some Bath-stone masons brought over from England to do some work in Cobh Cathedral and they were amazing to watch. They used to do more work in a few days with a handsaw and drags than our fellas could do in a week; they had never worked anything else so, of course, they knew the nature of the stone."

In this respect Bath stone is particularly soft but, as Murphy went on to acknowledge, masons and carvers working in a variety of materials were compelled to be adaptable.

> "That's the worst of this trade, the material is different wherever you go, and even here [Cork] you are expected to work the native, the Kilkenny stone, Bath-stone, beer-stone, marble – and all sorts of marble at that, from the local to the foreign. Sure a man that would get a slab of Belgian Black [Tournai marble] to cope with would shatter it like a piece of plate glass unless he had some experience of it."[105]

Supplementing the natural colours of these materials, polychromatic treatment was also deployed, and for this purpose alabaster was particularly receptive. Polychromatic work of this kind, including the application of gold leaf, was generally the work of specialists. As we have seen in 1605/7 Maximilian Poultrain (or Colt) created the monument to Elizabeth I in Westminster Abbey; an edifice that was then painted and gilded by John de Critz, the Sergeant Painter to the Crown.[106] This North Sea school of sculptors were largely responsible for introducing a third tonal element in addition to alabaster and Tournai marble – namely white Italian marble.[107] The taste for these variegated materials ran concurrently with the persistent use of polychromy. Nevertheless painted decoration was sometimes excluded from monuments of this period as with Poultrain's tomb to the first Earl of Salisbury of 1612 which is confined to black Tournai and white Italian marble (Hatfield Church, Hertfordshire).[108]

The use of various materials and pigments on one sculptural undertaking persisted into the seventeenth century and beyond. In 1743 when the Bristol High Cross had recently been re-erected it was "Painted in imitation of Grey Marble, ye Ornaments are Gilt, & ye Figures Painted in their proper Colours" although this may, in part, have been an almost archaeological approach. Despite such aberrations white marble was to become dominant for 150 years to the extent that it came to be used with almost tiresome predictability. In a northern climate statuary in Italian marble was generally destined for a setting inside a church, a public building or a country house – for the good reason that it does not survive very well out of doors in English winters. So standardised did imports of this material from Carrara become that it came to be known as "statuary marble". A highly successful sculptor like Joseph Wilton (1722–1803) was importing it in such vast quantities that he was able to: "Enter into arrangements with the merchants of Carrara by which he acquired a large supply of the best marble [much of which] he re-sold to his brother artists".[109]

In this respect Wilton was following a long established tradition, common in many of the building trades, in which a master craftsman would supplement his income by retailing the materials of his craft.[110]

On 12 December 1795 John Flaxman mentioned that he had visited "Carrara to purchase [for £600] marble for the monument of the late Lord Mansfield", which was destined for Westminster Abbey. Flaxman went on to report that:

> "The Town of Carrara contains about 9,000 inhabitants and the people are chiefly employed in working the Quarries in that neighbourhood. Some of these Quarries are very large, equal in space to Grosvenor Square. These are the only quarries from which we can import White Statuary marble [via Leghorn/Livorno]. The Greek quarries [Pentelic marble], now in the hands of the Turks not being allowed to be worked, by that ignorant and superstitious people".[111]

This explains why English sculptors, who wished to follow the precedent of antiquity, were compelled to use the austere or even sterile whiteness of Carrara rather than the more sympathetic cream-coloured Pentelic marble of Greece.[112]

The sculptors of late Tudor and Stuart England, both native and immigrant, were trained, at least in part, through family traditions and connections – connections that could be trans-national. As outlined above (p. 302) the Devonian Nicholas Stone (1586/7–1647) was not only partly trained as a journeyman by Hendrik de Keyser in Amsterdam but married the Dutchman's daughter so that the children of that union continued that connection across the North Sea into the next generation. In addition de Keyser worked extensively for Christien IV in Denmark resulting in bilateral associations that became trilateral. This was a situation of consequence for many others in addition to the Keyser/Stone school of mason/sculptor/architects. In this respect the Danish-born "English" sculptor Caius Cibber (1630–1700) may be seen as one of the last highly significant members of that "North Sea" group.

In the following century a new Franco-Flemish school of sculptors would reach these shores. Of these the most important were Peter Scheemakers (1691–1781) and Michael Rysbrack (1694–1770) who were both born in Antwerp and also the Lyon-born Louis François Roubiliac (1705?–1762). In 1752 the latter's studio in England was visited by the engraver George Vertue (1684–1756) who admired "the inventions" which he saw there and considered them to be "very copious free and picturesque – as light and easy as painting".[113] This observation is reminiscent of Walpole's later praise of the marriage of art and skill to be seen in the woodcarvings by Grinling Gibbons (see p. 347 above). Some have argued that Roubiliac was more a modeller than a carver.[114] If true this could explain why this eminent French-born sculptor failed to secure the job to create a relief in stone within the pediment of the Mansion House in the City. This commission was in fact won in 1744 by the 30 year old Robert Taylor (1714–1788) – and Taylor could certainly carve. He was the son of a stone-mason and had been apprenticed, for a premium of £105 in 1732, to the sculptor Sir Henry Cheere Bt (1703–1781). It was Taylor's custom, when working on portrait busts, "to hew out the heads from the block [of stone or marble] and, except for a few finishing touches, leave the rest to his "workmen".[115] From 1753 onwards he increasingly turned to architecture in which capacity he emerged as Sir Robert Taylor.[116]

The relationship between masonry, sculpture and architecture could be close. Take, for example, Nathaniel Ireson (1686–1769). Following his apprenticeship to Francis Smith of Warwick (1672–1738), Ireson worked in all three fields.[117] As a sculptor he made a number of church monuments. Among these he carved the figure of himself in Wincanton churchyard (Fig. 120) "keeping it ready to be erected after his death".[118] For Ireson, as for Pierce and many others, sculpture was closely related to architectural enrichment. His surviving drawings for a proposed refacing of the north front of Corsham Court, Wiltshire includes pilaster capitals with inward turning volutes – which derive from Boromini.[119] Although this scheme was never realised some capitals of this type were subsequently built into a small cottage in nearby Lacock (Figs 121 and 122).

Even in London, the relatively small communities of craftsmen there, coupled with the apprentice-

FIGURE 120. Nathaniell Ireson's carved Bath stone *Self Portrait* (now lacking its head) in the churchyard at Wincanton, Somerset. In 1748 Ireson re-roofed and re-windowed the nave of the church at his own expense. As a benefactor he was recorded inside the church as an "Architect" but in the inscription on the plinth of his memorial outside Ireson gives his occupation as "Master Builder" – with the tools of his trade carved in relief on the plinth.

FIGURE 121. Two details of a drawing of 1747 for Ireson's unrealised proposals for Corsham Court – note the distinctive pilaster capitals with their inward turning volutes. As a stone carver and architect Ireson had been apprenticed to Francis Smith of Warwick (1672–1738).

ship system, resulted not only in the transmission of skills but also in the communication of the latest fashions. This was true of Roubiliac who introduced his English apprentices to a French idiom. Among those who were trained by Roubiliac were Nathaniel Smith (*c.* 1741/3–after 1800) and John Atkins (or Adkins: fl. 1761–1777). Of these two Atkins received a prize in 1761 from the Society of Arts for a carved stone relief.[120] Contrary to some reports this strongly suggests that his master Roubiliac was himself a carver. Certainly both Smith and Atkins were to move on to work as carvers for other sculptors – most notably Wilton. Despite these examples there is some possibility that Roubiliac was resistant to taking on apprentices. For example, Nicholas Read (*c.* 1733–1787) was only accepted into the Frenchman's studio as a result of the forceful representations of Read's father. On the other hand this resistance may have had more to do with young Read's inadequacies for he was considered to be "the most deficient in talent of all Roubiliac's pupils".[121] Following his master's death in 1762 Read was said to advertise himself "like a trunk-maker or plumber and glazier … as the successor to Mr Roubiliac".[122]

Nathaniel Smith would later work as a principal assistant to the sculptor Joseph Nollekens (1737–1823). The latter was the son of the painter "Old Nollekens" (1702–1748) who, like the sculptors Scheemakers and Rysbrack, were all Catholics and natives of Antwerp. All three settled in London. Young Nollekens was to be apprenticed with some inevitability, to his late father's

FIGURE 122. *Pilaster capitals* in the manner of Boromini carved in Bath stone by Nathaniel Ireson (1686–1769). Although reused rather improbably in a cottage in Lacock, they were probably intended to grace Ireson's proposed refronting of nearby Corsham Court.

old friend and compatriot Scheemakers. In later life Nollekens was to claim that he began his apprenticeship at the early age of eleven which was very likely as this would have been just after his father's death in 1748. His formal apprenticeship to Scheemakers, at his workshops in Vine Street, Piccadilly, began in 1750 at the more usual age for agreeing an indenture.[123] In this case the master was a highly accomplished carver, a facility he passed to his disciple. Nevertheless, so numerous were the commissions accepted by sculptors as successful as Scheemakers or Nollekens, that they became, to varying degrees, dependent on assistants. For this reason these sculptors would reserve their efforts to modelling in clay which was then converted into plaster. These casts formed the basis from which highly skilled carvers such as Smith worked. So important was such an amanuensis that good quality carvers were highly valued.

> "What an acquisition ... an excellent carver must be [for] the classic sculptor of high fame, whose mind must necessarily be engaged upon his designs; and whose hand, had it once been master of the tool, for want of practice, could not manage it with so much ease as that of the artist who is continually employed on the marble".[124]

In this respect it is a matter of record that in Nolleken's studio the work proceeded as follows:

> "The model was the work of his own hands [and that a portrait bust] might cost him six or eight sittings before he gave it to his moulder to cast in Plaster

of Paris – a mason rough hewed it – a sculptor [then] carved it as far as the model enabled him to go".[125]

Masons were highly experienced in cutting away large quantities of stone or marble and were therefore quicker than sculptors in dressing back the chosen material. It was consequently logical that masons were employed to "rough hew" the work on the basis of "boasting drawings". These were full size representations of the prospective work on paper showing two elevations and a plan. For roughing-out sculpture these drawings took the form of a series of straight lines drawn from one salient point to the next. Working to such drawings was defined in the 1770s as follows: "*Boast*: among workmen, is the taking off the superfluous part of carving, mouldings, etc", a definition that correctly leaves open the nature of the material – wood, stone or marble.[126] For this type of work Nollekens employed a "brute of a mason" named Finney who, from that description, evidently possessed the appropriate strength for this activity. For those who worked in stone and marble this was an important attribute. As Nollekens aged "his strength failed [and] he gradually withdrew himself, first from marble and next from clay, and finally from making drawings".[127] This reminiscence confirms that the sculptor was indeed a carver – although the huge number of works in marble that carry Nollekens's name far exceed what his hands alone could have made. Among his known assistants were "Plara" (probably Joseph Plura II b. 1753), the elder Gahagen (Laurence Gahagan *c.* 1753–1820) and John Hippisley Green (b. 1753) who was one of "his best workmen".[128] In addition he sometimes employed Giovanni Battista Locatelli (1734–1805) and, as a sub-contractor, the mason George Lupton (b. 1792).[129] These assistants could earn "upwards of 5gns a week"; a considerable sum if compared with the 25 guineas that the sculptor would pay one of his carvers to translate a bust into marble complete with its socle.[130] For a highly skilled carver speed was important if any sense of spontaneity was to be maintained through the procedures that were involved. Despite such expeditious work it is unlikely that a bust on its plinth could have been carved within five weeks (25 guineas @ 5 guineas per week). By 1812 Nollekens commanded a fee of 150 guineas for a marble bust.[131]

As a carver himself Nollekens was to recognise the debt that he owed to those who worked for him. In his will he left to his then principal carvers Lewis Alexander Goblet (b. 1764) and Sebastian Goblet (1773–1855) the tools, bankers and marble in his yard and also "the jack I lent [George] Lupton". Goblet's children, Henry and Louisa were left £100 and £30 respectively.[132] All these carvers would have used pointing machines for this work. For carving

Nollekens's full-length figure of William Pitt (1808), which must have taken at least a year to translate into marble, Gahagan received £300.[133] This important commission resulted in Nollekens being paid a fee of £7,000, a sum which included modelling the figure in clay, casting it in plaster, supplying the marble, paying the masons and carvers, transporting the finished work and its plinth from London and installing the entire work in the Senate House of Cambridge University. The sculptor's overheads should also be taken into consideration together with the cost of employing a letter-cutter for the inscription on the plinth. Letter-cutting could become something of a speciality even if many carvers viewed this two-dimensional art with some contempt as "scratching for a living".[134] Not that it was lacking in difficulties in terms of drawing, the spacing of letters or the nature of the material into which letters were cut; wood, stone, marble or slate. Take for example a ledger stone in Westminster Abbey "a pavement square in blue marble" which carried the simple inscription "O RARE BEN JONSON". This modest monument to the great Jacobean playwright was paid for by Jack Young who, in *c.* 1637 "gave the fellow eighteen pence to cut" this brief inscription. At just over a penny a letter this was a high fee suggesting that this "blue marble" tablet was of an intractable material like Purbeck "marble". By the eighteenth century Henry Quayle of the Isle of Man (*c.* 1683–1765) charged ¾d per letter compared with James Hazlegrove in Sussex who, in 1714 was paid 1d a letter.[135] One important feature associated with cutting letters in stone, marble or slate, as in other aspects of the stone-working trades, is the ability to "hold a bite". That is to say the skill to cut an intended line or form without permitting the edged tool to be deflected by any inconsistencies in the material which is being cut. It was also advisable that a letter-cutter should be literate. The somewhat specialist nature of letter-cutting is indicated by the career of William Arminger (1752–1793) who moved from Norwich to work in Nollekens's London studio as a letter cutter; although he later moved on to more challenging work.[136] In America another such specialist was John Frazee (1790–1852) who had begun as a bricklayer and via letter-cutting, was to become a sculptor.[137]

In addition to all these specialist activities involving cutting there was one final stage that was important for marble and some limestones – namely polishing. This work involved the use of abrasives, of ever diminishing strength, which were used in conjunction with water. This procedure was something of knack involving some secrets of the trade but care had to be taken to avoid blurring details like the crisp edge of drapery. Nollekens employed "old John Panzetta" in this capacity and also a man named Lloyd. In some cases the sculptor's polishers doubled as sawyers since the two activities involved considerable strength.[138] The polishing of statuary was sometimes undertaken for reasons that had little to do with aesthetics. A case in point concerns Roubiliac's seated figure of the Lord President Duncan Forbes (d. 1747) which was placed in what was then the Faculty of Advocates Library, Edinburgh. For this sculpture: "the marble out of which it was cut is very hard, and of a bluish tinge, with delicate veins. The surface of the drapery was polished till it shone, to preserve it from stains – for polish is not easily penetrated".[139]

The presence of so many assistants, sub-contractors and visitors in a sculptor's marble workshop or showroom could make such locations very busy – the sort of turmoil shown in W. H. Pyne's drawing (Fig. 123). The sculptor Benjamin Carter (1719–1766) employed over 100 men, according to his son John (1748–1817).[140] In contrast the workshops of John Bacon the elder employed between 15 and 20 assistants at any one time. This rather small number, the sculptor believed, was sufficient to form a "home guard" in the event of hostilities with Revolutionary France.[141] In effect the most successful sculptors in Georgian England were the architects of the works that bear their names. For this reason some commentators were of the view that many of the carved memorials that issued from a studio such as Flaxman presided over: "cannot be considered as works of art, but as marble carved per-contract emblazoned with heraldry, and explained by means of inscriptions".[142]

As businesses, these studios were composed of a range of workshops and employed sufficient master craftsmen to provide practical training for apprentices and journeymen. All these individuals were engaged in a wide variety of activities from modelling and preparing clay and armatures to carving and polishing. Hence the large workforce that a successful sculptor's establishment would employ.

The use of various types of pointing machine made possible the posthumous realisation of a work in marble. Following Nollekens's death on 23 April 1823 an auction of the contents of his workshops was held (3–5 July 1823) by "Mr Christie" at which the Earl of Egremont purchased Lot 21. This was a seated figure of Venus; a plaster cast that was yet to be converted into marble. Accordingly the Earl commissioned J. C. F. Rossi RA (1762–1839) to produce a marble from the plaster. Rossi was an odd choice for this commission as he was primarily a modeller and in fact the work was undertaken by a man named Williams – almost certainly Richard Williams (b. 1799) who is known to have worked as an assistant to Rossi. The instructions to Rossi from Lord Egremont were very clear for no attempt was to be made to "improve on the plaster" although:

FIGURE 123. William Henry Pyne (1770–1843), *A Sculptors Show-room*, watercolour on paper (6½ × 9¼ in/16.5 × 23.5 cm) *c*. 1785. Although the carvers shown in this drawing are giving the appearance of working the absence of marble chips and the presence of about a dozen well dressed gentlemen suggests that this is a show-room for finished works. The lifting tackle may be explained as the means by which sculpture could be moved out of this room for onward shipment. The reverse of this watercolour carries a slight drawing by Pyne's father (J. B. P.) of Joshua Reynolds's painting room, Leicester Square. Both the Pyne and Reynolds families were Devon-born. (British Museum, London)

> "In giving this order, his Lordship was in my [J. T. Smith's] humble opinion, perfectly correct; for if improvements had been made it could no longer have been esteemed as a production of Nollekens's mind; though I am perfectly convinced that, had the figure been carved under his own eye, it would in many instances have benefitted by those corrections which most sculptors are induced to make whilst they are executing finished carvings from models".[143]

As Smith observed this would certainly have been the case had Nollekens been alive for it was said of him that he wrought portrait busts "with pleasure but his Venuses with enthusiasm". This was partly because these "goddesses" were modelled from the naked figure of individuals such as Bet Balmanno a woman whose attractions were such that "Mrs Nollekens was not without fears that her husband might ... forget himself".[144]

In contrast to Nollekens, it seems that neither Wilton (1722–1803) nor Flaxman (1755–1826), as the sons of decorative plasterers, ever gained a full command of the hammer and chisel. On the other hand their "trade" background meant that they were less likely to discriminate between the "applied" and the "fine arts". For example, Wilton "did not refuse to embellish chimney pieces for the mansions built by his intimate friend, Sir William Chambers". Work of this kind had, for some years, been undertaken by many eminent sculptors. In some such works Atlantides or caryatides formed part of their composition. These were presumably the cause of Isaac Ware's (1756) concern that: "Modern sculptors are fond of nudities; but in a chimney-piece ... they would shock" and therefore be inappropriate.[145]

As noted above, Wilton was dependent on his marble carvers, individuals such as John Atkins (or Adkins fl. 1761–1777), A Beaupre (fl. 1764–1783) and Nathaniel Smith (*c.* 1741/3–after 1800). For Wilton's decorative work on Chambers's Somerset House his two assistants Atkins and Smith "modelled and carved ... directly from the drawings, he [Wilton] never having put a tool to them".[146] Flaxman was no less dependent upon his studio workforce since at any one time he employed between 12 and 15 individuals. In such circumstances sculptors such as these came close to becoming administrators running a business rather than executants of their art. Indeed in adopting the outlook of an executive Flaxman was pretentious enough to employ his marble polisher John Burge as a footman whom he "caused to stand behind his chair" at Royal Academy dinners.[147]

Although men like Wilton and

FIGURE 124. Joseph Nollekens (1737–1823) marble bust of *Sir George Savile*, signed and dated 1784. Savile died in that year and it is known that Nollekens produced this bust from a death mask – a tribute to the sculptor's ability to offer vitality to his work (see also Fig. 2). (Victoria & Albert Museum, London)

Flaxman were reliant on their carvers such skilled men were even more indispensible for amateurs. The well-connected and indeed aristocratic Mrs Anne Seymour Damer (1748–1828) is an example of the type. As noted above Nathaniel Smith was outspoken on this lady's claims to be a sculptress. Mrs Damer did however receive some instruction from both Cerrachi and Bacon – but nothing like the years of grinding effort that is demanded to acquire such a complex skill.[148]

Despite the very considerable demands of carving as a craft not all true sculptors commenced their careers in the most propitious circumstances. John Bacon (1740–1799) was apprenticed to Nicholas Crisp the silversmith and proprietor of the Bow Porcelein manufactory. Bacon therefore began as a modeller but may have developed some skill as a carver. This much is indicated by the very practical observations that he made regarding the proposals for a statue of Lord Cornwallis to be erected in Madras, India (see p. 322 above). Ultimately the Royal Academy, as the organisers of this competition, decided to restrict the candidates to two Academicians – namely Wilton and Bacon. Wilton quietly withdrew from these proceedings and Bacon accepted the commission – for a fuller account of this episode. A similarly practical approach was applied by Bacon in relationship to the number of works that Academicians were expected to show in their annual exhibition. In October 1796 "Bacon proposed on acct. of the nature of their work Sculptors should be allowed once in 3 years to exhibit" – this being very much the view of a practical carver.

As Mrs Esdaile noted (1946) most of this kind of work was undertaken, down to about the age of George II, by individuals who were "at once architect, sculptor and designer".[149] This is more than an historical observation but the description of a circumstance that gave a unity of purpose between a concept and its realisation. From the late eighteenth century the division of these activities would cause fragmentation which the early twentieth century belief in a "truth to materials" would never quite restore.

By 1830 there was a growing recognition that the ability to carve was not only of value in itself but that to witness a skilful carver in action could be a joy to behold:

> "There is nothing more beautiful in the whole range of art than to see a skilled person hold the chisel upon a piece of fine sculpture – to observe the perfect confidence with which one hand guides the tool, while the other gives the blow, and this in places, requiring such neatness and delicacy of handling, that the smallest chip would be fatal".[150]

Perhaps one of the last of the great Neo Classical sculptors to retain this linkage with the crafts of his art was Sir Francis Chantrey RA (1781–1841). He was born at Jordanthorpe near Sheffield, the son of a man who was both a tenant farmer and carpenter, a background that gave young Chantrey an understanding of working in wood. He was to be apprenticed to the Sheffield woodcarver and gilder Robert Ramsay in 1797 at the slightly advanced age of sixteen. In 1802, a couple of years before he was out of his time, he left his master for a fine of £50 paid by a group of benefactors. Once free, Chantrey moved to London with the ambition of becoming a portrait painter although at first he subsisted on his wood carving skills. Among those who employed him in this capacity was Thomas Hope (1769–1831) – the connoisseur and proponent of Neo Classicism.[151] On the basis of his practical skills coupled with his natural abilities Chantrey was to emerge as one of the most significant sculptors of his generation.

In some ways, Chantrey's craft-based values were carried forward by John Gibson RA (1790–1866) who was apprenticed in 1804 to the Liverpool cabinet makers Southwell and Wilson. In their workshops Gibson was employed as an ornamental wood carver. Like Chantrey, his indentures were cancelled for a fine (of £70) although, in Gibson's case, this was paid by his next employers, the Liverpool statuaries Samuel and Thomas Franceys. This was the point at which Gibson probably transferred his allegiance from wood to marble. By 1817 he was in Rome where he was to spend much of the rest of his life in the Neo Classical orbit of Canova and Thorvaldsen. Despite these associations Gibson, on occasion, went beyond the conventions of that idiom. It was in the "Eternal City" that his archaeological tendencies were to appear in the shape of his "tinted marbles", statuary which saw a contentious return to polychromy following the precedent of Classical Antiquity. Alternatively Gibson's source for such "tinted marbles" may have come from closer to home. In 1658 the sculptor-architect William Byrd of Oxford (1624–1690?) "invented a method of staining or painting marble by sinking a colour of considerable depth into the body of polished white marble, by the application of it to the outside only ..."[152] (for another account of Byrd's process see p. 360 above).

Although sculptors like Chantrey retained their skill as carvers this became increasingly rare in Victorian England where there was an ever greater reliance on immigrant Italians. Gibson was something of an exception and so too was Sir George Frampton RA (1860–1928). In his early years, Frampton had worked as a commercial ornament carver. At times, when work was lacking, he like others, were reduced to "field ranging". This was a term, used in the nineteenth century by out of work stone- and marble-carvers, who sought out the fields round the expanding towns of Victorian England where masoned stone was stored. This could then be given its carved decoration by these itinerant tradesmen, the "field rangers". Masoned and carved stonework of this kind would ultimately be used to embellish the serried rows of speculative urban housing then being built. Frampton was to emerge from such humble repetitive work, to fulfil his vocation as a sculptor, partly as a consequence of "marrying well".[153]

The widespread use of carving assistants by Victorian sculptors was to be rejected by artists of Eric Gill's (1882–1940) generation. In this respect he was following the lead of Adolf von Hildebrand in Germany with his cry "Back to Stone" – with the implication that clay and marble had been dominant for too long.[154] In England Gill was to reject "those persons ... who are only executants in the material of which the design or model, and not the finished work, is made". He goes on to explain that clay is used because it "produces quick results". In contrast Gill reserves his respect for those "who are not merely designers [but] are free and able to translate their own ideas or designs ... into stone". At a utilitarian level he notes that "the use of stone in art schools is too expensive ... it necessitates very strong benches and floors [and] many more tools". In conclusion he regrets that "art schools are *art* schools and must therefore have *art* masters. But 'artists' are rarely stone carvers and stone carvers are rarely artists. So stone carving is not taught".[155]

In late Victorian Britain a gulf was opening up between carvers and artists, between craft and art. By contrast there was in early modern pre-industrial Britain a continuum between art and craft, between artist and artisan. The traditional apprentice carver, in wood as in stone or marble, worked under the close supervision of his master and was also influenced by the journeyman in the workshop or lodge. In such circumstances a trainee was functioning in competition with his fellow apprentices which further motivated his will to succeed. Furthermore, in the past, the comprehensive nature of a successful sculptor's studio was such that it enabled his apprentices to widen their horizons to the full extent of their abilities. At the very least these youths could emerge, at the end of their time, capable of earning a living. As for the possibility that some amongst them might have the potential to emerge as artists – that was a question that was beyond either training or education.

Notes

[1] Johnson's *Life of the Author* was written in 1777 and published in 1795. This very rare work has been reprinted with an introduction by Jacob Simon in *Furniture History* XXXIX, 2003, pp. 1–55

[2] Ambrose Heal (1953) 1988, p. 97–98 and fig. on p. 88

[3] Florentine wood carvers were an exception in giving their edged tools a single bevel

[4] McDermott and Berry eds of *Edmund Rack's Survey*, 2011 see Crowcombe. This information is not included by Collinson 1791; Jenny Uglow 2006, p. 238, Brian Read and Doug Morgan 2010, p. 59.Today Washita stone from the USA is often used as an alternative. James Ayres 1985, pp. 192–195; Eleanor Rowe 1907, pp. 7–14

[5] Joseph Moxon, first published in parts from 1677, complete edition of 1703, p. 185

[6] Pers. comm. Arthur J. J. Ayres (1902–1985). The author does not share Geoffrey Beard's assertion (1981, p. 66) that "carvers were usually skilled joiners" although they generally belonged to the same guild

[7] Ingrid Roscoe *et al.* eds 2009

[8] Ambrose Heal (1953) 1988 – John Linnell Jnr (1792–1882) was from a later generation and an easel painter

[9] Victoria & Albert Museum, *Rococo*, 1984, G41, G42

[10] Simon Jervis 1992, p. 101

[11] James W. P. Campbell 2002, p. 216; Victor Chinnery 1979, chapter 2: fig. 2.1 illustrates the Joyners's Hall in St Ann Street, Salisbury

[12] *Ibid.*, p. 43, citing Jupp and Pocock 1887 – both quoting the London regulations

[13] *Ibid.*, p. 168

[14] *Ibid.*, pp. 550–551. This carved panelling had disappeared by the late nineteenth century

[15] Benno Forman *Furniture History* VII, 1971

[16] James W. P. Campbell 2002, p. 216

[17] Howard Colvin 1995 – also *DNB*

[18] Margaret Whinney 1964, pp. 45–46

[19] For Pierce and the Painter Stainers see Borg 2005, pp. 76, 80; For the weathervane Pierce received £4 – see Howard Colvin 1995 and also for Pierce's work as an architect. Ms.Rawl.B.387.fol.125 and B.388.fol.134v – also *DNB*

[20] Michael Baxandall *The Limewood Sculptors of Renaissance Germany*, New Haven & London, 1980

[21] Horace Walpole 1786, Vol. III, pp. 148–149

[22] James Ayres 1985, fig. 193

[23] Horace Walpole 1786, Vol. III, pp. 149, 155. Ingrid Roscoe *et al.* eds 2009. Seldon lost his life attempting to save some of the wood-carving when part of Petworth House caught fire in 1715

[24] Ingrid Roscoe *et al.*

[25] Howard Colvin 1995; Ingrid Roscoe *et al.* eds 2009

[26] Eleanor Rowe 1907, p. 14

[27] Pers. comm. A. J. J. Ayres (1902–1985)

[28] William Dunlap (1834) 1969, Vol. II, Pt I, p. 134

[29] Ingrid Roscoe *et al.* eds 2009; Ambrose Heal (1953) 1988, p. 200 gives Whittle's address as King Street, Covent Garden

[30] Jacob Simon ed. 2003, pp. 36–37

[31] Examples in Pinto Collection of Treen, Birmingham Museum

³² In the 1920s some carvers, working in London, had walked, by stages, from as far away as Vienna. Thse men gathered in the Continental restaurants in Carlotte Street, London. Pers. comm. A. J. J. Ayres (1902–1985). For Irish experience of this see Seamus Murphy (2005) 2010, p. 17

³³ Henry Broadhurst *The Story of his Life: from a Stonemason's Bench to the Treasury Bench, Told by Himself*, London, 1901. Broadhurst was born at Littlemore near Oxford in 1840. This extract from his autobiography is included in John Burnett's anthology, London (1974) 1994, p. 323. I am grateful to Paul Smith of the University of Keele for drawing my attention to this

³⁴ George Sturt (1923) 1993, p. 13. Workshops retained this feature, with shutters, down to the late nineenth century

³⁵ Knight of Glin and James Peill 2007, pp. 70–71

³⁶ Jacob Simon ed. 2003, pp. 45–49

³⁷ Howard Colvin 1995, although designed by the elder Wood the Exchange (now the Town Hall) was supervised by his son John Wood the Younger (1728–1781). The interiors of the Exchange were lost in a fire in 1795 and rebuilt by John Foster (1758–1827)

³⁸ Knight of Glin and James Peill 2007, pp. 87, 170

³⁹ For Hennekin see British Museum Dept of P&D, Trade Label 32.31 and Ambrose Heal (1953) 1988, who also lists a later Hennekin (George) of 9 Marlebone Street, Golden Square, London. For Hartley see the Trade Label reproduced in James Ayres 1998, fig. 239

⁴⁰ William Kelby (1922), 1970, p. 4 quoting the *New York Mercury*, 22 September 1755

⁴¹ Jacob Simon ed. 2003, pp. 50–51

⁴² *Twelve Gerandoles* 1755 and *A New Book of Ornaments* published in parts between 1756 and 1757

⁴³ Vile and Cobb were prominent cabinet makers and upholders in George III's reign; Ambrose Heal (1953), 1988, p. 189

⁴⁴ Jacob Simon ed. 2003, pp. 43–44

⁴⁵ The *Jenny* was registered by Seel on 22 September 1747 as a vessel of about 200 tons "built in this present year" by a consortium headed by Seel. The ship was named after Jenny Cameron of Glendessary (1699–1790) who as a Jacobite raised a substantial force of men in 1745 – whose emblem was The White Rose: *Alba Maxima*

⁴⁶ J. T. Smith (1828) 1919, Vol. II, p. 355; Ingrid Roscoe *et al.* eds 2009; Francis Greenacre *et al.* 2011, p. 169

⁴⁷ Ivan and Elizabeth Hall, *Georgian Hull*,York, 1978/79, p. 73

⁴⁸ Edwin O. Christiensen (1952) 1972, p. 18

⁴⁹ See Hogarth's illustration of the Royal Oak, in his series of paintings/engravings *The Election* 1754; John Trusler 1768, p. 48

⁵⁰ Mungo Murray ("Shipwright in His Majesty's Yard, Deptford") *A Treatise on Ship Building*, 1754

⁵¹ James Ayres 1996, pp. 143–144

⁵² Joseph Farington, p. 814 2 April 1797

⁵³ William Dunlap (1834), 1969, Vol. I, p. 315

⁵⁴ Carving axes continue to be made in Sweden by Gränsfors Bruks of Bergsjo

⁵⁵ William Dunlap (1834) 1969, Vol. I, pp. 315, 319

⁵⁶ M. V. Brewington, 1962, p. 31

⁵⁷ *Ibid.*, p. 33, quoting Scharf and Westcott *History of Philadelphia*, Vol. III. In these circumstances these plaster casts must have been based on clay "squeezes" of details

[58] Sylvia Leistyna Lahvis "William Rush's Indian Trader", *Antiques*, New York, December 1999

[59] M. V. Brewington 1962. This figurehead was replaced for a third time in 1834 by a figure of Andrew Jackson carved by Laban S. Beecher, also of Boston. In the late eighteenth, early nineteenth century the Atlantic Seaboard of North America boasted some eight hundred master ship-carvers

[60] Jean Lipman (1948) 1972, pp. 25–33

[61] Jean Lipman and Alice Winchester, *The Flowering of American Folk Art 1776–1876*, New York, 1974, p. 129

[62] William Sutherland, *The Ship Builders Assistant*, 1711

[63] For a summary of this commission see Michael Snodin and Elspeth Moncreiff eds, 1984, Cat. L.76 and L.77. For Kent and the State Barge see G.W. Beard "William Kent and the Royal Barge *Burlington Magazine*, Aug 1970. Also Ingrid Roscoe *et al.* eds 2009.

[64] John Ford 2005, pp. 46–47

[65] Knight of Glin and James Peill 2007, p. 179

[66] William Bridges Adams 1837, pp. 177–178

[67] Anthony à Wood, Oxford 1674, p. 56; Christopher Morris ed. 1982, p. 178. For an account of Continental painted sculpture see Xavier Bray *et al. The Sacred Made Real Spanish Painting and Sculpture 1600–1700*, New Haven & London, 2009

[68] Thornton and Cain eds 1981, p. 23, citing the Salisbury MS.119-8, 1606

[69] H. M. Colvin *et al.* eds. 1975, Vol. III, p. 120

[70] Richard Bebb 2007, Vol. I, p. 255

[71] Eg *Figure of a mendicant*, St Alban's Abbey and a charity figure in the parish church, Cirencester – both eighteenth century

[72] John Watts was a trustee of the school from 1722–1738 – see P. J. Hughes *Oliver Whitby School, Chichester*, Chichester, 2002, p. 115. The figure is now in Chichester Museum; Christopher Morris 1982, 114 (8) citing Mission – the French traveller.

[73] In the heraldic sense of the word

[74] Michael Snodin ed. 2010, p. 337, Cat.256

[75] William Salmon (1672) 1701, chapter xx, p. 910

[76] Josephine Walpole 1997, pp. 109–110 citing Marjorie Allthorpe-Guyton

[77] *Ibid.*, p. 111

[78] *Ibid.*, p. 26

[79] Horace Walpole 1786, Vol. III, pp. 91, 139, quotes Vertue as describing B. Flesshier as "Another obscure painter … and a frame-maker too [who] lived in the Strand near the Fountain-tavern". Alternatively this could be Tobias Flessier – see Christopher Rowell ed. 2013, p. 23

[80] Peter Thornton (1979) 1981, p. 274 and fig. 262

[81] Ambrose Heal (1953), 1988, pp. 50, 51; Tessa Murdoch *et al.* 1985, Cat. 292 and James Ayres 1986, p. 158

[82] J. T. Smith (1829), 1919, Vol. II, p. 174

[83] Jacob Simon 1996, p. 130. At the Restoration Geldorp was appointed "picture mender" and cleaner to the King

[84] Jacob Simon ed. 2003, p. 52

[85] Isaac Ware, 1756, p. 256

[86] An example of Carpenter's work is in the Holburne Museum, Bath. For Wyatt and Carpenter see Ingrid Roscoe *et al.* eds 2009

[87] Richard Holmes *The Age of Wonder*, Harper, London, 2008, pp. 237, 353. A chimney

piece tablet by Robert Davy: *The Fox and the Stork* is said to be in the Victoria & Albert Museum

[88] Michael Snodin ed. 1984, pp. 73, 207, Cat.E.23, M.25. Morrison H. Heckscher and Leslie Greene Bowman1992

[89] Michael Snodin ed. 1984, p. 163, Cat.L.4

[90] W. H. Pyne 1823–24, Vol. I, pp. 38–39

[91] Allan Cunningham 1830, Vol. III, p. 84. Also J. T. Smith (1828) 1919, Vol. II, p. 122

[92] Jacob Simon ed. 2003, p. 54

[93] J. R. Kirkup "The History and Evolution of Surgical Instruments …" *Annals of the Royal College of Surgeons* LXIV, pt 2, 1982

[94] A situation of which Rudolf Wittkower (1979, p. 38) was apparently unaware

[95] J. T. Smith (1828), 1919, Vol. II, p. 76

[96] *Ibid.*, Vol. I, p. 129, which quotes Chantrey's belief in the judicious use of the drill in representing hair in marble

[97] Murphy (2005) 1996, p. 23

[98] Alec Clifton-Taylor and A. S. Ireson 1983, pp. 40–41, 46–50

[99] Schools of letter cutting developed in various regions. For example, in Leicestershire the best slate letter cutters included James Winfield (fl. 1790–1800) and a man named Wirmadge: Ingrid Roscoe *et al.* eds 2009

[100] The author's personal experience of working these materials is also offered by way of empirical evidence

[101] Samuel Izacke *Antiquities of the City of Exeter*, London, 1741, p. 151

[102] Margaret Whinney 1964, p. 21

[103] Alec Clifton-Taylor and A. S. Ireson 1983, pp. 50–51

[104] Margaret Whinney 1964, p. 29 and endnote 29

[105] Seamus Murphy, (2005) 1966, p. 46. I am indebted to Claudia Kinmonth for giving me a copy of this book

[106] H. M. Colvin ed. 1975, Vol. III, Pt I, p. 120

[107] This should perhaps be described as a reintroduction as Italian white marble was used in Roman Britain

[108] Margaret Whinney 1964, p. 20

[109] Inscription on an engraving by Robert West and William Toms of *The Bristol High Cross* 25 March 1743. Allan Cunningham 1830, Vol. III, p. 79

[110] James Ayres 1998, p. 110

[111] Joseph Farington, p. 438 12 December 1795, for the reference to Leghorn see p. 398 2 November 1795

[112] Roger Ling ed. *Making Classical Art*, Stroud, 2000, p. 21; Carl Bluemel *Greek Sculptors at Work*, London, 1955

[113] Horace Walpole 1786, Vol. III, p. 149

[114] W. T. Whitley 1928, Vol. I, pp. 88–89

[115] Rupert Gunnis 1953

[116] Ingrid Roscoe *et al.* eds 2009. Taylor was made free of the Mason's company of London by patrimony in 1744, the year he received the job for the Mansion House

[117] Andor Gomme 2000, p. 26

[118] Ingrid Roscoe *et al.* eds 2009

[119] Christopher Hussey *English Country Houses, Early Georgian 1715–1760* (1955), Woodbridge, 1984, p. 228

120 Nathaniel Smith also received a prize from the Society of Arts for a model entitled *Bringing Down the Stag* 1760

121 W. H. Payne 1823–24, Vol. I, pp. 396–397, see also J. T. Smith (1828) 1919, Vol. II, p. 34

122 J. T. Smith (1828) 1919, Vol. II, pp. 34–35

123 Joseph Farington, p. 287 2 January 1795 gives Nolleken's age at the start of his apprenticeship as 11 years. Allan Cunningham 1830, Vol. III, p. 123 gives the later date

124 Cunningham, Vol III, p. 159. Much of this passage also occurs in J. T. Smith's account (1828), 1919, Vol. II, p. 353–354

125 J. T. Smith (1828) Vol. II, pp. 353–354

126 Anon *The Elements of Architecture*, Edinburgh, 1773 and 1778 – see the Glossary in the 1778 edition

127 Allan Cunningham 1830, Vol. III, p. 187

128 J. T. Smith (1828) 1949, pp. 54, 57

129 As in the installation of Nollekens's figure of William Pitt in Cambridge – J. T. Smith (1828) 1919, Vol. II, p. 369

130 Allan Cunningham 1830, Vol. III, pp. 188, 160 and J. T. Smith (1828) 1919, Vol. I, p. 232

131 J. T. Smith (1828) 1949, Vol. I, p. 246

132 *Ibid.*, p. 218 and edition of 1919, Vol. II, p. 223. For George Lupton see Vol. II, p. 230

133 *Ibid.*, Vol. II, p. 230

134 Pers. comm A. J. J. Ayres (1902–1985)

135 Ian Donaldson *Ben Jonson: A Life*, Oxford, 2011, pp. 1–5. The tablet was said to be triangular;. J. T. Smith (1828) 1949, p. 232; Jonathan Kewley 2011, p. 94–105; Frederick Burgess (1963) 1979, p. 271

136 J. T. Smith (1828) 1949, p. 232

137 William Dunlap (1834) 1969, Vol. II, Pt I, pp. 266–269

138 J. T. Smith (1828) 1949, p. 54. "Old Panzetta" was probably the father of the sculptor Joseph Panzetta (fl. *c.* 1787–1830) and J. T. Smith (1828) 1919, Vol. I, p. 196 for Lloyd, for Nollekens's "sawyer and polisher" see Vol. I, p. 174

139 Allan Cunningham 1830, Vol. III, pp. 47–48

140 Bernard Nurse "John Carter FSA (1748–1817) 'The ingenious and very accurate Draughtsman'" *Antiquaries Journal* 91, 2011, p. 212 footnote 7. Carter's father was Benjamin Carter (1719–1766) – see Ingrid Roscoe *et al.* eds 2009

141 Bernard Nurse *ibid.* in note 140, 211–252; Holger Hoock (2003) 2009, p. 189 citing Allan Cunningham 1830, Vol. III, pp. 233, 237

142 *Ibid.*, Vol. III, p. 138

143 J. T. Smith (1828) 1949, p. 240. Rossi had worked for the Derby porcelain factory in 1789 and even for the clockmaker Vulliamy. Richard Williams carved a bust of Rossi which was exhibited at the RA in 1824

144 Allan Cunningham 1830, Vol. III, pp. 160, 146. For the model Bet Balmanno who also sat for Fuseli and Tresham see J. T. Smith (1828) 1919, Vol. I, p. 189

145 *Ibid.*, Vol. III, p. 71; Isaac Ware 1756, p. 574

146 J. T. Smith (1828) 1919, Vol. II, p. 110

147 Allan Cunningham 1830, Vol. III, pp. 48, 359

148 *Ibid.*, Vol. III, pp. 248, 271, 272

149 *Ibid.*, Vol. III, p. 674, 7 October 1796; Katharine A. Esdaile 1946, p. 82

150 Allan Cunnigham 1830, Vol. III, pp. 90–91 in connection with the work of Thomas Banks RA

[151] Margaret Whinney 1964, p. 217. Whinney describes Chantrey as self-taught – a strange assertion

[152] Ingrid Roscoe *et al.* eds 2009. Gibson's most famous example of a painted marble was his *Tinted Venus* of 1851–1856. However a still earlier example would be Roubiliac's *Sir John Cass* which J. T. Smith objected had (in 1828) "lately been most villainously painted of various colours" – see Smith (1828) 1919, Vol. I, p. 235; Robert Plott 1677, p. 277 and J. C. Cole *Oxoniensia* XVII, XVIII, 1952 and 1953; see also Nicholas Kiessling ed. *The Life of Anthony Wood in his own Words,* Oxford, 2009

[153] Pers. comm. A. J. J. Ayres (1902–1985). For this type of housing and its decoration see Stefan Muthesius *The English Terraced House,* New Haven & London (1982), 1990, figs 185, 219

[154] Rudolf Wittkower, 1979, pp. 244–245

[155] Eric Gill (1929), 1934, pp. 83–84, 88

Chapter 18

METAL CASTING
& THE FOUNDRY

T he sculptor Sir Francis Chantrey RA (1781–1841) was the proprietor of
his own foundry in Eccleston Place, Westminster (Fig. 125) despite which
he was not entirely convinced that bronze looked its best in the English light.[1]
This reservation was based on its appearance when deployed externally rather
than when shown in the more directional light found in an interior. A bronze
when placed out-of-doors in a bosky English landscape, all but disappears from
sight. Even for purposes of interior decoration bronze was sometimes made
more visible by fire gilding – as for example Le Sueur's bust of *King Charles I*
of *c.* 1636 at Stourhead.[2] In the following century the same gilding technique
was widely adopted for bronze furniture mounts and other items. This ormolu
was less a matter of ostentation than visibility. In England work of this type
was to become, particularly in the years between 1768 and 1782, the great
speciality of Matthew Boulton's Soho manufactury, Birmingham. Among the
sculptors who supplied master patterns for this venture the most significant
were Bacon and Flaxman.[3]

The visibility of bronze in the northern light and damp climate of the British
Isles was, as noted above, a central concern for sculptors. This may explain why
so many of the earlier exponents of the use of this material in England came
from more southerly latitudes where the light is stronger and the air clearer.
Among these immigrant artists brief mention has been made of Torrigiano's
effigies (of 1512–1518) of Henry VII and his consort in Westminster Abbey, Le
Sueur's busts of Charles I (*c.* 1633) and Rysbrack's figure of William III (1735).
In Hanoverian Britain bronze sculpture and woodcarving had fallen from
favour as a consequence of the primacy of marble; although the deployment
of cast lead statuary and ornament persisted from the late seventeenth century.
Bronzes were to return to fashion in the nineteenth century particularly in

FIGURE 125. George Scharf (1788–1860) *The Foundry of Sir Francis Chantrey RA* in 1830. This drawing shows the sculptor's figures of William Pitt (right) and George IV (left) – the latter with the right arm yet to be attached. (British Museum, London)

relationship to portrait figures of individuals who embodied civic pride or national prestige.

In landscaped gardens statuary of stone or lead was favoured as visible, and therefore effective, "eye catchers". Of these materials the cheapest by far was lead. This was not simply because, like other casts it could be produced in editions, but was also because of its low melting point (612°F, the melting point of bronze depends on the alloy but is at least twice that temperature).[4] Lead was also particularly receptive to painted and oil gilt decoration – a polychromatic treatment that was widely used.[5] Because of the relative technical simplicity of casting in lead some sculptors became founders specialising in that material. This was certainly the case with John Nost I (or van Ost, d. 1710) and his successor Andrew Carpenter (or Charpentiere c. 1677–1737). Bronze casting, by comparison was, in effect, a specialist near industrial trade.

Although sculptors might be expected to be skilful in working clay, making plaster casts and carving in wood, stone and marble; bronze casting was generally a highly technical trade that, with exceptions like Chantrey and Bacon, who owned their own foundries, was distanced from the sculptor's studio.[6] There was, of course, a tradition for artists attending the almost ceremonious "pour" of the hot and liquid metal, but this was very different from participating in the actual work. Despite this semi-detached relationship to these procedures the waxes for the *cire-perdu* or lost wax process were generally worked by the artist. Larkin (1892) insisted that since this "lost wax … process required great care [modelling in wax] it could only be carried out effectively by the sculptor or modeller himself".[7] Once the bronze was cast, the best sculptors, working in a pre-industrial early modern context, were responsible, directly or indirectly, for the most elaborate and systematic chasing of the metal casting. This could result in a bronze as a unique object, one that was not simply part of an edition of a given number of copies (Fig. 128). An occasional bronze that emerged in all the perfection of the original wax was regarded as miraculous – but even these would be given a consolidated surface by means of chasing.

The alternative to *cire-perdu* was sand casting, a somewhat less refined method suitable for larger works. It was also a rather cheaper system and was therefore widely adopted. The sand moulds used for this purpose were contained in iron boxes which, collectively, formed a piece mould. In some cases the master pattern that was impressed into the sand, could be of carved wood. For example, in 1682 Sir Christopher Wren, writing to the Bishop of Oxford, describes the equestrian group of Charles II at Windsor as follows: "the horse … was at first cut in wood by a German and then cast by one Ibeck a founder in London".[8] As a foreigner Josias Ibeck (fl. 1679–1710) is known to have been granted denization in London on 22 June 1694.

For the purposes of sand casting a fine loamy variety was used and this was mixed with varying proportions of fullers earth. For best results the mould was given a facing of finely ground charcoal or rottenstone. It was essential that these moulds were "sufficiently strong to withstand the action of the fluid metal and, at the same time, must be so far pervious to the air as to permit the egress of the gases".[9] For some castings, and for the lost wax process, an

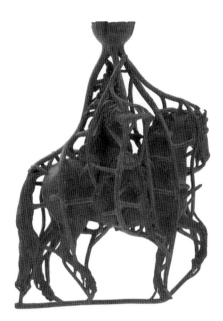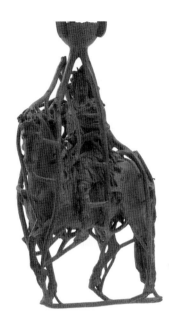

FIGURE 126. Half-finished bronze of an *Equestrian Group – Louis XIV* (ht 22 in/56 cm) by Martin Desjardins. Having just been released from its investment (the mould) the resulting bronze cast retains its runners and risers. In finishing these would be sawn off and discrepancies would be fettled and chased over. (Statens Museum f. Kunst, Copenhagen)

elaborate system of "risers" was used to release these noxious fumes. There was also a corresponding network of "runners" to deliver the molten metal to every part of the mould (Fig. 126).

With three-dimensional works, or those in very high relief a "core", or inner mould, was necessary. This core was suspended within the outer mould at a distance which corresponded to the thickness of the ultimate metal casting (allowing for shrinkage). Various materials were used for the core, as for the outer mould, but could be a mixture of two parts brick dust to one part plaster of Paris. An alternative composition for the core was comprised oak charcoal and a little clay diluted with horse dung.[10] For lead casting the core was sometimes omitted which further reduced its cost. This was possible, if inadvisable, not only due to its low melting point, but also because molten lead solidifies rapidly. For such a casting the mould, when assembled without a core, could be rotated as the lead was poured. This method generally resulted in a dangerously thin-walled cast. As a consequence lead statuary became notorious for collapsing which prompted Lord Burlington to dismiss them as so many "crooked billets", although the Earl certainly deployed such figures in the grounds of Chiswick House. The potential structural weakness of lead statuary was recorded by Lawrence Weaver (1909) who described such a sculpture of *Flora* at Syon House which suddenly subsided. On inspection this approximately twice life size figure was found, in places, to be a casting with walls that were only $3/16$ in (0.5 cm) thick. Its survival for over a century was attributed to its having been supported internally by a "fill" of "brick rubbish" held together with cement.[11] For good reason high quality lead castings involved the use of a core which established a reasonable wall thickness reinforced by the internal support of a wrought iron armature. Once the casting had cooled it was released from its "investment" (the mould) by means of a hammer and chisels. With the casting fully revealed the finishing could begin – although with lead castings this amounted to little more than the odd patch and general fettling.

For high quality work in such metals as bronze, silver and gold this was the point at which chasing began. By means of punches it was possible not only to establish a well-wrought surface or create incidental detail and texture but also, for a true artist, to model fundamental form. This was carried out in the cold metal which was annealed at intervals to prevent it becoming brittle. Chasing of this kind was what Celia Fiennes was attempting to describe in *c.* 1697 when writing about a bronze cannon that she had seen at Dover Castle which was "finely carv'd and adorn'd with figures".[12] Unlike a plain cast surface a chased one is denser and more permanent. Most importantly a chased metal casting assumes the character of its material and therefore becomes true to itself and not simply a pale imitation of the wood, clay or wax from which it derives.

There is evidence to suggest that in England the tradition for bronze casting was centred on the West Country; Devon and Somerset. This was based on the availability of some, if not all, of the ingredients that this trade required. In particular Somerset provides zinc (calamine), the special green sand (used for sand casting), and fullers earth. The somewhat oily texture of the sand chosen for this process enables it to maintain a shape and remain compacted. This probably explains why the floor of the bowling alley at Hampton Court (*c.* 1535) was made of a mixture of "founders yerthe" and "soope asshes".[13] Another resource found in Somerset is lead from the Mendip Hills small quantities of which, along with zinc, were sometimes added to the alloy which is bronze.[14] These and other raw materials formed the basis for bronze manufacturers in Georgian Bristol and elsewhere and accounts for certain street names like Brassmill Lane, Bath. Many of these West Country products were exported to form one leg of the "triangular trade" – bronze cooking vessels, etc. to West Africa, slaves to the Americas and molasses to Britain. This West Country tradition for bronze casting persisted into the twentieth century. The Singer foundry that was once based in Frome, Somerset, and its related company Morris Singer at Nine Elms, London (now in Basingstoke) are examples.[15]

The technical demands of casting a large bronze figure were immense. For those who specialised in this work it was presumably an advantage if metal working was a family trade. The sculptor, Hubert Le Sueur, a Frenchman who worked for Charles I, was the son of a master armourer.[16] He may therefore have been familiar from childhood with the repoussé techniques used for parade armour. This would have introduced him to some aspects of the chasing with which he finished his bronze casts. The contract for his equestrian bronze of Charles I in Trafalgar Square is dated 1633, an agreement which emphasises Le Sueur's role as a foundryman. His contemporaries seem to have had a greater respect for his technical skill rather than his artistic abilities. In general Le Sueur's work exhibits a rather stiff symmetry but in all cases his bronzes are well chased and sometimes fire gilt.[17] For this equestrian group he was expected to take advice from the grooms in the Royal Mews concerning "great horses, for the shape and action". For the more technical aspects of the commission the specifications in the contract were precise:

> "for the casting of a horse in Brasse bigger than a great Horse by a foot; and the figure of His Maj: King Charles proportionable ... which the aforesaid Hubert Le Sueur is to perform with all the skill and workmanship as lieth in his power ... of the best yealouw and red copper and carefully provide for the strengthening and fearm upholding of the same".[18]

The skills of the foundry were continued into the eighteenth century under the auspices of John Bacon RA (1740–1799). In some ways Bacon established the precedent, which Chantrey would later follow, in maintaining workshops for both marble and bronze but the "men who wrought his marble were not permitted to acquaint themselves with the arrangements of the foundry" which therefore preserved its art and mystery. Despite this secrecy it is known that it was Bacon's practice to have "his figures [cast in bronze] in many pieces and then into an entire whole by the process of burning or fusing the parts together".[19] This basic principle was one that he may have learnt from the way in which large Coade stone figures were assembled from their component parts (see p. 327 above). This system gave chasers greater access to each element in a bronze so that most of their work could be completed before the parts were finally united.[20] Any such advantage was offset by the difficulty of "fusing the parts together" for bronze is a notoriously difficult metal to weld. In classical antiquity this was resolved by cutting channels in the bronze on each side of the joint. The relevant components were then placed together and molten bronze was poured into these channels thus uniting the individual segments.[21] In the face of these advantages, and the countervailing difficulties, simpler, if strategically more difficult methods were deployed. We are, for example, told that: "In the foundries of Chantrey and Westmacott colossal statues twelve feet high are cast at a couple of heats".[22] These foundries were, in effect, wholly owned subsidiaries of the great sculptors' studios. It seems they were established because of their dissatisfaction with the poor quality of the work in the commercial establishments although the profit motive was almost certainly present.[23]

In 1854 legislation was introduced which would bring public statuary in London under the care of the Board of Works. This measure was brought in partly because of the poor condition of the equestrian statue of George I in Leicester Fields, a lead group modelled in John Nost's workshops by Burchard in 1716.[24] With public money at stake the bureaucrats, with this precedent in mind, were to favour the permanence of bronze, rather than the frailty of lead, for the civic statuary which was to be maintained by the public purse.

As noted by Jekyll and Hussey (1918) the fashion for lead garden statuary seems to have reached Britain with the Dutch court of William and Mary. In particular the leader of this trend was William III's cousin Nassau-Zulestein, Earl of Rochford. It was he who took possession of Powys Castle in Wales from 1696 to 1722 and it was in the gardens there that he introduced lead statuary on a grand scale.[25] The arrival of the sculptor John van Nost of Malines (d. 1710) in London sometime before 1686 was well timed in that it enabled him to meet this burgeoning demand for lead statuary – although he had initially come to England to work for his compatriot Arnold Quellin (1653–1686). On Quellin's death, van Nost married his master's widow. Thus established with a going concern van Nost was well placed to develop his business. As a carver of wood, stone and marble he was a true sculptor although he was to build his reputation on the production of lead statuary and other garden and architectural ornaments.[26]

Nost's home was in the Haymarket but his studio and workshops were located at Hyde Park Corner. There his many assistants were presided over by Anthony Hart (fl. 1686–1734). In 1694 a general search by the Mason's Company of London established that "William Colbourne [fl. 1694–c. 1726] was then at Mr Nest's [sic] in the Haymarket" indicating that Nost also had a workshop at his home address although his apprentices would certainly have lived at their master's home. This inspection may have concluded that Colbourne was working illegally as he was still "bound to Mr Bumstead" as an apprentice – probably

FIGURE 127. *The London Apprentice*, cast lead, sculptor unknown but presumably from one of the Hyde Park Corner workshops.

John Bumstead (or Bumpsteed) who died in 1683. Colbourne's offence was probably caused by his failure to inform the Company that he had transferred to another master, presumably van Nost, on Bumstead's death. Alternatively he had completed his apprenticeship but had not submitted his masterpiece to the guild.[27]

Because of the high levels of skill involved in metal casting, not to mention the necessary equipment, great advantage accrued to those who were born into such a *mileau*. Significantly John van Nost was followed by his cousin John van Nost II who in turn was succeeded by his son John van Nost III – although the latter moved across the Irish Sea to work in Dublin. The second van Nost ran the business at Hyde Park Corner until his death in circa 1729 when it was continued by Andrew Carpenter (or Charpentiere *c.* 1677–1737) who may have come from a French-speaking region of the Low countries. Like the Nosts, Carpenter was a proficient carver.

From the late seventeenth century, and onwards into Hanoverian London, Hyde Park Corner was to become a centre for a number of statuaries including Edward Hurst (fl. 1691–1714), Henri Nadauld (1653–1724) and Richard Osgood (d. *c.* 1724).[28] Of these Carpenter's workshop was to become much the most significant. This is noted in Thoresby's *Diary* for 11 May 1714: "walked down Piccadilly to Mr Carpenters the carvers" where the diarist saw "curious workmanship of his in marble and lead".[29] So well-known had these sculptors' workshops become in this locality that the joiner-architect-property-developer John Wood the Elder was to describe Claverton Street, Widcombe as having become "the Hyde Park Corner of Bath for small ornaments in Free Stone" by Thomas Greenway (fl. 1707–1720) and his family.[30] In the London area the association of this part of town with statuary was to persist. In *The Clandestine Marriage* (1766) one character in the play, Lord Ogleby, remarks on the "wonderful improvements" in Mr Stirling's garden which included "the four seasons in Lead, the flying Mercury, and the basin with Neptune in the middle, are in a very extreme of fine taste". Ogleby concluded by congratulating Mr Stirling on possessing "as many rich figures as the man at Hyde Park Corner".[31]

Carpenter continued the business until his retirement in 1736. The following year John Cheere (1709–1787) took over the yard which he maintained for some 50 years. Like his predecessors in this venture Cheere was a capable carver but he also established a market for plaster busts and statues for interiors. He insisted that these should be "painted over carefully with Flake White [white lead] and Turpentine Oile …", a treatment that he also applied to some of his lead statuary so that it might resemble stone or marble.[32]

A number of other sculptors working in the Hyde Park Corner area at this time included William Collins (1721–1793), Richard Deckenson (d. 1736) and Thomas Manning (d. 1747). Of these, Collins appears to have been employed as an assistant to the sculptor Sir Henry Cheere Bt (1703–1781), the elder brother of John Cheere. Manning produced statuary not only in lead but, as early as 1735, in artificial stone.[33] The decline in the fashion for statuary and architectural ornament in lead may be associated with the increasing use of Coade Stone – and similar materials. This decline was to result in "old stock" languishing in the Hyde Park Corner yards. In these circumstances potential bargains could be struck. Certainly Samuel Whitbread (1764–1815), the brewer, purchased a "job lot" of "the Piccadilly leaden-figures" for the pleasure grounds at his country house Southill Park, Bedfordshire. To facilitate the transport of these works Whitbread sent his carpenter to London to crate-up this lead statuary "with as much caution as if they had been looking glasses of the greatest dimensions for his drawing room".[34] That this was no idle comparison is confirmed by the invoice for crating-up a mirror for dispatch as cited above (see p. 15).

Much of this lead statuary was coloured naturalistically. In 1753 John Cheere supplied the Duke of Atholl with a figure of a gamekeeper "painted in proper coulers", the word "proper" being used here in the heraldic sense. He advised that in terms of maintenance it should be washed every other year and treated with linseed oil. Alternatively lead statuary, such as the equestrian George I which, as we have seen, once stood in Leicester Fields (Square), was "doubly gilt". By the 1760s the fashion for cast lead sculpture, painted or gilded, began its slow decline. When J. T. Smith accompanied Joseph Nollekens on a visit to the garden of "a very aged lady who resided near Hampstead Heath …" they gazed with wonder at the old fashioned taste that they encountered there including "Cheere's leaden painted figures of a Shepherd and Shepherdess".[35]

The reversal of fortune in this fashion is all the more remarkable when one considers Benjamin Rackstrow's trade label. This states that, from his address in Fleet Street, he "Makes and Mends Leaden Figures, Vases, &c" (see Fig. 102). His trade label is dated 1738 and its Rococo character demonstrates that these statuaries could be in the vanguard of taste. By 1777 the poet William Shestone expressed surprise "that lead statues are not more in vogue in our modern gardens" for although these castings may be imperfect "a statue in a garden is to be considered as part of a scene or landskip" whereas "a statue in a room challenges examination".[36]

Chasers & chasing

As the technology of the foundry burgeoned in the course of the nineteenth century the need for fettlers remained as the demand for chasers declined. Perhaps as a consequence the art of the chaser is now almost as close to extinction as an understanding of the term. This represents a serious cultural loss, a reduction in the range of possibilities that remain available to the art of sculpture. A skilful chaser did far more than simply finish a cast metal object for that was the role of the fettler. Such craftsmen were capable of transforming a metal cast by extinguishing all traces of its origins in clay, plaster or wood, and thus asserting its newly-found metallic condition. The best chasers were capable of creating form in a metal "blank". For these reasons a metal object, worked in this way, could be or become, a unique item and not simply part of an edition. Furthermore a chased metal surface was particularly receptive to fire gilding. In many cases the same individuals would chase the bronze mounts for furniture and refine a work of sculpture cast in bronze – yet another instance of the historical absence of a distinction between the "fine arts" and the "applied" or "decorative arts".

In working the cold metal with punches or *ciselets* the chasers were, in effect, sculptors.[37] Generally speaking this work was carried out on the external face of a cast. However the chasers art was often combined with *repoussé* work. This was a technique in which a sheet of metal was worked from behind with punches to produce a relief. When working in softer materials like gold or silver, sheet metal was place on a bed of pitch to offer some resistance to the craftsman's punches. Once this operation was completed the sheet metal was removed

FIGURE 128. *Arione and his Violin*, solid-cast bronze statuette, Italian, late fifteenth century. Most of the significant and subtle form has been created, direct in the cold metal, by means of chasing. Such a bronze becomes a unique object. (Museo Nazionale, Florence)

from the pitch to reveal the front face of the work so that finishing could be done by means of chasing. Through all these procedures in both chasing and *repoussé*, the metal was annealed at regular intervals to prevent it from becoming brittle. The twin crafts of chasing and *repoussé* involved the use of similar skills and tools to those employed in die-sinking which resulted in some of these artists being adept in all three skills. Of these individuals a few extended their potential still further by including seal and gem cutting in their portfolio of activities.

It seems that the auxiliary nature of the chasers' art has limited our awareness of its presence. And yet, where an individual and his work is identifiable, it is evident that some of these practitioners were artists of very great distinction. Despite this possible anonymity, mid-eighteenth century London boasted at least 20 such individuals. Some of their names have come down to us because the work they produced was of sufficient importance to carry their signatures.[38] Among these were George Parbury (fl. 1760–1791) and Albert Pars (fl. 1759–1767) whose father was also a chaser.[39] Of even greater importance than either of these were two German-speaking immigrants: John Valentine Haidt (1700–1780) and George Michael Moser RA (1706–1783).[40] Moser was born in Schaffhausen, Switzerland and probably received his first training from his father, Michael Moser Snr (1683–1739), a coppersmith. In 1725 the younger Moser moved to Geneva but was in the British capital by 1726, having travelled there via Paris. His first employment in London was with a coppersmith.[41] He then moved on to the cabinet maker

John Trotter where he worked on the production of ormolu mounts to which his travels to Geneva and Paris enabled him to introduce the latest French fashions. Trotter his employer in London was based at 43 Frith Street, Soho and was Upholder to George II. This demonstrates that Moser was now working at the most exalted level of his craft.[42]

Perhaps the most remarkable of all Moser's later employers was Nicholas Crisp (1704–1774). As J. V. G. Mallet (1992) has shown Crisp was a considerable figure in that the products of his enterprises brought together art, science and industry (see p. 326 above).[43] Crisp's interests were so extraordinarily wide that he was, almost certainly, more the entrepreneur than the working craftsman. His business concerns encompassed: jewellery, chemistry, dye-making, and the porcelain made by his Bow manufactory – for which he is now chiefly remembered (see Fig. 99 above). It was Crisp who, together with Henry Baker and a man named Messiter, formed the trio with practical experience that helped bring the (Royal) Society of Arts into existence in 1754. As an employer Crisp was something of a patron of the arts for, in addition to Moser as a chaser, painters like "Old Nollekens" and Sir James Thornhill produced designs for his porcelain.[44]

FIGURE 129. Design for a *repoussé* and chased watch-case together with the resulting object of vertu. Both the drawing and the metalwork are by George Michael Moser RA (1704–1783). (Drawing: Victoria & Albert Museum, London; Watch-case: Ashmolean Museum, Oxford)

From the production of ormolu furniture mounts Moser was to move on to the creation of such items as candlesticks and watch cases in gold and silver. Many of these products involved a combination of chasing and *repoussé*. These objects were, in their day, recognised as works of art and in this respect it is significant that the wife of the sculptor Joseph Nollekens RA (1737–1823) is known to have owned items of this kind.[45] For the consumerist taste of Georgian England these products could be irresistible. Lord Chesterfield, in one of his letters to his son, advised that "A fool cannot withstand the charms of a toy shop [in the sense of *etui*] ... snuff boxes, watches, heads of canes, etc. are his destruction".[46] The general importance that was attached to this type of work is reflected in the rules that were drawn up in January 1769 for the newly formed Royal Academy and its annual exhibitions. As noted above, these regulations stipulated that:

> "No Picture copied from a Picture or Print, a Drawing from a Drawing, a Medal from a Medal, a Chasing from a Chasing, a Model from a Model or any other species of Sculpture, or any Copy be admitted in the Exhibition".[47]

In placing the work of the die-sinker and chaser between painting and sculpture these two arts were accorded their due recognition. In contrast the Academy's President, Sir Joshua Reynolds, could not bring himself to refer directly to chasing in the eulogy he composed on Moser:

> "Few have passed ... a more inoffence or perhaps a more happy life; ... if happiness or the enjoyment of life consists in having the mind always occupied, always intent upon some useful art, by which fame and distinction may be acquired. Mr Moser's whole attention was absorbed either in the practice, or something that related to, the advancement of art".[48]

Despite this circumspect admiration for such work some Academicians acknowledged a respect for chasing by acquiring items made in this way for their own homes. In addition to Nollekens's wife, the opulent lifestyle of the painter Francis Cotes RA (1725–1770) was indicated by the "most elegant wrought and chased plate" in his home, items that were sold following his death.[49] Outside the possibly somewhat rarefied confines of the Royal Academy and the London art scene the importance of chased plate at this time may be traced obliquely through the inventories of great households. In this respect two London establishments – namely Montague House (Inventory of 1733) and Thanet House (1760) – and a country house Ditchley Park, Oxfordshire (1772) are significant. In these documents it is notable that far greater emphasis is accorded to chased silver and gold than to those items that are merely engraved.[50]

Chasing was an important trade in Matthew Boulton's Soho manufactory in Birmingham. His establishment was dependent upon a number of London-based artists. Amongst these was the chaser George Parbury who had been apprenticed to Moser, and was later employed by Boulton as a designer of coins and medals.[51] At Boulton's manufactory a chasing shop is recorded in an inventory of 1782 which shows that it contained chasing punches and hammers, cutting tools, rifflers, scalpers, etc. Unusually these implements seem to have belonged to the manufactory but in addition each craftsman is likely to have owned his own kit of tools. When Wedgwood visited Boulton's manufactory in 1770 he noted that the chasing shop housed no less than 35 of these specialist craftsmen. As this indicates Wedgwood and Boulton were not simply fellow tradesmen but, as both were members of the Lunar Society, they were close friends.[52] Consequently Bolton was well aware of the success of Wedgwood's London shop. This probably encouraged Boulton to sell a selection of his products through Mr Christie – a method of sale that Wedgwood had rejected on the grounds that "everybody would be apt to stroll into an auction room". Consequently Boulton instructed Christie to confine admittance to "persons of rank and fashion" and to exclude, among others, "all the dirty journeymen chasers, silversmiths, etc. etc." Whilst Boulton may have been at pains "to prevent the Nobility and Gentry from being incommoded" by the presence of workmen in Mr Christie's rooms, chasers and others were central to the manufacturers success. In examining the quality of the products made under Boulton and Fotheringill's supervision it is evident that the standard of the chasing is closely related to the importance of the object.[53] Despite Boulton's rather condescending attitude towards his chasers, as reflected in his instructions to Mr Christie, the industrialist was certainly aware that the success of his enterprise was dependent upon the quality of the artists he employed. In the furtherance of that fundamental consideration he set up a school for drawing and modelling ornament in his Soho Workshops in Bimingham.[54]

In this coming together of craft, art and industry a number of now conventional divisions were crossed. Another example of this concerned the son of the chaser Albert Pars. The younger man, William Pars, followed in his father's footsteps but was to cross the Rubicon and its tributaries between craft, art and archaeology. From 1764 to 1766 he was to accompany Nicholas Revett (1720–1804) as the draftsman on his expedition to record the *Antiquities of Iona* (2 vols 1769, 1797).[55] Rather poignantly it was of course Stuart and Revett's *Antiquities of Athens* of 1762 that did so much to herald a change of taste. This was the volume that would help to eclipse the fashion for Rococo, a visual language which was characterised by the fluid forms that chasing was so adept at creating. The Neo Classicism that followed was a more geometric idiom for which the chasers of the old school, Pars among them, had less to offer. Despite this aesthetic shift the work of the chaser persisted and continued to be passed down through the generations by means of apprenticeships. In this respect William Pitts the Elder did his time with George Moser and in 1811 Pitts was to take his own son, William Pitts the Younger (1789–1840) as his apprentice at the advanced age of 22. This demonstrates a decline in the place of apprenticeships a situation which was compounded when young Pars was enrolled as student at the Royal Academy Schools before he was out of his servitude. Possibly as a result of this concurrent training and education Pitts continued to practice as both a chaser and as a sculptor throughout his career and was to be described as a clever modeller "for silver work, in which he was an able manipulator".[56]

In contrast to Pitts, the chaser William Pars Jnr turned increasingly to drawing, not only in Iona but also as a teacher in William Shipley's drawing school. Even the great Moser, though:

> "originally a chaser … when that mode of adorning plate, cane-heads and watch-cases became unfashionable he, by the advice of his friend Mr Thomas Grignion [1721–1784] the celebrated watch-maker, applied himself to enamelling watch-trinkets, necklaces, bracelets, etc …"[57]

Moser was also to devote more of his time to the teaching of drawing at the St Martin's Lane Academy and later at the Royal Academy Schools where he was to become that institution's first Keeper (from 1768 to his death in 1783).

Another member of this London-based group of craftsmen was Richard Morton Paye (1750–1821). At the start of his career chasing was:

> "a branch of art at that time much in vogue … when the decorations of the table, the appendages of the toilet, together with trinkets and other ornaments of dress were, principally of precious metals and … derived their beauty and excellence from the hands of the chaser".

One authority argued that Paye's work as a chaser was superior to that of Moser whose work it was believed by some to be disfigured by "the French flutter". This opinion may reflect Paye's ability to move from a Rococo to a Neo-Classical idiom. Although painting had always been part of his *oeuvre* it "later became his exclusive pursuit" so perhaps even Paye fell victim to this shift in taste.[58]

* * * *

As chasing was seen to decline or become industrialised these artists either changed direction in terms of their craft or they followed John Valentine Haidt's example and emigrated to Colonial or early Federal America. Philadelphia was to become host to two English chasers; namely John Anthony Beau who arrived in 1772 and Thomas Beck who reached Pennsylvania in 1774.[59] Another of these migrant craftsmen was William Rollinson (1762–1842) who arrived in New York in 1783. In England he had been "brought up in the business of chaser of fancy buttons". At that date there was "little of nothing of the kind … practiced or sought after" in America, despite which he found employment with a silversmith. In the New World his most important commission came from General Henry Knox, the Secretary of War in the Federal Government. This job concerned the chasing of "the Arms of the United States upon a set of gilt buttons for the coat worn by General Washington on the memorable day of his inauguration as President" in New York in 1789. Despite this level of recognition Rollinson was eventually reduced to establishing a reputation as a stipple engraver.[60]

* * * *

As outlined above it is evident that a number of chasers were compelled to find alternative employment as the demand for their work declined. The qualities that they had brought to their art was, in many ways, emphasised by the subsequent employment of many of these individuals as teachers of drawing. Not that a painter like Edward Edwards (1738–1806) was capable of comprehending these qualities in this craft if the following observation is anything to go by: "As an artist Mr Moser ranked very high, for his abilities were not confined merely to chasing; he also might be considered one of the best medallists".[61]

Die-sinking & seal-cutting

To cut a die in steel for striking a coin or medal, or to sink a matrix in hardstone for a wax seal, are extraordinarily difficult procedures. These are activities that demand the ability to think in relief both inside-out and back-to-front. To ameliorate these challenges artists who engaged in such work would take "squeezes" in clay at intervals as the work progressed. In this way it was possible to judge the quality of the relief in its ultimate form. It should be noted, in passing, that wood carvers did much the same when working the moulds (Fig.

112) for the composition ("compo") ornament that was used to embellish chimneypieces and picture frames. The dies for coins and medals were cut in mild steel which was then case hardened for use once the intaglio was completed. The Swedish industrial spy Reinhold Rücker Angerstein described this process in some detail. On his visit to Woodstock, Oxfordshire in 1753 he noted that metal workers there undertook this procedure by applying to the worked mild steel, a special compound. This was a paste which was used to treat the work in hand before reheating it in an iron box – the "case" of case-hardening. According to his account this paste was "made by charring old leather until it can be pulverised in a mortar, after which it is mixed with brine or urine". An alternative preparation used in those same workshops consisted of horses' hooves, cow or sheep horns, "burnt till they will pound in a mortar, mixed with a little salt and urine or brine".[62]

The fundamental similarity between cutting an intaglio for a seal, or a die for a medal or coin, resulted in many of these artists being active in both fields. Despite the differing nature of hardstones (for seals) and steel (for dies) the ultimate objectives were comparable – the ability to create negatives with positive results. This type of work, with its emphasis on form should not be confused with the linear nature of engraving. Accordingly the term "die engraving", although widely used, is an oxymoron. Curiously die-sinkers of the importance of John Pingo (1738–1827) and Lewis Pingo (1743–1830) described themselves on their trade card as "Engravers to His Majesty".[63] Such a misnomer presumably inspired the gem-cutter Nathaniel Marchant RA (1739–1816) to write to the Society of Arts on behalf of himself and his old master Edward Burch RA (1730–1814) arguing that, as die-sinkers, they should both be described as sculptors. They reasoned that "The word Sculptor is more applicable to our profession than Engraver".[64] As this representation was made on the eve of the foundation of the Royal Academy in 1768 these two die-sinkers were evidently anxious that their craft should be understood as the art that it remains to this day – and it was as sculptors that they were to be recognised by the RA. Their case may have encouraged the Society of Arts to continue to offer prizes for work in intaglio although both Burch and Marchant left the Society and transferred their allegiance to the Academy.[65] Even before Marchant became an ARA in 1791 he initiated a lobby of Parliament with the aim of persuading the Government to grant exemptions to artists on the import duties due on works of art. As a respected artist, connoisseur and antiquarian, Marchant gained the support of Baron Camelford who approached his cousin William Pitt, the Prime Minister, on this matter. These representations were to prove effective and the exemptions were granted and were later extended.[66]

Die-sinking and seal-cutting in miniature were predicated on remarkably good eyesight. In this respect Farington records a rather sad meeting in 1796 with Burch whose "eyes failed him" (see p. 83).[67] In the long history of this *metier* its fundamentally miniature nature is exemplified in the work of the limner Nicholas Hilliard (*c.* 1547–1619) who, as a goldsmith by trade, concluded his career as medallist to James I.[68] His "Amada Jewel" (*c.* 1600) reflects both aspects of his craft and art. Later in the century die-sinking in England was to be dominated by immigrants. In 1625, the year of Charles I's accession, Nicholas Briot, a Parisian, moved to England. His arrival was to have both aesthetic and technological significance. From 1616 Briot had experimented with mechanical means of striking coins and medals which would displace the somewhat rough and ready methods of the past.

Inevitably the Civil War was to disrupt royal appointments such as Briot's. Nevertheless he was able to pass through the lines of the Parliamentary forces to reach Charles I's refugee court and the Royalist forces centred on Oxford. It was there that coinage was minted, under Briot's supervision, from melted down college plate.[69] The continental sophistication of which Briot was adept was not lost on English-born artists like Thomas Rawlins whose "Oxford crown" of 1644 closely matches the Frenchman's achievements. Rawlins, it should be noted, was made free of the Painter Stainers Company in 1647. All these artists, native and foreign, were to be outdone by the work of Thomas Simon (*c.* 1623–c1665). In 1645 he was appointed, together with another artist, to the London Mint. By 1648 he was in sole command. It was there, following the execution of the King in 1649, that Simon produced his superb portrait of Cromwell, one of the finest manifestations of this art ever to have been created. On the Protector's death in 1658 Simon walked in the cortège as one of the officers of state.[70] He was thus indelibly linked to Cromwell which was to inhibit his advancement with the return of the monarchy. Following the Restoration (1660) Thomas Simon presented his "Petition Crown" in 1663. The rim of this coin bears the following submission: "Thomas Simon most humbly prays your Majesty to compare this tryall piece with the Dutch and if more truly drawn and emboss'd, more gracefully order'd and more accurately engraven to relieve him [from his post at the Mint]".[71]

Despite the remarkable artistic qualities of the "Petition Crown" Simon was neither confirmed in his appointment at the Mint nor removed from it – he was side-lined. His treatment had nothing to do with the very considerable merits of his work as an artist. During Charles Stuart's years of exile in the Low Countries, the Prince had become obligated to the Roettiers, a family of Antwerp die-sinkers. Following the Restoration in 1660 Jan Roettiers moved

Figure 130. Thomas Simon's *Petition Crown*, obverse (diam. 1¾ in/3.9 cm) submitted to Charles II in 1663. Despite the self-evident quality of this work Simon's role at the Royal Mint was marginalised. It is believed that about a dozen of these silver crowns were minted. (British Museum, London)

to England to take up his appointment as a die-sinker to the Mint in London; a post he was to share, in a dominant position, with Simon. In effect Simon was demoted but he was able to pass on his skills to Thomas East and through him to East's nephew, John Roos. The latter became seal-cutter to George I much as his uncle had served James II in that capacity.[72] Significantly both had transferred their skills from one dynasty to another and from die-sinking to the cutting of intaglios for seals. At a later date Jan Roettiers's brother Joseph moved to England to work at the London Mint. Simon was effectively out-manoeuvred. It was Jan (or John) Roettier who Pepys was to visit at the Mint on 26 March 1666 "to the Tower [of London] to see the famous engraver to get him to grave a seal for the office". Although Pepys's position at the Admiralty would have meant that this was an official job artists at the Mint were permitted to use the machinery there to produce private commissions out of hours – a "perk" that persisted into the nineteenth century.[73]

The Roettiers artistic dominance of the Mint persisted even after the brothers returned to Antwerp for they were succeeded at the London Mint by Jan's sons James and Norbert Roettier. Although the work of these seventeenth century Continental artists was "undistinguished" the transition from the Protectorate to the Restoration of the monarchy was to result in the best candidate for the position at the Royal Mint in London failing to secure the appointment. This was despite Simon's manifest superiority as an artist whose work Sutherland (1955) described "as the high peak of English monetary design".[74]

In the following century the Mint was, once again, employing English artists like Crocker, Tanner and Richard Yeo (d. 1779), the latter being a founder

FIGURE 131. Richard Yeo's *Culloden Medal* (diam. 2in/5.1 cm) commemorating the brutal 1746 defeat of the Highlanders in Scotland. The obverse of this medal carries a portrait bust, in profile, of the Duke of Cumberland (1721–1765) who lead the English army. The reverse (shown here), being emblematic of victory, is centred by Hercules flanked by Britannia and a figure personifying the vanquished. The die sinker Richard Yeo (d. 1779) was evidently a sculptor of considerable ability and yet, though a founder member of the Royal Academy, he remains somewhat obscure. (Royal Academy of Arts, London)

member of the Royal Academy.[75] The quality of Yeo's work is manifest in his two inch diameter bronze medal that was struck to commemorate the brutal battle of Culloden of 1746 (Fig. 131). Yeo was probably trained by his father who was also a die sinker. Nevertheless despite Richard Yeo's importance as an artist and founder of the RA he is not listed in either of the two existing dictionaries of sculptors in Britain.

Although the visual arts were centred on London some craftsmen of this type would later work for provincial enterprises like Boulton's Soho Mint in Birmingham. In Sheffield Jonathan Watson combined his work as a die-sinker with the teaching of drawing, one of his pupils being the youthful sculptor Sir Francis Chantrey RA (1781–1841).[76]

The eighteenth century saw a number of seal intaglio-cutters in business in London, many of whom were of Continental origin. These included a seal-cutter named Tassie and also Christian Reisen who, in 1711, attended Kneller's Academy.[77] Of Reisen (d. 1725) it was noted by Horace Walpole that the "magic" of his work was revealed "by the help of glasses [which brought into focus] … all the beauties of statuary and drawing …"[78] An English specialist in this field was James Wickstead (or Wicksteed, fl. 1779–1824) of London. His father may have been the goldsmith Thomas Wicksteed of Long Acre, London who is recorded as taking on two apprentices – namely Richard Abery (5 Sept 1770) and Thomas Smith (8 Jan 1772) both of whom were sons of Carpenters. Another relative of the goldsmith's family may have been John Wicksted of Bath, a craftsman cited by John Wood the Elder of Bath (1704–1754) as follows:

"The Art of Engraving Seals was brought to Bath, about seventeen Years ago [*c.* 1725], by Mr John Wicksted; and he fixed his Machine at Hamton, removing it afterwards to the Junction at the lower Parts of Widcomb and Lyncomb, where it now remains in a small Building, for which I made a Design on the 15th of August, 1737, every Way suitable to the Taste and Spirit of our Artist; but a Proposal by his Engineer, and others, to erect it with common Wall Stone to be first Plaistered; and then Painted to imitate Brickwork; was such an Instance of Whim and Caprice, that when I got the Draughts I had made into my Possession, I never parted with them again."[79]

The seal-cutter Edward Burch RA (1730–1814), was a Thames waterman by guild affiliation or trade and claimed to have been self-taught in his art. This was a very remarkable assertion for such a fiendishly difficult art. Nevertheless it could be argued, in support of this contention, that the strength gained as a waterman, if that is what he was, would have developed the manual power that this craft demands – the ability to apply and yet restrain force when working in miniature. Although there was barely a decade between them in terms of age Burch took as his apprentice Nathaniel Marchant RA (1739–1816). Of the two men Burch seems to have been a difficult personality and ended his days in financial distress. In contrast the popular Marchant left a fortune of £24,000.

Across the Atlantic William Bateman of New York City advertised that he "cut coats of arms, crests, ciphers, figures and fancies in the neatest manner and on the most reasonable terms" in cornelian. Significantly Bateman stated that he was from London. Not to be outdone Thomas Reynolds his fellow New Yorker boasted that as a "stone seal cutter" he had worked in both London and Dublin; claims that were thought to indicate high quality work. Reynolds also undertook to create "all sorts of devices [for] state and public seals cut on brass".[80] This is yet another example which demonstrates that, on both sides of the Atlantic, many hardstone gem-cutters also worked in metal as die sinkers.

In Britain Nathaniel Marchant was appointed in 1797 as deputy to Lewis Pingo (1743–1830) at the Royal Mint in London.[81] Pingo had the advantage of being a die-sinker from the start of his career for that was the *metier* of his father Thomas Pingo (1714–1776).[82] As so often in these craft-based arts the required level of skill may only be achieved over several generations. By 1794 the Royal Academy was considering the production of a medal to celebrate its twenty-fifth anniversary. In March of that year the painter Robert Smirke RA (1752–1845) produced a design that was approved by the RA Council and in June "Bolton [*sic*] of Birmingham" was proposed for its production. For the cutting of the die or, alternatively, the master pattern, a limited competition was held involving Edward Burch, Lewis Pingo and Joseph Wilton all of whom were invited to submit examples of their work as contenders to execute this commission. On the basis of this trio of submitted samples it was concluded that Burch's medal expressed "more knowledge of the Art". However his submission had been created some years earlier and, as we have seen, the 65 year old's eyesight was failing. For this reason a compromise was agreed; Burch would make a model based on Smirke's design but the die would be cut by Pingo with Marchant's assistance. No further mention was made of the rather strange choice of Wilton as one of the original competitors. Pingo estimated that the die would take between six and seven months to cut and would cost 150 guineas. As Smirke was ignorant of this type of work, Pingo inevitably concluded "that Burch had improved on Smirke's model in his copy of it small".[83]

For die-sinkers the gradual introduction of machinery in the chief mints was to have a greater impact on this art form than the intrusion of painters like Smirke as designers, or the sensibilities of a committee of Academicians. As indicated above the Frenchman Briot was experimenting, as early as 1616, with mechanisms that would replace the rather informal hammered coins and medals of the past. This machinery was first applied to medals but, from 1629 began to be used by the Royal Mint for the production of coins.[84] These new machines would result in milled coinage, a feature intended to inhibit clipping (cutting the edges of coins to steal bullion). Celia Fiennes refers to this on a visit to Norwich in about 1698: "Here was also a Mint which they coyn'd at, but since the old money is all new coyn'd into milled money that ceases".[85]

Before the introduction of mechanisation dies were cut at the intended size of the coin or medal in mild steel which, when finished, was case hardened. Consequently a die created in this way was conceived and cut at its ultimate size so that both the dimensions and the scale were in keeping one with another.[86] This relationship, so important in artistic terms, was destroyed once the reducing machine was introduced. *En passant* it should be added that the distinction between dimensions and a sense of scale was and remains of great importance to the visual arts. In England much of the responsibility for the introduction of the reducing machine for coins and medals may be placed with Matthew Boulton and his Soho Mint. In 1789 he instructed Foucault, his agent in Paris, to recruit a mechanic to make such a mechanism. By 1790 Jean Baptiste Barthélémy Dupeyrat (1759–1834) was commissioned to build one and install it in the Soho works in Birmingham.[87] It was now possible for coins and medals to be produced that carried far more detail than their size could justify in aesthetic terms. Furthermore, from a commercial point of view, relief could also be reduced enabling a single die to remain useable for longer.

By 1795 Boulton was sending medals to London "as specimens of his capability" a public relations exercise that had more to do with commercial profit than artistic quality. Productivity was promoted at the expense of sculptural values. At this time it was acknowledged that "At the Royal Mint only 46 pieces can be coined in an Hour [whereas at Boulton's] 16 times 46 [736] can be coined at the same time..."[88] The mechanisation of the production of coins and medals would eventually transform what had been craft-based studios into manufactoring enterprises. In these changed circumstances managers and entrepreneurs, rather than artists and craftsmen, triumphed.

The client economies of the past were predicated on a system of informed patronage. In this respect a gentleman such as Sir Andrew Fountaine (1676–1753) was typical in that, among his scholarly interests were coins and medals. Influential individuals such as Sir Andrew were therefore to have a posthumous influence with the emergence of consumerism. As late as 15 July 1798 the Privy Council maintained the view that the production of coins and medals remained a primarily artistic matter. Accordingly this Council of State of the British sovereign approached the Royal Academy for advice on "the new coinage". A number of Academicians produced designs and on 27 March 1799 "The Committee of Coinage" met under the President's chairmanship – namely Benjamin West. On seeing the various proposals Farington was of the opinion that "West's design was very poor, – Bacon's quaint, Cosway's not proper but nicely executed. In short none so well as Flaxman's" – and yet his was "pedantick".[89] In November 1798 Joseph Farington overheard a bad tempered conversation on this matter between Sir Joseph Banks and John Flaxman. This exchange was concluded by Banks who responded to Flaxman with a barbed comment: "Oh! ... you perhaps wd. not afford your advice to the Privy Council unless your designs are adopted ... This stopped Flaxman short". When the sculptor left Sir Joseph turned to Farington remarking that "this was a rather pushy business".[90] The dominance of painters at the Academy and on this particular committee is another indication of the declining importance of die sinkers and other craft-based arts. Somewhat inevitably Parliament gave up on the Academy's committee of competing artists. This dominance of painters over die sinkers was not confined to Britain but appears to have been equally true of early Federal America. There is, for example, some evidence to suggest that the "Washington Season Medals" of 1796 were designed by the Conneticut-born painter John Trumbull (1756–1843) although the die was cut by C. H. Kuchler and produced by Boulton and Watt in Birmingham, England.[91]

Following the debacle with the Academy's "Committee of Coinage" the Privy Council determined by the end of December 1799 to throw "the whole into the hands of Bolton [sic] of Birmingham".[92] Then, as early as 1803, the

Government was issuing export licences for machinery for foreign mints.[93] The intervention of Government bureaucracy, designers and the reducing machine were distancing die-sinkers from their craft and its potential as an art. As early as December 1796 Farington noted that "This branch of Art [is now] at a low Ebb".[94] Despite this despairing tone this was an activity that was to be restored to some health in the nineteenth by the Wyon dynasty of artists.

The Wyon family were of German origin and the first to settle in England was probably Peter George Wyon (1710–1744). His son George Wyon (d. 1797) was apprenticed to Thomas Heming (fl. 1745–1795) of Bond Street, who, as George II's goldsmith displayed the Royal Arms as his sign.[95] By 1775 the Wyons were undertaking work for Matthew Boulton. Accordingly this family became established as die-sinkers, a craft that members the dynasty continued to practice into the twentieth century. Thomas Wyon the Elder (1767–1830) was active as both a chaser and die-sinker – sometimes working at the behest of designers. His sons, Thomas Wyon the Younger (d. 1817), Benjamin Wyon (1802–1858), and Edward William Wyon (1811–1885) were all trained in the family trade by their father but they also attended the RA Schools to become independent artists. All the brothers, including Edward William Wyon, became known for a wide range of work as sculptors, but maintained their skills as die-sinkers. The last member of the family to retain this tradition was Allan G. Wyon (1882–1962).[96]

Those members of the Wyon family who had undertaken work for Boulton were well-placed to maintain artistic standards within an industrial context. Their resolve was probably stiffened by the arrival in England from Rome in 1815 of Benedetto Pistrucci (1783–1855). By 1816 this Italian seal- cutter had found employment at the Royal Mint and, in the following year on the death of Thomas Wyon the Younger, he became the chief die-sinker. Pistrucci's superb George and the Dragon, which first appeared on the reverse of the sovereign of 1817 has been used, intermittently, ever since.[97]

Despite the best efforts of the Wyons and of Pistrucci, the minting of coins and medals was becoming an overwhelmingly industrial activity. Stuart and early Hanoverian monarchs had appointed die-sinkers in person so that these individuals enjoyed some authority under the crown. The decline in this situation was probably inevitable but may have begun when a man named Harris was appointed to the Royal Mint in the eighteenth century. According to Horace Walpole this person was "incapable of the office" and therefore "employed workmen to do the business". Fortunately one of these "workmen" was a "Mr Crocker who afterwards obtained the place of chief die-sinker".[98]

* * * *

In early Federal America the newly independent nation was in need of a coinage but for which this young Republic was dependent upon immigrant artists. One such was the Slovenian die-sinker Moritz Fürst (b. 1782) who had been trained by Würt at the Vienna Mint. In 1807 the American consul in Leghorn (Livorno) appointed Fürst as die-sinker to the United States Mint and the artist emigrated to America. As a sculptor working in metal Fürst's scope could be wide. According to Dunlap this die-sinker "executed some work under my direction for the swords presented by the state to military and naval officers who had distinguished themselves". Quite what a painter like Dunlap would have known about working metal is unknown.[99]

At a rather earlier date the English-born die-sinker James Smithers (d. 1797) emigrated to Philadelphia in 1773. This man had trained as a gem engraver but he later had some experience preparing dies at the Royal Mint in London. In Philadelphia, with the approach of the War of Independence, Smithers "engraved the blocks for the continental money" – a paper currency issued by the seceding Colonies.[100] As a new country with a relatively small population, early Federal America deployed the available skills as widely as possible.

*　*　*　*

As outlined above nineteenth century mints were becoming increasingly dependent upon mechanisation. Rather whimsically this was seen by some as a means of achieving "a superior degree of excellence" which would "set at defiance the imitation of ordinary workmen". The deterrence of counterfeiting rather than the promotion of artistic values had become the overriding concern. By the twentieth century industrialisation had curtailed this once proud art-form so that its practitioners were reduced to "workmen" following a "designer's" instructions. In the 1950s Walter J. Newman was the principal die-sinker to the Royal Mint – then still on its historic site on Tower Hill. In this employment Newman worked factory hours in contrast to the office hours of the administrators.[101]

In summary, these changing circumstances explain why die-sinking, and by extension seal cutting, are no longer seen as significant aspects of sculpture. This probably explains why, in examining the past, the names of Thomas Rawlins, Thomas Simon and Richard Yeo RA are largely forgotten. One authority has gone so far as to describe die-sinking as "a historical no-man's land between sculpture and engraving",[102] despite the distinguished place that this art once occupied in early modern Britain.

Notes

[1] Margaret Whinney 1964, p. 222
[2] Charles Avery "Hubert Le Sueur's Portraits ..." in Gervase Jackson-Stops, ed. *National Trust Studies 1979*, London, 1978, pp. 133–137
[3] Nicholas Goodison (1974) 2002, pp. 97, 98. Wedgwood described Boulton's business as "the most complete manufacturer in England in metal"; *ibid.*, p. 6, see also F. J. B. Watson "Sculpture on Furniture: An aspect of French eighteenth century technique", *Apollo*, June, 1965
[4] James Larkin (1892), 1914, p. 19
[5] J. T. Smith (1828), 1919, Vol. I, p. 35
[6] For a summary of metal casting techniques see James Ayres 1985, pp. 162–170
[7] James Larkin (1892), 1914, pp. 105–106
[8] Josias Ibeck or Iback may have come from Hanover; Margaret Whinney 1964, p. 248, endnote 27. A hoof on this horse is inscribed "Josias Iback Stadti Blarensis"
[9] James Larkin (1892), 1914, pp. 105–106
[10] *The New Universal Dictionary of Arts & Sciences* (1754) recommends "a mixture of clay, horse dung and hair" or alternatively "parget [plaster] and brick dust"
[11] Lawrence Weaver (1909) 2002, pp. 196, 182, 175
[12] Christopher Morris ed. 1982, p. 123
[13] L. F. Salman (1952) 1992, p. 148, "soope asshes" was, presumably, the residue resulting from soap-making
[14] Bronze mainly consists of copper to which is added zinc, and less than 2.14% of lead; James Larkin (1892), 1914, p. 258; James Smithson (1765–1829) the founder of the Smithsonian Institute in Washington DC, wrote scientific papers on Somerset calamine
[15] Down to the 1950s the manager of Morris Singers in London was a man from Somerset with the regional name of Parrott
[16] Charles Avery "Hubert Le Sueur's Portraits ..." in Gervase Jackson-Stops ed. *National Trust Studies 1979*, London, 1978, p. 129
[17] For parade armour see Stuart W. Pyhrr and José A. Godoy *Heroic Armour of the Italian Renaissance*, New York 1999; Allan Cunningham 1830, Vol. III, p. 241; Margaret Whinney 1964, p. 36
[18] Charles Avery "Hubert Le Sueur's Portraits ..." in Gervase Jackson-Stops ed. *National Trust Studies 1979*, London, 1978, p. 137 "fearm upholding" is a reference to the wrought iron armature
[19] Allan Cunningham 1830, Vol. III, pp. 240–241
[20] Nicholas Penny, 1993, p. 248. Assembling bronzes in this way is paralleled by the Gibbons school where wood carvings were assembled as each layer was finished
[21] *Ibid.*, p. 228
[22] Margaret Whinney 1964, p. 222
[23] Peter Jackson 1987, p. 91
[24] Rupert Gunnis 1953, index "Burchard, C."
[25] Gertrude Jekyll and Christopher Hussey (1918) 1927, p. 116. Nassau-Zulestein displaced the Jacobite Marquis of Powys
[26] Ingrid Roscoe *et al.* eds 2009 – Nost is known to have carved in wood a series of equestrian figures of monarchs for the Tower of London
[27] Rupert Gunnis 1953; Ingrid Roscoe *et al.* eds 2009; Bunstead was Upper Warden of the Mason's Company in 1676

28 Ingrid Roscoe *et al.* eds 2009
29 Quoted by Lawrence Weaver (1909) 2002, p. 170
30 John Wood (1765) 1969, p. 433. Claverton Street, Bath was the location of Thomas
    Greenway's (fl. 1740–1752) workshops. As a mason and carver he was to be followed by
    Benjamin and Daniel Greenway (fl. 1740–1752) and Joseph Greenway (fl. 1757)
31 Quoted by Lawrence Weaver (1909) 2002, p. 187. *The Clandestine Marriage* was written
    by George Coleman and David Garrick
32 As, for example, his River God at Stourhead
33 Ingrid Roscoe *et al.* eds 2009
34 J. T. Smith (1828) 1919, p. 234
35 J. T. Smith (1829) 1949, p. 35
36 Quoted by Lawrence Weaver (1909) 2000, p. 172
37 Nicholas Penny 1993, p. 257, for his reference to *ciselets*. See also F. J. B. Watson "Sculpture
    on Furniture: An aspect of French eighteenth century technique". *Apollo*, June 1965
38 Richard Edgcumbe "Gold Chasing" in Michael Snodin ed. 1984, p. 127
39 Rupert Gunnis 1953; Ingrid Roscoe *et al.* eds 2009
40 W. H. Pyne 1823–4, Vol. I, p. xxi. In addition Horace Walpole cites a still earlier chaser
    – namely Christien Van Vianen of Nuremberg who worked for Charles I in England
    (*ibid.*, Vol. II, p. 252). Haidt was to migrate to North America where he, like Moser back
    in London, was to produce easel paintings – example in National Gallery, Washington,
    DC.
41 Edward Edwards 1808, pp. 91–92 and *DNB*
42 Ambrose Heal (1953) 1988, p. 187
43 J. V. G. Mallet "Nicholas Crisp, Founding Members of the Society of Arts", chapter 4 in
    Allan and Abbot eds 1932, pp. 56–74
44 Allan Cunningham 1830, Vol. III, pp. 158–159
45 J. T. Smith (1828) 1949, p. 93
46 Quoted by Amanda Vickery 2009, p. 128 and endnote 61 citing Chesterfield's letter No.
    132. An *etui* was an elaborately wrought metal container or similar "object of *virtù* and
    vertue"
47 Sidney C. Hutchinson 1968, p. 54
48 Richard Wendorf 1996, p. 94 citing Edmund Malone, London, 1797, 1:XXVI, n.
49 W. T. Whitley 1928, p. 267
50 Tessa Murdoch 2006
51 Ingrid Roscoe *et al.* eds 2009
52 Jenny Uglow 2002
53 Nicholas Goodison (1974) 2002, pp. 133–135, 171
54 Holger Hoock (2003) 2009, p. 92
55 W. H. Pyne 1823–24, Vol. I, p. xxi; Edward Edwards 1808, pp. 89–91; Jason M. Kelly
    2009, p. 181 – also Stuart and Revett *The Antiquities of Athens*, 1762
56 Ingrid Roscoe *et al.* eds 2009; C. Drury E. Fortnum 1877, p. 153, F. Saxl and R. Wittkower
    1948, p. 76 – Revett produced the measured drawings, Richard Chandler supervised the
    archaeological work and William Pars took the views
57 J. T. Smith (1828) 1949, p. 30
58 The Library of Fine Arts, 1831, Vol. III, pp. 95–96
59 Morrison H. Heckscher and Leslie Green Bowman, 1992, p. 245 and endnote 36. For
    Haidt see endnote 4 above

60 William Dunlap (1834) 1969, Vol. I, pp. 158–159. Henry Knox (1750–1806) was a trusted companion of George Washington

61 Edward Edwards 1808, p. 92. Some histories of the Royal Academy list Moser as a painter (e.g. Sidney Hutchinson 1968, p. 222). The last exponent of quality chasing working in London was J. E. Clark who retired in c. 1953 – see James Ayres 1985, p. 170

62 Torsten and Peter Berg 2001, pp. 17–18. Angerstein was here describing the dies used in the manufacture of buckles, buttons and similar items stamped in bright steel

63 Trade Label: British Museum Dept of P&D

64 Gertrude Seidmann "A Very Ancient, Useful and Curious Art …" in Allan and Abbott 1992, chapter 7, p. 130

65 Ibid., p. 129

66 Holger Hoock (2003) 2009, pp. 240–245

67 Joseph Farington, p. 473 18 January 1796

68 Thornton and Cain 1981, pp. 23–33

69 C. H. V. Sutherland 1955, p. 183. To this day colleges in Oxford own far less pre-Civil War plate than their Cambridge counterparts

70 Alan Borg 2005, p. 60; Horace Walpole 1786, Vol. II, p. 286

71 C. H. V. Sutherland 1955, p. 188

72 Horace Walpole 1786, Vol. III, p. 192

73 Daniel Fearon 1984, pp. 7–8

74 C. H. V. Sutherland 1955, pp. 183, 187 (for Rawlings) and pp. 187–188 (for the Roettiers)

75 Ibid., p. 189 – although neither Rupert Gunnis (1953) nor Ingrid Roscoe et al. eds (2009) list Yeo

76 Margaret Whinney 1964, p. 217; David Symons "Bringing to Perfection the Art of Coining …" in Shena Mason ed. 2009, chapter 11, pp. 89–98

77 W. T. Whitley 1928, Vol. I, p. 8

78 Horace Walpole 1786, Vol. IV, p. 99

79 Thomas Wicksteed and his apprentices are listed in the Binding Book of the Painter Stainers demonstrating that Wicksteed was of that fraternity though being by trade a Goldsmith; John Wood (1765) 1969, p. 423. For dating purposes the edition of 1742 would suggest that seal-cutting was introduced to Bath in c. 1725

80 William Kelby (1922) 1970, pp. 12–13 citing Rivington's New York Gazetteer 20 Oct 1774 and p. 26, 27, 30 – and also The Daily Advertiser 21 Jan 1786 and 15 Jan 1725

81 Gertrude Seidmann 1992, p. 125

82 Ingrid Roscoe et al. eds 2009

83 Joseph Farington makes regular reference to this project in his Diary but see 3 Feb 1974, 21 March 1794, 20 June 1795, 18 July 1795, 17 Dec 1796, 26 Dec 1796, 31 Dec 1796, 8 March 1797, 23 March 1797

84 C. H. V. Sutherland 1955, p. 178

85 Christopher Morris ed. 1982, p. 137. In 1696 a series of provincial mints were established (e.g. Exeter) where this new machinery was put into use. Each coin was marked with the initial of the city to identify its origin. Gertrude Rawlings 1898, p. 99

86 "Dimension" and "scale" are far from synonymous

87 J. G. Pollard "Matthew Boulton and the Reducing Machine …" Newmismatic Chronicle 7 Ser. XI, 1971, London; James Ayres 1985, pp. 172–176. See also Shena Mason ed., 2009, chapter 10: Sue Turngate "Matthew Boulton's Mints…,"

88 Joseph Farington, pp. 557, 361 20 June 1795 and 4 July 1795, also p. 801 19 March 1797

89 Tim Richardson (2007) 2008, 103; Joseph Farington, p. 1096 26 Nov 1798

90 *Ibid.*, p. 1096 26 November 1798

91 Harriet Ropes Cabot 1979, p. 38 citing Theodore Sizer *The Works of John Trumbull*, New Haven, 1950

92 Joseph Farington, p. 1331 25 December 1799

93 Act of Parliament *To enable His Majesty to authorise the Exportation of the Machinery necessary for erecting a Mint in the Dominions of the King of Denmark*, pp. 677–679, Act of Parliament. *London: George Eyre and Andrew Strahan, 1803.* A similar Act was passed in 1816 for the export of machinery for the Mint in the United States of America

94 Joseph Farington, p. 726 22 December 1796

95 Michael Snodin ed. 1984, G49 for the trade card. For Heming's work see G40 and G44

96 The author was acquainted with Allan Wyon (1882–1962) at meetings of the Art Workers Guild in London. Rupert Gunnis 1953, Ingrid Roscoe *et al.* eds 2009

97 C. H. V. Sutherland 1955, p. 195

98 Horace Walpole 1786, Vol. III, p. 177 and C. H. V. Sutherland 1955, p. 189

99 William Dunlap (1834) 1969, Vol. II, Pt I, pp. 220–221

100 *Ibid.*, Vol. I, p. 156

101 Prince Hoare 1813, p. 108, W. J. Newman's brother Sidney was a well-known London letter-cutter in the second half of the twentieth century

102 Ingrid Roscoe *et al.* eds 2009 – see under Edward Burch RA

Part 4

THE EMERGENCE OF
ACADEMIES OF ART

Chapter 19

THE EMERGENCE
OF ACADEMIES OF ART

T here can be little doubt that at its best the apprenticeship system was the most effective way that has ever been devised for providing the young with instruction in the crafts as in other occupations. In Joseph Conrad's *Lord Jim* (1900) we are offered a glimpse into the heart of this form of enlightenment by an author who had himself served an apprenticeship as a seaman. In this account he observes that "the craft of the sea" may be one in which the "whole secret could be expressed in one short sentence, and yet it must be driven afresh every day into young heads till it becomes the component part of every waking thought – till it is present in every dream of their young sleep".[1] The notion that skill or expertise should be "driven" into a young apprentice is a theme which recurs. As we have seen, William Hogarth, who served his time as a silver engraver, was later to select the subject of an apprentice weaver for one of his pictorial parables. His chronicle of *Industry and Idleness* (1747) demonstrates most graphically both failure and success (see Fig. 10). In general, and at the most basic level, an apprentice had the potential to be equipped, at the conclusion of his time, to be employable. Of these a fortunate and conscientious few would become highly successful and employers in their own right. Tradesmen who successfully completed a craft apprenticeship were generally, in social terms, of "the middling sort". The cost of their premium as apprentices placed them well above the unskilled labouring masses – a situation that has often been elided in studies of "the working class".[2] This "middling" status was also enjoyed by those who were apprenticed to their fathers where the cost of the premium was circumvented. This commonplace situation offers some justification for the well-worn eighteenth century phrase which referred to individuals being "bred" to a particular trade. Others were fortunate enough to owe their apprenticeships to the sponsorship of charity.

420

The more complex crafts were, inevitably, a matter of lifelong learning and were dependent on more than one generation of experience. These issues are reflected in Batty Langley's *Builder's Jewel* (1742) which is subtitled *The Youth's Instructor or Master's Remembrancer*.

In great contrast to the traditional methods of training, the so-called "pauper apprenticeships" were a corrupt and exploitative source of cheap child labour that conveniently removed the offspring of the poor from the parish rate. Even within the context of a trade apprenticeship the master's tyranny, or an indentured youth's insolence, could result in failure. An example of the latter concerned the American painter John Wesley Jarvis (1780–1817) who recalled with horror the time that he spent bound, from 1788, to Edward Savage (1761–1840) whom Jarvis described in the most unflattering terms as:

> "The most ignorant beast that ever imposed upon the public. He painted what he called fancy pieces and historical subjects ... He was not qualified to teach me any art but that of deception ... at drawing or painting I was *his* master".[3]

As the previous chapters have indicated the diversity of trades that could lead to a career as a "polite painter" or as a "liberal sculptor" were remarkably diverse. Easel painters may, in the past, have been apprenticed as stainers, limners, plumbers, sign or house painters and as engravers. Similarly, statuaries may have evolved from the artisan traditions of masons, decorative carvers of wood or stone, as ornamental plasterers, chasers, die-sinkers or seal cutters. Some may have been fortunate in being apprenticed to the art that they hoped to follow.

Comprehensive though any one of these trade activities could be for an aspiring artist there was one highly significant element that long remained missing from such a training – namely drawing. Some informal out of hours attempts were made by individuals to overcome this deficiency. One example of this, as we have seen, was exemplified in the experience of Thomas Johnson (1723–1799) who was given instruction in drawing and modelling by his fellow wood carver Matthias Lock (*c.* 1710–1765) when both were employed in the London workshops of James Whittle. In Birmingham Matthew Boulton established a school for drawing and modelling ornament within his Soho Works.[4] That drawing was seen as a central concern, for both artists and artisans, there may be no doubt. The carpenter turned architect John Gwynn RA, writing in 1747, was very certain on this point: "There is scarce any Mechanic, let his Employment be ever so simple, who may not receive advantage" from learning to draw.[5] Just seven years later the embryonic Society of Arts acknowledged that drawing was the basis for the arts and manufacturers.[6]

The chief limitation with much of the existing in-house workshop tuition in drawing was that it was predicated on ornamental work with all its attendant conventions. For a decorative painter, plasterer, carver or silversmith the representation of an acanthus leaf is both more, and less, than a matter of botany. Of the numerous surviving drawings by various members of the Rose family of ornamental plasterers, most are notable for their very accomplished designs for ornament which contrast with their often dire representations of the human figure.[7]

For these reasons there existed amongst both artists and craftsmen a real need for drawing from "the naked". Drawing from a nude living model was, as it remains, a very considerable challenge. Consequently beginners would start to draw from plaster casts of antique statuary. This was marginally less difficult to do since the human form, as represented by sculptors had, to some extent, been interpreted and simplified. This explains why "Probationers" at the RA Schools were first expected to demonstrate their abilities as draftsmen by working from casts. Having achieved the necessary standard a Probationer would gain accreditation as a student, be permitted to draw from life, and admission to one of the three schools – of painting, sculpture or architecture. Before the foundation of the RA, students in most of these drawing schools worked exclusively from the male nude. This was a great disadvantage since drawing from the undraped female figure was the greater challenge simply because the subcutaneous fat, most evident on the female form, results in greater subtlety than is characteristic of the male body.

In practical terms eighteenth century drawing schools spread the cost of employing models amongst those who had signed-up as members of such associations. Inevitably this expense would otherwise have been prohibitive for an individual apprentice, journeyman or even a master craftsman. Indeed the costs were such that a highly successful artist like Sir James Thornhill (1675–1734) was accused of posing the models at Kneller's Academy to correspond to the figures in his great mural scheme at Greenwich Hospital – a ploy that did not go unnoticed by Sir Godfrey Kneller (1649–1723).[8] These early drawing schools generally functioned in the evening at the end of the working day. They were therefore accessible in terms of time, if not always cost, to both artisans and artists.

Compared to Continental Europe, academies of art were slow to take root in Britain. In Italy an institution of this kind was founded in Florence in 1562 and in France, despite the hostility of the guilds, an Academy was established by 1648.[9] In Britain the first moves towards such an institution was to be reserved for the aristocratic elite. One of the earliest of these was the Academy Royal

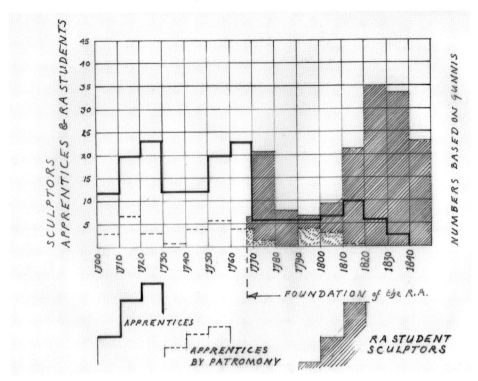

FIGURE 132. Graph based on details in Gunnis (1951) showing the decline in the number of sculptors who served time as apprentices and the rise in the number of student sculptors who enrolled in the RA Schools from 1769. Although the Schools were in London students were drawn from all over the British Isles. (Drawing: author)

proposed, but not realised, by Edmund Bolton in 1617. His "Academ Roial" was to be based in Windsor Castle and its members were to be entitled to wear special ribbons and badges and to amend their coat of arms to show this distinction (rather like the Order of the Garter). This honour was to have three levels of membership. The lowest and most significant in terms of scholarship were, appropriately known as "the Essentials". Inigo Jones was to be numbered amongst this category, but although such luminaries were to be included, the visual arts were not intended to be the primary concern of this Academy. More relevant for our purposes here was the *Museum Minervae* proposed by Prince Charles in 1636 which was to be confined to those "who could prove themselves gentlemen". The syllabus was to be wide, encompassing both the arts and the sciences and including: modern languages, mathematics, painting, architecture, riding, fortifications, antiquities and "the science of medals". This Academy, with its emphasis on the liberal arts (non-manual occupations) was placed under the direction of Sir Francis Kingstone whose house in Covent Garden provided a home for the institution.[10] The inclusion of painting and architecture ties in with Castiglione's belief that visual beauty may only be understood by those who were capable of representing it graphically.[11] This opinion was to persist into the nineteenth century by which time it had become a matter of both virtu and virtue. For Lord Kames (1817) "A taste in the fine arts goes hand in hand with the moral sense".[12]

The Museum Minervae founded in 1636 was, quite literally, a noble venture which was inevitable snuffed out by the Civil War. In the same decade, in 1640, the designer Sir Balthazar Gerbier established an academy at Whitefriars on similar lines except that the emphasis was on modern languages.[13] These somewhat general educational Academies would have had little relevance to an ordinary apprentice or journeyman – indeed they would have been excluded from them The great value of these aristocratic educational institutions was that they had the capacity to establish a visually educated elite, the potential patrons of the arts.

In London the first Academy that was inaugurated specifically for the visual arts was set up by the painter Sir Anthony Vandyck. It was he "who appointed one evening a week in Winter Time for the several branches [of art]: Painting, Sculpture, etc".[14] These gatherings were intended primarily for connoisseurs and on Vandyck's death in 1641 they ceased although "Vandyck's Club" as it became known, was not forgotten. At the Restoration this "Club" was revived by Sir Peter Lely as the Society of Virtuosi of St Luke, a Society that was to long outlive Lely, who died in 1680. From 1697, if not before, this "club" met at the *Rose Tavern* in the City where it continued to meet until 1703 and possibly later. Subsequent venues included *The Three Tuns, The Bumper Tavern, Spring Gardens, The Swan Tavern* and elsewhere. From this list, and indeed Gawen Hamilton's painting of one of these gatherings at the *Kings Arms* in 1735 the social, and indeed convivial nature of these meetings is evident.[15]

The first stirrings towards the establishment of a practical drawing school, rather than a "Society Academy", occurred in January 1657 when the "Picture Makers" affiliated to the Painter Stainers of London, sought to use the Lower Parlour in the Company's Hall "for an attendance to make use of drawing to the life". Sadly the Company did not agree to this request to establish an "Academy".[16] Another proposal, for a more generalised art school, was made by John Evelyn in his *Sculptura* (1662). His scheme was doubtless based upon the academies that he had seen on the continent in the course of his Grand Tour (1643–1647). Evelyn proposed:

"that a house be taken with a sufficient number of rooms: two contiguous to each other for drawing and modelling from life; [another] one for architecture and perspective, one for drawing from plaster; one for receiving the works of the school; one for the exhibition of them, and others for a housekeeper and servants. That some fine pictures, casts, bustos, bas-relievos, intaglios and prints be purchased".[17]

All this, and much more, was to prove remarkably close to the specification for the foundation, over a century later, of the Royal Academy Schools (Appendix XVI). John Evelyn's proposal did not come into being although in 1697/1698 William III "resolved to settle an academy to encourage the art of painting where are to be 12 masters" and for which admittance was to be "gratis". Despite Royal sponsorship this scheme also failed to materialise.[18] Although these earlier proposals were not to be realised a number of private schools in

FIGURE 133. Johann Zoffany, *A Life Class*, possibly at the St Martin's Lane Academy in *c.* 1761. The amphitheatre of seating has been a constant feature in the Academy's life drawing schools. The figure at the centre foreground shown looking out of the canvas may be the chaser George Michael Moser who taught drawing at St Martin's Lane and later at the RA. (Royal Academy of Arts, London)

which drawing formed an important part of the syllabus were established in the early eighteenth century. For example, Major John Ayres and Thomas Ayres ran a college in London which included gunnery, navigation and surveying; all these being disciplines in which drawing was of central importance.[19] Drawing as an aesthetic activity was a feature of the school run by the engraver Hubert Gravelot from his arrival in London in 1732 or 1733. this was based on his home address at the sign of the Pestle and Mortar, St James's Street, Covent Garden.[20] Small independent drawing schools and individual drawing masters were to become numerous in the course of the century and in late Georgian and early Victorian Britain they were omnipresent.

Many of these schools were intended primarily for amateurs for whom drawing was often a social accomplishment. In general middle class parents would seek to employ a tutor to teach these skills to their daughters. According to Wilkie Collins some fathers argued that these drawing tutors for young women should be selected with care: "We don't want genius in this country unless it is accompanied by respectability". In contrast sons could be submitted to the moral hazards of a drawing school. In Georgian England a more relaxed attitude prevailed. James Vertue (fl. 1744–1760), the brother of the engraver George Vertue (1684–1756: the "English Vasari"), ran a drawing school in Bath. Its social nature is indicated by the fact that it only functioned during "the season" – Vertue being away from the Spa between August and Michaelmas.[21] Although these establishments were attended by women, male students were also present as drawing was important for a commission in the army or navy. Furthermore the surviving Trade Directories show that drawing masters also taught fencing and French. Early in his life, whilst living in York, the young George Stubbs RA (1724–1806) "practiced French and fencing" suggesting that he may have had thoughts of becoming such a tutor.[22]

Following on from the "Clubs" established by Vandyck (d. 1641) and Sir Peter Lely (d. 1680) the fashionable portrait painter Sir Godfrey Kneller (1649?–1723) inaugurated an academy for life drawing. The membership met in his house in Great Queen Street, Lincoln's Inn Fields in London. The first meeting took place on St Luke's Day (18 October – patron saint of painters) in 1711. More than 60 men attended this gathering to select a "Governor", Kneller being elected for the role with some inevitability. To give some semblance of democracy to the proceedings 12 Directors were also chosen by ballot. Among these were Louis Laguerre, James Thornhill, Jonathan Richardson Snr, Thomas Gibson, Francis Bird and Nicholas Dorignay. Others who were present on this occasion included James Gibbs, George Vertue, Michael Dahl, Bernard Lens, John Wootton, Peter Tillemans, Joseph Goupy and John Vanderbank. Although the membership fee was 1 guinea for the season (presumably Autumn to Spring) not all who joined this club-of-a-school were established independent professional craftsmen or artists. For example, three of Kneller's assistants attended – namely Byng, Weedman, and Surartz; but they may have been granted concessionary rates. Despite the practical nature of these academies, some of the social features of the "clubs" formed by Vandyck and Lely were retained. For example, James Seymour the banker (and father of the sporting painter), and Owen McSwiney, Irish dramatist and theatre manager, were members, as was Sir Richard Steele.[23]

In an "anonymous" letter in *The Spectator* (4 Dec 1712) Steele makes reference to his membership of this body. Indeed he goes further and retells the story of the Virgin Mary descending to earth to have her portrait painted by St Luke. The essayist then goes on to suggest that, should she return, a visit to England would be advisable because this country abounds with "face-painters" of distinction. Above all, the "present President, Sir Godfrey Kneller, from his improvement since he arrived in this kingdom, would perform that office better than any foreigner living", an opinion shared by Alexander Pope (see p. 110 above).[24]

Sir James Thornhill was to succeed Kneller as "Governor" of this Academy on St Luke's Day 1716, despite the large minority who supported Laguerre's claim to the position. Thornhill's academy for drawing "from the naked" was located at his own home in James Street, Covent Garden. Here on the east side of the house this school was adjacent to "the back office" of the house and the "painting room [which] abutted ... Longford's [later Cock's] auction room in the Piazza".[25] Even before Kneller's death in 1723 conflicts surfaced amongst the membership of this "club". According to Hogarth these "Jealousies" reached such a pitch that "the first proprietors put a padlock on their door" to exclude other subscribers. There followed a confusing situation in which a number of different drawing schools emerged and competed, one with another. Jan Vanderbank and his old master Louis Cheron headed a "rebellious party" that abandoned the Great Queen Street establishment and, in October 1720, set up a new school in an old meeting house in St Peter's Court (Fig. 134). According to Hogarth the Vanderbank Academy "introduced a female figure to make it more inviting" a feature which confirms that earlier life drawing schools had been confined to studying male models. Despite these attractions this Academy lasted only a few years before it was brought down by its treasurer who had embezzled its funds. As a consequence the vital equipment of the Vanderbank Academy was sequestrated to pay the rent. Among the items removed by the bailiffs to help reimburse the creditors was the great lamp without which evening classes could not function and the stove on which nude models relied for warmth.[26]

Kneller's Academy had included many foreign-born artists, not least its first "President". Despite this, yet another academy was established primarily for foreigners. This was based in the home of the painter Peter Hyde in Greyhound Court, Arundel Street in the Strand. Here the chasers John Valentin Haidt and George Michael Moser were recruited to teach drawing – a role that Moser would later fulfil at the St Martin's Lane Academy and then at the RA Schools. The Greyhound Court School was probably rather short-lived partly because Haidt "went as a missionary with a party of Moravians to Philadelphia" (see p. 400).[27] The school was to have an afterlife of far greater importance when it moved to new premises, a move that was duly announced in the public prints in October 1722:

> "This week the Academy for the improvement of Painters and Sculptors by drawing from the Naked, open'd in St Martin's Lane and will continue during the Winter as usual.
>
> N.B. The company have agreed not to draw on Mondays and Saturdays".[28]

The "N.B." in this announcement demonstrates the importance of the weekend and the residual tendency of this Academy to retain the social character of its predecessors. A matter of weeks after this move to St Martin's Lane, the Prince of Wales, attended by Sir Andrew Fountaine, visited this Academy in the evening when the model was sitting.[29] By this means some tacit royal approval was granted to the establishment.

Back in 1724 the factions that emerged following Kneller's death eventually resulted in Thornhill losing control of that Academy.[30] Despite which, on Thornhill's death in 1734, his son-in-law Hogarth inherited the "apparatus" from this establishment which included not only its plaster casts but also "a proper table for the figure [the nude model] to stand on, a large lamp, iron stove and benches in a circular form" (Fig. 133).[31] It seems that the old premises were too small to accommodate the many students that wished to attend. In 1734 it was proposed that "a number of artists should enter a subscription for the hire of a place large enough to admit thirty or forty persons drawing from the naked figure". This was agreed and a room was taken in Peter Court, St Martin's Lane (Fig. 134).[32] Hogarth certainly attended the St Martin's Lane Academy for his name occurs in one of the membership lists next to that of the enameller Alexander Gamble. Hogarth had served his apprenticeship as a silver-engraver with Ellis Gamble of Blue Cross Street, Leicester Fields, who was related to the enameller.[33] Associations of this kind show that master craftsmen and apprentices co-existed in these drawing schools. The membership lists also reveal the types of individuals, from a variety of backgrounds, who attended these classes. They ranged from Allan Ramsay to Charles Catton "the prince of coach painters", to John Linnel "an excellent carver in wood" (see Appendix XV).[34] The painter Francis Hayman encouraged his pupils to draw in this institution where they immodestly and collectively dubbed themselves "the seven British Worthies". Reynolds, although not a subscriber, is known to have painted a *"Candlelight"* at this school and encouraged his assistants Marchi, Parry, Berridge and Beach to attend between 1760 and 1767. With the foundation in 1768 of the Royal Academy and the opening of its Schools in 1769 most of these individuals transferred their allegiance.[35]

The St Martin's Lane Academy admitted a wide range of craftsmen and artists for whom drawing in the evening would have done much to develop and enrich their work. Perhaps inevitably painters working in these evening classes by artificial light developed a strong chiaroscuro. This was a feature which would later emphasise the revolutionary nature of *plein air* painting as it emerged in the train of more easily dispensed and used manufactured watercolours and tube oil paints.

In contrast to the artists and artisans, of which the membership of the St Martin's Lane Academy was composed, mention should be made of the Dilettanti Society which was founded in 1734. As its name implies this was an organisation most of whose members belonged to the elite and, like the earlier Society of Virtuosi, held assemblies that were primarily social events. Despite these somewhat limited objectives it was at one of these gatherings that, in 1738, the Society proposed the foundation of a "Grand Clubb for promoting the Arts of Drawing, Painting, etc". This newly formed "Clubb" held its

FIGURE 134. *The Old Academy*, St Peter's Court, St Martin's Lane, London. This woodcut appeared in William Sandby's *History of the Royal Academy* (Vol. I, 1862). (Private Collection)

first meeting at the *Alfred's Head* in Southampton Street, Covent Garden in November 1749.[36] In that year Robert Dingley (bapt. 1710–d. 1781), the son of a jeweller and goldsmith (Robert Snr, 1678–1741) proposed that the Society should found an Academy of Arts.[37]. He argued that such an institution should contain "works of art, particularly casts from the antique". This institution was to be situated "at the upper end of the King's Mews, Charing Cross … with apartments for professors". For this purpose a site was acquired together with "supplies of Portland Stone" for an edifice which was to be built "according to the exact measurements of the Temple of Pola" for a total cost of £3,189. A design for this building was drawn up by Stephen Riou in 1753. Despite these very practical steps and the support of Lord Halifax, the Treasury refused to contribute to the cost of this scheme which was therefore abandoned.[38]

As noted above a St Martin's Lane Academy was founded in the same year as the Dilettanti Society's proposals (1734). Some years later on 13 November 1753 members of the St Martin's Lane establishment held a meeting at the Turk's Head Tavern in Greek Street, Soho, to elect 24 individuals with a view to establishing a public academy. The successful candidates comprised 13 painters, three sculptors, one chaser, two engravers and two architects. This produced a total that was half a dozen short of the intended number but the relative numbers, representing each vocation, were later reflected in the composition of the membership of the Royal Academy. Following a few convivial meetings this group eventually voted to join forces with the Dilettante Society which seems to have become more "clubable" as its artistic ambitions declined or were deferred to others.[39]

In addition to these schemes a drawing school was established and supervised by the artist William Shipley (1715–1803), a gentleman who, like his father before him, had served an apprenticeship as a Stationer. He was to become, with his influential connections, a significant figure in the foundation of the [Royal] Society of Arts within which his school played an important part.[40] The Society was formed in 1754 – the very year that the Royal Danish Academy was established in Copenhagen.[41] Shipley was appointed the [Royal] Society of Arts' first Registrar and teacher of drawing for which: "it will be Mr Shipley's endeavour to introduce Boys and Girls of Genius to Masters and Mistresses in … Manufactures and for which the knowledge of Drawing is absolutely necessary".[42]

This emphasis on youth, both boys and girls, and this marriage of art and industry, was reflected in the "premiums" or prizes offered by the Society to youths under the age of 14 years – thus preceding the age at which most apprenticeships began. Other prizes were offered to individuals between the ages of 14 and 17.[43] The connection with commerce was well represented both by Shipley, as an ex-Stationer, and by the manufacturer Nicholas Crisp, who served as Trustees. Crisp's trade as a silversmith and owner of the Bow porcelain works offered a practical understanding of the importance of drawing. Both were significant figures in the foundation of the Society of Arts.[44]

Judging by the range of individuals who are known to have attended Shipley's drawing school the Society's educational activities were a success. Its students included artists of the distinction of the painter Richard Cosway (1740–1821) and the sculptor Joseph Nollekens (1737–1823). In recognition of Shipley's endeavours the Society of Arts awarded him its first gold medal: "For his public spirit which gave rise to its foundation" – the Society and the drawing school.

In addition to the drawing schools at St Martin's Lane and the Society of Arts there was a third centre in London of some importance. This was the Duke of Richmond's Gallery which was located in His Grace's town house in the Privy Garden, Westminster. This gallery was fitted-up "as a gratuitous school" for the reception of students "above twelve years of age" and was "furnished with a number of gesses or casts in Plaster of Paris moulded from the most select antique and modern figures". This gallery opened on 6 March 1758 and students who wished to attend were admitted on the recommendation of either Wilton or Cipriani, the two artists who were charged with its supervision. As a youth the painter Edward Edwards was admitted under the terms of the following reference.

> "To the Porter of the Statue Room at Richmond House:
>
> This is to certify, that the bearer Edward Edwards is above twelve years of age: that he is recommended by Mr Wilton as a sober diligent person who is desirous of drawing from the gesses and has promised to observe the rules of the room. He is therefore to be admitted.
>
> Joseph Wilton"[45]

The collection of casts in this gallery included 24 figures, five heads and three reliefs.[46] These casts survived the fire at Richmond House on 21 December 1791 but, by this date, the Gallery had lost something of its value as a result of the foundation of the Royal Academy in 1768. Casts from the antique were the *raison d'être* of the Duke of Richmond's gallery, and were an important part of the the Kneller/Thornhill and St Martin's Lane Academies. Furthermore it had been the intention that such casts would have formed a significant feature in the Dilettanti Society's proposed establishment. In this respect the RA was following a long established tradition, with its own collection of casts which by 1810, comprised no less than 250 examples.[47]

About the same time as the emergence of these various drawing schools and Academies there was a parallel growth of public exhibitions of contemporary art. In the first decades of the eighteenth century one of the nearest approximations to such shows were the street signs which enlivened the thoroughfares in the capital and other urban centres. At that time "the place of show and sale" for these emblems "was found in Harp Alley, Shoe Lane, where from end to end of that place the works of the candidates for public favour and employ were to be found".[48] These signs took both sculptural and pictorial form. With regard to the public exhibition of what was considered to be "polite art", the more successful artists at this time exhibited their work in the exhibition rooms that were often attached to their "painting rooms". The Italian word "studio" did not fully enter the English language until the nineteenth century. André Rouquet (1755) noted that "Every portrait painter in England has a room to shew his pictures, separate from that in which he works. People who have nothing to do, make it one of their morning amusements to go and see their collections".[49] A watercolour after Rowlandson of 1809 illustrates this type of arrangement very fully showing the artist emerging from his painting room to see the throng of visitors in his "shew room". The most successful painters of the day could afford rooms of this kind which were sometimes very substantial spaces – Gainsborough's exhibition room in Bath measured 20 ft 8 in × 24 ft (6.30 × 7.32 m).[50] As Rowlandson's illustration demonstrates (Fig. 135), these galleries often accommodated a great number of pictures, some of which were probably painted as "exhibition pieces", others might be "bought-in" old masters. The majority of these exhibits though were probably newly painted commissioned works which were customarily held back for some five months or more before they could receive their final varnishing. This was the origin of "Varnishing Day", the artist's pre-private view at the Royal Academy's summer exhibitions. With artists' "shew rooms" a charge was sometimes made for admission but their primary purpose was that of a "shop window" to attract future commissions, rather than for the sale of ready-made works.

The London-born painter Robert Edge Pine (c. 1730–1788) spent some years in Bath where his Westgate establishment boasted a "shew room".[51] Following peace with the rebellious Colonies, he crossed the Atlantic in 1783 "on speculation" with a view to painting portraits of "the heroes and patriots of the American Revolution". Inevitably Pine was to open a "shew room" in Philadelphia in 1786, possibly the first such establishment in the young Republic.[52] The American jurist Joseph Hopkinson (1770–1842) remembered visiting Pine's room where he saw the artist's canvas of *Media* murdering her children.[53] Similarly, the American painter Rembrandt Peale (1778–1860)

FIGURE 135. Thomas Rowlandson (1756–1827), *A Portrait Painter's Show Room* (1809). Watercolour drawing on paper (5 × 7 ⅞ in / 12.4 × 20.1 cm). The painter is shown, brush in hand emerging from his painting room to see the assembled visitors to his exhibition. (Ashmolean Museum, Oxford)

reminisced that on his final visit to England in 1832–33 he divided his time in London between his "painting room and the various galleries of pictures and rooms of the artists".[54]

These "shew rooms" were, in effect, one-man exhibitions but by the second quarter of the eighteenth century the artistic community in London began to develop a wish for mixed shows of contemporary art. One of the first such venues was to be the Foundling Hospital (established in 1739). Here in the reception rooms of the orphanage a permanent collection of recent work was to be shown and used as part of a multi-pronged fund raising device, a public gallery that attracted the rich and powerful. The architect to the Hospital, Theodore Jacobsen (d. 1772) contributed his "ground plot and front" as a gift and this established something of a precedent.[55] The chapel was embellished by the decorative plasterer William Wilton (d. 1768) and the wood carver Henry Keene (1726–1776) who designed and made the pulpit. The wrought iron was the gift of its smith, a "Mr Wragg".[56] The marble chimneypiece and overmantle in the Court Room was donated by its mason John Devall I (1701–1774) and the carved relief it contains was the gift of its sculptor John Michael Rysbrack (1694–1770).[57]

The orphanage was founded by Capt. Thomas Coram, and he was the subject of Hogarth's grand, yet sympathetic, portrait of 1740 which the artist presented to the charity. Those artists who contributed works to the Hospital were elected as special Governors who met annually on 5 November "to consider what further Ornaments may be added" to the burgeoning collection. As a result, Francis Hayman, Joseph Highmore, Thomas Hudson, George Moser, John Pine, Allan Ramsay, Samuel Wale, James Wills and Richard Wilson all presented "Performances in their different Professions for Ornamenting the Hospital". At a somewhat later date both Joshua Reynolds and Thomas Gainsborough were to contribute examples of their work but they were not destined to become Governors of the Charity.[58] This collection survives to this day, a reflection of the taste of its times.

In addition, and improbable though it may seem, another exhibition of contemporary works of art was located in the Vauxhall Pleasure Gardens on the south bank of the Thames in Lambeth and very accessible to London and Westminster. This commercial enterprise was established by Jonathan Tyers who acquired a lease of the land in *c.* 1728. As a focus for resort and amusement the Garden's pavilions were decorated with a collection of pictures which eventually totalled some 150 canvases – many by Francis Hayman whose principal patron was Tyers. This enlightened proprietor also commissioned Roubiliac to create (in 1738) his very fine seated marble figure of Handel now in the Victoria and Albert Museum.[59]

These two very different examples show that George II's London did not lack collections of contemporary art on continuous public display. However, for practising artists, what was most needed was an annual and temporary show in which they could exhibit their latest works. Accordingly, at their annual dinner at the Foundling Hospital on 5 November 1759, those assembled determined to announce that:

> "A general meeting of all Artists in the several branches of Painting, Sculpture, Architecture, Engraving, Chasing, Seal Cutting and Medalling, be held at the Turk's Head Tavern in Gerrard Street, Soho, on Monday the 12th inst. at Six in the evening to consider of a proposal for the honour and advancement of the Arts ..."[60]

In response to the meeting at the Turk's Head, it was agreed that an exhibition should be organised. For this purpose the Society of Arts provided its "Great Room" as the venue. The exhibition was comprised of works by the "principal artists" of the day and these were "blended" with works submitted for the Society's premiums.[61] The exhibition, the very first of its kind in Britain, opened on 21 April 1760 and admittance was free but the catalogue was priced at six pence. This "blending" of work by established artists, students and others was not seen as a success, and the whole ensemble was described as being "far from select".[62] Partly for this reason another group of individuals was formed in 1762 which by 1765 was known as the Free Society of Artists. Their exhibitions became annual events and these continued down to 1783 at various addresses.

Even before the formation of the Free Society a rather more significant exhibiting group was established under the leadership of Sir William Chambers and Sir Joseph Wilton. This organisation, known as the Society of Artists of Great Britain, opened its first show in Spring Gardens on 9 May 1761.[63] The catalogue, with its frontispiece by Hogarth, provided the "mode of admission".[64] Although Hogarth exhibited in the first show he did not do so the following year. In that year (1762) he conspired with Bonnel Thornton to set up an exhibition of sign-board art as a persiflage of the "serious" art exhibitions (see p. 211).[65]

In contrast to the well-established shows of "old master" paintings organised by art dealers, these temporary exhibitions of contemporary work were "a spectacle new to this kingdom". So new in fact that the organisers were compelled to find suitable venues in pre-existing spaces.[66] Almost invariably it was found that auction rooms met this need. For example, when the Society of Artists of Great Britain asked Joshua Reynolds and James Paine to locate premises for their first exhibition of 1761 they identified Mr Cock's auction rooms in Spring Gardens as a suitable venue – which, as we have seen, was to be the location that was used.[67] In 1764 and, again in 1765, the Free Society of Artists exhibited in the rooms of the auctioneer "Mr Moreing" in Maiden Lane, Covent Garden.[68] In following years, the Free Society's exhibitions were held in "Mr Christie's" rooms in Cumberland House, Piccadilly (1767–1774), near the Black Bear Inn, also in Piccadilly (1775–1776) and intermittently thereafter at Spring Gardens and at the Lyceum.

Contemporaries were of the opinion that the exhibitions organised by the Free Society were "insignificant" and this became very apparent once the Royal Academy exhibitions commenced in 1769. In contrast to the RA's summer exhibitions those of the Free Society included items: "that could not be classed as works of art, such as pieces of needlework, subjects in human hair, cut paper and such similar productions as deserve not the recommendation of public exhibition".[69]

Neither was the Free Society alone in sponsoring shows of such miscellaneous material. By the mid-1760s, the Society of Arts was offering premiums "for the best examples of quilting in the Indian manner".[70]

Any confusion that may well have existed between the Free Society with its "indiscriminate" shows by "inferior practitioners", and the more polite exhibitions organised by the Society of Artists of Great Britain demanded a clear distinction. This was most easily achieved by a fresh start. This radical step took the form of a mass departure from the Society of Artists of Great Britain by many of its principal members. Their group letter of resignation was dated 10 November 1768, a matter of days before the first steps were taken towards the foundation of the Royal Academy. Among those who resigned were Joseph Wilton, Edward Penny, Richard Wilson, Benjamin West, William Chambers, George Michael Moser, Paul Sandby and Francis M. Newton.[71] Days later a delegation comprised of Cotes, Moser, West and Chambers visited the King in person carrying a "Memorial" or petition dated 10 December 1768. It proposed the establishment of a Royal Academy of Artists.[72] This foundation was to include painters, sculptors and architects which, as a body, was to establish "a well regulated School of Design". From this it is evident that "Design" was to take precedence over the processes of making. This shift in emphasis, from the making of a work of art to its conception, provided some individuals with an opportunity to improve their status. For example Reynolds had complained that "the place which I have the honour of holding, of the King's principal painter, is a place of not so much profit and of near equal dignity with his Majesty's rat-catcher".[73]

The crafts which had provided the fundamental basis on which many of these artists had built their careers, were to be relegated for reasons that were not always idealistic. In addition to the Schools, the petition also stated that the Academy was to organise "an Annual Exhibition, open to all artists of distinguished merit". Eventually, in response to this "Memorial", Sir William Chambers drew up a constitution for the Academy and this document was duly signed by the King at the meeting of 10 December 1768. With the Monarch's imprimateur the Academy held its first assembly that same day.[74] For George III royal patronage of this institution was far more than a matter of conferring his name and the Royal Arms to the Academy's stationery. The King's involvement was to be active for his Majesty was to retain "in his own hands" the right of approving all artists elected to the RA. Furthermore on 13 April 1796 Farington noted in his *Diary* that "The King passed a morning in considering" the RA's accounts.[75] This was not without self-interest. Although by this date the Academy was financially independent, as a result of the revenues from its exhibitions, the King had met its financial shortfall down to 1781. Essential though this support had been the King's subventions to his foundation over that first dozen years represented an enlightened yet comparatively modest total of £5,116.[76]

The next step was to find premises for this newly-founded institution. At first "*pro tempore*" the RA Schools occupied Aaron Lambe's auction rooms in Pall Mall opposite Market Lane.[77] In January 1769 it was agreed that the first of the RA's exhibitions would be held from 21 April to 27 May that year. The hanging committee for that first show comprised Paul Sandby, Edward Penny, George Barret, George Michael Moser and Francis Milner Newton – with the exception of Moser, all were painters.[78] The exhibition consisted of 136 works of which 79 were contributed by RAs and 57 by others. The show included 40 portraits, 48 landscapes, 22 history pieces, 5 animal or flower pieces, 9 sculptures, 2 specimens of die-sinking and 10 architectural designs.[79] Watercolours appeared in these exhibitions under sufferance in that the RA's constitution did not allow artists who worked exclusively in this medium to become Academicians.[80] In some ways the second division status of this art form is analogous to the disdain that Stainers had laboured under in earlier centuries.

The Academy's accommodation in Pall Mall may have been *pro tempore* but the programme of lectures delivered there were far from extempore. As these were to be approved by the RA Council before they were delivered, this inevitably resulted in written dissertations. The first of these was given by the anatomist Dr William Hunter at the Pall Mall address on 6 October 1769.[81] A more permanent home was found for the Academy when George III provided rooms in Somerset House where his foundation moved on 14 January 1771. At this address a library was established and in 1773 George Michael Moser moved into an apartment there as the Academy's first Keeper; a post he retained until his death in 1783. The exhibitions continued to be shown for some years at the old Pall Mall address until these too were moved to Somerset House; the first of which opened on 1 May 1780 – see Appendix XVI.

Concurrent with these developments the Incorporated Society of Artists continued with their exhibitions and instituted their own rival art education establishment. Furthermore the Society petitioned the King for support which, in his genial way, George III granted. He did so on the grounds that he had no wish "to encourage one set of men more than another". As a mark of good faith the King visited the Incorporated Society's next exhibitions. Further support for the Society came from the Duke of Richmond who placed his gallery of casts under its supervision.[82] Significantly, the Society retained the loyalty of some of the finest artists of the day. In 1769, the year of the Academy's first exhibition, Zoffany exhibited ten works with the Society and both Wright of Derby and Stubbs showed canvases there.[83] Although these three painters were to become Academicians there was a view that it was not possible to remain loyal to both organisations simultaneously. At a somewhat later date Sir Joseph Banks adopted a similar position with regard to membership of scientific establishments like the Royal Society and the Royal Institution.[84] There was certainly, at best, a sense of competition between the Academy and the Society. Edward Edwards (1808) makes disparaging reference to "the turbulent gentlemen of the Society" – notwithstanding the presence of female members, but perhaps they were less fractious.[85]

In contrast to the Academy the exhibitions organised by the Incorporated Society admitted works by amateurs. This resulted in it showing items like "An Old Man's head done with a hot iron [poker work], a "vase of flowers in shell-work" and a portrait of a lady "composed of human hair".[86] These were exactly the types of exhibits that the Academy sought to exclude. In 1769 the RA Council determined that "no needlework, artificial flowers, cut paper, shell-work, or any such baubles be admitted" to their exhibitions and that all easel paintings should be framed (see Fig. 16).[87]

Although, as noted above, the Academy received support from the crown its exhibitions generated an important source of income. Also the cost of setting up the Schools was minimised. On its foundation George Michael Moser, with some slight-of-hand, removed the "furniture, anatomical figures, statues, etc." from the St Martin's Lane school and transferred them to the RA Schools in Pall Mall.[88] In addition, the royal purse spared no expense in equipping the Academy schools. For example, the RA commissioned a lay figure from a man named Addison for an estimated cost of £80 which, after negotiations, cost on delivery £90.[89] By way of comparison, the Incorporated Society purchased an articulated figure of this kind for just £20. It seems that by the late 1790s French craftsmen had developed a fine reputation for making such manikins. This may explain why studio props of this type were to be included amongst works of art exempted from duty when imported by artists – see p. 168 above.[90]

The whole emphasis of the Academy Schools at their foundation, like that of its precursors, was drawing. For this reason the Schools employed Moser to teach this discipline and also recruited, in addition to the anatomist Dr Hunter, the surgeon William Cheselden to assist with the study of bones. Some of the osteological drawings made under Cheselden's supervision remain in the Academy's library. At its foundation it was agreed that "an antique academy [plaster casts] and a school for [drawing from] the living model" should be set up. These schools were described by John Deare (1759–1798) as follows: "There is one large room for the Plaster Academy, one for the Life, where two

FIGURE 136. Benjamin West (1738–1820). A sketch design for the installation of the artist's vast canvas (16 ft 9 in × 22 ft/510 × 671 cm) *Christ Rejected by the Jews*. The cinematic scale and presentation of this ambitious work served, in effect, as its world premier. Even before it was shown publically West claimed to have been offered 8000 guineas for the canvas (Farington *Diary* 18 January 1813). *Christ Rejected* was eventually shown, from June to late autumn 1814 in the Great Room at 125 Pall Mall, Westminster, which had previously served as a home for the Royal Academy. (Pierpont Morgan Library, New York City)

men sit two hours each night by turns every week ... [and] the plaster figures are placed on pedestals that run on casters".[91]

During their probationary term students were compelled to spend some time in the plaster academy before graduating to the life class. If, after drawing from the living model, students failed to reach the required standard they were ejected and returned to the plaster academy or even rusticated. Students were admitted to the schools as Probationers on the basis of the merits of a drawing, a model or an architectural design that was submitted to the Keeper for evaluation.[92] In theory attendance as a full-time student was for six years – a year less than for most apprenticeships. In practice students remained at the Schools for four or five years although their status as students lasted a lifetime. For this reason prizes continued to be won by individuals who may have left over a decade before. After 1800 this position was regularised and student status was limited to ten years.[93]

The hours during which the schools were open to students were laid down with some precision:

> "The schools shall be open every day (excepting Sundays and times of vacation), the Antique school from ten o'clock in the morning until three in the afternoon; and both schools [the antique and the life schools] shall be open in the evening for two hours., viz. from five o'clock to seven in summer, from six to eight in the winter. The Painting school from nine o'clock in the morning until four in the afternoon in winter and from nine till five in the summer".[94]

The reference to the evening hours for the life class followed the practice of earlier schools like the St Martin's Lane Academy. The American painter Thomas Sully (1783–1872) was to recall that in the months he spent in London between 1809 and 1810 "he laboured painting through the day, and drawing at the academy in the evening".[95] The hours for the other Schools were presumably comparable to those for Painting. A further regulation stipulated that "None but members of the Academy, or students of the school shall be admitted when the female model is sitting; nor shall any student under twenty years of age (unless he be married) be allowed to study from that model".[96] Members of the royal family were necessarily exempted from these restrictions on their Academy. Outside the academy some successful artists could afford to employ models privately – Romney famously recruited Emma Hart, Lady Hamilton, to sit for him.[97] Although the whole question of nude female models may arouse some curiosity, the Academy also employed male models.

At the RA Schools, its first porter John Malin also worked as one of its models, twin jobs that he had previously fulfilled at the St Martin's Lane Academy – and before that he was a Thames waterman.[98] Another of those early Academy models was James Dyer, a trooper in the Horse Guards. George White was a favourite model of Sir Joshua Reynolds' who would refer to him as his "beggarman". In fact he was, as Moser described him, a paviour by trade "exerting himself in the laborious occupation of thumping down stones in the street". For male models a pronounced musculature was evidently in demand;

attributes that the earlier occupations of these men would have developed.[99] This was taken to absurd lengths by Roubiliac for his figure of Hercules in which, it was alleged, the legs of a sedan chairman were combined with the arms of a waterman.[100]

It seems that male models were employed at the RA at 2s-6d an evening. In 1796 Edwards Edwards proposed that this should be increased to 3s, and this was agreed – a substantial sum for a couple of hours work.[101] Female models were even better paid, a prodigious half a guinea an evening. Some of these models were employed by both the Academy and the Incorporated Society. One female model was paid by the Society as much as £1-12-6d to model, but then she was also instructed to spy on the RA. In general the Society paid its female models 7s-6d an evening. In both institutions it was established practice "That the artist who sets the model shall preside … every evening … [and] take care that due decorum be preserved".[102] This was no idle observation and accounts of indiscipline amongst the students were recorded. Note was taken in 1795 that some of the youths behaved "very rudely; and that they have a practice of throwing bread, allowed them by the Academy for rubbing out, at each other". This lack of discipline increased the bread bill for the schools by some 16 shillings a week.[103] The following year it was reported that "The Plaister Academy is now in a very well regulated State" in accordance with the expectations of the "Memorial" or petition of 1768.[104]

The emphasis on drawing from casts of classical statuary and from the naked male and female figure accorded well with the burgeoning of Neo-Classicism and, some decades later, the Greek Revival. This was reinforced by Reynolds who, though primarily a portrait painter, subscribed to the prevailing view that history painting and, by extension, classically inspired sculpture, were the most important themes for the "liberal" artist. Such a mind-set also implied a degree of Classical learning. For a man like Reynolds this academic vantage-point could result in a blinkered outlook. On a visit to Brussels in 1785 to see the pictures from the 66 suppressed monasteries and other religious houses he wrote to the Duke of Rutland describing these works of art. In this letter Reynolds stated that he was "much disappointed in the pictures … they are the sadest trash that ever were collected together" works by Rubens and Vandyck being "the only tolerable pictures".[105] Evidently the fifteenth century panels painted by Jan van Eyck or Roger van der Weyden did not accord with the taste of the President of the Royal Academy.

Having looked at the training of artists via various apprenticeships, or their education in the Academy in London, an alternative regional route became possible for painters. In this respect the Norwich School is particularly significant. In contrast to Norwich, Bristol supported many artists but in that West Country port city there was simply a concatenation of individuals, rather than a school as such.[106] There are several possible explanations for the cohesiveness that was achieved by artists in Norwich by the early nineteenth century. In the late eighteenth century civic portraiture was shown in the city's St Andrew's Hall – an early provincial example of a public exhibition space. Also the Norwich Society of Artists was founded in 1803 one of the first such organisations to be established in England outside London.[107] With the benefit of hindsight the Norwich School can be seen to have been founded by John Crome (1768–1821). His training had taken the traditional route of a seven year apprenticeship with a coach- and sign-painter named Whistler.[108] However "Old Crome's" son John Berney Crome (1794–1842) received a Classical education at Norwich Grammar where he distinguished himself academically and, as the School Captain, delivered the annual oration in Latin. Nevertheless he was to follow in his father's footsteps and become a painter. This brings us to the important part that this Grammar School played in the emergence of these painters in Norwich. The headmaster, Dr Foster, took an active interest in the visual arts to the extent that, in 1805, he was elected Vice President of the Norwich Society of Painters.[109] Furthermore the teacher of mathematics, Charles Hodgson (*c.* 1770–1856), was himself a distinguished artist who exhibited not only locally but also at the Royal Academy and the British Institution.[110] Most significant of all was "Old Crome's" presence as the art master in the school.[111] In these circumstances it is no coincidence that, in addition to the younger Crome, many other artists who were to form part of this group attended this particular educational establishment. In sequence, by date of birth, these included: John Sell Cotman (1782–1842), James Stark (1794–1859), George Vincent (1796–*c.* 1835), Joseph Stannard (1797–1830), John Berney Ladbroke (1803–1879) and Edward Thomas Daniell (1804–1842).[112] Of these, Vincent and Ladbroke were to serve apprenticeships with "Old Crome" whilst Stannard trained with the elder Ladbroke. The cohesiveness of this group of painters was reinforced when John Crome (1768–1821) and Robert Ladbroke (1769–1842) married a pair of sisters whose maiden name was Berney. Consequently in the next generation these artists were united by familiar connection, old school friendships, or apprenticeships.

One member of this group of artists was Edward Daniell (1804–1842). He initially pursued an academic course graduating from Balliol College, Oxford in 1828. By 1832 he was made a deacon in the Church of England, and in 1833 was admitted to the priesthood in Norwich Cathedral. Following his ordination, he was appointed curate of St Mark's, North Audley Street, London, a church in a fashionable district close to Grosvenor Square. Nevertheless Daniell was to abandon his calling as a clergyman and develop his true vocation as a painter, not that he had ever ceased to paint. During his vacations as an undergraduate he continued to receive training as an easel painter from Joseph Stannard.[113]

In provincial Norfolk, many of these artists, even at this late date, experienced a thorough training through apprenticeships with local painters. This nexus of friendship, education and training established a recognisable regional idiom. In the long run the national, and even international, trends established by the Royal Academy and similar institutions would reduce the potential for such localised styalistic idioms or schools of painting. As early as 1801 Richard Warner, writing from Bath, observed that London was "the central point where the arts originate, and from whence they ramify".[114]

The governance of the Royal Academy, in its first decades, was a matter of curiosity and comment by contemporaries. For them Sir William Chambers was George III's viceroy over that institution, Joseph Farington was compared to "Warwick the Kingmaker" and Reynolds its duly elected President.[115] Beneath this triumvirate the "other ranks" were no less remarkable. At its inception the Academy was composed of 25 men and two women, both of Germanic origin. As a body these individuals were from socially differing backgrounds, many having served apprenticeships in a variety of trades. The resulting cross-fertilisation of ideas and skills offered a dynamic vitality that was destined to be vitiated. In this respect Reynolds's role may be seen as ambivalent. Under his presidency the Academy developed a focus, and yet his *Discourses* may be seen to have cultivated a doctrine which, by the same token, narrowed its horizons.

If the educational role of the RA was to prove somewhat stifling, what of the exhibitions that this institution, along with others, organised? As part of the London social season portraiture inevitably loomed large on the walls of Somerset House and elsewhere. Of even more significance was the growing tendency amongst artists to produce "exhibition pieces" speculatively which encouraged the production of works that were highly visible. Notoriously artists such as Turner, seeing their canvases almost disappear from sight amongst a multitude of works, famously used "varnishing day" to add a startling touch. Shock value had become a consideration.

Perhaps the first example of a truly provocative exhibition was organised by the fictitious Society of Sign Painters and opened in Bonnel Thornton's rooms in Bow Street on 23 March 1762 (see p. 211 above). This show of "wooden originals" was put together with William Hogarth's active participation with many of the works being by Hagarty – a self-evident pseudonym. The press reports of this event which appeared at this time reveal both consternation and confusion.[116] Admittedly specialist art criticism was in its infancy as were the exhibitions on which it was to become reliant. Similarly specialist art journals would emerge in concert with these public shows. Amongst these first publications were the *Artist's Repository* (from 1785), the *Annals of Fine Arts* (1816–1820) and *The Library of Fine Arts* (1831–1834).[117]

Apprenticeships offered training in numerous crafts, a surprising number of which were applicable to many aspects of the visual arts in the client economies of pre-industrial Britain. In such a context the maker was generally subordinate to the patron; a situation in which the client actively participated in the realisation of a commissioned work. With the rise of consumerism and industrialisation apprenticeships declined and the purchaser of a given product may have influenced, but did not take part in, its creation. Concurrent with this evolving situation, the Academies of art attempted to secure the position of artists both socially and in terms of their work. This historical progression was far from neutral in its impact but the response of artists and their art to changed circumstances is beyond the scope of this book.

Notes

[1]   Joseph Conrad *Lord Jim*, Blackwood's Magazine, 1900: 2008 reprint, p. 33. The youth of these nautical apprentices is emphasised in this account where they are referred to as being "no higher that the back of [a] chair"
[2]   E. P. Thomson (1963) 1991
[3]   William Dunlap (1834) 1969, Vol. I, p. 321, Vol. II, Pt I, p. 75
[4]   Jacob Simon ed. 2003, pp. 1–21 for Johnson/Whittle and for Boulton see Holger Hoock (2003) 2009, p. 92
[5]   John Gwnn 1749, pp. 22–31
[6]   D. G. Allan "Artists & society in the eighteenth century" in Allan and Abbots eds, 1992, chapter 6, p. 92
[7]   James Ayres 1998, fig. 309 for a reproduction of a drawing by Joseph Rose II (1744–1799)
[8]   William Sandby1862, Vol. I, p. 13. The Greenwich murals were painted between 1708 and 1727
[9]   Nikolaus Pevsner 1940
[10] Ian Donaldson 2011, pp. 365–366; W. H. Pyne 1823–24, Vol. II, pp. 37–38
[11] Baldassare Castiglione's *The Courtier* first published in English in 1561
[12] Henry Home, Lord Kames *Elements of Criticism*, 9th edition, 2 vols, London, 1817, Vol. I, p. 6; cited by Trevor Fawcett 1974, p. 4
[13] William Sandby 1862, p. 19, citing Horace Walpole
[14] James Fenton 2006, p. 49 citing George Vertue
[15] W. T. Whitley 1928, Vol. I, pp. 74–76, Vol. II, p. 242 – Hamilton's *Conversation of Virtuosi* ...
[16] W. A. D. Englefield (1923) 1936, p. 94; Alan Borg 2005, p. 63

[17] William Sandby 1862, p. 19 citing Evelyn 1662 – see also James Fenton 2006, chapter 2

[18] James Fenton 2006, p. 50

[19] Kim Sloan 2000, p. 105; Ewan Clayton 2013, pp. 164–165

[20] W. T. Whitley 1928, Vol. I, p. 94; Hans Hammelman 1975, pp. 38–46

[21] For drawing masters of "respectability" see Wilkie Collins *The Woman in White*, 1860, First Epoch, chapter 3. Collins's grandfather was an art dealer and writer, his father William Collins a well known painter. For Bath see Susan Sloman 2002, pp. 6–7.

[22] Ozias Humphry and Joseph Mayer *A Memoir of George Stubbs*, Anthony Mould ed., London, 2005, p. 36. In the 1920s when the author's mother attended the Byam Shaw School of Art in London, fencing was on the curriculum for purposes of improving the strength of the brush hand and arm

[23] William Sandby 1862, p. 21; W. T. Whitley 1928, Vol. I, p. 8

[24] *The Spectator* edition of 1793, Vol. VII, pp. 327–330. This letter reflects Steele's broad knowledge of painting across Europe "Italy may have the preference of all other nations for history painting; Holland for drolls and a neat finished manner of working, France for gay, jaunty, fluttering pictures; and England for portraits ..." p. 328

[25] William Sandby 1862, Vol. I, pp. 13, 21–23

[26] *Ibid.*, Vol. I, pp. 21, 22, 25; W. T. Whitley 1928, Vol. I, p. 15

[27] Edward Edwards, 1808, p. xxi

[28] William Sandby 1862, Vol. I, p. 21; W. T. Whitley 1928, Vol. I, p. 18

[29] *Ibid.* Sir Andrew Fountain was a well-known connoisseur of the arts whose seat, Narford Hall, Norfolk, contained his collection which was dispersed by Christies in 1884

[30] William Sandby 1862, Vol. I, p. 22 – quoting Hogarth in John Ireland's *Hogarth Illustrated* 1791

[31] *Ibid.*, Vol. I, p. 24; Martin Postle ed. 2011, p. 214

[32] W. H. Pyne 1823–24, Vol. I, pp. 23–38

[33] W. T. Whitley 1928, Vol. I, p. 17; Jerry White 2012, p. 101

[34] W. H. Pyne 1823–24, Vol. I, pp. 38–39

[35] W. T. Whitley 1928, Vol. I, p. 150; Nicholas Penny ed. 1986, pp. 57–58

[36] W. T. Whitley 1928, Vol I, pp. 24–25, 157

[37] See *DNB*

[38] William Sandby 1862, Vol. I, pp. 24–25; Charles Saumarez-Smith 2012, p. 26

[39] Edward Edwards 1808, p. xxii and W. T. Whitley 1928, Vol. I, pp. 157–159

[40] Shipley's brother Jonathan Shipley was Dean of Winchester and later Bishop of St Asaph. The elder brother's home, Twyford House, Hampshire was where Benjamin Franklin began his autobiography in 1771. For the Royal Society see Allen and Abbott eds 1992, p. 220. For Shipley's apprenticeship see Jerry White 2012, p. 101.

[41] Allen and Abbott eds 1992, p. 56; W. T. Whitley 1928, Vol. I, p. 351

[42] *Ibid.*, Vol. II, p. 249

[43] Edward Edwards 1808, p. xii citing the regulations of the Society of Arts at its foundation in 1754

[44] Allan and Abbott eds 1992, p. 56

[45] William Sandby 1862, Vol. I, p. 31; W. T. Whitley 1928, Vol. I, p. 237

[46] Edward Edwards 1808, p. xvi, lists each of the plaster casts

[47] Holger Hoock (2003) 2009, p. 55

[48] "Paul Sandby and his Times" *The Library of Fine Arts* 1831, Vol. I, No. 11

[49] André Rouquet *The Present State of the Arts in England*, 1755, cited by Susan Sloman 1996, p. 132

50 *Ibid.*, p. 145
51 *Ibid.*, 1996, p. 148
52 William Dunlap (1834) 1969, Vol. I, p. 318. It is possible that James Sharples (*c.* 1751–1811), who was to produce a series of portraits of America's founding fathers, was inspired to venture across the Atlantic in 1798 following the precedent established by Pine in 1783. Certainly the two portrait painters were in Bath, England in 1781–82; Robin Simon 1987, p. 228
53 William Dunlap (1834) 1969, Vol I, p. 318 quoting Hopkinson's letter to Dunlap of 6 May 1833
54 *Ibid.*, Vol II, Pt I, p. 57. Rembrandt Peale was the second son of Charles Wilson Peale
55 Howard Colvin 1995
56 *Ibid.*, Keene, though "bred to the profession of architecture" probably received his early training from his father Henry Keene, a woodworker
57 Ingrid Roscoe *et al.* eds 2009
58 Kit Wedd 2004, pp. 18, 19, 14, 25, 69
59 Michael Snodin ed. 1984, pp. 82–83 and 87–93. Also H. A. Hammelmann "The Art of Francis Hayman *Country Life* 14 Oct 1954. The number of paintings at Vauxhall is given in Holger Hoock (2003) 2009, p. 7. See also p. 227
60 W. T. Whitley 1928, Vol. I, p. 165. *The Turk's Head* was a regular meeting place for such ventures. It was there on 13 November 1759 that a group or artists met with a view to establishing an Academy – see p. 434 above
61 William Sandby 1862, p. 33
62 Edward Edwards 1808, pp. xxiv–xxv
63 Sidney C. Hutchinson 1968, pp. 37, 38. In 1765 this Society gained a Royal Charter and as such became "The Incorporated Society of Artists of Great Britain"
64 Edward Edwards 1808, pp. xxiv; William Sandby 1862, p. 34
65 W. T. Whitley 1928, Vol. I, pp. 174–180. Much of the catalogue and some of the reviews of the exhibition of signboard art is reprinted in the Appendix to Jacob Larwood and John C. Hotten 1866; see also James Ayres 1996, pp. 14–15
66 Edward Edwards 1808, Vol. I, p. xxvii
67 W. T. Whitley 1928, Vol. I, p. 172. The Society was charged £40 for renting this space for one month
68 William Sandby 1862, pp. 35–36. John Moreing is listed, at that address, as a cabinet maker in 1768; Ambrose Heal (1953) 1988
69 Edward Edwards 1808, p. xxxix
70 W. T. Whitley 1928, Vol. I, p. 192 – a probable reference to quilted Indian chintz
71 Sidney C. Hutchinson 1968, p. 40
72 *Ibid.*, p. 43 which quotes the "Memorial" in full
73 Iain Pears (1988) 1991, p. 137
74 Edward Edwards 1808, pp. xxxiv–xxxv
75 William Sandby 1862, pp. 59–60; Joseph Farington, p. 523 13 April 1796
76 Holger Hoock (2003) 2009, p. 34
77 Sidney Hutchinson 1968, p. 51
78 Edward Edwards 1808, pp. xxxvi–xxxvii
79 William Sandby 1862, p. 131
80 D. Clifford (1970) 1976, p. 28
81 Sidney C. Hutchinson 1968, p. 51
82 W. T. Whitley 1928, Vol. I, p. 237

[83] *Ibid.*, Vol. I, p. 229

[84] Richard Holmes *The Age of Wonder*, London, 2008

[85] Edward Edwards, 1808, pp. xxxi–xxxii. Female members of the Society included Catherine Read, Miss Benwell, Mrs Grace, Miss Gardiner and Miss Black. Two of the founder members of the Royal Academy were female, namely Angelica Kauffman and Mary Moser (Mrs Hugh Lloyd)

[86] W. T. Whitley 1928, Vol. I, p. 229

[87] Robert C. Alberts 1978, p. 96

[88] William Sandby 1862, Vol. I, p. 41

[89] W. T. Whitley 1928, Vol. I, pp. 189, 236, 278. The maker may have been Robert Addison a cabinet maker of Hanover Square; Ambrose Heal (1953) 1988

[90] James Ayres 1985, p. 42. The American painter and writer William Dunlap acquired his lay figure in Paris sometime between 1784 and 1787

[91] W. T. Whitley 1928, Vol. I, p. 276. The pedestals continued in use in the RA schools down to the 1960s and beyond

[92] Joseph Farington, p. 1317 4 December 1799

[93] Holger Hoock (2003) 2009, p. 53

[94] *The Library of Fine Arts* 1831–32, Vol. III, pp. 436–438

[95] William Dunlap (1834) 1969, Vol. II, Pt I, p. 122

[96] *The Library of Fine Arts*, p. 437, Resolution of the RA of 1769

[97] W. T. Whitley 1928, Vol. II, p. 144

[98] James Fenton 2006, p. 65; W. T. Whitley 1928, Vol. I, p. 183

[99] *Ibid.*, Vol. I, p. 281, Vol. II, p. 265

[100] J. T. Smith (1828) 1919, Vol. II, pp. 27–28

[101] Joseph Farington, p. 729 24 Dec 1796

[102] W. T. Whitley 1928, Vol. I, pp. 236, 237, 280

[103] Joseph Farington, p. 461 31 Dec 1795

[104] *Ibid.*, p. 703 27 Nov 1796

[105] W. T. Whitley 1928, Vol. II, p. 53

[106] A conclusion arrived at by the author as a result of conversations with Francis Greenacre who does not necessarily share this view

[107] Holger Hoock (2003) 2009, pp. 84, 89; Trevor Fawcett 1974, fig. 9

[108] Josephine Walpole 1997, p. 16

[109] *Ibid.*, pp. 16, 29, 64

[110] *Ibid.*, pp. 136,157

[111] *Ibid.*, p. 19

[112] *Ibid.*: for Cotman, p. 63, Stark p. 34, Vincent p. 43, Stannard p. 53, Ladbroke p. 47 and Daniell p. 157

[113] *Ibid.*, p. 157. Daniell's interest in painting had, as with others, begun at Norwich Grammar School

[114] Richard Warner, *History of Bath*, 1801, p. 224

[115] Kenneth Garlick and Angus Macintyre 1979, Vol. I, Introduction, p. xxv. See also Richard Wendorf 1996, p. 185 also citing Farington

[116] Jacob Larwood and John Camden Hotten 1866, pp. 512–526

[117] Holger Hoock (2003), 2009, p. 132

Chapter 20

CONCLUSION

"Art History" tends to encompass a relatively narrow band of human endeavour in that it may be more about "Art" than it is about "History". This is due to a tendency for Art History to be based upon a selection of examples of material culture that are exceptional culturally but are not necessarily characteristic in terms of history. In contrast, a history of the crafts may, by definition, be more inclusive and therefore has a greater potential to be based on what is historically typical of a given time and place.

Here the preceding chapters have been primarily concerned with the training of individuals and their creation of handmade objects. By extension some consideration has been given to the procedures that the various crafts deployed. The designation of some of the resulting products as "works of art", and thus their makers as "artists", is a subjective matter. Any such verdict, aesthetic or otherwise, is inevitably conditioned by the cultural attitudes of a given time and place. For William Morris (1892) "a work of utility might also be a work of art if we make it so". Similarly for Lethaby (1904) "art is man's thought expressed in his handwork" and consequently "art is more than picture painting".[1] This view was to be shared by the sculptor Eric Gill (1929) for whom "art is simply the well-making of what needs making". This notion was followed by Seamus Murphy (2005) who believed that "Art grows out of good work done by men who enjoy it."[2] These ostensibly simple statements challenge the whole notion of the "fine arts" in contradistinction to the "applied" or "decorative arts". The search for a frontier between these two realms is futile. Of more practical value is a consideration of the intrinsic and extrinsic influences on material culture in general. Such an approach has the capability of according greater emphasis to the prospective processes of making than is customary for the generally retrospective nature of art histories. By such means it may be possible to draw a distinction between two categories of objects. These may be considered in terms of man-made items, created on the basis of craft values, in which making and designing are simultaneous activities. By contrast the products of mechanisation are generally achieved by a separation of design from manufacture. In a pre-industrial context a strong case may be made to argue that "the medium was the message" to the extent that the resulting product was conditioned very directly by the tools, techniques and materials used in its realisation.[3] With industrialisation the earlier unity of means and ends has been lost or diluted.

A parallel argument has been advanced by Matthew Crawford (2009) where he observes that "standards of craftsmanship issue from the logic of things rather than the art of persuasion". Consequently "manual competence" relieves an individual "of the felt need to offer chattering *interpretations* of himself to vindicate his worth".[4] In the crafts the unity of making and designing is exemplified by the way in which the values of the bench may determine the product by means which may not have evolved on the drawing board. The fluting of Maximillian armour or a Georgian silver tea pot is present, in each case, for purposes of strengthening sheet metal; any decorative effect being a serendipitous consequence. Craft-based details with "design" implications of this kind abound in building history. Examples include the mason's mitre, in timber as in stone, the fielded panel, the architrave surrounding a window or door opening and many of the features found in rusticated stonework. All these details have their origins in workshop practice or structural necessity. In numerous often oblique ways empirical decisions were arrived at which have shaped our material culture. These issues bring us to the distinction, if distinction it is, between art and craft. In this respect Michael Owen Jones (1975) has noted that "such dichotomies as 'artist' versus 'clever craftsman'" are little more that "value judgements" rather than absolute definitions.[5] In North America these observations stem from a long tradition for thinking through issues of this kind. George Ripley (1802–1880), who founded the Utopian Brook Farm, Massachusetts in 1841, wished:

> "to ensure a more natural union between intellectual and manual labour than now exists; to combine the thinker and the worker, as far as possible, in the same individual … and thus to … permit a more wholesome and simple life than can be led amidst the pressure of our competitive institutions".

Clearly these objectives were far wider than the later "Arts and Crafts Movement" but then Ripley had taught mathematics at Harvard and was an ordained Unitarian minister.[6]

Within the early modern pre-industrial British tradition these matters did not arise. A patron simply wanted something made to his or her specifications.[7] In so far as visual concepts may be reduced to words the contracts that were drawn up for such ventures conditioned the resulting work. In this way the "idea", as represented by the patron's demands, carried varying degrees of significance. Even so the interpretation, the subtlety of expression, was chiefly in the hands of the maker. For example, many artists, under the direction of their clients, have endeavoured to give expression to such timeless and universal themes as the mother and child – and yet only a minority of such representations have come to be recognised as "works of art".

The patron, in the client economy of early modern Britain was, in most cases, an individual even where they were ostensibly representing a corporate body of church or state.[8] This was a situation that persisted, to some extent, in later centuries. The patrons of the past would simply commission an "artist", at the head of a whole team of artisans, to fulfil a given contract. When a noble lord sought to have a portrait of himself, his wife or mistress, he would instruct an artist as the principal contractor – for example the painter Sir Godfrey Kneller (1649–1723). Although Sir Godfrey might create the face; the clothes, the hands, background (landscape or interior) and other details were generally rendered by one or more specialist sub-contractors. In early modern England the patron of a work of art would be likely to have been in possession of a cultivated taste as this was considered to be central to the whole notion of gentility. This though was a form of behaviour that was not to be taken too far. In Addison's play *The Haunted House* (1719) Lady Truman exclaims "Really, Mr Tinsel, considering that you are so fine a gentleman, I am amaz'd where you got all this learning! I wonder it has not spoil'd your breeding". More substantial gentlemen than Tinsel may have had a hands-on understanding of a craft and many more were likely to have travelled, most notably on the Grand Tour. Much of this is reflected in Lord Chesterfield's letters to his son. On 10 May 1748 the Earl wrote quoting Ovid: *"Materiam superabat opus"* (the work excelleth the material). Chesterfield went on to add that this Latin tag was often used with reference to sculpture "where, though the materials were valuable as silver, gold, etc., the workmanship is still more so". In a later correspondence he advised his son that he should avoid "knick knackically" items like *"Intaglios* and *Cameos* [but to] form a taste of Painting, Sculpture and Architecture" for the good reason that "beyond certain bounds, the Man of Taste ends, and the frivolous Virtuoso begins".[9] In this way the gentleman connoisseur of the mid-eighteenth century developed an eye for what were seen as the masculine arts in contrast to the fripperies of the day. The age of patronage saw the artist meet the demands of a generally well informed employer. In the post-industrial consumerist context of the twenty-first century this position is often reversed. The artist has become the *prima donna* and the commission will be from a corporate body – the committee or advisor to a bank, a college or school. More often a work will be produced by the soloist, the artist, on speculation in the hope that it will eventually be purchased – often again as the mediated or collective decision of an institution. The transition of clients from patronage to consumerism and of artists from training to education, may be associated with the decline of the connoisseur and the rise of the aesthete, as exemplified in the essays of Anthony Ashley Cooper, third Earl of Shaftesbury (1671–1713). In a sense his work was a manifestation of a situation that had yet to come into being. For example, Cooper argued that only when art was shown publicly in galleries would "the true ambition in the artist" be realised, a situation that was decades away; although there was a long tradition for sculpture and painting being displayed in locations open to a wide community.[10] Nevertheless aesthetes were to blossom with the emergence of temporary public art exhibitions. An early example of this was Theophilius Marcliffe's ("a feigned name" probably William Godwin): *The Looking Glass; a True History of the Early Years of an Artist; calculated to awaken the attainment; particularly in the Fine Arts* (1805).[11] This was republished in 1889 and just two years later Oscar Wilde's *Picture of Dorian Gray* (1891) appeared. In the novel, the mirror image of Dorian Gray retains a constancy which the oil portrait does not, a canvas that anticipates Wilde's own fall from grace.[12]

As discussed in Chapters 3–5 the guild structures were originally designed to ensure the employment of the brethren, the quality of their work and the training of apprentices. In this way, the interests of both the producers and consumers were maintained. Accordingly the permanence of a man-made object was a demonstration of its quality; a feature that contrasts with the "built-in obsolescence" of industrialised consumerism. The importance of the longevity of pre-industrial material culture was most often expressed in relationship to architecture. To Sir Balthazar Gerbier (1663) a well-fabricated building was "like a stock of children" perpetuating the names of those who conceived and gave them birth.[13] In much the same spirit Sir Christopher Wren believed that a good building "ought to have the attribute eternal".[14]

As these chapters have attempted to demonstrate, some individuals, who had been apprenticed to their craft, were able to extend their reach, from their origins as artisans, to their emergence as artists. With the foundation of Academies of Art painters and sculptors, painting and sculpture, retreated into a *milieu* of aesthetics and academic tenets. This was far removed from the practical, the craft-based values of the guilds. Despite the craft origins of some, and the sense of intellectual superiority indulged in by many, the early

Royal Academicians may be seen, in retrospect, as meeting the demands of industrialisation, of consumerism. The annual RA exhibitions included works produced on speculation – ready-made art available for purchase. Some of these artists appear to have had a subliminal sense that their annual exhibition was a commercial undertaking. For this reason an attempt was made to exclude pictures that were for sale from the Great Room. Despite measures of this kind William Hazlitt (1816) was not alone in seeing the Academy as "a mercantile body ... consisting chiefly of manufacturers of portraits".[15]

This commercialism was predicated, so far as paintings were concerned, on those "products" that were created using commercially available canvases and manufactured paints. In these circumstances many painters were able to ignore the "mechanic" part of their art and promote the "liberal" nature of their vocation. No such industrially produced materials were available to sculptors, not that this prevented them from taking part in commercial ventures. For them, employment in manufacturing beckoned. Consequently, many of the more significant Neo-Classical and Greek Revival sculptors like Bacon, Flaxman and Wyon produced master patterns for industrialists like Coade, Wedgwood and Boulton.

The distancing of artists from their craft could become something of a dilemma. For Reynolds, with his declared repudiation of the "mechanic" aspects of painting, the deficiencies in his craft could become all too apparent, even during his lifetime. His portrait of Sir Walter Blackett faded so badly that the sitter's family saw it as a premonition of death. In response, Reynolds was gracious enough to acknowledge the criticism and sent the client a verse with the cadencies of Alexander Pope rather than the didactic character of the PRA's *Discourses*.

> "The Art of Painting clearly was designed
> To bring the features of the dead to mind,
> But this damned painter has reversed the plan
> And made the picture die before the man".[16]

In great contrast, other canvases by Reynolds have darkened with age as a result of his extensive use of bitumen. This pigment would have given his work great richness when first applied but with age these pictures have blackened with a *craqueleur* of sufficient seriousness to result in "cupping". This innocence of his craft was to result in Reynolds becoming all the more susceptible, between the years 1795 and 1797, to the blandishments of Thomas Provis's "Venetian Secret".[17] Despite this apparent disdain for the practicalities of painting he occasionally implies some respect for such matters. In his sixth

Discourse, delivered in 1774, Reynolds observed that "it is very natural for those unacquainted with the *cause* of any thing extraordinary, to be astonished at the *effect*, and to consider it as a kind of magic". He then goes on to say that the practice of the visual arts is developed by much "labour and application" and that any given work is achieved by small increments. Surely Reynolds is here declaring the importance of what he too often denied.[18]

With Reynolds's first *Discourse*, delivered on 2 January 1769, a secular theology of taste was inaugurated. This was exactly what William Hogarth had anticipated and feared would be the consequence of the establishment of an Academy. In his hostility to the foundation of such a formal institution he recognised that it would have the potential to be a harbinger of an absolute and intolerant aesthetic.[19] Hogarth's worst expectations were to be fulfilled. Indeed as President of the Academy Reynolds, in his first *Discourse* came close to arguing for the "divine right" of the visual arts as seen from that royal foundation. It was his view that there should be an "implicit obedience to the *Rules of Art*" and that the work of the "the great Masters" should be seen as "infallible Guides".[20] Authoritative though the *Discourses* were to become following their publication in 1778 they did not go unchallenged by individuals like Richard Payne Knight (1750–1824). Furthermore in 1810 Charles Lamb objected that academies resulted in the "inculcation of system" and in the suppression of individual feelings and ideas.[21]

Criticism of this kind was, in effect, a recognition of the power and influence that the Royal Academy had garnered unto itself. As Holger Hoock has observed the RA was at the height of its power between *c.* 1790 and 1820.[22] Moreover George III's active participation in the work of his foundation was to be reinforced by Parliament which came to see the Academy as a source of advice on the visual arts. Consequently Academicians were regularly invited to offer their views on such questions as the commissioning of sculptures for St Paul's Cathedral to commemorate war heroes (for some decades from 1782),[23] the design of "the new coins" (1798)[24] or the acquisition of the Parthenon marbles for the British Museum (in 1816 for £35,000).[25] In addition, under the leadership of the die-sinker and intaglio-cutter Nathaniel Marchant RA, Parliament was lobbied from 1792 to exempt artists from the import duty due on works of art brought into the country. This exemption was granted in 1797 (38 Geo III c.16) on the grounds that the Academy had improved public taste without recourse to public funds. The following year further influence was exerted on the legislature to grant sculptors copyright on their works, a provision that was duly granted (38 Geo III c.71).[26] Although sculptors formed a small minority of the Academy's membership they seemed to develop some importance in its deliberations at this time, a probable result of the Classical Revival.

Following Admiral Rodney's defence of Jamaica from attack by the French the RA was invited to give advice on a statue, to be erected in Spanish Town, to commemorate the Admiral. With some inevitability the RA proposed one its own, namely John Bacon the Elder who duly carried out the commission.[27] Much the same sequence of events followed with Thomas Banks's marble figure of the 1st Marquis Cornwallis for Madras, India (see p. 322 above). This commission came from the East India Company. For comparable monuments in Britain, notably St Paul's Cathedral in London, the treasury was to provide funding (between 1794 and 1823). With public money involved the official "The Committee of Taste" was established in 1802 so that, to a large extent, the Academy was to be bypassed and responsibility for officially commissioned works was to reside with Parliament. It was this Government Committee that was to offer fees, in the shape of prizes, of between 3,000 and 5,000 guineas for each work. In this way British sculptors became the beneficiaries of state sponsored art.[28]

By 1834 the Royal Academy, now a mature 66 years of age, had retained sufficient prestige to come under the scrutiny of Parliament. In that year William Ewart, the Member of Parliament for Liverpool, moved that the House of Commons should examine the position of the RA as occupants of Somerset House. This placed the then President, Sir Martin Archer Shee, in a difficult position, one that might jeopardise the independence of the Academy. With diplomatic skill Sir Martin sought the advice of the King regarding his foundation. In response, William IV gave the President permission to answer the Parliamentary enquiries.[29] A Select Committee of the House of Commons was duly established and met in two session – in 1835 with 49 Members of Parliament and again in 1836 with just 15 Parliamentarians. Among the objections that were raised was the tendency of academies of art to standardise taste. Furthermore it was noted that many of the founder members of the RA and its schools of painting, sculpture and architecture, had successfully evolved as artists with no such education.[30] The Select Committee was mindful of the many distinguished artists who had served a pupilage, among them Reynolds, Barry, Wilson and Flaxman. However in the spirit of the Great Reform act of 1832, which coloured their deliberations, this partiality would have been more fully apparent in those Academicians who had served apprenticeships; individuals like Chantrey and Stothard.

In some senses the preoccupation with status which concerned many artists was irrelevant in relationship to art, bourgeois concerns which were of little relevance. The essayist William Hazlitt (1814), who in his youth had been a painter, argued that the notion of "Professional Art" and thus "professional" artists, was "a contradiction in terms, Art is genius and genius cannot belong to a profession".[31] It therefore followed that art, unlike the material issues of a craft, could not be taught. This explains how it was that such a wide range of craft skills were capable of providing a natural artist with the means of translating a concept into a physical reality. In this context the evidence that was put before the Select Committee of the House of Commons in 1835–36 was highly significant. Of particular importance here was the testimony of Gustav Waagen (1794–1868) the Director of Berlin Museum. He argued that Academies of Art were "a poor substitute for the medieval workshop and guild".[32] His evidence was based on what were seen as the deficiencies in an ever increasing number of art schools. Despite Waagen's observation little reference was made to the surviving apprenticeships where craft-based values persisted in workshops, here and there, down to *c.* 1914/18.

Shared experience of an apprenticeship could result in a community of individuals with a background in common. Where two or more tradesmen spoke the language of a given craft these bonds were often significant. For example the American Benjamin Franklin (1706–1790), during the many years he lived in Craven Street, Westminster, became a close friend of William Hogarth (1697–1764). Both men had experience of servitude in their respective *metiers*, each was concerned with printing and both were to magnify their natural abilities on the basis of their trade origins. These two careers demonstrate that it was possible for an apprenticeship to provide a training capable of evolving into an education and that both, taken together, created the foundation for real achievement.[33]

Notes

1 Morris quoted by Ewan Clayton 2013, p. 268; H. H. Peach 1943, pp. 62 and 63 citing W. R. Lethaby (1857–1931)
2 Eric Gill (1929) 1934, p. v; Seamus Murphy (2005) 2010, p. x
3 Marshall McLuhan and Quentin Fiore, *The Medium is the Message*, London, 1967
4 Matthew Crawford (2009) 2010, pp. 18, 15
5 See James Ayres in Henig and Paine eds 2013, pp. 179–188; Michael Owen Jones 1975, p. 203
6 James R Mellow "Brook Farm an American Utopia" in *Dialogue* 13, No. 1, 1980, published by the International Communication Agency of the United States, Washington DC
7 Walter Cahn, 1979, eg. p. 55
8 There were exceptions, the magnificent pre-Reformation painted screen of 1528 in

Bradninch Church, Devon was commissioned by a sub-committee of the Parish Church using its own funds

9   Tim Richardson (2007) 2008, 138. David Roberts ed. (1992) 1998, p. 82, Chesterfield letter 10 May 1749 and pp. 164–165, letter of 27 September 1749

10 John Brewer 1997, p. 95

11 J. T. Smith (1828) 1919, Vol. II, p. 128 – see editor's footnote. William Godwin's partner/ wife was Mary Wollstonecraft

12 Oscar Wilde *The Picture of Dorian Gray* (1891), Penguin Classics, London, 2010. References to this mirror image occur at regular intervals in this short novel, e.g. chapter vii, p. 104; chapter xi, p. 125; and chapter xx, pp. 215, 217

13 Balthazar Gerbier 1663

14 Keith Thomas 2009, p. 240

15 Holger Hoock (2003) 2009, pp. 71, 209 citing *The Examiner* 3 November 1816 and David H. Solkin (ed.) "The Great Mart of Genius" exhibition Catalogue *Art on the Line: The Royal Academy Exhibitions at Somerset House 1780–1836*, New Haven & London, 2002

16 W. T. Whitley 1928, Vol. I, pp. 369, 370

17 Robert C Alberts 1978, chapter 17 "The Venetian Secret". Not all were so gullible: Sir Francis Bougeois "said he would not give Ten Shillings to know it" – Joseph Farington, p. 739 6 January 1797

18 Joshua Reynolds 1778, pp. 196–197

19 John Brewer 1997, p. 229

20 Joshua Reynolds 1778, p. 13 2 January 1769

21 Holger Hoock (2003) 2009, p. 74 citing Ernest Fletcher *Conversations of James Northcote* … 1901

22 Holger Hoock (2003) 2009, p. 74

23 *Ibid.*, pp. 237, 257. See also the Act of Parliament of 21 June 1798 *For encouraging the Art of making new Models and Casts of Busts, and other things* …

24 Joseph Farington, p. 1045 12 August 1798, p. 1121 28 Dec 1798

25 Holger Hoock (2003) 2009, pp. 288–290

26 *Ibid.*, pp. 242, 247, 250

27 *Ibid.*, pp. 237–239

28 *Ibid.*, pp. 250. 257–276

29 James Fenton 2006, pp. 183–184

30 Holger Hoock (2003) 2009, pp. 300–301, 303

31 Nina Fletcher Little (1954) 1972, p. 131. As a teenager the British-born Hazlitt spent some years in Hingham, Massachusetts where he appears to have worked as a painter; Holger Hoock (2003) 2009, p. 76 citing *The Examiner* 3 Nov 1816

32 *Ibid.*, 263, 300–303; James Fenton 2006, pp. 183–184. For a further account of Waagen's opinion of European Academies see Appendix XXI

33 In Hogarth's final hours of life on 25 October 1764 the artist received a letter from Benjamin Franklin – and even drafted a reply. Although Franklin only served part of his apprenticeship as a printer Hogarth's series of engravings *Industry and Idleness* must have struck a chord. See Jenny Uglow *Hogarth*, New York (1997), 1998, p. 697 and also W. J. Rorabaugh 1986

APPENDIX I

INDENTURE of 1788: ISAAC DELL to serve JOHN FLAXMAN Snr as APPRENTICE in the trade of "Moulder and Caster of Plaister Figures". Details written in by hand in the original document are printed in italics. From this it will be noted that this document was printed so as to be applicable to either male or female apprentices – e.g. h*is* / h*er*. – see Fig. 11

This Indenture Witnesseth that *Isaac Dell Son of Harriot Dell*
Widow of the Parish of Berkhamsted St Peter's in the County of Hertford
doth put h*imself* Apprentice to *John Flaxman of the Parish of St Martin's in the*
Fields in the County of Middlesex Moulder and Caster of Plaister Figures
to learn h*is* art and with h*im* after the manner of an Apprentice to serve from the
day of the Date hereof from the twentysixth day of April 1788 unto the full End and
Term of *Seven* years from thence next ensuing and fully to be compleat and ended During
which Term the said Apprentice h*is* M*aster* faithfully shall or will serve h*is* Secrets
keep h*is* lawful Commands everywhere gladly do so. H*e* Shall do no Damage to h*is* said
M*aster* nor see it be done of others but to h*is* Power shall let or forthwith give Notice
to h*is* said M*aster* of the same. The Goods of h*is* said M*aster* H*e* shall not
waste nor the same without Licence of h*im* to any give or lend Hurt to h*is* M*aster.*
H*e* shall not do cause or procure to be done H*e* shall neither Buy nor Sell without H*is*
M*aster's* Licence. Taverns Inns or Ale-Houses H*e* shall not haunt. At Cards Dice Tables or
any other unlawful Game H*e* shall not play nor from the Service of h*is* said M*aster*
nor from the Service of h*is* said M*aster* Day or Night absent h*imself* but in all Things
as an honest and faithful Apprentice shall and will demean and behave h*imself* towards
h*is* said M*aster* and all h*is* during all the said Term. And the said *John Flaxman for and in*
Consideration of the Sum of Thirty One Pounds and Ten Shillings in hand
well and truly Paid by the said Harriot Dell.

[Flaxman Snr shall instruct] h*is* said Apprentice in the Art of *Moulding*
and Casting of Plaister Figures which H*e* now useth shall teach and instruct
or cause to be taught and instructed the best Way and Manner H*e* can *finding unto*
the said Apprentice sufficient Meat Drink and Lodging during the said
Term of Seven years.

[There follows a standard clause followed by the date 26 April 1788]

A codicil reads as follows:

Mem[oran]dum: This agreed that Harriot Dell

    the Mother shall at her Expense   *Isaac Dell* [signed]
    during the 7 years find her Son
    Isaac in Washing. Mending and
    Apparel of all Sorts.

APPENDIX II

Advertisement for a Stationer and Picture Dealer c. 1750–1759

THOMAS BUTLER was a mid-eighteenth century bookseller and stationer in Pall Mall "nearly opposite St James's Palace". He later assumed the role of an easel painter of "sporting pieces" in which capacity he was dependent upon his "assistants".

> "He and his assistants, one of which takes views and paints Landskip and figures as well as most, propose to go to several parts of the Kingdom to take Horses and Dogs, Living and Dead Game, Views of Hunts, etc. in order to compose sporting pieces for curious furniture in a more elegant and newer taste than has been yet. Specimens of the Landskips and other performances may be seen at my house. Any Nobleman's or Gentleman's own fancy will be punctually observed and their commands strictly observed by applying or directing as above. Will be at Newmarket this meeting and continue in the country adjacent until after the Second Meeting, and the painting of the beautiful Foreign Horse taken by Captain Rodney, Lord Northumberland's, also the more eminent Stallions will be finished this summer, with many other Curiosities in the Sporting way".[1]

[1]   W. T. Whitley 1928, Vol. I, pp. 78–79. See also Stephen Deuchur 1988, p. 140, fig. 112

APPENDIX III

Samuel Wale (? – d. 1786) as sign painter

"Mr Wale painted some signs; the principal one was a whole length of Shakespeare, about five feet high, which was executed for, and displayed before the door of a public house, the north-west corner of Little Russel-street in Drury-lane. It was enclosed in a most sumptuous carved gilt frame, and suspended by rich iron work; but this splendid object of attraction did not hang long before it was taken down, in consequence of the Act of Parliament which passed for paving and also for removing the signs and other obstructions in the streets of London. Such was the total change of fashion, and consequent disuse of signs; that the above representation of our great dramatic poet was sold for a trifle to Mason the broker in Lower Grosvenor-street, where it stood at his door for several years, until it was totally destroyed by the weather and other accidents.

Before this change took place, the universal use of signs furnished no little employment for the inferior rank of painters and sometimes even the superior professors. Mr Catton painted several very good ones: But among the most celebrated practitioners in this branch, was a person of the name Lamb, who possessed a considerable degree of ability: His pencil [brush] was bold and masterly, well adapted to the subjects on which it was generally employed. At that time there was a market for signs, ready prepared, in Harp-Alley, Shoe-Lane".[1]

[1] Edward Edwards 1808, p. 117–118

APPENDIX IV

Charles Catton (1728–1798) "The Prince of Coach Painters"

Catton was born in Norwich, the son of a schoolmaster and apprenticed on 5 June 1745 to the coach-painter Thomas Maxfield of Little Queen Ann Street, St Giles' in the Fields, Middlesex.[1]

* * * *

"It should be observed that the profession of coach-painting might some years ago boast itself as holding rank among the arts; but, since the opulent coach-makers have taken this branch of decoration into their own hands, the herald-painters are become not more than their journeymen, consequently the most ingenious among them have no stimulus to exert their talents, or seek improvement, when neither honour nor profit can be obtained by their exertion.

Hence it is, that while carriages have been in the highest degree improved both for elegance and comfort, the painted decorations have degenerated into a state of frivolity and meanness, from which it is not probable they should emerge, until the profession can be restored to that independent state which it enjoyed at the time Mr Catton began his career".[2]

[1] The Binding Book of the Company of Painter Stainers of London, 1666–1795
[2] Edward Edwards 1808, p. 260

APPENDIX VIII

Prices of house-painters' work of 1799

In 1799 the Painter Stainers of London held a special meeting to resolve the "inconveniences existing between the Masters and Journeymen as to their wages and conduct". The following Resolutions were agreed at that meeting. (Document in Sir John Soane's Museum, London).

> "(1) That fair, equitable and liberal wages as between Master and Journeyman should be paid, namely at a rate of one guinea per week for good and able workmen – a day's work being reckoned from 6 o'clock in the morning till 6 o'clock in the evening – and inferior workmen according to their abilities.
>
> (2) That the 'Act to prevent unlawful combinations of workmen' be enforced [NB proto-Trade Unions – *The Unlawful Societies Act* 1799 – 39 Geo III, c79].
>
> (3) That an abstract of such Act with the above resolutions be printed and delivered to the Masters and Journeymen and occupiers of houses of call for the trade for their full information".

"Houses of call" were public houses which, in effect, served as labour exchanges and had been in existence from at least 1769.[1]

---

[1] W. A. D. Englefield, (1923) 1936, pp. 173, 184–191 and Alan Borg 2005, p. 123. In February 1803 a price list for individual jobs and materials was drawn up – and a revised price list was published in April 1816

APPENDIX IX

Stained hangings: early seventeenth and eighteenth century

In the following list I omit the earlier and more sophisticated examples at Coughton Court, Warwickshire and Hardwick Hall, Derbyshire, as also those in The Lockers, Hemel Hempstead, Hertfordshire, and the *Golden Cross Inn*, Oxford, the last of which are combined with wall paintings. The following were identified by Elsie Matley Moore, with the exception of those marked thus: +

Surviving examples in the house where first hung
Yarde Farm, Malborough, Devon
Owlpen Manor, Uley, Gloucestershire
+ Donore, High Street, Sherborne, Dorset (possible remains *in situ*)
+ Le Marinel, St John, Jersey (in a ruined house)

Surviving examples no longer in context
Gainsborough Old Hall, Lincolnshire (from Brandeston Hall, Framlingham)
Luton Museum (from a demolished house)
Mildenhall and District Museum (source uncertain)
+ Sherborne Museum, Dorset (sample from Donore, Sherborne)
+ Shakespeare Birthplace Trust, Stratford-on-Avon, Warwickshire (from a house in Bude, Cornwall)
+ Chichester Museum – from 43 North Street, Chichester
+ Rutland Gallery, London (unknown source, present whereabouts unknown)
+ In the London "trade" (from 43 North Street, Chichester, West Sussex, present whereabouts unknown

Recorded examples
Munslow Farm, Munslow, Shropshire (present whereabouts unknown)
Jenkyn Place, Bentley, Hampshire, formerly loaned to Victoria & Albert Museum, London
See Figs 74, 75, 76.

APPENDIX X

A sampling of individual painters or sculptors who left the English Provinces for apprenticeships in London, Westminster or Southwark

	PLACE OF BIRTH	TRADE
John BOSON (*c.* 1696–1743)	Suffolk	Woodcarver
Charles CATTON (1728–1798)	Norfolk	Coach painter
Luke (Marmaduke) CRADOCK (1660–1712)	Somerset	House painter
Richard DALTON (*c.* 1713–1791)	Cumbria	Coach painter
Robert DAVY (late eighteenth century)	Cornwall	Woodcarver
Epiphanius EVESHAM (1580–after 1632)	Herefordshire	Stone-carver
Nicholas HILLIARD (*c.* 1547–1619)	Devon	Goldsmith/ limner
John HUNT (*c.* 1682–1754)	Northampton	Woodcarver
John Joshua KIRBY (1716–1774)	Suffolk	Coach painter
Peter MONAMY (*c.* 1670–1774)	Channel Islands	House painter
Nicholas STONE (1587–1647)	Devon	Mason/carver
Samuel WATSON (1715–1778)	Derbyshire	Woodcarver

APPENDIX XI

Some of the many woodcarvers who later worked in stone and marble

SEFFERIN ALKEN	1717–1782
THOMAS BANKS	1735–1805
WILLIAM BARLOW II	fl. 1733–1754
JOHN BOSON	*c.* 1696–1743
ROBERT CARPENTER of BATH	1750/51–after 1817
Sir FRANCIS CHANTREY RA	1781–1841
CAIUS GABRIEL CIBBER	1630–1700
GRINLING GIBBONS	1648–1721
JOHN GIBSON RA	1790–1866
JOHN HUNT	*c.* 1682–1754
JAMES PATTY I of BRISTOL	d. 1747/8
EDWARD PEARCE	*c.* 1635–1695
EDWARD POYNTON of NOTTINGHAM	b. *c.* 1685–1737
RICHARD PRESCOTT of LIVERPOOL	fl. 1702–d. 1747
JAMES RICHARDS	1671–1759
RICHARD SAUNDERS	b. *c.* 1661–1735
JOHN VAN NOST	fl. 1684–1710
THOMAS VENTRIS of YORK	fl. 1620s–1630s
SAMUEL WATSON I	1662–1715
EDWARD WYATT	1757–1833

APPENDIX XII

The construction of an armature in John Flaxman's Studio

"... a constant practice with those who feel it to be wiser to work in a soft and pliable material [namely clay], than commit themselves with small models in the difficulties of marble. By means of this skeleton of wood the naked figure is raised; and farther framework is constructed to support hanging draperies. Wire and bits of wood ["butterflies"] will suspend arms or folds [in draperies]; while the whole skeleton is kept in position by an upright piece of timber resembling the mast of a ship which rises out of the centre of the turning banker on which the statue is modelled."

Allan Cunningham 1830, Vol. III, p. 327

APPENDIX XIII

*Prices in 1797 for shipcarving on Royal Navy vessels
in relationship to tonnage*

The following listing demonstrates that a First Rate Ship of the Line was given more lavish decoration (3 shillings per ton) than a modest Sloop (1 shilling and 6 pence per ton).

"Lysons & White of Deptford dined with me ... White states to me the tonnage and expense of carving ships of the following rates in the Kings Yards.

Victory, of 100 guns – 2162 ton, carving at 3s. a ton.
    Hull of a first rate costs abt. £47,500.
Neptune of 90 guns is 2110 ton at do. 3s. a ton.
    of 74 guns is 1600 ton at 2s. a ton costs carving £160.
Raisonable of 64 guns is 1376 tons at 2s. do.
Salisbury of 50 guns is 1043 tons at 2s.do.
Naiad of 38 guns is 1013 ton at 1s.6d. do. – £76.
Venus of 36 guns is 728 ton at 1s.6d. do. this is a small sized frigate.
Alarm of 32 guns is 683 ton at 1s.6d. do.
Active of 28 guns is 594 ton at 1s.6d.do.
King fisher *Sloop* of 18 guns is 300 ton at 1s.6.

The saving by not allowing ships to be carved as formerly, does not amount in all the Kings Yards to £6000 a yr".

Joseph Farington, RA (1747–1821) *Diary* p. 814 2 April 1797

APPENDIX XIV

Price List for Lead Statuary

Andries Carpentière (Andrew Carpenter 1677–1737) sent the following PRICE LIST for LEAD STATUARY to Lord Carlisle in 1723.

	HEIGHT	PRICE IN FEET
Narcissus	7½	£25
Hercules and Wild Boar	6	£20
Cain and Abel	6	£20
Diana and Stag	6	£20
Venus de Medici	6	£15
Antinous	6	£18
Bacchus sitting	6	£18
Faunus	6	£20
Melagor	6	£20
Adonis	6	£18
Apollo	6	£18
Flora	6	£16
Gladiator	6	£12
Duke of Marlborough	6	£28
Roman Wrestlers	6	£20
Neptune	5½	£9
Bagpiper	5	£7
An Indian	5	£8
Cleopatra	5	£7
Daphne	5	£8
French paisant and paisanne	4ft. 2in.	£12
Winter and Autumn	4½	£8 8s.
4 signs of ye Zodiac	4	£16
Faunus and Nymph	4ft. 2in.	£8 8s.

From a similar price list Lord Carlisle ordered in 1723 "Hercules of Farnese, Spartan Boys, Sitting Venus and Faunus" paying a total of £84. The cases to house these figures for transport to Castle Howard, Yorkshire took a carpenter nine and a half days to construct for a total cost of £9-7s-9d. The fragile nature of lead evidently demanded particularly well-made packing cases.[1]

[1]   Rupert Gunnis 1953

APPENDIX XV

Some Members of the St Martin's Lane Academy

"G M Moser
Francis Hayman
G B Cipriani
Allan Ramsay
F M Newton
Charles Catton: the prince of coach painters
J Zoffany: the Wilkie of his day
Collins: a sculptor [William Collins 1721–1793]
Jeremy Meyer
William Woolet: an engraver [William Woollett 1697–1764]
Anthony Walker: also an engraver
Linnel: an excellent carver in wood, a branch of art now almost obsolete. [William
   Linnel *c.* 1703–1764]

John Mortimer ... cut off in his prime ...
Rubenstein: the drapery painter, an ingenious drudge to the portrait painters
James Paine: son of the architect who built the Lyceum
Tilly Kettle: who went to the East, and gathered riches by painting the Nabobs

William Pars: who was sent to Greece by the munifcence of the Dilenttanti Society
   ... and returned with stores of rich materials for the improvement of our rising
   architects ...

Vandergutch: a painter, transformed into a picture dealer ... and whose word 'was
   not worth a straw'

Charles Grignon [engraver]
Samuel Wale [painter and engraver]
C Norton ⎫
Charles Sherlock ⎬ an honest triumvirate practicing the calcographic art
Charles Bibb ⎭

Richmond ⎫
Keeble ⎬ all known in their day
Evans ⎭

473

Black

Richard Cosway: whose elegant sketches and tasteful fancy in many departments of his
  art, shall stand recorded long after his harmless eccentricities have been forgotten,
  and all his ghosts quietly laid in the Red Sea.

W Marlow: a very respectable landscape painter, neither resembled nor regarded
  according to his disserts.

Messrs Griggs, Rowe, R Dubourg, J Taylor, J S Dance, J Seton and T Radcliffe, pupils
  and inmates with our gay Frank Hayman, seven British worthies, as good, if not so
  wise, as the seven of Greece, said one of their number.

Richard Earlom: engraver
J A Gresse: the most corpulent of all the sons of St Luke
Giusepi Marchi: a sort of deputy spare right hand to the great Reynolds
Thomas Beech
Lambert [James, fl. 1761–1773] a sculptor, pupil of Roubilliac
Reed [Nicholas d. 1787] another pupil of his [Roubiliac's] a conceited spark who used
  to annoy the great sculptor ...

Biagio Rebeca: the facetious painter whose original humour ... had begotten much
  innocent mirth at Windsor.

Richard Wilson: alas! The greatest genius, the least understood.
Terry
Lewis Lattifere
David Martin
Burgess
Burch [Edward, 1730-1814]
John Collet: an imitation of Hogarth
Hogarth himself
Joshua Reynolds [who attended but was not a member]
John Taylor: whose unfailing reminiscence has obligingly helped us ... in drawing
  up this list"

NB This list is printed in Pyne 1823–24, Vol. I, pp. 38–39. Its strange wording makes it
unclear if Nollekens was a member of the St Martin's Lane Academy. He certainly attended
William Shipley's drawing school in The Strand.

APPENDIX XVI

*Proposed Accommodation and Prospectus
for the Royal Academy Schools*

- That a house be taken with a sufficient number of rooms: two contiguous to each other for drawing and modelling from life; [another room] for architecture and perspective, one for drawing from plaster; one for receiving the works of the school; one for the exhibition of them, and others for a housekeeper and servants.
- That some fine pictures, casts, busts, bas-relievos, intaglias, antiquity, history, architecture, drawings, and prints, be purchased.
- That there be professors of anatomy, geometry, perspective, architecture, and such other sciences as are necessary to a painter, sculptor, or architect.
- That the professors do read lectures at stated times on constituent parts of their several arts, the resources on which they are founded, and the precision and immutability of the objects of true taste, with proper cautions against all caprice and affectation.
- That living models be provided of different characters to stand five nights in the week.
- That every professor do present the academy with a piece of his performance at admission.
- That no scholar draw from the life until he has gone through the previous classes, and given proof of his capacity
- That a certain number of medals be annually given to such students as shall distinguish themselves most.
- That every student, after he has practiced a certain time, and given some proofs of his ability, may be a candidate for a fellowship.
- That such of the Fellows as choose to travel to Rome to complete their studies, do make a composition from some given subject, as proof of their ability. He who shall obtain the preference shall be sent with a salary sufficient to maintain him decently a certain time, during which he is to

475

be employed in copying pictures, antique statues, or bas-relievos, drawing from ancient fragments or such new structures as may advance his art, such pieces be the property of the Society.

- That other medals of greater value, or some badges of distinction, be given publicly to those who shall manifest uncommon excellence.
- That some professors should be well skilled in ornaments, fruits, flowers, birds, beasts, &c., that they may instruct the students in those subjects, which are of great use in our manufactories.
- That drawing-masters for such schools as may be wanted in several parts of the kingdom be appointed by the professors, under the seal of the Academy.
- That a housekeeper shall continually reside at the Academy, to keep everything in order, and not suffer any piece to go out of the house without a proper warrant."

William Sandby 1862, Vol. I, pp. 19–20

APPENDIX XVII

Part of Gustav Waagen's (1794–1868) evidence before the Select Committee of the House of Commons in 1834, on the value of Academies of Art

"On comparing a number of specimens of the different schools, such as those in Paris, St Petersburg and other places, all exhibited a striking similarity of manner; while in earlier times, and in the earlier method of teaching, the character of the schools of different nations, and that of each individual artist, was entirely original and distinct ... By this academic method, which deadened the natural talent, it is sufficiently explained why, out of so great a number of academic pupils, so few distinguished painters have arisen".[1]

[1] Ralph N. Wornum ed. *Lectures on Painting by Royal Academicians*, London/Bohn, 1848; also cited by Sandby 1862, p. 69

GLOSSARY

According to custom this Glossary lists a large number of nouns but also includes a series of verbs, a consequence of the focus on making. Inevitably craft activities took place within a context that was far wider than the workshop or building site. For this reason, the traditional interdependence of art and architecture explains the use here of the glossary in Joseph Gwilt's *Encyclopaedia of Architecture* (edition of 1876) and the anonymous *Rudiments of Architecture* (1778)[1] which also includes a "Builder's Dictionary". In addition to such essential sources as *The Shorter Oxford Dictionary* (1979) and Kurt Wehlt's *The Materials & Techniques of Painting* (1967) 1983.[2] Historical perspective has been gleaned from James O. Halliwell's *Dictionary of Archaic Words* (1850)[3] and *Cassell's Latin Dictionary* (1979). Of even greater relevance to any of the above is the presence of many historic terms and usages in the surviving vernacular language of traditional craftsmen – a verbal idiom that is no less at risk from extinction than many of the skills with which these crafts were associated.

AERIAL PERSPECTIVE: Much used with reference to landscape painting and drawing in which progressively paler tones are used to suggest distance.

AESTHETIC: In this context a pleasurable reaction to something of visual beauty. "An aesthetic" may also be a reference to a single idiom.

AMATEUR: In this context, and in the exact meaning, an art lover. Also a person who indulges in the visual arts as an amusement or an accomplishment.

ANNEAL: The heating of metal to reduce its tendency to become brittle as it is worked.

APPLIED ART: See *Decorative Art.*

APPRENTICE: From the French *apprendre*: to learn.

ARRAS TAILOR: A craftsman concerned with the preparation, hanging, maintenance and cleaning of tapestries.

BANKER: Amongst sculptors and masons the bench or block of stone on which these tradesmen place their stone for working.

BANKER MASONS: The highly skilled masons who shape stone on a *Banker* in a *Lodge*. Much of the work on site was carried out by *Rough Masons* or *Fixer Masons.*

BALK or BAULK OF TIMBER: A large scantling of timber – defined in 1773 as "pieces of fir-timber coming from beyond the seas by floats".[1] such a definition implies timber that has been imported across the North Sea – in keeping with the Old Norse origins of the word.

BED: In stonework this refers to the way in which a sedimentary rock was laid down in the geological past. When stone is built-in as found in the quarry it is said to be "laid on-bed" – alternatively, for technical reasons, some stone is "edge bedded".

BISTRE: A dark brown pigment prepared from soot. Often used as a tonal wash on drawings.

BLADDER COLOURS: Pre-prepared oil paint contained in small leather bladders – the precursors of collapsible metal tubes for oil paint.

BLOCK BOOK: A book of woodcuts in which the text and any pictorial or decorative elements are cut from a single block of wood for each page. This was a mid-fifteenth century German innovation that was the precursor of moveable type for printing.

BLOOM: In painting or varnishing a clouding of the surface caused by adverse humidity.

BOAST: "Among workmen, is the taking off the superfluous part in carving or mouldings" 1773.[1] Boasting was also important for carved sculpture and for this purpose boasting drawings were produced for assistants to work to.

BOASTING DRAWING: For stone or wood carving or masonry, simplified drawings were produced as the basis for the roughing-out work. For three-dimensional work two elevations and a plan were necessary. These drawings generally consist of a series of straight lines running from one salient point to the next.

BODY COLOUR: See *Gouache.*

BOW DRILL: The motive power for drills of this kind is provided by a bow the string for which is wound round the chuck. Drills of this kind revolve clockwise and anticlockwise and thus shed dust at each reversal.

BOZZETTO: See *Maquette.*

CASE HARDENING: Or carburizing is a process applied to such items as steel dies after they have had their *intaglios* cut. The process involves a thermochemical heat treatment which, through the diffusion of carbon into the surface of the metal, results in great hardness. This procedure enables dies to remain useable for longer – see p. 406 above.

CASEIN: A size derived from cheese or milk. When used as a medium with powder colours and water such a distemper, when dry, is not soluble with water. To inhibit the tendency of these distempers from turning sour, ammonia is generally added – in the convenient form of urine.

CAST: (1) The production of a positive from a negative mould. (2) "Among workmen, a piece of timber or board or the like … by its own drought or moisture … becomes crooked".[1] Such a board may also be described as being "in winding".

CHARCOAL: (1) Calcinated Wood used for drawing. (2) The same material, in a less refined form, may be used as the fuel in a smith's forge.

CHASED: Metal that has been worked with punches by a chaser to create form in cold bronze, silver, gold, etc.

CHEF D'OEVRE: The French term for a *Masterpiece* or "proof piece".

CHIAROSCURO: In painting and drawing the use of strong light and dark tones.

CIRE-PERDUE: French for "Lost Wax" and a term used by founders to refer to a system of metal casting.

CLAUDE GLASS: A small dark convex mirror used by painters to reflect and reverse a landscape and simplify the tonal and chromatic values. Named after the French painter Claude Loraine (1600–1682).

COCKS COMBE: See *Drag*

COLLAGE: A picture composed of elements such as cut paper, sand, straw, cloth, etc that are stuck down on a *support* to create a picture. From the French *collage*: to paste down.

COLOUR CLOTHLETS: Small pieces of cloth soaked in a given colour and dried so as to "lock-up" the pigment for later use. Suitable for translucent washes. Much employed from the mid-fifteenth to the sixteenth centuries for colouring woodblock book illustrations, maps and engravings.

COLOUR WHEEL: A diagram showing the disposition of *Complementary Colours.*

COLOURMAN: An early modern term for a shop that supplied both "liberal and mechanic" painters with their materials. Also known as "Oil & Colourmen".

COMPLEMENTARY COLOURS: Colours that appear on the opposing sides of a colour wheel, e.g. red opposite green. See *Laws of Simultaneous Contrast.*

CONTÉ CRAYONS: A black or red crayon made by Conté of Paris for drawing on paper.

CRAQUELURE: A network of small cracks in the surface of a painting, a problem to which oil paintings are most subject.

CROCODILED PAINT: Paint may be so described when it has a strong *craquelure,* sometimes in association with *Cupping.*

CUPPING: Where a painting suffers from a *craquelure* the perimeter of the paint within each zone between the cracks may lift, to result in "cupping".

CUSTOM OF LONDON: In relationship to a craft training this was an exemption found in the English capital whereby the guilds permitted a craftsman to practise a trade other than the one for which he was qualified, and be affiliated to a guild whose craft he did not practice.

DÉCOR: "Or more properly DECORUM: this is perfect Latin, and signifies the keeping of a due respect between the inhabitant and the habitation".[1] Despite its classical origins this term implies some residual respect for the sumptuary laws, of medieval Europe in relationship to interior decoration.

DECORATIVE or APPLIED ART: Art that is applied to, or forms a central part of, an object that serves some practical purpose.

DIE-SINKING: Cutting an intaglio in a steel die for coins, medals or seals – the latter often being cut in a hardstone. Dies cut in mild steel were *Case-hardened* before use.

DISTEMPER: Pigments suspended in water and bound with a size.

DRAG: A comb-like steel implement designed to drag across stonework with a
   rasping action to establish a true form or surface. Shaped miniature versions
   of these tools are known as *cocks' combs.*

DRAWN-OUT: The edge tools used by sculptors and masons on stone and marble
   lose their temper and shape as a consequence of use and sharpening on a
   whetstone. At this stage such tools are sent to a smith to be "drawn-out".

DRYERS or SICCATIVES: Some media inhibit or accelerate the drying of certain
   paints and distempers. For example, linseed oil drys well and for this reason
   housepainters sometimes add a spoonful of linseed oil to a bucket of limewash
   as a "dryer". Other catalysts that are added for this purpose include Synourin
   (derived from castor oil) and lead-hexanate (although the latter has a tendency
   to darken oil paints).[2]

ECORCHÉ: A flayed human or animal figure cast in plaster and used for the study
   of anatomy.

EGG TEMPERA: A *Medium* or tempera derived from the white of eggs and used
   to bind pigments. Also known as *Glair* when used as a *Mordant.*

ENGRAVING: 1) To cut a line in metal (gold, silver, steel, wood etc) for decorative
   effect – as with engraved silver, armour or furniture. 2) To cut a line in metal
   or wood for purposes of holding ink for printing on paper.

ETUI: From the French *etui:* a small case or chatelaine. This term came to be used
   to signify all sorts of small "objects of virtu". In English usage the word *etui*
   was transformed into "toy" – hence the "toy shops" which sold such items to
   a sophisticated elite in fashionable centres of resort like Bath Spa.

FELLING OF TIMBER: "The proper season usually commences about the end of
   April because then the bark rises most freely; and if there be a quantity to be
   felled; the Statute obliges to fell then, the bark being so useful to tanners".[1]
   This account of 1773 fails to add that, for good quality timber, trees were best
   harvested in the Autumn when the sap was low.

FETTLING: The minimal finishing of metal castings by means of rasps, *Rifflers* and
   punches. For more systematic work in cold metal see *Chasing.*

FIELD-RANGING: A term used amongst stone carvers in the nineteenth century.
   This related to the fields surrounding the expanding towns where masoned
   stone was stored. When work was slack carvers would seek out these fields to
   carve ornament that would later be built into speculative terraced housing.

FIRE-SHARPS: Edge tools (punches, claws, chisels, boasters, etc) for working stone
   which, when worn down by sharpening past their temper, were sent to the
   smith to be "*drawn out*".

FLOGGERS: Large long horsehair brushes used to "flog" wet paint as a preparation
   for the use of combs for graining.

FOLK ART: See *Vernacular Art.*

FRESCO: Mural painting on plastered walls – takes two forms. These comprised
   fresco secco, painting on dry plaster, and *fresco buono,* painting on wet plaster,
   zone by zone.

FROWEY TIMBER: "Timber is said to be frowey when it is evenly tempered all the way and works freely without tearing".[1]

GADROON: A silversmith's term for which the masonry equivalent is known as the *Knull & Flute*.

GALLETS: Stone chips, from the French *gallet:* a pebble.

GESSO: A mixture of whiting (chalk) and size, used to prime *supports* for paintings. If built up, gesso may be carved in low relief and/or punched.

GLAIR: A size from white of egg – sometimes used as a *mordant*.

GLAZE: (1) Amongst painters the application of a tinted yet transparent layer of paint or *Varnish*. (2) Amongst plumbers and glaziers, the installation of glass.

GLYPTIC ARTS: Those sculptural arts involving the carving of stone, marble or gems.

GOTHIC ARCHITECTURE: "Is that which is far removed from the manner and proportions of the antique, having ornaments wild and chimerical, and its profiles incorrect".[1] That was a subjective definition in 1773. Today medieval architecture is generally divided into three phases: the "Early English", "Decorated" and "Perpendicular".

GOUACHE: The opaque use of watercolour paints – as, for example, in *Limning*.

GRISAILLE: Painting in monochrome in which a range of tones are used to create form or imply *"Local Colour"*.

GUM: the gums are used as an alternative to the sizes as "binders" in various media – e.g. gum arabic. Most characteristic of the watercolours.

HALF-LENGTH: In portrait painting the representation of a person from the head to the waist – a canvas size that was typically 25 × 30in (63.5 × 76.2 cm).

"HOLD A BITE": In carving and masonry the ability to guide an edged tool to maintain a cut in stone or marble without skating over the surface.

IMPASTO: Paint, especially oil paint, used thickly so that the strokes of the brush or the working of the palette knife leaves the paint in relief on the *Priming* of the *"Support"*.

INDENTURE: Any legal agreement written or printed in duplicate, on parchment or paper, which is then cut in half along an irregular line (the indent). An indenture for an *Apprentice* was drawn up between the parents or guardian of a youth and the prospective master, each party to the agreement keeping one copy. From the French: *endenture:* toothed.

INTAGLIO: Negative form cut into steel or some other material from which coins, medals, coins or seals could be struck. Signets were generally cut in a hardstone – carved wood intaglios were used to cast composition ("compo") ornament.

INTARSIA: Designs inlaid in wood.

INVESTMENT: In metal casting the covering of a model or master pattern with a mixture (such as refractory clay and brick-dust) to create a mould for the *Lost Wax* or *Cire-perdu* process.

ISINGLASS: A size derived from fish. Used in various forms for *Stained Hangings* or *Transparencies* and for watercolour painting.

JOURNEYMAN: A craftsman paid by the day (from the French: *journée*). Once an apprentice had completed "his time" he usually spent some years travelling as a journeyman before aspiring to become a master craftsman.

KIT-CAT FRAME/CANVAS: A frame or canvas size measuring 36 × 28 in (91.5 × 71 cm).

KNULL & FLUTE: A term used by carvers and masons to signify a moulding enriched across its axis by a sequence of alternating convex and concave forms – known to silversmiths as *"Gadrooning"*.

LAWS OF SIMULTANEOUS CONTRAST: These "laws" were promulgated by Michel-Eugène Cheverul in his *De la loi du Contraste Simultane des Couleurs*, 1839 and formed the basis for the theory of *Complementary Colours*. Chevreuls' book was first published in England in 1854.

LAY-FIGURE: An articulated figure (human or animal) in wood, *papier maché*, etc. used by artists to clothe or drape as a model for their work. Human figures of this type were most useful if life-size but they may be smaller.

LEVIGATION: To reduce a material such as a pigment to a fine smooth powder.

LIBERAL ARTS: In classical antiquity these were comprised of the occupations of the mind which were considered suitable for free-born men. These liberal arts were divided into the *quadrivium*: arithmetic, astronomy, geometry and music and the *trivium*: grammar, rhetoric and logic. Manual activities were mainly confined to slaves.

LIMNING: This was defined by William Salmon (1672) 1701, as "an Art whereby, in water colours, we strive to resemble Nature in everything to the life". The precision of this usage began to decline in the mid-eighteenth century.

LIME-TREE: An example of the retention, into the twenty-first century, of historic usage amongst wood-workers – reference to "lime wood" is more typical of those outside the trade.

LOCAL COLOUR: In painting *"en Grisaille"* where tone is used to imply local colour. The use of shadow as local colour in sculpture to suggest such details as a pupil in an eye.

LODGE: The open-sided shed in which a *banker-mason* worked.

LOST WAX or *CIRE-PERDU*: Metal-casting. This is a process in which a wax model is *Invested* with a mould and the wax melted out ("lost") so that the resulting cavity may be filled with molten metal.

MAHLSTICK: From the Dutch "paint stick" – a rod with a pad at one end used by painters to support the brush-hand for extra precision.

MAQUETTE: A sketch or model for a work of art – see also *Patron*.

MASTER CRAFTSMAN: The member of a guild who trained apprentices and employed journeymen and others. Such individuals worked as independent masters.

MASTERPIECE: A specimen of work made by an apprentice for submission to his trade guild to assess his level of skill. Masterpieces may have been more commonly made on the continent of Europe than in the British Isles. These exemplars of skill were also known as "proof pieces", and in the north of England as "humbling pieces".

MEDIUM: In painting, the combination of liquids used both to carry pigments and bind them. For example, in oil painting the carrier could be turpentine and the binder linseed oil

MEGILP: A thickening medium which enabled paint to be manipulated – often used for graining and marbling.

METAL POINT: A small metal rod used for drawing – as in silver point. So-called "lead pencils" are generally made of graphite.

MEZZOTINT: An elaborate system of engraving employing serrated "rockers" which were deployed to engrave copper plates with areas that would become tone when printed. The process was devised by Ludwig von Siegen of Utrecht in 1642. This method of print-making may have been introduced to England by Prince Rupert of the Rhine (nephew of Charles I).

MORDANT: A size used to hold a powdered pigment or leaf metal to a surface – as with strewing smalt or gold leaf.

MOULDS: (1) Negative casts, etc used to make positive form. (2) Templates used by *banker masons*, etc – hence moulding.

OBJECTS OF VERTU: Small well-finished works of art or artistry see *etui.*

OFFER-UP: Amongst craftsmen the trial placing of a work in its final position to ensure that it is in scale etc, with its surroundings.

OIL & COLOURMEN: See *Colourman.*

OIL OF SPIKE: Oil of Lavender.

OILSTONE: Close grained abrasive stones used with oil for sharpening woodworking tools.

ORMOLU: Fire-gilt bronze.

OVERMANTLE & OVERDOOR ENRICHMENTS: The panel over a door or chimneypiece was often embellished with carved or painted decoration.

PAINT: In essence paint of all kinds is comprised of ground and powdered pigment suspended in a *medium* (vehicle and binder).

PAINTER STAINERS: The Guild of the Painter Stainers was formed in London in 1502 by uniting the two previously independent fraternities. Although the most significant of these organisations was based in London this company had great influence across Britain and beyond to Colonial North America.

PALETTE: A small wooden board, or thin slab of some other material, on which painters prepared their paints, or rehearsed chromatic or tonal values before applying them to the work in hand. The small rectangular palettes of the seventeenth century and earlier evolved into an elliptical shape in the following century. Small ivory or porcelain palettes were used by limners working in miniature. Amongst oil painters palettes seem to have grown in size as manufactured paints became cheaper.

PANTOGRAPH: A device for reproducing a two-dimensional drawing or for enlarging or reducing the same.

PAPER: Paper appeared in northern Europe from the east in the fifteenth century.

PARCHMENT: An animal skin derived from various sources – e.g. sheep, calf, etc – vellum sharing the same route as veal was derived exclusively from calf skins. Parchment was used for illuminated manuscripts and legal documents – including an apprentice's *Indenture*.

PARGETTING: (1) Decorative relief plasterwork particularly popular on the external walls or domestic buildings in the south-east of England in the seventeenth century. (2) Also "signifies the plasistering of chimney funnels; sometimes it is used to signify the plaister itself".[1]

PATRIMONY: In terms of training in a craft this was a guild dispensation whereby a son could be admitted to his father's fraternity on the payment of a fine rather than by serving an apprenticeship in his father's trade.

PATRON: (1) In medieval and early modern England a pattern or *maquette* for an artistic scheme. (2) A person who commissioned a work of art, etc – in this historic role a patron played an active part in the realisation of a given scheme. Patronage in this creative sense was to decline with industrialisation and consumerism and the purchase of ready-made works.

PENCIL: Down to the eighteenth century a pencil was a synonym for a brush.

PENTIMENTO: With age paint, especially oil paint, has a tendency to become translucent revealing earlier work beneath later layers of paint. These "ghosts" are referred to as *pentimento*.

PIGMENTS: The colouring matter used by painters. These pigments derive from animal, vegetable and mineral sources and were traditionally purchased from *Colourmen* in lump form which was then reduced to powder colour, either by the Colourman or in the painter's studio.

PLASTER: Various types of plaster were used. These include the coarser lime plasters and the more refined plaster of Paris, a gypsum. The latter was used by modellers for making moulds and casting positives of their work.

PLASTIC ART: In 1773 this was "comprehended under sculpture but is indeed the very sculpture itself; but with this difference, that the plaisterer, by his plastic art, makes figures by addition, but the carver by subtraction"[1] – see also *Sculpture*.

PLEIN AIR: From the French "*en plein air*": in the open air – a phrase used to describe landscape paintings that have been created out-of-doors in the presence of nature rather than in the studio. This innovation became more possible with the introduction of easily used watercolour cakes (1770s) and tube oil colour (1841).

POINTING MACHINE: A device used by sculptors for locating a point in three-dimensional space. By means of this mechanism a point located on a maquette could be transposed to the final work. In effect these so-called "machines" were three-dimensional pantographs, and could be used to repeat work at the same size of to reduce or enlarge them. Three types of pointing machine were in general use by the early nineteenth century: "the cage", the "ball and socket device" and the "long-arm".

POLYCHROME: Literally "many colours", as for example when sculpture is painted in multicolours.

POPPY OIL: In oil painting the clarity of poppy oil is valued as are its *Siccative* properties.

POUNCING: A drawing was sometimes pricked and "pounced" with a bag of charcoal dust so as to transfer an image to another surface.

PROOF PIECE: See *Masterpiece*.

PROPER COLOURS: In the heraldic sense the painting of a crest, or some similar device, in an heraldic "achievement", in naturalistic colours.

PREMIUM: 1) The sum of money paid to a master craftsman by a parent or guardian to train a youth. 2) The name given to prizes presented by the [Royal] Society of Arts.

PRIMING: The preparation of gesso etc applied to a "*Support*".

PULL: As a noun, in the context of print-making, a pull is a synonym for a print – from the verb "to pull" the paper from the engraved plate, woodblock, etc …

REDEMPTION: The means by which an apprentice, by paying a fee or fine, could gain admission to a guild.

REFLECTED COLOUR: The way in which a colour may be observed in nature to be modified by the proximity of another colour.

REGRATING: The purchase of goods for stockpiling and later re-sale at a profit. To "corner the market".

REPOUSSÉ: A method of working relief designs in cold metal by punching from the reverse face of sheet-metal sustained on a temporary bed of pitch.

RESIST: A preparation, such as a size, a wax or varnish, applied to a surface to *resist* the application of subsequent preparations.

RIFFLER: A small curved file much used in fettling metal – also used by stone carvers.

RISERS: See *Runners & Risers*.

RUNNERS & RISERS: The channels within a mould for metal casting. These are designed to deliver molten metal to every part of the mould (runners) and to vent gases (risers).

ROOD SCREEN: A screen in a church which separates the chancel from the nave. Such a screen carried a cross or rood – hence its name.

SCANTLING: The cross-sectional dimensions of lengths of timber or stone.

SCULPTURE: Defined by John Evelyn (1662) as being "in Propriety of speech" those visual arts that involved "cutting". This exact definition persisted to some extent to 1773 when "sculpture" was defined as "the art of carving in wood and stone, etc." in contrast to "plastic" which was based on addition.[1]

SERVITUDE: The time (usually seven years) that an apprentice was bound to a master. At the completion of their time and subject to approval of their work, apprentices were free to practice their trade.

SGRAFFITO: From the Italian "to scratch". For mural schemes the scratching through of one coloured layer of plaster to reveal a second colour or colours. The term is also used with regard to comparable work in pottery.

SICCATIVES: See *Dryers*.

SIGHT: In a picture frame, the internal dimensions that leaves the picture visible.

SIGNIRON: Wrought iron bracket from which street signs were suspended.

SIZE: A binding material used in media for paints and distempers. Size may be derived from various animal sources, including bones (Scotch glue), rabbit skins, parchment, fish, white of egg, cheese or milk. Resins were also used for this purpose.

SKEWINGS: Small particles of gold leaf.

SLIPS: Shaped *oil-stones* used by woodcarvers to sharpen the internal bevel of gouges, etc.

SMALT: A pigment composed of powdered blue glass. This was known as "strewing smalt" and was sprinkled on a *Mordant* of goldsize or a similar preparation.

SOCLE: A pedestal or plinth as for a portrait bust in sculpture – may be rectangular or circular on plan.

SPRIGS: Small wedge-shaped headless nails used by glaziers to secure glass within timber glazing bars in association with putty.

STAINED HANGINGS: These were intended to resemble the far more expensive dyed-in-the-wool woven tapestries. Stained hangings were the work of the Stainers but fell from favour in the course of the 17th century.

STATUARIES: An early modern term for sculptors.

STRETCHER: The straining frame for a canvas *support* for a painting.

STROP: A leather strop was used to finish the sharpening of wood working tools (or razors). Its purpose was to remove the burr or *Swarf* that developed in the course of sharpening an edged tool on an oil stone.

STUDIO: An Italian term widely adopted in Britain in the nineteenth century to refer to a "painting room" or a sculptor's workshop. The French term "atelier" is less often used.

SUPPORT: The fundamental surface (panel, canvas, etc) to which a painter applies the preparation (gesso etc) and then his paints.

SWARF: The miniscule particles of the material that result from working metal – as in the particles of steel that are the consequence of sharpening an edged tool.

TEMPER: The steel edge given to cutting tools. Stone and marble working tools were regularly re-tempered by being "*Drawn-out*" by the smith, for this reason such tools were known as "*Fire-sharps*".

TEMPERA: An Italian term that once meant any fluid medium used by painters – it is now often confined to *Glair*.

THREE-QUARTER LENGTH: A portrait painting of an individual from the head to the knees – a canvas size that was typically 40 × 50 in (101.5 × 127 cm) – although for Reynolds these dimensions were used for a "half-length" see p. 169.

TOY SHOP: An eighteenth century term for a retail shop specialising in small luxury goods – see *Etui*.

TRANSPARENCIES: Transparent window blinds (or shades) of cotton that were stained with pictorial or decorative devices. These were intended to be seen within a room during the day, or externally at night when they were back-lit by candles, etc.

TROMPE L'OEIL: From the French "to cheat the eye". Used to describe paintings with a very high degree of verisimilitude in relationship to their subject matter.

TUBE PAINTS: Collapsible metal tubes to contain paints. These were the successors to *bladder colours*. Tubes for paints were patented in London in 1841 by the American portrait painter John G. Rand.

URINE: As a natural source of ammonia urine was added to milk-based distempers to reduce their tendency to turn sour.

VARNISH: A resinous solution applied, as a protective film, to paintings etc. For oil paintings a varnish derived from amber, copal or sandarac was used. These preparations were washed over oil paintings to protect them and were applied at least six months after their completion.

VEHICLE: In painting the volatile liquid in paint – e.g. water or turpentine. See also *Medium.*

VELLUM: Fine *Parchment* derived exclusively from calf skin – "vellum" shares the same route as veal.

VERNACULAR ART: An artisan art based on generations of tradition and the use of local materials and idioms.

VIRTU: "Objects of virtu" exhibited high quality craftsmanship – see also *Etui.*

WHETSTONE: An abrasive grit stone (such as York stone) used, in conjunction with water, to sharpen edged tools for working stone or marble – in contrast to the finer grained *Oil-stones* used to give an edge to woodworking tools.

WRITERS & STRIPERS: Long-haired brushes used for writing and striping.

Notes

[1]   Anon. (George Jameson?) (1773) 1778, reprint 1992
[2]   Kurt Wehlt (1967) 1982
[3]   James O. Halliwell (1850) 1989

ACKNOWLEDGEMENTS

The architect and historian A. L. N. Russell (1887–1969) was educated at Rugby – an exact contemporary of the poet Rupert Brooke. That great school formed the basis for Russell's classical learning, a feature reflected in his sketchbooks and accompanying notes – which are now in the RIBA Drawings Collection in the Victoria & Albert Museum. During the First World War Russell sustained a severe head wound which marked him for life. Despite some paralysis he, together with two friends, established the architectural practice Knapp-Fisher, Powell & Russell. In short, he battled-on in a thoroughly admirable fashion. I gratefully acknowledge Russell as my first benefactor. In a well-intended avuncular fashion I recall this survivor of the Great War once remarking, only half in jest, that the most important decision in life was the selection of one's parents. How true – yet how impossible. Aside from the biological reality mine were both actively engaged in the visual arts and thus shaped both me and my vocations. Father was the architectural sculptor Arthur J. J. Ayres (1902–1985). Elsa Ayres (1899–1985), my mother, was a portrait painter and daughter of the Danish-born ornithologist and artist Henrik Grönvold (1858–1940) whose work has given me some understanding of art in the service of science.

All this was to lead inexorably to my childhood apprenticeship in workshops and studios and then, at the advanced age of 12 years, to working on building sites. This training extended well beyond the immediate family. For example, I remember working as a boy with a stonemason named Woollett who had begun his apprenticeship in 1878 as one of "the hands" working on the installation of "Cleopatra's Needle" on the Thames Embankment in London. Another was a Welshman named Conway Jones. He came from a long line of sea captains sailing square rigged ships. However, having lost an eye in childhood, Jones was not permitted to sail before the mast. He became a fine stone-mason and carver working in three dimensions, but his monocular vision hampered his work in the subtleties of relief. Others who were to serve as my exemplars included the letter-cutter Sidney Newman and his brother Walter, the chief die-sinker at the Royal Mint – then still on its historic site on Tower Hill in the City. This roll-call of the artisan artists whom I sought to emulate include the woodcarver Cerrio Fiaschi and J. E. Clark who was probably the very last fully skilled chaser in Britain – he retired in 1952.

In the pre-industrial past the tools used by craftsmen were generally made by tradesmen whom they knew. As a consequence their implements were finely adjusted to the purposes for which they were intended. This continuity of thought and action was disrupted by mechanisation with its centres of production distanced from the "end user". One exception to this general rule concerned the maintenance of the edged tools used by stone-carvers and masons. For some four or five decades in mid twentieth century London these "fire sharps" were "drawn-out" by two specialist smiths – namely Pound in Vauxhall and Grimes in the north of the capital; Dickensian names that aptly fitted the nature of their occupations.

The various tools, materials and techniques deployed in working stone, wood and paint were thus the focus of my teenage years. This made me sufficiently useful to work for sculptors like Philip Bentham and Arnold Machin RA and also the architect E. Vincent Harris (1876–1971).

Although such a background is all very well it is the foreground that ultimately assumes greater importance and in my case a fellowship in the United States was to alter the direction of my life. On return to Britain this was to result in the Directorship of the Judkyn Memorial (since absorbed into the American Museum at Bath) which circulated exhibitions on various aspects of American cultural history.

Whilst living in Massachusetts the sculptor Khalil Gibran (nephew of the writer of the same name) helped me with the production of a lost wax bronze cast and also introduced me to welding in steel. This was one of many examples of the assistance and hospitality that I received in the USA. Others in North America whose help and friendship over the years I would like to acknowledge include: Mary Countess of Bessborough (née Drexel), Abbott Lowell Cummings, Susan Fisher, Kathleen Foster, James Gaynor, Henry Glassie, Isabella Halsted, Morrison Heckscher, Bernard Herman, Nina Fletcher Little, Carl Lounsbury, Keith Marshall, Charles Montgomery, Richard and Jane Nylander, Tyler Potterfield, Dallas Pratt, Perry Rathbone, Curtis Roosevelt, Beatrix Rumford, John Sweeney, Alexander Vietor, Richard Wendorf, Robin Winks and Richard Worth.

In Britain many craftsmen generously demonstrated their art and mystery for my edification whilst others shared their expertise in various relevant fields. Despite all this knowledge and experience offered by numerous individuals I am, inevitably, entirely responsible for the use to which I have put their skills and learning. Among these are N. W. Alcock, John Allan, Stephen Astley, Christopher Bibby, Peter Brears, Ian Bristow, Marcia Brocklebank, Richard Constable, Jeanne Courtauld, Timothy Easton, Kate Eustace, Paul Evans, Trevor Fawcett, Ian Fleming-Williams, John Gall and Rosy Allan, Ian Gow, Michael Gray (of Marlborough), Francis Greenacre,

Desmond Guinness, John Harris, Kenneth Hudson, Andras Kalman, Tony Lewery, Peter Lord, Sir Nicholas Mander, Sir Frances le Marchant, Dan Miles, Lillian Moore, Martin Myrone, Charlie Oldham, Steven Parissien, Terrance Pepper, Mark Pomeroy, John Rhodes, Treve Rosoman, Tina Sitwell, Jeremy Smith, Mary Spencer-Watson, Marianne Sühr, Melissa Thompson, Jeremy Uniacke, William Vaughan, Michael Weaver, Arnold Wilson and Kate Woodgate-Jones.

A number of private collectors have been good enough to permit me to illustrate works in their ownership. The institutions that have assisted in this way are acknowledged in the captions to the illustrations. Every effort has been made to identify the copyright owners of the images in this publication but if any have been overlooked this will be corrected in subsequent editions. Many photographs were sent to me via email and, but for the help of my good friend Michael Gray in nearby Beckington I doubt that they would have reached me safely. Similarly in typing-up my far from clear handwriting I am grateful to Ruth Holding and Sandra McPherson for the initial typescripts and to Jo Laurence for pulling the whole thing together in the final versions. None of this would have been realised in print but for my publishers Oxbow – and I am grateful to John Steane for introducing me to that Oxford-based publishing house. At Oxbow the design of the book has been in the capable hands of Val Lamb whilst Clare Litt and Julie Gardiner have brought their customary learning and expertise to the project.

In researching this book I have been dependent upon numerous museums and art galleries. Inevitably *things* are more difficult to read than *words* – a reality that has only served to emphasise the limitations of libraries, invaluable though these have been. My enquiries therefore extended beyond reading rooms and the workshops cited above to encompass the supply of materials from quarries, timber yards and a paint factory. Of utmost importance were the people in these various establishments, all of whom offered valuable insights.

More challenging was the need to orchestrate these various strands of information into what aspires to be a coherent whole. At this stage my physical presence at home did not compensate my nearest and dearest for my absent thoughts – thoughts that inhabited this book whilst it was under construction. I am therefore indebted to my wife and family for their forbearance.

James Ayres
Bath, Spring, 2014

SELECT BIBLIOGRAPHY

Books primarily published in London unless otherwise stated. Manuscripts are identified as being in the collections in which they are located. Dates of original/first edition publication are given in parenthesis.

Abbott, John. n.d. *Notebook & Sketchbook.* Manuscripts: Devon Record Office (404 M/B1, B2)

Adams, W. B. 1837. *English Pleasure Carriages*

Addison, Joseph. 1714. *The Spectator* – edition of 1793

Addy, Sidney O. (1898) 1933 *The Evolution of the English House*, chap 12 note 66

Airs, Malcolm, 1995. *The Tudor and Stuart Country House: A Building History*, Stroud

Alberts, Robert C., 1978. *Benjamin West: A Biography*, Boston MA

Allan, D. G. C. and Abbott, John L. 1992. *The Virtuoso Tribe of Arts & Sciences*, Athens GA

Allderidge, Patricia. 1977. *Masterpieces: Cibber's Figures from the Gates of Bedlam*

Anderson, J. H. *Notes on Exhibitions etc from 1769.* Manuscript: Royal Academy Library

Angerstein, R. R. *See* Berg and Berg 2001

Anon. (George Jameson? "a carver") (1773–4) 1992. *Rudiments of Architecture* (1773, 1778). Reprint, Edinburgh

Anon. (1875) 1995. *The Coach-Makers Illustrated Hand-book.* Reprint, Mendham NJ

Arnold (publisher). 1831. *Library of Fine Arts*

Arts Council of Great Britain. 1974. *British Sporting Art*

Avery, Charles (1978). *"Hubert le Suer's portraits"* in *National Trust Studies* 1979, pp. 128–147

Avery Tipping, H. 1914. *Grinling Gibbons and the Woodwork of His Age: 1648–1720*

Ayres, James. 1976. "Edward Hicks and his sources", *Antiques,* New York (February)

Ayres, James. 1980. *English Naïve Painting 1750–1900*, New York

Ayres, James. 1985. *The Artists' Craft: A History of Tools Techniques and Materials,* Oxford

Ayres, James. 1986. *The Art of the People*, Manchester

Ayres, James. 1996. *Two Hundred Years of English Naïve Art 1700–1900*, Alexandria, Virginia

Ayres, James. 1998. *Building the Georgian City*, New Haven & London

Ayres, James. 2003. *Domestic Interiors: the British Tradition 1500–1850*, New Haven & London

Ayres, James. 2009. "The stained hangings at Yarde Farm, Malborough", Exeter Archaeology Report 09.131

Ayres, James. 2013. "Empirical design as a product of the logic of craftsmanship", In M. Henig and C. Paine, (eds), *Preserving and Presenting the Past in Oxfordshire* ..., Oxford, 179–188

Ayres, John. 1700. *The Accomplish't Clerk or Accurate Penman*

Bagnoli, Martina, Klein, Holger A., Mann, C. Griffith and Robinson, James. 2010/11. *Treasures of Heaven: Saints Relics and Devotion in Medieval Europe*

Baker, Malcolm. 2000. *Figured in Marble*

Baldwin, Mike. 2006. "'Graviti in publicke places and yet inwardly licentious' the Custom House, Exeter", Exeter

Bankart, George. (1908) 2002.*The Art of the Plasterer*, Shaftesbury

Barber, Tabitha. 1999. *Mary Beale: Portrait of a Seventeenth-century painter and her family*, London

Bardwell, Thomas. 1756. *The Practice of Painting*

Barnard, John. 1747. *A Present for an Apprentice: A Sure Guide to Gain Esteem & Estate with Rules For his Conduct to his Master & the World*

Barnard, Thomas. 1784. "Working Goldsmith & Jeweler" of Adam St, Adelphi, London. *Receipt* of 23 April 1794 to Rev Mr. Le Marchant for the purchase of plate and flatware – total £90-19-0, Manuscript: Author's Collection

Barnwell, Paul, Palmer, Marilyn and Airs, Malcolm. 2004. *The Vernacular Workshop: from Craft to Art*, York

Barrell, John. (1986) 1995. *The Political Theory of Painting from Reynolds to Hazlitt* (1986), New Haven and London

Bath, Michael. 2003. *Renaissance Decorative Painting in Scotland*, Edinburgh

Beale, Charles. 1647–1663. *Experimental Secrets found out in the Way of Painting.* Manuscript, Glasgow University Library (Ferguson 134)

Beale, Mary. 1984. *A Study of Richard Symonds: His Italian Notebooks and their Relevance to Seventeenth Century Painting Techniques*, New York and London

Beard, Geoffrey. 1981. *Craftsmen and Interior Decoration in England 1660–1820*, Edinburgh

Beard, Geoffrey. 1997. *Upholsterers & Interior Decoration in England: 1530–1840.* New Haven & London

Beatty, C. J. P. 2007. *The Architectural Notebook of Thomas Hardy*, Dorchester

Bebb, Richard. 2007. *Welsh Furniture* (2 Vols). Kidwelly

Bellony-Rewald, Alice and Peppiatt, Michael. 1983. *Imagination's Chamber; Artists & Their Studios*

Beltramini, Guido and Burns, Howard (eds). 2009. *Palladio*

Benjamin, Walter. (1936) 2008. *The Work of Art in the Age of Mechanical Reproduction*, Harmondsworth

Berg, Maxine. 1985. *The Age of Manufacturers 1700–1820*

Berg, Torsten and Berg, Peter. 2001. *R. R. Angerstein's Illustrated Travel Diary 1753–1755*

Bewick, Thomas (1862) 1981. *My Life*, reprint Iain Bain ed.

Black, Jeremy. 1991. *The Grand Tour in the Eighteenth Century*, Stroud

Blair, Claude. 1958. *European Armour*

Blair, John and Ramsey, Nigel. 1991. *English Medieval Industries*

Bliss, Carey S. 1965. *Some Aspects of Seventeenth Century English Printing with Special Reference to Joseph Moxon*, Los Angeles

Bluemel, Carl. (1927) 1955. *Greek Sculptors at Work*

Bodleian Library. 2001. *A Nation of Shopkeepers: Trade Ephemera 1654–1860: The John Johnson Collection*, Oxford

Bonehill, John and Daniels, Stephen (eds). 2009. *Paul Sandby: Picturing Britain*, Nottingham & London

Borg, Alan. 2005. *The History of the Worshipful Company of Painters*, Huddersfield

Boutet, Claude. 1730. *Traite de mignature …1684 The Art of Painting in Miniature*

Brewer, John. 1997. *The Pleasures of the Imagination: English Culture in the Eighteenth Century*, New York

Brewington, M. V. 1962. *Ship Carvers of North America*, New York

Bristow, Ian C. 1996. *Interior House Painting: Colours and Technology 1615–1840*, New Haven & London

Brooks, E. St John. 1954. *Sir Hans Sloane*

Brownell, Morris. 2001. *The Prime Minister of Taste*, New Haven & London

Bullen, Simeon. 1813. Manuscript: *School Exercise Book*, Ilminster, Somerset, author's collection

Burgess, Frederick. (1963) 1979. *English Churchyard Memorials*

Burke, Peter. (1978) 1994. *Popular Culture in Early Modern Europe*, Aldershot

Burke, Thomas. 1941. *The Streets of London*

Burnett, John (ed.). (1974) 1994. *Useful Toil: Autobiography of Working People from the 1820s to the 1920s*

Bushman, Richard L. (1992) 1993. *The Refinement of America: Persons, Houses, Cities*, New York

Byrne, Patrick. n.d. Concerning the lease for three years of "Timber and Quarry Land" at Prior Park, Bath, to John Thomas for £235-10-0; 1813–1816. Manuscript: Author's Collection

Cabot, Harriet Ropes. 1979. *Handbook of the Boston Society*, Boston, MA

Cahn, Walter. 1979. *Masterpieces: Chapters in the History of an Idea*, Princeton, NJ

Campbell, James W. P. 2002. "The carpentry trade in seventeenth century England" *Georgian Group Journal* XII

Campbell, R. 1747. *The London Tradesman*

Catton, Charles. 1790. *The English Peerage*

Cennini, Cennino D'Andrea. (Earliest manuscript 1437) 1933 and reprint n.d.. *Il Libro Dell'Arte: The Craftsman's Handbook* Daniel V. Thompson transl., New York

Cescinsky and Gribble 1922, *Early English Furniture and Woodwork* 2 vols

Chalkin, C. W. 1974. *The Professional Towns of Georgian England: A Study of the Building Processes: 1740–1820*, Montreal

Chambers, W. and Chambers, R. 1860. *Chambers Encyclopaedia*, Edinburgh & London

Chaney, Edward. 1998. *The Evolution of the Grand Tour*

Cheetham, Francis. 1984. *English Medieval Alabasters*, Oxford

Chesterfield, Lord. Letters to his son, see David Roberts ed. 1992

Chevreul, M. E.. 1839. *De la Loi du Contraste Simultane des Couleurs*, Paris; and *Chevreul on Colour* (translation) London 1876

Chinnery, Victor, 1979. *Oak Furniture: The British Tradition*, Woodbridge

Christienson, Edwin O. (1952) 1972. *Early American Woodcarving*, New York

Clayton, Ewan 2013. *The Golden Thread: The Story of Writing*

Clifford, D. (1970) 1976. *Collecting English Watercolours*

Clifton-Taylor, Alec, and Ireson, A. S. 1983. *English Stone Building*

Cobbett, William (1821) 1979. *Cottage Economy*, see also Morris, Christopher

Collinson, John 1791. *History of Somerset*, Bath, see also *Rack* under McDermott and Berry

Collyer, J. 1761. *The Parents and Guardians Directory*

Colvin, Howard. 1995. *Biographical Dictionary of British Architects 1600–1840*, New Haven & London

Colvin, Howard *et al.* eds 1975 and 1976. *The History of the King's Works* Vols 4 and 5

Connely, Willard. 1955. *The Monarch of Bath & Tunbridge Wells*

Constable, W. G., 1954. *The Painters Workshop*, Oxford

Cooke, Arthur, O. n.d. *c.* 1905. *Work and Workers shown to Children*

Coombs, Katherine. 1998. *The Portrait Miniature in England*

Coombs, Howard and Coombs, Peter. 1971. *Journal of a Somerset Rector 1803–1834: John Skinner*

Cooper, George. 1821. Carver & Gilder of "36 Piccadilly opposite St James's Church", London. Receipt for the sale of a chimney glass, 12 June 1821, author's Collection

Cooper, Nicholas. 1999. *Houses of the Gentry 1480–1680*, New Haven & London

Crawford, Matthew. (2009) 2010. *The Case for Working with Your Hands* (2009)

Credland, Arthur G. 1993. *Marine Painting in Hull through Three Centuries*, Hull

Croft-Murray, Edward. 1962. *Decorative Painting in England 1537–1837* (2 vols)

Cummings, Abbott Lowell. 1979. *The Framed Houses of Massachusetts Bay 1625–1725*, Cambridge, MA

Cunningham, Allan. 1830. *Lives of the Most Eminent British Painters* – incl. sculptors (5 vols)

Davidson, A. S. 1986. *Marine Art & Liverpool … 1760–1960*, Wolverhampton

Davies, Kathryn. 2008. *Artisan Art: Vernacular Wall Paintings of the Welsh Marches 1550–1650*. Almeley

Davies, Philip. 2009. *Lost London 1870–1945* (in photographs), Croxley Green

Deauchur, Stephen. 1988. *Sporting Art in Eighteenth Century England*, New Haven & London

Defoe, Daniel. 1715. *The Family Instructor*

Defoe, Daniel. (1724) 1991. *Tour Throu' the whole Island of Great Britain*, Furbank, P. N., Owens, W. R. and Coulson, A. J. (eds), New Haven & London

Defoe, Daniel. 1727. *The Complete English Tradesman*

Dellow, E. L. transl., see Svedenstiera

Dickens, Charles. 1842. *American Notes*

Doerner, Max. (1963) 1979. *The Materials of the Artist and their use in Painting*

Dolan, Brian. 2004. *Josiah Wedgwood: Entrepreneur to the Enlightenment*

Donaldson, Ian. 2011. *Ben Jonson: A Life*, Oxford

Dossie, Robert. 1764. *The Handmaid to the Arts*

Du Fresnoy, Charles Alfonse. (1684, 3rd edn) 1695 (transl.) *Remarques sur l'art de Peinture*

Duffy, Eamon. (1992) 2005. *The Stripping of the Altars*, New Haven & London

Dunlap, William. (1834) 1969. *The History of the Rise & Progress of the Arts of Design in the United States* Vol. I and Vol. II Parts 1 and 2, New York

Dunlop, O. Jocelyn. 1911. *English Apprenticeship & Child Labour*

Dyer, Christopher. 2003. *Making a Living in the Middle Ages*

Earle, Peter. 1989. *The Making of the English Middle Class ... 1660–1730*

Easterly, David. 1998. *Grinling Gibbons and the Art of Carving*

Eastlake, Charles Lock (1847) 1960. *Materials for a History of Oil Painting* (2 vols), New York

Edkins, Michael. 1761–1787. *Letter Books & Ledger*, manuscript, Bristol Central Library B20196

Edwards, Edward. 1808. *Anecdotes of Painting*

Elsum, John. 1704. *The Art of Painting after the Italian Manner with Practical Observations of Principal Colours and Directions how to know a Good Picture*

Englefield, W. A. D. (1923) 1936. *The History of the Painter Stainers of London*

Esdaile, Katherine A. 1946. *English Church Monuments 1510–1840*, New York

Evans, Monica. 1997. *The Place of the Rural Blacksmith in Parish Life 1500–1900*, Bristol

Evelyn, John. 1662. *Sculptura: or the History and Art of Chalcograhy and Engraving on Copper*

Evelyn, John. (1664) 1670. *Sylvia: A Discourse of Forest Trees ...*

Evelyn, John. 1706. *An Account of Architects & Architecture*

Farington, Joseph, see Garlick and Macintyre (eds)

Fawcett, Trevor. 1974. *The Rise of English Provincial Art: Artists, Patrons and Institutions outside London 1800–1830*, Oxford

Fawcett, Trevor. 2008. *Georgian Imprint: Printing and Publishing at Bath 1729–1815*, Bath

Fearon, Daniel. 1984. *Spinks Catalogue of British Commemorative Medals 1558 to the Present Day*, Exeter

Fenton, James. 2006. *School of genius: A History of the Royal Academy of Arts*

Fiennes, Celia, See Morris, Christopher (ed.)

Fishlock, Michael. 1992. *The Great Fire at Hampton Court*

Flaxman, John. 1865. *Lectures on Sculpture*

Flaxman, John, Snr. 1788. Indenture to train Isaac Dell as a "Moulder and Caster of Plaister Figures", manuscript, National Art Library, London

Fleming, Michael. 2012. "Woodworking tools in early modern Oxford", *Oxoniensia* 77, 107–116

Foister, Susan. 2006. *Holbein in England*

Ford, John. 2005. *Coach maker: The Life and Times of Philip Godsal 1747–1826*, Shrewsbury

Forester, Ann. 1963. "Hogarth as an engraver of silver", *Connoisseur* 152, 113–116

Fortnum, C. Drury E. 1877. *Bronzes*

Foster, Kathleen A. 2008. *Thomas Chambers: American Marine and Landscape Painter 1808–1869*, New Haven & London

Fox, Celina (ed.). 1992. *London: World City, 1800–1840*, New Haven & London

Fox, Celina 2009. *The Arts of Industry in the Age of Enlightenments*, New Haven & London

Frere-Cook, Gervis. 1974. *The Decorative Art of the Mariner*

Frith, Henry. n.d. *c.* 1895. *The Romance of Engineering*

Furbank, P. N., Owens, W. R. and Coulson, A. J. (eds) 1991, see *Defoe, Daniel* 1724

Garlick, Kenneth and Macintyre, Angus (eds). 1978. *The Diary of Joseph Farington*, New Haven & London

Gatrell, Vic. 2006. *City of Laughter: Sex and Satire in Eighteenth Century London*

Gaunt, William. 1975. *Marine Painting*

Gaynor, James M. 2001. "Tools for Gentleman", *Antiques* 159, New York (January) 134–141

Gaynor, James M. and Hagedorn, Nancy L. 1993. *Tools: Working in Wood in Eighteenth Century America*, Williamsburg, Virginia

Gerbier, Balthazar. 1663. *Council and Advice to all Builders*

Gerbino, Anthony and Johnson, Stephen 2009. *Compass and Rule: Architecture as Mathematical Practice in England*, New Haven & London

Gibson-Wood, Carol. 2000. *Jonathan Richardson: Art Theorist of the English Enlightenment*, New Haven & London

Gill, Eric. (1929) 1943. *Art Nonsense and Other Essays* (1929)

Glanville, Philippa and Goldsborough, Jennifer Faulds. 1990. *Women Silversmiths 1685–1845*, Washington DC & London

Glin, Knight of and Peill, James. 2007. *Irish Furniture*, New Haven & London

Gomme, Andor. 2000. *Francis Smith of Warwick*, Stamford

Gooddy, John. 1974. "Paintings, drawings, plans, and Sculpture", in Medvei and Thornton 1974, chapter 15

Goodison, Nicholas. (1974). 2002. *Matthew Boulton: Ormolu*

Green, Chris. 1999. *John Dwight's Fulham Pottery: Excavation 1971–1979*

Greenacre, Francis *et al.* 2010. *Public Sculpture of Bristol*

Greenwood, Martin. n.d. *c.* 2008. *Frederick Thrupp*, Torquay

Griffith, David. 2006. "The Scheme of Redemption on the Later Medieval Painted Panels in Bradninch Church, Devon", in Devon Buildings Group: Research Paper 2, Exeter, 45–66

Griffiths, Anthony. (1980) 1986. *Prints and Printmaking* (1980)

Guillery, Peter. 2000. "Further adventures of Mary Lacy", *Georgian Group Journal* X, 61–9

Gunnis, Rupert. 1953. *Dictionary of British Sculptors 1680–1851*

Gwilt, Joseph (1842) 1876. *An Encyclopaedia of Architecture*

Gwnn, John. 1749. *An Essay on Design: Including Proposals for Erecting a Public Academy*

Hadley, Guy. 1976. *Citizens and Founders*, Chichester

Halliwell, James Orchard. (1850) 1989. *Dictionary of Archaic Words*

Hambly, Maya. 1988. *Drawing Instruments*

Hammelmann, Hans. 1975. *Book Illustrators in Eighteenth Century England*, New Haven & London

Hammond, J. L. and Hammond, Barbara. 19191. *The Skilled Labourer 1760–1832*

Hardcastle, E. see Pyne, W. H.

Harley, R. D. 1971. "Oil colour containers: development work by artists and colourmen in the nineteenth century", *Annals of Science* 27, No. 1 (March), 1–12

Harley, R. D. (1970) 1982. *Artists Pigments c. 1600–1835*

Harris, John. 1976. *Gardens of Delight*

Harris, John. 1979. *The Artists and The Country House*

Harris, Tim (ed.). 1995. *Popular Culture in England c. 1500–1850*

Harvey, John. 1946. *Henry Yevele*

Harvey, John. 1950. *The Gothic World*

Harvey, John. 1975. *Medieval Craftsmen*

Haskins, Charles. 1912. *The Ancient Trade Guilds and Companies of Salisbury*, Salisbury

Hawksley, Lucinda. 2013. *The Mystery of Princess Louise*

Hawthorne, J. G. and Smith, C. S., see Theophilus

Haydocke, Richard. 1598. *A Tracte Containing the Artes of Curious Paintinge, Caruings & Buildinge* Oxford. "Englished" from G. P. Lomazzo's *Trattato dell'arte …* (Milan 1584),

Hayter, Charles. (1813) 1832. *An Introduction to Perspective, Practical Geometry, Drawing and Painting*

Heal, Ambrose. (1953) 1988. *The London Furniture Makers … 1660–1840*

Hearn, Karen. 1995. *Dynasties: Painting in Tudor and Jacobean England*

Hearn, Karen. 2002. *Marcus Gheeraerts II: Elizabethan Artist*

Heckscher, Morrison and Bowman, Leslie Green. 1992. *American Rococo*, New York

Henig, Martin and Paine, Crispin (eds). 2013. *Preserving and Presenting the Past in Oxfordshire and Beyond: Essays in Memory of John Rhodes*, Oxford

Hilliard, Nicholas n.d. Manuscript on *Limning*, Edinburgh University Library, Laing III, 174; see also Thornton and Cain

Hillick, M. C. (1898) 1997. *Practical Carriage & Wagon Painting*, Mendham, N. J.

Hoare, Prince. 1806. *Arts of Design in England*

Hoare, Prince. 1813. *Epochs of the Arts*

Hobhouse, Hermione. 1971. *Thomas Cubitt: Master Builder*

Hogarth, William 1753. *Analysis of Beauty* (1753); see R. Paulson 1997 and Trusler 1786

Honeybone, Diane and Honeybone, Michael. 2010. *The Correspondence of the Spaulding Gentleman's Society 1710–1761*, Woodbridge

Hoock, Holger (2003) 2009. *The King's Artists: The Royal Academy of Arts & the Politics of British Culture 1760–1840*, Oxford

Howarth, David. 1997. *Images of Rule*

Hunt, William Morris, see Movalli (ed.) 1976

Hussey, Christopher. 1967. *English Gardens and Landscapes 1700–1750*

Hutchinson, Sidney. 1968. *The History of the Royal Academy*

Icher, François. 2000. *The Artisans & Guilds of France*, New York

Ingamells, John and Edgcumbe, John (eds). 2000. *The Letters of Joshua Reynolds*, New Haven & London

Jackson, Kevin. 2012. *Constellation of Genius: 1922 Modernism Year One*

Jackson, Peter. 1987. *George Scharf's London*

James, Lawrence. 2006. *The Middleclass: A History*

Jameson, George, see Anon (George Jameson? "a carver")

Jekyll, Gertrude and Hussey, Christopher. (1918) 1927. *Garden Ornament*

Jervis, Simon. 1992. "Rudolph Ackerman" in Fox (ed.) 1992, 97–110

Johnson, Thomas. 1793. *Autobiography of a Woodcarver*, see also Simon, Jacob 2003

Jones, Michael Owen. 1975. *The Handmade Object and its Maker*, Berkeley, CA

Jupp, E. B. and Pocock, W. W. 1887. *An Historical Account of the Worshipful Company of Carpenters*

Kahl, William F., see Unwin, George

Kelby, William. (1922) 1970. *Notes on American Artists 1754–1820*, New York

Kelly, Alison. 1990. *Mrs. Coade's Stone*, Upton on Severn

Kelly, Jason M. 2009. *The Society of Dilettanti: Archaeology and Identity in the British Enlightenment*, New Haven & London

Kemp, Martin. 2009. *The Science of Art*, New Haven & London

Kewley, Jonathan. 2011. "Henry Quale: A Georgian stonecutter and his work", *Georgian Group Journal* XIX, 94–105

Knoop, Douglas and Jones, G. P. (1933) 1967. *The Medieval Mason*, Manchester

Krill, John. 1987. *English Artists' Paper*

Ladis, Andrew, Wood, Carolyn, and Eiland, William U. 1995. *The Craft of Art*, Athens, GA

Lane, Joan. 1996. *Apprenticeship in England 1600–1914*

Lang, Jennifer. 1975. *Pride Without Prejudice: The Story of London's Guilds and Livery Companies*

Larkin, James. (1892) 1914. *The Practical Brass & Iron Founders Guide*, Philadelphia

Larwood, Jacob and Hotten, John Camden. 1866. *The History of Signboards*

Laurie, A. P. 1930. *The Painter's Methods & Materials*

Lauring, Palle. 1960. *A History of the Kingdom of Denmark* D. Hohnen transl., Copenhagen

Less-Milne, James. 1962. *The Earls of Creation: Five Great Patrons of Eighteenth Century Art*

Lewis, W. L. (ed.). 1973. *Selected Letters of Horace Walpole*, New Haven & London

Lindley, Phillip. 2003. *Making Medieval Art*, Donington

Lindley, Phillip. 2007. *Tomb Destruction and Scholarship: Medieval Monuments in Early Modern England*, Donington

Lipman, Jean. (1948) 1980. *American Folk Art in Wood, Metal, Stone*, New York

Lipman, Jean. (1968) 1980. *Rufus Porter Rediscovered: Artist, Inventor, Journalist: 1792–1884*, New York

Lippincott, Louise. 1983. *Selling Art in Georgian London: The Rise of Arthur Pond*, New Haven & London

Lipski, L. L.. 1984. *Dated English Delftware...1600–1800*

Liszka, Thomas R. and Walker, E M. (eds). 2001. *The North Sea World in the Middle Ages*, Portland, OR

Little, Nina Fletcher. (1952) 1972. *American Decorative Wall Painting 1700–1850*, New York

Little, Nina Fletcher. 1976. *Paintings by New England Provincial Artists 1775–1800*, Boston

Lloyd, Nathaniel (1931) 1975. *A History of the English House*

Long, Derek A. 2013. *"At the Sign of Atlas": The Life and Work of Joseph Moxon*, Donington

Loudon, J. C. 1836. *Encyclopaedia of Cottage Farm and Villa Architecture*

Louw, Hentie. 1989. "Demarcation disputes between English carpenters and joiners from the sxteenth to the eighteenth centuries", *Construction History* V

Lubbock, Jules. 1995. *The Tyrany of Taste*, New Haven & London

McCallum, Iain. 2003. *Thomas Barker of Bath: The Artist and His Circle*, Bath

McCoubrey, John W. (ed.). 1965. *American Art 1700–1960 Sources & Documents*, New Jersey

McDermott, M. and Berry, S. 2011. *Edmund Rack's Survey of Somerset (1781–1787)*, Taunton, see also Collinson 1791

McKendrick, Neil, Brewer, John and Plumb, J. H. 1988. T*he Birth of a Consumer Society: The Commercialisation of Eighteenth Century England*

McKendrick, Scot, Lowden, John, and Doyle, Kathleen. 2011. *Royal Manuscripts: The Genius of Illumination*

Maclehose, Louisa (trans.) and Baldwin Brown, G. (ed.). 1907. *Vasari on Technique*

Mancall, Peter C. 2007. *Hakluyts Promise: An Elizabethan's Obsession for an English America*, New Haven & London

Mander, Nicholas. 1997. "Painted cloths: history, craftsmen and techniques", *Textile History* 28 pt 2, 119–148

Mandy, Venterus. Auction catalogue of *Mandy's Library* 557 lots, 1713/14 British Library Sc301 (2)

Marks, Richard and Williamson, Paul (eds). 2003. *Gothic: Art for England 1400–1547*

Martin, Joanna. 2004. *Wives and Daughters: Women & Children in the Georgian Country House*

Martin, John *c.* 1690–1701. Manuscript *Notebook*, Sir John Soane's Museum, London, AL/41c

Mason, Shena (ed.). 2009. *Matthew Boulton: Selling what the World Desires*, Birmingham, New Haven & London

Matther, George Marshall. 1840. *The Elements of Drawing*, Edinburgh

Medvei, Victor Cornelius and Thornton, John L. 1974. *The Royal Hospital of St Bartholomew 1123–1973*, see also Gooddey 1974

Merrifield, M. P. 1849. *Original Treatises Dating from the XII to the XVII Centuries on the Arts of Painting*

Merritt, Douglas, Greenacre, Francis, and Eustace, Katherine. 2001. *Public Sculpture in Bristol,* Liverpool

Mitchel, Brigitte and Penrose, Herbert. 1990. *Letters from Bath 1766 –1767 by the Rev. John Penrose,* Gloucester

Montgomery, Charles F. 1973. *A History of American Pewter,* Winterthur, Delaware/ New York

Montgomery, Charles F. and Kane, Patricia (eds). 1976. *American Art 1750–1800: Towards Independence,* Boston, MA

Montias, John Michael. 1982. *Artists & Artisans in Delft: A Socio-Economic Study of the Seventeenth Century,* Princeton, NJ

More, Charles. 1989. *The Industrial Age … 1750–1985*

Morris, Christopher (ed.) 1982. *The Illustrated Journeys of Celia Fiennes 1685–1712,* Exeter

Morris, Christopher. 1992. *Selections from William Cobbett's Rural Rides 1821–1832,* Waltham Abbey

Movalli, Charles. 1976. *William Morris Hunt on Painting & Drawing,* New York

Moxon, Joseph. (1678 in parts; 1703 as book) 1975. *Mechanic Exercises or the Doctrine of Handy–Works,* Mendham, NJ

Murdoch, Tessa (ed.). 1985. *The Quiet Conquest: The Huguenots 1685–1985*

Murdoch, Tessa (ed.). 2006. *Noble Households: Eighteenth Century Inventories of Great English Houses,* Cambridge

Murphy, Seamus. (2005) 2010. S*tone Mad,* Cork

Murray, Isabel (ed.). 1979. *The Complete Shorter Fiction of Oscar Wilde,* Oxford

Myers, Harris. 1996. *William Henry Pyne and his Microcosm*

Myrone, Martin (ed.). 2011. *John Martin: Apocalypse*

Neal, R. S. 1981. *Bath 1680–1850: A Social History*

New York Historical Society 1938. *The Arts & Crafts in New York 1726–1776: Advertisements and News Items from New York City* (Newspapers), New York

Nichol, J. 1866. *Some Account of the Worshipful Company of Ironmongers*

Nurse, Bernard. 2011. "John Carter F.S.A. (1748–1817) …", *Antiquaries Journal* 91, 211–252

O'Day, Rosemary. 2000. *The Professions in Early Modern England 1450–1800,* Harlow

O'Dwyer, John and Le Mage, Raymond. 1950. *A Glossary of Art Terms*

Onalaja, A. O. and Claudio, L. 2000. "Genetic susceptibility to lead poisoning", *Environmental Health Perspectives* 108 Supple. I (March) 23–28

Osbourne, Harold, ed. 1970. *The Oxford Companion to Art,* Oxford

Ousby, Ian. 2002. *The Englishman's England: Taste, Travel and the Rise of Tourism* 1990

Pacey, Arnold. 2007. *Medieval Architectural Drawing,* Stroud

Painter Stainers Company. *The Binding Booke of the Company of Painters Stainers of London 1666–1795,* Manuscript: Guildhall Library, London

Parshall, Peter (ed.). 2009. *The Woodcut in Fifteenth Century Europe.* New Haven & London

Pasquin, Anthony (alias of John Williams). 1796. *Memoirs of the Royal Academy: Being an Attempt to Improve the National Taste*

Paulson, Ronald. 1979. *Popular and Polite Art in the Age of Hogarth and Fielding*, Notre Dame, Indiana

Paulson, Ronald. 1991 and 1992. *Hogarth: The Modern Moral Subject 1697–1732* Vols I and II, New Brunswick

Paulson, Ronald (ed.) 1997. *Hogarth: Analysis of Beauty* (1753), New Haven & London

Paty, Thomas and Paty, William 1712/13–1789 and 1758–1800. Manuscript *Copybook*, Bristol University Library

Payne, Christiana. 1993. *Toil and Plenty: Images of the Agricultural Landscape in England 1780–1890*, New Haven & London

Peach, H. H. 1948. *Craftsmen All: An Anthology* with a foreword by Pick, Frank, Leicester

Peake, Mervin. 1939. *The Craft of the Lead Pencil*

Pears, Iain. (1988) 1991. *The Discovery of Painting*, New Haven & London

Penny, Nicholas. 1993. *The Materials of Sculpture*, New Haven & London

Penny, Nicholas (ed.). 1986. *Reynolds*

Peterson, Charles E. (ed.). 1992. *Rules of Work for the Carpenters' Company of the City and County of Philadelphia – 1796 Rule Book*, Mendham, NJ

Pevsner, Nikolaus. 1940. *Academies of Art*, Cambridge

Physick, John. 1969. *Designs for English Sculpture 1680–1860*

Pilkington, M. 1769. *The Gentleman's & Connoisseurs Dictionary of Painters*

Plaisterers Price Book. 1798. *The Master Plaisters of London* price book, Sir John Soane's Museum

Platt, Colin. 2005. *Marks of Opulence: The Why, When and Where of Western Art 1000–1914*

Pleasants, Jacob Hall. (1943) 1970. *Four Late Eighteenth Century Anglo-American Landscape Painters*, Freeport, NY

Plott, Robert. 1677. *The Natural History of Oxfordshire*, Oxford

Poesch, Jessie, 1983. *The Art of the Old South: Painting, Sculpture, Architecture and the Products of Craftsmen 1560–1860*, New York

Pollard, J. G. 1971. "Matthew Boulton and the Reducing Machine in England", *Numismatic Chronicle* (7th ser.) XI, 311–317

Pooley, Ernest.1947. *The Guilds of the City of London*

Porny, Mark Anthony. (1765) 1771. *The Elements of Heraldry*

Postle, Martin (ed.). 2011. *Johan Zoffany RA: Society Observed*, New Haven & London

Potter, Jennifer. 2006. *Strange Blooms: The Curious Lives and Adventures of the John Tradescants*

Preston, Arthur. (1929) 1994. *Christ's Hospital Abingdon*, Oxford

Priddy, Sumpter. 2004. *American Fancy: Exuberance in the Arts 1790–1840*, Milwaukee, Wisconsin

Priest, Gordon. 2003. *The Paty Family: Makers of Eighteenth Century Bristol*, Bristol

Primatt, Stephen. 1667. *The City & Country Purchaser & Builder*

Prothero, Iorwerth. 1979. *Artisans and Politics in the early Nineteenth Century: John Gast and His Times*, Folkestone

Pye, David. 1971. *The Nature & Art of Workmanship*

Pyne, W. H. [alias Ephrain Hardcastle] 1823–1824. *Somerset House Gazette & Literary Museum* (2 vols)

Quimby, M. G. ed. 1978. *Material Culture & the Study of American Life*, Winterthur, Delaware/New York

Rawlings, Gertrude B. 1898. *The Study of British Coinage*

Read, Brian and Morgan, Dong. 2010. *Natural 19th and early 20th Century Sharpening Stones and Hones*, Dorchester

Redfield, Robert. (1956) *Peasant Society & Culture*, Chicago

Rees, Jane and Rees Mark (eds). (1994), 2012. *The Tool Chest of Benjamin Seaton*, Swanley

Reynolds, Joshua. *Journals* eg for 1765, Royal Academy Library, Manuscript R1I/1/8

Reynolds, Joshua. 1778. *Seven Discourses Delivered in the Royal Academy by the President*

Richardson, S. 1785. *The Apprentices Vade Mecum*

Richardson, Tim. (2007) 2008. *The Arcadian Friends: Inventing the English Landscape Garden*

Roberts, David, (ed.). (1992) 1998. *Lord Chesterfield's Letters*, Oxford

Robinson, Cook & Holdway 1859. Coach Builders & Harness Makers 11–12 Mount Street, Grosvenor Square, London, Receipt listing materials etc dated 27 Sept 1859, manuscript: author's collection

Rodwell, W. 2012. *The Archaeology of Churches*, Stroud

Rorabaug, W. J. 1986. *The Craft Apprentice: From Franklin to the Machine Age in America*, New York

Roscoe, Ingrid, Hardy, Emma and Sullivan, M. G. (eds). 2009. *A Biographical Dictionary of Sculptors in Britain*, New Haven & London

Rose, Jonathan. 2009. *The Interlectuctual Life of the British Working Class*, New Haven & London

Rose, Walter. (1937) 1946. *The Village Carpenter,* Cambridge

Rosen, William, 2010. *The Most Powerful Idea in the World: A Story of Steam*

Rouquet, Jean Andre. 1755. *The Present State of the Arts in England*

Rowe, Eleanor. 1907. *Practical Woodcarving*

Rowell, Christopher (ed.). 2013. *Ham House: 400 Years of Collecting and Patronage*, New Haven & London

Salmon, William (1672) 1701. *Polygraphice: or the Art of Drawing Engraving, Etching, Limning, Painting, Varnishing, Japanning, Gilding &c.* (2 vols)

Salzman, L. F. (1949) 1992. *Building in England down to 1540*, Oxford

Sandby, William. 1862. *The History of the Royal Academy* (2 vols)

Saumarez-Smith, Charles 2012. *The Origins of the Royal Academy of Arts in London*

Saxl, F. and Wittkower, Rudolf 1948. *British Art and the Mediterranean*, Oxford

Seidmann, Gertrude. 1992. "'A very ancient, useful and curious art': the Society and the revival of gem-engraving in eighteenth century England" in Allan and Abbott (eds), 120–131

Sennett, Richard. 2008. *The Craftsman*

Shanes, Eric. 1981. *The Genius of the Royal Academy*

Simon, Jacob. 1996. *The Art of the Picture Frame*

Simon, Jacob (ed.). 2003. "The Life of the Author Thomas Johnson" 1793, *Furniture History* XXXIX

Simon, Robin. 1987. *The Portrait in Britain and America*, Oxford

Sitwell, Sacheverell. 1945. *British Architects and Craftsmen*

Skinner, John – see Coombs and Coombs (eds) 1971

Skovgaard, Joakim A. 1973. *The King's Architecture: Christian IV and His Buildings*

Sloan, Kim. 2000. *A Noble Art, Amateur Artists and Drawings masters c. 1600–1800*

Sloan, Kim. 2007. *A New World : England's First View of America*

Sloman, Susan Legouix. 1996. "Artists picture rooms in eighteenth century Bath", *Bath History* VI

Sloman, Susan. 2002. *Gainsborough in Bath*, New Haven & London

Smith, John. 1676. *The Art of painting in Oyl*

Smith, J. T. (1828) 1919 (2 vols) and 1949 (1 vol.). *Nollekens and His Times*

Snodin, Michael (ed.). 1984. *Rococo: Art & Design in Hogarth's England*

Snodin, Michael (ed.). 2010. *Horace Walpole's Strawberry Hill*, New Haven & London

Snodin, Michael and Moncrieff, Elspeth. 1984. *Rococo: Art & Design in Hogarth's England*

Snodin, Michael and Styles, John. 2001. *Design and Decorative Arts: Britain 1500–1900*

Society of Antiquaries. 2007. *Making History*

Solkin, David H. 1993. *Painting for Money*, New Haven & London

Solkin, David H. (ed.). 2002. *Art on the Line: The Royal Academy Exhibitions at Somerset House 1780–1836*. New Haven & London

Spiers, Walter Lewis (ed.). 1919. "The Diary of Nicholas Stone Jnr", *Walpole Society* VIII, Oxford

Stalker, John and Parker, George (1688) 1971. *A Treatise on Japanning & Varnishing*

Steane, John. 1998. *The Archaeology of the Medieval English Monarchy*

Steane, John. 2001. *The Archaeology of Power*

Steane, John and Ayres, James. 2013. *Traditional Buildings in the Oxford Region*, Oxford

Steegman, John. 1936. *The Rule of Taste*

Stein, Roger B. 1975. *Seascape & the American Imagination*, New York

Stevens, John. (1705) 1958. *His Book 1705*, facsimile of manuscript, Newport RI

Stone, Lawrence. 1955. *Sculpture in Britain in the Middle Ages*

Strong, Roy. 1969. *The Elizabethan Image 1540–1620*

Stroud, Dorothy. 1961. *The Architecture of Sir John Soane*

Sturt, George (1923) 1993. *The Wheelwrights Shop*. Cambridge

Sutherland, C. H. V. 1955. *Art and Coinage*

Svedenstiera, E. T. (1802–3) 1973. *Tour of Great Britain 1802–3*, trans. E. L. Dellow, Newton Abbot

Theophilus. (1963) 1979. *On Diverse Arts*, trans John G. Hawthorne and Cyril Stanley Smith, New York

Thomas, Keith. 2009. *The Ends of Life: Roads to Fulfilment in Early Modern Britain*, Oxford

Thompson, Daniel, see Cennini, Cennino D'Andrea

Thompson, E. P. (1963) 1991. *The Making of the English Working Class*

Thomson, Christopher. 1847. *The Autobiography of an Artisan*

Thomson, D. 1975. *Painting in Scotland 1570–1650*, Edinburgh

Thornton, Peter. (1978)1979. *Seventeenth Century Interior Decoration ...*, New Haven & London

Thornton, Peter. 1984. *Authentic Décor: The Domestic Interior 1630–1920*

Thornton, R. K. R and Cain, T. G. S. (eds). 1981. Hilliard, Nicholas: *A Treatise Concerning the Arte of Limning*, Ashington

Tingry. P. F. (1803) 1816. *The Painters & Varnisher's Guide*

Tingry, P. F. 1830. *Painter's & Colourman's Guide*

Tipping, see Avray Tipping

Townley, Charles 1799. Letter written on 28 Oct 1799 on behalf of Townley from Park Street, Westminster to Mr Sastres at Upper Seymour Street concerning some medals & gems and Visconti's "dissertation" on a head of Jupiter, manuscript, author's collection

Townsend, J. 2011. *Watercolour* (exhibition booklet)

Tressell, Robert [Robert Noonan] (1914) 1991. *The Ragged Trousered Philanthropists*

Trusler, John. 1768 *Hogarth Moralised: Being a Complete Edition of Hogarth's Works Containing Near Fourscore Copper Plates ...*

Uglow, Jenny. 2002. *The Lunar Men: The Friends who made the Future*

Uglow, Jenny. 2006. *Nature's Engraver: A Life of Thomas Bewick*

Unwin, George (1908) 1966. *The Guilds & Companies of London*. Introduction by William F. Kahl in 1966 edition of

van de Wetering, E. (1997) 2004. *Rembrandt: the Painter at Work (1997)*, Berkeley, CA

Vickery, Amanda. 2009. *Behind Closed Doors: At Home in Georgian England*, New Haven & London

Walpole, Horace. 1762 and 1786. *Anecdotes of Painting in England*, Strawberry Hill edn of 1762 and 4th edn in 5 vols of 1786, see Lewis and also Snodin

Walpole, Josephine. 1997. *Art and Artists of the Norwich School*, Woodbridge

Ware, Isaac. 1756. *The Complete Body of Architecture*

Waterfield, Giles. 2009. *The Artists Studio*, Norwich

Waterfield, Giles, French, Anne and Craske, Matthew. 2003. *Below Stairs: 400 Years of Servant Portraits*

Watt, Tessa. (1991) 1996. *Cheap Print and Popular Piety 1550–1640*, Cambridge

Weatherill, Lorna. (1988) 1996. *Consumer Behaviour & Material Culture in Britain 1660–1760*

Weaver, Lawrence. (1909) 2002. *English Leadwork*, Shaftesbury

Weber, Susan. 2013. *William Kent:* Designing Georgian Britain (Bard Graduate Center for Studies in the Decorative Arts, Design & Culture), New Haven & London

Wedd, Kit. 2004. *The Foundling Museum*

Wedd, Kit; with Peltz, Lucy and Ross, Cathy. 2001. *Creative Quarters: The Art World in London, 1700–2000*

Wehlte, Kurt. (1967) 1982. *The Materials and Techniques of Painting*, New York

Weinreb, Ben, see Wrightson, Pricilla

Wells-Cole, Anthony. 1997. *Art and Decoration in Elizabethan & Jacobean England*, New Haven & London

Wendorf, Richard. 1996. *Sir Joshua Reynolds: The Painter in Society*, Cambridge, MA

Whinney, Margaret. 1964. *Sculpture in Britain 1530–1830*

Whitaker, John. 1998. *The Best: A History of H.H. Martyn & Co., Carvers in Wood, Stone and Marble; Modellers of Decorative Plaster Enrichment. Sculptors...*, Gloucester

White, Jerry. 2012. *London in the Eighteenth Century*

Whitley, W. T. 1928. *Artists & Their Friends in England* (2 vols)

Whittock, Nathaniel. 1827. *The Decorative Painters' and Glaziers' Guide*

Wilde, Oscar. (1891) 2010. *The Picture of Dorian Grey*

Wilde, Oscar, see Murray, Isabel

Williams, John, see under his pseudonym: Pasquin, Anthony.

Williams, William. 1787. *Essay on the Mechanic of Oil Colour*, Bath

Wittkower, Rudolf. (1977) 1979. *Sculpture, Processes and Principles*

Wood, Anthony à. 1674. *History & Antiquities of Oxford*, Oxford

Wood, John. (1742) 1765, 1969. *Towards a Description of Bath*, Bath

Woodman, Francis. 1986. *The Architectural History of Kings College Chapel*, Cambridge

Worsley, Giles. 2007. *Inigo Jones and the European Classical Tradition*, New Haven & London

Wotton, Henry. 1624. *Elements of Architecture*

Wrightson, Priscilla. 1978. *The Art and Practice of Drawing and Painting*

INDEX

All places are in England unless otherwise stated. Dates are provided against a few names to avoid confusion with other artists of the same name

pauper apprenticeship 40
premium, for an apprenticeship 51, 52, 54, 55, 62
women 70–1
architectural drawing 9, 84
aristocracy x, 114, 160, 284
armour & armourer 99, 282
Arras tailor 81, 99, 153
Astley, John 91, 151
Art & Mystery 2, 41, 44, 46
artisan/artificier 2, 3, 15, 28
Arundel, Lord 7, 289
Atkins (or Adkins), John 374, 380
Atlantic Ocean x, 19, 186, 237, 238
Aubrey, John 279
Audubon, John James 69
Avis, Isabella 291, Fig. 91
Ayres, John 289, 426

Bacon
  John 22, 72, 88, 92, 94, 311, 314, 326, 327, 330, 337, 338, 378, 381, 390, 392, 395, 412, 454, Fig. 95
  Sir Nathaniel 114, 161
Badminton House, Gloucestershire 285, 309
Bagshaw, William, of Rugby 108, 193
Baker, John 94, 201, 209, 218, 222, 228, Fig. 69
Baltic 18
Banks
  Sir Joseph 412, 438
  Thomas 300, 309–10, 322, 323–4, 327, 341, 355, 366, 454
Bard, James & John 239–40
Bardwell, Thomas 85, 190, 191, 209
Barker, Benjamin, of Bath 9, 175, 191, 194, 222, 271
Barlow
  Francis 174, 366
  William 300, 309, 323
Barnard, Sir John 69
Baroque 47, 265
Barret, George 437
Barry, James 4, 24, 56, 454
barter 65
Basire, James 22, 93
Baskerville, John 156, 195, Fig. 52
Bateman, William 410

Bath, city of 38, 82, 168, 194, 212, 222–3, 260, 271, 285, 293, 310, 353, 394, 426, 432, 443
Baxter, Thomas (Snr & Jnr) 155, Fig. 32
Beale
  Charles 83, 113
  Charles Jnr 282
  Mary 67, 83, 113, 119, 126, 184
Beaumont, Sir George 81, 105
Beechey, Sir William 81, 101, 161, 222
Beilby, Ralph, of Newcastle 23, 69
Bentley, Rev. William 77
Bernini, Gianlorenzo 346
Bewick, Thomas 23, 24, 69–70, 344, Fig. 4
Bird, Francis 305–6, 436
Birmingham, city of 32, 49, 156, 195, 222, 267, 421, Fig. 52
Blackfriars, City of London 33
blacksmith and smithing 11, Figs 54, 56
bladder colour 18, 113, 116–17
Blair, Eric see Orwell, George
Blake, William 22, 72, 93, 271–2
blockbook 287
boasting drawing 376
Bobbin, Tim see Collier, John
Bodley
  John 279, 303
  Thomas 303
Bossam, John 266, Figs 85, 86
Boston, Massachusetts USA 90, 101, 170, 171–2, 194, 264, 351
Boulton, Matthew 65, 222, 258, 330, 390, 402, 403, 409, 410, 411–2, 413, 421, Fig. 78
Bourgeois, Sir Peter 17, 92, 101, 125
Boutet, Claude 282–3, Fig. 87
bow drill 367, Fig. 119
Bow porcelain 22, 72, 88, 326, 401, 431, Fig. 99
Bowles, Thomas 206, Fig. 58
bozetto see maquette
Briot, Nicholas 407, 411
Bristol, city of 38, 62, 64, 67, 155, 159, 195, 198, 233, 237, 263, 267, 371, 394, 442
British Institution 442
bronze 299, 390–3, 395, Fig. 126
Brooking, Charles 235